University Textbook Series

February, 1980

Especially Designed for Collateral Reading

HARRY W. JONES

Directing Editor

Professor of Law, Columbia University

———————

ADMIRALTY, Second Edition (1975)
Grant Gilmore, Professor of Law, Yale University.
Charles L. Black, Jr., Professor of Law, Yale University.

ADMIRALTY AND FEDERALISM (1970)
David W. Robertson, Professor of Law, University of Texas.

AGENCY (1975)
W. Edward Sell, Dean of the School of Law, University of Pittsburgh.

BUSINESS ORGANIZATION AND FINANCE (1980)
William A. Klein, Professor of Law, University of California, Los Angeles.

CIVIL PROCEDURE, BASIC, Second Edition (1979)
Milton D. Green, Professor of Law Emeritus, University of California, Hastings College of the Law.

COMMERCIAL TRANSACTIONS, INTRODUCTION TO (1977)
Hon. Robert Braucher, Associate Justice, Supreme Judicial Court of Massachusetts.
Robert A. Riegert, Professor of Law, Cumberland School of Law.

CONFLICT OF LAWS, COMMENTARY ON THE, Second Edition (1980)
Russell J. Weintraub, Professor of Law, University of Texas.

CONSTITUTIONAL LAW, AMERICAN (A TREATISE ON) (1978) with 1979 Supplement
Laurence H. Tribe, Professor of Law, Harvard University.

CONTRACT LAW, THE CAPABILITY PROBLEM IN (1978)
Richard Danzig.

CORPORATIONS, Second Edition (1971)
Norman D. Lattin, Professor of Law, University of California, Hastings College of the Law.

CORPORATIONS IN PERSPECTIVE (1976)
Alfred F. Conard, Professor of Law, University of Michigan.

CRIMINAL LAW, Second Edition (1969)
Rollin M. Perkins, Professor of Law, University of California, Hastings College of the Law.

ESTATES IN LAND & FUTURE INTERESTS, PREFACE TO (1966)
Thomas F. Bergin, Professor of Law, University of Virginia.
Paul G. Haskell, Professor of Law, Case Western Reserve University.

EVIDENCE: COMMON SENSE AND COMMON LAW (1947)
John M. Maguire, Professor of Law, Harvard University.

EVIDENCE, STUDENTS' TEXT ON THE LAW OF (1935)
John Henry Wigmore.

JURISPRUDENCE: MEN AND IDEAS OF THE LAW (1953)
The late Edwin W. Patterson, Cardozo Professor of Jurisprudence, Columbia University.

LEGAL CAPITAL, Second Edition (1980)
Bayless Manning, Former Dean, Stanford Law School.

LEGAL RESEARCH ILLUSTRATED (1977)
J. Myron Jacobstein, Professor of Law, Law Librarian, Stanford University.
Roy M. Mersky, Professor of Law, Director of Research, University of Texas.

LEGAL RESEARCH, FUNDAMENTALS OF (1977), with 1980 Assignments Pamphlet
J. Myron Jacobstein, Professor of Law, Law Librarian, Stanford University.
Roy M. Mersky, Professor of Law, Director of Research, University of Texas.

PROCEDURE, THE STRUCTURE OF (1979)
Robert M. Cover, Professor of Law, Yale University.
Owen M. Fiss, Professor of Law, Yale University.

THE PROFESSION OF LAW (1971)
L. Ray Patterson, Dean of the School of Law, Emory University.
Elliott E. Cheatham, Professor of Law, Vanderbilt University.

PROPERTY, Second Edition (1975)
John E. Cribbet, Dean of the Law School, University of Illinois.

TAXATION, FEDERAL INCOME, Second Edition (1979)
Marvin A. Chirelstein, Professor of Law, Yale University.

TORTS, Second Edition (1980)
Clarence Morris, Professor of Law, University of Pennsylvania.
C. Robert Morris, Professor of Law, University of Minnesota.

TRUSTS, PREFACE TO THE LAW OF (1975)
Paul G. Haskell, Professor of Law, Case Western Reserve University.

WILLS AND TRUSTS, THE PLANNING AND DRAFTING OF, Second Edition (1979)
Thomas L. Shaffer, Professor of Law, University of Notre Dame.

MORRIS ON TORTS

Second Edition

By

CLARENCE MORRIS
Emeritus Professor
University of Pennsylvania Law School

and

C. ROBERT MORRIS, JR.
Professor of Law
University of Minnesota Law School

Mineola, N. Y.
THE FOUNDATION PRESS, INC.
1980

Library of Congress Cataloging in Publication Data

Morris, Clarence, 1903–
    Morris on torts.

    (University textbook series)
    Includes index.
    1. Torts—United States. I. Morris, C. Robert, 1928–   joint author. II. Title.
III. Series.
KF1250.M67   1980   346.7303   80–170

ISBN 0-88277-002-0

Morris on Torts 2d Ed. UTB

To
Bill
and
Sandy

*

PREFACE TO SECOND EDITION

The first edition of this book was published in 1953. It, like this edition, was written primarily for first year law students taking a course in Torts. As "outside reading" this book may help them to understand better some of the topics covered in class and may orient them to some topics not otherwise covered. Since some stress is placed on advocacy, the book may be of interest to practicing lawyers as well.

Contemporary studies in the law of Torts have increasingly stressed procedure and policy. Perhaps these trends are advanced a little in this book. In addition to the usual emphasis on division of functions of judge and jury and on the importance of jury charges, we have stressed the problems and processes of proof. A policy analysis of all topics covered is stated; it may prove orienting and useful.

The book covers most of the central, traditional subjects; it is not intended to be exhaustive. It cites many of the leading cases and, as illustrative of the current state of the law, many quite recent ones. It is not a search book, although it may prove to be useful as a starting point for research. Few references will be found to the voluminous literature on Torts (from which we have learned most of what we know) because once we started, we would have covered too many pages before a stopping place was reached.

We are grateful to the many people who helped us whip this book into shape.

CLARENCE MORRIS
C. ROBERT MORRIS, JR.

Philadelphia, Pa.
Minneapolis, Minn.
February, 1980

*

SUMMARY OF CONTENTS

*

TABLE OF CONTENTS

Chapter V. Negligence—Proof of Negligence and Proof of Due Care

Chapter VI. Duty—The No–Duty Rules and Immunities

Chapter VII. Extent of Liability for Negligence: Duty, Negligence and Causation

xiii

Chapter XI. Misrepresentation

Chapter XII. Defamation

Chapter XIII. Malicious Prosecution and False Imprisonment

MORRIS ON TORTS

Chapter I

INTRODUCTION

Table of Sections

---

§ 1. THE LAWYERS' ROLE IN TORT LITIGATION

Automobile accidents, falls in stores, fights, bursting water mains, bad food processing, swindling, slanders, and many other unpleasant events touch off tort litigation. Torts is a branch of private law; both the plaintiff and the defendant are usually either private citizens or business corporations. Most of the cases are damage suits—the plaintiff prays for a money judgment to compensate him or her for personal injuries or property damages inflicted by the defendant. No terse definition can meaningfully describe all that falls within the four corners of the law of torts; no short catalogue of misdeeds can exhaust the field. If a quick phrase is needed, torts can be called the law of private wrongs.

Clients seldom consult lawyers on tort problems before claims arise. Lawyers are rarely asked how to avoid committing torts. Sometimes governmental agencies, large private enterprises, safety engineers, and liability insurance underwriters undertake preventive work in special fields. The lawyer's work usually starts when he or she is consulted by a claimant or a client resisting a claim.

The most spectacular part of a torts lawyer's work is advocacy in courtrooms. This role is a climax reached after a lot of time-consuming and unspectacular preparation. Painstaking investigation of the law and the facts, and careful sifting and planning must be done if courtroom advocacy is to be effective.

Most of the advocate's important work has been done before the trial begins. Nearly all of this book will be directed toward an understanding of the trial process and what the advocate does to get ready for it.

Many torts claims, however, are never referred to lawyers. The bulk of collectable claims run against persons or firms who are either insured or are corporations so large that they need no insurance. Soon after an accident, a claim adjuster investigates and often either settles with the claimant or convinces the claimant that the claim is groundless. Lawyers are brought in only when the claimant retains counsel. Tort lawyers' most important function is to champion their clients in negotiations for settlement. They meet with claim adjusters and discuss the cases with them, and advise their clients on what offers of settlement should be put forth, accepted, and rejected. A high percentage of all claims referred to lawyers are settled by them for their clients—sometimes after litigation is under way. Many plaintiffs' lawyers settle more than ninety percent of their clients' claims.

Defense counsel are not usually retained unless litigation seems likely. When claim adjusters think that a lawsuit may be unavoidable, defense counsel are brought in. Even at this late stage, negotiations for settlement are likely to continue, and defense counsel often advise and help in continued negotiation for settlement.

Forces that favor or block settlements are subtle and hard to analyze, but some of the more obvious can be sketched.

A major factor is the lawyers' estimate of the case—their guesses on the plaintiff's chances to win if it is tried, and their guesses on the probable size of the judgment if the plaintiff does win. Experienced advocates after fully investigating the law and the facts can often make canny evaluations. Of course settlement is more likely when plaintiff's and defendant's lawyers make about the same estimates of the worth of the claim. The number of instances in which they reach similar estimates is quite high; a fact which may account for the prevalence of settlements.

Even when the lawyers are not far apart in sizing up the value of the claim, settlement is not assured. Other factors affect negotiations.

It costs money to defend a lawsuit. In American litigation defendants must pay their own lawyers even when defendants win. Rather than spend a thousand dollars fighting an unfounded claim, a defendant may be willing to pay the plaintiff five hundred. So almost any claim is said to have at least a "nuisance value." But a defendant who buys peace may attract a flood of demands. Sometimes defendants spend many times the small sum for which a claim could be settled in resisting it—to discourage those who might otherwise press weak or fraudulent demands. Certain kinds of businesses become special prey if they give in to nuisance claimants. A lawyer who defends bottlers of soft drinks against claims for injuries alleged to have come from foreign matter in their product said long ago (when the price, as well as the product, both were more modest than they now are) that he never recommended a settlement. "After all," he said, "all a man needs to go into business against us is a bug and a nickel."

Most plaintiffs' lawyers accept cases on a contingent fee basis —they get a percentage of the sum collected, and nothing at all if nothing is realized. Both plaintiffs and their lawyers are willing to settle for less than what can be won by going to trial. No lawsuit is a sure thing—witnesses die or give unexpected testimony, unanticipated prejudice affects juries, defendants develop proof of some fact that catches the plaintiff totally by surprise, and so on. Rather than run such risks, nearly all plaintiffs and their lawyers are willing to take less in settlement than they believe they would get from the jury.

Furthermore, lawsuits take time. Cases often hang fire for months and years before a valid claim is reduced to final judgment. Money available only in the remote future is rarely as attractive as a solid but smaller sum in hand. Most claimants are people of small means and are especially pinched when they have suffered a severe injury. Need may be so urgent that the claimant is willing to take a great deal less than his or her due to get it immediately. Even when a claimant's lawyer thinks that the poor client is almost sure to recover a much larger judgment than the defendant offers, the lawyer often hesitates to recommend that the client forego a substantial settlement.

Personal interests of lawyers and their clients do not always coincide. Lawyers should, of course, put their clients' interests above their own, and no doubt a great many do. But not all of them always defer to their clients' interests. A busy plaintiffs' lawyer may be able to make more money by bringing about a large volume of substantial but inadequate settlements than he or she would make by pressing fewer claims more effectively. Some stubborn plaintiffs' lawyers may subject needy clients to unwise risks of litigation on the ground that the lawyers' total take will be greater if they litigate a large fraction of their cases. Contingent fee contracts sometimes provide that the claimant's counsel fee will be higher if a suit is filed, and these contracts give the lawyer an incentive to stall negotiations until the case is docketed. Defense counsel fees usually depend, at least in part, on the amount of time spent on their cases, and a defendant's lawyer can make more out of a trial than out of a settlement. But even utterly selfish lawyers want good reputations. This desire for respect probably tends to check flagrant abuses by lawyers who otherwise might not be sensitive to their professional obligations.

The art of negotiating settlements is different from the art of courtroom advocacy, but both arts are built on the same sort of preliminary work. By readying for trial, a lawyer also acquires the information needed to negotiate settlements soundly. Only when the lawyer knows what proof can be marshalled and how the courts will apply the law to it can the lawyer estimate the value of a claim properly and negotiate a settlement soundly. So the approach to an understanding of the process of settlement is through an understanding of the process of litigation. However undergraduate law students seldom see trial advocates in action and do not study firsthand reports of trials. Legal education in America converges with advocacy by an indirect route.

§ 2. THE LAW STUDENT'S APPROACH TO STUDY OF TORTS

The practice of law is learned by practicing, but the untutored would seldom know where to start. Legal education should supply a base for learning how to be a lawyer. At its best it gives students some understanding of the processes in which lawyers function and some clues about the way lawyers act.

The standard course in torts relies in lart part on reports of appealed cases, and therefore throws most of its light on the workings of appellate courts; but the materials are better than they seem. Students who try only to reduce case materials to rules of substantive law (which is, of course, an important part of their work—though doomed to prove somewhat disappointing), tend to overlook the trial process in which those rules must function, and thus fail to grasp even the appellate process as well as they should. Appellate courts focus only on the correctness of rulings that were made by the trial judge at various stages of the trial. Each of these rulings was made in a procedural setting which affected the problem raised. Unless that setting is appreciated, neither the trial nor the appellate process can be understood. As that understanding ripens, students begin to learn about both the trial and the appellate processes. The first and most important advice to novice case-readers is this: Learn to read cases with due attention to procedure.

There is, of course, a substantive law of torts. Procedure is only a means to an end. If a claim is utterly without merit no honest use of procedure can make it meritorious. If a claim is soundly founded, procedure indicates the approved method of getting it recognized. But lawyers' arts are built on use of the substantive law, and substantive law cannot be understood completely apart from its use. No client wants a treatise. Clients want favorable results.

Law students are eager to know "what the law is." A questioner who asks, "What is the substantive law of torts?" normally makes two unfounded assumptions: (1) that there is a clear, recognized, complete, and static set of rules, readily applicable to any set of facts that occur, and (2) that the facts of cases can be authoritatively and readily described, once and for all, and in only one way.

Rules and principles of tort law are a changing body of materials. This does not mean that all rules are good for one case only. In 1348 when a rowdy customer wielded a hatchet at a tavern keeper who refused to open up and serve him in the middle of the night, he committed an assault and had to pay damages. Similar facts would produce a similar holding today or a hundred years from now. But only a few years ago manufacturers' liability for harms caused by defects in their products was much more limited than it is now; and only in the last thirty-two years has any defendant been held liable for bodily injuries inflicted on a child before its birth.

Law students are not going to practice in the past, or even in the present. They are going to practice in the future. They are primarily concerned with what will happen when they appear in court and how they can properly serve clients who will retain them later on. What courts have done (precedents) and what courts and learned authorities say the law is (rules and principles) are good, but not infallible, guides to what courts will do. When past decisions or pre-formulated rules are poor guides to the wise solution of problems, they may still control decisions of judges, but they are less sure to do so. In the last half century judges have often (without the intervention of legislatures) changed tort law.

Judges are magistrates and technicians. As magistrates they have the job of deciding cases justly for live litigants of their own times. As technicians they are trained to justify their decisions by reliance on precedents and doctrines which embody the accumulated wisdom (and the accumulated mistakes) of the ages. Their respect for authoritative legal materials is high; they will not act at all without looking for and at precedent and principle. However, their desire to decide cases justly is such that from time to time impolitic rules and unwise precedents are repudiated, manipulated, interpreted or developed to serve society. Therefore students who want to know what courts will do must concern themselves with policy problems inherent in tort law. Even students who are pathetically uninterested in making the world a better place must give thought to what the law ought to be if they are to evaluate claims, determine whether they should be litigated, and seek favorable rulings from courts. Concern with policy not only helps lawyers to anticipate some breaks with the past; it also bears on recognizing areas in which change is unlikely. When a well-established rule is clearly applicable to settled facts and produces an obviously just result, the law of the case is not uncertain.

Many tort doctrines which are staples of opinions, briefs, and arguments lack sufficient meaning to dictate the results that will be reached by courts "using" them. Principles couched in such words as "duty," "negligence," and "proximate cause" may point in the general direction of an acceptable solution without clearly identifying the destination. When they are "applied" to new cases their meaning is often far from clear. Unique cases are constantly occurring. Principles harboring words of inexact meaning cannot always control decision of cases that were never dreamed of by their authors. Behind such principles the intuitions and conceptions of judges and jurors about the needs of society often operate.

The "facts" of tort cases are hard to determine. Some accidents happen quickly and may be described months later by witnesses who are neither skilled observers nor trained narrators. They may not have good memories; they are often biased; and they are sometimes dishonest. Many jurors are not able to understand testimony well or to remember it for long. Furthermore, between law and facts is a twilight zone—an area in which a fact-determining jury may have much to do with attaching legal consequences to events. In these areas, jury charges are vague and abstract and seldom indicate more than the general nature of the problems turned over to the jury.

A law student must learn much more than rules and precedents. A student must learn how they function in the process of disposing of torts cases. A student must learn that they indeed often control decision, but also that they often do not. Another determinant of some judgments is the judge's (and jurors') views on the social problems raised and on policies that *should* affect decisions.

§ 3. A POLICY APPROACH TO TORTS

"Policy" is an evocative word, easily and sometimes piously said. Some of those who propound theories about how law does or should advance the common good build models and propose paradigms which are intended to throw light on the understanding of sound legal values and on the improvement of judicial and legislative law making. Other evaluators of the law have been more factually oriented and have sent observers and questioners "into the field." We will not be much concerned (in this book for beginning students) with the techniques and fruits of either of those two methods except insofar as they seem to bear trenchantly on everyday law—now and in the next rising generation. This book is little calculated to throw much light on *novel* legal constructs that have been recently developed in schematic detail from the perspectives of analytical economics, ecology, or logical analysis. Our policy analyses will deal mostly with the crude normative views that are likely to influence judges and juries. We also lack confidence in our ability to probe into deep, unarticulated, emotional forces that affect the decisions of tort problems, and we shall not deal with arcane aspects of motivation. Insofar as we discuss policy, then, we shall deal mostly with commonly held, non-technical ideas on the relation between tort law and the common good.

The central problem in most torts cases is: whether the plaintiff or the defendant should bear a loss. Our own basic axiom in approaching such problems is: A loss should lie where it has happened to fall unless some affirmative public good will result from shifting it. This axiom is bottomed on a predilection against use of the power of government in the absence of some perceived likelihood that legal intervention will, at least in some slight way, advance the public good by ordering one litigant to pay money over to another.

Judicial conformity to this axiom often will not prevent futile litigation. One does not know whether affirmative good can come from reordering affairs without finding out just what those affairs are. A claimant's counsel will often seek redress from courts even though the claim is unfounded. Conformity to our axiom will, however, prevent some unprofitable governmental activity that might otherwise go on—the energy spent in collection of judgments. When a defendant wins a case, that is an end of the matter. When a money judgment is entered for a plaintiff, the full process is not complete until that judgment has been paid. Of course in many, if not most cases, the defendant writes the plaintiff a check once final judgment has been entered and closes the case. But if the defendant is obdurate, further proceedings may start—such as levy of execution, garnishment, and so on. These proceedings involve expense to the litigants and the public. If the total situation after the defendant has been forced to pay is no improvement over leaving the plaintiff to bear his or her own loss, the expense of enforcement of judgments should be saved.

A corollary of the axiom is: The fact that the plaintiff has suffered a loss is no reason, in and of itself, for taking money from the defendant. Security and stability are desired by most people, and repairing the fortunes of those who have suffered an unexpected loss is normally a social good. But the security and stability of persons who happen to be plaintiffs are no more important than the security and stability of persons who happen to be defendants. A shift is justified only when affirmative policy reasons can be given for requiring the defendant to bear a loss. Reasons for taking money from defendants differ sharply in various types of cases and can be discussed profitably only in connection with specific problems. An attempt will be made at appropriate places throughout this book to develop them.

Unless and until the facts of a case are settled no one knows what doctrines and what policies can operate on them. Since the process of establishing facts is far from efficient and sure, and since the understanding of those facts by judge and jury is fallible, someone who knows both what the abstract law is and what it should be still may be unable to predict the outcome of a case. But even if the facts of a case are admitted, and all relevant doctrines and policies are known, the outcome of litigation continues to be uncertain. Many variables play a part: The talents of advocates, the prejudices and lack of prejudices of judge and jurors, the ability of judge and jurors to perceive the implications of doctrine and policy, the personality and health of judge and jurors, and a myriad of other determinants too subtle to list.

Much remains to be known about factors that crucially affect judgments and verdicts, and what is known is hard to organize and state. In this book no attempt will be made to study more than (1) the application of some important rules and principles, (2) an evaluation of the results of some of these, and (3) an occasional indication of methods of developing the proof to which doctrine and policy are applied. These are main currents in the judicial process, but their sum falls short of the judicial process itself. The more subtle determinants of verdicts and decisions have to be learned by the lawyer in practice, and are not now profitable materials for the study of torts in the classroom.

Chapter II

ENTRIES ON AND DAMAGES TO REAL PROPERTY

Table of Sections

---

§ 1. TRESPASS QUARE CLAUSUM FREGIT

Laymen use the word "trespass" to mean intrusion on private premises. The legal meaning is much broader. Trespass *vi et armis* [trespass with force and arms] is one of the English forms of action used in medieval times for redress for assault and battery, false imprisonment, and many other kinds of tort cases. One variety of that form of action is trespass *quare clausum fregit* [trespass because he has broken the close] that lay in cases of unlawful entry on land. "Close" originally meant enclosure, but trespass may be committed on unenclosed tracts of land.

The basic legal doctrine applicable to trespass *q. c. f.* is this: An occupant in possession of land may maintain an action against any intruder who makes an unauthorized entry.

§ 2. A POLICY ANALYSIS OF TYPES OF TRESPASS Q. C. F. CASES

Mr. Alden and Mr. Standish pay court to Priscilla. Alden wins Priscilla's hand, and the newly married couple buys a house in which there is a large picture window. Standish gives vent to his rancor by throwing a rock through the pane.

The Aldens have suffered an economic loss. Their window will be repaired out of their savings (if they have any) [1] or out

---

1. "[Twenty percent] of all families in the United States had no liquid assets . . . . 8% of American families had negative net worths, while another 17% had net worths below $1,000." Census Bureau, Survey of Financial Characteristics of Consumers, 50 Fed. Reserve Bull. 285, 286 (1964), cited by Franklin, When Worlds Collide: Liability Theories and Disclaimers in Defective-Product Cases, 18

10

of their future savings (if they have credit) or out of the proceeds of insurance (if they have the window insured against breakage). Their savings, or their thrift program, or the insurance fund to which they contribute can be put back in status quo if Standish is forced to pay for the window. Stability and economy are furthered by judgment for these plaintiffs. Stability and economy are worth protecting; therefore reparation of the Aldens is politic.

This is not the way lawyers and judges talk; this is not traditional legal language. But the idea expressed accords with the way courts act; plaintiffs have been compensated for similar losses since the beginnings of tort law. The desirability of mending some losses with compensatory damages will be recognized as long as we have our present system of tort liability.

Of course tort liability cannot compensate for all unfortunate losses. Some losses result from storms and floods, and storms and floods cannot be sued. And some losses that flow from individuals' acts should not be charged to them. Modern legislation provides for less than full compensation in some fields. Under Workers' Compensation Acts a laborer injured at work is entitled only to a predetermined sum which often falls short of full reparation. The Compensation system of limited but widespread protection was originally rationalized on two grounds: administrative expediency and economic necessity—though of course there is much room for debate on how large these payments should be.

The reason for compensating the Aldens does not justify doing so at Standish's expense. However, Standish was *at fault* —that is, he was guilty of undesirable behavior appropriately discouraged by civil liability. Standish and others who are tempted to do similar acts should be deterred. Formally and publicly finding Standish guilty of misconduct and requiring him to pay compensatory damages may discourage such behavior. No scientific guarantee is available for this conclusion. In fact, some psychological studies tend to throw doubt on its validity; but penologists and psychologists have not studied the deterrent effects of civil liability, and the assumption that liability may discourage wrongdoing seems worthy of some respect. That assumption has commanded the respect of courts and seems likely to continue to do so. In any event, the only overall social loss that can be incurred in acting on the assumption is

Stanford L.Rev. 974, 1009 n. 210 (1966). Of course these figures are already out of date. Do they still indicate patterns of consumer wealth?

the disruption resulting from shifting a loss. Liability based on fault works valuable reparative results; if it sometimes also discourages wrongdoing, an over-all social gain is accomplished.

This discussion of fault is closer to traditional legal language than was our discussion of reparation. Though statements can be found in opinions and textbooks that expressly repudiate the ideas stated, statements in judicial opinions to the effect that faulty conduct is an appropriate basis of tort liability are common. When cases like the hypothetical one are litigated, the holdings are consistently for plaintiffs, and the policy of discouraging such wrongdoers as Standish by civil liability is so well accepted that such holdings are to be expected in the future.

Landowner has a tract of unfenced commercial timber. Rancher, in good faith and reasonably believing that he is on his own land, enters Landowner's tract and cuts and removes a few trees, to repair his corral.

The policy reason for giving money to Landowner is the same as the one for compensating the Aldens for their broken window —restoration of the status quo. However, ordinary people about to do sporadic acts in their own interest, who have no reason for suspecting that they are about to act illegally, will not be deterred from undesirable action by tort liability. Since Rancher had no notion that he was violating Landowner's legal rights, he and others so situated may not be discouraged by law from making similar mistakes. People are not likely to be more circumspect than they are when they act in good faith and with due care. "Good faith and due care" are legal argot for honesty and appropriate consideration for others. We are not unaware that, in some settings, the refusal to accept any excuses may raise the level of performance. But this casual case probably does not fall into that class.

Rancher, however, has taken property that belongs to Landowner. If he gives it back his status quo is restored rather than disturbed; he is merely losing the fruits of his mistake. If he pays for what he took, much the same result is reached—money compensation is often a good substitute for specific reparation. This simple result is reached by courts and approved in language of property law; they talk in terms of recognizing Landowner's title, and characterize Rancher's taking as wrongful— not in the sense that it is wayward, but in the sense that it is inconsistent with Landowner's title.[2]

2. See Jeffries v. Hargus, 50 Ark. 65, 6 S.W. 328 (1887); Masters v. Stone, 134 Vt. 529, 367 A.2d 686 (1976).

Had Rancher either intentionally taken Landowner's trees or negligently failed to use care to cut only his own, there would be an additional policy reason for mulcting him in damages. In that case, however, a judgment for no more than the value of timber cut would have no deterring effect, for such a judgment merely requires Rancher to pay for what he got and might give him a bargain that he is eager to make. In most jurisdictions juries are permitted to assess punitive damages, in addition to compensatory damages, against those who commit intentional and oppressive wrongs.[3] If Rancher's expropriation were planned, a punitive damage verdict could have a deterring effect. Unfortunately punitive damages have not been allowed against any defendants whose only fault was mere lack of care.[4]

Jones and Smith are neighbors living on adjoining lots. Jones honestly and reasonably believes that she is standing on her own property when told by Smith that she is over the line, as in fact she is. Jones denies Smith's claim and asserts that she intends to occupy that spot whenever she feels like it.

If Jones has made a passing entry of no real value to herself, she is not enriched at Smith's expense. And since she reasonably and honestly believes that she is on her own land, she is not at fault. Furthermore, Smith has suffered no loss. The policy justifications given above for liability in the window and timber cases are irrelevant. Yet there are two other reasons for the entrant's liability in this case: (1) The boundary dispute should be settled once and for all so that the parties will know their rights in the future and can live in peace; (2) By the law of adverse user, if Jones persists in her claim for a sufficient length of time, Smith will lose title to that part of his property. The pronouncement of judgment in Smith's favor interrupts the period of adverse user and prevents this result. Both of these functions are served by a judgment for nominal damages (6¢ or $1). The judgment should not be for a substantial amount, for there is neither fault to deter nor loss to shift.

Our discussion of this case has followed traditional lines. Courts have long recognized trespass *q. c. f.* as properly used to

---

3. See Nyzio v. Vailancourt, 382 A. 2d 856 (Me.1975) in which a Maine Statute provides for double damages for several kinds of willful trespasses resulting in harm to trees and other physical harms.

4. But see Withers v. Ferrero Constr. Co., 21 Md.App. 550, 320 A.2d 576 (1974), in which a negligent shade-tree cutter had to pay damages for reducing the value of residential property; the judgment was for a sum greatly exceeding the value of the timber cut.

settle boundary disputes and to prevent acquisitions of title by adverse user.[5]

Mammoth Construction Co. makes a contract with the State of Magenta to dig a ship canal which will pass Farmer's modest farm. A hard layer of rock underlies the soil, and the only practical way of digging through involves blasting. Mammoth honestly and reasonably believes that blasting can be done without injury to the farm, and proceeds to do it. The contractor takes every reasonable precaution, but nevertheless a large rock hits Farmer's barn and damages it.

Clearly Farmer has suffered a shock loss which is similar to the Aldens' broken window and Landowner's loss of timber, and compensation for Farmer is desirable. But are there policy grounds for taking money from Mammoth? By assumption Mammoth is not at fault—more careful blasting is not possible. No boundary is in dispute, and no title is threatened by adverse possession.

Nor is Mammoth unjustly enriched at Farmer's expense. True, the loss arose from the prosecution of Mammoth's money-making enterprise; but Mammoth has nothing that belongs to Farmer, and Farmer too is engaged in a money-making enterprise.

Mammoth's liability is not warranted by saying that its acts were the cause of the loss. Digging-a-canal-next-to-a-farm is no more the cause of the injury than farming-next-to-a-canal-construction is the cause of it. The risk does not result from Mammoth's activities alone; the risk is a product of the activities of both parties.

In the last seventy years increasing attention has been paid to risk bearing abilities of enterprisers. The theory advanced is: As between two possible risk bearers, risk should be allocated to the one who can better plan to disperse it. Farmers, as a class, are not so likely to be able to deal effectively with the risk of damage from nearby construction blasting as are contractor-blasters. Most farmers are not subjected to damage by such activities and therefore will make no plans to deal with such losses. Since most farm properties are not subject to damage from blasting, a particular farmer who suffers a blasting loss is not able to raise prices and pass that loss on to the farmer's customers. When blasting damages a farm the farmer is unlikely to be able to take such a loss in stride. On the other hand, contractors planning blasting operations know that they are considering

---

5. A comparable holding in a slightly different problem is found in Maganini v. Coleman, 168 Conn. 362, 362 A.2d 882 (1975).

a chancey venture. Even proper and careful blasting may damage nearby property, and builders appreciate this risk. If they know that they are liable for all blasting damage they do, they can and probably will take steps to carry the risk—such as buying liability insurance or setting up reserves. Once the law is settled against such defendants as Mammoth, financially sound and foresighted contractors will regard the cost of carrying blasting damage risk as one of the costs of operation which should not be ignored in figuring bids. Since all bids tendered will probably reflect this view, the contract price of the canal will include the cost of carrying the risk. The State of Magenta disperses this cost along with the other costs of building the canal by collecting canal tolls or taxes. The dispersed cost is borne without serious dislocation anywhere. Moreover, the law may induce the reduction or prevention of some risks. Of course, a contractor who failed to take known and available safety precautions would be guilty of fault, but saddling the contractor with the burden of the risk even in the absence of fault may induce research and development to discover new safety techniques. Projects may be redesigned to avoid dangers, and some projects may never be undertaken because the cost of this risk makes their total cost too large in relation to the expected benefits of the project. These results are more politic than saddling Farmer with the loss.

Until the last half of the twentieth century, a litigant's special ability to absorb or spread a loss was rarely mentioned in judicial opinions, nor did judges often mention the desirability of inducing faultless enterprises to redouble their safety efforts. Advocates formerly skirted these topics in appellate arguments as unlawyerlike, if not downright irrelevant and prejudicial. Recent developments of new liabilities without fault (to be discussed in later chapters), however, have resulted in professional recognition of these theories.[6] Perhaps this aspect of policy is not mentioned in judicial opinions because well accepted rules of law seem to be sufficient justification for results that are, in

---

6. Perhaps most influential was Traynor, J.'s concurring opinion in Escola v. Coca Cola Bottling Co., 24 Cal.2d 453, 150 P.2d 436 (1944) (a products liability case). An interesting contemporary instance is the opinion handed down by Lord Denning M.R. in the English Court of Appeal in Spartan Steel & Alloys Ltd. v. Martin & Co., [1972] 1 Q.B. 27, 34 (Denying an ingot maker—who recovered some damages against an excavator for negligently interrupting its power supply—a further recovery for a short business interruption which had caused the plaintiff to lose £1,767 [$4,000] in profits, Lord Denning said that such losses are often prevented by standby systems, insurance or programming a short term speed up. None of these social facts were proved, of course; Lord Denning just "knew" them.)

opinion writers' unarticulated views, consonant with good policy. If, however, risk-bearing and risk abatement abilities are to be a major determinant of some tort cases, they (in our opinion) should be openly discussed by judges who take them into account. Judges' assumptions concerning these capacities deserve scrutiny; they may be far from obviously accurate.

Trimmer owns a tall shade tree which is near the boundary of his property. An upper branch dies. It looks unsightly and threatens to fall on his neighbor's house. Trimmer climbs the tree to cut it off. He works amateurishly but carefully, and reasonably supposes that his ropes will guide the branch's fall onto his own property. Fate decrees otherwise and the branch falls through the skylight of neighboring Artist's studio.

Artist has suffered a loss and is as deserving of compensation as any of our hypothetical plaintiffs. But all of the reasons given for taking money from our hypothetical defendants seem inapplicable to Trimmer. Unless some other reason is forthcoming—and we know of none—we conclude that the loss should lie where it has fallen—on Artist.

This does not mean that no one in Trimmer's boots would feel he or she ought to pay. Many who accidentally do harm pay for it, whether they are legally liable or not—out of sympathy, out of a desire to avoid offense, or simply because they are accidentally the authors of harm. But a legal obligation to pay is not necessarily politic. Society has no reason for preferring Artist's economic security over Trimmer's. If Trimmer were held liable, the good done for Artist would be no greater than the harm done to Trimmer, and the energy used in shifting the loss would be wasted.

§ 3. POLICY, DOCTRINE, AND PRECEDENT IN TRESPASS Q. C. F.

The discussion of policy in section two was directed toward what courts *should* do, with passing mention of what courts have decided and are likely to decide in the future. Legal doctrine and precedent influence the decision of cases. The basic principle in the traditional analysis of trespass *q. c. f.* is the unauthorized entry rule: An occupant in possession of land may maintain an action against any intruder who makes an unauthorized entry.

In the newlyweds' window case, the timber case, and the boundary dispute case, the unauthorized entry rule produces the results that are also justified by our policy analysis. In the canal case the uninitiated might have difficulty in finding an entry since no intruder's foot stepped on the plaintiff's soil. The courts have uniformly held, however, that casting a tangible object on land is an entry, and the unauthorized entry rule, so interpreted, calls for the same decision as the one justified by our policy analysis.

The tree trimmer case cannot be so easily brought into line. Our policy analysis calls for judgment for defendant, but the principle calls for judgment for plaintiff. A famous old English case, The Case of the Thorns,[7] decided in the fifteenth century, arose on almost identical facts and was decided for the plaintiff in conformity with the unauthorized entry principle. No authority earlier than 1695 even suggests a contrary result. As late as 1914, in Louisville Ry. Co. v. Sweeney,[8] the claimant asked for compensation for personal injuries in these circumstances: a derailed streetcar uprooted a telephone pole, which fell so that the plaintiff was hurt on her own land. The Kentucky court held, on the unauthorized entry principle, that the transit company was liable without proof of negligence, because (the court said) the defendant trespassed on land. Injuries caused by traffic mishaps have traditionally not resulted in liability without fault (though, of course, proposals for no-fault legislation have borne fruit). A sporadic exception when vehicular force causes harm in a private close makes little sense. This streetcar case has not only been repudiated in Kentucky, but has no contemporary following elsewhere. A Maine court, for example, refused to hold a non-negligent truck driver liable in trespass *quare clausum fregit* for damages to a house when his errant truck left the road, made an unauthorized entry, and knocked a house off its foundation.[9]

One value of a sound policy analysis is that it identifies areas in which a traditional doctrine with some judicial recognition may not be an entirely reliable basis for evaluating claims. If the problem of the tree trimmer case were to arise for the first time today in one of those states whose courts have happened not to pass on it, the court might still be impressed by the holding in The Case of the Thorns, by the many other cases that have followed it, and by the constant judicial reiteration of the unauthorized entry rule. But there are a few modern cases to the contrary. These cases in turn are probably based on the notion that, in the absence of an opportunity to do a positive over-

---

7. Y.B. 6 Edw. 4, f. 7, pl. 18 (1466).

8. 157 Ky. 620, 163 S.W. 739 (1914). Overruled expressly by Randall v. Shelton, 293 S.W.2d 559 (Ky.1956).

9. Hayes v. Bushey, 160 Me. 14, 196 A.2d 823 (1964).

all good, the fact that a defendant's entry has happened to cause a loss is no reason for shifting that loss to the defendant. If a legal researcher suspects the policy soundness of an apparently unqualified principle and a mass of decisions in conformity to it, he or she has reason to believe that further research may lead to some authority favoring a different result. On the other hand, when initial research leads to a line of cases conforming to unquestionably sound policy and to accepted rules as well, extended search for conflicting authority is more likely to be unprofitable.

Even in the face of much adverse authority, a claim or defense based on sound policy usually has some value if the advocate knows how to present the case. Seldom can counsel call on the court to ignore the past and start afresh by righting old wrongs. Judges are hesitant to act as they did in the Maine errant truck case and repudiate traditional doctrine. They are more likely to sidestep undesirable rules either by making significant some unique aspect of the facts, or by reformulating the rule ever so slightly. In Kank Realty Co. v. Brown,[10] the facts were like those in the tree trimmer case, and the court refused to find a trespass. The opinion (1) emphasizes the tree trimmer's motive to safeguard his neighbor's house and (2) reformulates the unauthorized entry rule to forbid only "wrongful or unjustifiable entry." It also cites cases like the one to be discussed next, cases which are arguably not quite in point but were nevertheless some support for its modified version of the rule.

The early cases of trespass *q. c. f.* could have been used to deal with feudal forays. When the unauthorized entry rule was invented for the purpose of holding hostile entrants liable, the judges did not think about emergency entries. When justifiable entries occurred, good sense required some qualification of the rule. For example, in Campbell v. Race,[11] the only road by which a traveler could reach his destination was blocked by snow. He passed over the edge of a landowner's adjoining field without doing any harm. Nevertheless the landowner sued him in trespass. The trial court found against the traveler, probably on the theory that the entry was unauthorized by the occupant. The appellate court reversed and found an "authority in law" to enter. By extending the conception of "authorized entry" to include legal authorizations, the court seemingly kept the principle inviolate and yet flexible enough to reach a politic result.

---

10. 114 Misc. 357, 187 N.Y.S. 556 (1921), aff'd, 198 App.Div. 958, 189 N.Y.S. 946 (1921).

11. 61 Mass. (7 Cush.) 408, 54 Am. Dec. 728 (1851).

The court in the Kank tree trimmer case noted the justice of the privilege to make emergency entries and the courts' recognition of the right to make them. It compared the defendant tree trimmer's lack of fault with the innocence of entrants acting in emergency as partial warrant for its reformulation of the rule and its holding that the tree trimmer was not liable.

Some judicial attempts to avoid the doubtful result of The Case of the Thorns have led to reformulations of the unauthorized entry rule that are worded so that the rule no longer can hold the better risk bearer liable in the absence of fault. An actual case like our canal hypothetical was decided on the unauthorized entry rule for the plaintiff.[12] Since the case was decided in 1849, which was long before the better-risk-bearer theory had modern recognition, the court probably was thinking only along doctrinal lines. But if our policy analysis of the canal case is sound, whatever the court's inspiration, the precedent should be followed. Compare what happened in Texas in 1936 when the court decided Turner v. Big Lake Oil Co.[13] An oil producer maintained a large pond of salt water—an unwanted by-product of its wells. The water escaped and did serious damage to property of a rancher. The jury acquitted the oil producer of negligence. The court repudiated the strict liability of the unauthorized entry rule, and held that no liability results from unintended, non-negligent entries. As long as this change was law some politic uses of liability without fault could not operate in land entry cases. One of the fortunate by-products of the holding is that cases like the tree trimmer case have been held for Texas defendants ever since that decision was entered.

Mr. Chief Justice Cureton's beetle-browed presence and his firm, sweeping repudiation of liability without fault for any unauthorized entry under any circumstances brooked no Texas holding to the contrary from 1936–64. After nearly three decades the memory of Cureton faded, ecology burgeoned, and not surprisingly, in Shronk v. Gilliam,[14] a Texas civil appeals court cut a nick in Big Lake's sweeping principle. The court held that the trial judge did not err when he allowed a farmer to recover without proof of fault for harm to his crops and pasture resulting from the aerial spraying of nearby cotton fields.[15] The day

---

12. Hay v. Cohoes Co., 2 N.Y. 159, 51 Am.Dec. 279 (1849).

13. 128 Tex. 155, 96 S.W.2d 221 (1936).

14. 380 S.W.2d 743 (Tex.Civ.App. 1964).

was won for putting pressure on crop sprayers to develop better techniques for protecting cotton without imperiling other crops.

We can generalize. A simple, single rule (like the unauthorized entry rule) can be applicable to several different kinds of cases involving several unrelated policy problems. Insofar as that rule tends to decide cases well, it is a reliable guide for evaluating claims and an apt tool of advocacy and decisions. Insofar as its meaning is vague, it must be interpreted—and interpretations of courts are often influenced by policy considerations. When the application of a rule results in decisions of doubtful wisdom, such decisions may nevertheless be reached; and when the quantity of decisions increases, precedents tend to father more questionable decisions. But judges may become dissatisfied with tradition; and when they do, respected techniques are available for change. Change is not necessarily advance. The law can deteriorate as well as improve. Sometimes judges remodel a rule to solve one policy problem and change it too drastically, thus increasing the likelihood that some other policy problem will be solved incorrectly. Policy problems may be hard problems. Social science is in its infancy. Human values and goals are far from uniform. Judges have little special training for making policy decisions, and partisan advocacy is not always calculated to throw light on social change. In areas in which men differ on the desirability of legal change, it is not surprising that judges also differ, and that this disagreement is reflected in the technical materials of the law.

15. Of course judges are often influenced by highly respected authority. A victim of crop spraying escaped the unauthorized entry rule in Loe v. Lenhardt, 227 Or. 242, 362 P.2d 312 (1961), because the court was impressed by the unofficial American Law Institute's Restatement of Torts I, § 165.

Chapter III

ASSAULT AND BATTERY, CONSENT, AND DEFENSE OF PERSONS AND PROPERTY

Table of Sections

---

§ 1. ASSAULT AND BATTERY

After the Norman Conquest of England the newly established King's Courts entertained actions of trespass *vi et armis* [with force and arms] for assault and battery. The Crown wrested jurisdiction from manorial and baronial courts on the ground that the misconduct charged was a breach "of the King's peace." In the early cases the courts made no clear distinction between criminal prosecutions and civil suits. After the distinction between crime and tort developed, assault and battery could be prosecuted by the Crown, and the victim could also sue in tort for damages. The second kind of suit is our present topic.

Nowadays one who accidentally and without fault injures another would hardly be called a disturber of the peace; but at one time he or she would have been civilly liable for assault and battery. In the fifteenth century Case of the Thorns,[1] discussed in the preceding chapter, the court said this: "[I]f a man lop a tree, and the boughs fall upon another [man] *ipso invito* [against the defendant's will], yet an action lies. If a man shoot at butts and hurt another unawares, an action lies. . . ." The courts of this period adopted a theory of liability for the harm done by acts, even though those acts were neither intended to harm nor negligently done. If injuries of various types "directly" resulted from an actor's conduct, he or she incurred liability in trespass *vi et armis*.

By 1700, imposition of liability without fault in personal injury cases seemed unjust to the courts.[2]

---

1. Y.B. 6 Edw. 4, f. 7, pl. 18 (1466).   2. See, e.g., Gibbons v. Pepper, 91 Eng.Rep. 922 (1695).

One who unjustifiably slaps, strikes, clubs, stabs, or shoots another commits an assault and battery. Much less spectacular disturbances may also be assaults and batteries.[3]

Battery can be defined as rude and inordinate contact with the person of another. The victim's flesh need not be touched; the prohibition runs against touching the clothes an individual is wearing, striking the cane a person is carrying, or slapping the horse he or she is riding. Battery implies action; those who merely stand in others' way and impede their passage may commit some tort, but they do not commit a battery.

Battery is not limited to serious injuries; those who suffer the indignity of having their coat lapels grabbed or of being spat on may recover. A hostile intent is not always necessary; a battery may be committed by kissing a woman without her consent or vaccinating a child without consent of the child's guardian. Nor need the aggressor intend to hit the person actually struck; under the rule of "transferred intent," an aggressor who wrongfully strikes at one person and hits another is liable to that other.[4]

A greeting-pat on a friend's back or a polite attention-attracting touch on a stranger's arm is no battery. One who shoves another out of the path of an oncoming train or carries another unconscious from danger commits no battery if the rescuer acts with reasonable regard for the rescued person's safety, even though serious injury happens to result.

Assault can be defined as an unjustifiable threat of force sufficient to arouse a well-founded apprehension of immediate harm. Typically an aggressor tries to strike but misses, or withdraws at the last moment. An assault may be committed by aiming a blow at a person, or advancing on a person and threatening a beating, or menacingly pointing a gun at someone. An assaulted plaintiff is given grounds for believing the time has come for self-defense or flight. Insulting words not coupled with an express or implied threat of harm are not an assault, but abusive language may constitute some other tort. Threat to

---

3. See, e.g., Estate of Berthiaume v. Pratt, 365 A.2d 792 (Me.1976); Marshall v. District of Columbia, 391 A.2d 1374 (D.C.App.1978).

4. Carnes v. Thompson, 48 S.W.2d 903 (Mo.1932). Bodily contact caused by fault totally unlike physical attack does not constitute assault and battery. In Madden v. D.C. Transit System, Inc., 307 A. 2d 756 (D.C.App.1973) an allegation of the complaint was as follows: The plaintiff while standing on a public sidewalk was assaulted by fumes and offensive oily substances which defendant permitted to spew from its buses with knowledge that its buses regularly emitted such discharges. Held: The complaint stated no cause of action in assault and battery.

injure in the future may not be an assault; an old case held that a defendant who said, "If it were not assize time, I would run this sword through you," did not commit an assault because his words negated a present intention to harm. An assault cannot be committed over the telephone because the speaker cannot immediately carry out the threats.

If one is close enough to make good a threat in the next moment, a threatener cannot escape liability by showing that he or she was barely out of striking distance. A conditional threat constitutes an assault when the aggressor has no right to impose the condition; a highwayman commits an assault when he says, "Your money or your life." An assault may be committed by wielding an unloaded gun, since reasonable apprehension of harm may be aroused. Assaults are not committed accidentally; the guilty defendant intends either to harm or to frighten.

Most batteries are preceded by an assault. Sometimes the word "assault" is used as an abbreviation of assault and battery, but better usage reserves the term for threatening conduct that may or may not be followed by a battery. A battery without an assault is theoretically possible; a person struck from behind without warning is battered without being civilly assaulted; but both in law and in life this subtlety is of no practical moment.

Some battered plaintiffs suffer severe injuries and receive large compensatory damage judgments to reimburse them for medical bills, loss of wages, on-going disability, and pain and suffering. Other batteries result in neither financial loss nor discomfort. In an assault action a plaintiff rarely proves any damages. Even in modern times, a plaintiff who establishes either an assault or a battery without proving any damages is nevertheless entitled to nominal damages.[5] In most jurisdictions when a plaintiff proves an intentional and over aggressive battery resulting in actual damages, the jury is allowed to enter an additional verdict for punitive damages (damages assessed for the purpose of discouraging the defendant and others from committing similar offenses in the future). When, however, a serious hurt has been proximately caused by a slight excess of force, an award of punitive damages (in addition to a substantial compensatory verdict) has been held improper.[6] Authorities are divided on whether or not punitive damages may be recovered when the victim makes no showing of an appreciable need for compensation. Claims for medical expense or loss of earnings often are not made in battery cases and are almost never made

---

5. Tessier v. LaNois, 98 R.I. 333, 201 A.2d 927 (1964) (per curiam).

6. Wanis v. Zwennes, 364 A.2d 1193 (D.C.App.1976) (per curiam).

in assault cases. Reported cases are scarce because victims suffering no financial loss are seldom willing to go to the expense of litigating their claims. Lawyers will rarely accept such a case if their fee is to be contingent on (and a fraction of) whatever may be recovered. Verdicts are not likely to be large. Defense lawyers are, of course, as knowledgeable as plaintiffs' counsel on the probability of a meager verdict; the claimant's attorneys, therefore, know that no substantial pre-trial settlement will be made, and that a lawyer who accepts such a case will spend valuable time which, at best, will produce only a small fee. Assault and battery clients are rarely willing, even if able, to agree to pay for a lawyer's time on a win-or-lose basis. Perhaps community service lawyers may, at some future time, be willing to pursue some of these claims against wrongdoers guilty of outrageous misconduct.

Policy justifications of liability for assault and battery follow the usual pattern of justifications for liability based on fault. A seriously injured plaintiff is a typically good candidate for reparation. It can be hoped that liability of misbehaving defendants has some deterrent force. Punitive damages may make this force all the more effective. Awards of punitive damages to plaintiffs give them windfalls that may encourage suits against wrongdoing defendants who might escape criminal prosecution. A defendant who is held both criminally and civilly liable may be treated too harshly, since the two kinds of procedures are not coordinated. Many prosecutors are not likely to press criminal charges of assault and battery when civil proceedings are contemplated. Most victims whose attackers are publicly prosecuted exhaust their indignation at the criminal trial.

Compensation in dollars for a battered plaintiff's mental pain and suffering—one of the elements of recoverable damages in some battery cases—is difficult to justify. But the same difficulty inheres in all personal injury suits and extends far beyond the liability for battery.

§ 2. CONSENT

Volenti non fit injuria [one who consents cannot receive an injury] has been a respected legal maxim for centuries. Consent, it is said, is a defense to all charges of battery. But cases and holdings that seem alike may raise different policy problems.

Strong and Wiry meet in a gymnasium and agree to a wrestling bout. Wiry throws Strong and breaks his arm. Wiry intends, of course, to throw Strong, but has no thought of injuring him seriously, and follows all of the rules of the sport.

Strong has suffered a loss; however, to compensate him at Wiry's expense would be impolitic. Had Wiry done the very act he did without Strong's consent to wrestle, his conduct might be faulty; but many intentional physical contacts that are wrong when done without permission become privileged when authorized.

That Strong did not say that Wiry could break his arm is of no legal consequence. Wiry's reasonable acts done with Strong's consent are and should be privileged. Of course if Wiry used the occasion with intent either to injure Strong or dangerously to depart from the rules of the sport, he would be at fault and sound policy would justify liability for damages.

Weak and Warpt are members of a queer fanatical sect which has promulgated the tenet, "Parts of the human body are capable of sin which can be expiated only by amputation." Weak confesses to Warpt that she stole a watch with her right hand and asks Warpt to cut it off. Warpt obliges.

Warpt is guilty of serious fault; she could be convicted of mayhem and sent to the penitentiary. Though Weak may be hard pressed to pay her medical expenses and suffers great financial loss because of her disability, her participation is also serious fault; actions like hers too should be deterred. Were people like Weak given a cause of action for damages, such misconduct might become commoner. Since Warpt can be punished as a criminal, the civil court need not concern itself with her escape from tort liability.

In both of these hypothetical cases, *volenti non fit injuria* calls for a judgment for the defendant. But the policy reasons for denying the plaintiff's claim lie in the strength of the injurer's position in the wrestling case, and in the weakness of the victim's position in the fanatic case. An understanding of this difference will focus attention on important considerations in other kinds of cases.

The *volenti* rule, like most legal principles, has been interpreted, elaborated and qualified. The discussion that follows tells about some of its judicial adventures.

The courts have recognized that the *volenti* rule means no more than it says affirmatively. It says that consent is a defense; it does not say that all unauthorized physical contacts are batteries. If a defendant is justified in touching, shoving, or carrying a person without permission, the action is not a battery.[7]

Courts have held that consent may be implied from acts, as well as expressed by words. When a plaintiff has given the defendant a reasonable impression that he or she authorizes a certain contact, the plaintiff's implied consent has the force of a spoken consent.

These last two points often bear on the practice of medicine. A patient may impliedly authorize chest thumpings and pulse takings without uttering special words of consent. A surgeon acting in an emergency is privileged without consent to perform a drastic procedure on an unconscious or irrational patient, if the surgeon reasonably believes that the operation is immediately needed to save the patient's life or to ward off serious harm. Only when a delay entailed in getting consent will not seriously endanger the patient need the surgeon either wait until the patient can personally give consent or seek the authorization of relatives. A reasonable surgical rescue is treated in the same way as any other kind of reasonable rescue.

On the other hand, unauthorized medical treatment in the absence of an emergency is a battery. Ordinarily doctors who impose treatment without their patients' informed consent are at fault, and their kind of conduct should be discouraged by liability.

Early in our century the courts were in conflict on one kind of medical consent case. In Mohr v. Williams,[8] a patient was anesthetized in pursuance of authority to operate on her right ear. Anesthesia enabled the surgeon to examine the patient's ears more penetratingly than before, and convinced him that her left ear needed unauthorized surgery. He postponed the planned operation and skillfully operated on her left ear. The court held that since there was no emergency, he committed a battery as a matter of law. Had the surgeon conformed to the original plan, he would have given, in his own estimation, inferior treatment. Had he performed no operation until his patient recovered from the anesthetic and consented to the preferable surgery, he would probably have been even more remiss and incurred the wrath of the patient as well. In this dilemma the course of action he followed seems reasonable (unless he should have realized and disclosed to the patient a considerable likelihood that examina-

7. See, e. g., Luka v. Lowrie, 171 Mich. 122, 136 N.W. 1106 (1912), in which a surgeon performed an immediately needed amputation on an unconscious accident victim.

8. 95 Minn. 261, 104 N.W. 12, 111 Am.St.Rep. 462 (1905).

tion under anesthesia might disclose a need for procedures different from those to which the patient had consented). The least the surgeon deserved was a chance to persuade the jury that he had acted reasonably under the circumstances. The court in the similar case of Bennan v. Parsonnet [9] would not even risk leaving the surgeon's fate to the jury, and ruled in his favor as a matter of law. The court said that the law constitutes the surgeon to be the representative of the patient who is anesthetized. The court's implication was that surgeons can give themselves the necessary consent. Thus a sensible result was reached, and the legalistics of the consent requirement were kept intact.

Modern styles of opinion writing are less concerned with legal niceties—but not detached from them. In the 1956 case of Kennedy v. Parrott [10] the appellate opinion dealt more candidly with the realities of unanticipated needs for surgical procedures that become evident after the patient is anesthetized. In the Kennedy case the patient expected an appendectomy. When a proper incision was made, the surgeon discovered ovarian cysts that threatened future serious surgery unless attended to by a simple, prudent puncture. The surgeon, in this situation, would have practiced surgery foolishly if he had not exceeded the patient's consent. The court held that the surgeon was justified in performing the unanticipated, medically correct procedure. The court said, "[O]rdinarily a surgeon is employed to remedy conditions without any express limitation on his authority [and when unanticipated] conditions . . . make consent impractical, it is unreasonable to hold the physician to the exact operation—particularly when it is internal—that his preliminary examination indicated was necessary. . . . Reason is the soul of the law; the reason of the law being changed, the law is also changed."[11] Compare this case to Lloyd v. Kull,[12] in which the surgeon saw a mole on his patient's leg while he was performing an abdominal operation and flicked it off. This bit of precautionary surgery could have been done about as well at a later time and after consultation. The court held this meddlesome therapy constituted an assault and battery.

The medical profession and its legal advisers sought to forestall liabilities for unauthorized treatment by including in hospital admission procedures a requirement that the patient sign a form purporting to authorize both the doctor in charge of the

9. 83 N.J.L. 20, 83 A. 948 (1912).   11. Id. at 360–61, 90 S.E.2d at 758.

10. 243 N.C. 355, 90 S.E.2d 754   12. 329 F.2d 168 (7th Cir. 1964).
   (1956).

patient and other doctors designated by the doctor in charge to perform diagnostic procedures, anesthesia, operations, and other medical or surgical treatments that they believe are either necessary or advisable for the health or well-being of the patient. The patient in the mole-excision case signed such a "boiler plate" consent. The patient sued the surgeon on two counts: first, for malpractice for untoward results of botched abdominal surgery; and second, for the unauthorized removal of the mole. The verdict returned for the surgeon's malpractice in the patient's abdomen was substantial. The jury also returned a $500 verdict for assault and battery committed when the surgeon excised the mole, even though the patient suffered no ill effects from the excision. The boiler plate consents probably discourage some unknowledgeable patients from charging doctors with assault and battery for unauthorized procedures. Formal consent, when not understood and not explained to the patient, is not likely to protect the doctor in modern litigation.[13] When medical procedures are beneficial or cause no real harm, few lawyers would be willing to put much effort into pressing the patient's claim on a contingent fee basis. When, however, careful but unauthorized procedures go sour, the patient's case may prove attractive to a contingent fee lawyer.

　　In the early 1960's the requirement of "*informed* consent" attracted the interest of the plaintiffs' bar. One of the first cases was Natanson v. Kline,[14] brought by a patient who had been subjected to cobalt radiation. This drastic treatment for cancer was appropriate in her case and was properly administered; nevertheless, she suffered terrible consequences. The radiologist testified that even though the treatment was highly desirable, he knew it might result in serious injury. He admitted that he had not explained the risk to the patient. The trial judge refused to rule that the radiologist owed his patient a duty of disclosure. This was held to be error. The case was remanded for a new trial at which the jury would decide what a reasonable radiologist would have disclosed under the circumstances. Recent litigation on what constitutes informed consent and how the issue should be tried has raised ancillary questions resulting in a detailed body of case law that is not always consistent.[15]

---

13. See Sard v. Hardy, 281 Md. 432, 379 A.2d 1014 (1977); Sauro v. Shea, 390 A.2d 259 (Pa.Super.1978).

14. 186 Kan. 393, 350 P.2d 1093 (1960).

15. See the detailed discussion of lines of authority in Sard v. Hardy, 281 Md. 432, 379 A.2d 1014 (1977). Cf., Starnes v. Taylor, 272 N.C. 386, 158 S.E.2d 339 (1968), in which perfunctory warning of remote risks was held sufficient to show negligence by the physician.

Fights by mutual consent have had a special history. A fight in dead earnest is different from the sport of boxing; brawlers break the peace and are wrongdoers. These fight cases seem, at first glance, analogous to the hypothetical fanatic case; but many courts have allowed an injured fighter to recover in an assault and battery action brought against an antagonist.[16] The opinions circumvent the *volenti* doctrine by stating that unlawful consent is no consent. If courts consistently took this view, many other kinds of plaintiffs who are also so seriously at fault could maintain assault and battery actions. In most of the other kinds of cases in which the plaintiff has been a guilty participant in wrongdoing, however, the plaintiff does not succeed and judges do not mention the legalism that unlawful consent is no consent. Fifty years ago a woman who had consented to sexual intercourse could not maintain a battery action against the man who seduced her.[17] Judges avoided saying that her unlawful consent was no consent, and in its place said that courts would not come to the aid of a wrongdoer whose misconduct resulted in injury.[18]

Some courts (probably a minority) apply this party-to-the-crime rule to fight cases and deny recovery to the vanquished.[19] At first blush this result may seem to be the more politic holding —since both parties are at fault, the plaintiff deserves deterrence as much as does the defendant. But in our opinion, a procedural accident makes the majority view the better. If consent does not bar the vanquished from bringing an assault and battery action, then the victor too has an action for the vanquished's threatening conduct or blows. The victor-defendant can assert this legal claim in the same lawsuit by filing a cross-action. Then the jury can be authorized to find a verdict for each litigant against the other, and the vanquished is almost sure to receive a net judgment smaller than full compensation. Such a judgment leaves each party a financial loser; the victor is required to pay something and the vanquished is not fully compen-

See also, Sauro v. Shea, 390 A.2d 259 (Pa.Super.1978), and other Pennsylvania cases cited therein.

16. See, e. g., McNeil v. Mullin, 70 Kan. 634, 79 P. 168 (1905).

17. See Oberlin v. Upson, 84 Ohio St. 111, 95 N.E. 511 (1911). She could, however, in those days get judgment in contract action for "breach of promise" to marry (an action then universally recognized, and seldom mentioned now). In

that kind of suit she could prove seduction to enhance damages.

18. Many people now think that sexual intercourse between consenting unmarried adults is a private matter of no concern to the public. Such an attitude is, of course, inconsistent with viewing "seduction" as a tort, or consent as "*particeps criminis*."

19. Cf., Hart v. Geysel, 159 Wash. 632, 294 P. 570 (1930).

sated. This is better than turning the victor scot free. Our analysis may be subtle, and in actuality the majority view may not always work out so neatly. In jurisdictions following the majority view, defense counsel who sees the worth of a cross-action preserves a chance to argue for a reduced net recovery and forestalls the jury's attempt to compensate the plaintiff fully at the defendant's expense.[20]

Another chance to give weight to policy factors occurs in a different kind of case. Though an adult woman does not usually have a good tort claim against her seducer, she will have one if the seducer knows he is diseased, does not disclose it, and infects her. The courts hold that she is not barred because the seducer has, without her consent, subjected her to a risk of harm of which he had knowledge and of which she was ignorant. The seduced plaintiff, who was herself at fault, nevertheless recovers compensation for the infection. Discouragement of conduct like his is more to be desired than discouragement of conduct like hers. Since the court must either compensate her or allow him to escape liability, the former is a better result. This comparative fault reasoning has been adopted by courts in such cases.[21] (Later discussion will show, however, that courts do not seize every opportunity to favor the lesser of two wrongdoers in all tort cases in which both parties are at fault. Comparative fault reasoning has had effect only in restricted areas of the common law of torts, and, more important for the present, has been applied only sporadically in cases of faulty consenting plaintiffs.)

Holdings in some statutory rape cases are in conflict. In Bishop v. Liston,[22] a seventeen-year old girl brought an assault and battery action against her fifty-year old seducer. A Nebraska statute provided that carnal knowledge of a girl under eighteen, even with her consent, was a crime. The plaintiff recovered judgment. The court inaccurately opined, "The statute says that up to a certain age [female children] are incapable of giving consent to the violation of their persons."[23] The court concluded that consent in fact was not consent in law, that therefore the *volenti* doctrine was inapplicable, and the seducer was liable.

20. The majority view was applied in McNeil v. Mullin, 70 Kan. 634, 79 P. 168 (1905).

21. For an example of express judicial statement see DeVall v. Strunk, 96 S.W.2d 245 (Tex.Civ. App.1936).

22. 112 Neb. 559, 199 N.W. 825 (1924).

23. Id. at 563, 199 N.W. at 827.

The Nebraska case was decided in 1924 by judges whose attitudes on sex were formed at the turn of the century. The girl's outraged (or greedy) family probably shared these same values. If the fifty-year old defendant had a deep pocket, the jury probably wanted to make his adventure costly. If the girl suffered no physical harm, damages in such a case must be assessed on a punitive rather than a compensatory basis. A judgment for the girl pays her cash for abandoning her "virtue." Comparative fault reasoning is clumsy in a case in which the plaintiff has suffered no financial loss, since a punitive damage judgment for her will be a financial windfall. Perhaps in 1924 many seventeen-year old girls were less knowing than they are now. Jurors nowadays probably would be unlikely to be generous with a willing plaintiff in a case like Bishop v. Liston. The claim against so mature a defendant as this fifty-year old man then may have had a sizeable hushmoney value. This seems to us to be all the more reason for favoring those authorities that leave this kind of problem where the legislature put it—in the legal processes of the criminal law. The statute does not say what the court says it says; the statute does not say that girls under eighteen must be treated as though they had not consented when they sue in tort; it defines a crime and is silent on the subject of civil liability. In a similar New York case,[24] the court held against the girl and said that it was one thing for society to protect itself, it was another to hold that such a plaintiff was to be rewarded.

Of course when the girl in a statutory rape case is in fact too young to understand what she is about, her words of consent should not constitute consent in law. In such a case she is not at fault and the man who abuses her is. She may have suffered serious but unprovable psychiatric trauma. A heavy award of damages even though entirely "punitive" seems called for.

A youth's consent to surgery presents problems. A surgeon who does a major operation on a child without consent of his or her guardian is at fault. Surgeons should be discouraged from depriving parents of their opportunity to exercise parental judgment. A child who consents on the advice of a surgeon is either innocent of fault or guilty of trivial fault. The adult surgeon should carry the responsibility of getting proper consent. Courts have generally held that an unemancipated minor's unratified consent will not protect the surgeon from liability.[25]

24. Barton v. Bee Line, Inc., 238 App.Div. 501, 265 N.Y.S. 284 (1933). See also, Braun v. Heidrich, 62 N.D. 85, 241 N.W. 599 (1932).

25. At just what age a child becomes old enough to consent is in some doubt; the cases for the most part involve children of obvious immaturity. In Bonner v.

The need for parental consent when a youth is treated for venereal disease presents a special problem. If a doctor to whom such a patient applies for treatment is subject to extended liability in the absence of parental consent, the diseased youth may be unwilling to seek out competent medical attention. To reassure those physicians whose fear of liability might deter them from proceeding without parental consent some legislatures have adopted special statutes. On December 1, 1971, a Pennsylvania act was passed that provided that if a minor consents to treatment for venereal disease, approval of his or her parents is not necessary and any physician who properly administers appropriate treatment shall not be liable.

The *volenti* rule privileges not only physical contact with persons; it applies also to entries on land and use of chattels. An invited guest does not commit a trespass by entering the host's house; a lender of a watch has no claim of conversion against the borrower who abides by the conditions of the loan.

Sometimes disputes arise over property rights in which a defendant who acts in conformity to consent nevertheless repudiates the authority which the consenter has attempted to give. For example, in Strang v. Russell,[26] the owner of a lagoon told a boater that he might cruise on it whenever he wished. The boater spurned the offer and said he would use the lagoon at his own pleasure because he had the right to do so. The owner brought a trespass action against the boater. The court properly viewed the owner's consent as irrelevant and tried the title dispute. Had the boater acquiesced in the owner's consent, his acquiescence would have been an implied admission provable against him as tending to show that he had no valid claim of title. Were the boater trying to mature a right by adverse user,

---

Moran, 75 U.S.App.D.C. 156, 126 F.2d 121 (1941), a fifteen-year old consented to a skin graft for the benefit of his cousin. The jury found that the child appreciated the nature and consequences of the operation. The court held, nevertheless, that the surgeon was liable. The language of the court indicates a distaste for any non-emergency surgery on a minor without parental consent, but the court was particularly concerned with this operation which was primarily for the benefit of another. In Bishop v. Shurly, 237 Mich. 76, 211 N.W. 75 (1926), the court held that a nineteen-year old was old enough to consent to the use of a local anesthetic in an operation authorized by his parent, even though the parent had specifically forbidden the local anesthetic and had arranged for a general anesthetic. There is a split of authority on the effect of the consent of a temporary custodian. Such consent was held adequate in Bakker v. Welsh, 144 Mich. 632, 108 N.W. 94 (1906). Contra, Moss v. Rishworth, 222 S.W. 225 (Tex.Com. App.1920).

26. 24 N.Z.L.R. 916 (1904).

his acquiescence would have interrupted the period of adverse use.

§ 3. SELF–DEFENSE

Early common law courts did not recognize self-defense as a justification for inflicting injury. A slayer who killed in self-defense was sent to death unless the Crown pardoned him. This position was, of course, repudiated centuries ago and in both criminal and civil cases courts have long allowed pleas of self-defense.[27]

The basic legal principle is: Those who reasonably believe that they are unwarrantedly attacked have a privilege to protect themselves, using only the force that a reasonable person would use under the circumstances. This principle is a general rule recognizing that appropriate self-defense does not result in liability. The rule points in the direction of proper decisions; it calls on courts to determine whether or not a defendant who claims the privilege was free from fault. But the rule does not itemize either the facts that justify use of self-defending force or the kinds of force that the self-defender may use. Cases may be submitted to a jury which will then have to decide (1) what, in fact, the defendant did, and (2) whether this conduct was what it should have been.

The courts have, however, developed specialized rules for various recurring types of self-defense cases. These rules supply more definite criteria of the propriety of some self-defenders' acts. Some examples of such rules are: Force calculated to wound or kill can be used only if the self-defender reasonably fears, and is trying to ward off, severe bodily injury or death.[28] Even then, a defender may have to retreat rather than use such force. Defenders may stand their ground in their dwellings and perhaps in other close personal premises, but otherwise they must retreat rather than use deadly or wounding force if an avenue of retreat is known or should have been known to them. (This rule was rejected in many western states by judges who shared the pioneers' views on honor and cowardice. In those states, self-defenders may stand their ground and oppose force with reasonable counterforce.) When an attack is repulsed and

---

27. The defendant who pleads self-defense has the burden of proving it. Stephens v. Dixon, 30 Md.App. 56, 351 A. 187 (1976).

28. Keep v. Quallman, 68 Wis. 451, 32 N.W. 233 (1887). The simplicity of nineteenth century and early twentieth century cases, which could be appealed and reported in those days, make some of them exceptionally valuable in this and the next section. For a later authority see Davis v. Freels, 583 F. 2d 337 (7th Cir. 1978).

the danger past, the self-defender's privilege to use force ends.[29] This last rule is sometimes called "the excessive beating rule."

These more specialized rules can cut down the scope of jury inquiry and, on occasion, preclude jury submission entirely. If, in a court following the eastern rule, the proof clearly established that an obviously safe avenue of retreat was open to a defendant who nevertheless shot the attacker, the trial judge can direct the jury to find the defendant guilty of assault and battery; or, if the proof raises doubt as to whether or not a reasonable person in the defendant's position would have known that he or she could retreat in safety, that issue can be expressly submitted to a jury. This jury's instructions will foreclose the question of whether or not self-defenders may stand their ground; the jury will be told expressly that the defendant was not privileged to do so. Of course jurors sometimes do not understand their instructions and sometimes accidentally or intentionally ignore them.

The workings of the privilege of self-defense are justified from a policy viewpoint when a defendant is exonerated; defendants not guilty of fault are not held liable. The rules of law orient the judicial process to trial of the issue of the defendant's fault.

When the law of self-defense imposes liability on a defendant who has exceeded the privilege of self-defense, a more difficult policy problem is posed. The law of self-defense was developed in criminal courts and taken over as an apt analogy in tort cases. A self-defender who uses force when none was justified or who uses unreasonably drastic force merits criminal punishment. But in a tort case for battery where the defense of self-defense is raised, the plaintiff is not in the position of the state dealing with a breach of the peace; the plaintiff is an aggressor who is clearly at fault. Such a claimant may be an undeserving candidate for compensation. Of course, the defendant may file a cross-action against the plaintiff-attacker and lay the ground-work for cutting down the plaintiff's net recovery. This may leave both parties bearing part of the loss and may tend to deter each kind of fault. But a plaintiff guilty of serious fault, who complains that the defendant made an error in judgment and dealt with the plaintiff too drastically, may be undeserving of even partial compensation. Though we know of no case in which courts have done so, comparative fault reasoning could be used to justify judgment for the self-defender in such a case.

---

29. McKenna v. May, 134 Vt. 145, 353 A.2d 359 (1976).

Perhaps would-be litigants have sensed that judges and jurors do not deal generously with plaintiffs guilty of serious fault; few of them have enough gall to bring civil actions for damages.

Sometimes courts may have a chance to refuse to classify some cases of resisted aggression as self-defense cases. Suppose Bellicose advances on Quiet, saying, "Quiet, put up your fists; I'm going to knock the living daylights out of you." Quiet meets this threat with a quick blow on the point of Bellicose's chin, and Bellicose goes down. Bellicose then stands and staggers, obviously *hors de combat*. Nevertheless, the aroused Quiet delivers a second blow that breaks Bellicose's nose. Bellicose brings an assault and battery action claiming damages for the broken nose.

Quiet was privileged to deliver the first blow in self-defense; Bellicose is suing for the damage done by the second blow, and claims no damages for harm done by the first. Under the excessive beating rule, Quiet is liable for the damage done by the second blow; Quiet exceeded the privilege of self-defense. A cross-action for Bellicose's original assault may reduce Bellicose's recovery. But is there any way to present Quiet's case within the framework of rules already discussed protecting Quiet from any liability?

The facts of the case are stated against a background of defense law, and engrossment with that context may blind Quiet's lawyer to another possibility. Counsel could argue that Bellicose's invitation to do battle amounted to an implied consent to a fight to the finish. This alternative classification would do Quiet no good in the jurisdictions in which consent to fight is held to be no defense; but in those jurisdictions in which consent to fight bars recovery, the alternative classification will preclude holding Quiet liable. In these jurisdictions the excessive beating rule has not been repudiated. These courts, then, accidentally have a choice of classification. If Quiet's counsel can persuade the trial judge to call the case as a consent case, the judge may direct a verdict for Quiet. If Bellicose's lawyer can persuade the trial judge to call the case as an excessive beating case, a directed verdict for Quiet becomes improper, and Bellicose will get the case to the jury. Of course, in either event the appellate court may reclassify and decide that the trial judge erred.

The lesson to be learned from Bellicose v. Quiet is that the body of the law is not always consistent. Inconsistencies sometimes leave courts with a choice, a choice that may be exercised with crucial effect on the outcome of litigation. A good advocate develops skill in discovering opportunities to cross doctrinal lines and does not assume that the first approved rules he or she finds are the only applicable rules that judges respect.

§ 4. PROTECTION OF PROPERTY

The formal principle recognizing the privilege to use self-help to thwart intrusion on land or seizure of chattels is much like the principle approving self-defense; "force reasonable under the circumstances" is the phrase often found in judges' opinions generalizing on the privilege. Severe harm inflicted on wrong-doers for the protection of property is, however, often held to be too drastic, and the courts have developed rules limiting privileged self-help in some kinds of property protection cases to the use of force calculated not to wound or kill.

At early common law when an intruder on land injured by forceful removal brought an action of assault and battery against a land occupant, the ejector's defense of privileged self-help was raised by a plea of *molliter manus imposuit* [he laid his hands on gently]. Gentleness is hardly to be expected from a person "bouncing" an obdurate trespasser; it is not in fact required by the courts.

Occupants are privileged to lead, pull, carry, or push intruders off of their outlying premises (as distinguished from their dwellings and close environs). Should occupants push intruders down, kick them out, or drop them hard, occupants may have used unreasonable and therefore unprivileged force. Even when intruders resist simple ejective force, or when occupants lack sufficient strength or courage to use simple effective force, occupants are not privileged to use wounding force to eject. If occupants intentionally wound or kill they clearly overstep their privilege; and they may overstep it even with a less violent ejectment. Should an intruder go on the offensive, the occupant's privilege of self-defense comes into play and may justify steps more drastic than could be used merely to protect property. There are occasions on which the privileged self-help is too mild to do the job of removing the intruder from outlying premises; then the occupant who does not look to the courts or to public officers for help runs a risk of liability to the intruder.[30]

Extreme measures may be reasonable when taken to protect an occupied dwelling from violent intruders who may injure the

30. See the old leading case of Mc-Ilvoy v. Cockran, 9 Ky. (2 A.K. Marsh.) 271 (1820), in which a land occupant exceeded his privi-lege when he beat and seriously injured a trespasser who was breaking down a fence on outlying property.

occupants. A householder can use reasonable force under the circumstances and may be justified in inflicting severe injury or killing. The law, however, puts a high value on human life and limb, and a householder irked by annoying visitors had better not resort to deadly force.[31] An intruder may, of course, be liable in a cross-action for trespass.

Some intruding animals may be shot to prevent mischief on outlying property. Shooting a dog worrying poultry or sheep is often reasonable and therefore privileged. Circumstances taken into account include the known or probable value of the dog as well as the value of the property threatened. A special consideration bears on defense against trespassing cattle, horses, and other livestock. In Ford v. Taggart,[32] the court held that a farmer was not privileged to shoot a trespassing mule caught trampling his crops, and was liable to the owner for its value. For centuries the common law has afforded an effective remedy for damages perpetrated by stray livestock; the trespassing animals may be impounded until their owner pays for the damage they have done. Since the occupant has this remedy, destructive force is ordinarily unreasonable.

Reasonable force under the circumstances may normally be used to thwart a wrongful appropriation of chattels; but killing or wounding is usually held reasonable only to thwart a heinous crime. The traditional attitude privileged wounding force to prevent theft; there is, however, a growing view that since life is more precious than property, the privilege should be narrower. If a misappropriation is not a crime or is only a misdemeanor, force calculated to kill or wound is not privileged.[33]

Once a chattel has been grabbed, some self-help may be used to retake the property if the owner acts immediately and prudently. This privilege to use self-help cloaks the owner as long as he or she is in "fresh pursuit";[34] but the owner may not stop and go about other business without losing this privilege. An owner of a chattel who delivers it over without duress or fraud is not privileged to use force to retake it, even though the receiver threatens to damage or destroy it.[35]

---

31. See McKenna v. May, 134 Vt. 145, 353 A.2d 359 (1976).

32. 4 Tex. 492 (1849).

33. The holding and opinion in Curlee v. Scales, 200 N.C. 612, 158 S. E. 89 (1931), is informative.

34. See Hodgeden v. Hubbard, 18 Vt. 199, 46 Am.Dec. 167 (1846).

35. Kirby v. Foster, 17 R.I. 437, 22 A. 1111 (1891). Compare footnote 36, infra.

If chattels are deposited without the owner's fault on land of an innocent third party, a peaceful entry to retrieve them is not a trespass—the law authorizes such an entry. Such an entry can be made even though the owner is not in fresh pursuit.

Policy factors involved in the protection of property are much like those bearing on self-defense. The law is designed to set limits on proper self-help, and does a good job of it. Those who stay within the scope of the privileges are not at fault, and even when they happen to injure they should not incur liability. Those who exceed these limits are at fault, and their kind of conduct should be discouraged. In these cases, however, an injured plaintiff is usually also guilty of fault. Again, a cross-action can be filed against claimants who have themselves committed torts, and the jury can be given an opportunity to enter verdicts allowing these plaintiffs less than full compensation. Some intruders or expropriators may be guilty of misconduct so gross that no court should be willing to permit any recovery in their favor; in these cases some defendants will be protected by privileges afforded by the rules—for attack on a dwelling or felonious theft of chattels may be repelled by reasonable force even in some cases though severe injury is inflicted.

Mechanical devices are occasionally used to protect property. Such simple artifices as barbed wire, broken glass mounted on walls, and so forth, may be used in customary ways and places without subjecting the occupant to liability for the scratches and cuts they inflict.[36] The electrified fence has not yet been considered by the courts. Its effectiveness in controlling cattle at low cost is impressive; if and when it threatens serious injuries to persons, liability may attach to its use. Spring guns and man traps are unreasonable protective measures under most circumstances; too often they get the wrong person. The courts say, "One may not do indirectly what he could not do directly," and they hold liable spring gun setters whose devices inflict wounds that they would not be privileged to inflict if they were present. But the principle is not properly reversible: spring gun setters will be held liable for some wounds they would have been privileged to inflict in person. An intruder intent on murder may be repulsed from a dwelling with deadly force, either in person or by spring gun. Moreover, an occupant who *erroneously* but reasonably believes that an intruder intends to murder may use deadly force in person. Spring gun setters who wound mere

---

36. See Quigley v. Clough, 173 Mass. 429, 53 N.E. 884 (1899), in which Oliver Wendell Holmes Jr. wrote the opinion holding a corner lot owner privileged to use barbed wire to discourage short cuts through his lawn.

trespassers, however, cannot justify such wounds on the irrelevant ground that they would have made the same reasonable mistake had they been present in person.[37] Even a criminal trespasser may be allowed damages against a spring gun setter who inflicts serious bodily injury on a petty wrongdoer. In a recent Iowa case, the owner of an unoccupied furnished house, remotely situated, became exasperated by petty marauders' break-ins, and set a spring gun. His victim, a hobbyist looking for old bottles, was seriously injured and recovered a $30,000 judgment.[38]

§ 5. DESTRUCTION OR USE OF PROPERTY TO PREVENT DISASTER

Private property is sometimes destroyed in the public interest. For example, spread of fire may be fought by dynamiting a building. The blast is usually set by public servants—firemen acting under orders of their chiefs or fire marshals. When destruction is reasonable under the circumstances, the dynamiters are, of course, not at fault. Nor are those whose property is saved unjustly enriched. They are not enriched at all: they have merely escaped impoverishment, and possess nothing that belongs to someone else. True, property situated in the path of the oncoming fire has been saved and it might otherwise have been lost. The problem is, who should bear the loss occasioned by destruction of the building? Most courts hold that the municipality is not liable and its servants are not liable unless they acted unreasonably.[39]

At first blush the municipality seems to be the better risk bearer; spread of sacrifice through taxation seems better than saddling the owner of the dynamited building with the loss. Nearly all improved urban real property, however, is insured. Property owners can usually settle claims with their own insurance companies more easily than with strangers liable to them in tort. Insurance policies deal in advance with the obligations of the parties and channel terms and techniques for settling losses. The insurance company and its policy holder have previously dealt with each other voluntarily and have some stake in getting along in the future. An insuring property owner can calculate the amount of protection needed and pay for just that protection. Advance planning to meet liabilities for damage to other

---

37. See Grant v. Hass, 31 Tex.Civ. App. 688, 75 S.W. 342 (1903).

38. Katko v. Briney, 183 N.W.2d 657 (Iowa 1971).

39. But see Bishop & Parsons v. Macon, 7 Ga. 200, 50 Am.Dec. 400 (1849), holding the city liable.

people's property is more difficult. A city cannot know how much reserve to set up or how much liability insurance to buy, and claims against it cannot be settled as simply as property insurance claims are usually settled. If the city is held liable, in all probability an insurance company will be subrogated to the owner's claim to the extent that it has paid the loss. This should reduce insurance rates but increase taxes. Taxpayers as a class are approximately the same people as those who pay fire insurance premiums. If the insurer is reimbursed from tax coffers, the ultimate burden will fall on the same people who will also have to pay the cost of shifting the loss. Non-liability of the municipality seems to be the more politic result.[40]

Courts have long recognized "the rule of necessity," which is: private individuals have the right to use property of others to save life or more valuable property. In the classic case of Ploof v. Putnam,[41] a boater alleged that he and his wife were caught in a tempest while sailing and tried to save themselves by mooring to a dock, but the dock owner cast them off and they were injured. The court held that these facts stated a cause of action under the rule of necessity. The rule modifies ideas of absolute ownership and recognizes a duty of sociality; it points to another variety of legal fault, and the holding in the Ploof case results in just liability for injuries caused by conduct that tort law holds impermissible.

A more difficult problem of policy arises in cases in which a property owner sues for the damage done by the imperiled person. When liability-for-acts was in vogue the courts did not hesitate to hold defendants liable in these cases. In the 17th century case of Gilbert v. Stone,[42] the defendant sought to justify his theft of the plaintiff's horse on the ground that he acted under orders of a gang that threatened him with death if he disobeyed. The court held his plea stated no defense.

In the twentieth century case of Vincent v. Lake Erie Transportation Co.,[43] a cargo vessel docked at the plaintiff's wharf; a storm came up and the ship's captain, exercising good seaman-

---

40. In the absence of an express provision courts have held that ordinary fire insurance covers the risk of destruction by civil authorities to prevent the spread of fire. Some fire insurance policies have expressly provided *for* such coverage. See W. Vance, Insurance (3 ed. 1951), 872. An interesting Texas statute provides for municipal liability, but sets up a procedure in which an insured claimant may be able to recover only for loss in excess of the insurance coverage. Vernon's Ann.Tex.Civ. St. art. 1070.

41. 81 Vt. 471, 71 A. 188, 130 Am. St.Rep. 1072 (1908).

42. 82 Eng.Rep. 539 (1648).

43. 109 Minn. 456, 124 N.W. 221 (1910).

ship, kept her fast even though the ship was battering the wharf. The majority opinion said that the captain was not at fault, but nevertheless held him liable on the ground that he had deliberately saved the ship at the expense of the dock owner. Perhaps this opinion justifies liability; under our property system, even if we may be willing to pardon a Jean Valjean who steals bread to feed his starving family, we still recognize his obligation to pay for the loaves taken. In a sense the mariner in the Vincent case "consumed" the dock. But the ship owner was not enriched; he merely escaped impoverishment. It will cost money to shift the loss to him, and the court enunciates no forward-looking justification for the shift. The ship owner is not the superior risk bearer; if either he or the wharfinger sets up reserves to cover such a loss, the cost will probably eventually be passed on to consumers served by shipping. Shipping costs will probably reflect either increased wharfage or increased freight rates.

A justification for liability may possibly be brought to light by comparing the Vincent case to Cordas v. Peerless Transportation Co.[44] In the Cordas case, a pursued armed bandit jumped into a taxi-cab and ordered the driver to get going. The driver started the cab, shifted into neutral, suddenly slammed on his brakes to throw the bandit off-balance, and leaped out. The cab veered onto the sidewalk and injured a pedestrian. The court held the driver was not liable to the pedestrian in spite of the great likelihood that the driver's intentional act, done in a congested downtown locale, would cause injury and was done to save his own hide.

The cab case differs from the dock case in several ways. The cab driver's conduct was fraught with only a possibility of injury; the ship captain's conduct was sure to injure the dock. The cab driver had much less time for deliberation than did the mariner. Another distinction may, however, have great significance. If the wharfinger could not hold the mariner responsible, he might have been tempted to cut the ship loose and risk liability for whatever harm might befall the ship or crew. That risk might not materialize; if the ship happened to weather the storm without damage, the dock owner would then incur no liability. He was sure that his dock would be harmed if the ship remained fast. But if he were assured of compensation for damage to the dock, he would have no incentive to cast the ship loose. In the cab case, however, the pedestrian could do nothing

44. 27 N.Y.S.2d 198 (N.Y. City Ct. 1941).

to impede the cab driver from executing his plan of escape. No promise of compensation is needed to affect the pedestrian's behavior; he need not be given assurance of compensation to encourage cooperation.

There is not one shred of language in judicial opinions showing awareness of the distinction we have just made. But decisions in actual cases seem to conform to it. Many cases in which cooperative conduct should be encouraged are decided for the plaintiff; many of those in which the plaintiff could not have impeded the defendant are decided for the defendant. This may be pure accident. It may be the result of subconscious or inarticulated judicial recognition of the difference. Perhaps our hypothesis biases our classification of the holdings.

In the Vincent case the court said, "The record in this case fully [substantiates] that in holding the vessel fast to the dock, those in charge of her exercised good judgment and prudent seamanship." If those exercising that judgment know that they must pay for the resulting harm to the dock, they might do even better. The opinion in the Vincent case says nothing about liability sharpening the ship captain's judgment. Modern developments of liability without fault for manufacturers of unsafe, defective products might be influential when a case similar to Vincent is next considered.

If, however, newly enacted statutory liability without fault runs from motorists to pedestrians, there is no good reason for exempting a taxicab's insurer from liability to an injured sidewalk user in a case like Cordas.

Time marches on.

Chapter IV

NEGLIGENCE—THE SUBSTANTIVE LAW AND THE JURY CHARGE

Table of Sections

---

§ 1. THE SUBSTANTIVE LAW OF NEGLIGENCE

Discussion now turns to a great variety of cases which were tried at common law as actions of trespass on the case for negligence—cases in which a defendant is charged with unintentionally but carelessly injuring a plaintiff's person or property.[1]

In negligence cases defendants are liable, theoretically, only if they have been at fault. Juries may illicitly depart from the fault theory, and courts have adopted some doctrines that may be squared with the fault theory only with difficulty. Later discussion will deal with defendants whose negligence is a formal or legalistic, but not a factual failure to use due care. When defendants in fact at fault are held liable for damage negligently done, the policy justifications for liability based on fault discussed in previous chapters may be applicable. We should be skeptical, however, about the deterrent effects of holding individual defendants liable for damages that result from momen-

---

1. Trespass on the case was *not* a variety of trespass *vi et armis* (discussed in Chapters II and III). It was an independent form of action that lay not only for negligent injury, but also for many other kinds of harms not now up for discussion, two of the most important of which were deceit (Chapter XI) and defamation (Chapter XII). It sometimes overlapped with tres-pass *vi et armis*; at one time either form of action lay when careless conduct resulted in "direct" injury to persons or property. If an injury was "consequential" then only trespass on the case would lie. Procedural reforms have wiped out most, if not all, of the importance of this medieval subtlety.

43

tary and sporadic clumsy acts that are human lapses of non-angelic men and women.[2] Of course many negligent acts are so inconsiderate of others that their characterization as fault is natural enough; liability for them may be as effectively deterrent as is liability for more dastardly deeds.

The nineteenth century American courts, almost inadvertently, backed into the affirmative policy of liability for negligence. The judiciary was eager to avoid liabilities for personal and property damages resulting from reasonably careful commercial and traffic activities; once the judicial tradition of characterizing carelessness as fault arose, common law judges did not question the suitability of basing defendants' legal liability on negligence and of debarring contributorily negligent plaintiffs from recovering judgments for damages.

Traditional analyses of negligence suits divide the plaintiff's case into four elements. Plaintiff may recover only if (1) the defendant was under a *duty* to the plaintiff to use due care, (2) the defendant was guilty of a *breach* of that duty, (3) the plaintiff has suffered *damages,* and (4) the breach of the duty *proximately caused* those damages. The subject of this chapter is the second element—what constitutes a breach of a duty to use due care? For present purposes we shall assume (inaccurately) that everyone has a duty to use due care all the time; later on, challenges to this assumption will be discussed. Discussion of proximate cause is also postponed. Damages, too, will be discussed in more detail at later junctures, but two aspects of damages in negligence cases should be quickly stated at the outset: (1) Plaintiffs who establish neither personal injury nor property damage cannot recover in an action for negligence—nominal damages are never assessed; (2) Plaintiffs who establish only negligence (as distinguished from reckless or willful misconduct) are never entitled to punitive damages, even if they prove personal injury or property damages.

The orienting legal principle of the law of negligence is the reasonably-prudent-person doctrine: One whose conduct is not as careful as a reasonably prudent person's conduct would be in like circumstances is guilty of negligence.

The word "prudent" is well chosen when the issue tried is the plaintiff's contributory negligence; claimants who have impru-

---

2. This does not mean that enterprisers who incur responsibility for the negligence of their servants (see p. 251, infra) do not try to reduce risks. They can (1) select and train their workers with the aim of reducing accidents; (2) replace or retain their employees whose safety records show a proneness to hurt others; (3) supply or redesign equipment so as to reduce negligent injuries.

dently failed to look out for themselves are sometimes barred by their own imprudence. But the word is slightly mischosen when a defendant's care is at issue. "Prudent person" tends to call to mind Benjamin Franklin, savings accounts, and the use of the ends of candles. The law of negligence has little to do with thrift; a motorist who cannot afford a Cadillac may nevertheless own and drive one with due care. Defendants use due care when they act with the well-being of others in mind—when they act as reasonably *considerate* individuals. This way of putting it may sound a little too soft; sometimes reasonable considerateness is almost no consideration. In some circumstances individuals may look out for themselves even though they imperil others; in this sense a defendant is entitled to be prudent, rather than over-considerate. A more accurate phrase that courts sometimes use is "the reasonably careful and prudent person," for which "reasonably prudent person" is the accepted abbreviation.[3]

Courts have concerned themselves with the relationship between negligence and foreseeability of harm. Some preliminary analysis may make this relationship clearer. Negligent conduct always is dangerous conduct. Danger is a *tendency* to cause harm. Dangerous acts sometimes do no harm; a motorist can drive much too fast down a perilous mountain road and still arrive safely at the bottom without suffering injury or injuring anyone else. Acts that are not risky sometimes happen to result in harm; a friendly handshake may transmit the germ that kills the friend. Though negligent conduct is dangerous conduct, not all dangerous conduct is negligent conduct. Even when some act does have a tendency to cause harm, if a reasonably careful person in the actor's situation would be excusably ignorant of that tendency, then the conduct is not negligent. Furthermore, even when a reasonable person would know that certain acts tend to cause harm, still those acts are not negligent if their worth justifies the risk of harm to others.

When an injury is unforeseeable to a reasonable person situated in circumstances like those in which the defendant acted the defendant's conduct is not negligent. This protects the defendant from liability in three different kinds of negligence cases:

(1) In Aune v. Oregon Trunk Ry.,[4] a railroad left an empty freight car on a spur track. That night hobos camped in the car

---

3. Until recently, the accepted phrase was "reasonably prudent man." No implication of gender was intended, but to emphasize that gender is irrelevant "reasonably prudent person" is now commonly used.

4. 151 Or. 622, 51 P.2d 663 (1935).

and built a fire. The car caught fire, and flames spread to the plaintiff's adjoining warehouse and burned it down. The court held that the railroad was not negligent. Spotting empty freight cars near warehouses is not very dangerous—it has virtually no tendency to cause harm. At the time the defendant acted, injury to others would not have been foreseen by a reasonably prudent person in defendant's position.[5]

(2) A blood donor gave blood for a transfusion to aid an ailing friend. Hospital authorities asked the donor whether or not he had ever had hepatitis, and he answered that he had not. The patient contracted hepatitis. Medical researchers found records showing that the donor, as a two-year old, had the disease while he was an inmate in an orphan asylum. He, however, had no knowledge of this childhood illness. He incurred no liability to the patient for negligence. The patient's mishap was unforeseeable to a person situated as was the donor. These facts, however, differ from those in the freight car case—in which harm was unforeseeable since the railroad's conduct was not particularly dangerous. In this hepatitis case, the blood donor's conduct was dangerous; he had so acted that he subjected his friend to a serious risk of infection. The donor, however, was at the time excusably ignorant of danger, and therefore was not guilty of negligence.[6]

5. See a similar modern holding in Stoskin v. Prensky, 256 Md. 707, 262 A.2d 48 (1970). Sometimes proof of a defendant's previous experience shows that the defendant appreciated a risk not discernable to ordinary jurors unfamiliar with a seemingly bland, but actually dangerous, situation. See, e. g., Nelson v. Union R. R. Co., 26 R.I. 251, 58 A. 780 (1904), in which proof showed that when a streetcar turned a corner its overhead trolley came off the power line and struck a street light globe. Glass fell and cut a passenger waiting to board the car. The passenger offered proof to show that light globes at this place had been broken several times before in the same way. The court held that the evidence was admissible since it tended to show danger rather than mere coincidence.

6. The classic case illustrating this point is Gould v. Slater Woolen Co., 147 Mass. 315, 17 N.E. 531 (1888), in which plaintiff was poisoned by on-going handling of cloth impregnated by a chemical commonly used at the time in dyeing cloth. Even learned scientists did not then know that cloth so impregnated was dangerous to handle. The court ruled that the dyer was not guilty of negligence, since injury was not foreseeable to a reasonable manufacturer situated as the dyer was.

In many, if not all jurisdictions, such a processor would now probably be held liable to those injured by his product without proof of negligence—under modern theories of products liability. See p. 237, infra.

A case illustrative of an unreasonable failure to recognize danger is Largess v. Tatem, 130 Vt. 271, 291 A.2d 398 (1972). In that case a general practitioner realized that his patient's broken hip required treatment beyond his competence and called in a specialist in ortho-

(3) Mr. Milquetoast tells his wife that he thinks installation of an electric cook stove in their house would be safer than a gas stove because gas sometimes explodes. Nevertheless, at her command he buys a gas stove which, though properly installed and used with due care, happens to explode and start a fire which spreads to a neighbor's house. Though Milquetoast's hunch proved correct, he was nevertheless not negligent. The injury was not "foreseen" in the sense that we have heretofore used the word; the requirement is an appreciation of a practical tendency to do harm and does not encompass clairvoyant visions of catastrophe. Of course, if Milquetoast had actual knowledge of real danger known only to him, the situation would be different; in that case, a reasonable person in his position would have knowledge of danger and injury would be foreseeable.

Thus far the negative aspect has been stressed; when injury is not foreseeable there is no negligence. When injury is foreseeable to a reasonable person situated like the defendant, the defendant's conduct is nevertheless not negligent if the worth of the defendant's conduct justifies the risk. Mr. Chief Justice Rosenberry of the Wisconsin Supreme Court illustrates the point this way: "One driving a car in a thickly populated district, on a rainy day, slowly and in the most careful manner, may do injury to the person of another by throwing muddy or infected water upon that person. Society does not hold the actor responsible because the benefit of allowing people to travel under such circumstances so far outweighs the probable injury to bystanders that such conduct is not disapproved. Circumstances may require the driver of a fire truck to take his truck through a thickly populated district at a high rate of speed, but if he exercises that degree of care which drivers ordinarily exercise under the same or similar circumstances, society, weighing the benefits against the probabilities of damage, in spite of the fact that as a reasonably prudent and intelligent man he should foresee that harm may result, justifies the risk and holds him not liable." [7] So dangerous conduct may be reasonable conduct even

pedic surgery. The orthopedist reduced the fracture by emplacing a pin. During all of the post-operative period, the surgeon gave strict written instructions on the patient's chart that the patient was not to put weight on the leg. She made fine progress and her care was returned to the general practitioner, who failed to find out that the leg should not bear weight until the healing process was complete. The general practitioner encouraged her to walk too soon with disastrous results. The court held that lack of knowledge of the danger was no excuse and that the general practitioner was negligent in failing to discover readily available knowledge of the danger.

7. Osborne v. Montgomery, 203 Wis. 223, 234 N.W. 372 (1931).

though risk is obvious. If an act should not be discouraged, by definition it is non-faulty and non-negligent.

§ 2. LAW AND FACT

Suppose that Hunter kept a small-bore shotgun for Hunter's fifteen-year old child to use in hunting under the parent's supervision. One day while Hunter was away from home, the child disobediently took the weapon out of the gun cabinet for unsupervised use and wounded Walker who was enjoying an afternoon stroll in suburban woods. Walker sues Hunter for negligence. Hunter disclaims negligence. Does the dispute generated raise a question of law or a question of fact?

If testimony adduced by Walker tends to show that Hunter left the gun cabinet unlocked, but Hunter nevertheless testifies that the cabinet was carefully kept locked at all times, this head-on contradiction raises a question of fact. The problem involves what happened; the litigants are at odds on past history. Let us now change the facts of the case and suppose that Hunter freely admits that the cabinet was left unlocked; Walker agrees that the child had for many years obediently never touched the gun cabinet in the parent's absence. Hunter further testifies without contradiction that since dangerous marauders infested the neighborhood, Hunter had kept arms for self-defense readily available. The dispute now does not involve what happened; it centers on whether or not admitted facts of Hunter's behavior are negligent misconduct. This question may not be answered by inquiring further into what happened—both of the litigants agree on all of the significant details of Hunter's behavior. The question is, what legal consequences should courts attach to these known facts?

We hesitate to call this a question of law for two reasons:

(1) When legal evaluation of known facts is in doubt, the problem generated is seldom nonfactual—even though the facts-of-the-case are known. Whoever decides whether Hunter was negligent should know something about the behavior of teenagers, the way in which marauders behave, the consequences, in fact, of impediments to access to firearms, and so on. The issue-trier must eventually determine, however, whether Hunter's conduct was legally satisfactory; and this decision is different from sifting historical facts—it is legal evaluation of facts. In the light of enough factual knowledge the decision may come so easily and be so embedded in fact that its *evaluative* aspect is hardly noticed.

(2) A respected procedural principle is this: Questions of fact are for the jury and questions of law are for the judge. Our question may properly be submitted to a jury for decision. If reasonable jurors could differ on whether Hunter was negligent, most courts would hold that each litigant is entitled, *if* he or she wants the issue submitted, to have the jury pass on the issue. If reasonable jurors could reach only one answer, then the litigant favored by that answer is entitled to have it entered by the trial judge. We do not know with certainty into which of these two categories this case falls, so we do not know, in terms of this procedural analysis, whether this should be called a question-of-law-to-be-decided-by-the-court or a question-of-fact-to-be-decided-by-the-jury.

Once the last two points are understood, further characterization of the issue is a matter of little moment. It has been called a question of fact, an administrative issue, a mixed question of law and fact, and a question of law. Each of these categorizations has some purely academic justification. But the lawyer's main interest should be in understanding how the issue will be tried—the procedure by which it is properly decided—rather than in how it should be categorized.

§ 3. THE JURY CHARGE—THE REASONABLY PRUDENT PERSON STANDARD

When jurors deciding an issue of due care are told only that negligence is a failure to use the care that a reasonably prudent person would use in like circumstances, they are not given a "test" of negligence. Their instructions may be too general to be decisive when difficult discriminations must be made. Such instructions work much more like a crude country guidepost than like a carefully kept laboratory scale.

One of the weaknesses of such a jury charge is that it does not identify the significant circumstances surrounding the defendant's behavior that should be considered under the "like circumstances" phrase. Some circumstances are ruled out by the nature of the issue and the common sense of the jury. A motorist who did not watch the road would hardly think of arguing that he or she used the care of a reasonably-prudent-person not keeping a proper lookout—a reasonably-prudent-person-not-keeping-a-proper-lookout is a contradiction in terms. Defendants who have voluntarily loaded themselves with liquor are not entitled to be judged by the standard of a reasonably prudent drunk;[8] but a defendant acting in an unexpected emergency may be acting under circumstances that should be taken into account.[9] In appropriate cases, the reasonably prudent person instruction can be and often is supplemented by instructions which, for example, rule out the defendant's voluntary drunkenness as an exculpatory circumstance or include emergency facts in the circumstances properly considered.

Strangely enough, most courts have taken the view that insanity (permanent or temporary) should not be taken into account.[10] Of course a reasonably-prudent-insane-person is also a contradiction in terms, but the misconduct of the mentally unbalanced may not be discouraged by civil liability. The way out is simply a recognition that insanity disabling a defendant from using due care is a proper excuse for conduct that would otherwise be negligent.[11] One court attempted to justify liability of the insane for negligence on the ground that liability will induce those responsible for restraining mental patients to take their responsibility seriously.[12] If guardians are to be controlled, this indirection is unfortunate; guardians who are negligent in caring for their charges, and consequently subject other people to risks

8. See McMichael v. Pennsylvania R. R. Co., 331 Pa. 584, 1 A.2d 242 (1938).

9. See Leo v. Dunham, 41 Cal.2d 712, 264 P.2d 1 (1953). See and compare Clayborne v. Mueller, 266 Md. 30, 291 A.2d 443 (1972), in which a traffic officer's status and duties were recognized in a jury charge as significant circumstances when he was injured by a passing car while handing out a ticket.

10. Johnson v. Lambotte, 147 Colo. 203, 363 P.2d 165 (1961); Sforza v. Green Bus Lines, 150 Misc. 180, 268 N.Y.S. 446 (1934). But see Buckley and Toronto Transportation Comm's v. Smith Transp. Ltd., [1946] O.R. 798 [1946] 4 D.L. R. 721 (Ontario Ct. of App.), and the recent intermediate court case of FitzGerald v. Lawhorn, 29 Conn. Sup. 511, 294 A.2d 338 (1972). By analogy, one court has even gone so far as to hold that sudden illness may not be taken into account. Leary v. Oates, 84 S.W.2d 486 (Tex.Civ.App.1935). Most of the authority on unexpected illness is

contra. See, e.g., Shea v. Tousignant, 172 Conn. 54, 372 A.2d 151 (1976); Moore v. Presnell, 38 Md. App. 243, 379 A.2d 1246 (1977). Cf. Lobert v. Pack, 337 Pa. 103, 9 A.2d 365 (1939), in which a sleeping passenger incurred no liability for unconscious acts which caused the driver to wreck the car. A motorist who should suspect he might black out, but drives nevertheless may be found negligent. Lutzkovitz v. Murray, 339 A.2d 64 (Del. 1975).

11. In tort actions in which liability is not based on fault, insanity should be no defense. In an action of trespass *q.c.f.* to settle a boundary dispute or to interrupt a period of adverse use, the insanity of the defendant is irrelevant. If motorists, because they are superior risk bearers, should incur no-fault liability to pedestrians whom they run over, the motorist who has such an accident while temporarily insane should not escape liability.

12. In re Guardianship of Meyer, 218 Wis. 381, 261 N.W. 211 (1935).

of harm, should be (and under some circumstances are) personally liable.

The famous English case of Vaughan v. Menlove[13] held that an adult defendant (who was apparently not very bright) was to be adjudged negligent if he failed to use the care of a reasonably prudent person, and was not entitled to an instruction relieving him from liability if he acted in good faith and to the best of his judgment. This holding attempts to exclude from the circumstances a jury may properly consider minor deviations from normal capacity to appreciate danger and act wisely in reducing risks. In a sense Menlove may have been held liable without fault. If one does the best one can, angels could do no more; surely St. Peter at the Pearly Gates forgave Menlove for not doing better than he knew how to do. Tort liability will not make dull people smart, any more than it will make crazy people sane. It might be difficult, but not impossible, to use the good faith test that Menlove suggested. It is sometimes hard to know whether a person has done the best he or she could do; but the issue of a defendant's good faith has often been decided, in deceit actions for example, with no great complaint about the difficulty of disposing of that issue. However, if liability for negligence is to be educative, perhaps the time had come to try to teach Menlove to do better. The severity of the example might have had some effect on others no brighter than he, and so liability for innocent misconduct may be justified. The courts, however, have not held that morons and idiots who do their best are nevertheless guilty of contributory negligence barring them from recovering damages from others who are negligently inconsiderate of the general public and happen to injure a mental defective.[14]

Vaughan v. Menlove has been hailed as establishing an "objective measure" of negligence—as setting up a standard that does not change with each defendant and that can be applied without taking into account each defendant's complicated personality and experience. A defense counsel will not be allowed to prove a relatively normal adult's history in minute detail or offer psychological evidence on the defendant's mental capacity. Nevertheless, the defendant is usually in the trial court and testifies before the jury. Inevitably much about defendant comes out in the trial—defendant's identification as a witness, testimony about the activity in which defendant injured someone, and defendant's appearance and actions in the courtroom all throw light on his or her discrete personality. The defendant's impact

---

13. 132 Eng.Rep. 490, 3 Bing. (N.C.) 468 (1837).

14. See Lynch v. Rosenthal, 396 S. W.2d 272 (Mo.App.1965).

as a unique person often affects jury deliberations. A jury charged to take circumstances into account seldom compares the defendant to an abstract reasonably prudent person having none of the defendant's attributes. Sometimes courts do not exclude evidence that bears on the defendant's experience and capacity —often a motorist-defendant is allowed to testify that he or she has been driving for only a short time, a plaintiff-worker is allowed to say on the witness stand that he or she was new on the job, and so on. The complete objectiveness of the standard is more academic than real. Sometimes jury charges purport to rule out proven circumstances; no one knows, however, how effective these instructions are.

§ 4. THE JURY CHARGE—VARIATIONS ON THE REASONABLY PRUDENT PERSON THEME

The capacities of some kinds of litigants charged with negligence are always specifically taken into account in jury instructions. When the physically handicapped are charged with negligence, instructions authorize the jury to take their significant infirmities into account. In an action against a deaf defendant, whose deafness has prevented him or her from acting as a careful person with normal hearing would act, the jury is told to determine whether the defendant used the care that a reasonably prudent deaf person would use in like circumstances.[15] Those with impaired hearing should compensate for their defect by using their vision as a partial substitute, and juries are often expressly charged that a deaf person is reasonably careful only if he or she keeps a sharper lookout than is required of a person who can hear.

Few children are sued in tort; they are likely to be judgment proof. In theory they are liable for their *intentional* wrongs without regard for their youth, and in the cases that have been litigated, courts have so ruled.[16] Occasionally youths have been sued for negligent injuries and held liable. Most of these cases are against young motorists covered by the omnibus coverage

---

15. Some courts prefer a slightly different version which amounts to the same thing, *viz.*, the care that a reasonably prudent person would use under like circumstances, and one of the circumstances to be taken into account is the defendant's deafness.

Similarly, a blind person's incapacity is a relevant circumstance. Hill v. City of Glenwood, 124 Iowa 479, 100 N.W. 522 (1904). A blind man who did not even take the precaution of feeling his way with a stick was held contributorily negligent as a matter of law in Smith v. Sneller, 147 Pa.Super. 231, 24 A.2d 61 (1942).

16. See Zuckerbrod v. Burch, 88 N. J.Super. 1, 210 A.2d 425 (1965); Garratt v. Dailey, 46 Wash.2d 197, 279 P.2d 1091 (1955).

clause in automobile liability insurance policies, which insures all who drive the car with consent of the owner. A popular new clause in homeowners' policies covers the liability of child members of the insured's household; extensive writing of this policy has increased the number of children worth suing. Child plaintiffs have always been numerous; their claims are as attractive to contingent fee lawyers as claims of adults. Often these child-plaintiffs are charged with contributory negligence, and jury instructions on the care required of children have been developed in submitting that issue.

Child litigants charged with failure to use due care are usually entitled to have the jury instructed that they were negligent only if they fell short of the care properly expected of a child of like age, experience, and capacity.[17] This formula opens the door for proof of the child's past and stage of development at the time of the accident. For example, in Dickeson v. Baltimore & Ohio Chicago Terminal R.R. Co.[18] a train-hopping fourteen-year old was permitted to testify that he had never before ridden on a train, and his expert witness, a psychologist, was permitted to testify that he was a dull normal child with less than average intelligence, since three tests showed he had an "I.Q." of 81.

An attempt to be slightly "objective" is made since jurors in these cases are asked to judge the particular child in comparison with an imaginary child of the same background and intelligence who makes reasonable use of his or her capacity in applying the lessons of the child's limited experience. This exercise can be understood by trained lawyers, but it is too fine-spun to affect most ordinary jurors. They would probably reach similar verdicts were they told merely to determine whether or not the child-litigant was as careful as he or she should have been.

Some courts hold that all children under age seven are incapable of negligence; these same courts also hold that youths over fourteen are presumed to have the full capacity of an adult and no mention of their youth in a jury charge is proper unless it is specially shown that they are immature.[19] In all jurisdictions, persons over twenty-one are not entitled to have their youth pointed out in instructions to the jury. Most courts treat chil-

17. See, e. g., Smith v. United States, 546 F.2d 872 (10th Cir. 1976). But see Neumann v. Shlansky, 63 Misc.2d 587, 312 N.Y.S.2d 951 (1970), holding an eleven-year old golfer (whose ball hit plaintiff) to an adult standard because he was engaging in an adult activity.

18. 42 Ill.2d 103, 245 N.E.2d 762 (1969).

19. See, e. g., Jones, J. in Kuhns v. Brugger, 390 Pa. 331, 135 A.2d 395 (1957).

dren under seven or over fourteen on the basis of the facts as they appear. Even children under seven may arguably be old enough to take some care, and an age-experience-and-capacity charge is often used to instruct the jury on the issue of their negligence. Of course infants in arms are incapable of caring for themselves or others, and children under some such age as four are almost invariably protected by a court ruling which states that they are incapable of negligence. Some courts have held that seventeen-year old youths are entitled to age-experience-and-capacity charges.[20]

Since eighteen-year olds have been enfranchised, and the public estimate of the capacity of youth is enhanced, it is not surprising to find that courts have lost their official tenderness for, say, young motorists. In Allen v. Ellis,[21] a sixteen-year old motorist was sued in a wrongful death action. The trial court, over the plaintiff's objection, instructed the jury that even though the young motorist was a licensed driver, this license did not oblige him to use the care and caution required of a licensed adult. The appellate court, however, equated the legislature's silence when it made minors eligible for drivers' licenses with giving no lenience to immature drivers, and held that the instruction was wrong. In the well-known 1961 case of Dellwo v. Pearson[22] a negligent twelve-year old motorboat operator to whom the trial judge gave the benefit of his youth lost this boon on appeal. The Dellwo opinion says that a minor perpetrating an injury while operating an automobile, airplane, or powerboat is required to use that care which is expected of an adult. Perhaps the likelihood that these children are covered by liability insurance disposes some courts to be strict. In 1976, however, the Supreme Court of New Jersey held that a seventeen-year old defendant, who skied into a bystander, was entitled to the protection of an "age, intelligence and experience" standard.[23]

Parents who themselves are guilty of no negligence are not liable, at common law, for the personal torts of their children; more than half of the states, however, have changed the common law rule by enacting statutes providing for some parental legal responsibility. The enactment of these statutes was probably stimulated by the hope that parental liability would result in better home training and supervision. Nearly all of the statutes

20. Mahon v. Heim, 165 Conn. 251, 332 A.2d 69 (1973). Contra, Dorais v. Paquin, 113 N.H. 187, 304 A.2d 369 (1973).

21. 191 Kan. 311, 380 P.2d 408 (1963).

22. 259 Minn. 452, 107 N.W.2d 859 (1961).

23. Goss v. Allen, 70 N.J. 442, 360 A.2d 388 (1976).

limit liability to cases of intentional wrongdoing, and most enactments limit judgments against parents to small amounts.

In several jurisdictions the care that a common carrier owes to its passengers is judged by a specially worded standard. Juries are told that a carrier has a duty to use "the highest degree of care,"[24] or "the care that a very cautious and prudent person would use." In other jurisdictions the courts have said that while a carrier should be very cautious indeed, the degree of care owed is only ordinary care under the circumstances, which however, call for great care.

Modifications of the reasonably prudent person instruction when the infirm, children, or carriers are charged with negligence may keep a few jurors on the track who would otherwise be derailed. But the discriminations made are usually either so obvious or so subtle that most jurors would probably reach the same verdicts if they were simply told to determine whether reasonable care was used. A lawsuit is an ongoing process; jurors hear proof for hours and often days before they are instructed, and the case as it develops orients them to fault issues. Before the jury is charged, jurors already have tentative ideas about which litigant was in the wrong; few jurors are likely to be close analysts of the phraseology of instructions, and fine-cut distinctions between various instructions on negligence are not likely to affect the verdicts of many jurors.

Nevertheless, appellate courts are likely to hold that any appreciable deviation from approved instructions is a reversible error. One of the important functions of plaintiffs' lawyers is to keep jury instructions straight. If they do not do this job right victories at trial may turn to ashes on appeal, even when their clients got no real advantage from instructions theoretically too favorable to them.

A novel form of jury charge was developed in the nineteenth century for trial of medical malpractice issues. The substantive law rule was that a patient is treated improperly by a physician, surgeon, or dentist only if the defendant has departed from the practice of other reputable practitioners in the same or similar communities. Such a rule calls for proof not required in other negligence cases. The jury instructions were based on this rule of liability rather than on the reasonably prudent person standard.

---

24. See, e. g., LeGrand v. Lincoln Lines, Inc., 253 Pa.Super. 19, 384 A.2d 955 (1978).

The malpractice rule was an anomaly. In negligence suits against railroads, banks, drovers, or any defendant other than a medico, the plaintiffs usually need not prove that the defendants departed from the ways of their craft, and the defendants do not escape liability, as a matter of law, merely by showing that they acted like others following the same occupation.[25]

The malpractice rule did not produce injustice in cases in which doctors were held liable; their agreements with their patients accounted for their liability in these cases. "[B]y undertaking to render medical services, even though gratuitously, he will ordinarily be understood to hold himself out as having the knowledge and skill commonly possessed by members of the medical profession under similar circumstances, and he will be liable if harm results because he does not possess it."[26] But this is no explanation of immunity from liability for injuries resulting from outmoded practices which a few others also have failed to discard. Patients do not in fact agree to excuse harmful medical mistakes like those made by other doctors.

This locality test of malpractice, nevertheless, remained legal orthodoxy well into the 1950's. In Powell v. Risser,[27] a jury which was critical of a psychiatrist who had ordered continued drastic methods to restrain a manic patient without bothering to observe him, found the psychiatrist liable for $5,000 for the resulting permanent harm to the patient's hands. On cross-examination the patient's own expert witness said that the "wet pack" restraints applied to the patient were in common use at state hospitals, and that they were generally applied by nurses and attendants without the presence or supervision of the doctor who ordered them. The appellate court reversed and rendered a judgment of no liability, saying that this jury of laymen must not be permitted to condemn any medical procedure carried out in accordance with accepted practice; since the patient had not proved any deviation from the profession's established procedure, he therefore had not established sufficient facts to prove

---

25. See, e. g., Cottingham v. Wells, 108 Ga.App. 40, 132 S.E.2d 215 (1963), in which a beauty parlor operator contended, unsuccessfully, that to prove negligence, an injured patron must offer testimony of departure from practices used by other operators. But see Dresco Mechanical Contractors, Inc. v. Todd-CEA, 531 F.2d 1292 (5th Cir. 1976), involving a "similar engineers" standard for a boiler design; and compare National Cash Register Co. v. Haak, 233 Pa.Super. 562, 335 A.2d 407 (1975), involving proof of an architect's negligence on a design not within the exclusive realm of architects.

26. W. Prosser, Handbook of the Law of Torts 237 (1st ed. 1941). Compare W. Prosser, Handbook of the Law of Torts 164 (4th ed. 1971).

27. 375 Pa. 60, 99 A.2d 454 (1953).

the psychiatrist liable. Oklahoma has followed this orthodox view into the 1970's.[28]

Perhaps the clearest call for change came when doctors practicing in rural neighborhoods sought refuge in the backwardness of the bucolic medicine of their own locality. In Brune v. Belinkoff,[29] a maternity anesthetic, administered in New Bedford, Massachusetts, injured the plaintiff. The patient's expert witness testified about the proper maximum dose. The defendant's experts testified that in New Bedford a much larger dose was customarily used. The trial judge told the jury that the anesthesiologist was not liable if he had followed New Bedford's customary medical practices, even though the New Bedford practice was inferior to Boston anesthesiology. The appellate court held the charge to the jury was wrong and ordered a new trial, saying that while the jurors could take into account the medical resources available in New Bedford, the defendant specialist should be held to the standard of care that was exercised by average specialists in anesthesiology under similar circumstances. In this view local facilities are significant, but local practice is no longer the sole criterion of due care.[30] Some courts have treated not only local, but all other aspects of customary medical practice as only evidentiary, and have taken the position that a showing of conformity to the usual procedures cannot prove that methods dangerous in fact are safe in law.[31] In at least one jurisdiction, the legislature provided that after April 26, 1976, malpractice plaintiffs can adduce the expert testimony only of witnesses "familiar with the

28. See Reeg v. Shaughnessy, 570 F.2d 309 (10th Cir. 1978).

29. 354 Mass. 102, 235 N.E.2d 793 (1968); see also Kronke v. Danielson, 108 Ariz. 400, 499 P.2d 156 (1972); Gambill v. Stroud, 258 Ark. 766, 531 S.W.2d 945 (1976).

30. Field researchers on the quality of medical care sponsored by Ralph Nader's Center for Study of Responsive Law issued a study which was reported in the N.Y. Times of November 9, 1970, at 46: "[T]he study said that the [medical] profession had an almost complete lack of internal quality control, and that this lack had allowed a very large measure of very poor medicine to be practiced . . . the medical profession's own system for policing its members' performance exists in theory but in fact is virtually non-existent." A U.S. Senate Committee report published in 1969 stated that in the previous year, state boards of medical examiners had revoked the licenses of only 64 of the 300,000 physicians licensed to practice in the U.S. See Franklin, Tort Law and Alternatives 82 (1971).

31. See, e. g., Helling v. Carey, 83 Wash.2d 514, 519 P.2d 981 (1974); Shilkret v. Annapolis Emergency Hospital Ass'n, 276 Md. 187, 349 A.2d 245 (1975).

degree of skill and care ordinarily employed in the community or locality where the alleged malpractice occurred. . . ."[32]

When the facts of a damage suit brought by a patient against a doctor are well within the understanding of ordinary jurors, departure from the practice of other doctors is not the test of fault. A case in which a doctor is charged with burning a patient with an instrument used too soon after it came from the sterilizer is tried in the same way as a case in which a doctor is charged with slamming an office door on a departing patient's arm—the reasonably prudent person instruction is used.

Even some technical medicine itself is so commonly understood that no expert testimony is required to establish a physician's malpractice. In Smith v. Yohe,[33] a seventy-year old man fell and hurt himself. The doctor called to attend this oldster did not order x-rays. Eleven days later, another doctor discovered that the old man's fall had broken his leg, and delayed bone setting had aggravated the patient's condition. No expert testified that the first physician should promptly have had x-rays taken. The appellate court held nevertheless that common knowledge could support a jury finding of malpractice in this case.

§ 5. THE JURY CHARGE—JUDICIAL EFFORTS TO DEVELOP STANDARDS MORE EXACT THAN THE REASONABLY PRUDENT PERSON STANDARD

Sometimes courts have developed tests of care that are less abstract and, therefore, more exact than the reasonably prudent person standard; use of these tests can reduce the jurors' function merely to determining what happened and exclude them from evaluating the defendant's conduct. For example, a court might take the view that motorists who, without extenuating circumstances, fall asleep at the wheel of their cars are negligent because they know both that they are drowsing and that they should not continue to drive.[34] If the proof in such a case throws doubt on whether the motorist did fall asleep, the only aspect of the negligence issue that need be submitted to a jury is one of fact—the jury is asked to determine only what happened.

32. Loftus v. Hayden, 391 A.2d 749 (Del.Super.Ct.1978).

33. 412 Pa. 94, 194 A.2d 167 (1963). See Suburban Hospital Ass'n, Inc. v. Hadary, 22 Md.App. 186, 322 A.2d 258 (1974); Carlsen v. Javurek, 526 F.2d 202 (8th Cir. 1975). Compare Marshall v. Tomaselli, 118 R.I. 190, 372 A.2d 1280 (1977),

in which the court held the plaintiff's case too technical for recovery without expert testimony.

34. See Theisen v. Milwaukee Automobile Mut. Ins. Co., 18 Wis.2d 91, 118 N.W.2d 140 (1962). But see Shanley v. Shanley, 27 Conn. Sup. 417, 241 A.2d 543 (1968).

The most prominent exponent of the desirability of this kind of procedure was Mr. Justice Oliver Wendell Holmes, Jr.   In Baltimore & O. R. R. v. Goodman,[35] in which Holmes wrote the opinion, the Court held that motorists approaching obstructed railroad grade crossings are negligent as a matter of law even though they look and listen for trains, unless they also stop. This stop-look-and-listen rule still has some following, but it has been rejected by many courts, including the Supreme Court of the United States, which overruled the Goodman case seven years later.[36]   The aspect of the Goodman case which is important for this discussion is not the soundness or unsoundness of the particular rule, but is the technique of stating a test of negligence in concrete terms for a special class of cases—a technique resulting in a standard more exact than the reasonably prudent person standard.

Holmes' technique in the Goodman case was not a procedural novelty.   Early common law courts had, on occasion, developed and refined concrete standards for judging propriety of conduct.   For example, under the plea of *molliter manus imposuit* courts developed the rule that force calculated to wound or kill could not be used to eject a mere trespasser.   The broader notion of reasonable conduct as a criterion of permissible behavior is a latecomer, and was formulated in negligence cases in the nineteenth century after various specific types of unreasonable conduct had been condemned by more exact standards in the kinds of torts suits which were not actions on the case for negligence.

Before the trial of the Goodman case, juries had often had the job of deciding what constitutes reasonable or unreasonable behavior.   In many courts, characterization of conduct as negligent or careful had often been left to juries, even in cases in which facts were not otherwise in dispute.   Jury trial of the reasonableness issue has much to be said for it: it is flexible; it can move with the times; it uses the judgment of lay individuals and bypasses mistakes that some too-cloistered judges might make.   But it has disadvantages: If concrete standards are not announced in advance, people may not know what is expected of them (a sixty mile per hour speed limit sign tells motorists not to drive faster); the area of jury function is extended and opportunities for playing on jurors' sentimentality and prejudices

35.   275 U.S. 66, 48 S.Ct. 24, 72 L. Ed. 167 (1927).

36.   Pokora v. Wabash Ry. Co., 292 U.S. 98, 54 S.Ct. 580, 78 L.Ed. 1149 (1934). Illinois law interest-

ingly modifies the Goodman rule by making it more flexible, and therefore more acceptable.   See McEvers v. Missouri Pacific R. R. Co., 528 F.2d 220 (7th Cir. 1975).

are multiplied by the more abstract test; important social questions are decided by a changing group of amateurs.

Just how far courts have used and will use Holmes' preferred technique is a difficult question. But Holmes' ideal (that the technique should be used at an accelerated pace until exact standards are developed by judges for all important types of cases) has not guided courts in the last half century. Lawyers preparing cases do their job well only when they have searched the precedents carefully for applicable judicially announced concrete standards, but they still will find few of them.

Perhaps the major curb on more extensive use of the Holmes technique is fear of reversal, entertained by both trial judges and plaintiffs' lawyers. If no exact standard has heretofore been approved by their appellate courts, trial judges who give the reasonably prudent person charge run no risk of reversal; but they know that the chances of appellate disapproval of an exact standard fabricated by the trial judge are fairly high. Plaintiffs' lawyers are even more fearful of reversal than trial judges and are not likely to espouse use of novel concrete standards. Defense counsel usually prize directed verdicts; they are especially likely to press trial judges to rule that plaintiffs have been guilty of contributory negligence as a matter of law in appropriate cases. Perhaps this accounts for the fact that most recognized concrete standards refer to contributory negligence and have been sponsored initially by defendants.[37]

Though some courts have virtually ruled out the Holmes technique there are nevertheless instances of its use in all jurisdictions. A bit of Texas history illustrates this point:

(1) In Trochta v. Missouri, Kentucky & Tennessee Railway,[38] the jury found specially (in answer to questions of fact submitted to Texas juries) that plaintiff's decedent drove his car onto a railroad grade crossing without looking, listening, or doing any other act to discover an oncoming and visible train, but nevertheless the jury also found that the decedent was not negligent. The intermediate court held that the jury's conclusion could not follow from its other findings of fact, and the decedent was negligent as a matter of law. The Supreme Court reinstated judgment for the plaintiff on the ground that failure

---

37. See, e. g., Haines v. Dulaney, 424 Pa. 608, 227 A.2d 625 (1967). After a jury has found that the defendant has used due care, the plaintiff has nothing to lose in seeking a judicial ruling that the defendant was guilty of negligence as a matter of law. Such an attempt succeeded in Tyrrell v. McDonald, 133 Vt. 389, 340 A.2d 99 (1975).

38. 218 S.W. 1038 (Tex.Com.App. 1920).

to look and listen or take any other precaution was not negligence as a matter of law, and that the jury had the function of determining whether or not the decedent was negligent.

(2) In all jurisdictions, including Texas, courts purport to honor this rule of procedure: When reasonable jurors can reach but one result, the litigant favored by that result is entitled to a directed verdict. This rule came into play in a case decided by the Supreme Court of Texas twenty-seven years after it had decided the Trochta case; the court ruled that a warned pedestrian who walked in front of an oncoming train was negligent as a matter of law.[39] This decision is now precedent for a similar ruling, if and when a similar case occurs; and Texas therefore has a concrete standard for a class of cases. The Texas inhospitality to the Holmes technique tends to hold down use of that technique to standards encompassing a very small class of cases; but the technique is not exiled from Texas so long as the court continues to honor the procedural rule. In jurisdictions less inhospitable the courts are sometimes emboldened to adopt concrete standards that cover larger classes of cases.

§ 6.   THE JURY CHARGE—CONCRETE STANDARDS BORROWED FROM CRIMINAL STATUTES

Most courts hold that breach of a criminal statute or ordinance is negligence *per se*. One of the classic cases is Bott v. Pratt.[40] The defendant-teamster, hauling a load of wood, in violation of a criminal law left his horses standing unhitched to make an inquiry about where he should deliver his cargo. The team took fright, ran away, and collided with the plaintiff's wagon, causing damages. The wood hauler believed his horses were gentle. They had never run away before. The trial judge, nevertheless, instructed the jury that they must find against the wood hauler if the runaway horses were left illegally unattended and unhitched. In this civil case, the more exact standard found in the criminal statute was substituted for the vaguer reasonably prudent person standard, and the jury was left with only a question of what happened.

The doctrine of negligence *per se* was invented by judges hearing civil cases. These tort judges injected into civil law standards which they borrowed from the criminal law. Legislatures can pass statutes expressly controlling civil litigation, and have done so from time to time, but such statutes are rare. The doctrine of negligence *per se* calls for use in civil cases of proscrip-

---

39. Texas & N. O. R. v. Burden, 146 Tex. 109, 203 S.W.2d 522 (1947).

40. 33 Minn. 323, 23 N.W. 237 (1885).

tions formulated in criminal statutes, even though those statutes say nothing about civil liability. When a legislature does not mention civil liability, it seldom has any intention to affect damage suit litigation. A few courts have rejected the doctrine of negligence *per se* on this very ground; their views will be discussed later, after the implications of the majority position are developed.

The orthodox analysis of the doctrine was written by Professor Thayer.[41] Thayer said the doctrine of negligence *per se* was logically inferred from accepted principles of tort law. He reasoned this way: one who acts affirmatively has a common law duty to act with the care of a reasonably prudent person; reasonably prudent people do not break the law; therefore one who violates criminal law is guilty also of a breach of the common law duty to use due care.

This analysis is almost acceptable without qualification, but one criticism must be made. Reasonably prudent people rarely break the criminal law, but sometimes they do. When prudence justifies conduct that is nevertheless technically criminal, civil liability for harm done is liability without fault. Draconian application of the doctrine of negligence *per se* will occasionally result in a finding that a defendant who was careful in fact was negligent in law.

The case of Day v. Pauly[42] bears out this criticism. A motorist was ruled guilty of contributory negligence because he had made a left turn as directed by highway lane markings inside of the center of an intersection. The turn violated a criminal statute. Had he complied with the statute and ignored the markings, his conduct would have dangerously surprised other motorists. His conduct was reasonable in fact and yet the court held that he was negligent in law.[43]

Other courts have obdurately applied the doctrine of negligence *per se* in cases similar to Day v. Pauly. But some courts use the doctrine and yet avoid holding reasonable behavior negligent; a holding opposite to Day v. Pauly could have been reached in either of two ways: (1) "interpretation" of the crim-

---

41. Thayer, Public Wrong and Private Action, 27 Harv.L.Rev. 317 (1914).

42. 186 Wis. 189, 202 N.W. 363 (1925).

43. See also, Hensel v. Beckward, 273 Md. 426, 330 A.2d 196 (1974).

Of course, literal interpretations of statute are not always sound. In Abood v. Hospital Ambulance Service, Inc., 30 N.Y.2d 295, 332 N.Y.S.2d 877, 283 N.E.2d 754 (1972), the court held that a non-literal interpretation of a traffic statute was the correct interpretation.

inal statute, or (2) recognition of an exception when the criminal law is justifiably violated.

A good case illustrating how interpretation can properly result in holding that the statute was not violated, and thereby side-tracking the doctrine of negligence *per se* is Deamer v. Evans.[44] In that case the plaintiff was driving his car behind a vehicle that stopped to avoid hitting a pedestrian. The plaintiff could not pull out and pass the stopped car because of traffic oncoming from the opposite direction; so he also stopped. The defendant driving third in line was negligently inattentive and plowed into the plaintiff, doing the damage for which plaintiff sued. The defendant argued that the suit was barred by the plaintiff's violation of a criminal statute providing that no one shall park or leave a vehicle, attended or unattended, on the paved portion of a highway. This defense was rejected on the ground that the statute did not cover the plaintiff's conduct.

Proper interpretation of criminal statutes reduces the number of misapplications of the doctrine of negligence *per se*. Sometimes, however, a non-faulty breach of the criminal law is nevertheless a breach, and an interpretation of the statute to the contrary would be a misinterpretation.

If negligence *per se* is to be restricted to cases of unreasonable misconduct, the courts should candidly recognize that there are justifiable violations of criminal statutes. Several courts have done so. The defendant proved an excuse in Taber v. Smith,[45] a rear-end collision case in which the leading car was driven without taillights in violation of criminal statute. Defendant's truck lights showed no signs of being out of order until darkness fell, when the driver turned the switch and his lights did not go on. He stopped immediately and tried for a long time to get a service truck to come to him and make repairs. After his summonses for help went unanswered, he proceeded very slowly and carefully toward a garage four hundred feet away. During this short trip the collision took place. The defendant was held liable in the trial court on a negligence *per se* theory. The appellate court reversed and remanded on the ground that the defendant was entitled to have the jury pass on whether or not he had acted as a reasonably prudent person would have under the circumstances.

---

44. 278 Ala. 35, 175 So.2d 466 (1965). See also, Tedla v. Ellman, 280 N.Y. 124, 19 N.E.2d 987 (1939); Rafferty v. Weimer, 36 Md.App. 98, 373 A.2d 64 (1977).

45. 26 S.W.2d 722 (Tex.Civ.App. 1930).

Violations of criminal statutes should not be excused on every pretext. Legislative judgment expressed in criminal statutes usually should command respect from both the civil litigant and the civil judge. The legislature has opportunities to investigate and deliberate, and it has the function of giving voice to an official view. One who knows the criminal law should not violate it lightly. In Bushnell v. Telluride Power Co.,[46] a land-clearing fire got out of control and destroyed nearby property. A criminal statute proscribed setting such fires without a permit from a fire warden. The fire setter testified that the warden told him to go out some morning and light up, and when the warden saw smoke he would fetch the permit to him. The court rejected this lame excuse and directed a verdict against the fire setter. Courts should assume that a breach of the criminal law is negligence in the absence of a strong showing of justification. If they do otherwise they are likely to allow jurors capriciously to ignore legislative proscriptions. A lame excuse is no warrant for abandoning a concrete standard and turning the jury loose with the reasonably prudent person standard.

Perhaps the best way of justifying departures from criminal safety rules in civil negligence cases is to keep in mind that civil courts, on proper occasions, *borrow* or *adopt* a rule formulated in a criminal statute for the purpose of deciding a fault problem in a civil case. When the legislature's particularized rule is, for the civil case in hand, a better criterion of fault than the jurors' extemporized evaluation (which the reasonably prudent person charge permits), the trial judge should rule using the criminal norm. When, however, a trial judge knows that, because of unusual circumstances, use of the criminal norm will result in the mistrial of the negligence issue, the criminal norm should not be adopted. The doctrine of negligence *per se* can, however, be properly extended and used against a defendant who has not technically committed a crime. For example, Cavalier v. Peerless Ins. Co.,[47] a trailer's tongue broke and dug into the ground, abruptly stopping the trailer, and as a result, a passenger riding in the trailer was hurled out and hurt. A criminal statute required trailer haulers to use safety chains (as well as the ordinary hitch) for an additional safeguard. No chains safeguarded this injured passenger. The hauler, however, committed no crime because the statute by its terms applied only to highway travel, and this trailer was operated along a private road. The court said that even though the lack of chains was no crime, logic required care on a private road no different from that appropriate for similar travel on a public highway, and therefore the

46. 145 F.2d 950 (10th Cir. 1944).   **47.** 156 So.2d 105 (La.App.1963).

norm of the criminal statute could properly be used as the criterion of negligence in a civil case.

Some courts have rejected the doctrine of negligence *per se* and have adopted in its place the rule that breach of a criminal statute is only evidence of negligence. This view seems simple and flexible; it can be used widely, since it permits problems of negligence to be decided for either litigant as the facts may appear. Liability without fault is avoided without abstruse interpretation of criminal statutes and without special exceptions for justifiable violations. Under this view, the jury can be (and usually is) told that breach of a criminal statute is not conclusive but should be taken into account in determining whether the violator used due care. Though the jury is given power to ignore the statute, it is at least warned not to do so lightly.

If in these courts violation of a criminal statute is *never* more than evidence of negligence, then violators are *always* entitled to try to persuade a jury that they used due care—even though the trial judge believes that reasonable jurors could not find that they did. This view prevailed in Sheehan v. Nims,[48] an automobile collision case in which proof conclusively showed that a trucker criminally failed to equip his truck with clearance lights for night operation. No proof tended to justify the trucker's breach. The trial judge ruled that failure to display clearance lights constituted negligence, and left other questions to the jury, which returned a verdict against the trucker. The appellate court (foolishly in our view) reversed on the ground that the jury submission was wrong, since the trucker had not been allowed to try to convince the jury that a reasonably prudent person might have acted as he did.

Fortunately, other courts have more soundly held that even though breach of a criminal statute is only evidence of negligence, unless proof tends to justify breach, the evidence of negligence may be strong enough to warrant a charge telling the jury that negligence has been proved. In Marsden v. Patane,[49] a motorist traveling down a side road ran through a stop sign and collided with a car traveling a main Florida highway. The collision killed a passenger in the car that was hit. The stop sign was plainly visible, the day was clear, and the decedent's car was driven with due care. The Florida courts had established the rule that violations of traffic law are only evidence of negligence, rebuttable by proof tending to show that the violator used due care. The motorist tried to excuse himself by offering to prove that the vehicle ahead of him had not stopped, that he was

---

48. 75 F.2d 293 (2d Cir. 1935).   **49.** 380 F.2d 489 (5th Cir. 1967).

unfamiliar with the intersection, and that he was distracted by the approach of the decedent's car from his left at unabated speed. The trial judge held that even though the rule of negligence *per se* had been rejected, the issue of the defendant's negligence should not be submitted to the jury. The appellate court affirmed this ruling, and said that the violator's proof was not strong enough to permit the jury to find that he had used due care.

The holding in this stop sign case is a special application of a well-settled procedure rule—a trial judge may direct a verdict on an issue on which jurors cannot reasonably differ. Substantively, the holding is a recognition that prudent individuals do not break the criminal law without justification. In an evidence-of-negligence state, once these rules of substantive law and procedure become controlling, the trial of the negligence issue differs little from that in courts recognizing the justifiable violation exception to the doctrine of negligence *per se*. In either kind of jurisdiction, a clearly inexcusable breach of a criminal safety statute is inescapably negligent, and a clearly justifiable breach will be excused. Perhaps the violator with a lame excuse may occasionally be a little better off in an evidence-of-negligence jurisdiction, since the use of the criminal criterion is less automated.

After plaintiff proves that the defendant's criminal act injured the plaintiff, may the defendant attack the soundness of the statute? If a criminal statute calls for unreasonable or unwise precautions, breach may be consistent with reasonable care. An arbitrary and capricious statute is likely to be held unconstitutional, and therefore not a proper criterion for civil liability. But misguided criminal legislation may nevertheless be constitutional and enforceable.

We have found no civil case in which a defendant accused of breaking a criminal *statute* has attacked the wisdom of the legislature. But many *municipal ordinances* have been so questioned. These cases need not be fought on constitutional battlegrounds; city councils are given statutory authority to pass only reasonable ordinances, and therefore unreasonable ordinances are *ultra vires* [beyond their powers] and void. In one of the older cases,[50] a streetcar motorman ignored an ordinance requiring continuous ringing of a bell. The court took judicial notice that constant clangor would become too familiar to serve as a warning and would dangerously frighten horses. The court held the

50. Stafford v. Chippewa Valley Electric R. R. Co., 110 Wis. 331, 85 N.W. 1036 (1901).

ordinance void as unreasonable and then ruled that breach could not be negligence *per se.* Several courts have refused to measure due care by ordinances limiting the speed of trains to a crawl in sparsely settled neighborhoods.

Courts that will listen to attacks of lawbreakers on the soundness of a criminal proscription are nevertheless hard to convince. Judges are likely to presume the wisdom of legislative judgment in the absence of a strong showing to the contrary. For example, half a century ago a railroad failed in its attack on a ten mile per hour speed limit.[51]

Some courts have refused to countenance any attack on the wisdom of a constitutional (or *intra vires*) criminal proscription. Holmes approved such a refusal in Nashville, Chattanooga & St. Louis Ry. v. White, [52] a case in which a grade crossing was guarded by an automatic signal instead of the watchman required by ordinance. The railroad offered proof that automatic signals guarded crossings better than watchmen. Holmes said that even if a signal were better than a watchman, the choice lay with the legislature and not with the court.

When a criminal court refuses to consider the wisdom of valid criminal legislation, it follows accepted principles of separation of powers. But if the legislation is calculated to define only *criminal* responsibility, *civil* judges who reject the criminal proscription as a measure of care in civil cases are not substituting their judgment for that of the legislature. If novel civil liability results from use of a criminal proscription as a measure of negligence, the responsibility for that result lies with the civil judiciary—for the holding flows from the application of the judicially invented doctrine of negligence *per se* and not from the criminal statute itself. If a criminal statute or ordinance is outmoded or a technological mistake, the civil judiciary compounds that mistake on its own power when it uses the criminal proscription as a measure of civil liability—the legislature has called for no such use, and the decision to make it is a decision of a civil court. Sometimes a criminal proscription may be wise when violators are threatened only with small criminal punishments administered with the safeguards and flexibility of criminal procedure and yet be an unsuitable criterion for heavy civil responsibility.

Effective advocacy calls for special alertness in some negligence cases in which a litigant is charged with breach of a crim-

51. Thompson v. St. Louis-San Francisco Ry. Co., 334 Mo. 958, 69 S.W.2d 936 (1933).

52. 278 U.S. 456, 49 S.Ct. 189, 73 L.Ed. 452 (1929).

inal proscription. The routine cases are tried in accordance with standard practices understood by experienced lawyers. In some areas, however, the practice may still not be solidified by reliable precedents in bulk. In negligence *per se* jurisdictions, authorities still may differ on whether excuses for breaches should be heard; [53] in evidence of negligence jurisdictions, authorities still may differ on whether breaches that are unjustified are conclusive proof of negligence.

Plaintiff's Strategy in Negligence Per Se Jurisdictions. A major goal of plaintiffs' lawyers is to get their cases to a jury without reversible error. Victory at trial is not worth much if an appellate court is likely to reverse. Plaintiffs can seldom afford the delay of retrial. Reversal often leads to settlement at bargain rates.

In negligence *per se* jurisdictions, the plaintiff's temptation to use risky tactics occurs when proof tends to show that plaintiff justifiably violated a statute and was not, therefore, guilty of contributory negligence. This plaintiff should be entitled to instructions allowing the jury to determine whether he or she used due care. Cases so holding are available to support this view. But even though acceptance of a good excuse for breach is supported by authority and sound in policy, plaintiff's lawyer may use bad strategy by asking for instructions based on the theory of justifiable violation. Authority for the opposite view may happen to appeal to the superior court—particularly since the doctrine of negligence *per se* is stated over and over in cases entailing no problem of excused breach, without mention of any justifiable violation exception.[54] The doctrine of negligence *per se* is neater when unmodified, and legalistic simplicity sometimes has greater appeal than it should have. The plaintiff may have other routes to a favorable verdict without running this risk. Three common possibilities of countering proof of contributory negligence *per se* are: (1) proof showing that the plaintiff did not in fact violate the criminal statute; (2) a showing that the plaintiff's breach was not a proximate cause of the injury;[55] (3) proof barring defendant from asserting the defense of contributory negligence because either defendant had the last clear chance to avoid the harm, or discovered the plaintiff's peril, or was guilty of willful misconduct.[56] If plaintiff

53. See, e.g., Albers v. Ottenbacher, 79 S.D. 637, 116 N.W.2d 529 (1962).

54. See Corona v. Pittsburgh Rys. Co., 418 Pa. 136, 209 A.2d 425 (1965).

55. Discussed in Chapters VII and VIII.

56. Discussed in Chapter VIII.

has a reasonably good chance to get a favorable verdict without a justifiable violation instruction, that instruction may prove an expensive luxury—an unneeded advantage at the trial which may prove fatal on appeal. Of course in some cases excused breach may be the plaintiff's only hope, and the risk must be run. Where, when, and if excused breach rules have been thoroughly approved by the courts, of course the plaintiff can use them safely.

For similar reasons, a plaintiff's lawyer should hesitate to oppose a defendant's request that the jury be allowed to consider defendant's excuse for breach. If the jury is clearly unlikely to honor the defendant's excuse, the plaintiff should not take the chance that an appellate court will hold that error was committed because the jury was not authorized to consider the defendant's excuse.

Plaintiff's Strategy in Evidence of Negligence Jurisdictions. In courts following the rule that violation of a criminal statute is only evidence of negligence, a problem of strategy arises when one of the litigants offers no shred of an excuse for the breach. Authority is divided. Some of the cases hold, as we have shown, that the jury should be instructed that violation is conclusive of negligence. These are the new authorities and are opposed by a substantial number of holdings. A plaintiff who asks for a jury charge that the defendant's unexcused breach is conclusive of negligence runs an unnecesary risk of reversal—for jurors are not likely to find that a lawbreaker used due care when the defendant has offered no shred of excuse for criminal conduct causing injury. This risk has disappeared in those jurisdictions in which courts have clearly recognized the emerging sounder view.

Plaintiff should hesitate to oppose defendant's request for instructions that plaintiff's unexcused breach is conclusive of contributory negligence. If plaintiff is fairly sure of winning even though such an instruction is given, plaintiff should accede rather than run the risk that a progressive appellate court will rule that the request should have been granted—even in a jurisdiction in which courts have taken the view theretofore that a lawbreaker is always entitled to a chance to persuade the jury that he or she used due care.

Defendant's Strategy in Negligence Per Se Jurisdictions. A major goal of defense lawyers in damage suits is to keep cases from going to the jury, since jurors are often likely to favor injured plaintiffs over the defendants who injured them. Of course defendants sometimes get verdicts, and they may have a very real stake in alternative theories of the proper jury charge. When a case must go to the jury, defendant wants favorable instructions; but defendants are much more interested in getting directed verdicts shielding them from the mercies of the jury—mercies which may flow toward the plaintiff. A judgment for defendant at the trial may be valuable even if obtained at some risk of reversal; it enhances the defendant's bargaining position in settlement negotiations even though likelihood of reversal is quite high. Therefore defense lawyers are not chary of use of novel theories that persuade a trial judge to direct a verdict in their favor. They are bolder than plaintiffs' lawyers in framing requests for novel instructions favoring their clients; if the instruction is given, they may get a worthwhile advantage at the trial; and more important, if it is refused, they may have a valuable argument for reversal.

The defense should not invariably urge the trial judge to recognize the justifiable violation exception when proof tends to show that the defendant has an excuse for breach of a criminal statute. An advantage gained on the negligence issue may be more than offset by a disadvantage on the contributory negligence issue. Of course if the defendant's case on excused breach is so strong that defendant has a substantial chance of complete victory at the trial by moving for a directed verdict, that opportunity is too good to pass up. But such opportunities seldom occur. If both parties charge each other with breach of a criminal statute and each gives some proof tending to establish an excuse, the defendant may lose more than he or she gains by espousing the justifiable violation exception. By urging the trial judge to consider defendant's excuses, counsel opens up the likelihood that the plaintiff's excuses will also be considered. Were the judge to rule that both parties' excuses are to be weighed, the jury might accept the plaintiff's and reject the defendant's. When the plaintiff has only a lame excuse, the defendant is particularly ill-advised to request a jury charge articulating the theory of justifiable violation. Of course if only the defendant is charged with breach of a criminal statute, counsel does not run this risk in advocating the excusable breach theory. If only plaintiff is charged with breach of a criminal statute, the defendant can usually afford the risks of a rigid negligence *per se* theory—especially when defendant succeeds in getting a directed verdict by doing so.

Defendant's Strategy in Evidence of Negligence Jurisdictions. In evidence of negligence jurisdictions, defendants may gain an advantage on the negligence issue if they are allowed to try to convince the jury that they used due care without offering any proof justifying their breach. But if the crux of a defendant's case is that the plaintiff's unjustifiable breach was contributory negligence, defendant will gain little from a ruling that his or her unjustified breach is not conclusive of negligence and lose much if the court does not rule that the plaintiff's unjustified breach cannot be excused. Defendant can well afford to urge novel authority in support of a motion for a directed verdict or in support of requests for instructions.

Courts often hold that even though a breach of a criminal statute is negligence *per se*, conformity to a criminal statute is not due care *per se*. Their theory is that since criminal acts are intolerable behavior, conduct less flagrant may still fall short of reasonable prudence.[57] Though this theory is based on a correct description of some criminal statutes, it is nevertheless an over-generalization. Some criminal legislation (as a practical matter, rather than a matter of formal logic) is intended to approve complying conduct.

In Turner v. Bennett,[58] a motorist was charged with negligence in driving without lights. A criminal statute required lights one hour after sunset. The sky was clear at the time of the accident, and the motorist had no special reason for turning high lights on earlier than the required time. The appellate court held that the motorist was entitled to an instruction telling the jury that lights were not due until 5:52 P.M., which was one hour after sunset on the day of the accident.

Of course when daylight fails at high noon, driving without lights is negligent; the legislature did not intend to approve of driving without lights on all occasions until one hour after sunset. The statute is, however, based on the legislative judgment that *under optimum conditions*, lights turned on one hour after sunset are lit soon enough. What incentive could the legislature have had for choosing the time named if they thought lights ought to be lit earlier? They could have no sensible basis for their choice other than a belief that it was right. The court was as much warranted in ruling that compliance with the traffic regulation was due care in the Turner case as it would have been in ruling that breach would have been negligent. In either case, the court is respecting and borrowing legislative judgment, and thereby getting a concrete criterion of due care.

57. See, e.g., Burch v. Amsterdam Corp., 366 A.2d 1079 (D.C.App. 1976).

58. 161 Iowa 379, 142 N.W. 999 (1913).

Defendants who abide by a criminal proscription applicable to one aspect of their conduct may be negligent in some other way. In Curtis v. Perry,[59] the motorist-defendant complied with a criminal statute requiring a hand signal for a left turn. Had the plaintiff contended that he should have signaled with a red flag or a flashing light, the court might have been willing to rule that the criminal statute implied a legislative judgment that hand signals were adequate for ordinary turns under optimum conditions. The motorist, however, came to grief when he tried to persuade the court that the statute warranted a turn without a glance into his rear vision mirror if the approved signal was given. Of course criminal proscriptions are not properly used as a criterion of due care in judging conduct that falls outside of the legislature's concern.

§ 7. THE JURY CHARGE—CONCRETE STANDARDS BORROWED FROM ADMINISTRATIVE SAFETY MEASURES

When a legislature decides that on-going technological regulation is needed to reduce danger, it may decide to enact law giving an administrative agency power to adopt rules to reduce danger. Injured claimants often bring suit against those who have departed from or conformed to safety measures formulated by governmental bureaus.

Some courts have held that a breach of an administrative safety measure is negligence *per se*, and have ruled that a jury should be so instructed. In Phoenix Amusement Co. v. White,[60] a theatre patron fell down stairs leading directly from an emergency exit. The Director of Insurance had adopted a regulation against exit doors opening directly on stairs, and required that doors open on landings of a specified size. The court held the jury should be instructed that failure to have such a landing was negligence as a matter of law. The courts of other jurisdictions (including some who hold that breach of a criminal statute is usually negligence *per se*) have ruled that deviation from an administrative safety regulation is only evidence of negligence. This is not surprising, since a sizeable minority of courts hold that breach of a criminal statute is not negligence *per se* but only evidence of negligence, and several other courts have

---

59. 171 Wash. 542, 18 P.2d 840 (1933).

60. 306 Ky. 361, 208 S.W.2d 64 (1948). See also, Ridley v. Boyer,

426 Pa. 28, 231 A.2d 307 (1967) (violation of I.C.C. regulation limiting hours of truck driver held negligence *per se*.)

refused to apply the doctrine of negligence *per se* to breaches of ordinances and traffic law.

Perhaps it makes little difference to a claimant represented by wise counsel which view the court takes. If a claimant demonstrates that the defendant has been guilty of departure from a duly promulgated safety regulation, the implication of the defendant's negligence is not likely to be rebutted by an argument that the defendant should nevertheless be found to have used due care.

In several cases in which plaintiff's counsel unwisely has insisted at the trial that departure from an administrative safety measure is negligence *per se*, the plaintiff has come to grief. In Schumer v. Caplin,[61] a case in which a workman fell while washing a window not equipped with the safety catches required by regulations of the Industrial Commission, the workman at the trial requested and got a jury instruction to the effect that the defendant's failure to install the safety catches was negligence as a matter of law. The appellate court reversed on the ground that the jury was improperly charged. The decision is unwise in policy and unsound on principle. When jurors have no basis for doubting the soundness of an official safety measure, they should not be authorized to disregard it and substitute their own untutored judgment. Nevertheless, the result is supported by a considerable body of authority with which advocates must reckon until it is repudiated.[62]

An administrator's focus is likely to be on correction of unsafe conditions rather than on reasonable precautions, and use of some administrative rules as criteria of due care would result in liability without fault. In Phillips v. Britannia Hygienic Laundry Co.,[63] an administrative traffic regulation provided that all cars shall be "in such condition as not to cause or be likely to cause danger." If an inspector found a nonconforming car, administrative enforcement of the regulation would be entirely proper. In the Phillips case, however, a careful trucker did not discover a defect in an axle until after another traveler was damaged. King's Bench rejected the contention that breach

61. 241 N.Y. 346, 150 N.E. 139 (1925).

62. The New York Court of Appeals was still of the same mind thirty-five years later in Major v. Waverly and Ogden, Inc., 7 N.Y.2d 332, 197 N.Y.S.2d 165, 165 N.E.2d 181 (1960), in which an apartment landlord had violated administrative state and local building codes requiring handrails and lighting of stairways. The court sustained a trial judge's ruling that these violations were simply some evidence of negligence for the jury to take into consideration with all the other evidence on that subject.

63. [1923] 2 K.B. 832.

of the regulation was negligence *per se*. Had the court done otherwise, the trucker would have been liable without proof of his failure to use due care.

Just as an unconstitutional criminal statute is not a proper source of concrete standards for judging negligence, so an unconstitutional administrative measure is not.[64] Administrative safety regulation, however, may be unwise without being so arbitrary and capricious that it is unconstitutional. In Woody v. South Carolina Power Co.,[65] the plaintiff's car was fouled in a span of power line that sagged across a road after a third party's truck had collied with a supporting pole. The span of wire crossed the road diagonally and was much longer than the width of the highway. A Public Service Commission rule said crossing spans "shall be as short as practicable." Power company experts were allowed to testify that changes in direction of power lines should be at the smallest practicable angle to avoid dangerous stress on poles, and that this crossing span was as short as was practicable. The plaintiff contended that this testimony should have been excluded since it contradicted the rule. The court held that the evidence was admissible as an aid to proper interpretation of the technical regulation and, once heard, supported a directed verdict for the defendant. The court expressly said that the expert testimony did not conflict with the rule. The defendant escaped liability because it conformed to the rule soundly interpreted—rather than on the ground that the rule was unwise.

Another aspect of the Woody case raises a more crucial question. The Commission had adopted another rule providing that spans next to crossings should "in general" be shorter than one-half the length of the crossing span. The plaintiff proved that the adjoining spans were much longer than one-half the length of the crossing span. The trial judge received over objection the power company experts' testimony asserting that if adjoining spans are short, a collision with a corner pole is likely either to tear a cross-arm from an adjoining pole or to break an adjoining pole or span. The appellate court approved admission of this evidence, saying that the phrase "in general" contemplated exceptions. The proof, however, supplied no basis for treating the crossing in question as exceptional; the theory of the experts was that the rule was technologically unsound for all crossings. Though the court does not say so, the power company was allowed to challenge the soundness of the rule and lay a predicate for its rejection as a criterion of due care. This inar-

---

64. See, e.g., Lone Star Gas Co. v. Kelly, 140 Tex. 15, 165 S.W.2d 446 (1942) and 166 S.W.2d 191 (1942).

65. 202 S.C. 73, 24 S.E.2d 121 (1943).

ticulate holding is the only authority we have found allowing a tort defendant to challenge the wisdom of an administrative safety measure without challenging its constitutionality. The result seems sound. In cases in which defendants have proved conformity to unsoundly lax administrative safety rules, however, several courts have simply rejected those measures as proper criteria of due care.[66]

In some damage suits defendants depart from or conform to standards promulgated by administrators who have no jurisdiction to regulate the defendants but who have official claims to the courts' respect for their expertise. In Polk v. City of Los Angeles,[67] a worn spot in the insulation on a city's power line was touched by a tree trimmer with disastrous results. A commission had authority to regulate private power lines throughout the state, but arguably had no authority to regulate municipal power lines. The jury's attention was directed to a rule of the commission requiring frequent and thorough inspection of insulation, and the jury was then charged that failure to conform to the rule would be negligence. The trial judge refused the city's request for an instruction that the commission's rules did not apply to it. The appellate court was not sure that the commission lacked authority to regulate city-owned power lines; but the court said that even on the assumption that the commission had no authority, the standard of care should not vary with the ownership of utilities, and no error was committed. Whatever ills municipal ownership may cure, it does not reduce the risks of defects in power line insulation; the commission's competence to judge the proper methods of insuring adequate insulation is not affected by municipal ownership. The plaintiff, however, probably took a chance of reversal that was not worth running. Defense counsel who shows that his client conformed to a rule promulgated by a commission that similarly has only parallel jurisdiction may more wisely run the same risks to get a directed verdict. In Dilley v. Iowa Public Service Co.,[68] a defendant used this strategy successfully and got the appellate affirmance it deserved.

---

66. See, e.g., Johnson v. Steam-Gauge & Lantern Co., 72 Hun. 535, 25 N.Y.S. 689 (1893), aff'd, 146 N.Y. 152, 40 N.E. 773 (1895), in which a factory inspector's approval of an obviously and inexcusably dangerous fire escape was held to be no protection against liability for injuries to a user.

67. 26 Cal.2d 519, 159 P.2d 931 (1945).

68. 210 Iowa 1332, 227 N.W. 173 (1929).

Defendants who comply with administrative safety regulations often deserve a court ruling that they have, as a matter of law, used due care. Administrators who address themselves to the problem of making some aspect of an installation safe are not likely to require less than the precaution they believe proper. Therefore most administrative regulations express or imply an administrative judgment on what should be done as well as on what should not be done.[69]

In Southwestern Gas & Electric Co. v. Deshazo,[70] a telephone operator sued both a power company and her employer, the telephone company, for electric shock injuries. The lines of two companies crossed some miles from the exchange where the operator was injured while at her work. Farmers felled a tree near the crossing. An unseen vine entangled in the tree-top thwarted their woodsmanship, and the tree unexpectedly fell on the crossing; the lines of the two companies touched and telephone wires became charged with high voltage current. The companies proved that the crossing was built in accordance with utility commission rules. The telephone operator offered no proof that the regulations were lax or failed to cover all significant safety aspects. The court held that, even though the regulations did state only the tolerable minimum of care, once the companies proved compliance the telephone operator had the burden of showing particular acts or conditions that constituted negligence, and that since she did not carry this burden the companies were entitled to judgment. An exhaustive and applicable regulation, therefore, was held to be the criterion of due care, in the absence of a showing justifying its rejection.[71] Even when the regulation has been adopted after the act complained of, proof that defendant's conduct met the standard in the regulation has been held to absolve defendant of negligence.[72] Of course, conformity to a safety regulation may

---

69. Cf. Nader v. Allegheny Airlines, Inc., 426 U.S. 290, 96 S.Ct. 1978, 48 L.Ed.2d 643 (1976).

70. 199 Ark. 1078, 138 S.W.2d 397 (1940).

71. It is not surprising to find that Federal courts have held that administratively promulgated rules for river navigation are fixed standards for judging collision cases. See, e.g., Weathers Towing, Inc. v.

M. V. Herman Pott, 570 F.2d 1294 (5th Cir. 1978) in which defendant's compliance protected it from liability for collision damages.

72. Stonehocker v. General Motors Corp., 587 F.2d 151 (4th Cir. 1978). Plaintiff claimed General Motors negligently designed a car with too weak a body. General Motors proved the car's strength met standards promulgated several years after the car was built.

not be determinative if the injury is not of the type which the agency was attempting to prevent.[73]

Courts should not give much weight to administrative silence.[74] Lack of regulation can be accounted for in one of two ways: either (1) the administrator has not considered safety at all, or (2) the administrator has considered the need for safeguards and decided that none is called for. Only in the latter case is silence significant.

In Grand Trunk Ry. Co. v. Ives,[75] a grade crossing collision case, the railroad contended that since a commissioner could have ordered a crossing flagman and had not done so, lack of a flagman was legally irrelevant. This contention was put forward even though approaching trains were not visible to highway users, until they came within fifteen or twenty feet of the tracks. The court properly rejected this unsound view.

In the Ives case, the court said, "The underlying principle . . . is that neither the legislature nor railroad commissioners can arbitrarily determine in advance what shall constitute ordinary care or reasonable prudence in a railroad company, at a crossing, in every particular case which may afterwards arise . . . . [E]ach case must stand upon its own merits and be decided upon its own facts and circumstances; and these are the features which make the question of negligence primarily one for the jury to determine . . . ." If the court meant (and it may well have not) that jurors should be allowed to reject an administrative judgment without grounds for doubting its soundness, its opinion is supported by neither reason nor authority. Unless an administrative judgment is shown to be unduly lax or unless significant circumstances were not considered

73. See, e.g., Turner v. American Motors General Corp., 392 A.2d 1005 (D.C.App.1978). Defendant was not entitled to a summary judgment on the ground that the design of its bus conformed to a safety regulation when the regulation required windows to be unobstructed to permit easy exit in case of accident but plaintiff was injured when she fell while reaching for a bell-rope placed high above the windows.

74. They were over-impressed by it. In Dyson v. New York & New Eng. R. R. Co., 57 Conn. 9, 17 A. 137, 14 Am.St.Rep. 82 (1889), the court held that since the legislature had instructed a railroad commission to require special warnings at grade crossings where they were necessary, a victim of a crossing accident could not complain of lack of special signals unless they had been ordered. In Pratt, Read & Co. v. New York, N. H. & H. R. Co., 102 Conn. 735, 130 A. 102 (1925), however, the same court held that administrative silence was at most evidential and was not conclusive. In some other jurisdictions the history has been similar.

75. 144 U.S. 408, 12 S.Ct. 679, 36 L.Ed. 485 (1892).

by the administrators, judges probably should not allow jurors to substitute their opinions for those of the administrative agency.

Even though an administrator has studied a particular installation and approved it the administrator may have made only a limited judgment and passed no judgment on the phase of the installation significant in a particular case. If, for example, a labor commission requires safety catches to guard window-washers against falls from sills, a conforming hospital may nevertheless subject window-washers to undue risks of contagion— a subject ignored by the commission. In less obvious cases the ambit of administrative judgment may be unclear. When a convincing case is not made that relevant administrative judgment has been passed, administrative silence should have no weight.

In Hubbard-Hall Chemical Co. v. Silverman,[76] two illiterate farm laborers died shortly after spreading a poisonous insecticide. They did not use the precautions printed on the manufacturer's label. The manufacturer had complied with federal law by submitting its proposed label to the Department of Agriculture and complying with a minor change the Department had ordered, but the label did not contain a skull and crossbones or other symbol which might have alerted the illiterate victims. The Court of Appeals, affirming a judgment against the manufacturer, said, "The approval of the Department of Agriculture merely satisfied the conditions laid down by the Congress for shipment in interstate commerce. Neither Congress nor the Department explicitly or implicitly provided that the Department's approval [meant] that the defendant had met the possibly higher standard of due care imposed by the common law of torts. . . . ."

In Southern Pacific R.R. Co. v. Mitchell [77] (a railroad crossing accident case in which a passenger in a motor car was injured), a few cars were being backed over the crossing late at night. The engine's headlight pointed away from the crossing and, of course, did not reach the crossing before the leading dark colored boxcar crashed into the automobile. Both the automobile driver's and the engineer's vision were impeded by buildings. Trainmen atop the slow moving boxcar saw the automobile and tried to warn the driver by swinging their lanterns. The train was moving slowly enough so that a trainman could have jumped off and guarded the crossing and reboarded after the train passed. The only warnings were, at most, bell and whistle signals to which the automobile driver paid no attention. Both

76. 340 F.2d 402 (1st Cir. 1965).   77. 80 Ariz. 50, 292 P.2d 827 (1956).

the maintenance of crossing safety guards and the operation of trains over crossing were subject to safety regulation by an Arizona administrative commission. At the trial the defendant asked the judge to tell the jury that, since the commission had neither ordered the railroad to install an automatic warning nor required the railroad to maintain a watchman at this crossing, the railroad was under no duty to take either of those precautions. The trial judge denied this request, and asked the jury to decide whether or not the railroad company had failed to use due care, even though the company had complied with all promulgated administrative regulations. The appellate court said, "[T]he duty of the railroad must be measured by reasonable care under the circumstances. . . . The reasonable need for crossing protection . . . is to be determined by the special and unusual dangers of the particular crossing. . . . [G]reater care must be exercised . . . when trains are being backed . . . particularly when the train's approach is obscured by obstructions. . . . [T]here is affirmative evidence from which the jury could have found that reasonable care would require additional warning of this train's operations over the instant crossing. Even in the absence of a requirement of special precautions by the public authorities the jury could have found a situation of unusual and particular danger herein which would be the basis for a finding of negligence in the failure of defendants to maintain additional safeguards. The problem herein is not whether the railroad should have permanently maintained at this crossing a watchman or other automatic warning device, but whether in view of the particular circumstances at the specific time of collision, it should have given some more adequate form of warning . . . ."[78]

78. In Ebel v. Board of County Road Comm'rs, County of Saginaw, 386 Mich. 598, 194 N.W.2d 365 (1972) the vehicle in which the injured plaintiff was a passenger collided at night with a stanchion maintained in the center of a road at a grade crossing. The stanchion supported warning lights which flashed whenever a train approached. None was approaching at the time of the accident. The defendant railroad had erected and maintained the stanchion in compliance with an order of the Public Service Commission in 1928, thirty-five years before the accident. The trial judge instructed the jury that they could find for the plaintiff only if the stanchion was "unusually dangerous" to highway users. The appellate court reversed, saying that the proper test of liability was not unusual danger, but lack of ordinary prudence; the jury, furthermore could hold that compliance with the ancient administrative order, issued to prevent grade crossing accidents, did not justify maintenance of an unreasonable hazard endangering passersby under changed conditions of motoring. The appellate court also ruled that the trial judge erred in charging that the administrative order prevented a finding that the stanchion was a nuisance.

Chapter V

NEGLIGENCE—PROOF OF NEGLIGENCE AND PROOF OF DUE CARE

Table of Sections

§ 1. THE OBJECTIVES OF PROOF

The substantive law of negligence points to the goals of proof of negligence. Claimants' lawyers offering proof try to lay predicates for detailed conclusions of fact which inescapably fall into the category of negligence in law. Legal negligence is a compound conclusion based on prior sub-conclusions; it can be broken down and its parts so stated that they throw light on the kinds of proof needed. Plaintiff's lawyer, when arguing the defendant's negligence to a trial judge or a jury, needs to have made proof which will back up these six assertions:

1. This (describing it) is what defendant did.

2. Such conduct is dangerous.

3. Either (a) the defendant knew it was dangerous, or (b) a reasonable person in the defendant's circumstances would have known of the danger.

4. The risk could feasibly have been reduced in such-and-such a way, for a comparatively small dollar cost, and with at most, tolerable inconvenience.

5. Defendant knew of (or had a reasonable opportunity to know of) a feasible way of reducing the risk.

6. Defendant's inconsiderate conduct fell short of the care required by law.

Proof which will justify these six statements varies in complexity. In some cases the proof which the plaintiff needs is only evidence picturing (in a common sense way) the scene of

80

injury and the defendant's conduct at the time of injury. Proof that a defendant discarded a banana peel on a busy walkway would sustain a verdict of negligence. Often, however, proof of what happened at the time of the accident is only a start, and other evidence must be adduced bearing on the last five of the above six statements. This discussion is designed to indicate the kinds of evidence sometimes needed to back up each of the six statements.

§ 2. PROOF DESCRIBING DEFENDANT'S CONDUCT AND THE SCENE OF INJURY

Automobile-collision witnesses are seldom asked the color of the defendant's coat or when defendant last bought gasoline. But if identity is in dispute, the color of a driver's clothing might be crucial; or if testimony on speed conflicts, a showing that the driver was pulling out of a filling station at the time of the collision may be determinative. Each law suit has individuality; details unimportant in one may be decisive in another.

In a negligence suit the plaintiff usually has the burden of coming forward with a credible and fairly specific version of what defendant did and of circumstances surrounding defendant's conduct.[1] The plaintiff usually proves what happened by calling eyewitnesses who testify to what they saw; for example, that the defendant drove through a red light, or that the defendant's circular saw was used without a guard, etc. Litigants themselves often take the stand and give this sort of testimony; occasionally they are called as witnesses by their opponents.

Testimony about prior or subsequent events may throw light on what happened at the time of accident. Witness testifies that Merchant's stairway had no handrail shortly before or shortly after Customer fell downstairs. If Witness's testimony stands uncontradicted, the trial judge and jury may infer that there was no handrail when Customer fell—unless Merchant explains how a handrail got there after Witness's pre-fall observation, or what became of the rail before Witness's post-fall observation.

1. Some common sense assumptions will aid plaintiff unless defendant comes forward with disproof; in a head-on collision case, for example, if plaintiff proves defendant drove on the wrong side of the road, plaintiff need not initially rebut possible excuses defendant may have had for doing so. See Pfaffenbach v. White Plains Express Corp., 17 N.Y.2d 132, 216 N.E.2d 324 (1966). Cf. Gift v. Palmer, 392 Pa. 628, 141 A.2d 408 (1958), in which a plaintiff parent who proved nothing more than that the defendant had run over his three-year old boy was held to have fallen short of proving negligence.

Conduct may leave tracks which can be fruitfully examined. An automobile braked at high speeds leaves skid marks which can be located, measured, and interpreted. Proof of the beginning of the mark establishes the point at which the brake was applied; proof of its length may establish speed; proof that the brake was applied tends to establish that the driver saw trouble ahead; etc.

Ordinary people cannot read some of the tracks left by certain events; only experts can decode their meaning. In Clark v. Standard Sanitary Mfg. Co.,[2] claimant had cut her hand on a sharp edge of a fracture in a porcelain faucet-handle which broke when she turned it. The defendant manufactured the handle. An expert testified that he found the handle brittle because it was improperly overbaked.

Experts may also be used to draw meanings from testimony of eyewitnesses. In Kelly v. McKay,[3] homeowners testified that a quarryman set off a blast which shook pieces off the rock walls of their house, and stated the distance between quarry and house. Then an expert took the stand and testified that a dynamite charge could have such an effect only if it was heavier than one hundred pounds.[4]

§ 3. PROOF OF DANGER

As a matter of substantive law, conduct that is not dangerous is not negligent for only when conduct is dangerous can resulting injury be foreseen. Injuries can be the upshot of reasonably safe conduct; a careful driver, for example, can run over a child who darts into the path of the car. No proof is needed to establish the dangerous character of those deeds that are commonly known to be hazardous; but many hazards not understood by ordinary judges and jurors lurk in technical activity. When one of these hazards takes its toll, the injured claimant who charges negligence needs expert testimony to show danger. In Wood v. Canadian Imperial Dry, Inc.,[5] a workman, newly employed in a carbonated-drink bottling plant, was hurt when a bottle exploded. Had the workman proved only these facts, jurors (who know little about bottling machinery) might have had difficulty in deciding whether the explosion was (1) a sporadic accident

2. 8 N.J.Misc. 284, 149 A. 828 (1930).

3. 149 Tex. 343, 233 S.W.2d 121 (1950).

4. See Mitchell v. Fruehauf Corp., 568 F.2d 1139 (5th Cir. 1978), in which experts testified on the change of a meat truck's center of gravity while rounding a curve, caused by swinging meat carcasses which impaired the trucker's control.

5. 296 Mass. 80, 5 N.E.2d 8 (1936).

unlikely to recur in bottling works, or (2) an instance of a tendency to cause harm inhering in the design or method of using the bottling machinery.

Danger or safety may be investigated in two different ways:

1.　An investigator (without inquiring into the past history of a bottling machine) may apply general knowledge about the design of the machine and adjudge it dangerous or safe. This general knowledge may bear on bottling machines as a class, mechanics, tensile strength of commercial bottle glass, gas pressures, etc. Those who have such knowledge are usually experts.

2.　An investigator may be able to adjudge a particular machine dangerous or safe by going into its past history. If bottles often have exploded in it, then its use is probably dangerous; if it has been used for a long time without mishaps both before and after a particular explosion it can be adjudged relatively safe. These conclusions are sometimes soundly reached by persons without special knowledge or training; their judgment is "practical" rather than "theoretical."

Each of these methods has its weakness. If a bottling machine is adjudged dangerous or safe on theoretical grounds without looking into its history, some practical aspect of danger or safety may be overlooked. If the machine is judged only on its bad or good record, happenstance may make it seem more dangerous or safer than it is. Often, of course, theory is enough; putting one's hand into an electric fan is dangerous. And practical experience can clearly warn of danger before the nature of a risk is fully understood; some swamps were known to be malarial before the role of mosquitos in spreading the disease was discovered. Sometimes, however, only a combination of theory and experience is convincing.

A good example of educating a trial judge and a jury on danger by use of expert testimony is Air Reduction Co. v. Philadelphia Storage Battery Co.,[6] a suit for fire damage to a factory. The defendant had designed and installed a system for distributing oxygen in the plaintiff's factory. Oxygen entered the system through a manifold which exploded soon after the system was put in operation. The fire ensued. The factory owner's experts testified that oxygen under high pressure is inflammable and will explode on contact with coal dust, waste, oil, or small steel clippings. When oxygen explodes in a copper or brass manifold, the fire burns itself out harmlessly inside the chamber. In a steel chamber, however, fire feeds on the walls, perforates them, and bursts out. This testimony, coupled with

---

6.　14 F.2d 734 (3d Cir. 1926).

proof that the manifold was made of steel, proved an impressive case of danger. If they are available, qualified experts can be used to give such testimony whenever ordinary jurors are not able to recognize danger without a specialist's help. For an interesting example of expert testimony establishing the safety of a defendant's conduct, see Dresco Mechanical Contractors, Inc. v. Todd-CEA Inc.[7]

Even though an accident happens in a technical setting, danger may be appreciated by jurors without expert testimony. In Missouri, K. & T. Ry. Co. of Texas v. Williams,[8] a passing locomotive engineer was killed when he struck his head on a mail crane near the track. The railroad contended that jurors could not intelligently decide where mail cranes should be located unless they had been informed by expert testimony, and that since the plaintiff offered none she had not proved negligence. The court held that danger was patent to ordinary people and plaintiff needed no experts to prove it.

Ordinary individuals do not always know the limits of their knowledge, and expert testimony may be used to warn jurors away from unsound lay assumptions of danger. In Johnson v. Detroit & M. Ry.,[9] an action against a railroad for running over cattle, the stock owner's non-expert witnesses described the cattle guard over which the stock had passed onto the right-of-way. The railroad offered expert testimony on the almost unfailing capacity of this type of cattle guard to prevent live-stock from passing. The appellate court ruled this testimony admissible. Such proof may keep jurors from assuming the existence of serious danger where there is little or no risk. There are times, however, when an expert's opinion would add little or nothing and should be rejected.[10]

Discussion now turns to proof of danger or safety by showing the past record of the site of the accident—safety history evidence. Most courts admit safety history evidence, but some

7. 531 F.2d 1292 (5th Cir. 1976). See also, Marshall v. Humble Oil & Refining Co., 459 F.2d 355 (8th Cir. 1972); Massey-Ferguson, Inc. v. Wells, 383 A.2d 641 (Del.1978). But see Geremia v. Benny's, Inc., — R.I. —, 383 A.2d 1332 (1978), in which the claimant's expert testimony did not go far enough to inculpate the defendant.

8. 103 Tex. 228, 125 S.W. 881 (1910). See also, Delmarva Power & Light v. Stout, 380 A.2d 1365 (Del.1977); Frazier v. Continental Oil Co., 568 F.2d 378 (5th Cir. 1978).

9. 135 Mich. 353, 97 N.W. 760 (1904).

10. See Stoler v. Penn Central Transportation Co., 583 F.2d 896 (6th Cir. 1978).

courts exclude it on the ground that it opens up a "collateral inquiry."

A factory inspector who had to decide whether or not a bottling machine is safe would not ignore either proof that it had already claimed fifteen eyes or proof that it had been used constantly for forty years without hurting anyone; but factory inspectors do not hear lawsuits and are not impeded by the three following aspects of litigation:

1. Trial judges and jurors cannot recheck partisan proof by active inquiry. The court hears only the history that advocates choose to present, and when safety history evidence is offered, it can only be heard or kept out. Partisan advocates are likely to prove only parts of the machine's record, parts which favor their clients. Cross-examination to develop completeness may be clumsy and time-consuming. Often safety history evidence has too little value to be worth the time it takes.

Sometimes, however, safety history evidence can shed crucial light on a central dispute. Many courts are willing to put up with it as a rule with these cases in mind. The most flexible practice allows trial judges to decide whether or not safety history is likely to be worth hearing and to admit or reject it accordingly. A few appellate courts expressly avow this flexible practice; others tacitly approve it by upholding virtually all trial rulings either way.

2. Litigants need special protection against surprise. A factory inspector who finds a clue to danger is at liberty to consider it until he or she understands it. A damage suit lawyer who is unexpectedly confronted with safety history evidence during a trial is rarely able to cope with it properly. Safety history evidence may encompass events happening sporadically over months and years; opposing counsel may be unprepared to meet fraudulent, partial, or mistaken testimony about other accidents or long periods of safe use.

If, however, lawyers know that safety history evidence is admissible, they have a chance to prepare to meet it; in no case which we have found does an objector make a convincing showing of unreasonable surprise. Modern pre-trial hearings probably make surprise even more unlikely.

3. Jurors may be misled by safety history evidence. Jurors impressed by a good safety record may fail to see that defendant nevertheless subsequently became negligent; jurors convinced of a defendant's guilt of negligence on earlier occasions may find for plaintiff even though defendant mended his or her ways before the accident in suit.

Courts receiving safety history evidence try to restrict proof to times when conditions were virtually the same as those surrounding plaintiff's injury. The logic of valid use of safety history evidence is simple, practical logic which adult jurors should understand. Trial judges can, and sometimes do, give enlightening jury instructions on the value and use of the proof.

Shopper falls while walking in Merchant's store. Eyewitnesses' description of the floor may be the only proof needed on danger—once described, the floor may be obviously too slippery or clearly safe. Proof of other falls or of long periods of safe use should be excluded as a waste of time. Fully described walkways, however, may still be arguably dangerous or safe; the scenes of some falls are described by unskilled witnesses so poorly that a jury can do no more than choose between conflicting dogmatic testimony. If Shopper claims the floor provided poor traction, plaintiff's witnesses are likely to testify, "the floor was slippery," or "the slickest I've ever seen," or "gave me a feeling of insecurity," or some other subjective statement of low probative weight. Proof of other falls (or of extensive use without falls) cogently bears on the quality of traction. Most courts admit safety history evidence in such cases.[11] An occupant's proof of safe use may be so convincing that it warrants a directed verdict. A faller's failure to prove other falls may be fatal in an already doubtful case—a lack which courts have occasionally noted when granting a nonsuit. Proof of other falls may not only forestall a directed verdict for the occupant but may also convince some juror otherwise inclined to believe a defense witness who testified that the floor afforded ordinary traction.

In these fall cases the scene of accident is described testimonially and safety history evidence is added to throw light on the safety of premises which are hard to describe objectively. In another type of case, safety history evidence is a substitute for detailed testimonial description. Baker v. Hagey,[12] was a suit against a junk dealer who processed steel scrap for market. Modern cutting torches had not yet been invented, and large pieces of steel were broken up with explosives inside a log structure. A steel fragment hit and injured a neighbor. The neighbor was allowed to prove that the junkman's operations had long been scattering missiles over the neighborhood. This evidence established that the junkman's operation was freighted with

11. See, e. g., Safeway Stores, Inc. v. Bozeman, 394 S.W.2d 532 (Tex. Civ.App.1965); Frazier v. Continental Oil Co., 568 F.2d 378 (5th Cir. 1978).

12. 177 Pa. 128, 35 A. 705, 55 Am. St.Rep. 712 (1896). See also, Gulf Hills Dude Ranch, Inc. v. Brinson, 191 So.2d 856, 861 (Miss.1966); Mitchell v. Fruehauf Corp., 568 F. 2d 1139 (5th Cir. 1978).

danger. Had the neighbor tried to prove the seriousness of risk without showing this bad record, he would have needed testimony describing in detail the chinks in the structure and proof showing the sizes, force, and likely paths of fragments scattered by the kind of blasts used. Safety history evidence was a simple and ample substitute for complicated eyewitness and expert testimony.

When eyewitnesses' description shows a high order of danger, proof of a long period of safe use is valuable and should be received. In Stark v. Allis-Chalmers and Northwest Roads, Inc.,[13] the claimant brought an action for the wrongful death of her husband which occurred while he operated a tractor. The machine, she alleged, was negligently designed by the defendant-manufacturer, and as a result, her husband was pitched between the front-loading bucket and the hood, where he was crushed to death. The trial judge allowed the tractor manufacturer to prove that no similar accident had ever occurred in the use of the 10,000 machines of the same design. Proof of the circumstances of the operator's injury might tend to dispose the jurors to find danger. Even though jurors may have been convinced of the soundness of the tractor's design by other kinds of proof, the manufacturer deserved the protective inference implied by the good record of 10,000 similar machines.

A good example of the use of a combination of expert testimony and safety history evidence is found in Muller v. A. B. Kirschbaum Co.,[14] a case in which a bystander was scalded when a restaurant coffee urn burst. The plaintiff proved by expert testimony that the urn could not withstand pressures above twenty-five pounds per square inch and that its valves would not forestall pressures higher than twenty-five pounds. The plaintiff thereafter proved the urn had burst three times before he was hurt, showing that his expert knew what he was talking about. So safety history evidence may corroborate expert testimony.[15]

13. 2 Wash.App. 399, 467 P.2d 854 (1970).

14. 298 Pa. 560, 148 A. 851 (1930).

15. Proof of other accidents sometimes tends to show that defendant knew (or should have known) that his or her conduct was dangerous—a topic that will be discussed shortly. But a showing of other accidents *after* plaintiff's injury has no bearing on defendant's knowledge at the time of plaintiff's injury. Some courts receive this proof of subsequent safety history for its bearing on danger; other courts exclude it and restrict safety history evidence to cases in which it bears on defendant's knowledge of danger. See C. Morris, Studies in the Law of Torts 76–77 n.5 (1952).

Discussion turns to another type of proof of danger or safety —admissions. An admission is a litigant's out-of-court statement inconsistent with his or her position at trial; it may be oral, written, or implied by conduct. Admissions are hearsay but are received under an exception to the rule that usually excludes hearsay. A plaintiff's admission of the safety of the site of the injury is inconsistent with the claim that the site was not maintained with due care; it may be proved against plaintiff. A defendant's admission of danger at the site is, of course, also admissible evidence.

Proof of an admission is not necessarily conclusive; it is only entitled to the probative weight it happens to have. Consumer is poisoned by eating Packer's product. If, in a moment of magnanimity, Consumer says that Packer's plant is run with all possible care, proof of this admission may be far from fatal to the claim. Safety of food processing can be judged reliably only by experts or those who know safety history. Unless Consumer has either special experience with food packing or knows about Packer's plant's record for safety, this admission may have little weight and probably will not sway a jury confronted with better founded proof to the contrary.

A defendant's admission of facts showing negligence, even though made on the witness stand, is not conclusive when other proof tends to show due care.[16] When, however, an admission involves danger readily discerned by ordinary people, it may be virtually determinative. In Reid v. Owens,[17] a young motorist driving his father's car ran down a pedestrian. The pedestrian sued the father, claiming that he negligently entrusted the car to the boy, knowing he was not competent to drive. The pedestrian proved that before the accident the father had said his son was a reckless driver. The court held this evidence was properly admitted to show that the boy was, in fact, incompetent, and established the danger of turning a car over to him.

§ 4. PROOF OF KNOWLEDGE OF DANGER OR OPPORTUNITY TO DISCERN IT

The topic of proof of danger, just discussed, is a significant part of a negligence case because the substantive law of negligence makes it so. This new topic—knowledge of danger—is, of course, equally rooted in substantive law. The law does not

16. London v. Perreault, 118 N.H. 392, 387 A.2d 342 (1978).

17. 98 Utah 50, 93 P.2d 680 (1939). See also, Arsenault v. Willis, 117 N.H. 980, 380 A.2d 264 (1977), in which a motorist's admission of inattention entitled his victim to a summary judgment.

make all dangerous conduct negligent; one who acts dangerously nevertheless does not fail to exercise due care when he or she is excusably ignorant of the risk. If a reasonably prudent person contemplating the same act in the same circumstances would not have discerned a likelihood of harm, the actor is not negligent. The reasonably prudent person is not omniscient; the actor sometimes is ignorant of dangers that in fact exist. Of course a defendant with knowledge of danger cannot plead excusable ignorance of it. And some defendants who are ignorant of danger are not *excusably* ignorant; they should know better.

In simple cases the only evidence needed to establish that the defendant was not excusably ignorant of a risk is eyewitness description of defendant's conduct. A normal adult who said, "I didn't know it was dangerous to light a cigarette while cleaning a rug with gasoline," would not be believed.

When novel operations in technological fields turn out to be unexpectedly dangerous, something more than eyewitness description is usually needed to prove that the defendant should have anticipated the harm which resulted. Illustrations of both adequate and inadequate pre-searches for risk were set out in Chapman Chemical Co. v. Taylor,[18] a suit for damages to growing cotton resulting from the use of 2, 4–D (a then recently discovered chemical killer of broad leaf plants) brought against a rice farmer and a chemical company. The manufacturing chemical company mixed 2, 4–D with talc and sold the mixture for dusting rice fields to kill weeds. The farmer, after getting assurances from the manufacturer and impartial experts that 2, 4–D dusting was unlikely to harm neighboring cotton fields, hired aerial crop-dusters to dust his rice fields. Much dusting had been done with other chemicals; these materials had never floated more than a hundred feet when properly applied. Unknown to either defendant (or anybody else, for that matter) the particles of dust were tiny air foils and glided far enough to settle on and kill a cotton crop three-fourths of a mile away. The court held that: (1) farmer was excusably ignorant of danger and not liable, but (2) manufacturer "was charged with knowledge which tests would have revealed." [19]

18. 215 Ark. 630, 222 S.W.2d 820 (1949).

19. The majority were willing to hold the manufacturer liable without proof of negligence, and they approved an instruction visiting liability without fault upon it—on a theory of "extra-hazardous activity." This result of course, would be routine under newer theories of products liability. See Ch. IX, infra. A dissenting judge thought the jury should have passed on whether or not the manufacturer was excusably ignorant of soaring qualities of the chemical. Cf. Walton v. Sherwin-Williams Co., 191 F.2d 277 (8th Cir. 1951), in which a manufacturer put 2, 4–

Actual knowledge of danger (or lack of it) can be proved by several kinds of evidence. The defendant can take the stand (or be called to it by the plaintiff) and admit or deny having such knowledge. Eyewitnesses who saw defendant observe the source of danger, or make a bungling attempt at safeguarding, or order an employee to take steps to reduce risk can give damaging testimony. Express admissions of knowledge of danger are occasionally proved; in the case in which a pedestrian proved that a car-lending father admitted knowledge of his son's reckless driving, the admission was received to prove (1) the son was not a competent driver (danger) and (2) the father knew of his son's recklessness (knowledge of danger).

Implied admissions of knowledge of danger are often proved. In Branson v. Northern Pacific Ry.,[20] a train hit a truck on a private grade crossing. No warning whistle was blown. Since the crossing was not public, highway crossing signal statutes were worded so that they were inapplicable. Some private crossings may be so little used and so relatively safe that absence of warnings is sensible. The trucker, however, was allowed to prove that until a short time before the accident, the railroad had maintained a sign directing engineers to blow their whistles at this crossing. The court held that this evidence tended to admit both danger and the railroad's knowledge of that danger.

Defendant's knowledge of danger need not be established if plaintiff can prove that defendant had an adequate opportunity to discover the danger and, if reasonably alert, would have discovered it. In Rosenthal v. Central Garage of Lynn,[21] a business guest slipped on a glob of grease on a stairway. Plaintiff proved neither that his host knew the grease was there nor how long it had been there. He failed to carry his affirmative burden of establishing that a reasonably alert garage operator would have discovered the hazard, and therefore lost his case. But in White v. Mugar,[22] decided by the same court in the same

D in oil and made tests which showed it would not injure neighboring broad-leafed crops if properly applied. The court said, "There is . . . solid foundation for the finding that 2, 4–D in an oil solution is not an inherently dangerous product." The court then analyzed the case as a negligence claim defeated by proof of the manufacturer's due care.

20. 55 Idaho 220, 41 P.2d 629 (1935). Compare Burdis v. Texas & Pacific Ry., 569 F.2d 320 (5th Cir. 1978).

21. 279 Mass. 574, 181 N.E. 660 (1932). See also Smith v. Safeway Stores, Inc., 298 A.2d 214 (D.C. App.1972).

22. 280 Mass. 73, 181 N.E. 725 (1932). See also Bohn v. Hudson & Manhattan R. Co., 16 N.J. 180, 108 A.2d 5 (1954).

year, proof of a slip on vegetable leaves after they had been on a market floor for an hour thwarted the retailer's motion for a directed verdict.

Safety history evidence can be used to prove knowledge of danger. In Dyas v. Southern Pacific Co.,[23] a workman was killed by a collapsing railroad derrick which fell because ties under the derrick car were rotten. The plaintiff was allowed to prove the railroad's knowledge of an earlier accident in which another derrick collapsed on the same stretch of track for the same reason. Proof of the detailed knowledge of the earlier accident established either knowledge of the rot that resulted in this death or an adequate opportunity to discern the dangerously decayed ties.

Does proof of prior accidents tend to establish the defendant's knowledge of danger when the plaintiff does not show the defendant's knowledge of the prior accidents? In Long v. John Breuner Co.,[24] a customer fell on an inclined concrete store entrance. The customer called a witness who was ready to testify to an earlier harmless fall he had experienced while using the same entrance. The defendant objected because the customer made no showing of the merchant's knowledge of the witness' fall. The appellate court affirmed a ruling admitting this evidence, saying the testimony not only tended to show the ramp's dangerous character, but also tended to bring home to the merchant knowledge of the danger. This court's theory seems wrong; storekeepers often may not hear of harmless slips on their premises; the probative weight of this proof to show knowledge of danger seems almost negligible. But viewed from a procedural angle the ruling takes on different light. The court did not bar the storekeeper from testifying that he neither saw nor heard of the witness' tumble. The merchant could have protected himself from an inference of knowledge by testifying convincingly that he had none.

In Bridger v. Asheville & S. R.,[25] a case in which a child was killed while playing on an unlocked railroad turntable, proof was offered to show that serious injuries had been inflicted by the turntable on several other children before the tragic accident in suit. The court ruled this evidence incompetent unless it was coupled with proof specifically showing the railroad's knowledge of these earlier accidents. This ruling seems doubtful on three

---

23. 140 Cal. 296, 73 P. 972 (1903). See a modern example in Pushnik v. Winky's Drive-In Restaurants, Inc., 242 Pa.Super. 323, 363 A.2d 1291 (1976).

24. 36 Cal.App. 630, 172 P. 1132 (1918).

25. 27 S.C. 456, 3 S.E. 860, 13 Am. St.Rep. 653 (1887).

grounds: (1) The evidence tended to prove the unlocked turntable dangerous. (2) Such accidents seldom go unreported, and the railroad probably knew they happened; proof of their happening is strong circumstantial evidence tending to show the railroad's knowledge of them. (3) The railroad can protect itself against a false inference of knowledge by showing that earlier accidents were neither reported to it nor seen by its servants. The likelihood that an occupant will know about earlier accidents on his or her property varies with circumstances. When many people have been seriously injured on the premises, the occupant is almost sure to know about some of those accidents. If only a few have been slightly injured (or barely escaped injury), the proprietor may well not be aware of the minute blemishes on the premises' record.

A proprietor's proof of a long period of safe use coupled with descriptive testimony tending to show safety may conclusively establish lack of danger—and, of course, no one can have knowledge of hazards that do not exist. Favorable safety history does not, however, establish excusable ignorance of danger when a clear hazard should have been discerned, even though it has happened to claim no victims. Between these extremes lies a group of cases in which a record of no accidents bears on the acceptability of excuses for failure to discern danger.

In William Laurie Co. v. McCullough,[26] a customer fell on an oiled floor in a dry goods store. The court held that the merchant should have been allowed to prove he had used the same floor dressing for a number of years without accidents. The court said the evidence tended not only to show the floor safe but also to show no lack of diligence on the part of the merchant in failing to discern whatever danger may have resulted from use of the floor dressing.

Other courts have taken a less sensible view. In Park Circuit & Realty Co. v. Coulter,[27] a child was injured in an amusement park when his foot caught in a "fun house" slide. The slide was a slanted series of free-rotating cylinders; the child's foot caught between two of them because the lower one was rotating the wrong way. Experts demonstrated with models and gave testimony showing (1) reverse rotation caused the accident, and

26. 174 Ind. 477, 90 N.E. 1014, reh. denied, 174 Ind. 477, 92 N.E. 337 (1910). See also, Stark v. Allis-Chalmers and Northwest Roads, Inc., 2 Wash.App. 399, 467 P.2d 854 (1970); Pippin v. Ranch House South, Inc., 366 A.2d 1180 (Del. 1976).

27. 233 Ky. 1, 24 S.W.2d 942 (1930). See also, Gravely v. Providence Partnership, 549 F.2d 958 (4th Cir. 1977). See generally, on safety history evidence, C. McCormick on Evidence § 200 (2d ed. 1972).

(2) reverse rotation could feasibly have been avoided by inexpensive rachets. The proprietor offered to prove use of the slide by 100,000 people a year without prior accidents. This evidence was excluded. The appellate court approved exclusion on the doubtful theory that jurors would assume there were no other accidents if none were proved, and therefore exclusion was harmless. This holding is unsound. The unheard evidence would have tended to show experience which might have warranted a reasonable belief in the slide's safety. As a matter of substantive law the proprietor, even though his slide was dangerous, was not at fault if he reasonably believed it safe. The excluded evidence, then, had an affirmative bearing on a point at issue.

Another kind of proof bearing on knowledge of risk is proof of warnings of danger. In Curd v. Wing & Co.,[28] a wall collapsed and damaged adjoining property. For the purpose of showing the defendant knew of the risk, the plaintiff was allowed to prove that the city engineer had told defendant that his wall was likely to fall.

Defendants are also allowed to prove assurances which lull them into reasonably (but mistakenly) believing their property safe. In Langdon-Creasy Co. v. Rouse,[29] a storekeeper's exploding gasoline lamp injured an employee. The court held that the storekeeper should have been allowed to prove he had investigated before buying the lamp and was told by a number of users that the brand of lamp that he bought was perfectly safe. The evidence, of course, bore on whether or not the employer was excusably ignorant of danger.[30]

---

28. 115 Ga. 371, 41 S.E. 580 (1902).

29. 139 Ky. 647, 72 S.W. 1113 (1903).

30. The case of Service v. Shoneman, 196 Pa. 63, 46 A. 292 (1900), raises a similar problem. Steam from a boiler sprayed a workman in a dry goods store. The trial judge allowed the merchant to prove that he knew little about boilers, and was assured by a number of boiler users before his purchase that the kind of boiler he was considering was a safe, good one. The jury was not impressed and returned a verdict for the workman on which the court pronounced judgment. The appellate court reversed and rendered judgment for the employer. Perhaps this case goes no further than the gasoline lamp case, plus a holding that reasonable jurors could not find negligence on the facts proved. The opinion, however, all but formulates a new rule of substantive law to this effect: an inexpert buyer of a complicated mechanical appliance who, in good faith, seeks out and relies on advice of qualified safety experts cannot be found guilty of negligence. At least one court has so interpreted the holding and then followed it. State Journal Printing Co. v. City of Madison, 148 Wis. 396, 134 N.W. 909 (1912). Such a rule must have at least two limitations: (1) A proprietor less competent to judge safety than experts relied upon may still know enough to make some independent intelligent investigations;

The proprietor of a dry goods store who may reasonably rely on advice of others in selecting a gasoline lamp must not be confused with the maker of gasoline lamps who is engaged in an enterprise that should be carried on only by experts. In the oxygen manifold case, discussed earlier,[31] experts called by the owner of the fire-damaged factory testified on danger resulting from use of steel manifolds, and then testified that this danger had long been known to science and to commercial suppliers of oxygen systems. As a matter of substantive law, the supplier who furnished the steel manifold was not entitled to claim excusable ignorance of this danger. Such an enterprise should be carried on only by those who have technical know-how. Even an uninformed beginner in such a trade is derelict unless the enterpriser engages, as servants for whose qualifications he or she is responsible, experts acquainted with dangers known to the craft and allied sciences.

Even careful experts are sometimes excusably ignorant of risks. In Grammer v. Mid-Continent Petroleum Corp.,[32] an occupational disease case, an employer went to great length to show that in spite of elaborate investigation and precaution, a risk of lung disease was not discerned until after the plaintiff workman contracted it. The majority of the court held that the employer established excusable ignorance of danger and was entitled to a directed verdict.[33]

§ 5. PROOF OF FEASIBLE SAFER ALTERNATIVES

An alarm-answering driver of a fire engine who speeds through crowded streets knows he is doing something dangerous. Yet, as a matter of substantive law, he may not be negligent. There is no other feasible way to perform his important service. It is, however, practical for him to give warning by blowing a siren; normally he would not be excused for driving a fire truck not equipped with one. He may, however, drive dangerously fast and still use due care.

Sometimes this aspect of the substantive law of negligence calls for no special proof. If a factory operator fails to fence an

---

the proprietor's failure to investigate may sometimes be an unreasonable disregard for the safety of others. (2) The off-hand opinion of an expert caught on the fly may be based on a flimsy submission of the problem; if the submitter ought to know that the expert has not considered the problem carefully, the expert's opinion cannot be prudently relied upon.

31. Air Reduction Co. v. Philadelphia Storage Battery Co., 14 F.2d 734 (3d Cir. 1926).

32. 71 F.2d 38 (10th Cir. 1934).

33. A dissenting judge was not convinced. Both opinions are illuminating.

elevator shaft, no evidence is needed to show that practical safeguards are available and that the operator should have known about their availability. A parent who entrusts the family car to a reckless child for a night on the town will not be heard to say there was no feasible alternative. But in some cases availability, practicality, and opportunity to know about safer alternatives is not so obvious and must be established by proof.[34]

A defendant's knowledge of feasible safeguards can be proved by admissions. Businessmen, however, are likely to guard their talk; they seldom admit (on or off the witness stand) that they neglected to use feasible safeguards of which they had knowledge. Some damning admissions of this kind are occasionally elicited on cross-examination. A rare example of an out-of-court admission occurred in Jones v. Raney Chevrolet Co.,[35] a suit against a second-hand car dealer for injuries resulting from inefficient brakes. The trial judge refused to allow proof that after the accident the dealer's shop foreman told the plaintiff that they had had trouble with the type of brake on the model sold and had replaced many of them with a better type. The appellate court held this to be error, commenting on the evidence's tendency to establish the dealer's knowledge of a feasible safeguard.

Cases on *implied* admissions of known feasible precautions are more common. In Warburton v. N. B. Thayer Co.,[36] a factory hand was injured when her dress caught in a revolving shaft under her workbench. She was allowed to show that skirt guards were used on similar benches in the same plant. This evidence tended to prove the employer's knowledge of a feasible safeguard. Practicality of better protecting the employee was in issue, and the Warburton holding is authority for the competence cf proof of implied admissions establishing knowledge of a feasible way of reducing a risk.[37]

Suppose that the employer had used no skirt guards before the accident but installed them afterwards. Proof of this fact would tend to show that the risk could feasibly have been reduced before the worker was hurt. It would not, however, tend to show that before the accident the employer discerned danger or was aware of a way of reducing the risk. Some accidents educate; they call attention to dangers theretofore reasonably overlooked and stimulate searches for safeguards.

34. See Mitchell v. Fruehauf Corp., 568 F.2d 1139 (5th Cir. 1978).

35. 217 N.C. 693, 9 S.E.2d 395 (1940).

36. 75 N.H. 592, 72 A. 826 (1909).

37. For a similar modern holding, see Larue v. National Union Electric Corp., 571 F.2d 51 (1st Cir. 1978).

Courts universally exclude proof of precautions taken after an accident when offered "to establish negligence." One judicial justification for this exclusion is fear that jurors will not understand the limited value of the proof. When, however, a lawyer offering proof of precautions adopted after injury states that the offer is solely for the purpose of showing that safer ways would have been practical, virtually all courts receive the evidence. Courts have ruled the following evidence competent: proof that a railroad changed its roadbed to keep sand from washing on its track, offered to show that a derailment which killed an engineer could feasibly have been prevented; [38] proof that a slaughterhouse glue vat was covered after an employee fell into it, offered to show that a cover would not have unduly interfered with the packer's business; [39] proof that a railroad discontinued use of a dangerous cross-over track, offered to show that its use was not necessary when a trainman was injured; [40] proof that an icy road was sanded shortly after the accident, offered to show that it could have been sanded before the accident.[41]

Even if offered only to show the practicality of the safeguard, exclusion of proof that some simple fence or rail was built after an accident would not be error. Jurors already know about feasibility of simple precautions. When, however, the setting of an injury is industrial, feasibility of safer alternatives is usually a technical question. If new precautions are taken after the accident, the claimant attempting to establish negligence should be allowed to prove the post-accident safety measure only for the limited purpose of showing it could feasibly have been adopted sooner. The claimant's lawyer should state this limited purpose clearly. Except when the defendant is willing to admit that the

38. St. Louis, A. & T. Ry. v. Johnston, 78 Tex. 536, 15 S.W. 104 (1890).

39. Carstens Packing Co. v. Swinney, 186 F. 50 (9th Cir. 1911). An industrial accident statute was involved, but the principle seems to be the same.

40. Derrington v. Southern Ry., 328 Mo. 283, 40 S.W.2d 1069 (1931), cert. denied, 284 U.S. 662, 52 S.Ct. 37, 76 L.Ed. 561 (1931). See also, Hyndman v. Pennsylvania R. R. Co., 396 Pa. 190, 152 A.2d 251 (1959) (proof of posting an informative warning after the accident); Brown v. Quick Mix Co., 75 Wash.2d 833, 454 P.2d 205 (1969) (proof of a safety guard on power augur to protect user's hand affixed after the accident); Brown v. Link Belt Corp., 565 F.2d 1107, 1109, n.2, (9th Cir. 1977) (proof of warning horns on cranes attached after crane ran over workman).

41. Kaatz v. State, 540 P.2d 1037 (Alaska, 1975).

See Federal Rule of Evidence 407 which provides that the rule excluding proof of safety measures after an accident does not apply when the feasibility of taking such precautions is controverted and the evidence is offered concerning that issue.

new precaution was a feasible way of avoiding the harm, plaintiff should not be heard to say that a showing of feasible precaution might be taken by the jury as an admission of negligence.[42]

One judicial justification given for exclusion of proof of post-accident precautions is this: If such proof were competent, proprietors would postpone adoption of new safeguards until claims against them are disposed of. If this reasoning justifies exclusion when the evidence is offered "to show negligence," it also justifies exclusion when the purpose of the offer is more limited. This reasoning, however, is based on a doubtful prophecy. Many claims are in the mill for a long time; threat of further harm resulting in new claims is much more frightening to defendants and their insurers than a minor threat of strategic disadvantage in a lawsuit which will probably never be tried. This is especially true since expert testimony may be used to prove that safer alternatives were open to the defendant. In the oxygen manifold case, discussed earlier, experts testified that copper and brass manifolds were safer than steel manifolds; that their safety had long been known to science and the trade; and that they were in general use. This proof established that (1) the defendant feasibly could have reduced the risk, and (2) he should have known he could.

A defendant whose experts testify that all practical precautions were taken completes this proof only if their testimony also accounts for the defendant's rejection of alternatives which seem safer to inexpert jurors. In Harris v. Central Power Co.,[43] a car struck a guy wire which ran from a power pole to pavement in an alley. Power company experts testified the guy wire was an indispensable support and had to be in the pavement if the pole was in the pavement. They then said the pole could not be moved off the pavement because its cross-arms would encroach on abutting property. But a non-expert can think of feasible safer alternatives. The power company's witnesses had not testified that an arm extending only on the alley side would be impractical, and the court was willing to allow a jury, in the absence of expert testimony to the contrary, to find such an alternative feasible. The opinion puts forth other suggestions of practical safer alternatives, such as condemnation of a wider right of way, and warnings on the guy wire.

---

42. Defendants in these cases are normally specialists who have obligations to discern dangers and seek out ways of reducing them. They seldom can claim, as a matter of substantive law, either excusable ignorance of existing danger or excusable unawareness of available practical safeguards. These, then, are cases in which practicality of safer alternatives is likely to be a central issue.

43. 109 Neb. 500, 191 N.W. 711 (1922).

Closely resembling both expert testimony and subsequently adopted precautions is proof of departure from custom. If most restaurateurs customarily use safety valves to control steam pressure in coffee urns, their use is probably feasible for a particular restaurateur; if they are used widely, this restaurateur probably had an adequate opportunity to find out about them. Of course a particular restaurateur should be allowed to show in rebuttal unusual circumstances which make customary safeguards peculiarly unnecessary or especially onerous.[44]

Unusual conduct is not necessarily unsafe conduct; proof that a defendant is merely different from other members of the craft is a waste of time and may be misleading. In Cunningham v. Ft. Pitt Bridge Works,[45] an industrial accident case, a heavy girder was moved by hand and dropped on a workman. The claimant was allowed to prove that structural iron was customarily moved by crane—without showing that crane-moving was safer than hand-moving. The trial judge told the jury that departure from ordinary methods was negligence. The appellate court held the instruction wrong and said, "The party charging negligence does not show it by showing that the machinery was not in common use. If it should be so held, the use of the newest and best machine, if not yet generally adopted, could be adduced as evidence of negligence. . . . [T]he evidence should not, in the first instance, be admitted on behalf of the plaintiff, unless it tends to show that the method pursued was not only unusual, but more dangerous in itself than the ordinary one." When evidence tends to show lack of a customary *precaution* it does tend to show a feasible, well-known alternative safer than the course followed.[46] Though the concept "custom" is often emphasized in opinions, a precaution may be less than customary and yet be required for a verdict of due care. Twenty-four children were injured when their school bus's brakes failed. The bus was mounted on a 1965 General Motors chassis which lacked a "dual hydraulic system." Some years before 1965 dual systems, though not yet customary, were widely used on motor vehicles—particularly on public transit buses. Detailed proof of

---

44. Proof of departure from business safety custom has another (and unusual) bearing. It tends to show that liability will not force widespread business change. Without it, jurors might erroneously assume that departer's conduct is representative of business. Some jurors (though not many) might hesitate to impose liability which would have widespread repercussions throughout an entire industry. Proof of departure divests the departer of undeserved prestige.

45. 197 Pa. 625, 47 A. 846 (1901).

46. See, e. g., McCollan v. Tate, 575 F.2d 509 (5th Cir. 1978); Pittsburgh, S. & N. R. Co. v. Lamphere, 137 F. 20 (3d Cir. 1905).

the extent of this use was held to justify a verdict of negligent design.[47]

Courts allow defendants charged with negligence to prove they used all customary safeguards. This proof does not necessarily show either that greater precaution was impractical or that a defendant was excusably ignorant of feasible precautions not yet adopted by defendant's craft. The whole craft may have inexcusably failed to use feasible and well-known safeguards. Nevertheless, this proof does have two permissible uses:

(1) It tends to point up the onus of the plaintiff's burden of proof. Proof of a defendant's conformity to custom sharpens attention on whether or not plaintiff *has established* that defendant had practical safer alternatives. When jurors know the ways of defendant's calling, they are less likely to accept academic or hasty suggestions that defendant could and should have acted differently. If none of defendant's craft has adopted suggested alternatives, the plaintiff must show clearly that these novel alternatives are both safer and feasible.

(2) Lack of opportunities to learn of safeguards from other members of defendant's craft is one of the circumstances to be taken into account in judging whether or not defendant was excusably ignorant of a feasible safeguard. Defendants who prove they followed standard usages prove they could not learn greater precaution from fellow craftsmen. Such a defendant still may be negligent; those who follow bad examples may be at fault even though their models are respectable and numerous. If the defendant should have learned about safeguards some other way, proof that defendant could not find knowledge of them in competitors' shops is no defense.

A business usage may be so obviously hazardous that negligence of those who follow it is clear; then proof of conformity to custom is a waste of time. In Mayhew v. Sullivan Mining Co.,[48] an industrial accident case, a mine operator cut a ladder hole in a platform located in a dark shaft and posted no guards and gave no warnings. A workman fell through, dropped thirty-five feet, and was seriously hurt. The trial judge rejected operator's offer to prove such openings were customarily left unguarded. Barrows, J., approved the exclusion and said, "If the defendants had proved that in every mining establishment that has existed since the days of Tubal-Cain, it has been the practice to cut ladder-holes in their platforms . . . without guarding or lighting them, and without notice to contractors

47. Spurlin v. General Motors Corp., 528 F.2d 612 (5th Cir. 1976).

48. 76 Me. 100 (1884).

or workmen, it would have no tendency to show that the act was consistent with ordinary prudence . . . . The gross carelessness of the act appears conclusively upon its recital." When a custom is outrageously dangerous, feasible greater precaution may be a matter of common knowledge.

Evidence of conformity to custom takes on added significance when coupled with proof that widespread usage has resulted in virtually no injuries; the combination has all of the usual force of proof of conformity plus all of the usual force of widespread favorable safety history. If, in a fall case, a grocer shows that the shop's floors were treated in the customary manner, and that customers have, without injury, walked on similar surfaces in hundreds of grocery stores, this evidence tends to prove not only that the grocer could discover no better way in the examples set by other grocers, but also that the floor was, in fact, safe. Proof of conformity alone does not go so far; usages may sometimes persist even though they result in injuries.

§ 6. EVIDENCE TO ESTABLISH CRITERIA OF DUE CARE

Normally proof tends to establish "facts"; that is, evidence about what happened, how it could or could not have been avoided, etc. On the negligence issue, both the plaintiff and defendant will have exhausted the possibilities of proof once they have presented all their evidence concerning: (1) what defendant did, (2) how dangerous it was, (3) defendant's opportunity to discern danger, (4) availability of safer alternatives, and (5) defendant's opportunity to know about safer alternatives. Sometimes, however, counsel are allowed to prove that in someone's estimation the defendant's conduct was *unreasonably* hazardous or *duly* careful, and the jury is permitted to respect these opinions for what they are worth. These are instances of exceptions to the "opinion rule," which normally requires exclusion of proof of opinions about the proper legal characterization of facts. Most of the following discussion will be concerned with exceptional cases in which such proof may be received.

One preliminary problem involves a kind of proof that is clearly admissible—but which implies an opinion on reasonableness that should be disregarded by the jury—viz., proof of business custom. The problem can be posed this way: should the jury be allowed to use a business custom *as a measure* of what the reasonably prudent person does, *as a test* of due care?

Early in the twentieth century a few courts took the position that the reasonably prudent person is the average person, and therefore a craftsman who proves that his or her conduct was like that of other members of the craft establishes the *fact* of due care. Even these courts, however, hesitated to exonerate conformers to obviously dangerous customs. These courts said that conformity is due care only when the custom followed is not obviously unreasonable.

Most courts now affirm that due care is what-ought-to-be-done rather than what-usually-is-done; proof of what people do is only an inconclusive aid in determining what should be done. Nevertheless a contrary notion—that the reasonably prudent person is a composite of actual people—seems to have great hardihood. Its persistence probably stems from the ambiguity of the phrase, "ordinary care," often used as a synonym for "due care."

An ordinary pin is a common pin, not easily distinguished from billions of others. An ordinary meal, though clearly different from some other ordinary meals, is a routine, passable repast and falls short of being a gourmet's delight. Similarly, "ordinary care" has two meanings: (1) a statistical meaning comparable to the pin example; that is, the care in fact taken by others acting in similar circumstances, or (2) a value-judgment meaning comparable to the meal example; that is, passable care, the care average persons *should* exercise. In the first sense ordinary care can be defined only by reference to what people do. In the second sense ordinary care can be defined only by reference to norms of acceptable conduct—conduct neither *unduly* solicitous nor *unconscionably* self-centered. These two ideas are not unrelated. Average care is likely to be duly considerate, and due care is likely to be average—people usually act passably. But we can ill afford to let those whose self-interest may run counter to paying the bill for adequate safeguards escape liability when all of them are guilty of the same shortcomings. While many business usages are satisfactory, some are not, and we should not make conformity to custom (average care) an automatic test of satisfactory care.

If a custom must be adjudged satisfactory before it can be used as a legal standard, the grounds of that judgment, rather than the custom itself, are the sources of the standard. Judging reasonableness of a custom is, after all, the same as judging reasonableness of behavior conforming to it. Custom used as a test of due care only after it has been found reasonable is, in itself, no test of care at all.

Usually when evidence of custom is received, jury instructions are bare of comment on this proof. Occasionally it is mentioned, and the jury is told nothing more helpful than that custom is not a conclusive test. Jurors instructed no more clearly than this may nevertheless substitute the judgment of a craft for their own judgment; claimants' lawyers should make clear arguments to keep jurors from doing so to the prejudice of their clients; these arguments should stress the other functions of the proof—its bearing on practicality of using a certain safeguard and on the opportunity of defendant to know that such a safeguard exists. Perhaps in the future courts will devise more trenchant instructions. A simple caution to use custom as a test of reasonableness only after the custom is itself adjudged reasonable is hardly enough.

Experts are used to testify on danger, feasibility of reducing danger, and availability of knowledge of danger and safeguards; this testimony is all factual. May an expert witness go further and characterize conduct as "reasonably prudent" or "unreasonably imprudent"? Usually such characterization is not permitted. Courts say it "violates the opinion rule" or "invades the province of the jury," or "goes beyond the qualifications of the expert." Nevertheless, there are some exceptions to this rule, *none of which is so firmly established that it can be relied on as a matter of course.*

Some facts are deeply imbedded in special techniques and cannot be exhumed for understanding of average jurors in the time available for trial of lawsuits. In Zarnik v. C. Reiss Coal Co.,[49] a dump car hopper door opened off schedule and discharged cargo on a laborer working beneath a trestle over which the car was travelling. The door's locking mechanism was complicated. The clarity of most of the opinion vouches for the judge's writing ability, but careful study of his description of the lock leaves the reader with only a muddled impression of its workings. Perhaps jurors understood better; they had raw testimony before them and they may have seen diagrams or exhibits not embalmed in the opinion. The claimant's counsel apparently feared jurors could not understand the risk; he asked his expert witness whether or not the hopper door was under the circumstances *reasonably* safely locked. The expert was allowed to testify that it was not. The appellate court affirmed and said jurors could not do as good a job of judging safety as the expert could.

The court in the Zarnik case impliedly approved of this proposition: When facts are too complicated to expect jurors to settle the negligence issue on purely factual evidence, an expert's opin-

49. 133 Wis. 290, 113 N.W. 752 (1907).

ion on reasonableness of risk may be given to the jury. When such evidence is received, expert testimony functions as argument; that is, the expert on the stand advises the jury that they ought (or ought not) to find the defendant was negligent. Of course such testimonial-argument may be fortified further or attacked by argument of counsel made at the usual time.

In spite of the good sense of the dump car case, many courts would not follow it; they would exclude the evaluational testimony as an incompetent "conclusion." A canny plaintiff's counsel, fearing reversal on appeal should this kind of testimony be admitted, will take the risk only if it appears that the plaintiff will lose on the negligence issue unless the expert testifies that the defendant acted unreasonably.

Evaluational expert testimony was not needed and brought a claimant to grief in Demarais v. Johnson.[50] Plaintiff's expert had testified that a truck wheel collapsed because of loose spokes. Then the trial judge allowed him to testify that reasonable inspection before the accident would have uncovered the defect. This ruling was held to be a reversible error. The appellate court said that the witness could properly have described methods of inspection and testified on their effectiveness and cost, but he was no more competent than the jurors to determine whether or not failure to inspect was unreasonable; the witness thus was not qualified to give expert testimony on what a reasonably prudent person would do. Plaintiff's lawyer could have avoided this risk of reversal and adduced more effective proof had he simply requested that the witness tell how inspections are usually made, how well they work, and what they cost.

On some subjects, experts are not able to state articulately the factual basis of their knowledge. In Christiansen v. McLellan,[51] a teamster working at a road-building site was ordered to drive down an incline. His wagon upset and he was hurt. His expert was allowed to testify that the grade was so steep that it could not be driven down in *reasonable* safety. The ruling was upheld on the ground that special knowledge and experience were involved. The witness did not elaborate on his judgment in any way. The factual basis of his dogmatic conclusion probably was not susceptible of fuller explication. An experienced teamster, however, has roughly accurate special knowledge on risks en-

50. 90 Mont. 366, 3 P.2d 283 (1931). In Corl v. Corl, 222 Pa.Super. 152, 292 A.2d 541 (1972), the court affirmed a trial judge's rejection of expert testimony on the standard of care required in constructing a flagstone walk on the ground that

the jury needed no expert guidance.

51. 74 Wash. 318, 133 P. 434 (1913). See also, Hill v. State — R.I. —, 398 A.2d 1130 (1979).

tailed in driving down grades. That knowledge is a composite of learning on traction, horse behavior, likelihood of load shifting, wagon centers of gravity, etc., all intertwined beyond possibility of unraveling. His testimony amounted to saying, "the contractor was wrong in ordering the teamster to drive down the grade"—a judgment for the jury to take or leave. Jurors unskilled in the teamsters' art might be incompetent to judge such an issue solely on proof of the angle of slope, condition of its surface, the type of wagon, content of load, etc. Without expert characterization of the grade as unreasonably dangerous, the teamster's case might have been too weak to withstand a motion for nonsuit. Nevertheless, the expert could have been questioned on a more "factual" level; he could have testified that driving down the incline was freighted with substantial risk of upset, and stopped there. Perhaps his statement (in its context) meant no more, and was not likely to be understood as an opinion on a controversial matter of social policy. Experienced plaintiffs' advocates usually caution experts not to use evaluative language, for many courts are less liberal than the one that decided the teamster case.[52]

In some circumstances, defendants' experts testifying on safety can hardly be expected to avoid evaluational language. In Stewart's Adm'x v. Louisville & N. R.R.,[53] an action for wrongful death of a trainman killed in a derailment, one fact in dispute was the place where the train left the tracks. The plaintiff's evidence did not touch on the condition of the tracks at the point where the railroad's evidence tended to locate the derailment. The railroad undertook to prove by experts that the tracks were in good order at that point. They were allowed, over objection, to testify that the tracks were reasonably safe and that they had not discovered the cause of derailment. The appellate court approved the trial judge's ruling without saying anything about the expert's evaluational language.[54] Practically no other form of testimony is natural in this context. If the experts had tried to detail the factual basis of their judgment, they would have had to wander over the whole professional field of proper roadbed building and care. Had the plaintiff attacked some aspect on cross-examination or by counter-proof (and so given focus to the inquiry) the expert's original testimony would have little value until supplemented by more specific testimony.

52. See, e.g., Pointer v. Klamath Falls Land & Transportation Co., 59 Or. 438, 117 P. 605 (1911), a contra decision on almost the same facts.

53. 136 Ky. 717, 125 S.W. 154 (1910).

54. See also, Gravely v. Providence Partnership, 549 F.2d 958 (4th Cir. 1977).

In contrast is the holding in Whitehead v. Wisconsin Central Ry.,[55] a suit for injuries incurred by a trainman struck by a low bridge. The bridge was guarded by telltales, but its ropes were fouled on a sheltering platform built over the telltales. Other roads used no such platforms. The court excluded testimony in general terms about the adequacy of these telltales. Proof before the court had already converged on the conclusion that the platform was an inexcusable fouling hazard; if there was a technical justification for the platform's use, defendant's experts should have gotten down to brass tacks and told about it.

The composite judgments of experts on safety standards are held admissible. In Nordstrom v. White Metal Rolling and Stamping Corp.,[56] a man using a ladder was injured when it collapsed. The defendant who manufactured the ladder was allowed by the trial judge to prove that the ladder's structure exceeded the safety standards set up by the American Standard Safety Code for Portable Metal Ladders. The manufacturer's witnesses described the make-up of the American Standards Association and showed that the Code was published after research by an Association committee on which personnel represented consumers, professional groups, insurance companies, and governmental agencies, as well as manufacturers. The appellate court said that if the committee's objectivity was not established by the committee's membership, evidence of its bias, if any, could presumably be offered by the claimant, who did not seriously challenge the committee's objectivity. This Code, said the appellate court, was promulgated before the accident and was not drawn to favor manufacturers in litigation; though the Code is only an expression of experts' opinions, the court continued, those opinions are relevant on proper design, and if those opinions were not the latest or best on the subject, that fact could have been brought out by the plaintiff.

However technologists develop approved practices to serve ends other than safety; these practices are not relevant to the determination of due care. In Norfolk & W. Ry. v. Gillespie,[57] a derailment case, the injured plaintiff claimed that the bank of a curve in the tracks was too shallow. The plaintiff introduced into evidence a standard engineering table which called for an outside rail elevation of $5\frac{3}{8}$ inches on such curves. An expert for the railroad testified that the figure in the table was the

55. 103 Minn. 13, 114 N.W. 254 (1907).

56. 75 Wash. 629, 453 P.2d 619 (1969). See also, Lewis v. Texas &

N. O. R. Co., 199 S.W.2d 185 (Tex.Civ.App.1946).

57. 224 F. 316 (4th Cir. 1915).

right elevation for comfortable riding, but that safety required only an elevation of 4½ to 5 inches. Plaintiff's counsel used bludgeoning cross-examination to get the expert to say, "The table sets out normal and correct elevations." The trial judge ruled that the jury could find the elevation negligently unsafe on proof of variation from the table. Perhaps this ruling was justified—on direct examination the railroad's expert did a poor job of demonstrating that the figures in the table were affected by considerations of comfort; he also admitted that construction conforming to the table would have been safer and gave no excuse for departure. But the appellate court's affirming opinion shows no glimmer of recognition of the possibility that objectives other than safety may have affected the table.

When craft judgment crystallizes on subjects well understood by laymen, courts differ on the competence of proof of craft judgment. In Hommel v. Badger State Inv. Co.,[58] a case involving a fall down a five inch step located four inches from a swinging door in an office building lobby, the claimant's expert was allowed to testify to a violation of "good architectural practice." Architects seldom use laboratory science to furnish guides to safe walkways; nevertheless, architectural interest in safe walkways has developed into craft lore crystallized in standard rules and charts. An architect explained to one of us, "The rule against close proximity of steps to doors is based on the commonly known fact that doors are opened with hands and attention is drawn away from feet." But many modern structures are built in disregard of the rule.[59] Though the appellate court held testimony on architectural practice was admissible in the office building case, some courts have excluded similar proof in other cases as non-expert opinion invading the jury's province.[60]

In most cases in which experts testify to the "reasonableness" (or "unreasonableness") of precautions used, they have come

---

58. 166 Wis. 235, 165 N.W. 20 (1917).

59. After the above conversation, four violations of the rule were noticed during a five minute walk back to the law school through a modern university campus.

60. See, e.g., Graham v. Pennsylvania Co., 139 Pa. 149, 21 A. 151 (1891). The court held that the trial judge erred in permitting an architect to testify that an unguarded nine-inch step between two levels of a railroad platform was unsafe. The court said every traveler who ever got out of a railroad car or used stairs was as capable of judging the alleged danger as the witness. Though this architect only gave his personal opinion, the court probably would have been no more favorably disposed to proof of violation of good architectural practice—the court wanted no expert judgment. Perhaps this view can be justified on the ground that architects try to protect the careless as well as the careful; architecture has no rule of contributory negligence and no doctrine of voluntary assumption of risk.

prepared to give useful and clearly admissible "factual" testimony. While laymen are often able without help of specialists to discern risks and their seriousness, they often know little about the practicality of alternative courses of conduct and the costs in money and inconvenience of adopting them. An advocate who thinks through the presentation in advance can plan to question expert witnesses so that their answers will bring out all of their relevant information and, at the same time, avoid the risk of reversible error lurking in eliciting their opinions on reasonableness. Of course, sometimes that risk may be worth running.

Discussion now turns to the litigants' own characterization of their own conduct or that of their opponents. Are such statements proper evidence as admissions? A witness overhears Trucker's statement that "a reasonably prudent motorist driving at high speed will not accelerate when entering a curve." The next day Trucker speeds up from 50 to 60 miles per hour while going into an appreciable curve on a country road, skidding the truck and killing several sheep grazing in a roadside pasture. Is this pre-accident statement admissible against Trucker in a suit brought by the shepherd?

A close approximation of this sheep killing case arises when damages result from a breach of an organization's own safety rules. Typical is Ryan v. Port of New York Authority.[61] The defendant-authority operated a bridge. It issued instructions that required the closing of the bridge to certain types of vehicles when north or south wind exceeded thirty miles per hour. A van about to cross the bridge came within this rule, but nevertheless was permitted to cross under the interdicted conditions with disastrous results to the plaintiff. The appellate court held that the plaintiff was properly allowed at the trial to prove a breach of the rule; this evidence tended to support the verdict he got.[62]

---

61. 116 N.J.Super. 211, 281 A.2d 539 (1971).

62. Many of the older cases in accord involved proof that railroad crew violation of company safety rules resulted in harm. See, e.g., Lake Shore & M. S. Ry. Co. v. Ward, 135 Ill. 511, 26 N.E. 520 (1891). In Dillenbeck v. City of Los Angeles, 69 Cal.2d 472, 72 Cal.Rptr. 321, 446 P.2d 129 (1968), the Supreme Court of California held that the trial court erred in rejecting proof that a police car on an emergency call went through a red light at a speed higher than that permitted by the police department's rules. In Pederson v. Dumouchel, 72 Wash.2d 73, 431 P.2d 973 (1967), the court held that a violation of a hospital's own rule forbidding surgery under a general anesthetic, unless an M.D. was in the operating theater and supervised the procedure, was negligence *per se*.

A well-known older case supporting a contrary minority view is Fonda v. St. Paul City Ry.,[63] in which the court said that the law fixes the standard of care, and the law cannot be varied by private rules. If private rules state standards different from legal standards, the rules are irrelevant; if they state the same standards, the rules are unnecessary. Of course the jury often has the function of deciding whether described conduct is negligent. Ordinary witnesses are never (and expert witnesses are seldom) permitted to testify on what a reasonably prudent person would do. Why should a railroad's views on reasonable conduct be singled out and held competent?

When a railroad fails to live up to its own concrete safety rule, the rule and its breach should be recognized as facts of the case. The legal conception of reasonable prudence entails the very considerations that normally guide draftsmen of company rules. *Reasonable prudence* means enough effort to discern risks and their seriousness, determination to reduce appreciable risks when feasible, diligent search for safer procedures, and so on. These considerations also prompt and guide drafting of safety rules. Promulgation of a safety rule is an implied admission by defendant that its draftsman (the railroad's servant) has discerned danger and knows of a feasible way to reduce it. Admissions of fact are normally competent evidence.

But a safety rule is something more than an admission of fact; it admits that a risk of harm *ought* to be reduced in a particular way. This ought-judgment is grounded in fact and grows out of fact—it is not a disembodied abstract principle of ethics. Surely a railroad should not be heard to say that its own realistic, informed opinion, based on its own professional qualifications and experience, should not be taken into account. A company rule is not likely to suggest a standard too high for practical enterprise; if and when it does, the trial judge should have discretion to exclude proof of its existence. Violations of safety rules should not necessarily be negligence *per se*. Some organizations have ideals impossible of accomplishment which may affect drafting of their rules. A company should be permitted to show that a violated rule was intended as an unattainable goal counseling perfection.[64] Such ideals, however, are not

63. 71 Minn. 438, 74 N.W. 166 (1898).

64. In Dillenbeck v. City of Los Angeles, 69 Cal.2d 472, 72 Cal. Rptr. 321, 326, 446 P.2d 129, 134 (1968), the court said that rules are admissible only as evidence of

requirements of due care, and the employer can explain that he acted from an excess of caution. In a footnote the court elaborated by calling attention to a police department bulletin which said, "[A]n officer operating an emergency vehicle should assume that

usually expressed in rules published as working instructions. "No Smoking" is not an ideal in an oil refinery; it is a condition of continued existence.

Sometimes company rules are designed to protect the careless. Courts should keep clearly in mind that a breach of such a rule should not deprive the company of contributory negligence defenses it would have had were there no rule to violate.

Admissions of proper standards of care can be implied by conduct as well as expressed in announced rules. In a case discussed earlier,[65] an injured factory hand was allowed to prove that workbenches other than hers in the plant had skirt guards. This evidence tended to show that her employer discerned danger and knew of a feasible way of reducing it. All of its benches except the plaintiff's had skirt guards. The employer's extensive use of skirt guards implied that, in its judgment, benches *should* have them. Of course the implication disappears if proof of special circumstances shows that the employer's implied judgment is inapplicable to the plaintiff's bench. Hunziker v. Scheidemantle [66] was an action for wrongful death which occurred when an airplane crashed while taking off from a rural airport in a dense fog. The plaintiff claimed that the airport should have been closed. The airport had no control tower, and therefore under FAA regulations departing aircraft were not required to receive clearance. Nevertheless, the defendant's airport manager had on three earlier occasions ordered aircraft pilots not to take off under similar conditions. The court held proof of these earlier occasions was admissible and tended to prove the manager's negligence in not closing the airport.

Plans to take precautions also imply the planner's judgment on what *ought* to be done. When execution of such a plan is unjustifiably delayed, and meantime an injury occurs, the implied admission that the planner departed from his own standards is clear. In P. J. Lewelling Constr. Co. v. Longstreth,[67] a quarry worker was hit by a rock which bounced out of a chute. Sides of the chute were about a foot high. The injured workman was allowed to prove that several days earlier his boss had ordered a foreman to make the sides higher, but the order was not carried

all other motorists are partially deaf, that they are inattentive . . ., that the windows of their vehicles are closed, that a radio is playing and conversation is taking place within their vehicles, and that they will become confused if and when they hear a siren."

65. Warburton v. N. B. Thayer Co., 75 N.H. 592, 72 A. 826 (1909).

66. 543 F.2d 489 (3d Cir. 1976).

67. 156 Ark. 236, 246 S.W. 19 (1923).

out. The proof showed discernment of danger and a feasible way to greater safety. It also tended to prove something more, *vis*, in the employer's judgment, the chute *should* have been safer.

After accidents, those involved in them may make admissions of fault or lack of it. The unelaborated statement, "I was in the wrong," is based on the speaker's unannounced version of facts and his unarticulated theories of responsibility. Witnesses on the stand are seldom allowed to testify in terms so general. Some courts have excluded proof of all such admissions, as "mere conclusions of law"; most courts, however, receive such proof in some circumstances. These admissions, viewed in isolation, purport to be based on declarant's theories of legal responsibility, but when viewed in their setting may be admissions descriptive of fact. In Robbins v. Weed,[68] an action against a motorist who ran down a pedestrian, the parties' testimony on what happened was in utter conflict. The pedestrian's witnesses testified that plaintiff was crossing the street, and the approaching motorist, whose view was unobstructed, gave no warning, did not change his course, and plowed into the claimant. The motorist testified that he saw the pedestrian, altered his course, and gave the pedestrian ample opportunity to pass in front of him, but the pedestrian jumped backwards into his car's path. The dispute involved only what happened; either party was probably willing to concede that if his opponent's version of the facts was correct his opponent was entitled to a verdict. The pedestrian was then allowed to prove that the motorist had admitted that he was to blame for the accident. This admission could have only a factual function; it tended to show falsity of the motorist's testimony on the facts. It had no bearing on a standard of conduct to be applied to the facts, for the standard was not in dispute. The motorist contended the admission should have been excluded because it was a mere conclusion following from his conceptions of law. In this setting the contention made little sense; obviously the bearing of the admission was on facts and not on the motorist's theory of law. The court held the evidence competent.

In other settings reference to a bare admission of fault is clearly legalistic and throws no light on what happened. In Rudd v. Byrnes,[69] members of a hunting party separated and took up positions at deer crossings on a stream. The plaintiff

---

68. 187 Iowa 64, 169 N.W. 773 (1918).

69. 156 Cal. 636, 105 P. 957 (1909). See also, Boshnack v. World Wide Rent-A-Car, Inc., 195 So.2d 216 (Fla.1967).

left his station and trailed a dog into brush across a stream from defendant's station. The defendant saw brush move, fired, and (since he had more skill than judgment) hit the plaintiff. Shooting at an unidentified moving object was so clearly negligent that the trial judge directed a verdict against the defendant on the negligence issue. The defendant had pleaded contributory negligence and offered to prove the plaintiff's out of court statement that he, too, was at fault. This evidence was held competent, but the court said it had little probative weight. Evidence of this admission served no fact-proving office—other proof clearly portrayed the facts and they were not in dispute. Plaintiff's post-accident qualms are worth little unless they show facts or are based on special competence or experience.

These two cases show the variability of worth of bare post-accident admissions of fault. When their reference is factual, admissions may valuably help in settling disputes of fact. When their reference is only moralistic, compassionate or legalistic, admissions are worthless. But if judges must discriminate between these two kinds of admissions in midtrial their rulings will often be wrong. Proof of admissions like the one in the hunting case is not calculated to do much harm; jurors aided by arguments of counsel should see their worthlessness.

There are, of course, cases that fall between these two extremes. For example, in Doerflinger v. Davis,[70] the claimant was hurt as she walked in an aisle in the defendant's store. A box, in which there was a bicycle, stood on the floor "beside the aisle." The box fell over on her. It was six feet tall and stood on an end which was two and a half feet wide. Neither party offered to show whether the box was resting on its own weight or was leaning against a nearby wall, or was secured in any way, or what caused the box to fall. At the time of the accident, however, the defendant said, "It [the box] shouldn't have been there in the first place," and after the accident he ordered its removal. On this scanty evidence of negligence, the trial judge submitted the case to the jury, and entered judgment on their verdict for the plaintiff. The Supreme Court of Pennsylvania affirmed, saying that the evidence of negligence, "though very slight," was sufficient to take the case to the jury. The wise solution on the admissibility of such statements is the one to which most courts are tending—receive proof of bare post-accident admissions of fault and trust to the abilities of jurors and counsel to see that they are properly weighed.[71]

70. 412 Pa. 401, 194 A.2d 897 (1963).

71. See, e.g., Gosselin v. Perry, 166 Conn. 152, 348 A.2d 623 (1974).

Three common forms of implied post-accident admissions of fault are flight from the scene of accident, rendering financial aid to the injured, and discharge of a servant who inflicts injury. They will be discussed separately.

Flight. In several cases a claimant has offered proof of a motorist's flight after a traffic accident. In none of them has the motorist objected. Criminal courts have universally permitted proof of an accused's flight from the scene of a crime. Perhaps this analogy has so settled the law that objection would be futile. In most cases proof of flight tends to establish facts, rather than legalistic conclusions. In Shaddy v. Daley,[72] a sideswipe collision case, dispute centered on whether or not the defendant (who was travelling toward the plaintiff) was on the wrong side of the road. Proof that defendant fled after the accident was received. The probative weakness of the evidence is that he may have fled in confusion, or to avoid involvement, etc. —explanations which, of course, he could prove in rebuttal. The likelihood that he fled because he held erroneous theories of substantive law is not high; surely he knew that driving on the left side of the road was improper.

Financial Aid. Proof that a defendant rendered or promised a claimant financial aid is often excluded on these grounds: (1) it is irrelevant, and (2) if it were admitted charitable impulses would be stifled.

There are those who will not offer to pay medical bills unless they believe themselves legally responsible for injury. Therefore proof of an offer to pay medical bills does have some tendency to prove consciousness of fault—a fact which can be proved in many courts, of course, by express admissions. Later discussion of specific cases will show that this kind of evidence is not necessarily irrelevant.

The second reason has more in it. If evidence of proffers of financial aid were received, those who might otherwise lend a helping hand may suppress their generosity. But the number of private citizens who volunteer financial assistance to those whom they injure without fault cannot be large, and growing availability of aid from other sources (charitable and govern-

---

72. 58 Idaho 536, 76 P.2d 279 (1938). Cf. Jones v. Strelecki, 49 N.J. 513, 231 A.2d 558 (1967), however, a more modern case involving the New Jersey unsatisfied judgment statute and an unidentified bolter in which flight was held to be evidence of negligence. Compare Brooks v. E. J. Willig Truck Transportation Co., 40 Cal. 2d 669, 255 P.2d 802 (1953), in which flight violated a criminal hit-and-run statute, in which the court held that if failure to summon aid aggravated the victim's condition, the fleeing motorist incurred liability even if he was not liable for the original injury.

mental) reduces the social importance of such sporadic bounty. Corporations (railroads, for example) whose rules instruct their employees to come to the aid of all persons injured on their property or by company operations, will be protected by the terms of their rules from making admissions of fault; if assistance must be given to all who are injured, an instance of assistance has no tendency to show consciousness of guilt. Many insurance claims departments have acted on the theory that generosity in aiding victims who may have large claims covered by liability policies is good business even though liability is doubtful.

Caution in receiving proof of financial aid is therefore supported by adequate reason. Since proof of financial assistance has some little probative weight, it might turn the scale in a close case. It could be the undoing of a humanitarian; a warm-hearted benefactor could suffer liability because of generosity. This seems to be reason enough for rejecting evidence of financial aid—even though its exclusion may occasionally favor those whose real concern is only for themselves.

Some offers to pay for harm done are on their face far from unsullied charity; exclusion of proof of these offers would unwarrantedly prevent a claimant from proving a damning admission of fault. In Rosen v. Burnham,[73] a landlord was remodeling part of his building; plaster fell on the stock of one of his tenants, a merchant occupying premises next to those worked on. The landlord was called in and said he would pay for the damage done. Proof of this offer was admitted without objection. Had the landlord objected, his objection should have been overruled. The merchant-tenant was not the kind of person likely to excite sympathy, and his landlord probably was not prompted by generosity. Of course the landlord could show in rebuttal, if such were the case, either that he was trying to satisfy a good tenant, whether or not he was liable, or that he acted on a mistaken theory of liability.

The rule emerging in case law on the admissibility of evidence showing proffers of financial aid is this: the proof should be excluded unless circumstances tend to show affirmatively that the proffer was not prompted by humanitarian impulses.[74] When such evidence is admitted, it may bear on disputes of fact; but

73. 272 Mass. 583, 172 N.E. 894 (1930). See also, Edwards v. Passarelli Bros. Automotive Service, Inc., 8 Ohio St.2d 6, 221 N.E.2d 708 (1966).

74. See Howell v. Hairston, 261 S. C. 292, 199 S.E.2d 766 (1973).

in some settings it will tend to show only the defendant's legal characterization of his acts and will be of little worth.

Discharge of servant. Proof that shortly after an accident a master fired the servant who did the harm tends to establish the master's belief that the servant was in the wrong. If the servant was let go for some other reason, the discharge is, of course, irrelevant. But in the absence of explanation, discharge following an accident tends to prove discharge because of the accident. Courts have uniformly excluded proof of dismissal or discipline of a servant—on the ground that proof of a remedial measure taken after an accident is never competent.[75] Firing a negligent truck driver is quite different from scrapping a flawed fly wheel. Fly wheels can become unsound and do harm without negligence of their owners or their servants; masters, however, are responsible for the negligence of their servants even though they have used every possible precaution in selection, training, and supervision. If a master expressly admits a servant's negligence, proof of that admission is competent. Nowadays, notions of fairness and union protection against unjust discharge may require express statements of misconduct when this is the reason for discharging an employee. There seems to be no acceptable reason for treating an admission of a servant's fault implied from dismissal any differently from an express admission to the same effect. With the authorities in their present state, however, plaintiffs' lawyers should hesitate to use such proof when other evidence will do the job.

§ 7. THE BURDEN OF PROVING NEGLIGENCE

In all civil litigation plaintiff starts the ball rolling; the trial of issues of fact does not start until plaintiff offers proof. Some issues are "defenses" and the plaintiff need offer no proof to negate them until and unless at a later stage of trial the defendant's evidence puts them in issue. Negligence, however, is a plaintiff's issue; plaintiff has the initial burden of coming forward with proof adequate to establish negligence. Unless the plaintiff carries this burden before resting, the defendant is entitled to a dismissal. Once the plaintiff has carried this burden of going forward far enough to thwart a motion for a dismissal, the defendant may offer evidence, including proof of due care.

One of the defense's major objectives is to keep the case from the jury. At the conclusion of plaintiff's case, the defendant usually tests its sufficiency by asking the judge to rule that plain-

---

75. The leading case is Gillet v. Shaw, 217 Mass. 59, 104 N.E. 719 (1914). Rynar v. Lincoln Transit Co., 129 N.J.Law 525, 30 A.2d 406 (1943), is a more recent but less articulate holding in accord.

tiff's case is too weak to go to the jury. If this request is denied and the defendant offers proof, defendant is likely to renew this request when all of defendant's evidence is in. Both requests may center on the negligence issue—although of course they may center on other issues in dispute.

In most jurisdictions, the judge can theoretically be called upon also to settle the negligence issue in the plaintiff's favor. If a reasonable juror after considering all of the evidence could come to no conclusion other than that the defendant was negligent, the plaintiff is entitled to a directed verdict on that issue —should the plaintiff ask for it. Plaintiffs seldom avail themselves of this opportunity.[76] If the proof of negligence is strong enough for a directed verdict, plaintiff is not likely to be afraid of the jury; but plaintiff should fear that the appellate court may not see the full strength of the proof. In allowing the issue to go to the jury, plaintiff runs virtually no risk of adverse verdict; but in asking for a directed verdict, plaintiff may run some substantial risk of reversal.

Negligence issues properly submitted to and decided by a jury are usually settled once and for all. In most states, however, trial judges may override verdicts even though they are supported by some evidence; when a verdict is "against the weight of the evidence," the trial judge may set it aside and order a new trial. In so doing the judge does not substitute his or her judgment for that of the jury; the judge merely cancels the verdict rendered and orders a new trial before another jury which may act more sensibly. Disappointed plaintiffs (as well as those defendants found liable by jurors) are likely to attack verdicts as against the weight of the evidence; once the jury has ruled for defendant, plaintiff has nothing to lose in asking for a new trial.

There are few procedural guides to help trial judges and jurors decide on the adequacy of proof of negligence. When a defendant asks a trial judge to keep the issue of negligence from the jury and rule on the issue in the defendant's favor, the judge can only apply the substantive law requirements to the proof offered and consider whether reasonable jurors properly instructed could possibly find for the plaintiff. If the answer is yes, the case must be submitted to the jury; if it is no, the defendant's request must be granted. The judge's legal learning bears on what evidence is worth considering, but rarely will it help determine the specific probative weight of the competent evidence in the case.[77] It is often said that a plaintiff must establish negli-

---

76. But see Stec v. Richardson, 75 N.J. 304, 381 A.2d 789 (1978).

77. One possible exception: A few courts have held that testimony on

gence "by a preponderance of the evidence," and this phrase is used in jury charges. The phrase points in the direction of adequate proof and has enough meaning to indicate that a plaintiff need not prove negligence "beyond a reasonable doubt," but it gives little comfort to trial judges or jurors faced with close problems of the adequacy of proof.

Substantive law points to what must be proved. If the evidence tends to show that a pedestrian was run down by a car owner's fifteen-year old child, and if, as a matter of substantive law, entrustment of an automobile to one so young is negligence, the trial judge and jurors need ask themselves only whether or not the plaintiff's evidence adequately proves the child's youth and the parent's entrustment. If, however, the substantive law furnishes no measure of negligence more exact than the reasonably prudent person test, the trial court must settle not only whether or not a fifteen-year old was in fact entrusted with a motorcar, but also whether or not the entrustment should be characterized as negligence.

Occasionally both parties to a damage suit are willing to go to trial without a jury. (In England, damage suit litigants seldom have any choice; they are rarely entitled to a jury trial.) Perhaps waiver of jury trial is more common than it once was. When a jury trial is waived, the trial judge determines the facts as well as the law. Waiver of jury trial, of course, has no theoretical effect on burdens of proof—though in fact, judges are likely to be more demanding than jurors in their evaluation of proof of negligence. Usually plaintiffs' counsel are willing to waive jury trial only when they fear that their clients are likely to fall victim to either the jurors' prejudices or their ineptness. Some judges are more likely to give adequate verdicts on large claims than are jurors unused to thinking in terms of large sums of money, amortization, etc. Defense counsel usually try to keep their cases from going to the jury in jury trials, but this does not mean that they are eager to waive jury trial whenever a claimant is willing to do so. Intricacies of jury trial multiply chances for error, and the likelihood that jurors will be misled predisposes appellate courts to hold errors harmful enough to require retrial.

out-of-court admissions of negligence uncorroborated by any other kind of proof of negligence will not support a verdict. Most courts have repudiated this view. See C. Morris, Studies in the Law of Torts, 57 et seq. (1952).

§ 8. RES IPSA LOQUITUR

One pattern of proof of negligence has been singled out by courts for special emphasis and is referred to in Latin as *res ipsa loquitur* [the thing speaks for itself]. In a famous nineteenth century English case, Byrne v. Boadle,[78] a pedestrian proved only that he was walking past a store and that a barrel of flour fell from a second story window, hit him, and seriously injured him. The trial judge ruled that the pedestrian did not establish the storekeeper's negligence and entered a nonsuit. this ruling was questioned before the full bench of the Court of Exchequer and held to be wrong.

Did the pedestrian prove negligence? A barrel can fall out of a storehouse window without negligence of the storekeeper. It is possible, for example, for an undiscoverable defect in a restraining rope to let a barrel loose in an utterly unforeseeable way.

The law does not require a plaintiff in a negligence case to prove negligence beyond a reasonable doubt; plaintiff needs only to establish by a preponderance of the evidence that the defendant failed to use due care. When a heavy object falls out of a window, the likelihood of its custodian's negligence is quite high. Chances are better than fifty-fifty that this storekeeper or his servants were negligent in their dealings with this barrel. Reasonable jurors could infer negligence by bringing their own worldly knowledge about such events to bear on the facts proved. The pedestrian's case was strong enough to escape a nonsuit; he adduced circumstantial evidence tending to show that the storekeeper was negligent. Baron Pollock, using the Latin phrase for the first time in negligence law, put it this way: "There are certain cases of which it may be said *res ipsa loquitur* [the thing speaks for itself], and this seems one of them. In some cases the Courts have held that the mere fact of an accident having occurred is evidence of negligence . . . . " A modern example of the same sort of circumstantial proof is found in the 1961 case of Gash v. Lautzenheizer,[79] in which the plaintiff testified to the following facts: he was in his car near, but off a highway; the defendant's car, moving at high speed, left the road, collided with the plaintiff's car, and injured plaintiff's back. The trial judge nonsuited the plaintiff because he

78. 2 Hurl. & Colt. 722, 159 Eng.Rep. 299 (1863).

79. 405 Pa. 312, 176 A.2d 90 (1961). See also, Pennsylvania Liquor Control Bd. v. City of Philadelphia, 32 Pa.Cmwlth. 423, 333 A.2d 497 (1975).

failed to show how or why the defendant careened off the road; in the judge's view, the plaintiff had not offered proof of the defendant's negligence adequate to escape a nonsuit. The appellate court reversed and held that the jury could have found that the plaintiff had shown a preponderant likelihood of negligence, sufficient to support a verdict in his favor.

In Capital Transit Co. v. Jackson,[80] a passenger was injured when a streetcar collided with a truck. The court said, "[T]he happening of such a collision . . . may permit an inference of negligence . . . sufficient to support the plaintiff's case *against* a motion for directed verdict." This court holds that if a passenger proves only a collision and his or her resulting injury, and then rests, the defendant carrier is not entitled to a directed verdict on the ground that the passenger has not carried the burden of proof of negligence. We cannot say, however, that a juror of common experience knows that when a streetcar collides with another vehicle, the likelihood that the carrier was negligent is greater than the likelihood that the carrier exercised due care. The court's refusal to presume negligence of the truck driver indicates that the court did not believe that proof of a collision is strong enough to show that the traction company's servants were negligent in fact. The passenger was excused from coming forward with proof of the motorman's negligence. The thing does not *in fact* speak for itself; only by fiction or legalistic presumption has the passenger proved the motorman's negligence by a preponderance of the evidence.

This analysis is not necessarily an attack on the result reached in the streetcar case. The opinion in the barrel case includes a relevant remark by Bramwell, B.: "Looking at the matter in a reasonable way it comes to this—an injury is done to the plaintiff, who has no means of knowing whether it was the result of negligence; the defendant, who knows how it was caused, does not think fit to tell the jury." In many cases, defendants' evidence-gathering opportunities are superior to plaintiffs'—particularly when defendants are in control of the premises, vehicles, or instrumentalities involved. On this ground some few courts do not permit the use of *res ipsa loquitur* circumstantial proof of a decedent's negligence when death prevents the defendant decedent's representative from giving exculpatory explanation; most courts, nevertheless, recognize whatever circumstantial force the happening of the accident has that tends to prove the decedent's negligence. More or less arbitrary convention usually allots to most plaintiffs a burden of coming forward with evi-

80. 149 F.2d 839, 161 A.L.R. 1110 (D.C. Cir. 1945).

dence of defendants' negligence, rather than allotting to the defendants a burden of coming forward with evidence of their own care. (The arbitrary nature of this allotment becomes clear when it is compared with the defendants' allotted burden of coming forward with evidence of (a) consent in a suit for battery, and (b) contributory negligence in a personal injury case.) No strong reason can be given against assigning the burden of proof to the defendant in the streetcar case, especially since common carriers' access to proof is usually superior to that of their passengers injured in collision cases.

The holding in the streetcar case does not make for tidy law —in virtually all other negligence cases the claimant has an initial burden of coming forward with proof of lack of due care. Modern practice provides increasingly effective pretrial procedures for discovering facts known to opponents; a passenger represented by skillful and vigorous counsel seldom needs the advantage of having the traction company present its evidence on the negligence issue first. In jurisdictions not following the Capital Transit case, passengers injured in collisions often sufficiently establish the negligence of carriers. So the justification for special treatment is far from conclusive. In some jurisdictions it has been expressly repudiated.[81] Nevertheless, there is a widespread tendency to advert from time to time to the defendant's superior access to proof in *res ipsa loquitur* cases.

In Mahoney v. Hercules Powder Co.,[82] a miner was killed when seven dynamite caps, used in a blasting operation, were set to go off in series—one after another in a period of about six seconds. The system misfired, however, and the last six caps went off simultaneously when the first charge exploded. The heavy blast dislodged a nearby boulder, which otherwise would have remained in place; it fell on and crushed the plaintiffs' decedent. If the miner's widow and children had proved only these facts, they would not have shown to the ordinary jurors that the accident resulted from negligence that occurred during the processes of manufacturing the caps. Jurors, who of course have no technical knowledge about explosives, are not likely to know that accidents like this one do not usually happen unless the caps are negligently manufactured. The plaintiffs' counsel feared that, without additional proof of the manufacturer's failure to use due care, the trial judge might agree with the cap maker's inevitable objection to adequacy of proof of his negligence. To avoid defeat, the claimants' lawyer called an expert

81. See, e.g., Sandler v. Boston Elevated Ry. Co., 238 Mass. 148, 130 N.E. 104 (1921).

82. 221 Cal.App.2d 353, 34 Cal.Rptr. 468 (1963).

witness who testified that concussion waves from the first explosion would cause other caps to detonate simultaneously whenever caps were too sensitive; hypersensitivity, he testified, results only from either metallic impurities or moisture in the caps, and neither of these defects ever occur when adequate precautions are taken during the manufacturing processes. The appellate court held that the jury should have been told that if they believed this expert's testimony, they could find that the plaintiffs had proved negligence. A similar decision was reached in a Washington malpractice case; the plaintiff's medical expert testified that the patient's injury would in all probability not have happened unless he had been subjected to negligent treatment.[83] In Stanolind Oil & Gas Co. v. Lambert,[84] a landowner whose property was damaged by blasting in nearby geophysical exploration for oil, did not offer expert testimony and did not fare so well. Norvell, J., said, "In a case such as this, the matter is one for proof and cannot be supplied by common knowledge, as it is in some *res ipsa loquitur* cases. We do not judicially know the details of exploratory operations by use of a seismograph, so that we can say that the damage . . . indicates a departure from the norm and raises an inference of negligence."

Once a court has ruled that, as a matter of common knowledge, a kind of injury is one not likely to happen without negligence, its ruling becomes a precedent, which can be used with some assurance that expert testimony is not needed in similar cases. In the bursting-carbonated-drink-bottle cases, for example, some courts have held that the bottler is not entitled to a dismissal when the consumer proves only the burst and his injuries. Though these holdings are bottomed on a doubtful proposition about common knowledge (carbonated-drink-bottles do not ordinarily burst when the bottler has used due care, unless abused after bottling), they seem to have the usual hardihood of precedent.

In the barrel case, defense counsel argued that no evidence connected the storekeeper or his servants with the runaway of the barrel. Pollack, B., answered: the presumption is that the storekeeper's servants were working with the barrel, and if they were not, the storekeeper could prove that fact. The pedestrian's proof tended to show not only negligence, but misconduct in the storekeeper's own organization.

83. ZeBarth v. Swedish Hospital Medical Center, 81 Wash.2d 12, 499 P.2d 1 (1972).

84. 222 S.W.2d 125 (Tex.Civ.App. 1949). For a similar medical malpractice case see Marshall v. To-

A plaintiff's burden of proof is, of course, not satisfied by a showing that an anonymous somebody was negligent; plaintiff must bring this misconduct home to the defendant. This requirement is formalized in the literature of *res ipsa loquitur*; it is generally said the plaintiff must show that the instrumentality causing the injury was under defendant's control at the time. When a runaway barrel escapes from the defendant's custody, proof of a resulting injury is circumstantial proof of negligence of the custodian. But if the control requirement is pushed too far, some defendants may unjustifiably escape liability. In Kilgore v. Shepard Co.,[85] a shopper sat in a merchant's chair while awaiting a saleswoman. The chair collapsed. On the ground that the customer, rather than the merchant, had control of the chair, the court held she could not rely on the doctrine of *res ipsa loquitur*. This is technicality gone wild. In Winfree v. Coca-Cola Bottling Works of Lebanon,[86] a bursting bottle case, the bottler argued that since his wares had been delivered to a retailer and he no longer had control over the bottle when it exploded, the claimant could not use *res ipsa loquitur* proof of negligence. The court said that the doctrine of *res ipsa loquitur* was inapplicable to this case; but nevertheless, since the proof tended to show the bottler's negligence, he was not entitled to a dismissal. This court refused to use Latin words but reached the proper result. In most jurisdictions this overly nice verbal discrimination is not made; when a plaintiff's proof tends to show an accident not likely to happen without negligence *on the part of the defendant*, the doctrine of *res ipsa loquitur* is applied even though the defendant no longer had custody of the damaging instrumentality when it did the harm.

Some courts have moved in the opposite direction and tend to apply the doctrine of *res ipsa loquitur* to cases in which proof does not bring negligence home to the defendant. In Vogt v. Cincinnati, Newport & Covington St. Ry. Co.[87] the court held that a passenger suing a traction company did not make out a case merely by showing that the streetcar collided with another vehicle. However, the court went on to say that under Kentucky authorities, if the passenger joined as defendants both the driver of the other vehicle and the traction company then proof of the accident thwarted dismissal. Two vehicles seldom do collide

maselli, — R.I. —, 372 A.2d 1280 (1977).

85. 52 R.I. 151, 158 A. 720 (1932).

86. 19 Tenn.App. 144, 83 S.W.2d 903 (1935).

87. 312 Ky. 668, 229 S.W.2d 461 (1950).

when drivers of both use due care. Proof of collision does tend to establish negligence of at least one driver; but the passenger is relieved from showing initially whether both or only one of the two drivers has acted negligently. Ordinarily a tort plaintiff suing several independent defendants has the burden of showing the fault of each defendant. (An assault and battery plaintiff who proves that only one of two identical-twin-defendants battered him would probably be nonsuited unless he identified the batterer.) But the Kentucky re-allotment of burdens is not necessarily unwise. When defendants, by a conspiracy of silence, may defeat a plaintiff who obviously has a good cause of action against one of their number, the burden of going forward with identifying evidence can justly be cast on each defendant. In Ybarra v. Spangard,[88] a malpractice case, the patient proved only that while he was under an anesthetic for an abdominal operation his shoulder was severely injured. Defendants were all of the attending doctors and nurses. They contended they were entitled to a nonsuit because the patient had not proved which of them was negligent. The court held that each defendant could escape liability only by adducing proof of exoneration.

Thus far the discussion has dealt with trials in which (a) a plaintiff rests after proving an accident, and (b) the defendant then questions the sufficiency of the plaintiff's proof of negligence by asking for a dismissal. The doctrine of *res ipsa loquitur* may thwart the defendant's request and the trial then continues. What happens subsequently?

In a number of states the doctrine of *res ipsa loquitur* is regarded as approving a kind of circumstantial proof of negligence *and nothing more*. In these states proceedings after refusal to dismiss when plaintiff rests are as follows:

1. *Cases in Which Defendants Offer no Proof of Due Care.* The trial judge's refusal to dismiss when plaintiff rests is at least a ruling that a reasonable juror could find plaintiff's proof of negligence adequate; it is not a ruling that no reasonable juror could find plaintiff's proof inadequate. Therefore, when the plaintiff requests the judge to rule that plaintiff has established negligence, a problem that has not yet been raised is posed. In theory, however, plaintiff's circumstantial proof can be strong enough to require a directed verdict on the negligence issue. In practice plaintiff seldom asks for it because (a) the proof is rarely, if ever, strong enough to merit a directed verdict,[89] and

---

88. 25 Cal.2d 486, 154 P.2d 687 (1944). Contra, Rhodes v. De Haan, 184 Kan. 473, 337 P.2d 1043 (1959).

89. Lehman, C.J., in George Foltis, Inc. v. City of New York, 287 N.Y. 108, 38 N.E.2d 455 (1941), said that where a plaintiff establishes

(b) even when it is, the plaintiff does not wish to risk an appellate finding of reversible error in the ruling. These cases, then, usually go to the jury.

2. *Cases in Which Defendant Gives Proof Tending to Rebut Plaintiff's Circumstantial Proof of Negligence.* Whenever the defendant adduces credible evidence tending to show due care, plaintiff has no right to a directed verdict. The best plaintiff can hope for is a favorable finding from the jury. But the defendant's proof of due care may be so compelling that defendant is entitled to a directed verdict, even though such a verdict would have been improper earlier when plaintiff rested. In Texas & N. O. R. Co. v. Schreiber,[90] a homeowner proved that a passing locomotive chuffed and chuffed and sprayed oil on his house. A railroad's expert then testified convincingly that engines often scatter oil without fault on the part of the railroad. The court held that on all of the evidence the jury could not be allowed to find proof of negligence. In other cases defendants' proof is less devastating and yet has the effect of raising a dispute on negligence appropriately submitted to a jury for decision—a decision which sometimes goes for the defendant.[91]

Jury charges in *res ipsa loquitur* cases are fertile breeders of trouble. If the only effect of the *res ipsa loquitur* doctrine is to give a technical Latin name to a special kind of circumstantial proof, there is seldom any reason for mentioning the doctrine to the jury; most instructions articulating a "rule" are likely to confuse ordinary jurors. In other kinds of negligence cases, standard instructions tell jurors that the plaintiff has a burden of proving negligence by a preponderance of the evidence. If standard instructions are given in a *res ipsa loquitur* case, claimant's counsel can make a legitimate argument on the weight and nature of the circumstantial proof. When trial judges attempt to explain *res ipsa loquitur* to the jury in terms of "presumption" or "inference," they may commit error; such instructions can seldom be framed without risking a jury im-

prima facie by direct evidence that injury was caused by negligence of the defendant, the court may seldom direct a verdict though the plaintiff's evidence is not contradicted or rebutted by the defendant. The practice should be the same where under the rule of *res ipsa loquitur* the plaintiff establishes *prima facie* by circumstantial evidence a right to recover. In Magner v. Beth Israel Hospital, 120 N.J.Super. 529, 295 A.2d 363

(1972), however, the appellate court held a malpractice plaintiff's *res ipsa loquitur* proof of negligence was so strong that the trial judge erred when he accepted a jury finding that the defendant doctor had used due care.

90. 104 S.W.2d 929 (Tex.Civ.App. 1937).

91. See, e.g., Rumbo v. Nixon, 241 S.W.2d 983 (Tex.Civ.App.1951).

pression that the defendant has a burden of proving due care. If the jury should be given special guidance, instructions limited to telling them that claimant's circumstantial evidence should be given the weight that it actually has seem desirable; instructions should not be capable of misleading jurors into believing that the defendant's burdens are more onerous than burdens of defendants confronted with other types of proof of negligence. In many jurisdictions a standarized form of instruction has passed muster many times in the court of last resort. That form is, of course, safe to use and is not likely to be overturned without judicial warning.

The foregoing description of procedural pattern is applicable only in jurisdictions in which *res ipsa loquitur* is merely a technical name for a kind of circumstantial proof. In some jurisdictions, courts have developed a doctrine of *res ipsa loquitur* which sometimes does shift burdens to the defendant—burdens that defendants ordinarily do not have. In the Capital Transit case (in which the streetcar passenger was injured when the car collided with a truck), the District of Columbia court intended to saddle the transit company with a burden of coming forward with evidence of its due care, even though the passenger, at the time he rested his case, had not offered adequate proof of the company's negligence. In the Ybarra case (in which the patient came out of an anesthetic with an injured shoulder), the California court intended to saddle each doctor and nurse with a burden of coming forward with proof of exoneration even though the patient had offered no proof tending to single out those personally guilty of negligence. These plaintiffs who did not prove particular defendants' negligence by evidence are held to have "proved" negligence by "legal presumption." In such cases, if defendants come forward with unrebutted proof of due care so strong and credible that reasonable jurors could not find against them, they deserve the protection of a dismissal entered by the trial judge. If a defendant offers no proof at all of due care, or proof that falls short of conclusively establishing due care, the plaintiff may be entitled to rulings and jury charges disfavoring the defendant. Just what these rulings should be is not made clear by the decisions. To be consistent, the decisions should probably reflect the view that the defendant has a burden, not only of coming forward with evidence of care, but of proving due care by a preponderance of the evidence. A halfway point is possible. The defendant could be saddled with the burden of coming forward with sufficient proof to raise a dispute on which reasonable jurors could differ, and then the plaintiff could be saddled with the burden of convincing the jury that the defendant was guilty of negligence. Until precedent settles the procedure in such cases, proper jury charges on allotment of burdens will be hard to frame. Unfortunately, the fate of litigants may turn on such jury charges; laymen are skeptical of the value of circumstantial evidence and instructions on who has burden of conviction may prove crucial.

Chapter VI

DUTY—THE NO–DUTY RULES AND IMMUNITIES

Table of Sections

§ 1. TWO KINDS OF NO–DUTY RULES

Earlier discussion of negligence in preceding chapters was based on the assumption that everyone has a duty to use due care all of the time. This assumption is somewhat inaccurate, and the discussion now turns to its correction.

Plaintiffs in negligence actions lose unless they establish that defendants were negligent. They also lose to defendants who owe them no duty to use due care. Over the years the courts have developed rules that shield some kinds of negligent defendants from liability. Some of these rules are couched in terms of lack of duty. Such rules expressly announce that a particular kind of defendant owes no duty of care to a specified sort of plaintiff in certain described circumstances. We shall call these rules "no-duty rules."

Two different varieties of no-duty rules operate in two different ways:

(1) Motorist is injured in a collision with Western Railroad's locomotive. The grade crossing is in open prairie country and can be seen for miles on a clear day by highway users approaching from either direction. The only warnings given by Railroad are stationary signs and whistle blasts. Motorist contends that Railroad should have installed flashing signals or automatic gates. Some courts might brush this contention aside, relying on this nineteenth century rule: A railroad is under *no duty* to give crossing warnings other than stationary signs and whistle signals unless the crossing is extraordinarily hazardous. This rule is a disguised (and probably outdated) concrete standard

126

for judging due care.[1] The rule would have the same effect were it phrased: A railroad is not negligent even though its crossing warnings are only stationary signs and whistle signals, unless the crossing is extraordinarily hazardous. The form used has significance; a standard for judging due care stated in terms of lack of duty is likely to escape criticism. The crossing rule may still govern decisions even though the time has come when grade crossings should be better guarded or closed. Some unduly lax concrete standards of due care couched in terms of duty, however, have long ago been abandoned. In Bender v. Welsh,[2] a motorist was injured when his car collided with a horse which had escaped from its pasture. The horse's owner argued that he was protected from liability by the common law rule that a stock owner has *no duty* to keep his animals off the highway. The court said that live stock on highways had not been a serious hazard when traffic was horse-drawn, but that the rule was no longer sound and would not be followed.

(2) Swimmer is seized with cramps while bathing near Mariner's boat. Mariner discerns Swimmer's plight, has a life preserver which could be thrown to Swimmer with a flick of the wrist, but shockingly decides to stand by and watch Swimmer drown. Swimmer's spouse brings a wrongful death action against Mariner. An ancient no-duty rule may protect Mariner from liability. One who sees a stranger in peril, it was said, is under *no duty* to render aid. This rule was never a standard for judging fault; the rule exonerates those who do not render aid, whether or not they are at fault. The rule interdicts trial of the fault issue; it relieves Mariner from liability even though Mariner is at fault. Rules of this sort present a new problem for discussion.

§ 2. NO DUTY TO RENDER AID TO A STRANGER

The action of trespass *vi et armis* was originally designed to cope with disturbance of "the King's peace." The peace was not disturbed by inaction; it was disturbed by active misconduct. The action of trespass on the case was developed to supplement trespass *vi et armis*. The newer action lay for misconduct "similar to" but not covered by the older one. Trespass *vi et armis* lay only for "direct" injuries; trespass on the case extended liability to "consequential injuries." But even after trespass on

---

1. The court clearly recognized it as a negligence rule in Stoler v. Penn Central Transportation Co., 583 F.2d 896 (6th Cir. 1978).

2. 344 Pa. 392, 25 A.2d 182 (1942). See also, Weber v. Madison, 251 N.W.2d 523 (Iowa 1977) (traffic accident caused by geese on roadway).

the case was developed, common law courts dealt gingerly with faulty inaction ("nonfeasance"), as distinguished from affirmative misconduct ("misfeasance"). The early common law refusal to recognize a duty to render aid to strangers is a specific manifestation of this history. It has been carried to extreme lengths and has produced some outrageous results.

At the turn of the century one of the leading cases was Union Pacific Ry. v. Cappier,[3] a wrongful death action in which the plaintiff alleged that employees of the railroad had failed to come to decedent's aid promptly after he was run over by defendant's locomotive, and as a result, he bled to death. The court held that the railroad had no duty to come to decedent's aid. With one exception,[4] other closely similar cases have, until recently, been decided in favor of defendant-railroads.

Unpalatability of the no-duty rule led to its early rejection in Missouri Pacific Ry. v. Platzer.[5] A fire set by a railroad damaged a farmer's property. The trial judge charged the jury that even though the railroad was not negligent in starting the fire, it was liable if its servants unreasonably ignored a chance to put the fire out before it reached the farm. This charge was approved by the appellate court. Nevertheless in the same jurisdiction, courts later held that a railroad was not liable for personal injuries resulting from its servants' unreasonable failure to render aid to a man run over by its train.[6]

The rule of Union Pacific Ry. v. Cappier was rejected in the Second Restatement of Torts. Section 322 provides that anyone who injures another, whether or not the injurer is liable for the original infliction, is obliged to use reasonable care to minimize the victim's harm. Injurers, even if they have good defenses against liability for the harm they originally inflicted, nevertheless incur liability for aggravation of their victims' initial harm by failing to use due care to render or summon aid.

There are two exceptions to the no-duty-to-render-aid rule: (1) if a relationship between the parties imposes on the defendant an obligation to act, or (2) if a wellwisher undertakes to render aid and thereafter fails to use due care.

---

3. 66 Kan. 649, 72 P. 281 (1903). See also, Yania v. Bigan, 397 Pa. 316, 155 A.2d 343 (1959).

4. Whitesides v. Southern Ry., 128 N.C. 229, 38 S.E. 878 (1901).

5. 73 Tex. 117, 11 S.W. 160, 15 Am.St.Rep. 771 (1889).

6. Riley v. Gulf, Colorado & Santa Fe Ry., 160 S.W. 595 (Tex.Civ. App.1913). Contra, Rains v. Heldenfels Brothers, 443 S.W.2d 280 (Tex.Civ.App.1969) (citing the Restatement, Second, Torts § 322 (1965)).

(1) A good example of a duty to render aid arising from a *Relationship* relationship is the duty of carriers to their passengers. In Middleton v. Whitridge,[7] a streetcar conductor thought a dying passenger was drunk and took no steps to care for him. Prompt medical attention would have saved his life. The traction company was held liable for its conductor's failure to use reasonable care. Courts have also held that employers owe a duty to render aid to injured or sick servants when others are unlikely to care for them.[8] Similarly, in the case of Depue v. Flatau,[9] the court held that a host incurred liability to a stricken social guest who was cast out on a stormy night.

An interesting 1976 case extended the ambit of psychotherapists' duty of care to others than their patients. In Tarasoff v. Regents of Univ. of California,[10] a patient revealed that he wanted to kill a young woman. The therapist gave no warning to the girl or her family. When the patient carried out his threat, the parents sued the therapist and his employer. The trial judge ruled that because the defendants owed no duty of care to the victim, the complaint stated no cause of action. The majority of the California Supreme Court reversed. Justice Tobriner said that psychotherapists who decide (or should have decided, according to the standards of their profession) that their patients' threats involve a serious risk of violence are obliged to use reasonable care to protect those threatened. The opinion emphasized that therapists are not required to give warning in all cases of threats, but need only exercise the reasonable skill ordinarily possessed and exercised in similar circumstances by members of their medical specialty; when professional opinion may differ, said that court, therapists are free to exercise their own best judgment without incurring liability.

(2) If in the Cappier case the railroad took charge of the injured man and then neglected to use reasonable care to succor *Good Samaritan* him, the railroad would incur liability. Those who adopt the role of the Good Samaritan fulfill their obligations only by being reasonably good Samaritans.[11] They are not forever responsible for the care of the injured; they may withdraw their bounty after taking steps to see that the plight of the stricken person is

---

7. 213 N.Y. 499, 108 N.E. 192 (1915).

8. Budd v. Erie Lackawanna R. R., 98 N.J.Super. 47, 236 A.2d 143 (1967).

9. 100 Minn. 299, 111 N.W. 1 (1907).

10. 17 Cal.3d 425, 131 Cal.Rptr. 14, 551 P.2d 334 (1976).

11. See, e. g., Weber v. Towner County, 565 F.2d 1001 (8th Cir. 1977).

called to the attention of the person's family or public authorities. A move enlarging the humanity required of the Good Samaritan was made in extending the liability of Wilmington General Hospital to a plaintiff (whose name, by poetic accident, was Manlove)[12] when a child was refused medical attention in the defendant hospital's emergency room. The court held the hospital liable for its refusal to treat an unmistakable emergency when the supplicant relied on the hospital's well-established custom of rendering aid in emergency cases.

In 1975 a volunteer's duty to use due care proved costly to a hydroelectric power company. The claimants were lower riparian owners who had harvested wild hay before the company built its dam. The wild hay thrived on riverside fields after inundation by spring floods. The company had no obligation to control spring runoffs, but nevertheless managed its water storage to protect downstream owners from flood damage for many years. This service, however, put an end to the claimants' wild hay harvests; consequently they planted other crops that flooding would damage. Then came a winter of extraordinarily deep snows. The power company neglected to prepare for torrential spring runoffs by winter water releases. The court held that the power company, by voluntarily undertaking to control spring floods, incurred a duty to use due care to protect downstream property from runoff damages.[13]

Even though the defendant is no legal stranger to a victim, a duty to use protective due care does not always arise; in Taylor v. Philadelphia Parking Authority,[14] the court held that the lessor of a "park and lock" automobile space was not a custodian of the parked car and therefore did not have a bailee's duty of due care to protect the car against theft.

One who quits voluntary service may have a duty to give notice of withdrawal. Suppose that Railroad has no duty to station a watchman at a certain crossing but nevertheless does so. Members of the traveling public come to rely on the watchman. Railroad withdraws the watchman without warning. Because no one is flagging down cars, Motorist believes it is safe to cross and comes to grief. On these facts a number of courts have held Railroad guilty of breach of a duty to give reasonable notice that the watchman has been withdrawn. Yet in slightly different circumstances, some courts have obtusely protected a silent with-

---

12. Wilmington General Hospital v. Manlove, 54 Del. (4 Storey) 15, 174 A.2d 135 (1961). See also Stanturf v. Sipes, 447 S.W.2d 558 (Mo.1969).

13. Kunz v. Utah Power & Light Co., 526 F.2d 500 (9th Cir. 1975).

14. 398 Pa. 9, 156 A.2d 525 (1959).

drawing volunteer from liability. In Hieber v. Central Kentucky Traction Co.,[15] a quarryman's blasting disquieted horses being shod in a nearby blacksmith shop. The quarryman followed the practice of warning the smith before he set off blasts. One morning no warning was given and a blast was set off while the smith held a hoof in his lap—with disastrous results to the smith. The court held for the quarryman on the ground that previous warnings were voluntary and the quarryman had no duty to continue them.

One who undertakes to perform a service as a favor has a duty to use due care. The word "undertake" is ambiguous; it may mean either a promise to do an act or commencement of performance of an act. In the early nineteenth century case of Thorne v. Deas,[16] one of two joint owners of a ship promised the other to arrange for insurance covering both of their interests. He did nothing. The ship was lost. The court dismissed the claim on the ground that the defendant had not commenced his undertaking and that failure to perform an unpaid for promise was not actionable. More than a hundred years later, in the same jurisdiction, a defendant who gratuitously promised to submit a bid at an auction sale of property especially valuable to the plaintiff was held to have made an undertaking and liable for failure to perform.[17]

A quotation from the Medicine section in *Newsweek*, published on October 9, 1972 says, "There probably isn't a doctor in the U.S. who has not on occasion gone past the scene of an accident without stopping, comforting himself with the thought that if he were to become involved he might well be slapped with a costly malpractice suit . . . . [N]ot a single suit of this type has ever been recorded . . . . [T]he editors of the magazine *Emergency Medicine* offered $100 to the first of its 106,000 readers who could document such a case . . . . [T]here has been only one response—and that turned out not to involve a Good Samaritan situation . . . . Nor has the legal department of the American Medical Association been able to discover any record of a Good Samaritan lawsuit . . . . [I]n most states the physician who volunteers his services to an injured person is at least partially protected from malpractice suits by special Good Samaritan laws that have been on the books for

15. 145 Ky. 108, 140 S.W. 54 (1911).

16. 4 Johns. 84 (N.Y.1809).

17. Kirby v. Brown, Wheelock, Harris, Vought & Co., 229 App.Div.

155, 241 N.Y.S. 255 (1930), rev., 255 N.Y. 274, 174 N.E. 652, reargument denied, 255 N.Y. 632, 175 N. E. 346 (1931). But see Comfort v. McCorkle, 149 Misc. 826, 268 N.Y. S. 192 (1933).

five to ten years . . . . [T]hese statutes generally protect any doctor who acts in good faith, is not guilty of gross negligence and doesn't collect a fee . . . ."

§ 3.   NO–DUTY RULES PROTECTING LAND OCCUPANTS FROM LIABILITY

Persons Injured Off the Premises.   Occupants of land owe their neighbors and passersby a duty of care.[18]   A shop owner negligently lets the shop's wall fall into disrepair; it collapses on a passing pedestrian or an adjoining greenhouse.   The shop owner incurs liability.   But when the source of danger is natural, rather than artificial, the occupant is sheltered from liability by a no-duty rule.   In the old leading case of Giles v. Walker,[19] an action for damages resulting from a failure to cut thistles which spread to neighboring fields, Lord Coleridge said, "There can be no duty as between adjoining occupiers to cut thistles, which are the natural growth of the soil."

Perhaps in the Giles case the no-duty rule functions only as a good concrete standard for judging due care.   The burden of cutting noxious weeds can be onerous.   A farmer whose land is lying fallow may not be unduly inconsiderate when he lets thistles go to seed.   Some legislatures have thought that railroads should keep weeds from spreading and have passed statutes calling on railroads to cut thistles and other noxious spreaders or suffer civil liability.

The principle of immunity for natural conditions shields some land occupants who have not used due care.   Householder's tree overhangs a public sidewalk; Householder knows or could readily discern that it is decayed and likely to topple in the next heavy breeze.   The tree falls on Pedestrian.   If the tree were *planted*, Householder has the duty to use due care, is guilty of breach, and is liable for Pedestrian's injuries.   If the tree had happened to grow in the same spot, Coleridge's theory set out in the thistle case would relieve Householder from liability.   But the botanical distinction is not a satisfactory basis for a legal difference.   Several modern courts have repudiated the no-duty rule in similar cases.[20]   When a landowner's property in its "natural condition" is unreasonably dangerous to travelers on adjoining roads, the force of justice should pierce the landowner's legalistic claim of immunity.   For example, in McCarthy v.

18.   See Lerro v. Thomas Wynne, Inc., 451 Pa. 37, 301 A.2d 705 (1973).

19.   24 Q.B.D. 656 (1890).

20.   See, e. g., Barker v. Brown, 236 Pa.Super. 75, 340 A.2d 566 (1975). See W. Prosser, Handbook of the Law of Torts 354–57 (4th ed. 1971), for ramifications.

Ference,[21] a steelmaker was irked by a public road that ran through its fabricating plant; the steelmaker eliminated this annoyance by building a detour which cut into an adjoining hillside. The company dedicated the new route to the county; the county accepted the hillside detour and closed the old route. The hillside was rocky, and after the new route was built, rocks in their natural site above the cut fell onto the road. In response to public protest, highway officials asked the steel company to allow them to enter the property above the road and pull down all dangerous rocks, with the condition that they be given permission and releases. The steelmaker knew of the danger but nevertheless refused the request. A huge boulder fell on a busload of people. The Supreme Court of Pennsylvania said that a land owner is not responsible to passersby for natural conditions even when the owner appreciates a substantial risk of injury to travelers. Though the rock that crushed the bus rolled from its natural setting, the court held that the situation had become artificial and ruled that the steelmaker was obliged to use reasonable care to prevent the injuries inflicted on the bus passengers by the rock fall. Similarly, a municipality or public authority may have a duty to use due care to inspect and maintain trees on publicly occupied land which, if they fall, may injure travelers on heavily traveled roadways.[22]

Entrants Injured on the Premises. In traditional common law, entrants were divided into the three following classes: (1) Trespassers, who enter the premises without authority, (2) Licensees, who are given permission to enter to further their own purposes, and Social Guests who are invited to enter for non-business visits, and (3) Business Guests, who usually enter for the mutual benefit of themselves and the occupant.

In most jurisdictions occupants owe their business guests a full duty of using reasonable care for their safety, and may incur liability either for failure to maintain the premises in reasonably safe condition or for negligent conduct in the presence of the entrant. However, in some jurisdictions the defense of voluntary assumption of risk (postponed for full discussion in Chapter VIII) has been rephrased in terms of duty, and some courts say that business hosts have no duty to keep their premises in safe condition—that their duty is only to warn guests of dangers that are not open and obvious. Later discussion will show that such a view may unwisely protect business hosts from

21. 358 Pa. 485, 58 A.2d 49 (1948).   22. See Husovsky v. United States, 590 F.2d 944 (D.C.Cir. 1978).

liability even though they are guilty of serious fault and even though the guests are not guilty of contributory fault.[23]

In years past, all courts have honored this rule: a land occupant owes *no duty* to trespassers to maintain the premises in safe condition. Sometimes this rule operates to protect occupants innocent of fault from liability to intruders guilty of serious misconduct. Suppose that an atomic energy plant maintains a supply of radioactive material dangerous to human life and limb. The plant guards this hazard by storing it in an appropriately situated and foolproof chamber. A foreign country's secret agent attempts to steal this fissionable material to obtain ingredients for a thermonuclear weapon. The agent suffers dire injuries. No court should or is likely to hold that the proprietor of the atomic energy plant is liable to pay damages for this intruder's injury.

This no-duty rule, alas, has also supplied immunity from liability in cases like Foley v. F. H. Farnham Co.,[24] an action for personal injuries to two wearied old pedestrians who, on their Sunday stroll, happened to sit for a momentary rest on the door sill of the defendant's shop. The defendant had not inspected an overhead sign for a long time; disastrously, it fell on the resting men. The court ruled that the oldsters had no legal claim because they had stepped off the sidewalk and become trespassers; as such, they assumed the risk of negligent maintenance of property they had entered without permission. In Murray v. McShane,[25] the facts were virtually the same, except that a pedestrian sat on the defendant's door step to tie his shoe. A brick, the pedestrian alleged, fell off the building's front wall and hit his head which protruded over the highway. The court legalistically, but justly, held that since the cracked skull was not trespassing, the allegations of negligence stated a cause of action.

Globs of overly technical law sometimes develop little swellings before they burst. A rule that relieves negligent occupants from liability to unlucky but inoffensive entrants not unnaturally nudged some judges into developing clever exceptions.

If a hazard lurks so close to a highway or public sidewalk that careful passersby may accidentally slip across the occupant's boundary and into trouble, nearly all courts have held that the

---

23. See Ch. VIII § 5, *infra.*

24. 135 Me. 29, 188 A. 708 (1936).

25. 52 Md. 217, 36 Am.Rep. 366 (1897).

innocent "technical trespasser" may nevertheless recover from an occupant who has been negligent.[26]

Some courts have adopted the "tolerated intruder" exception. In Franc v. Pennsylvania R.R.,[27] an adult pedestrian crossing a walkway on a private railroad trestle fell through a hole in that walkway and suffered personal injury. A center plank in the walkway had disappeared three weeks earlier, leaving the hole through which the victim fell; two days before her accident snow had fallen, and a drift concealed the gap through which she fell. At that time, the public had been crossing the trestle for thirty years. The court refused to invoke the no-duty rule protecting landowners against liability to trespassers for negligent maintenance, citing the "tolerated intruders" exception to the no-duty rule in section 335 of the Second Restatement of Torts. This exception to the no-duty rule applies only to very dangerous conditions of which the landowner has or should have knowledge, and only when the landowner knows of and tolerates many intrusions. The tolerated intruder exception now is relatively well received; however, many courts have had no recent occasion to accept or reject it.

In most jurisdictions immunity from liability to trespassers runs only in favor of a principal occupant, and the no-duty rule cannot be asserted by others whom the principal occupant allows to use the land. In Humphrey v. Twin State Gas & Electric Co.,[28] a trespassing hunter touched a wire fence charged with high voltage electricity by a sagging power line. The power company was only a licensee on the property. The court held that the power company could not invoke the no-duty rule and was liable for its failure to use due care.

A court's interesting display of discomfort with the rule sheltering landowners from liability to trespassers for dangerous conditions on their premises surfaced in Gould v. DeBeve.[29] In

---

26. See, e. g., Puchlopek v. Portsmouth Power Co., 82 N.H. 440, 136 A. 259 (1926). Contra, Lioni v. Marr, 320 Mass. 17, 67 N.E.2d 766 (1946). In Paquette v. Joyce, 117 N.H. 832, 379 A.2d 207 (1977), the claimant was an automobile passenger injured when the car missed a sharp curve on a country road and collided with a tree stump six feet off the highway. Chief Justice Kenison said, "we are not prepared to say that defendant's conduct [that is, leaving the stump when they cut the tree] introduced a risk that was appreciable enough to be foreseen and that would give rise to a duty to avoid."

27. 424 Pa. 99, 225 A.2d 528 (1967). See also, Vickers v. Gifford-Hill & Co., Inc., 534 F.2d 1311 (8th Cir. 1976); Hammond v. Maine Central R. R., 390 A.2d 502 (Me.1978).

28. 100 Vt. 414, 139 A. 440 (1927). Contra, McPheters v. Loomis, 125 Conn. 526, 7 A.2d 437 (1939).

29. 330 F.2d 826 (D.C.Cir. 1964).

that case the defendant leased an apartment, contracting with
the tenant to keep the premises in repair. The tenant promised
in the lease to take in no subtenants; nevertheless, the tenant
rented half of the apartment to the child plaintiff's mother. A
window screen next to the child's bed warped and cracked. The
landlord was notified that the screen was in a precarious state,
but he neglected to fulfill his obligation to repair the screen.
The child fell out of the window and was hurt. The trial judge
ruled that since the tenant had no right to sublet, the child was a
trespasser; nevertheless, this trial judge submitted the child's
claim to the jury, charging that it could give the child a verdict
if the landlord's conduct was willful or wanton. The jury returned a verdict in favor of the child. The court of appeals affirmed a judgment in favor of the child; speaking through
Judge McGowan, the court said that there are trespassers and
trespassers, and that this child should not be identified with the
English poacher who would not be heard to complain that the
landed gentry had neglected to keep their game preserves in safe
condition.

An exception to the no-duty rule is usually made for child
trespassers who wander onto unreasonably unsafe premises. In
the leading case, Sioux City & Pacific R.R. v. Stout,[30] a six
year-old child trespassed on an unlocked railroad turntable and
was injured when his playmates spun the turntable. The turntable was unfenced, near a depot, and not far from a public
road. The Supreme Court of the United States held that the
railroad could not escape liability by proving that the child was
a trespasser. The court announced the simple theory that a land
occupant whose negligently maintained premises seriously endanger children violates a duty of care owed to children. About
fifty years later the Supreme Court dealt more legalistically
with child trespassers in United Zinc & Chemical Co. v. Britt,[31]
and reached a snide result. Two children were poisoned by
swimming in a pool on a chemical company's land. The pool
was the abandoned cellar of a building in which sulfuric acid
had been manufactured. The building was torn down, and the
cellar had filled up with water that became impregnated with
sulfuric acid. It looked like an inviting swimming pool but was
in fact a seething death trap. It lay on the outskirts of a town
near the camp of the children's touring family. The land was
unfenced and no warnings of danger were posted. The court
held in favor of the chemical company on the ground that the
children did not discover the dangerous attraction until after

30. 84 U.S. (17 Wall.) 657, 21 L.Ed.
745 (1873).

31. 258 U.S. 268, 42 S.Ct. 299, 66
L.Ed. 615 (1922).

they had crossed the chemical company's boundaries. Justice Holmes equated attractions to children with invitations to enter, which changed their status from trespassers to invitees. When children enter first and discover the attraction later, Holmes said, they enjoy no invitation and the no-duty rule must be applied. This theory produced a shocking result in the sulfuric acid case. Nevertheless, its legal symmetry attracted a small following. One court that adopted the theory later returned to the simpler, more just, prevailing view of the Stout case.[32] The courts that do specially protect children are willing to do so only when the child is relatively young; rarely has a child trespasser over twelve been accorded protection greater than that given to adults.[33]

Licensees and social guests injured by unreasonably dangerous conditions have, in the past, fared little better than trespassers. An occupant it was said has *no duty* to make the premises safe for licensees or social guests.[34] However, the occupant has long owed a duty to licensees and social guests that is not traditionally owed to trespassers, the duty to warn them of hidden dangers of which the occupant has knowledge. A breach of that duty can result in liability. Some modern authority extends the duty to warn of hidden dangers to instances in which the occupant has "reason to know" of dangers fraught with risk of injury.[35]

The occupant's immunity from liability to licensees is especially unappealing when police or firemen in performance of their duty fall prey to an unreasonable hazard. These entrants are

32. See Gotcher v. City of Farmersville, 137 Tex. 12, 151 S.W.2d 565 (1941); compare Banker v. McLaughlin, 146 Tex. 434, 208 S.W.2d 843 (1948). Prosser said in 1971 that only six jurisdictions still adhered to Justice Holmes' view. W. Prosser, Handbook of the Law of Torts 366 (4th ed. 1971).

33. See, e. g., Hashtani v. Duke Power Co., 578 F.2d 542 (4th Cir. 1978). A few states still make no exception for children. See, e. g., Hensley v. Henkels & McCoy, Inc., 258 Md. 397, 265 A.2d 897 (1970). Of course, a child trespasser can recover for injuries arising out of the condition of the premises only if the occupant's negligence is proved. For example, if the occupant has no reason to believe that any youngster will enter the premises, the occupant is not obliged to take precautions to promote child safety. See, e. g., Shell Petroleum Corp. v. Beers, 185 Okl. 331, 91 P.2d 777 (1938). This defense has also been successful when the trespasser was an adult. Bennett v. Public Service Co. of New Hampshire, 542 F.2d 92 (1st Cir. 1976). The duty of care to children may not apply to "natural" conditions; one court has recently so held. See Loney v. McPhillips, 268 Or. 378, 521 P.2d 340 (1974).

34. See, e. g., Derby v. Connecticut Light & Power Co., 167 Conn. 136, 355 A.2d 244 (1974).

35. See, e. g., Marchello v. Denver & Rio Grande Western R. R., 576 F.2d 262 (10th Cir. 1978). For the definition of "reason to know" see Restatement, Second, Torts § 12 (1965).

not trespassers—their entry is authorized by law. But even when they are called to the premises by the occupant, they enter "on public business," and are not the occupant's business guests. Most courts have classified them as licensees and have held that the occupant owes them no duty to maintain the premises in reasonable safety. Some courts have rejected this reasoning. Long ago in Meiers v. Fred Koch Brewery,[36] the court said that an entering fireman is not a licensee of the occupant, since this right to enter is conferred by law, and therefore the occupant's immunity to one who enters with permission is irrelevant. The court held that occupants do owe firemen a duty to use care to keep their premises reasonably safe, and permitted a recovery. Recently, a court has created a new category for police and firemen entrants. It has called them "public safety visitors" and held that occupants whose premises were in negligent disrepair could not invoke the no-duty rule applicable to licensees.[37] The "public invitee" is also a newly created category (recognized in the Second Restatement of Torts, section 332) and is used typically in McKinnon v. Washington Federal Sav. & Loan Ass'n.[38] In that case a scout leader was injured at a scouting meeting held in a bank's meeting room. The bank welcomed, as a public service, use of its meeting room without charge by various civic and community organizations. The trial judge ignored evidence of the bank's negligence proximately causing the victim's harm because, said he, the bank owed her no duty of due care. The Supreme Court of Washington reversed, holding that the scout leader was no mere social guest but a "public invitee," and therefore the bank owed her a duty of due care in maintaining its premises.

Discussion has centered on injuries resulting from dangerous conditions—failures to maintain safe premises. Most courts hold that an occupant acting affirmatively after discovering the presence of an entrant has a duty to act with due care. Even trespassers have recovered in most jurisdictions for injury negligently inflicted by activity of an occupant who knows they have entered. Courts say that the presence of a licensee or guest should be anticipated since the occupant knows he or she has granted the license or issued the invitation; and the courts hold that active negligence of the occupant injuring a licensee or guest may result in liability even though the occupant acted

36. 229 N.Y. 10, 127 N.E. 491 (1920). See also the opinion in Shypulski v. Waldorf Paper Products Co., 232 Minn. 394, 45 N.W. 2d 549 (1951).

37. Cameron v. Abatiell, 127 Vt. 111, 241 A.2d 310 (1968).

38. 68 Wash.2d 644, 414 P.2d 773 (1966).

without noticing the entry.[39] A few courts have held that occupants have no duty to act with due care in the presence of trespassers or licensees, but need refrain only from injuring them intentionally or wantonly.

Some jurists have long been impatient with the legalistic results that automatically attach to characterizations of entrants. In England a Law Reform Committee's report to the Parliament resulted in passage of a statute in 1957; the enactment in general imposed the "common duty" of due care under the circumstances on all land occupants to likely entrants. The contributory fault of entrants can, no doubt, sometimes affect occupants' liability to them. In an admiralty case, the Supreme Court of the United States repudiated the distinction between shipboard business and social guests and held that the ship owed a duty of due care to all on board whose interest was not inimical to the ship owner.[40] The majority in a five to two decision in a California case, Rowland v. Christian,[41] allowed a social guest to recover damages for serious injuries to his hand inflicted when he turned a defective porcelain faucet handle which broke and cut him. His host had knowledge of the defect and gave him no warning; the court recognized the host's knowledge and failure to warn as an established source of liability to the social guest. Nevertheless, the majority of the court, citing the admiralty rule, went on to say that "the classifications of trespasser, licensee, and invitee, the immunities from liability predicated upon those classifications, and the exceptions to those immunities, often do not reflect the major factors which should determine whether immunity should be conferred upon the possessor of land. Some of those factors . . . bear little, if any, relationship to the classifications . . . and the existing rules conferring immunity." After citing the 1957 English statute, the court noted that the common law distinctions had been repudiated by the jurisdiction of their birth. The majority concluded that continued adherence to the distinctions would perpetuate injustice, and that the invention of a new fiction would enhance complexity and confusion; therefore they declined to follow and perpetuate "the rigid classifications." The minority preferred

39. See, e. g., Marchello v. Denver & Rio Grande Western R. R., 576 F. 2d 262 (10th Cir. 1978); Pridgen v. Boston Housing Authority, 364 Mass. 696, 308 N.E.2d 467 (1974); Mailloux v. Steve Soucy Constr. Co., 116 R.I. 348, 356 A.2d 493 (1976), a borderline case of "passivity."

40. Kermarec v. Compagnie Generale Transatlantique, 358 U.S. 625, 79 S.Ct. 406, 3 L.Ed.2d 550 (1959).

41. 69 Cal.2d 108, 70 Cal.Rptr. 97, 443 P.2d 561 (1968). See also Mounsey v. Ellard, 363 Mass. 693, 297 N.E.2d 43 (1973); Mariorenzi v. Joseph DiPonte, Inc., 114 R.I. 294, 333 A.2d 127 (1975).

to leave such a sweeping modification to the legislature. The majority seems to us to be the more prophetic view.[42]

§ 4. NO–DUTY RULES SHIELDING LAND SELLERS AND LESSORS

Some courts have held that a seller of land owes no duty to those injured by hazards on the land after the title passes—even though the seller knows of the dangerous conditions at the time of sale. When a seller knows of a hidden hazard that is not likely to be discovered by the buyer, the seller is under a duty to disclose the hazard. A seller who fails to do so may incur liability to the buyer and others. In most cases these rules exonerate only sellers who, though once negligent, are no longer at fault. After title to property passes, the proper person to take care of it is the new owner. In unusual circumstances a culpable defendant may be relieved of liability and a deserving plaintiff may be denied a recovery. In Palmore v. Morris,[43] a seller sold a foundry one afternoon; the next morning, a heavy gate in negligent disrepair fell on a bystander. The court held that the sale relieved the seller from liability. The bystander would have fared no better had he sued the buyer; even if the buyer had known that the gate was out of repair, he would not have had time to fix it.

After time to repair has passed, the buyer alone should be liable. The theory that the seller's duties vanish at the moment when title passes is legalistically neat but impolitic in the Palmore case. At least one sort of vendor of real estate has been singled out for different treatment. In Schipper v. Levitt & Sons, Inc.,[44] the court held that the builder of a vast housing development was not unlike the manufacturer of automobiles; when the developer marketed a defective and dangerous house, the developer was held accountable for negligence to the purchaser or others injured on the premises.

At common law landlords enjoyed a similar immunity. Landlords who do not covenant to maintain real property, the courts held, incur no liability for injuries resulting from hazards on the leased premises. This rule does not protect landlords from liability if they do not disclose a hidden danger known to them but not likely to be discovered by the tenant. When tenants or those properly on private premises are injured by the lessor's failure

---

42. See, e. g., Ouellette v. Blanchard, 116 N.H. 552, 364 A.2d 631 (1976); Scurti v. City of New York, 40 N.Y.2d 433, 387 N.Y.S.2d 55, 354 N.E.2d 794 (1976).

43. 182 Pa. 82, 37 A. 995 (1897).

44. 44 N.J. 70, 207 A.2d 314 (1965).

to use reasonable care for the safety of occupants and entrants, such a landlord may be at fault, but nevertheless immune from liability. This immunity has been enjoyed in all courts except in cases governed by local legislation that puts the legal burden on some landlords to take greater precautions to furnish safe premises. In a recent case, the court expanded landlords' obligation; it held that landlords who fail to use due care may be liable to persons rightfully on the premises.[45] This case seems to us to be a prophetic holding likely to be adopted by other courts in the near future.

Lessors who rent property to be used for a "public purpose" do not enjoy the immunity. Danger to a large number of people with no correlative responsibility in the landlord is too high a price for legal symmetry, and the courts have held that lessors of theatres, public lecture halls, and amusement parks are under a duty to patrons to turn the property over to their tenants in reasonably safe condition. In Webel v. Yale Univ.,[46] the Connecticut court classified a beauty parlor as a public place and held the landlord liable for injuries resulting from a hazard that was on the property when rented. The Connecticut court stoutly enlarged the obligation of landlords to be considerate of the safety of their tenants' guests. Since that time most courts have followed and held that lessors of shops, garages, taverns, and so on are under a similar obligation.

Landlords who rent offices or apartments to several tenants, retaining control of lobbies, elevators, halls, etc., have a duty to use due care to prevent injury in "common passageways." They are subject to liability to tenants and tenants' families, employees, invitees, etc., for breach of this duty. They may be obliged to pay not only for injuries resulting from physical defects,[47] but also, when they know or should know that marauders prowl their buildings, for injuries resulting from negligent failure to thwart marauders' attacks.[48]

A landlord's covenant to keep rented premises in repair is a promise on which the tenant may bring a contract action should the landlord default. The covenant might be construed as a contract for the benefit of others than the tenant, but certainly many entrants or passersby injured by disrepair would be only

45. Sargent v. Ross, 113 N.H. 388, 308 A.2d 528 (1973); Contra, Givens v. Union Investment Corp., 116 R.I. 539, 359 A.2d 40 (1976).

46. 125 Conn. 515, 7 A.2d 215 (1939).

47. See, e.g., Taneian v. Meghrigian, 15 N.J. 267, 104 A.2d 689 (1954).

48. See, e.g., Scott v. Watson, 278 Md. 160, 359 A.2d 548 (1976).

"incidental beneficiaries" and not entitled to bring an action for breach of this contract. Furthermore, the contract measure of damages may not cover all personal injuries proximately resulting from dangerous disrepair. In the past many courts took the view that a covenant to repair in no way increased the tort liability of a landlord. The law, however, sometimes shakes off old mistakes and starts anew. Pennsylvania was a die-hard state until 1968. In Reitmeyer v. Sprecher,[49] decided in 1968, a landlord relied on a 1937 precedent to avoid tort liability for personal injuries arising out of his failure to make repairs he had promised at the time he rented the premises. The Pennsylvania court overruled its earlier precedent; the court adopted the view of liability for negligence of landlords who contract to repair set out in section 357 of the Second Restatement of Torts. This illustrates a modern trend.[50]

Perhaps the most satisfactory technical explanation of covenanting landlords' obligations in tort is found in an analogy to the duty of those undertaking to render aid to a stranger. Assuming landlords have no duty to repair in the absence of a covenant, once they covenant they are responsible for all damages proximately flowing from their failure to act with reasonable prudence. Of course, landlords cannot be expected to make constant and recurring inspections, and unless they are notified of dangerous disrepair or happen to have knowledge of it, they may not be unreasonable in failing to perform their covenants.

§ 5. THE REPUDIATED NO–DUTY RULE WHICH ONCE SHELTERED MANUFACTURERS, BUILDERS AND OTHER SUPPLIERS FROM LIABILITY

In 1842 the English Court of Exchequer decided Winterbottom v. Wright.[51] A coach driver plaintiff in that case alleged that a wheelwright defendant contracted with the Postmaster General to furnish and maintain the mail coaches used on the driver's route, that the wheelwright negligently supplied a coach in disrepair which broke down, and that as a result the driver was lamed for life. The court held that since the source of the

---

49. 431 Pa. 284, 243 A.2d 395 (1968).

50. See Merchants' Cotton Press & Storage Co. v. Miller, 135 Tenn. 187, 186 S.W. 87 (1916), in which the court held the covenanting landlord liable for an injury suffered by a servant of the tenant after the tenant notified the landlord of disrepair and demanded performance of the covenant. The court discussed the whole problem well and marshalled authorities. See also, Arledge v. Gulf Oil Corp., 578 F.2d 130 (5th Cir. 1978).

51. 10 M. & W., 109, 152 Eng.Rep. 402 (1842).

wheelwright's duty to act was a contract with the Postmaster General, the duty was owed only to the Postmaster General.

This case spawned a line of holdings in which negligent suppliers of chattels under contract were relieved from liability to injured users who were not parties to the contracts. Manufacturers escaped liability to consumers whenever their contractual dealings were with retailers or middlemen—which in modern times is the normal course of business.

The first move of the courts away from this impolitic rule was the development of two exceptions: (1) The courts held that manufacturers of food, drugs, and firearms—"articles intended to preserve, destroy or affect human life"—do have a duty to consumers to use reasonable care and are liable to consumers for negligence. (2) Manufacturers who know their product is dangerous to life and limb are under a duty to give notice of the danger. These two exceptions did not cover those manufactured goods which were neither food, drugs, nor firearms, or which were marketed without knowledge of their dangerously defective condition.

Radical repudiation of Winterbottom v. Wright came in 1916 when Cardozo wrote his famous opinion in MacPherson v. Buick Motor Co.[52] A motorcar manufacturer sold an automobile to a dealer, who in turn sold the car to the plaintiff. One of the wheels was defective; its spokes crumbled and the plaintiff was injured. The wheel was bought by the manufacturer from a reputable parts supplier, but the plaintiff's evidence tended to show that its defects would have been discovered by the manufacturer had it made a reasonable inspection. Cardozo extended the food, drug, and firearm exception to cover all articles that imperil life and limb when negligently made. His holding was eminently sensible; it has been followed by virtually all courts.

Cardozo expressly refused to discuss liability of suppliers of component parts sold to manufacturers, and his theory was not broad enough to hold manufacturers liable for negligence resulting in damage to property. In the next four decades other courts filled in these gaps in manufacturers' duties; no negligent manufacturers now escape liability by invoking the doctrine of Winterbottom v. Wright.

Manufacturers' civil liability for negligence has become a major protection against dangerous exploitation of the public by inconsiderate or grasping enterprisers. One of the most striking instances is disclosed by Rheingold in the MER/29 Story,[53] an

---

52. 217 N.Y. 382, 111 N.E. 1050 (1916).

53. The MER/29 Story—An Instance of Successful Mass Disaster

article describing the filing of more than fifteen hundred private civil suits, which eventually cost a pharmaceutical manufacturer and its insurers over twenty-two million dollars. The same misconduct resulted in comparatively trifling public punishment; i. e., only the maximum allowable eight thousand dollars in criminal fines and two suspended sentences of imprisonment.

One of the last battlegrounds of manufacturers' limited liability for negligence involved so-called "second collision" injuries in automobiles. For example, in Larsen v. General Motors Corp.,[54] the plaintiff was driving a Corvair. The steering mechanism was dislodged and pushed back when the Corvair collided head-on with another car; as a result, the claimant received severe head injuries which he claimed were caused or aggravated by negligently unsafe design of the steering assembly. The trial judge, relying on earlier authority, gave General Motors a summary judgment on the theory that since the car manufacturer had no duty to eliminate head-on collision, it was not liable for the consequences of such collisions. The appellate court reversed, holding that even though accident-proof cars cannot be made, manufacturers must be careful to design cars to afford reasonable protection from injury in those accidents that are bound to happen.

The manufacturer's liability for injuries resulting from negligence in design or manufacture is not limited to consumers of the wares he produces. A bystander or traveler who suffers an injury proximately caused by a manufacturer's negligence may also be entitled to compensation.[55]

Another modern line of development has extended products liability beyond responsibility for negligence and holds manufacturers and others liable without proof of fault. We postpone discussion of this development until later in chapter IX, so that we can make some significant comparisons with other instances of liability not based on fault.

Another field in which the privity requirement of Winterbottom v. Wright had influence was building construction. In Ford v. Sturgis,[56] a theatre roof collapsed on an audience because of the building contractor's negligence. The court relieved the builder from liability to playgoers and said, "There was, of course, no privity of contract existing between Ford and the de-

Litigation, 56 Cal.L.Rev. 116 (1968).

54. 391 F.2d 495 (8th Cir. 1968).

55. See Passwaters v. General Motors Corp., 454 F.2d 1270 (8th Cir. 1972).

56. 14 F.2d 253 (D.C. Cir. 1926).

cedent, and the general rule is well established that the negligence of a contractor in constructing a building will not render him liable to a third person, who is injured in consequence thereof after the work has been completed and accepted by the owner of the building." But the force of the MacPherson case has been felt in this field too, and the "well-established rule" has crumbled. It was repudiated long ago by Judge Goodrich in his spendid opinion in Moran v. Pittsburgh-Des Moines Steel Co.,[57] and several other holdings are in the same camp.

Different considerations may come into play when avowedly imperfect and secondhand articles are sold "as is." Financially responsible traders might not be able to afford to traffic in these goods if they incurred liability for failure to inspect and repair them. In Bergstresser v. Van Hoy,[58] a secondhand car dealer sold an obviously unsafe car to a buyer who later ran over a pedestrian. The court held for the dealer since the pedestrian did not show that the dealer knew of and willfully concealed hidden defects. The cause of safety might be better served if dealers in secondhand cars had to make them reasonably safe or break them up for the junk market. Costs of inspection, repair, and risk-carrying would raise the price of hulks. There are, of course, some ingenious buyers who do not have money enough to buy old cars already put into good condition, but who are themselves able to recondition them. The danger is that unsafe cars will be sold to buyers who lack ingenuity, means, or desire to make them safe. This danger can be reduced by compulsory inspection, criminal prosecution, etc. Many secondhand cars in apparent running order are sold as suitable for operation. Dealers in these wares have, at the least, a duty to use reasonable care to make them safe, especially when the dealer represents the car as roadworthy, as most secondhand car dealers do. In Egan Chevrolet Co. v. Bruner,[59] a dealer sold vehicles as "O.K.'d used cars and trucks." A buyer's truck went out of control the day after he bought it because of a faulty steering mechanism readily discoverable when inspected by an ordinary mechanic using reasonable care. The truck collided with the claimants' car and inflicted serious injuries. On proof of these facts the court held that the rule of MacPherson v. Buick Motor Co. should be extended, and that a retail dealer in used trucks who undertakes to recondition them for resale owes

---

57. 166 F.2d 908 (3rd Cir. 1948). Accord, Cosgriff Neon Co. v. Mattheus, 78 Nev. 281, 371 P.2d 819 (1962).

58. 142 Kan. 88, 45 P.2d 855 (1935).

59. 102 F.2d 373 (8th Cir. 1939).

the public a duty of reasonable care to seek out defects which would make the wares a menace.[60]

§ 6. CRIMINAL STATUTES AND CIVIL NO–DUTY RULES

In Parker v. Barnard,[61] a Massachusetts court decided this case: A patrolling policeman came upon a suspiciously open back door. He went into the building to investigate and stepped into an unguarded elevator shaft. The trial judge classified the policeman as a licensee and found for the occupant on the ground that he owed no duty to a licensee to keep his premises safe. The appellate court reversed on the ground that the occupant had broken a criminal statute by leaving the shaft unfenced and so incurred civil liability.

Fifty years later, the facts recurred in the Massachusetts case of Wynn v. Sullivan.[62] The court refused to follow its earlier decision and held that the policeman had no cause of action. The court said that immunities of common law no-duty rules are not affected by criminal statutes unless the legislature also provides for civil liability in express terms or by clear implication. This view has some support in other jurisdictions, but the weight of authority supports the earlier holding.

Both Massachusetts holdings purported to be statutory interpretation—the earlier court inferred that the legislature had changed the civil law; the later court held that the legislature was not concerned with tort liability. If the problem were only one of statutory construction the later view would be the sounder one. When private rights go unmentioned in a criminal statute, the legislature probably does not intend to change private law.

The problem is not, however, simply one of statutory interpretation. When criminals seek sanctuary behind a common law no-duty rule, the time has come to reexamine the soundness of the rule. Many no-duty rules are legal heirlooms which courts have relegated to the attic without legislative prompting—witness judicial abandonment of the doctrine of Winterbottom v. Wright. Once the legislature sees fit to punish the very conduct shielded by a no-duty rule, surely the value of the rule should be reconsidered. Neither the earlier nor later Massachusetts view

---

60. See Turner v. International Harvester Co., 133 N.J.Super. 277, 336 A.2d 62 (1975) indicating that dealers in dangerously defective secondhand vehicles may incur liability without proof of fault as developed in Ch. XI § 6.

61. 135 Mass. 116, 46 Am.Rep. 450 (1883).

62. 294 Mass. 562, 3 N.E.2d 236 (1936).

Tort law should follow civil

is acceptable. The advance of criminal responsibility into areas of civil immunity raises a question (which may be answered either way): Should tort liability follow the criminal law?

Many criminal statutes should be backed with civil responsibility even though the legislature has not ordered courts to furnish it. Penal statutes dispel at least two objections to extension of civil liability:

(1) Sudden abandonment of some common law no-duty rules might trap people whose conduct has been scrupulously law-abiding. But after criminal legislation proscribes conduct, those held civilly liable for breach of the criminal law are not likely to be caught innocently off guard. Criminal statutes serve a warning function. That all people know the law is a fiction; but they do in fact have a fairly good chance to know much of it.

(2) The legislature's opportunities to investigate and debate tend to vouch for feasibility of compliance with criminal statutes. A court creating a novel tort liability without investigation runs a risk of demanding impractical or undesirable precaution. But criminal statutes are not likely to interdict conduct which most people cannot forego in everyday affairs.

Civil liability should not always follow criminal responsibility. Administration tempers criminal responsibility in ways unparalleled in civil courts. Enactment of statutes may happen to go unpublicized, and so no adequate warning of impending drastic changes in the law of negligence is given by their passage. Some criminal statutes may be unwisely severe. Potentially ruinous civil liability is often inappropriate for infraction of petty criminal regulations.

In cases in which a no-duty rule grants impolitic immunity from liability, several courts have held that civil liability follows new criminal responsibility into areas of common law immunity.

The legislatures of several jurisdictions have passed criminal statutes penalizing landlords who fail to keep up certain kinds of rented premises. In several damage suits landlords guilty of criminal failure to maintain these rented premises have been held liable to tenants, subtenants, tenants' customers, and tenants' employees, even though the landlords would have escaped liability under a common law no-duty rule had the injuries happened before the criminal statute was enacted.

In Pine Grove Poultry Farm, Inc. v. Newton By-Products Mfg. Co.,[63] a manufacturer adulterated poultry feed and sold it

63.   248 N.Y. 293, 162 N.E. 84 (1928).

to a retailer, who sold it to a poultry raiser, whose ducks died from eating it. Ten years earlier Cardozo had decided in the Buick case that a manufacturer owes consumers a duty to use care to prevent harm to human life and limb. But no court had yet questioned careless manufacturers' immunity from liability for damages to property. The feed manufacturer was held liable, but the court did not boldly overrule old precedents. Instead, the court rationalized its decision by referring to a criminal statute interdicting sale of feed likely to injure animals and analogizing civil and criminal responsibility. The careless manufacturer which was sued for damages in the next property damage case happened to have broken no criminal law.[64] Nevertheless, it too was held liable. The court cited the adulterated feed case as support for its repudiation of the no-duty rule of Winterbottom v. Wright (the coach driver case). This court, prompted by a criminal statute to find civil liability in the feed case, pushed ahead in the next case to repudiate immunity of manufacturers who had not broken the criminal law.

When a civil court is first confronted with a breach of a new criminal statute, and when the violator's conduct falls within the immunity of an old tort law no-duty rule, the case is unprecedented—for in no precedent recognizing the immunity has the defendant also committed the new crime. In this novel situation the court cannot avoid judicial lawmaking. Some courts have refused to extend civil liability in cases in which the extension would be unwisely harsh. Some courts have refused to relieve serious criminal wrongdoers from civil liability in cases in which a common law no-duty rule, standing alone, exonerates the wrongdoer from a duty of reasonable care. But few, if any, courts have expressly and clearly recognized that criminal legislation is neither binding nor irrelevant and that civil courts have the problem of discriminating between (a) cases in which civil liability should be extended to cover the criminal breach and (b) cases in which civil immunity should be reaffirmed even though defendant has broken a criminal law.

A cluster of precedents purports to mark out one kind of case in which a no-duty rule should not give way in the face of criminal legislation. Most courts do not hold abutters who criminally fail to clear naturally deposited ice, snow, and mud from public sidewalks civilly liable to passersby who fall. Courts say that an abutter owed no duty at common law to act affirmatively for the safety of sidewalk users and the criminal ordinances create no such duty.

---

64. Genesee County Patrons Fire   Inc., 263 N.Y. 463, 189 N.E. 551
Relief Ass'n v. L. Sonneborn Sons,   (1934).

Professor Thayer in his classic article generalizes the abutter cases in this fashion: When criminal legislation calls for affirmative action, civil liability should not follow the criminal law.[65] Thayer reasons that mere omissions are not usually actionable at common law. Criminal statutes do not create civil duties; they merely formulate new and more exact standards for trying the issue of breach of existing duties. An issue of breach arises only where the common law of torts recognizes a duty of due care.

Thayer proves too much. He builds not only on the acceptable proposition that criminal statutes are not a legislative change of the law of torts; he builds also on these unstated and unacceptable assumptions: (1) when the legislature does not change the law of torts it should remain static; and (2) criminal legislation is irrelevant to the solution of civil duty problems.

The abutter cases—which are numerous and fairly uniform— will not be overruled lightly. But some other holdings are inconsistent with Thayer's conclusions. We said in the second section of this chapter that, shortly before Mr. Thayer wrote his famous article on negligence *per se*, injurers who were not liable for harm originally caused were under no duty to come to the aid of their victims; but more recently, courts have held that those actors who know or should know that their conduct has put victims in need of aid must exercise care to prevent further harm—regardless of liability for the original injury. One of the mechanisms facilitating the change in tort law is the holding that a violation of a criminal hit and run statute is negligence *per se* and, therefore, violators are criminally liable for any damages proximately caused by their criminal failure to see to the care of their victims.[66] At common law one carefully using a highway had no duty to other highway users to report or remedy a dangerous highway defect, even if the user was the cause of the defect. But a motorist who collided with a trolley pole which another motorist had, without fault, knocked into the highway, recovered damages for his injuries.[67] One of the announced bases of the decision was a criminal statute penalizing those who cause to be left on the street a broken substance likely to cause injury. These examples cast doubt on the reliability of Thayer's analysis either as a description of what courts have

65. Thayer, Public Wrong and Private Action, 27 Harv.L.Rev. 317 (1914).

66. See, e. g., Brooks v. E. J. Willig Truck Transportation Co., 40 Cal. 2d 669, 255 P.2d 802 (1953); Hallman v. Cushman, 196 S.C. 402, 13 S.E.2d 498 (1941); Battle v. Kilcrease, 54 Ga.App. 808, 189 S.E. 573 (1936).

67. Simonsen v. Thorin, 120 Neb. 684, 234 N.W. 628 (1931).

done or a prophecy of what courts will do. Tort liability based on seriously culpable criminal nonfeasance seems justifiable on policy grounds and is not interdicted for all cases by established principle or precedent.

In 1978 the Oregon Supreme Court decided an interesting case, Burnette v. Wahl.[68] Several infants brought damage suits against their mothers who had abandoned them, praying for money damages to compensate the plaintiffs for the emotional and psychological harm resulting from their desertion. The children alleged that their mothers' desertions were intentional, willfully malicious and cruelly disregarded the emotional and psychological harm that was likely to result to the plaintiffs. Child abandonment is a felony in Oregon. The mothers demurred to their childrens' complaints. The trial judge held that the children had failed to state any cause of action. On appeal, the Supreme Court upheld the trial judge's ruling by a vote of three to two. The opinion supporting the dismissal of the childrens' suit begins by reviewing the many statutes enacted by the Oregon legislature to protect "dependent" children, including, of course, the statute declaring abandonment to be a felony. The opinion notes the legislature's silence on claims like those put forth by the child-plaintiffs. The opinion continues, "If there is any chance that . . . the court's establishment of a [new and novel] civil action might interfere with the total legislative scheme [for dealing with the subject of dependent children] courts should err on the side of non-intrusion . . . courts should exercise restraint in fields in which the legislature has attempted fairly comprehensive social regulation . . . . If there is ever a field in which juries and trial courts are ill equipped to do social engineering, it is in the realm of emotional relationship between mother and child." One of the dissenting judges said that the legislature had not preempted this field; he cited many studies of economic, psychiatric, and sociological injuries suffered by abandoned children and concluded that judicial action to compensate these plaintiffs should implement the community's values. The second dissenting judge (with whom the first concurred) based his argument on an extended view of the "statutory purpose rule," first announced in 1874 by the English Court of Exchequer and discussed at length in section 5 of Chapter VII of this book. The dissenting judge said that when criminal legislation is silent on civil liability, then civil liability should depend on "whether the plaintiff belongs to the class for whose special protection the statute was enacted

68. 284 Or. 705, 588 P.2d 1105 (1978).

. . . . ." He characterized the statutory duty arising out of the felony statute as a sanction for breach of "a preexisting duty to the child." The duty, he said is not owed to the state; the child's rights deserve "governmental reinforcement . . . . To hold the plaintiffs cannot invoke this duty, one must assume a legislative policy that a deserted and abandoned child . . . should ask a district attorney to seek the criminal punishment of the parent . . . but that the child should have no claim that would be of any benefit to itself." We recommend reading the court's opinions in this case to those interested in the judicial process in tort cases.

§ 7.   IMMUNITIES FROM TORT LIABILITY

Certain injuries that would ordinarily result in tort liability were not actionable at common law because the perpetrator was said to be "immune" from liability. These immunities operated in the same way that the no-duty rules did; [69] even when an "immune" defendant's negligent conduct proximately caused damage, this defendant escaped liability. The two most important immunities were those enjoyed by charities and by governmental units.

Judge Fuld, in his opinion in the leading case of Bing v. Thunig,[70] said that the first American case recognizing the charitable immunity was decided in Massachusetts in 1876.[71] The Massachusetts court justified its holding by citing earlier nineteenth century English common law already abrogated by the English courts. Fuld pointed out that every American case decided after 1940 in those jurisdictions in which the courts were unfettered by precedent had refused to recognize the charitable immunity and that many courts in states that had followed Massachusetts' false lead had later reversed themselves. After characterizing the historical and analytical reasons given for the immunity as specious, Judge Fuld said, "The rule of nonliability is out of tune with the life about us, at variance with modern-day needs and with concepts of justice and fair dealing. It should be discarded." At this writing most, if not all, American courts

---

69. There may be a slight, but unimportant, analytical difference. Courts have said that an immunity can be waived. See, e.g., Collins v. Memorial Hospital of Sheridan County, 521 P.2d 1339 (Wyo.1974). It would sound curious to say, for example, that a land occupant waived the lack of legal duty to trespassers to use reasonable care in maintaining the premises. Of course, the no-duty rule protecting occupants from liability to trespassers has many limitations and exceptions.

70. 2 N.Y.2d 656, 163 N.Y.S.2d 3, 143 N.E.2d 3 (1957).

71. McDonald v. Massachusetts General Hospital, 120 Mass. 432, 21 Am.Rep. 529 (1876).

have agreed with him and no longer cloak charities with this unwarranted immunity.

States, it was thought, could not be sued at all without their consent.[72] Some remedies against the federal and state governments have long since been conferred by statutes establishing Courts of Claims or by Torts Claims Statutes. Many of these statutes impose special limits on state liability so that the state avoids some obligations which bind private defendants. The Federal Torts Claims Act, for example, denies liability for punitive damages, for claims arising out of assault, battery, false imprisonment and a number of other intentional torts, for claims arising out of combatant activities in time of war, etc.[73] In earlier times some courts held that the state incurred no tort liability other than that explicitly provided for by legislative enactment.[74] One of the most sweeping judicial inroads on the states' immunity (completely independent of legislative sanction) is the 1972 case of Campbell v. State of Indiana,[75] in which the court held in two consolidated cases that Indiana incurred tort liabilities for its failure to mark the center of a highway with a yellow line and its failure to use care in maintaining a pedestrian crosswalk over a roadway.

Local governmental units enjoyed an immunity from tort liability arising out of "governmental" as distinguished from administrative acts. The first English case to recognize this immunity was Russell v. Men of Devon, in 1798.[76] In that case, the court thought that the claim was embarrassed by the lack of any public purse from which the claimant could be paid by the unincorporated group which was sued and that (in those days) injury was better borne by the person hurt than by the public. These reasons have not protected local governments in our times, and their immunity from ordinary tort liability has virtually vanished in many American states.[77] Legislatures, however, have been somewhat disturbed by this judicial lawmaking and have restored or modified the immunity of local governments to some extent. There are areas of local government in which activities are not comparable to private business or indi-

72. See Maguire, State Liability for Tort, 20 Harv.L.Rev. 22 (1916).

73. See 28 U.S.C.A. §§ 2674, 2680 (1970).

74. See, e.g., Riddoch v. State, 68 Wash. 329, 123 P. 450 (1912).

75. 259 Ind. 55, 284 N.E.2d 733 (1972). The Pennsylvania Supreme Court has done the same. See Mayle v. Pennsylvania Dept. of Highways, 479 Pa. 384, 388 A. 2d 709 (1978).

76. 2 Term Rep. 667, 100 Eng.Rep. 359 (1798).

77. See, e.g., Muskopf v. Corning Hospital Dist., 55 Cal.2d 211, 11 Cal.Rptr. 89, 359 P.2d 457 (1961).

vidual behavior.   In some of these, courts still hold the governmental unit immune.[78]

One other immunity deserves mention—the intra-family immunity.   At common law, minor children and parents could not sue each other for negligent personal injury, and spouses were likewise immune from liability to each other.   The theory behind this immunity was twofold.   Courts said (1) that litigation between members of a family would disrupt the family and (2) that when the liability asserted was covered by insurance, named defendants were likely to perjure themselves in favor of plaintiffs.   Modern courts are unwilling to accept either of these rationalizations, and many of them have reversed older cases establishing these immunities.[79]

78. See for example, Riss v. City of New York, 22 N.Y.2d 579, 293 N. Y.S.2d 897, 240 N.E.2d 860 (1968), in which the plaintiff, who alleged that the police acted improperly when they refused special protection against a threat of violent injury, failed to state a cause of action.

79. See for example, Plumley v. Klein, 388 Mich. 1, 199 N.W.2d 169 (1972), rejecting a parent's claim of immunity against liability to her children, and Brooks v. Robinson, 259 Ind. 16, 284 N.E.2d 794 (1972), rejecting a husband's similar claim in an action brought by his wife.   Each of these cases cite much supporting authority from other states.   The opinion in Merenoff v. Merenoff, 76 N.J. 535, 388 A.2d 951 (1978), gives careful and extensive coverage of the history, social theories and policy problems involved in intraspousal immunity and virtually destroys the remnants of the immunity lingering in New Jersey personal injury law.   It is well worth reading.   But see Holodook v. Spencer, 36 N.Y.2d 35, 364 N.Y.S.2d 859, 324 N.E.2d 338 (1974).

Chapter VII

EXTENT OF LIABILITY FOR NEGLIGENCE: DUTY, NEGLIGENCE AND CAUSATION

Table of Sections

---

§ 1. THE RELATION BETWEEN DEFENDANT'S WRONG AND PLAINTIFF'S INJURY

Imp acts carelessly and Angel is seriously injured. Imp is a wrongdoer who acted without due consideration for the safety of others—Imp is negligent. Angel has suffered bodily injury—a kind of damage which is often compensable in tort actions. But suppose that an average person would have trouble deciding whether or not Imp, though blameworthy, is to blame for Angel's injury. When an average person would entertain such a doubt, courts too are likely to be bothered. The roots of doubt may lie in one (or both) of two kinds of soil:

(1) There may be doubt about what happened, about whether or not Angel's injury was *in fact* a consequence of Imp's wrongdoing. In such a case, proof may resolve that doubt and settle the issue.

(2) Even though Angel's injury is, in fact, indisputably a consequence of Imp's act, doubt that Imp is to blame for Angel's

154

injury may still persist. Such a doubt cannot be resolved by proof of more facts, for connection between the wrong and the injury is already understood from every point of view but the legal one. The issue remaining is solved by deciding the proper limits of liability. Such an issue has been formulated by courts in four alternative forms: (a) was Imp under a duty to Angel to avoid the injury? (b) was Imp negligent towards Angel? (c) was Imp's wrong the proximate cause of Angel's injury? (d) was the harm inflicted a kind of injury for which the law allows compensatory damages? The differences between these four formulations is largely verbal, but a choice of one, rather than another, sometimes affects procedural or substantive rulings.

§ 2. ACTUAL CAUSE—PROOF PROBLEMS

A tort plaintiff usually (but not invariably) has the burden of proving that the defendant's wrong was a cause in fact of plaintiff's injury. For example, in Stubbs v. City of Rochester,[1] the plaintiff claimed that negligent pollution of the defendant city's drinking water had infected him with typhoid fever. It was adequately proved that the city had negligently introduced sewage into the plaintiff's drinking water. Typhoid was, at that time, spread in many ways, only one of which was polluted water. Other modes of bacilli transmission were associated with several forms of food contamination and contact with human and insect carriers. Unless the city's water carried typhoid germs to the plaintiff, the city was not, in fact or in law, responsible for the plaintiff's injury. Statistics showed that the incidence of typhoid was abnormally high in the plaintiff's neighborhood during the time when the city distributed polluted water. These statistics won the plaintiff a judgment. Counsel who have recognized actual cause problems usually try to get a preliminary understanding of the connection (or lack of it) between the defendant's conduct and the plaintiff's damages without too much thought on strategy. After counsel begin to understand the facts, they start planning proof. The reader of reported cases can seldom retrace the process to learn why one program of proof, rather than some other, was adopted. A checklist of methods of establishing (and disproving) actual cause and a discussion of some of their practical implications may be useful.

Eyewitnesses. The testimony of an eyewitness may foreclose a dispute on causation. If a credible and credited witness saw an identified motorist run over a pedestrian who was then cart-

---

1. 226 N.Y. 516, 124 N.E. 137 (1919).

ed off to the hospital with a broken leg, defense counsel is likely
to concede causal relation between the accident and the injury.
A pedestrian who can find no eyewitness may have difficulty in
identifying the injuring motorist.   A defendant's eyewitness
may be able to testify that the motorist who ran over the pedestrian was not the defendant; or a simple factual description
may establish that a litigant's misbehavior in fact had no significant relation to an accident.   In Rouleau v. Blotner,[2] a north-
bound truck driver made a left turn across the path of a southbound motorist.   The truck driver, it was claimed, negligently
failed to give a left turn signal.   The southbound motorist, however, admitted on the witness stand that he was not watching
and would not have seen the signal had the truck driver put out
his hand; the truck driver's negligence, it was held, had no factual (and therefore, no legal) significance.

Expert Testimony. Sometimes the need for expert testimony
is patent.   Patient dies in Exodontist's dental chair while under
a total anesthetic administered to allow Patient to avoid the pain
of a tooth extraction.   Plaintiff's medical experts testify that
the cause of death was asphyxia; defendant's experts testify
that Patient died of heart failure unrelated to administration of
the anesthetic.   Such a causation issue will be decided by the
jury after each side has tried to persuade the jurors that its experts are the more credible.[3]

Sometimes knowledge of medical etiology is common enough
so that lay jurors can reasonably conclude (without expert guidance) that some physical condition resulted from an earlier experience.   In Wilhelm v. State Traffic Safety Comm.,[4] plaintiff
proved that the defendant's negligent act resulted in a cut on
her face and the resulting disfigurement was aggravated by a
loss of pigmentation in the skin surrounding the scar.   The
court held that jurors were knowledgeable enough to find that
depigmentation was a consequence of the cut, even though no expert witness had so testified.

A claimant's failure to adduce expert testimony may, however,
be fatal.   In Christensen v. Northern States Power Co. of Wis.,[5]
a lake owner proved that his lake was well stocked in the au-
tumn but bare of fish in the spring.   He proved a power compa-

2. 84 N.H. 539, 152 A. 916 (1931).

3. Cf. Montgomery Ward & Co.,
Inc. v. McFarland, 21 Md.App. 501,
319 A.2d 824 (1974), in which the
plaintiff needed, but did not adduce, adequate expert medical testimony on factual cause. Compare plaintiff's adequate expert
proof in Jones v. Treegoob, 433
Pa. 225, 249 A.2d 352 (1969).

4. 230 Md. 91, 185 A.2d 715 (1962).

5. 222 Minn. 474, 25 N.W.2d 659
(1946).

ny's 66,000 volt line passed through a tower resting on the lake bed; in mid-winter ice pressure tipped the tower and current was grounded for four seconds. The lake owner did not adduce expert testimony to show that his fish were electrocuted, and he lost his case. It is common knowledge that high voltage electricity destroys life; but it is not commonly known—if it is true in fact at all—that electricity grounded in a large lake charges all of its waters.

Common beliefs are sometimes dispelled by defense experts. In Western Telephone Corp. of Texas v. McCann,[6] the plaintiff's decedent was struck by lightning and killed on her front porch. The defendant telephone company, it was alleged, negligently failed to dismantle an abandoned drop line which ran from its trunk line into decedent's house. Lightning struck a pole some distance from the house. The plaintiff's theory was that lightning traveled along the telephone company's lines to the drop line and then along the drop line until it came close to decedent and struck her. The telephone company's four lightning experts gave convincing testimony that lightning, unlike ordinary electricity, is not likely to follow metallic conductors. The court held that the company was entitled to a directed verdict.

On the other hand a jury may, in some circumstances, be convinced by credible lay testimony in conflict with expert testimony. In Ward v. H. B. Zachry Constr. Co.,[7] a blaster exploded his charge more than four thousand feet away from the plaintiff's house. The blaster's expert witnesses testified that the distance and other facts were such that the blast could not have damaged the house. The householder, however, testified that she heard the explosion, felt vibrations and saw and heard mortar falling from the walls and ceiling of her house. The jury found for the householder and the court held its verdict was acceptable.

Circumstantial Evidence. In all cases and on all issues of fact, the trier of fact draws some inferences. Normally the process goes on without special notice. In some cases, however, the circumstantial qualities of proof are spectacular. Particularly may this be so in the trial of some causation issues. In Paine v. Gamble Stores,[8] a woman proved that her husband left home one afternoon and was found dead the following morning at the bottom of a stairwell affording entrance to a store basement.

---

6. 128 Tex. 582, 99 S.W.2d 895 (1937).

7. 570 F.2d 892 (10th Cir. 1978).

8. 202 Minn. 462, 279 N.W. 257 (1938).

The stairwell abutted on a public alley. It was originally guarded by a two-pipe railing, but as a consequence of the storekeeper's negligence, the top rail guarding the deep end had been missing for some time. Plaintiff's counsel was faced with the problem of proving: (1) decedent's entry was over the improperly guarded end, and not over the properly guarded side or through the gate at the head of the stairs; and (2) decedent was not pushed, but stumbled over the bottom rail into the well. (Plaintiff did not have the burden of coming forward with evidence that decedent was free from contributory negligence in this jurisdiction.)

Proof which tended to show entry over the end was: the position and condition of the body was consistent with a fall over the end; prongs of the deceased's ring setting were scratched, and a fresh scratch on the end wall matched spacing of the prongs; and undisturbed dust and rubbish on the steps were inconsistent with a fall down them. There was also proof which tended to show decedent was not pushed into the well: his body showed no marks of violence other than a broken neck, which apparently resulted from the fall; and no signs of struggle near the stairwell could be found. This evidence was held sufficient to support the jury's verdict for the plaintiff.

Preparation of such a case is detective work. Fortunately for this plaintiff, the body was found by policemen who reported on a detailed investigation made before the site was disturbed and who could be called to testify.

Sometimes history of the site yields circumstantial proof of causation. In Hoyt v. Jeffers,[9] a property owner claimed that his building was damaged by fire as a consequence of a neighboring woodworker's failure to equip his sawmill smokestack with a proper spark arrester. The property owner could find no eyewitness who saw sparks travel from the sawmill stack to his building, but he did prove that before his loss the mill's stack emitted sparks constantly and that these sparks had started other fires. This proof was held admissible and adequate to support the jury's verdict for plaintiff.

§ 3. SUFFICIENT CONNECTION IN LAW— THE QUESTION

Engineer, driving Railroad's locomotive, does not keep a proper lookout, and runs the train into an obstruction. Tank cars overturn and spilled oil catches fire. This flaming oil flows down a hill and into a stream, which carries it for a mile. Dry

---

9. 30 Mich. 181 (1874).

grasses on downstream banks are then ignited, and fire spreads to Farmer's barn a quarter of a mile from the stream. Farmer brings a damage suit against Railroad for loss resulting from the destruction of the barn and proves all of these facts. Even though these facts are fully established, this question remains: Is Engineer to blame for Farmer's loss? That Engineer is blameworthy is clear—failure to keep a proper lookout is negligence. That destruction of the barn is, in fact, a consequence of Engineer's negligence also is clear—at least in the sense that the barn would not have been destroyed had Engineer watched where the train was going. The facts are understood from every point of view but the legal one—experts on railroading, chemistry of oil, the law of gravity, spread of fire, wind, behavior of streams, etc., have nothing to add. The problem is whether or not liability for Engineer's negligence extends to Farmer's loss. Facts substantially like those set out were established in two cases. In Hoag v. Lake Shore & M. S. R.,[10] a Pennsylvania court directed a verdict in favor of the railroad. Three years later in the New Jersey case of Kuhn v. Jewett,[11] the property owner recovered a judgment for damages. If the question were one of actual cause, science could tell which of these results is correct. But non-legal sciences do not deal with the proper extent of legal liabilities; they supply no answers to this question. Only the law can formulate criteria for judging such cases.

The four legal concepts used in formulating questions on the extent of liability are (a) duty, (b) negligence, (c) proximate cause, and (d) damages. There are four alternative formulations for the assumed case:

(a) Duty. Engineer had a legal duty to keep a reasonable lookout. To whom does this duty flow? Certainly to passengers and fellow employees, to shippers whose chattels were on the train, and to the railroad company. Perhaps Engineer owes this duty to owners of property close to the right of way whose property is likely to be damaged. But is this duty also owed to owners of property outside of the normal zone of risk of harm from breach—owners whose damages are the consequence of a number of coincidences which happen, in fact, to link up with Engineer's negligence? Should not Engineer's duty extend to owners of property in the neighborhood even though insignificant details of the accident are somewhat unusual, and even though the fire does spread a little further than such a fire ordinarily would?

10. 85 Pa. 293, 27 Am.Rep. 635 (1877).   11. 32 N.J.Eq. 647 (1880).

(b) Negligence. Engineer was negligent. But negligent toward whom? Surely Engineer was negligent toward those who were likely to be injured by this misconduct. But was there negligence toward Farmer whose property, over a mile away, was not likely to be injured by Engineer's misconduct? Should Engineer be permitted to say that since those more likely to be injured miraculously escaped injury, therefore there was no negligence toward Farmer whose property was, after all, relatively close by?

(c) Proximate Cause. Farmer's loss was a consequence in fact of Engineer's negligence. The scope of Engineer's liability must be limited, however, to an ambit less than responsibility for all damage which might forever after result from Engineer's misdeed. Was Engineer's negligence a cause legally too remote for liability, or was it sufficiently proximate? Was Engineer's negligence—which is admittedly a cause in fact of Farmer's loss —a cause in law, a legal cause, of the injury?

(d) Damages. Engineer's negligence was a cause in fact of Farmer's damages, but not all losses are legally recoverable damages. Did the loss of Farmer's barn fall within the ambit of those damages that are legally recoverable from Engineer on account of the negligent misconduct, or must Farmer make independent financial plans to deal with such a contingency?

Any of these questions poses a problem of extent of liability. Before discussion turns to the way in which such answers are reached, clarity may be served by identifying the kinds of cases in which such questions are crucial. Most cases in which an extent of liability problem (the "blame for" problem) is still troublesome even after the facts of the case are known fall into one of the two following classes:

(1) Cases in which connection between the wrong and the injury is fortuitous, even though the plaintiff's injury is in fact an aftermath or consequence of the defendant's wrong—cases in which the actual outcome of the defendant's misconduct seems persistently peculiar or unique. The common sense form of the question raised by these cases is: is the defendant to blame for such a queer consequence, or is the injury just an accidental upshot of the misconduct for which defendant is really not to blame and should not be held legally responsible? When injuries are routine this question is not raised. If a motorist negligently runs down a careful pedestrian and breaks the victim's leg, which mends in the ordinary way, no one would doubt that the break, resultant routine medical and hospital expenses, loss of time at an ordinary occupation and typical mental pain and suffering are all within the proper ambit of responsibility.

(2) Cases in which the plaintiff's injury is the aftermath of both the defendant's wrong and some other contributing force —such as misconduct of a third person or a malevolent turn of nature. The other antecedent competes with the defendant's wrong for authorship of the plaintiff's harm. Of course a wrongdoing defendant is not necessarily relieved from responsibility even though someone else (or something else) is responsible—both may be responsible. But sometimes the overwhelming impact of some other force eclipses the defendant's contribution. The common sense form of the question raised by these cases is: is the defendant at least partially to blame for this injury, or should not the other antecedent be adjudged solely responsible for it? In these cases, even though the defendant's wrong fortuitously sets the stage for some other antecedent (which might have been harmless had the defendant not misbehaved), yet defendant's part in the misadventure may—or may not—pale into insignificance.

These two described classes of cases are not mutually exclusive. Some cases fall into both classes. The classification is only a descriptive aid in identifying most scope-of-liability problems; it is no help in solving them. Since such problems call for a determination of legally recognized consequences, the lawyer must turn to the legal process for solutions.

§ 4. IS THE DEFENDANT LIABLE FOR UNFORESEEABLE CONSEQUENCES?

A few courts have said that once defendants are shown to be wrongdoers they cannot escape liability for consequent damage merely on the ground that such injuries could not be anticipated. Perhaps the two jurisdictions in which this view was stated most vigorously are England[12] and Minnesota.[13] The courts of both of these jurisdictions have had trouble maintaining this position consistently, for reasons to be discussed later. Most courts frankly admit that foreseeability in some sense has some bearing on the ambit of some liabilities. In the famous Palsgraf case,[14] in which the plaintiff was denied a recovery on the ground that the defendant's behavior was not breach of a *duty* owed *to* the plaintiff and the defendant's negligence was not *negligence toward* her, Cardozo said (subject to some excep-

12. See Smith v. London & S. W. Ry., L.R. 6 C.P. 14 (1870); In re Polemis, [1921] 3 K.B. 560. Contra, Overseas Tankship, Ltd. v. Morts Dock & Engineering Co., [1961] A.C. 338 (Privy Council 1961).

13. See, e.g., Christianson v. Chicago, St. P. M. & O. Ry., 67 Minn. 94, 69 N.W. 640 (1896).

14. Palsgraf v. Long Island R.R., 248 N.Y. 339, 162 N.E. 99 (1928).

tions), "The risk reasonably to be perceived defines the duty to be obeyed." In many jurisdictions, courts are firmly of the view that foreseeability of the injury is normally prerequisite to liability. Particularly is this so in courts that call the problem "*proximate cause*" and also define legal proximity in terms of natural and probable consequences of wrongful conduct. This way of describing proximate cause is interpreted to mean that a negligent wrongdoer is responsible only for foreseeable consequences.

Usually, courts—even those which hold a negligent defendant liable for unforeseeable injuries—hold that when a reasonable person in the defendant's position could foresee no harm to *anyone or anyone's property*, the defendant is not negligent. Only when damages to someone could have been anticipated by a reasonable person in defendant's position is the defendant negligent. If defendant's conduct was not likely to visit untoward consequences on someone, then usually the conduct is not wrongful and should not be discouraged. Conduct may, however, be negligent even though a reasonable person acting in similar circumstances could not foresee with great particularity the harm likely to flow from it. Motor travel at excessive speed, for example, causes a variety of accidents, injuries, and damages. Even without foreknowledge of the exact harm that may result, the reasonable person recognizes unjustifiable risks of harm from excessive speed. Excessive speed which happens to cause no injury at all nevertheless subjects the speeder to a *criminal* penalty.

In a sense, then, a dispute over whether or not the defendant was negligent can be (and often is) settled before a question involving the ambit of liability for negligent conduct is considered. Householder keeps an unloaded hand gun and a box of shells in a locked top bureau drawer. Householder's despondent adolescent child manages to get hold of the gun and attempts suicide. Fortunately, the youth jerks the gun at the last minute and misses, but the shot damages a valuable antique chair left by Baylor in Householder's safekeeping. The issue, "Did Householder act as a reasonably prudent person would act in similar circumstances in guarding the weapon in this manner?" can be decided before settling (and without reference to) the scope of Householder's liability. If Householder is not at fault, and therefore would not be liable for any kind of damages, then of course Householder is not liable for damages to Baylor's chair. If Householder is at fault, then the problem of whether or not Householder is liable to Baylor can be raised and settled. Such a procedure is actually followed—at least in theory—in many courts. The negligence issue entails the problem of scope of liability only when it is differently formulated. When it is put in the form, "Did Householder fail to use due care for the safety of Baylor's chair?" then the issue entails not only decision of whether or not Householder's conduct merits discouragement, but also decision of whether or not the ambit of responsibility includes damages to objects in Householder's safekeeping.

When a defendant's conduct is not likely to result in harm to anyone, an attempt to discuss the ambit of defendant's groundless liability is confusing and senseless. In Aune v. Oregon Trunk R.R.,[15] a railroad "spotted" unlocked, empty freight cars on a siding next to a warehouse. Hoboes camped in a car and started a fire which spread to the warehouse. The court decided that these facts did not constitute a cause of action against the railroad. The court properly said, "None of the acts alleged in the complaint was negligent or wrongful." This statement sufficiently disposed of the case; it could have been developed further only by a discussion of the insignificant likelihood that any injury would result from the way the railroad made use of the siding. The important idea is that the railroad's conduct was not dangerous and therefore was not negligent. But the court went on to say, "Moreover if the acts of the defendant were negligent, they were too remote and not the proximate cause of the injury." The court embroidered on this theme for four columns of the Pacific Reporter. Of course when no kind of damage to anyone is foreseeable, the particular damage that results is necessarily unforeseeable. But dismissal in the Aune case is properly justified on the actual ground that the railroad was not at fault, rather than on the hypothetical ground that, if the railroad were at fault, this is not the kind of result for which it would be responsible. An abstract assumption of the railroad's fault without specifying what constituted that fault makes discussion of the ambit of the railroad's responsibility meaningless. If it is not known in what way a defendant is blameworthy, it usually is impossible to discuss whether or not the defendant is to blame for a particular consequence.

Once misconduct causes damage, a specific accident has happened in a particular way and has resulted in a discrete harm. When, after the event, the question is asked, "Were the particular accident and the resulting damages foreseeable?", the cases fall into one of three classes:

(1) In some cases, damages resulting from misconduct are so typical that judges and jurors cannot be convinced that they

15. 151 Or. 622, 51 P.2d 663 (1935).

were unforeseeable. Builder negligently drops a brick on Pedestrian who is passing an urban site of a house under construction. Even though the dent in Pedestrian's skull is microscopically unique in pattern, Builder could not sensibly maintain that the injury was unforeseeable.

(2) In some cases freakishness of the facts refuses to be downed, and any description that minimizes that oddity is viewed as misdescription. For example, in a Louisiana case [16] a trucker illegally and negligently left his truck on a traveled lane of a public highway at night without setting out flares. A car crashed into the truck and caught fire. A passerby came to the rescue of the car occupants—a husband and wife. After the rescuer got them out of the car, he returned to the car to get a floor mat to pillow the injured wife's head. A pistol lay on the mat that the rescuer wanted to use. He picked it up and handed it to the husband. Unbeknownst to the rescuer, the accident had deranged the husband, and he shot the rescuer in the leg. Such a consequence of negligently failing to guard a truck with flares is so unarguably unforeseeable that no judge or juror would be likely to hold otherwise. (Incidentally, the Louisiana court held the trucker liable to the rescuer on the ground that foreseeability is not a requisite of liability in Louisiana.)

(3) Between these extremes are cases in which consequences are neither typical nor wildly freakish. In these cases unusual details are arguably—but only arguably—significant. If they are held significant, the consequences are unforeseeable. If they are held unimportant the consequences are foreseeable. For example, in Hines v. Morrow,[17] two men were sent out in a service truck to tow a stalled car out of a mud hole. One of them, the plaintiff, made a tow rope fast and tried to step from between the vehicles as the truck started. His artificial leg slipped into the mud hole in the road, which would not have been there had defendant-railroad not disregarded its statutory duty to maintain this part of the highway. He was unable to pull out his peg-leg and was in danger of being run over by the stalled car. He grabbed the tailgate of the service truck to use its forward force to pull him loose. A loop in the tow rope lassoed his good leg, tightened, and broke his good leg. As long as these details are considered significant facts of the case, the accident is unforeseeable. No doubt some judges would itemize the facts and hold that the railroad's neglect was not the proximate cause of the injury. As a matter of fact, courts have on occasion ruled that much less freakish injuries were unforeseeable. But in the

16. Lynch v. Fisher, 34 So.2d 513 (La.App.1948).

17. 236 S.W. 183 (Tex.Civ.App. 1922).

peg-leg case, the court quoted with approval the plaintiff's lawyer's "description" of the "facts," which was couched in these words, "The case, stated in the briefest form, is simply this: Appellee was on the highway, using it in a lawful manner, and slipped into this hole, created by appellant's negligence, and was injured in undertaking to extricate himself." The court also adopted the injured man's answer to the railroad's attempt to stress unusual details: "Appellant contends [that] it could not reasonably have been foreseen that slipping into this hole would have caused the appellee to have become entangled in a rope, and the moving truck, with such dire results. The answer is plain: The exact consequences do not have to be foreseen." [18]

In this third class of cases, foreseeability can be determined only after the significant facts of the case have been described. If official description of the facts of the case as formulated by the court is detailed, the accident can be called unforeseeable; if it is general, the accident can be called foreseeable. Since there is no authoritative guide to the proper amount of specificity in describing the facts, the process of holding that a loss is—or is not—foreseeable is fluid and often embarrasses attempts at accurate prediction.

This third class of cases includes most, but not quite all, of the arguable cases on the scope of liability for negligence. Cases which fall in the first class—in which the resulting damages are so typical that arguments of unforeseeability sound nonsensical—are almost invariably decided for the plaintiff. Cases which fall in the second class—in which the utter freakishness of the coincidental connection between the defendant's wrongdoing and the plaintiff's injury cannot be suppressed—are almost invariably decided for the defendant (except in those jurisdictions which try to rule out foreseeability as a requirement of liability;

---

18. In Larue v. National Union Electric Corp., 571 F.2d 51 (1st Cir. 1978), the eleven year-old plaintiff's penis was amputated while he rode on the canister of a vacuum cleaner manufactured by the defendant. The manufacturer negligently failed to shield fast moving fan blades. The court said, "The hole was large enough for insertion of fingers and similar parts of the body . . . . [The manufacturer] argues . . . this accident results from unforeseeable misuse of the product for which the manufacturer cannot be charged . . . . [T]he vacuum cleaner presented an unreasonable risk of harm to children who might reasonably be foreseen to explore and fiddle with the device. The inadvertent intrusion of [plaintiff's] penis into the fan . . . fell within this class of dangers, even though the precise circumstances of the accident might have been improbable . . . . [T]he district court had a sufficient basis for refusing to rule that as a matter of law the injury . . . was so unforeseeable as to be outside the scope of [the manufacturer's] duty . . . ."

even in those jurisdictions, most wildly freakish cases are decided against the plaintiff on some other rationale). Arguable cases usually fall in that class three, in which the foreseeability requirement cannot function as a "test." In these cases advocates and judges can and do state logical and acceptable analyses of either foreseeability or unforeseeability.

Even though foreseeability of the injury will not function as a definitive test of the scope of liability, the idea that responsibility should be limited to foreseeable consequences is properly potent—an idea that will continue to have some influence on decisions and to demand respect. Close problems on the scope of liability-for-fault call for judgments on whether the defendant is to blame for the plaintiff's injury. Those who make such a judgment—regardless of what doctrines or rules they purport to use—often view freak injuries as the workings of malevolent fate rather than as injuries legally caused by the wrongdoer's misconduct. A plaintiff, therefore, is likely to dispose judges and jurors favorably if they can be persuaded that unusual aspects of the case are insignificant details. On the other hand, if the defendant can convince judges and jurors that the freakish details are a prominent and significant part of the case, psychological support may be induced for the defendant's position. Such advocacy is a fine art. Counsel who overdo it strengthen, rather than weaken, their opponents. A plaintiff's lawyer who insists on a too-general description appears to be trying to suppress important facts; a defense counsel who insists on a too-specific description appears to be taking advantage of mere technicality.

Foreseeability will not be downed as an important fact in the eyes of courts. The English and Minnesota courts have tried to rule expressly that once fault is established a claimant may recover for unforeseeable consequences of that fault; but the psychological pressure to dismiss the freak claim is so strong that in both of these jurisdictions courts have backtracked, at least in part. The details of these retreats are complicated and their extent is not yet clear. The story has been told elsewhere, if the reader cares to read it.[19]

Yet there are some cases in which even the most unforeseeable damage constitutes an injury for which, in the view of ordinary people, the defendant is to blame and for which the defendant is

---

19. On the English developments see Overseas Tankship, Ltd. v. Morts Dock and Engineering Co., [1961] A.C. 388 (Privy Council 1961); Further Retreat from the Polemis Doctrine, 17 U. of Chi.L. Rev. 379 (1950). On the Minnesota developments see, C. Morris, Proximate Cause in Minnesota, 34 Minn.L.Rev. 185, 196–198 (1950), reprinted in C. Morris, Studies in the Law of Torts 259–261 (1952).

almost sure to be held legally liable. In Wyant v. Crouse,[20] an impudent interloper broke into a blacksmith shop and used it. He was not negligent in any way, but nevertheless, as a consequence of his use, the shop burned down. He was held liable for property destroyed. Even though proper use of a blacksmith shop was not likely to destroy it, liability of the interloper hardly seems arguable.

The point may be strengthened by this hypothetical case: Stronghead appropriates a car knowing the owner would not lend the car to anyone. Stronghead's route of travel goes past a zoo. An elephant gets out of hand, sits on the hood of the car, and squashes it. Stronghead returns the car to its owner, who accepts it and sues Stronghead for damages. What kind of injury could be more unlikely? Yet Stronghead's liability is clear. One who usurps and uses the property of another, in common judgment, is usually to blame for damage that results from the use, regardless of the oddity of the events that produce the accident. Judges probably share this generally accepted apperception. *Chain of causality goes further + intentional Torts*

§ 5. THE STATUTORY PURPOSE RULE

In Gorris v. Scott,[21] sheep carried on the deck of a ship were washed overboard and lost. The shipper sued the carrier and sought to establish negligence by reference to the Contagious Diseases Act, which carried criminal penalties for transporting sheep without supplying pens and footholds. The carrier's violation of the act was clear—he was guilty of negligence per se. Nevertheless, the court held for the carrier on the ground that the injuries were not of the type that the statute was designed to prevent.

In Kelly v. Henry Muhs Co.,[22] a fireman fell down an unguarded elevator shaft while battling flames in a factory. The common law at the time of the fall classified firemen engaged in fighting fires as entrants by license; the occupant of the burning building, therefore, owed them no duty to use care to keep the premises in safe condition. The firemen sought to establish the manufacturer's duty to guard the elevator shaft by referring to a labor statute which carried criminal penalties for failure to guard elevator shafts in factories. The manufacturer's violation of this statute was clear, and it was guilty of negligence per se; the court, nevertheless, relieved it from liability on the ground

---

20. 127 Mich. 158, 86 N.W. 527 (1901).

21. L.R. 9 Ex. 125 (1874).

22. 71 N.J.Law 358, 59 A. 23 (1904).

tor statutes → negligence per se

that the purpose of the statute was to protect factory workers, and the fireman was not within the class of persons the statute was designed to protect.

These two holdings are applications of a rule which may be stated in this way: Plaintiffs may not claim that violation of a criminal statute is negligence toward them unless (a) they are within the class of persons the statute was designed to protect, and (b) their injuries are within the class of injuries the statute was designed to prevent.[23]

The rule has been treated with respect by virtually all courts. Nevertheless, the basis for the rule is difficult to understand. Criminal statutes in which tort liability is not mentioned do not purport to change civil law. The effect criminal statutes have on civil liability usually works through tort judges' respect for legislative judgment, rather than through tort judges' obedience to legislative command. Driver breaks a criminal statute by driving fifteen minutes after sunrise without turning on headlights and as a result runs over Shepherd's little lamb. A judge rules that Driver's breach of the criminal law is negligence per se—respectfully borrowing the criminal proscription as a measure of Driver's lack of reasonable prudence. Motorist drives carefully, but nevertheless runs down Walker. Motorist then breaks the criminal hit-and-run statute, and as a result Walker suffers from exposure. A judge holds Motorist liable for exposure injuries—prompted by the judge's respect for legislative judgment to reexamine and reject the old common law immunity of those who fail to render aid in such circumstances. In these hypothetical cases the legislature has considered problems akin to those raised in the civil trial. But in Gorris v. Scott (the deck cargo case) and Kelly v. Henry Muhs Co. (the fireman case), the legislature had not considered any problem remotely like that decided by the court—both defendants were guilty of criminal misconduct and subject to prosecution. Yet each defendant escaped civil liability by "reference" to criminal statutes which they had clearly broken! Surely this result cannot be rationalized as respect for, or help from, the legislature; at most what can be said is that the legislature was not concerned with the problems raised in the civil cases.

23. Both aspects of the rule are exemplified in the more modern case of Erickson v. Kongsli, 40 Wash.2d 79, 240 P.2d 1209 (1952). The defendant motorist made a left turn without yielding the right of way to a car coming in the opposite direction, violating a traffic statute. The on-coming car knocked the defendant's car off the highway and into a wall of plaintiff's building. Neither this kind of plaintiff nor this kind of damage, the court thought, were objects of legislative solicitude.

The criminal statute to which the sheep shipper referred had nothing to do with guarding cargo from rough seas. The carrier could have complied with the statute by building pens open on the outboard side which would have kept sheep apart even though such pens would not guard sheep from being washed overboard. The statute is a clumsy measure of the care the carrier owed the shipper for the safety of his cargo. The court was right in deciding that the statute was passed without thought on proper protection of cargo against rough seas and expressed no legislative judgment applicable to the case before the court.

Analysis of the fireman case is different. The legislature challenged the wisdom of unguarded elevator shafts and decided that they should be fenced—for the purpose of keeping people rightly near them from falling down them. No doubt the legislature was thinking of the safety of employees when the statute was passed and expressed no concern for anyone else. But the legislative judgment is applicable to all persons imperiled unless there is some special reason for disfavoring them over employees. In the fireman case the statutory purpose rule calls for disregarding legislative judgment rather than for intelligent respect for it.

The opposite result was reached in Hyde v. Maison Hortense, Inc.[24] A customer of a tenant in search of a toilet fell down an unfenced elevator shaft and brought an action for injuries against the landlord. The legislature had adopted a labor law carrying criminal penalties for landlords who leave elevator shafts unguarded in this kind of building. The court held that the breach of statute resulted in the landlord's liability to the customer's tenant. The result is utterly inconsistent with the statutory purpose rule. But the court does not expressly repudiate the rule; the court does not mention it.

"Intention of the legislature" is not the crispest of concepts. Some courts find "intentions" to protect classes of persons or prevent classes of injuries that have never crossed legislators' minds—and thus foil the unduly restrictive effect of the statutory purpose rule. In La Point v. Hodgins Transfer Co.,[25] a teamster broke a criminal ordinance by leaving his horses unhitched near a sidewalk. One of the horses stepped on the sidewalk, bit, and knocked down a passerby. The teamster plausibly but vainly contended that the only purpose of the ordinance was to prevent runaways and resulting traffic accidents. The appellate

24. 132 Misc. 399, 229 N.Y.S. 666 (1928). See also the discussion in Spence v. Funk, 396 A.2d 967 (Del.1978).

25. 48 N.D. 1032, 188 N.W. 166 (1922).

court found that one legislative purpose was to protect pedestrians from injuries that were like the passerby's. Perhaps the holding the court wished to reach had something to do with its discernment of this obscure intention of the legislature.

Not all plaintiffs fare so well. In Mansfield v. Wagner Electric Mfg. Co.,[26] a workman was injured when a particle from an unhooded emery wheel got into his eye. A criminal statute penalized use of emery wheels not equipped with a hood and blower sufficient "to carry off dust and prevent its inhalation." The court found a legislative purpose to prevent only respiratory injuries, and therefore held the employer was not liable—even though compliance with the statute would have prevented the injury that the workman incurred.

The statutory purpose rule limits civil liability to foreseeable harms. The prevision required, however, is prevision of the legislature rather than that of a reasonably prudent person situated as was the defendant. The legislature's prevision is gathered from words of the statute, judicially construed. When a legislature focuses either on one risk inherent in dangerous conduct or on the protection of one class of persons, it often passes a criminal statute without bothering about other risks inhering in that kind of conduct or other classes of persons imperiled by that conduct. Since violation of criminal statutes requiring safeguards is punishable even though no one is injured, enforcement of the criminal law will tend to eliminate other risks and protect other classes of persons, and the criminal law is in no way hampered by the setting in which the legislature happened to enact the statute. But the judicially invented statutory purpose doctrine can produce highly restrictive and somewhat irrational limitations on civil liability flowing from breach. The blame for such irrational restrictions lies with the courts, rather than the legislature, for the legislature has not dealt with the scope of civil responsibility nor intended that the criminal statute be put to any such use.

When a legislature happens not to evince any express concern for a particular class of people or some special kind of harm, the legislature's foresight will not differ from that of a reasonably prudent person in the defendant's position. Then only a freak accident will call the statutory purpose rule into play. In Larrimore v. American Nat. Ins. Co.,[27] phosphorus rat poison was set out in a restaurant; it exploded when a waitress lighted a nearby gas burner. A criminal statute forbade the setting out of

---

26. 294 Mo. 235, 242 S.W. 400 (1922).   **27.** 184 Okl. 614, 89 P.2d 340 (1939).

poison except in a safe place. The phosphorus poison was probably not put where it was likely to get into food or be eaten by mistake. But suppose that it was—that the restaurateur clearly ran a risk of poisoning his patrons and therefore clearly violated the statute. In her personal injury suit against her employer, the waitress did not prove that the restaurateur had any reason to suspect the poison was inflammable or explosive. In this assumed case the restaurateur was at fault, and the waitress was injured as a result of his misconduct. But the accident was freakish. The question, "Did the legislature intend to prevent such accidents as this?" raises the same inquiry as "Would a reasonable person in the defendant's position have foreseen such an accident as this?" Identity of the two questions results from posited reasonableness of the legislature in dealing with the problem of proper care in setting out poisons—the same reasonableness as that which would be attributed to a reasonable person in the defendant's position. The court in the Larrimore case said that the legislature did not intend to prevent such accidents as this. It is not surprising that the court also said in another paragraph that the restaurateur's negligence was not the proximate cause of the waitress's injury, after defining proximate cause in terms of foreseeability.

The point is this: When a legislature displays no specially restrictive interest in condemning dangerous conduct in a criminal statute, the statutory purpose rule is a foreseeability requirement. In these cases the statutory purpose rule has virtually the same justifications, the same psychological impact, the same disadvantages and limitations, and calls for the same sort of advocacy as the foreseeability doctrines previously discussed. One slight difference may, however, affect the outcome of some cases. The statutory purpose rule requires that the plaintiff be within the class of persons the legislature intended to protect and that the injury be within the class of injuries the legislature intended to prevent. Sometimes the foreseeability requirement is stated in this way: The defendant is liable if a reasonable person could foresee the likelihood of the injury that happened. No specific injury is ever foreseeable in every detail, and all courts which hold foreseeability prerequisite to liability, at some time or other, say that the injury need not be foreseen in exact detail. If an injury need not be foreseen in exact detail, then only a kind of injury to a kind of person injured must be foreseeable. "Kind" is after all a synonym for "class." Nevertheless the proposition that the injury need not be foreseen in exact detail is only an ancillary rule—one that need not be (and is not always) stated every time a foreseeability rule is applied to an extent of liability problem. Courts sometimes emphasize fairly specific details of a specific injury and then hold that injury was unforeseeable. These same courts might well have reached the opposite result in many cases if the problem were phrased in terms of foreseeable classes of injuries to foreseeable classes of persons happening in a foreseeable kind of way.

Up to this writing, when torts defendants who have broken the criminal law invoke the statutory purpose rule, they seek to avoid civil liability. Occasionally, however, a case arises in which the plaintiff's lawyer may effectively use the statutory purpose rule to justify an extension of liability to the advantage of the claimant; counsel may be able to convince a court that the criminal statute's history involved legislative concern for persons like plaintiff, who have suffered the kind of injuries that plaintiff suffered. For example, in De Haen v. Rockwood Sprinkler Co.,[28] a radiator standing close to an unguarded hoistway shaft in a building under construction was knocked down the shaft and injured a man at the bottom. Failure to guard the shaft violated a criminal statute that was enacted primarily for the purpose of preventing construction workers from falling down shafts. One of the statutory requirements, however, was that shaft gates should be at least two feet from the shaft edge. The radiator that fell was left standing parallel to the shaft edge, only ten or twelve inches away from the opening. In his opinion, Cardozo said that if the legislature had given no thought to protection against falling objects, it could have omitted this requirement of a two foot margin between guard and shaft. "Workmen, who may otherwise be tempted to store material in dangerous proximity to the edge of an open shaft, will be reminded of the danger. . . ."[29]

§ 6. "CLASS FORESEEABILITY" WHEN NO STATUTE IS INVOLVED

Modern analysts have often espoused extent of civil liability criteria resembling the statutory purpose rule—absent criminal statutes. They reason that no negligent act threatens all imaginable harms; unreasonably dangerous conduct is dangerous because it threatens particular kinds of harms to particular kinds of persons in particular kinds of ways; responsibility should fol-

---

28. 258 N.Y. 350, 179 N.E. 764 (1932).

29. See also the heretofore minority holding in Ross v. Hartman, 78 U. S.App.D.C. 217, 139 F.2d 14 (1943); compare the explanatory comments and text of Motor Vehicle Safety Standard no. 114, 33 Fed. Reg. 6471 (1968).

low the pattern of the risk.[30] Dynamite stored in a teeming urban center creates unreasonable risk of explosion that may destroy nearby life, limb, and property; it is no threat to chasity;
the storer should not be responsible if a night watchman guarding it happens to seduce a child living in the neighborhood.

Limitation of liability to the pattern of risk can be expressed
either in terms of duty (the risks to be perceived delimit the
duty of care), negligence (negligence must be judged in terms of
the risk involved), or proximate cause (only foreseeable injuries
are proximately caused; the requirement, however, is foreseeability in general form). All of these formulations attempt to
limit liability in terms of purposes served by discouraging the
defendant's *kind* of misconduct.

Analysts who espouse these forms of analysis do not always
agree on their application. In Paris & G. N. R. Co. v.
Stafford,[31] a trainman was killed by a derailment. A switch
stand was mounted on a single, decayed tie; it was so unstable
that a small force would dislodge it. Had the railroad taken due
care, the switch stand would have been mounted on two sound
ties. An automobile missed a curve on a nearby highway and
traveled fifty feet from the roadway, across a ditch and up the
railroad embankment. It collided with the switch stand. Spikes
came out of the rotten tie, and the switch was knocked into
split-switch position, sure to derail the next train that passed.
One view taken on the case is this: the railroad's duty with respect to its ties is not to guard against any such hazard, and
therefore the railroad is not liable for the trainman's death.
Another view is phrased in these terms: the risk of accident
from rotten ties, as that risk would be described before the trainman was killed, is a risk of derailment; a person describing
that risk before the accident would not try to predict the exact
force that would displace the spikes; since derailment did result
from the railroad's negligence, the railroad should be held responsible.

Why are both of these contradictory analyses available? Every accident is a specific accident. When it is not something of
a freak, no problem of extent of liability is likely to arise. If it
is something of a freak, an analyst who stresses its freakishness
will conclude that it falls outside of the purpose generally served
by condemning the kind of misconduct of which the defendant

---

30. See L. Green, Proximate Cause
(1927), especially p. 20. See also,
Maltman v. Sauer, 84 Wash.2d
975, 530 P.2d 254 (1975).

31. 53 S.W.2d 1019 (Tex.Com.App.
1932). Noon v. Knavel, 234 Pa.Su-
per. 198, 339 A.2d 545 (1975), is a
similar case; see both the majority and minority opinions.

was guilty. If it is not too freakish, an analyst who minimizes unusual detail can conclude that it falls within the purpose generally served by condemning the kind of misconduct of which the defendant was guilty. There is neither authoritative premade classification of patterns of the risk, nor authoritative guide to proper descriptions of the facts.

The basic problem in the decayed tie case is whether or not the railroad is to blame for the death of the trainman. Unusuality of the facts raises the problem but may not solve it. Is this loss too unusual, too much of a freak, so much of a freak that the mismanaged railroad should escape responsibility? The problem is hard. The court that tried the case had to decide whether the railroad deserved a directed verdict; it held that the railroad did. The opposite decision would have had as much and as little to be said for it.

§ 7. THE PROXIMATE CAUSE RULES

Courts until comparatively recently called most scope of liability problems, problems of "proximate cause," and courts still extensively use that phrase and its opposite, "remote cause." Judges and text writers have often tried to frame general rules or tests for distinguishing between proximate and remote causes. One of these rules has been discussed—the defendant's wrong is the proximate cause of the plaintiff's injury only if the injury is a natural and probable consequence (a foreseeable consequence) of the wrong. We now will discuss other rules which have received judicial approval.

The Substantial Factor Rule. Professor Jeremiah Smith, one of the great tort teachers at the turn of the century, formulated this rule.[32] The test he proposed is, in substance: A defendant's wrong is a proximate cause of an injury only if it was a substantial factor in producing that injury. Several courts purport to apply this rule, and the Second Restatement of Torts makes the substantial factor "test" its keystone formula for dealing with legal cause.[33]

The rule throws little light on the problem. A factor in producing an injury is a cause of that injury. The relation of cause to consequences is, in fact, an *all-or-none* relationship—an event in fact either *is* a cause *or is not* a cause of another event. No

---

32. See Smith, Legal Cause in Actions of Tort (pts. 1–3), 25 Harv. L.Rev. 103, 223, 303 (1911–1912).

33. The basic section in the Restatement, Second, Torts (1965) is

§ 431. See, e.g., Gibson v. Garcia, 96 Cal.App.2d 681, 216 P.2d 119 (1950) and Noon v. Knavel, 234 Pa.Super. 198, 339 A.2d 545 (1975).

event can be, in fact, an insubstantial cause of another event. The reference, then, of the word "substantial" is not factual. A cause that is substantial-in-fact can be insubstantial-in-law—a necessary factual antecedent is not necessarily legally proximate. The reference of the word "substantial" is to legal substantiality. Professor Smith's rule, restated in light of this analysis, becomes: a legally substantial cause is a proximate cause.

But since by definition only proximate causes are legally substantial, the test supplies only a new synonym for a troublesome legal phrase. This synonym is put forward to solve difficulties not rooted in a lack of words but rooted in a lack of understanding. Since the synonym is itself undefined, it throws no new light on the nature of legal remoteness. When the question, "Is this defendant to blame for this injury?" is hard to answer, we get no more help from the substantial factor "test" than from "proximate cause" used raw.

Illustration may make the difficulty clearer. Railroad carries a carload of goods to a rail center from which they should go forward over another line. Railroad negligently fails to turn the car over to the connecting carrier and allows it to remain in the yards. The yards are ordinarily a safe place, but an unforeseeably disastrous flood sweeps down a nearby river, the yards are inundated, and the goods are damaged. Shipper sues Railroad for this damage. Railroad's negligence is clear, shipper's damage is clear, proof that the car would have been forwarded to safety but for Railroad's negligence is clear. But is Railroad's negligence a substantial factor in producing the loss?

Argument for the affirmative: Since Shipper's goods would not have been damaged had it not been for Railroad's negligence, surely Railroad's negligence is a substantial factor in producing the loss. Argument for the negative: The concurrence of Railroad's negligence and the flood is mere coincidence—if the timing had been slightly different or if delay had happened at a similar but different place, the goods would not have been damaged by floodwaters.

Both of the conclusions have support in the precedents.[34] The substantial factor rule calls for one as much as for the other. When scope of liability problems are puzzling, the rule merely puts the question and does not supply an unequivocal answer. The draftsmen of the Second Restatement of Torts recognized this when they stated, "The word 'substantial' is used .   .   .

34. See W. Prosser, Handbook of the Law of Torts, 285–86 (4th ed. 1971).

in the popular sense, in which there always lurks the idea of responsibility. . . . " [35] Since the problems to be decided are scope-of-responsibility problems, a word that does no more than denote the idea of responsibility is of no great help; what is needed is words that will identify cases of responsibility.

Independent Intervening Force or Superseding Cause. Another approach to proximate cause is an attempt to distinguish between "independent intervening forces" which break the chain of causation and mere "concurring causes" which do not. Some courts prefer "superseding cause" to "independent intervening force." [36] Sometimes courts attempt to draw a distinction between proximate causes and "mere conditions." These verbally differing techniques all are legalistic approaches to the common sense problem, "Is defendant at least partially to blame for this consequence of his misconduct, or is some other person (or force), which is another cause of the harm incurred, solely responsible for it?"

The two following cases illustrate the impotency of this analysis:

In Brauer v. New York Central & H.R.R. Co.,[37] the plaintiff was hauling some property when his vehicle was negligently struck at a grade crossing by the defendant's train. The accident stunned the plaintiff, and thieves soon stole the cargo that he was unable to protect. The railroad contended it was not liable, as a matter of law, for the depredation that intervened between its negligence and the loss. The appellate court affirmed a judgment including damages for the stolen goods, although the dissenting judge said that, in his opinion, the railroad should not be liable for damages caused by "the active intervention of an independent criminal actor."

In Purchase v. Seelye,[38] a railroad was liable for a hernia contracted by one of its workmen. The workman engaged a surgeon to operate on him. The surgeon came to the operating room and mistook the workman for another patient with a different ailment. As a result of this negligence, the surgeon performed the wrong operation. The workman sued the surgeon. The surgeon pleaded a release given by the workman to the railroad. This pleading raised the question of liability of the railroad for improper surgery, for as the law then stood, if the railroad were legally responsible for the improper surgery, the re-

---

35. Restatement, Second, Law of Torts § 431, Comment a (1965).

36. See Restatement, Second, Law of Torts §§ 440–453 (1965).

37. 91 N.J.Law 190, 103 A. 166 (1918).

38. 231 Mass. 434, 121 N.E. 413 (1918).

lease discharged both the railroad and the surgeon. The court held that the surgeon's mistake was a "wholly wrongful, independent and intervening cause for which the original wrongdoer [the railroad] was in no way responsible."

The point is not that the cases cannot be distinguished; thievery differs from negligent mistake of identity and virtually none of the facts of these cases are the same. But bare causal aspects of these two cases are identical. In both cases the first wrongdoers (both of the railroads) were responsible for getting the plaintiffs (the hauler and the workman) into positions in which the second wrongdoers (the thieves and the surgeon) had an opportunity to injure the plaintiffs. Therefore it can be argued that the first wrongdoers' misconduct concurred with misconduct of the second wrongdoers in producing the harm. In both cases the second wrongdoers acted, at the time of their misconduct, with complete independence. Therefore it can be argued that their misdeeds were independent intervening forces. In any case in which conduct of two wrongdoers is related in this fashion, "independence" or "concurrence" can be emphasized. Sometimes courts emphasize one; sometimes the other.

An attempt has been made to rid the independent intervening force "test" of its ambivalence by defining independent intervening forces as unforeseeable forces, and concurrent forces as foreseeable ones. This is the route by which Minnesota, which earlier excluded foreseeability as a test of proximate cause, returned to giving foreseeability importance. In Robinson v. Butler,[39] a motorist overtook and passed another car in the face of nearby traffic coming from the opposite direction. He cut back into line so sharply that the passed car was forced onto the right-hand shoulder of the highway. A panicky front seat passenger in the passed car grabbed the steering wheel and pulled the car back onto and across the road, where it collided with a telegraph pole. The court held the passenger's act was an intervening, legally efficient cause which relieved the passing motorist from liability. The court justified this holding on the ground that the passenger's act was unforeseeable—that it was not the normal response to the situation created by the defendant and was so extraordinary that it constituted an intervening efficient cause. Of course this form of foreseeability "test" is no less fluid than other forms of foreseeability "tests." If the accident is described a little more generally ("One who forces a car off the road at high speed can foresee that the occupants of that car

39. 226 Minn. 491, 33 N.W.2d 821 (1948).

may become panicky and fail to act with calm detachment"), the passenger's act could be put in a class of foreseeable events and become a concurring, rather than an independent, cause.

§ 8. PROOF AND EXTENT OF RECOVERABLE DAMAGES

In the Second Restatement of Torts, Illustration 8 of Section 433A states, "A suffers from arthritis in his arm, as a result of which he has a 50 percent disability in the use of the arm. He is struck by an automobile negligently driven by B, and the injury aggravates the arthritis so that he loses the use of the arm entirely. B may be held liable for 50 percent of the disability." If proof substantiated such a case, the Restatement clearly approves application of the orthodox principle governing liability for compensatory damages, i.e., the negligent defendant is obliged to compensate his victim only for the damages he has inflicted.

In Dillon v. Twin State Gas & Electric Co.,[40] the defendant utility's transmission wires carried electricity to light fixtures that illuminated a bridge. The electric company negligently and insufficiently insulated its wires, and as a result electrocuted a boy who fell from the bridge and grasped the wires to save himself. The appellate court, while ruling on damages, said that if the boy would have fallen to his death had he not been electrocuted in midair, his life or earning capacity had no value at the instant of his death. If, however, his fall would have caused only serious injury, but for the electrocution, damages for lost earning capacity should be measured by their value in his crippled condition. Even though the victim need prove damages only "by a preponderance of the evidence," these rulings impose on the plaintiff an insurmountable burden of coming forward with adequate proof of any substantial damages.

In Hamil v. Bashline,[41] a wrongful death action, the decedent had a heart attack and was rushed to the defendant hospital. The hospital's emergency unit obviously failed to follow proper procedures, and the decedent's wife hurried him to a nearby doctor's office where prompt treatment was unable to save him. Plaintiff's expert witness outlined the procedures which the hospital should have followed and testified that had it done so, decedent would have had a seventy-five percent chance of surviving but that this chance was lost by the delay. Defendant's witness disagreed, testifying that decedent would have died regardless of

40. 85 N.H. 449, 163 A. 111 (1932).   **41.** 481 Pa. 256, 392 A.2d 1280 (1978).

any treatment the hospital might have provided. The Pennsylvania Supreme Court decided that if the jury believed the plaintiff's expert, his testimony was adequate to establish causation, and the jury could find that the increased risk was a substantial factor in bringing about the resultant harm.

Injured claimants whose previous physical weaknesses are probable life shorteners and whose death is hastened by a negligent wrongdoer's injury may have an actionable claim. In McCahill v. New York Transportation Co.,[42] a negligently driven taxicab struck a pedestrian. He died in a hospital the next day of delirium tremors. The attack of D. T.'s, according to the plaintiff's medical expert, was precipitated by the accident; the injuries, the expert testified, could not have lead to delirium tremors unless the victim was already suffering the ravages of alcoholism. "The principle," said the court, "is . . . that one who has negligently forwarded a diseased condition, and thereby hastened and prematurely caused death, cannot escape responsibility, even though the disease probably would have resulted in death at a later time. . . . [The] probability of later death from existing causes for which a defendant was not responsible would probably be an important element in fixing damages, but [in this case] it is not a [complete] defense."

In many cases, the extent of actual loss is decreased by insurance, gifts or gratuitous care. Under the "collateral source rule," however, defendants may not take advantage of such matters. Tortfeasors are subject to liability to compensate their victims fully for all the economic harm they proximately cause, even though those victims also receive benefits from their own insurers or free care from family, friends, charity or public institutions.[43]

§ 9. IS THE DEFENDANT LIABLE FOR ALL FORESEEABLE CONSEQUENCES?

Previous sections concerned cases which, when they involved a chain of causes and effects, were arguably freakish. In a crowded, interrelated world, however, many chains of causation are ordinary and the victims at the end of them foreseeable. Motorist negligently runs down Pedestrian, whose resulting paralysis worsens the lives of her husband and her children. Builder's excavating crew negligently cuts a gas main, interrupt-

---

42. 201 N.Y. 221, 94 N.E. 616 (1911).

43. See, e. g., Werner v. Lane, 293 A.2d 1329 (Me.1978). Automobile no fault statutes and legislation dealing with malpractice is not always consistent with the collateral source rule.

ing production at a nearby bakery, spoiling the cakes in the oven, depriving the bakery of one day's production and profits and its employees of one day's pay. Boater negligently rams and sinks a barge, blocking the channel and closing the port until the barge can be raised, causing losses to shippers whose goods cannot leave or be brought into the harbor. None of these events appear freakish. Are the wrongdoers liable for all these consequences?

"[T]here can be no doubt that a foreseeable result of an accident in the Brooklyn Battery Tunnel [a major artery of traffic under the East River in New York City] during rush hour is that thousands of people will be delayed. A driver who negligently caused such an accident would certainly be held accountable to those physically injured in the crash. But we doubt that damages would be recoverable against the negligent driver in favor of truckers or contract carriers who suffered provable losses because of the delay or to the wage earner who was forced to 'clock in' an hour late. And yet it was surely foreseeable that among the many who would be delayed would be truckers and wage earners." [44] The judge who uttered this dictum apparently thought it self evident. He did not articulate a reason, merely quoting, "It is all a question of expediency . . . of fair judgment, always keeping in mind the fact that we endeavor to make a rule in each case that will be practical and in keeping with the general understanding of mankind." [45]

Lord Denning, in denying a manufacturer recovery for profits lost when a nearby contractor negligently cut the electric cables supplying the plaintiff's factory, said, "[T]he cutting of the supply of electricity . . . is a hazard which we all run. It may be due to a short circuit, to a flash of lightning . . . or even to the negligence of someone or other. . . . Such a hazard is regarded by most people as a thing they must put up with—without seeking compensation from anyone. There are some who install a standby system. Others seek refuge by taking out an insurance policy against breakdown in the supply. But most people are content to take the risk on themselves. . . . They just put up with it. They try to make up the

---

44. In re Kinsman Transit Co., 388 F.2d 821, 825 (2d Cir. 1968). The court stated this example in explanation of its holding that defendants who had blocked a river for two months as a result of an accident involving two ships and a bridge were not liable to shippers for the losses they suffered because navigation was impeded.

45. Id. This language was quoted from Judge Andrews' dissent in Palsgraf v. Long Island R. R., 248 N.Y. 339, 354–355, 162 N.E. 99, 104–105 (1928).

economic loss by doing more work the next day. This is a healthy attitude which the law should encourage." [46]

There is, of course, some truth in Lord Denning's observations, and similar factors may help explain the New York traffic-jam hypothetical as well, but these are only descriptive statements which do not define which kinds of claims ought not be satisfied. For instance, the untimely death of a breadwinner may be the result of disease, a flash of lightning or even the negligence of someone or other. The loss may be endured without complaint. Other members of the household may take over the breadwinner function to make up for the loss. Often the risk is insured. Yet it is not generally thought that the dependents of a negligently slain breadwinner ought to show self-reliance by not suing the wrongdoer. Of course, their attitudes usually are different from the norm described by Lord Denning, but his description was not completely accurate. The plaintiff in the case before him thought it proper to seek judicial relief. If such relief were generally available, it is probable a great number of those injured by negligent interruption of power would sue. The general stoicism concerning some kinds of losses may be in part a healthy reaction to the laws' refusal to permit recovery.

In Rickards v. Sun Oil Co.,[47] defendant's barge negligently rammed and destroyed a drawbridge, cutting the only access to the island town of Brigantine, New Jersey, and isolating the town until a new bridge could be built. Merchants in the town sued the barge owner for the resulting lost profits but their complaints were dismissed because "It is obvious that the alleged wrong was not the natural and proximate result of defendant's negligence." In contrast, when a similar accident damaged a railroad bridge and isolated plaintiff's blast furnaces for slightly more than two days, the vessel owner was held liable for the difference between the cost of steel which would have been pro-

---

46. Spartan Steel Ltd. v. Martin & Co. [1972] 3 All E.R. 557, 563–564 (C.A.). The electricity heated plaintiff's furnace in which molten alloy was processed. Defendant admitted liability for physical damage caused when the heat went off and hardly questioned plaintiff's claim for profits lost because the melt in process was damaged. The contested issue was defendant's liability for profits which could have been made from four batches of alloy which could have been processed had power not been interrupted. One member of the three judge panel would have permitted that recovery. The case, therefore, is not a precedent for the rule that negligent interruption of electricity is non-justiciable nor is it a very strong precedent for the denial of lost profits in such cases.

47. 23 N.J. Misc. 89, 41 A.2d 267 (1945).

duced and the higher price the steel company paid to purchase steel elsewhere.[48]

The main problem which troubles the courts in many of these cases is illustrated by Stevenson v. East Ohio Gas Co.[49] The defendant gas company negligently set an immense fire at its plant in an industrial neighborhood. As a result, a neighboring factory was closed for eight days. An employee of the factory sued the gas company for lost wages. Though the claim was small, the court feared the precedent would lead to a crushing burden. Not only other employees but many other persons had probably been injured by the factory closing. "Cases might well occur where a manufacturer would be obliged to close down his factory because of the inability of his supplier due to a fire loss to make prompt deliveries; the power company [supplying the factory] would be deprived of the profit which it would have made if the operation of the factory had not been interrupted . . . .; the neighborhood restaurant which relies on the trade of the factory employees may suffer a substantial loss. The claims of workmen for loss of wages . . . represent only a small fraction of the claims which would arise if recovery is allowed in this class of cases. . . . [T]he courts generally have reached a wise result in limiting claims for damages in this class of cases to [those] who may have sustained personal injuries or physical property damage. . . ." [50]

One who negligently rams and closes a bridge probably ought not to be liable for the economic stagnation of an entire town. Liability for damage to the bridge is probably a sufficient deterrent. On the other hand, liability for the loss of a few hours' steel production is not too crushing a burden, and so the blast furnace case is correctly decided. The court in the blast furnace case, however, did not consider this issue. As the court in the gas works fire case pointed out, the fear of crushing judgments has limited claims for economic loss to those who have also suf-

48. National Steel Corp. v. Great Lakes Towing Co., 574 F.2d 339 (6th Cir. 1978).

49. 47 Ohio Law Abs. 586, 73 N.E. 2d 200 (1946).

50. In arguing that an accountant who certified a balance sheet of company which showed the company to be financially strong when, in fact, was insolvent, should not be liable for negligence to those who advanced credit to the company in reliance upon the balance sheet, Cardozo said, "If liability for negligence exists, a thoughtless slip or blunder . . . may expose accountants to a liability to an indeterminate amount for an indeterminate time to an indeterminate class. The hazards of a business conducted on these terms are so extreme as to enkindle doubt whether a flaw may not exist in the implication of a duty that exposes to these consequences." Ultramares Corp. v. Touche, Niven & Co., 225 N.Y. 170, 174 N.E. 441 (1931).

fered personal injuries or property damage. The plaintiff steel company owned the bridge and so it could recover its economic loss as well as the expense of repairing its bridge. Had a railroad company owned the bridge, the steel company may have been unable to recover.

This mechanistic approach, of course, is typical of many areas of the law in which courts "must draw the line somewhere." But occasionally the courts have drawn the line in a completely nonsensical manner. Pennsylvania courts once held that liability for negligently set fires extends only to the first building burned.[51] But the first building may be a shed or a palace; and fires are improperly set by such diverse activities as careless smoking and improper storage of gasoline. Many potential sources of danger can insure against a greater loss. The rule proved much too arbitrary, and it was soon repudiated.[52]

The court in the gas works fire case was arbitrary too. It may be that common law courts could not easily permit recovery for wages lost when defendant's negligence closes a plant without permitting a myriad of other claims, but a distinction could be made if it were deemed appropriate. Admiralty courts, citing the principle that "seamen are the favorites of admiralty," have permitted members of fishing vessel crews to recover income lost when the vessels are laid up due to negligence,[53] though other remote economic losses are not recoverable in admiralty.[54]

The danger of crushing damages can only be avoided by arbitrary solutions. No formula can draw the line properly. The courts, without data, are making arm-chair guesses concerning the ability of various classes of defendants to absorb or spread these losses. Because these limits are set arbitrarily, it is not too difficult for later courts to set them differently as their estimate of the strength of various classes of defendants or the worthiness of various kinds of plaintiffs changes. The step-by-step repudiation of the no-duty rule which once sheltered manufac-

51. Pennsylvania R. R. v. Kerr, 62 Pa. 353, 1 Am.Rep. 431 (1870).

52. Pennsylvania R. R. v. Hope, 80 Pa. 373, 21 Am.Rep. 100 (1876). New York originated the first building rule in Ryan v. New York Central R., 35 N.Y. 210 (1866), and struggled with its arbitrariness for a long time.

53. Carbone v. Ursich, 209 F.2d 178 (9th Cir. 1953). The respondent's vessel negligently fouled a fishing boat's purse seine net. Crewmen of the fishing boat were permitted to sue for the three days' income lost while the net was repaired.

54. Robins Dry Dock & Repair Co. v. Flint, 275 U.S. 303, 48 S.Ct. 134, 72 L.Ed. 290 (1927). The defendant which negligently damaged a ship's propeller was not liable to a charterer of the ship who suffered loss because the ship was out of service for repairs.

turers, Chapter VI, Section 5, is an example of this. A similar development may be occurring concerning liability for negligent misrepresentation, discussed in Chapter XI below.

One set of recurring cases involves family relationships, when one member of a family suffers a loss because of injury to another. Since the claims involve only members of an immediate family or household, there is little danger of crushing judgments and the courts have not been chary to recognize some of them. In simpler times, when the household was the primary economic institution, the head of the household could recover his losses resulting from tortious injury to his servants, apprentices or children (loss of services) or to his wife (loss of consortium). A wife, of course, had no such remedies. With the emancipation of labor, the status of suits for loss of services of a servant has become uncertain.[55] The suit for loss of services of children, which at one time may have been primarily a suit for economic loss, has evolved into suit for loss of the child's society and affection. The suit for loss of consortium is also a suit for the loss of affection, companionship and sexual relations with the wife. The Married Women's Acts deprived husbands of any right to their wives' earnings, and so that economic loss could no longer be an element of the husband's damage. A few states held that those acts abolished the cause of action, but most have decided that the emancipation of women has given them standing to sue for the loss of their husband's companionship.

The right of dependents to recover for injuries to their breadwinners has not been generally recognized. Breadwinners who recover their lost earnings will be able to provide support for their dependents and any recovery by those dependents would be redundant. The four ways in which extent-of-liability questions are formulated—duty, negligence, proximate cause and damages—all bar the dependents' recovery. The defendant breached no duty owed them, was not negligent toward them, did not proximately cause their injury, and they have suffered no compensable injuries.

When the breadwinner dies as a result of the wrongdoer's negligence, all is changed. If, but for death, the breadwinner could have recovered from the wrongdoer, wrongful death statutes permit the dependents to recover their economic loss.[56]

---

55. See Restatement, Second, Agency § 316, Comment b (1958).

56. The complexities of suits for wrongful death are beyond the scope of this text. They are all creatures of statute and there are a number of variations. It does not appear that American common law was hostile to such actions, and a number of early common law recoveries are reported. But there was also considerable early legislation. Some statutes pro-

That the victim died, of course, is often fortuitous. But the wrongdoer is blameworthy and only the dependents' losses can be repaired. At one time, many statutes imposed a maximum dollar amount which could be awarded, again, to prevent ruinous judgments. Most of these have been repealed.[57]

§ 10. CERTAINTY OF THE LAW ON SCOPE OF LIABILITY

The general rules of proximate cause do not tend in borderline cases to make the law certain or the results predictable. This uncertainty persists even though the issue is discussed as a problem of duty or negligence, rather than as a problem of proximate cause. Experienced trial lawyers are accustomed to this uncertainty and take it in their stride as a peril of litigation and a factor affecting settlement.

Even though *generalized* legal analysis has not fostered certainty, the outcome of borderline scope-of-liability cases is not always unpredictable. In some cases *specialized* rules and precedents lay a sounder basis for prediction. In certain kinds of cases the law has become more structured by precedent or rule in various jurisdictions. The following are examples:

a. Defendant drives a vehicle or train in such a way that X is negligently imperiled. Plaintiff makes a reasonable attempt to rescue X and is injured while doing so. Defendant is liable for typical injuries so caused.[58]

b. Defendant negligently sets fire to plaintiff's property under such circumstances that defendant is liable for loss of the property. Plaintiff makes a reasonable attempt to put out the fire and suffers burns while doing so. In a few jurisdictions de-

---

vided that awards to the bereaved would be made in criminal proceedings. Others specifically provided for the liability of common carriers. In the face of these statutes, it is said, some courts considered the common law preempted by legislation and began denying all common law claims for wrongful death. See W. Malone, The Genesis of Wrongful Death, 17 Stan.L.Rev. 1043, 1066–1076 (1965).

57. W. Malone, Torts in a Nutshell, Injuries to Family, Social and Trade Relations 43–44 (1979).

58. See, e.g., Wagner v. International Ry., 232 N.Y. 176, 133 N.E. 437 (1921), relying on Eckert v. Long Island R. R., 43 N.Y. 502, 3 Am.Rep. 721 (1871), and saying the rule is the same in other jurisdictions. The rule may not apply to professional rescuers in some cases. A helicopter crew killed while flying to remove a traffic victim was not covered in Maltman v. Sauer, 84 Wash.2d 975, 530 P.2d 254 (1975). See also, Gillespie v. Washington, 395 A.2d 18 (D.C.App.1978).

fendant is not liable for plaintiff's personal injuries, but most courts have held defendant liable.[59]

c. Defendant wrongfully injures or confines X, causing such mental distress that X becomes deranged and, while insane, commits suicide. Defendant is usually liable for X's death.[60]

d. Defendant throws a missile or strikes at X under circumstances such that defendant would be liable to X for assault and battery had X been hit. The attack miscarries, however, and the missile or blow strikes a bystander. Even though defendant does not suspect the bystander's presence, defendant is liable to bystander, at least for typical injuries. This kind of case falls under the "rule of transferred intent." [61]

The list could be expanded to include hundreds of different kinds of cases in which the doctrine of stare decisis has some tendency to settle the law. But many cases raising scope of liability problems are freak cases, unique and not ruled by cases closely in point. Common sense is the only guide to the likelihood that research will turn up valuable precedents or specialized rules. Some cases are so patently unusual that experienced counsel know offhand that they are not likely to find authority closely in point. Other cases are almost sure to raise a question which has already been considered by some court, and therefore protracted research is almost bound to turn up an earlier decision. Unusual cases do sometimes recur. In 1896 the Supreme Court of Texas decided a case in which a railroad received cattle for shipment and directed them to a pen entered through a gate with a defective latch; the shipper was trying to fasten the gate when the cattle were frightened, plunged through the gate and injured him. The railroad escaped liability.[62] Virtually the same facts recurred in 1931. The court saw no significant difference between the cases and decided the second case as it had the first—for the defendant.[63] The Supreme Court of Pennsylvania has twice considered and both times ruled against a claimant who was injured when the defendant negligently ran into a third person whose flying body struck the claimant.[64]

---

59. See W. Prosser, Handbook of the Law of Torts, 277 (4th ed. 1971).

60. Id. at 280–281. See also, Falkenstein v. City of Bismarck, 268 N.W.2d 787 (N.D.1978).

61. See, e.g., Carnes v. Thompson, 48 S.W.2d 903 (Mo.1932).

62. Texas & Pacific Ry. v. Bigham, 90 Tex. 223, 38 S.W. 162 (1896).

63. Union Stock Yards v. Peeler, 37 S.W.2d 126 (Tex.Com.App.1931).

64. Wood v. Pennsylvania R. R., 177 Pa. 306, 35 A. 699 (1896); Dahlstrom v. Shrum, 368 Pa. 423, 84 A.2d 289 (1951). Inexact anal-

Of course precedent and specialized rules are no more sacrosanct in this field than in any other branch of the law; if they yield obviously unjust results, they are likely to be repudiated. In Vicars v. Wilcocks,[65] a vilifier slandered a workman and as a result the workman's employer discharged him in violation of a contract of employment. The English court of King's Bench held that since the master had committed an intervening unlawful act, the vilifier was not liable for the loss of wages. This case initiated a rule sometimes called "the last wrongdoer's rule," requiring an injured person to seek his recovery from the last of a series of wrongdoers. The result of the slander case is obviously unjust—though the master was liable to his servant, the slanderer was also to blame for plaintiff's loss. The rule in this inflexible form has been repudiated in virtually all jurisdictions.

§ 11. CAUSE–IN–FACT RELATION AS A PREREQUISITE OF LIABILITY

Thus far in this chapter, we have assumed that cause-in-fact is crucial to a claimant's case. It is almost accurate to say that unless a defendant's misconduct in fact causes plaintiff's loss, the defendant is not liable for the loss. But there are exceptions and qualifications.

In Summers v. Tice,[66] two of three hunting companions simultaneously and independently mistook the third for game, and each fired on him. One pellet of shot hit the unfortunate hunter in the eye. The injured man could not prove which of his companions hit him. (The science of ballistics has not developed a technique for identifying the shotgun from which a pellet has been fired.) The court had two alternatives: hold liable both or neither of the two triggerhappy hunters. It chose the former, which seems the more sensible. One defendant's conduct, however, did not in fact cause the injury.[67]

ogy may, however, be unavailing. See the similar case of Mellon v. Lehigh Valley R. R., 282 Pa. 39, 127 A. 444 (1925), in which the defendant railroad, which struck a car that hit a nearby pedestrian, unsuccessfully tried to rely on Wood v. Pennsylvania R. R.

65. 8 East 1, 103 Eng.Rep. 244 (1806).

66. 33 Cal.2d 80, 199 P.2d 1 (1948).

67. In the similar case of Oliver v. Miles, 144 Miss. 852, 110 So. 666 (1926), the court reached the same result. But in *Oliver*, the plaintiff was a stranger to the hunting party, and the court was able to dub the two hunters joint-enterprisers and thus justify, on an agency theory, the liability of the hunter who did not hit the plaintiff. The plaintiff in *Summers* was a member of the hunting party. If the defendants were liable for each other's wrongs as joint-enterpris-

The connection-in-fact between misconduct and harm is arguably not causal when two independent forces, each of which would have produced the whole injury alone, strike simultaneously or after merging. In the classic case of Corey v. Havener,[68] two motorcyclists whizzed past and scared a horse with resulting injuries to the driver. Noise made by either cyclist was frightening enough to cause the runaway that ensued. It cannot be said that the misconduct of both or each cyclist caused the harm, since the harm would have happened if either were absent. It cannot be said that the misconduct of neither caused the harm, because the harm would have happened unless both were absent. All that can be said is that either was sufficient to cause the harm—which means that the misconduct of each would have been a cause of harm if the other were absent,

ers, such liability would run only to strangers, and not to another joint-enterpriser.

Professor Frank Goodman, University of Pennsylvania Law School, has suggested verbally that the defendant in *Summers* who did not hit the plaintiff was guilty of negligence, which prevented the plaintiff from proving a clear case of liability against the other defendant; the defendant who missed should therefore be liable to the plaintiff.

A related problem was dealt with as a problem of proof in Ybarra v. Spangard, 25 Cal.2d 486, 154 P.2d 687 (1944), a medical malpractice case, in which the patient proved that while he was under an anesthetic during an appendectomy he suffered a traumatic injury to his neck. Suit was brought against all of the attending medical people —doctors and nurses. Defendants contended that they were entitled to the nonsuit entered at trial because, even though the plaintiff had circumstantially proved that one of the defendants was negligent, he failed to prove which one, and none of the defendants was liable for the others' torts. Nevertheless, the appellate court reversed and held that each defendant could escape liability only by affirmatively proving exonerating facts. Thus the penalty for silence or unconvincing proof of exoneration was liability for harm

not caused by the innocent defendants. A similar result was reached in Fosgate v. Corona, 66 N.J. 268, 330 A.2d 355 (1974). In Anderson v. Somberg, 67 N.J. 291, 338 A.2d 1 (1975), a patient who was injured when a surgical implement broke during an operation sued the surgeon, the hospital that owned the tool, the tool manufacturer, and the tool supplier. The claims against the surgeon and the hospital were based on negligence. The claims against the manufacturer and distributer were based on products liability without fault (see Ch. IX § 5, infra). The patient's proof tended to show that either the surgeon or the hospital was negligent, or that the implement was defective. The court held that each defendant who failed to prove exoneration was liable.

Compare McCreery v. Eli Lilly & Co., 87 Cal.App.3d 77, 150 Cal.Rptr. 730 (1978). Plaintiff, aged 25, sued one of 142 pharmaceutical manufacturers who marketed a drug taken by her mother during her gestation for prenatal injuries caused by the drug. Because plaintiff was unable to prove which of the 142 companies made the specific capsules her mother had taken, a summary judgment for defendant was affirmed.

68. 182 Mass. 250, 65 N.E. 69 (1902).

that is, if the facts were different from what they were. The court felt no difficulty, however, in holding them jointly liable. In spite of confusion generated by thinking of the problem as one of cause-in-fact, obviously both were to blame for indivisible harm, and they easily fitted into the established legal category of co-tortfeasors.

Cases of simultaneous or merging forces are not always so intuitively obvious. In Cook v. Minneapolis, St. P. & S. S. M. Ry.,[69] two fires merged and swept over a landowner's property, doing great damage. A railroad had negligently set one fire; the other fire was not set by the railroad and its origin was unknown. The landowner would have suffered the same devastating loss had the railroad not set its fire. The Supreme Court of Wisconsin held the railroad not liable. Other courts have reached the opposite result in similar cases.[70] Contrast these fire cases with Thompson v. Louisville & Nashville Ry.,[71] an action brought for the wrongful death of a trainman seriously injured by negligence of the railroad. Medical testimony tended to show that his injuries were mortal and that he had a short time to live. His wife mistook poison for medicine and gave him a lethal dose. He died almost immediately, instead of lingering on for a few short hours. The wrongful death statute provided for liability only when negligent injury results in death. The appellate court held that the trial judge erred in charging the jury that the railroad was not liable if the poison caused death. The court said, "If the wound was mortal, the person who inflicted it cannot shelter himself under the plea of a new, intervening cause. . . ."

In these multiple cause cases, the notion that actual causation is prerequisite to liability is a misleading nuisance. The central problem is: Should the defendant be held to blame for the injury, even though, in some abstract sense, causal connection in fact may be lacking? Such issues are sometimes easy and sometimes hard. They raise problems involving the proper scope of liability; the facts are thoroughly understood from the point of view of physical occurrence, and further concern with the cause-in-fact relationship will not move toward solutions. These problems do not differ significantly from the other problems dealt with under the heading of (1) the scope of duties, (2) the ambit of negligence, or (3) the legal proximity of an established

69. 98 Wis. 624, 74 N.W. 561, 67 Am.St.Rep. 830 (1898).

70. See, e.g., Anderson v. Minneapolis, St. P. & S. S. M. Ry., 146 Minn. 430, 179 N.W. 45 (1920).

71. 91 Ala. 496, 8 So. 406 (1890).

cause-in-fact relationship. Defense counsel should be prepared to and permitted to stress the lack of cause-consequence relationship. That lack is not totally irrelevant, for it bears on—but does not foreclose—the question of whether or not the defendant is to blame for the injury. What should be borne in mind is that liability can, and sometimes does, encompass harms which would have occurred even if the defendant had abstained from misconduct.

§ 12. DISTINGUISHING BETWEEN ACTUAL–CAUSE PROBLEMS AND OTHER SCOPE–OF– LIABILITY PROBLEMS

Advocates who have actual cause problems usually know with assurance that they need proof of what happened; advocates who have scope of liability problems usually realize that, once the facts are established, they will need arguments persuasive to judges and, perhaps, to jurors. Normally the difference between these two kinds of problems is so apparent that the chance of confusion is small.

There are at least two kinds of cases in which suspected unreliability of proof of cause-in-fact has in earlier times affected the law on scope of liability: (1) prenatal injury cases, and (2) cases in which bodily injuries have resulted from emotional disturbance.

Until a few decades ago all courts held that a child injured before birth had no cause of action against its injurer. Typical is Magnolia Coca Cola Bottling Co. v. Jordan,[72] in which the court justified such a holding on three grounds: (1) there were no precedents permitting such a recovery, (2) an unborn child has no legal personality and can therefore acquire no rights, and (3) courts are incapable of distinguishing between prenatal injuries and inherited or congenital defects. These rationalizations have now been rejected by most, if not all, courts; the third one is of particular interest in this discussion; it is given in support of a rule of law that limits liability because courts cannot trust proof tending to show actual causal connection.

In 1946 in Bonbrest v. Kotz,[73] a bold judge entered one of the first judgments repudiating the long established rule. He was not impressed with either the lack of precedents or the legal personality argument. More important, he decided that proof of causation should be heard and weighed. This was simply a recognition, perhaps long overdue, of an advance made by medical

---

72. 124 Tex. 347, 78 S.W.2d 944 (1935). **73.** 65 F.Supp. 138 (D.D.C.1946).

science. In most, if not all, cases tried since the Bonbrest case, the courts have followed it.[74] The child may have, however, a difficult problem in proving that the defendant's negligence injured the child and in fact caused defects with which the child was born.[75] Some courts have said, (but they did not so hold) that the injury is actionable only when the child was viable (or at least quick) at the time of the contact that caused the injury. The many holdings we have found are all contra.[76] If the fetus or child dies as a result of the injury, then liability depends on the court's construction of the applicable wrongful death statute.[77]

Even though a court is willing to try actual cause issues in prenatal injury cases, liability does not extend to all prenatal injuries. Leafburner negligently sets fire to a neighbor's house; a fire engine en route to the fire collides with a butane truck; the truck explodes; a violent concussion breaks a plate glass window a mile away; glass falls on Enceinte, injuring the child she carries. The court that decided the Bonbrest case removed the bar against proof that prenatal injuries in fact result from wrongdoing; it did not extend liability to every prenatal injury occurring as the result of misconduct.

A similar problem arose in those cases in which physical injuries may possibly have resulted from emotional disturbance. The early common law view prevailed in Spade v. Lynn & Boston R. R.,[78] in which a woman passenger was so frightened by the way a streetcar conductor handled a drunk that she suffered physical injury. One ground on which the court justified a nonsuit was that liability "would open a wide door for unjust claims, which could not be successfully met." The courts feared that by faking physical injury, or falsely attributing it to emotional upset, plaintiffs might impose on courts and defendants.

During the last seventy-five years, courts have held intentional wrongdoers liable for *physical* injuries resulting from conduct calculated to produce severe emotional upset. The classic case is

---

74. See, e. g., Leal v. C. C. Pitts Sand & Gravel, Inc., 419 S.W.2d 820 (Tex.1967). In a few cases the courts have allowed recovery for injuries resulting from negligence in treating the child's mother before the child was conceived. See, e. g., Bergstreser v. Mitchell, 577 F.2d 22 (8th Cir. 1978).

75. See, e. g., Sinkler v. Kneale, 401 Pa. 267, 164 A.2d 93 (1960).

76. In addition to *Sinkler*, id., see Sylvia v. Gobeille, 101 R.I. 76, 220 A.2d 222 (1966).

77. See, e. g., Marko v. Philadelphia Transportation Co., 420 Pa. 124, 216 A.2d 502 (1966). Compare Rice v. Rizk, 453 S.W.2d 732 (Ky. 1970).

78. 168 Mass. 285, 47 N.E. 88, 60 Am.St.Rep. 393 (1896).

Wilkinson v. Downtown,[79] in which a practical joker with a perverted sense of humor frightened a woman by saying that her husband had been seriously hurt. The "joke" brought on severe illness resulting in her permanent disability—for which the joker was held liable.

Some courts have nibbled at the early common law rule with exceptions. A Mississippi court, for example, held an insurance company liable for aggravating a policy holder's illness when a claim adjuster accused the insured man of malingering. The court said that the common law defense is inapplicable when the defendant's misconduct takes place in the injured person's home, where the victim is specially entitled to peace and quiet.[80] Five years after Massachusetts had reaffirmed the early common law view in the streetcar case, the court recognized an exception in Homans v. Boston Elevated Ry.[81] A negligent collision threw a passenger against the seat of a streetcar. The passenger was bruised and shocked and became paralyzed. The traction company asked for jury instructions to the effect that the passenger could recover for paralysis only if the disability resulted from the physical impact. These instructions were refused. The trial judge told the jury that the traction company, under the circumstances, should be held liable for the paralysis even though it resulted from nervous shock rather than from the physical bump. This ruling was affirmed, and in an opinion written by Holmes the court approved of liability for physical injury resulting from emotional disturbance when that disturbance is contemporaneous with physical trauma, however slight. This view was followed by several other courts and significantly expanded liability.

In most jurisdictions, reform is now more wide-sweeping. In Orlo v. Connecticut Co.,[82] a motorist became seriously ill after a streetcar trolley wire dropped on his car, and he found himself sitting under a shower of electric sparks and a barrage of hissing. He offered no acceptable proof that he had received an electric shock or any other contact. The trial judge instructed the jury, over the motorist's objection, that he could recover a verdict for damages only if he suffered some physical contact

79. [1897] 2 K.B. 57. But see, Harris v. Jones, 281 Md. 560, 380 A.2d 611 (1977), in which a judgment awarding of $3,500 actual damages and $15,000 punitive damages to a ridiculed plaintiff was reversed and rendered for his tormentor, on the ground that proof failed to show "severe" emotional distress.

80. Continental Cas. Co. v. Garrett, 173 Miss. 676, 161 So. 753 (1935).

81. 180 Mass. 456, 62 N.E. 737, 91 Am.St.Rep. 324 (1902).

82. 128 Conn. 231, 21 A.2d 402 (1941).

along with the emotional disturbance. The appellate court held that the instruction was wrong. Chief Justice Maltbie said, "Some of the reasons given for denying recovery, particularly in the older cases, have little if any weight now. One is the difficulty in tracing with any certainty the resulting injury back through the fright or nervous shock to the claimed negligent conduct. The steadily increasing advance in medical knowledge has tended to minimize this difficulty." Now in Connecticut and many other jurisdictions, liability for physical injuries produced by emotional disturbance and proximately resulting from misconduct is no longer specially limited.[83]

Of course, physical injuries arising out of emotional upset can be too remote from defendant's misconduct to justify liability. Sometimes the shock does not arise from fear of injury to the claimant, but results from horror as a consequence of actual or potential harm to someone else. In some of these cases the defendant's negligence is so directed toward harm to the plaintiff that liability to the claimant seems obvious. For example, in Price v. Yellow Pine Paper Mill Co.,[84] a blood-besmeared injured workman was sent home in an automobile by his employer. He recovered his wits sufficiently to insist that the driver should not subject his wife, who was in an advanced stage of pregnancy, to the shock of seeing him covered with blood. The battered husband futilely demanded that his employer's driver let him out of the car. The company's servant, nevertheless, obdurately took the victim home and so shocked his wife that she miscarried and suffered severe aftereffects. The appellate court held

---

83. In a recent bizarre case, plaintiffs suffered emotional distress but no physical injury when they were held hostage by a criminal attempting to extort money from the husband's employer. Plaintiffs sued the telephone company for divulging their address even though their phone was unlisted. Although the court held the defendant not liable because the injury was not foreseeable, the court added that "there is no logical reason for making a distinction, for purposes of determining liability between those cases where the emotional distress results in bodily injury and those cases where there is emotional distress only." Montinieri v. Southern New England Telephone Co., 175 Conn. 337, 398 A.2d 1180 (1978).

One of the last die-hards was Pennsylvania, which did not relax the contact requirement until 1970 in Niederman v. Brodsky, 436 Pa. 401, 261 A.2d 84 (1970). Niederman has been extended to allow award of damages for mental pain and suffering even though emotional upset has not resulted in severe physical damages. See Plummer v. United States, 580 F.2d 72 (3d Cir. 1978) (applying Pennsylvania law). The D.C. Court of Appeals held in 1978 that the contact requirement is still the law of the District of Columbia. Garber v. United States, 578 F.2d 414 (D. C.Cir. 1978).

84. 240 S.W. 588 (Tex.Civ.App. 1922).

the evidence of the driver's negligence adequate to take her claim for damages to the jury.

Difficult proximate cause problems can arise, however, when the wrong complained of injures or imperils someone other than the plaintiff. In Hambrook v. Stokes Bros.,[85] a 1924 English case, the defendant's truck driver negligently left the engine running when he parked the vehicle. This unattended truck started and ran down a narrow street. The runaway truck stopped when it smashed into the house of a woman whose children had, a moment before, started up the narrow street. The children might well have been, but in fact were not, run over. The mother's shock caused her death. The court held the jury was wrongly charged when the trial judge told them that if her shock arose out of fear for the children, the claimant had no cause of action. Compare Tobin v. Grossman,[86] a 1969 New York Court of Appeals case: A mother in her house heard the screech of a motorist's brakes, went outside to check on the safety of her son, and found him lying dead on the roadway. The court held that the mother had no legal claim for physical injuries resulting from her shock. Judge Breitel said that until 1968 no upper court in this country had followed the English case, and he held that a mother could not recover for her own injuries resulting from fear for the safety of her child injured out of her presence. In 1975 the Supreme Courts of New Hampshire and Hawaii followed Judge Breitel's lead, and held that death negligently caused out of the presence of the shocked and physically injured plaintiff is too remote for liability of the negligent defendant.[87]

In 1968 a divided California court did allow a woman to recover for physical injury resulting from the shock produced when her child was negligently killed in her presence.[88] A more unified but not unanimous Rhode Island court exceeded the California lead in 1975.[89] The Supreme Judicial Court of Massachusetts in 1978 held that a complaint alleging that a mother who "lived in the immediate vicinity of the accident and who went to the scene . . . and witnessed her daughter lying injured on the ground . . ." stated a cause of action for the moth-

85. [1925] 1 K.B. 141.

86. 24 N.Y.2d 609, 301 N.Y.S.2d 554, 249 N.E.2d 419 (1969).

87. Deem v. Town of Newmarket, 115 N.H. 84, 333 A.2d 446 (1975); Kelley v. Kokua Sales & Supply, Ltd., 56 Haw. 204, 532 P.2d 673 (1975).

88. Dillon v. Legg, 68 Cal.2d 728, 69 Cal.Rptr. 72, 441 P.2d 912 (1960).

89. D'Ambra v. United States, 114 R.I. 643, 338 A.2d 524 (1975).

er's death resulting from shock as a result of her experience.[90] Thus more than fifty years later than the decision of Hambrook v. Stokes, an American court of last resort extended liability as far as the English law.

While courts have usually been guided by the theory that negligent defendants must take plaintiffs as they find them, courts have displayed a reluctance to hold a defendant for mental illness precipitated by the defendant's negligence when the plaintiff's previous condition made him or her unusually susceptible to this kind of harm.[91] Potential mental illness, however, has recently become more closely identified with physical defects. At this writing a claimant who can produce expert testimony to show that a defendant's negligence in fact precipitated, say, schizophrenia, which would not otherwise have occurred at that time, has been held to have a case adequate for jury consideration.[92] Of course, wise defendant's counsel should offer proof on which to base an argument that even if the jury does find for the plaintiff in assessing damages, it should take into account the likelihood that some other event might have had the same effect on the plaintiff in a relatively short time.

In prenatal injury and emotional disturbance cases the courts clearly understood that they were dealing with cause-in-fact problems, even when they specially limited legal liability by refusing to try a cause-in-fact issue. But in some cases judges seem to have mistaken extent-of-liability problems for cause-in-fact problems. In Geisen v. Luce,[93] a passenger in a motor car was injured. The defendant had left his stalled car on a traveled portion of the highway. The car in which the plaintiff was riding approached the stalled car from the rear at a high rate of speed. The driver of the plaintiff's car did not have a clear view ahead but nevertheless pulled out to pass the stalled car. A third car was approaching from the opposite direction. The plaintiff's host saw that a head-on collision was imminent and drove off the left side of the highway. The car upset and the plaintiff was injured. The court held for the defendant who had left the stalled car on the highway. The court properly analyzed the case as one in which the defendant was not negligent under the circumstances in leaving his car where he did, and went on to say properly that even if the defendant were negligent, his negligence was not the proximate cause of the plain-

---

90. Dziokonski v. Babineau, —— Mass. ——, 380 N.E.2d 1295 (1978).

91. See, e. g., Williamson v. Bennett, 251 N.C. 498, 112 S.E.2d 48 (1960).

92. See Steinhauser v. Hertz Corp., 421 F.2d 1169 (2d Cir. 1970).

93. 185 Minn. 479, 242 N.W. 8 (1932).

tiff's injury. But then the court continued in this fashion: the accident would have happened even if the stalled car had been moving slowly; had it, however, been moving slowly, the passing-time of overtaking cars would have increased and danger to overtaking cars would have been prolonged; since slow movement of the stalled car would not have been unlawful, leaving it on the highway was not a cause-in-fact of the accident.

The unsoundness in this rationalization is this. If lawful slow travel of a car contributes to a head-on collision between a passing car and a car coming from the opposite direction, the slow traveler escapes liability because slow driving is not negligent; the traveler does not escape liability because the slow motion is not a cause of the accident. It does not follow that if a car left on the highway were not there it would be moving slowly; and if it were, a different case would be up for decision. The cause-in-fact relationship between leaving the car on the highway and the upset was not insufficient for liability. The sound basis for deciding this case for the defendant was not that the plaintiff's injury did not result from the presence of the stalled car. The sound basis was that the defendant excusably left the car there in the first place; and even if he were negligent in leaving the car there, the plaintiff's host's negligence so overshadowed defendant's fault that the host alone should be held liable.

§ 13. JUDGE AND JURY

A significant dispute in a damages suit on whether or not the plaintiff's loss is an actual consequence of the defendant's misconduct raises a question of fact; it should be and usually is tried in the same way as other disputes of fact. If reasonable jurors could draw different conclusions from the proof, the issue should be submitted to the jury. If reasonable jurors could come to but one conclusion, the litigant favored by that conclusion is entitled to a directed verdict—if the party asks for it. The defendant usually need not establish that the plaintiff's loss was not a consequence-in-fact of the defendant's conduct—plaintiff nearly always has the burden of proof, so the defendant is usually entitled to a directed verdict if reasonable jurors could not find that plaintiff has affirmatively established causal connection between the defendant's conduct and plaintiff's loss.

Once plaintiff has established that defendant's misconduct in fact caused the plaintiff's injuries, should the jury play any part in determining whether the plaintiff's loss falls within the ambit of defendant's legal responsibility? A quick answer to this question is yes and no; juries sometimes do and sometimes do not have the function of deciding whether the defendant who has in fact caused a loss should nevertheless escape liability for it. The only helpful guide to allocation of this function (in arguable cases) is precedent closely in point, which, of course, is usually, but not always, followed.

Defendants' Strategy. When proof tends to show either that a person was so situated that injury by the defendant's kind of wrongdoing was somewhat unlikely, or that the kind of injury or the way it happened was somewhat unusual, the defendant is almost sure to ask the trial judge to direct a verdict against the plaintiff. The defendant will ordinarily support a request with arguments to the effect that (1) defendant owed no duty of care to the plaintiff, or (2) defendant was not negligent toward the plaintiff, or (3) defendant's misconduct was not the proximate cause of the plaintiff's loss.

Two different kinds of cases present different problems in advocacy:

(1) Cases in which the defendant relies on precedent or authority closely in point. Landowner excavates a hole near a public sidewalk and negligently fails to put up a railing sufficient to keep people from falling into it. Villain intentionally shoves Pedestrian into this hole. Pedestrian sues Landowner for consequent injuries and these facts are proved. Landowner moves for a directed verdict. In support of this motion Landowner can cite clear authority. In the virtually identical cases of Miller v. Bahmmuller,[94] and Alexander v. Town of New Castle,[95] courts held that the defendants were entitled to directed verdicts. In the case at bar, Landowner's attorney's argument will be that kind of argument which lawyers usually make when they have cases in point on an issue of law. In absence of authority to the contrary, Pedestrian's lawyer's chances are dim— though, of course, the law does occasionally change, and courts do not always follow authority.

(2) Cases in which the defendant has no authority closely in point. Retailer negligently fails to pick up a banana peel dropped in an aisle in the store. Shopper, who has just bought a heavy electric iron, hurries down the aisle, slips on the banana peel and flings the iron some distance; the iron strikes and injures Customer. Customer sues Retailer, proves these facts and rests. Retailer moves for a directed verdict. Suppose that defense counsel can find no cases closely in point, and the most fa-

---

94. 124 App.Div. 558, 108 N.Y.S.   **95.** 115 Ind. 51, 17 N.E. 200 (1888).
924 (1908).

vorable cases involve only arguably similar facts—such cases as Dahlstrom v. Shrum,[96] in which the court held that a motorist was entitled to a directed verdict against a bystander who proved he was injured when struck by the body of X hurled against him when the motorist negligently ran into X. This cited case is relevant and convincing authority only if the general principle on which it rests calls clearly for a directed verdict in the electric iron case. But earlier discussion has shown that principles which the courts purport to use do not dictate the decision of a novel scope-of-liability case—which by hypothesis our flung iron case is. An argument for a directed verdict based on traditional principles stated in the opinion of the flying body case or implicit in the holding of that case can be countered with an argument based on the same principles but reaching a contrary conclusion.

The electric iron case is one in which the dispute does not center on what happened; dispute centers on the legal consequences that follow from the described facts. In this sense it is not a dispute of fact, and courts emphasizing this point often hold that it is not a question for the jury. Nevertheless this kind of question is often submitted to juries. The situation is viewed by some courts as analogous to trial of a negligence issue in which facts of the defendant's behavior are not in dispute, but reasonable jurors could differ on whether the defendant acted with reasonable prudence; in such cases jurors are often asked whether or not the defendant was negligent. If the scope-of-liability problem in the iron case is viewed as a question of whether or not Retailer's failure to pick up the banana peel was "a substantial factor in producing Customer's injury," or a question of whether or not Customer's injury was a "natural and probable consequence of Retailer's negligence," some courts are likely to dub the issue one of fact on which reasonable jurors can differ and hold that the issue should be decided by the jury. On the other hand, if the problem of the iron case is viewed as a question of whether or not Retailer violated a duty owed to Customer, the court is almost sure to hold that the responsibility for settling the issue is that of the trial judge, since determination of "the existence and scope of duties" has, by tradition, long been a judicial function. In some jurisdictions the duty approach is popular (although in no jurisdiction is it universally used to solve scope-of-liability problems). In these jurisdictions, the likelihood that a novel question of scope of liability will be settled by the judge, rather than by the jury, is relatively high. The likelihood is perhaps somewhat lower in jurisdictions where

96. 368 Pa. 423, 84 A.2d 289 (1951).

other forms of analysis are used; but in these jurisdictions also courts have often granted defendants' motions for directed verdicts.

Prophesying whether or not a court will direct a verdict for a defendant in an arguable scope-of-liability case is simply a special form of prophesying the outcome of that kind of case. Earlier discussion has indicated the difficulties. In the absence of precedent closely in point, prophesy cannot reach great accuracy. Lawyers with experience and insight can estimate the likelihood that a particular judge will grant a defendant's motion for a directed verdict; but lawyers with experience also know that judicial temperament is most mercurial when judges deal with arguable scope-of-liability problems.

Plaintiffs' Strategy. In theory, some plaintiffs too may be entitled to trial judges' rulings in their favor concerning the scope-of-liability. As a practical matter, plaintiffs' advocates usually are not likely to take advantage of this theoretical possibility; they are usually satisfied when the defendant's motion for a directed verdict is overruled and the jury is given an opportunity to decide in their favor. A plaintiff whose case is strong enough for a favorable scope-of-liability ruling usually has little fear that the jury will find against him or her on that issue. Likelihood of appellate reversal of a trial judge's ruling in the plaintiff's favor is usually much, much greater than the likelihood that the jury will find for the defendant. Tactical wisdom usually restrains plaintiffs from asking the trial judge to settle the issue by instruction. If the jury does find for defendant, a plaintiff sometimes tries to salvage the case by moving for a new trial, or seeking a reversal on appeal.

§ 14. POLICY CONSIDERATIONS

In the kinds of cases discussed in this chapter, misconduct of the defendants has been proved or assumed, and the usual policy justifications for basing liability on fault tend to justify taking money away from them. Compensible damages of the plaintiffs have also been proved or assumed, and the usual policy justifications for repairing fortunes of those who suffer personal injuries or property damages tend to justify giving money to them. In these scope-of-liability cases, however, courts have an additional problem: granted that this defendant's conduct, viewed in isolation, is a kind of conduct that merits tort liability, and granted that this plaintiff's loss, viewed in isolation, is a kind of loss that merits tort recovery, would or would not judgment for the plaintiff extend the ambit of responsibility unwisely?

Most troublesome cases involve neither especially crushing liabilities, nor chains of losses extending through time and space. In Gilman v. Noyes,[97] a trespasser left a stock raiser's pasture gate open; a few sheep strayed and were eaten by bears. Even if the bears were licking their chops within the hour, and even if the sheep were worth only several dollars, the case would still involve a scope-of-liability problem. Why?

On the other hand, there are cases in which negligent acts cause expectable injuries, but nevertheless liability of the wrongdoer seems unthinkable. For example, in Phipps v. McCabe,[98] the infant plaintiff alleged that the defendant motorist negligently collided with a car carrying his mother; that five days later, because of the collision, she suffered a dizzy spell and dropped and injured the child while carrying him downstairs. The Supreme Court of New Hampshire held *per curiam* that the petition stated no cause of action, on the ground that the injury was too unrelated in time, place, and circumstance for liability.[99]

Deeply rooted in our culture is the postulate that wrongdoers should pay for the harms they do. That notion seems so natural and right that other alternatives seldom occur to us. An injury contemporaneous with but not caused by a wrongful act is an injury for which the wrongdoer usually has no legal responsibility. A scheme which allowed all injured persons to seek reparation from wrongdoers who had nothing to do with their injuries would seem to us arbitrary, disorderly and unworkable. We would not be happy with some system in which injuries and misdeeds were paired on a chance scheme or on numbering, alphabetizing or propinquity. Our general acceptance of the notion that the blame-for relation is usually the proper measure of the scope of responsibility is reflected in both (1) the usual holding of no liability unless the defendant's misconduct is a cause-in-fact of the plaintiff's injury, and (2) limitation of liability to those consequences appropriately attributable to the defendant. If the blame-for relation is our starting point, it is not unnatural that when ordinary laymen are uncertain about the existence of that relation, the law, too, may be similarly infected with uncertainty. Decisions of cases tend to settle the law because of the tra-

---

97. 57 N.H. 627 (1876).

98. 116 N.H. 475, 362 A.2d 186 (1976).

99. Had the mother's fall resulted in her injury, the defendant's liability would be routine. "[I]f the plaintiff's weakened condition . . . subjects him, while he is exercising proper care, to the risk of a fall . . . he may recover if the accident was one normally to be expected in view of his condition, even though the second accident injures some entirely different part of the body." W. Prosser, Handbook of the Law of Torts, 280 (4th ed. 1971).

dition of stare decisis—when closely similar cases recur, courts are likely to do again what they have done before (particularly when they have no affirmative reason for doing otherwise). The stabilizing force of precedent has often not operated because new queer cases raise the problem.

There have been, and there will probably continue to be, many cases in which the scope-of-liability problem can be decided for either litigant. Nevertheless, the number of cases raising arguable scope-of-liability problems is insignificant when compared to the number of damage suits in which no such issue is disputed. The general run of tort liability will be relatively unaffected by decision of unusual scope-of-liability problems.

Beneficial effects of the law of torts as an instrument of social control and security are limited; other institutions take up where the law of torts leaves off. That the legal boundaries of liabilities should be fringed or vague seems inevitable; and in cases close to the boundaries, potent policy reasons seldom indicate proper decisions. Though text writers have often said that problems on scope of liability are at bottom problems of policy, they have thrown virtually no light on how these problems can be best solved to serve society. When claims are for unspectacular sums, when a novel case raises the question of whether a consequence is, or is not, too freakish to call for reparation from the wrongdoer whose misconduct caused it, usually little of profit can be said about policy considerations. It is clear that the prejudices and assumed social values of judge and jury may affect the results they reach—but the instances in which a rational program of social betterment can be served by the solutions of borderline scope-of-liability cases rarely occur.

Chapter VIII

CONTRIBUTORY FAULT

(as a defense to claims based on fault)

(In the earlier edition of this book, the title of this chapter was simply Contributory Fault. Two decades ago products liability in tort was based on proof of negligence, and compulsory no-fault automobile liability insurance was still only an academic possibility. Changes in those fields have already reduced the significance of contributory negligence and may make further inroads in the near future. Contributory fault in those two kinds of cases will be discussed later.)

§ 1. ALTERNATIVES WHEN PLAINTIFF'S LOSS RESULTS FROM FAULT OF BOTH LITIGANTS

Cyclist rides a bicycle across a bridle path without looking to the right or left. Equestrian, approaching on horseback, is unable to stop the horse. A collision results and Cyclist is injured. Equestrian's spirited horse is bridled with a snaffle, though reasonable prudence dictated use of a curb bit. What effect should Cyclist's own fault have on Equestrian's liability? Five different kinds of disposition can be made when both litigants are at fault:

(1) Disregard the plaintiff's fault if plaintiff's case is otherwise meritorious.

If the function of liability for fault is only to discourage wrongdoing, uniform disregard of the plaintiff's misconduct is hard to justify. Nevertheless, something of a case can be made for this disposition. Personal injury plaintiffs virtually always suffer pain and confinement, and even if they are fully compensated in money their discomfort may have deterring effect. Those suffering property losses at least experience inconvenience and upset, and are subjected to the unpleasantness of collecting their claims. A counter argument can be made: many people enjoy the drama of misfortune and its accompanying sympathy, limelight, and opportunity to talk about their problems; disregard of plaintiff's misconduct may stimulate such misconduct.

No Anglo-American court has ever espoused a general policy of invariable disregard of all plaintiffs' fault, but workers compensation statutes and some other forms of specialized legislation have abolished contributory fault defenses in a variety of cases. No doubt jurors sometimes consciously or subconsciously disregard instructions stating that contributory negligence is a complete defense because they feel that the injured or damaged plaintiff has already paid for his or her folly.

(2) Hold that the plaintiff's fault bars recovery in all cases.

This practice would at least save the expense of shifting losses when both parties are at fault. While some wrongdoing defendants will escape liability, the threat of liability for similar conduct when innocent plaintiffs happen to be injured may still be an effective deterrent. The practice has the virtue of not condoning misconduct like plaintiff's.

This system is closer to the common law tradition. In a great many cases, though not all of them, contributory fault is (in theory) a complete defense to an action based on fault. Many observers say that juries often disobey their instructions and return verdicts for plaintiffs whose own misconduct constituted a legal defense. Certainly some jurors are moved by sympathy for an injured plaintiff, prejudice against a corporate or insured defendant, a feeling that in justice the misbehaving defendant should pay for at least part of the loss his or her wrongdoing has caused, etc., etc. Proponents of "special issue" practice believe that these tendencies to ignore the jury charge can be damped down if juries are required to answer a series of specific questions, one of which is: Do you find that the plaintiff exercised the care of a reasonably prudent person? When faced with the duty to answer such a direct question, jurors may be less likely to substitute their own ideas on justice for instructions given them by the trial judge. Special issue procedure affords defense counsel a better psychological base from which to argue that the jury should respect the limits on jury functions; defense counsel can and often do tell jurors that their sworn duty is to return correct answers to questions asked, without regard to legal consequences. In jurisdictions in which juries are asked to apply the law stated in general instructions to the specific facts of the case and return a single decisive verdict, an argument calling on the jury to do its duty and obey its instructions may be unwise—it may carry antagonizing innuendoes of lack of confidence, which may injure the cause of the defense counsel making the argument.

The likelihood in a particular case that the trial judge will direct a verdict against a plaintiff proved guilty of contributory fault, or that a jury will follow its instructions and find against plaintiff, is probably an important factor in inducing plaintiffs to accept offers of settlement.

(3) Permit the plaintiff to recover damages whenever and only if the defendant's fault is greater than the plaintiff's.

This more flexible practice holds liable the defendant whose misconduct is more serious than the plaintiff's misconduct, but disfavors the wrongdoing plaintiff whose misconduct is more serious than the defendant's; the court is thus enabled to castigate the more serious of the two wrongs at the expense of disregarding the less serious—provided the court can tell which wrong is the more serious. Often the problem of deciding which one of two wrongdoers is more at fault is so hard that its solution may result in capricious decision of many cases on hairline distinctions.

Courts have uniformly rejected this alternative in negligence cases; contributory negligence is a defense in a negligence case even though the defendant may have been more negligent than the plaintiff. When, however, a defendant has been guilty of something worse than negligence, when defendant has been guilty of reckless, wanton, or intentional wrongdoing, mere contributory negligence is not a defense. So a defendant is not discharged in a contributory fault case when the defendant's misconduct is outrageous and the plaintiff's is only negligent.

(4) Permit the plaintiff to recover half of the loss.

This system visits part of the economic sting on each litigant; the defendant has to pay something and the plaintiff does not get full reparation. Both are given a financial incentive to do better in the future.

The common law courts have not adopted this system, but it has been followed in some admiralty courts in maritime collision cases.

(5) Reduce the verdict to less than plaintiff's total loss on the basis of a comparison of the seriousness of the fault of the parties.

The fourth alternative reduces the judgment to half of plaintiff's loss even though plaintiff's negligence is only trivial and defendant's fault is substantial; it reduces recovery only by half even when plaintiff's fault is serious and defendant's is almost insignificant. This fifth alternative allows finer adjustment of responsibilities and may, therefore, produce more politic results. It does not suffer from the defect of the third alternative, in which the incidence of liability depends on the comparison, so that a defendant may escape liability by a hair. Under the fifth alternative, when the two faults are about equal in seriousness, recovery is reduced to about one-half of plaintiff's loss, and a small miscalculation either way is of little moment.

Up to the date of this writing common law courts have adopted the fifth alternative, "comparative negligence," in four jurisdictions. The Supreme Courts of Florida, California, Michigan and Alaska have held that contributory negligence is no longer a complete defense to an action based on negligence; a contributorily negligent plaintiff may recover a verdict reduced by a proportion representing plaintiff's share of the blame.[1] A comparative negligence rule is also applied in admiralty courts. Many observers believe that jurors are often likely to divide damages illicitly in damage suits. Several legislatures have enacted statutes calling for variations on this kind of disposition of negligence cases in which both litigants were guilty of fault, and partisans of this solution will no doubt persuade other legislatures to follow suit.[2]

1. See, e.g., Hoffman v. Jones, 280 So.2d 431 (Fla.1973); Nga Li v. Yellow Cab Co., 13 Cal.3d 804, 119 Cal.Rptr. 858, 532 P.2d 1226 (1975); Placek v. City of Sterling Heights, 405 Mich. 638, 275 N.W.2d 511 (1979); Kaatz v. State, 540 P. 2d 1037 (Alaska 1975). Cf. United States v. Reliable Transfer Co., 421 U.S. 397, 95 S.Ct. 1708, 44 L. Ed.2d 251 (1975) (adopting a comparative negligence rule in admiralty cases). And see the *Bradley* case described in the next footnote.

2. A Wisconson statute, for example, combines alternatives (3) and (5). The plaintiff recovers damages reduced on a comparative fault basis unless plaintiff's fault is equal to or greater than defendant's in which case plaintiff recovers nothing. See Cameron v. Union Automobile Ins. Co., 210 Wis. 659, 246 N.W. 420 (1933). The statute is a curious failure to take full advantage of the comparative fault principle. Some statutes enact the full principle, e.g., the Federal Employers' Liability Act, 45 U.S.C.A. §§ 51–59.

As this was being prepared for press, the West Virginia Supreme Court of Appeals adopted the Wisconson statutory rule as a matter of common law. It rejected the unrestricted comparative fault principle because it did not want plaintiffs who were substantially to blame for their injuries to recover any part of them from defendants who were less blameworthy. Bradley v. Appalachian Power Co., — W.Va. —, 256 S. E.2d 879 (1979).

The hypothetical collision between the horseman and the bicycle rider may mislead. Cyclist's fault has a dual aspect; failure to keep a proper lookout endangered both the cyclist and others. When contributorily negligent plaintiffs fall on improperly kept floors or stick their hands into unguarded machinery, defendants have been unduly inconsiderate of the safety of others; but these plaintiffs have usually endangered only themselves. The justification for denying them recovery must be based on the desirability of discouraging imprudent self-exposure. Should that goal prevail over the goal of discouraging a wrongdoing defendant who has threatened the safety of careful people but happened to injure only a careless one? In these cases, particularly, the fifth alternative seems more politic and just, and in these cases, particularly, jurors may be likely to disregard instructions stating that contributory negligence is a complete defense.

§ 2. THE DEFENSE OF CONTRIBUTORY NEGLIGENCE— SUBSTANTIVE LAW

The key judicial principle of contributory negligence is usually stated this way: Contributory negligence is a defense whenever the plaintiff's claim is based on negligence of the defendant. This principle does not bar a contributorily negligent plaintiff who establishes that the defendant has intentionally harmed the plaintiff or has acted in reckless, wanton, or willful disregard of the plaintiff's safety.[3]

In McFarlane v. City of Niagara Falls,[4] the plaintiff unsuccessfully argued that the defense of contributory negligence was not open to the defendant because she proved that the defendant was maintaining a nuisance. The plaintiff-pedestrian stumbled when she caught her heel on an irregularity in a curb constructed by the defendant-city. The court said that even though the defect was properly characterized as a nuisance, some (though not all) nuisances originate in negligence. The court held that this particular nuisance originated in negligence, and therefore, contributory negligence barred plaintiff's claim.

---

3. Kasanovich v. George, 348 Pa. 199, 34 A.2d 523 (1943), is a leading case in which a contributorily negligent pedestrian recovered a full judgment from a transit company whose motorman was guilty of reckless disregard of the pedestrian's safety. See also, McLaughlin v. Rova Farms, Inc., 56 N.J. 288, 266 A.2d 284 (1970).

In Carr v. Case, — Vt. —, 380 A. 2d 91 (1977), a dog owner knew his beast was vicious and tied it up. The dog seriously injured a visitor who tried to pet it. The court said that Vermont law requires a vicious dog owner to restrain the dog and failure to do so is negligence; therefore contributory negligence of the dog's victim was properly considered.

4. 247 N.Y. 340, 160 N.E. 391 (1928).

There is some confusion in cases in which the defendant has violated a criminal statute. Motorist carelessly fails, in violation of criminal law, to stop at a stop sign and runs down Pedestrian, who has stepped into the roadway without looking for approaching traffic. In most jurisdictions Motorist is guilty of "negligence per se; " but this misconduct is, after all, only a form of negligence. Pedestrian's claim is based on negligence, and Pedestrian's own negligence cannot be excused on the ground that Motorist broke a criminal statute. Fiend, in violation of a criminal statute, builds a man-trap in a public sidewalk; Preoccupied, carelessly inattentive, walks into it and suffers severe injury. Fiend contends that since violation of criminal law is "negligence per se," Preoccupied's contributory negligence is a defense. The answer to this argument is obvious; inexcusable violation of the criminal law is at least negligence per se, but it can be something worse—intentional or wanton misconduct which entails liability even when those injured are guilty of contributory negligence.

In one kind of case courts hold that a merely negligent violator of a criminal statute cannot assert the plaintiff's contributory negligence as a defense. In Karpeles v. Heine,[5] an apartment house owner put a thirteen year-old boy in charge of his elevator in criminal violation of the child labor law. The boy ran the elevator negligently and hurt himself. The court held that the child was not barred by his contributory negligence. The child labor law was a special legislative recognition of the incompetence of a class of persons to take proper care of themselves. The court respected this legislative judgment even though the statute did not purport to control civil liability. Such a holding is sound only when the criminal statute is designed to protect an especially incompetent class of persons; therefore the defense of contributory negligence is peculiarly inappropriate in cases is which the defendant has violated the criminal statute and thereby injured the very kind of person who, in the legislature's judgment, is unable to care for himself.[6]

In another special situation courts are divided on whether or not contributory negligence is a defense to a suit based on a claim of negligence. In Leroy Fibre Co. v. Chicago, M. & St. P.

5. 227 N.Y. 74, 124 N.E. 101 (1919).

6. Compare Majors v. Brodhead Hotel, 416 Pa. 265, 205 A.2d 873 (1965) (defendant civilly liable for criminally serving liquor to a clearly intoxicated plaintiff). Contra, Berdos v. Tremont & Suffolk Mills, 209 Mass. 489, 95 N.E. 876 (1911), one of the few cases holding that a defendant who criminally employs a child laborer nevertheless is not liable if the child's negligence contributes to its injury.

Ry.,[7] a railroad negligently set fire to flax straw piled on land adjoining its right-of-way. The jury found that the landowner had negligently piled his straw so close to the right-of-way that carefully operated trains were likely to set it afire. The Supreme Court of the United States held that the straw owner's negligence was no defense. Justice McKenna, speaking for the majority, said, "It will be observed, the use of the land was of itself a proper use. . . . [T]he rights of one man in the use of his property cannot be limited by the wrongs of another. The doctrine of contributory negligence is entirely out of place. . . . The legal conception of property is of rights. When you attempt to limit them by wrongs, you venture a solecism." Justice Holmes dissented. He said, "If a man stacked his flax so near to a railroad that it obviously was likely to be set fire to by a well-managed train, I should say he could not throw the loss upon the railroad by the oscillating result of an inquiry by the jury whether the road had used due care. . . . [L]iability of the railroad for a fire was absolutely conditioned upon the stacks being at a reasonably safe distance from the train." According to Holmes, then, the fact that land is used in an otherwise lawful manner is no reason for shielding the user from the usual effects of contributory negligence. Some courts have followed Holmes' view.[8]

The flax straw case should not be confused with a similar but different kind of case. In Donovan v. Hannibal & St. J. Ry.,[9] a stock-raiser demanded that a railroad whose right-of-way crossed his pasture comply with a statute requiring railroads to fence their tracks. The railroad did nothing. The stock-raiser was faced with the alternatives of not using his pasture or running a risk of injury to his stock. He chose the latter course and his cattle were run over. The stock-raiser was reasonable in running the risk; he was not guilty of contributory negligence. Holmes' analysis would not bar him from recovery, and the stock-raiser does not need McKenna's rule, which shields land occupants from the usual effects of contributory negligence.

A plaintiff's negligence is not "contributory"—and therefore does not bar recovery—when it is not a proximate cause of the injury. In Smithwick v. Hall & Upson Co.,[10] an action against an employer by a workman injured when a negligently main-

7. 232 U.S. 340, 34 S.Ct. 415, 58 L. Ed. 631 (1914).

8. See cases cited in Comment, Failure of Landowner to Protect his Premises from Outside Harm, 26 Tex.L.Rev. 345 (1948).

9. 89 Mo. 147, 1 S.W. 232 (1886).

10. 59 Conn. 261, 21 A. 924 (1890). See also, Lee v. Wheeler, 130 Vt. 624, 298 A.2d 851 (1972).

tained wall fell on him, the workman had been warned against working on an unrailed part of a platform because of the danger of slipping on its icy floor and falling off. He nevertheless worked in the dangerous place. He did not slip, but he was knocked off the platform when the wall fell on him. The court held that the workman's negligence was not a proximate cause of his injury and therefore was not a defense. In Brazel v. McMurray,[11] a drunk pedestrian *en route* to a bus stop was struck by an automobile. The motorist went off to call for an ambulance, leaving his passenger to warn oncoming vehicles of the presence of the injured man on the roadway. The defendant failed to heed the passenger's warning and, therefore, negligently ran over the injured man again. The trial judge entered a judgment against this negligent motorist for the additional harm he inflicted on the injured drunk. The appellate court affirmed this judgment on the ground that the victim's negligence that caused the first accident was not a "juridical cause" of the second injury. Cases like these raise the same kind of question as that posed by other superseding cause cases.

An interesting cause-in-fact problem bearing on contributory negligence comes up in the "seat belt" cases. For example, in Miller v. Miller,[12] the claimant's petition alleged that the defendant-motorist drove so carelessly that she overturned the car, and as a result, the plaintiff-passenger suffered a compressive fracture of his vertebrae. The motorist pled several paragraphs in defense, including allegations to the effect that the plaintiff failed to use his seat belt, which was (1) the proximate cause of his injury and (2) aggravated any injury that the plaintiff would have otherwise suffered. The plaintiff moved to strike these defenses. The appellate court affirmed the trial judge's ruling that struck these defenses out of the defendant's answer. One of the grounds of this decision was the unavailability of reliable medical testimony to support either of these defenses. No doctor, said the court, could say what injuries would have been suffered had the claimant been wearing a seat belt. There are, however, well-considered cases recognizing the possibility of findings of both negligence and its causal relation to the unbelted victim's injuries on adequate proof of these issues.[13] Technologi-

11. 404 Pa. 188, 171 A.2d 151 (1961).

12. 273 N.C. 228, 160 S.E.2d 65 (1968). See also, McCord v. Green, 362 A.2d 720 (D.C.App. 1976).

13. See Bentzler v. Braun, 34 Wis. 2d 362, 149 N.W.2d 626 (1967); Spier v. Barker, 35 N.Y.2d 444, 363 N.Y.S.2d 916, 323 N.E.2d 164 (1974).

cal and legal changes in automobile safety and automobile liability law will probably reduce the significance of the issue.

All of the difficult law and lore on the scope of responsibility may swing into play when there is doubt about whether or not careless plaintiffs are to blame for their own injuries.

§ 3. THE DOCTRINE OF LAST CLEAR CHANCE AND ALLIED DOCTRINES

In 1842 the English Court of Exchequer's holding in a simple traffic accident case started a special development in contributory negligence law. In Davies v. Mann,[14] an ass with its forefeet fettered was turned onto a highway to graze; some time later it was run down by a team and hurt. The ass's owner was negligent—a fettered animal on a highway is a traffic hazard and furthermore is likely to be injured. The teamster was also negligent; he had become tired of sitting on his wagon seat and was walking behind—out of reach of brake handle and reins. The wagon picked up speed on a slight slope and forced the horses into collision with the ass.

The jury found against the teamster after the trial judge told it to hold the teamster liable if he was negligent—that his negligence was the "proximate cause" of the accident even though the owner of the ass was also at fault. The trial judge did not discuss proximate cause. "Proximate" can mean "nearest." The teamster was acting negligently at the time of the collision; his negligence was nearer the accident in point of time than the act of turning the fettered ass onto the highway. Had the trial judge asked the jurors whether or not the ass's owner was partially to blame for the collision, they might well have said that he was. There was no freak connection between his fault and his loss; there was nothing in the facts that should have shielded the ass's owner from responsibility for his own misconduct. Nevertheless judgment was pronounced on the verdict and approved by the full bench.

The judges who decided Davies v. Mann were probably echoing the now-discredited "last wrongdoer's rule" of Vicars v. Wilcocks,[15] an English case decided not many years earlier. In that case a vilifier slandered a workman to his employer, and the workman's employer fired him in violation of a contract of hire. The court decided that the workman could not look to the vilifier for redress since his loss resulted from a later wrongful act of his employer. If a defendant is not liable when another's

14. 10 M. & W. 546, 152 Eng.Rep. 588 (1842).   **15.** 8 East. 1, 103 Eng.Rep. 244 (1806).

wrong intervenes between defendant's misconduct and the plaintiff's injury, should not a plaintiff also escape responsibility for misconduct when the defendant's wrong intervenes between the plaintiff's misconduct and injury? The judges in Davies v. Mann stressed the time sequence of the wrongdoing of the parties.

Thirty-four years later, in Radley & Bramall v. London & N. W. Ry.,[16] the House of Lords decided a similar case and followed Davies v. Mann. The House of Lords also stressed the plaintiff's helplessness at the time of the accident and the subsequent negligence of the defendant. Lord Penzance said, "[T]hough the Plaintiff may have been guilty of negligence, and although that negligence may, in fact, have contributed to the accident, yet if the Defendant could in the result, by the exercise of ordinary care and diligence, have avoided the mischief which happened, the Plaintiff's negligence will not excuse him."

Davies v. Mann is now generally thought of as engendering the "doctrine of last clear chance," which withholds the defense of contributory negligence from defendants who have, but fail to seize, the last clear chance to prevent loss.

"Clear chance" is, however, an ambiguous phrase, and the ambiguity has resulted in differing interpretations and reformulations. Walker is strolling along a path which crosses a railroad track. A train is bearing down on the crossing. Walker is about to enter and stroll absentmindedly through a zone of danger. The speed of the train is such that if brakes are not applied before the train reaches a point some distance from the crosswalk, the train is sure to hit Walker—unless Walker comes to and realizes the danger. After that critical point for braking has been passed, there will still be several seconds in which Walker, if aware of the danger, could jump clear. The engineer sees Walker but negligently fails to brake until after the critical point; Walker obliviously continues on and is struck. Did Walker have the last clear chance? Some courts have held that Walker's opportunity to jump clear, though undiscerned, is nevertheless the last clear chance and that Walker is not shielded from the defense of contributory negligence by the rule of Davies v. Mann.[17] Other courts have held that a person oblivious to danger has no more chance to avoid injury than one who is asleep or drunk, or one who has left property in a dangerous place and gone away; these courts withhold the defense of con-

16. L.R. 1 App.Cas. 754 (1876).

17. See, e. g., French v. Grand Trunk Ry., 76 Vt. 441, 58 A. 722 (1904).

tributory negligence from defendants like the railroad that ran over Walker.[18]

Suppose the engineer was absentmindedly failing to keep a lookout and had only an undiscerned opportunity to avoid injuring Walker. Would the engineer have the last clear chance? Courts have divided on this point too. In the famous English cases (Davies v. Mann and the Radley case) the defendants did not discern danger and thereafter fail to use care; the defendants were simply guilty of on-the-spot careless inadvertence injuring the property of plaintiffs who had earlier negligently left that property where it was likely to be harmed. Some courts, however, have rephrased the doctrine of last clear chance so that the defense of contributory negligence is not withdrawn from the defendant who has only an undiscerned opportunity to avoid injury; in these jurisdictions the rule of "discovered peril" withholds the defense of contributory negligence only from those defendants who discover and appreciate the plaintiff's plight in time to avoid an accident and are thereafter negligent. In St. Louis S. W. Ry. v. Watts,[19] a wrongful death action, the decedent negligently jumped from a moving train, fell, and lay stunned on railroad tracks where he was run over and killed. The court held that the decedent's own contributory negligence barred the claim unless the trainmen saw him, appreciated his peril, and thereafter failed to use reasonable care.

The doctrine of discovered peril should not be confused with the rule that withholds the defense of contributory negligence from defendants who act in willful or wanton disregard of plaintiff's safety. A defendant who discerns the perilous position of a negligent plaintiff and thereafter willfully or wantonly fails to use the means at hand to keep from injuring the plaintiff is barred from asserting the plaintiff's contributory negligence as a defense by both principles. But defendant's mere negligence after discovery of the plaintiff's peril activates the doctrine of discovered peril in the plaintiff's favor. In Houston, E. & W. T. Ry. v. Sherman,[20] a grade crossing collision case, the engineer testified that he saw the decedent pulling onto the tracks when the locomotive was 250 feet from the crossing, and immediately did the following acts in the stated order: (1) braked, (2) shut off the power, and (3) blew the whistle. The court held that the jury could properly find that the engineer was negligent after

---

18. See, e. g., Cavanaugh v. Boston & Me. R. R., 76 N.H. 68, 79 A. 694 (1911).

19. 110 Tex. 106, 216 S.W. 391 (1919).

20. 10 S.W.2d 243 (Tex.Civ.App. 1928), rev'd, 42 S.W.2d 241 (Tex. Com.App.1931).

discovery of peril because he failed to blow the whistle first. This error in judgment was not willful or wanton disregard of the plaintiff's safety.

The willful-or-wanton-disregard rule does not require discovery of peril. If an engineer and fireman play cards instead of keeping a lookout, their conduct is wanton, and the railroad would be liable to a contributorily negligent plaintiff even though the trainmen never saw the victim before the accident.

In discovered peril jurisdictions these two rules overlap, but each has a sphere of independent operation.

In some jurisdictions courts have developed a rule which withholds the defense of contributory negligence in traffic cases from defendants who have either a discerned or an undiscerned opportunity to avoid injury—even when plaintiffs are guilty of on-the-spot negligence or have got themselves into positions from which they cannot avoid their own injury. In these jurisdictions, defendants who either discover the plaintiffs' peril or could have discovered it by keeping a proper lookout cannot assert the defense of contributory negligence. Plaintiffs are barred only if they wantonly or intentionally throw themselves in harm's way.[21]

In practical effect, "discovered peril" and "opportunity to discover peril" may not be as different as they seem. The major practical disadvantage of the discovered peril doctrine to the plaintiff is plaintiff's burden of showing that the defendant, in fact, discerned plaintiff's peril in time to avoid accident. The more favorable doctrine is satisfied when the plaintiff proves that the defendant did or could have discovered plaintiff's peril in time to avoid the injury—undiscerned opportunity is enough. But in a discovered peril jurisdiction, the plaintiff who shows that the defendant could have discovered plaintiff's peril if defendant was keeping a proper lookout, offers proof tending to show, circumstantially, that the defendant did, in fact, discover the plaintiff's peril. Some courts have permitted a jury to find actual discovery from evidence showing an opportunity to dis-

---

21. Contra, Latta v. Caulfield, 79 N.J. 128, 398 A.2d 91 (1979).

Both the first and second Restatements of Torts distinguished between the rights of absentminded and helpless plaintiffs. An absentminded plaintiff's carelessness may be disregarded only when plaintiff's peril was in fact discovered in time to avoid the injury.

A helpless plaintiff's carelessness may be disregarded if plaintiff's peril either was or could have been discovered in time to avoid the injury. See Restatement of Torts §§ 479, 480, applied in Independent Lumber Co. v. Leatherwood, 102 Col. 460, 79 P.2d 1052 (1938).

cover which was likely to have been seized.[22]   When such an issue is submitted to a jury, defense counsel has difficulty in per-
suading the jury that plaintiff has not proved that defendant
discerned plaintiff's peril—even though the defendant truthfully
testifies to not seeing the plaintiff in time.   Thus a major difference in substantive law may be of little importance to lawyers
and litigants.

Another interesting variation on the doctrine of last clear
chance was developed in British Columbia Electric Ry. v.
Loach,[23] a grade crossing collision case.   A train was dispatched
with defective brakes on the morning of the accident.   The defect would have been discovered and fixed had the train been
properly inspected.   Hours later the accident happened.   The
plaintiff was contributorily negligent.   The engineer was speeding, and the poor brakes could not hold the train out of the collision, which would not have happened had the brakes been in order.   The court withheld the defense of contributory negligence
from the railroad, saying, "Were it otherwise the defendant
company would be in a better position, when they had supplied a
bad brake but a good motorman, than when the motorman was
careless but the brake efficient."   This court treated negligence
depriving a defendant of the last clear chance as equal to negligent failure to seize a last clear chance.   Most courts do not accept this equation.[24]

The foregoing discussion shows that the aftermath of Davies
v. Mann is complicated.   A few courts have repudiated "last
clear chance" and all variants that followed in its trail;[25] they
treat the contributorily negligent traffic accident victim like any
other kind of plaintiff guilty of contributory negligence.   But in
most jurisdictions, Davies v. Mann has generated some practice
of withholding the defense of contributory negligence from some
traffic accident defendants.   The exact scope of these practices
varies widely, and this discussion has only outlined major patterns.

Is there any policy justification for those practices that single
out some traffic accident plaintiffs for specially favorable
treatment?   A large fraction of the cases are grade crossing accidents; nearly all the rest involve trains, streetcars and automobiles.   Most of the defendants are large corporations or in-

22. See cases cited in Comment,
Proof of Discovered Peril by Cir-
cumstantial Evidence, 27 Tex.L.
Rev. 375 (1949).

23. [1916] 1 A.C. 719 (Privy Council
1915).

24. See, e. g., Andersen v. Bingham
& Garfield Ry., 117 Utah 197, 214
P.2d 607 (1950).

25. See the court's opinion in Kasanovich v. George, 348 Pa. 199, 34
A.2d 523 (1943).

sured motorists. Perhaps the loss-distributing abilities of these defendants has affected the attitudes of some judges.

It has been suggested that once these cases go to juries, jurors are likely to reduce the plaintiff's recovery—that they will calculate the size of plaintiff's verdict by determining what proportion of blame is properly attributed to the plaintiff and withholding that proportion of a full recovery. No doubt juries sometimes do this. When a plaintiff fails to convince jurors that the defendant had a last clear chance, jurors may be sorely tempted to give the plaintiff who is entitled to nothing a verdict inadequate to cover the entire loss. The jurors are, however, clearly told that a plaintiff who is entitled to recovery is entitled to full recovery. When a disabled ordinary person is entitled by law to a full recovery from a defendant with deep pockets, it seems to us that few jurors are likely to disobey their instructions and give the plaintiff less than the law allows and requires; in these cases only jurors who do not understand their instructions are likely to disfavor a contributorily negligent plaintiff.

Perhaps these anomalous doctrines are omens of a time when more attention will be paid to the superiority of a system of reduced damages for the contributorily negligent over a system in which the contributorily negligent recover nothing. Perhaps they presage recognition of the risk-distributing abilities of enterprisers and motorists, and development of new liabilities without fault of defendants and in spite of fault of plaintiffs. (Witness the no-fault automobile liability statutes.) Maybe these anomalous doctrines are merely an example of a complicated legal development, triggered by technical, legalistic considerations, which may preoccupy and ensnare judges—a development in which judges, working case by case, reach holdings best described in terms of relatively arbitrary doctrine, holdings which cannot be rationalized in terms of policy. Certainly the general principle denying all recovery to all contributorily faulty plaintiffs in negligence cases has a distastefully gross quality almost bound to stimulate exceptions. In any jurisdiction in which the legislature decides to provide in a "comparative fault" statute that plaintiffs partially to blame for their own injuries are entitled to recover for only a part of their loss, contributorily negligent traffic accident victims should not be given specially favorable treatment.[26] When cases are governed by such statutes,

26. The court so held in Loftin v. Nolin, 86 So.2d 161 (Fla.1956). The same result was reached and discussed in Kaatz v. State, 540 P.2d 1037 (Alaska 1975), in which the doctrine of comparative fault was, without legislation, adopted by the court.

courts have, not unnaturally, held that the defendant's last opportunity to avoid the plaintiff's injury is a factor increasing the defendant's share of the blame for the plaintiff's harm.[27]

§ 4. TRIAL OF CONTRIBUTORY NEGLIGENCE ISSUES

Most courts hold that contributory negligence is a defendant's issue—whenever no evidence is submitted tending to show that the plaintiff failed to use due care, no contributory negligence issue arises; if the proof develops a dispute over whether or not the plaintiff exercised due care, the defendant has the burden of convincing judge and jury that plaintiff's contributory negligence has been adequately established. In a few jurisdictions the burdens may be reversed, and plaintiffs do not prove their full case unless they make an adequate showing that they were not contributorily negligent.

Formal aspects of trial of an issue of contributory negligence follow patterns modeled on formal aspects of trial of an issue of primary (defendant's) negligence. Jury charges are patterned in the same style, with the same definitions; the same effects are given to breach of criminal statutes, physical infirmities, age, etc.

Proof of primary negligence often involves complicated facts, because the defendant is often engaged in technological enterprise involving engineering, electricity, chemistry, and the like. Proof of contributory negligence seldom is more than a nontechnological proof of what the plaintiff did at the time of the accident—technological considerations rarely are involved in judging care of those injured. Occasionally supplementary proof bearing on plaintiff's special ability (or lack of special ability) to discern risk is relevant and crucial.

Plaintiffs rarely ask for directed verdicts on any issue, including the contributory negligence issue; they do not wish to run the risk of reversal involved in such a ruling and generally assume that they do not need such a ruling because jurors will favor them once the case is submitted. Defendants usually ask for directed verdicts on all issues on which they think they have a slight chance to get one, including contributory negligence issues; they often assume that jurors are against them and a directed verdict may be their best hope for a complete victory at trial.

27. See, e. g., Macon v. Seaward Constr. Co., Inc., 555 F.2d 1 (1st Cir. 1977).

When a court holds a plaintiff contributorily negligent as a matter of law, that holding formulates (expressly or by implication) a standard more exact than the reasonably prudent person standard. Motorist does not look and listen for approaching trains before driving on a railroad crossing into the path of an oncoming train whose engineer negligently fails to use means at hand to avoid a collision. The railroad moves for a directed verdict on the ground that Motorist was negligent. The railroad's chance of getting a directed verdict will be improved if precedent or authority closely in point supports its motion, and dim if precedent or authority is against it. Cases "on all fours" are specially important for advocates at this juncture. But lack of authority is not decisive. The trial judge still must determine whether reasonable jurors can differ. An appellate ruling on this finding becomes a precedent which may well be followed in future similar cases.

§ 5. VOLUNTARY ASSUMPTION OF RISK

The defense of voluntary assumption of risk was formerly used most often in industrial accident cases—cases in which workers sued their employers for injuries incurred on the job. Worker's Compensation laws and Employers' Liability statutes have withdrawn that defense from most employers, and it is now outmoded in industrial accident claims made by employees against their employers. Products liability claims against manufacturers of machinery used by workers on the job, however, are not uncommon; and in such suits the manufacturer often raises the defense of voluntary assumption of risk.[28] The law of voluntary assumption of risk was never confined to industrial accident cases and still has a bearing on many forms of personal injury litigation.

Usually when voluntary assumption of risk defeats a plaintiff's claim, a defendant guilty of fault escapes liability. In one kind of case, however, the defendant is not guilty of fault, and the defense of voluntary assumption of risk is appropriately used to justify a judgment in defendant's favor. In Murphy v. Steeplechase Amusement Co.,[29] the defendant operated "The Flopper," an undulating belt which challenged amusement park patrons to show their skill at standing on its erratically moving surface. The Flopper was designed to make footing and balance unsure—that was the fun of the thing. A patron took the dare, paid his admission, and tried to stand on the belt. He was

---

28. E. g., Lambert v. Wall Brothers Co., 596 F.2d 799 (8th Cir. 1979).

29. 250 N.Y. 479, 166 N.E. 173 (1929).

thrown off and hurt. The court found against the patron. The amusement park operator was not at fault; the amusement value of The Flopper justified its use in spite of the minor danger involved. One element of justification was the obviousness of danger—patrons could be expected to discern risk and decide whether or not they chose to run it. The ordinary meaning of the words "voluntary assumption of risk" made the phrase appropriate for use in supporting this holding. Other common examples of similar cases arise out of injuries resulting from taking part in or watching legitimate sports; when well understood risks materialize and a player or spectator is hurt, lack of fault on the part of the promoter or participants is often the reason for denying liability.[30]

Express or implied consent that would constitute a defense is sometimes called voluntary assumption of risk, and it involves the considerations discussed in Chapter III.[31]

In another type of case the defendants are guilty of fault, but the plaintiffs intentionally and unreasonably expose themselves to understood dangers. Such a plaintiff's fault is not appropriately called contributory negligence; plaintiff is foolhardy, not merely careless. This form of contributory fault is a defense open to a wrongdoing defendant even though the defendant is guilty of reckless misconduct.

Plaintiffs who intentionally run a risk of injuring themselves or damaging their property may nevertheless not have acted unreasonably. In the classic case of Clayards v. Dethick & Davis,[32] a contractor dug an excavation across the exit from a stable-yard. The stableman had use for his horses and could get them out in time only by leading them over the ditch. He saw the likelihood that his horses would slip into the ditch, but decided to run the risk. He got one out safely; the second horse slipped and was hurt. The trial judge ruled that reasonable jurors could differ on whether or not the stableman was at fault and charged the jury to find for him unless they found that he had acted imprudently under the circumstances. The jury found in the stableman's favor and the full court held he was entitled to judgment. This plaintiff understood a risk and chose to run it; he nevertheless recovered a judgment. Had he been unreasonable in choosing to run the risk, he would have lost his case. The

---

30. See, e. g., Kennedy v. Providence Hockey Club, Inc., —— R.I. ——, 376 A.2d 329 (1977); McPherson v. Sunset Speedway, Inc., 594 F.2d 711 (8th Cir. 1979).

31. Supra, pp. 24–33.

32. 116 Eng.Rep. 932, 12 Q.B. 439 (1848). For a later affirmation see, e. g., Sulack v. Chas. T. Miller Hosp., 282 Minn. 395, 165 N.W.2d 207 (1969).

case turned on an issue of contributory fault; the choice to run a risk, as such, was not decisive.

Courts have not always understood the problem so well. In Hunn v. Windsor Hotel Co.,[33] a woman slipped on stairs leading from a hotel to the street. The steps were newly cemented, and soft concrete was covered by protective loose boards. One of these boards moved when she stepped on it and she fell. Proof of the innkeeper's fault was clear; he knew before the accident that the loose boards had caused other falls to users of the newly poured stairs, but nevertheless he did nothing to prevent likely injury. There were other safe routes out of the hotel that the woman could have taken with a little inconvenience. She said on the witness stand that she realized the steps were dangerous before she started down them. With his eye on this testimony, the trial judge directed a verdict for the defendant. The appellate court affirmed. Had the court said reasonable jurors could not find that the woman was not guilty of contributory fault, the court's position would have been understandable and defensible. What the court did say was, "The essence of contributory negligence is carelessness; of assumption of risk, venturesomeness. Thus an injured person may not have acted carelessly; in fact, may have exercised the utmost care, yet may have assumed, voluntarily, a known hazard. If so, he must accept the consequence." This court did not distinguish (as did the court in the stableman's case) between reasonable venturesomeness and foolhardy imprudence; it adopted the theory that one who appreciates a risk "consents" to run it, and held that such consent bars a tort claim. This theory blocks concern with whether or not a plaintiff who intentionally runs a risk is at fault in doing so.[34] Plaintiffs, denied a recovery because they discerned risks before acting, may or may not have been guilty of imprudence; therefore deserving plaintiffs may be denied recovery for injuries caused by misconduct of defendants.

33. 119 W.Va. 215, 193 S.E. 57 (1937).

34. The Supreme Court of Texas had pushed this irrationality a step further and held that a plaintiff who had an adequate opportunity to discover a risk voluntarily assumed it whether or not she in fact discovered the danger. Houston Nat. Bank v. Adair, 146 Tex. 387, 207 S.W.2d 374 (1948). Happily the court has retreated from this position, and now eschews use of the phrase "voluntary assumption of risk"; it now holds that a plaintiff who reasonably runs a risk is not barred thereby from recovering damages for resulting injuries. See, e. g., Farley v. M. M. Cattle Co., 529 S.W.2d 751 (Tex.1975); Parker v. Highland Park, Inc., 565 S.W.2d 512 (1978).

An alternate legal analysis works the same way. For example, in Paubel v. Hitz,[35] a postman was hurt when he slipped on a snow-covered ramp. The ramp was the only means of access to a business establishment run by the merchant to whom the mail was addressed. The merchant did not bother to remove ice and snow from his ramp. The court discussed the duties of land occupants to various kinds of entrants and said that the merchant owed a duty to the postman-entrant either to use care to keep the ramp safe or to warn the postman of dangers. The court noted that the danger of slipping was obvious, and, since a warning would not give the postman information that he did not already have, the obviousness of danger excused the merchant from posting warnings. The court concluded that since danger was open and obvious, the merchant violated no legal obligation owed to the postman. This analysis bars consideration of two issues: (1) was the merchant at fault in doing nothing to rid his ramp of slippery ice? and (2) was the postman at fault in traveling over such an icy ramp instead of refusing to deliver mail until it was made safer? According to Thurman Arnold, "On the New York Post Office we find carved in stone the following sentiment: 'Neither snow nor rain nor heat nor gloom of night stays these couriers from the swift completion of their appointed rounds.' All this means is that mail will be delivered even in the winter." [36] We like mail delivery in the winter. Should our courts refuse to recognize a cause of action accruing to postmen injured while reasonably brooking minor hazards to deliver mail, a cause of action against addressees who have not used reasonable care to eliminate those hazards?

In McCready v. Southern Pac. Co.,[37] the owner of an industrial building in course of construction electrified wires close to a place where a contractor's employees were working. The owner had no use for electricity at the time, and the contractor had asked that current be cut off. His request was turned down. The contractor warned his workmen of the danger and told them to go ahead with the job. A carpenter touched a wire and was severely injured. The owner contended that an occupant of property is entitled to maintain his own private premises as he sees fit; the duty he owes to all entrants who can refuse to enter if they wish to stay out does not extend beyond disclosure of dangers. The court rejected that contention. Its reasoning does not entirely sweep away the holding in the postman case, be-

---

35. 339 Mo. 274, 96 S.W.2d 369 (1936).

36. T. Arnold, The Symbols of Government 95 (1935).

37. 26 F.2d 569 (9th Cir. 1928).

cause it stressed extreme, useless hazard and the special relationship of the parties. But the court did quote with approval this statement: "Thus one who voluntarily assumes a position of danger, the hazard of which he understands and appreciates, cannot recover for resulting injury, unless there is some reason of necessity or propriety to justify him in so doing. If by the exercise of care proportionate to the danger one might reasonably expect to avoid the danger, or if reasonably prudent men might differ as to the propriety of encountering it, or where the way used is the only way, a recovery is not barred." [38] Most modern cases hold that a business entrant injured while running known and appreciated risks on negligently maintained or improperly designed premises is not barred from recovering damages from the proprietor.[39]

There are, of course, cases in which it should not lie in the mouth of one favored to complain of his or her benefactor's failure to offer more than the benefactor intended to give. Borrower accepts from Lender a free loan of a car which Borrower knows has defective brakes. Even though Borrower's need for transportation is urgent and justifies running the risk of driving the defective vehicle, Borrower has no cause of action for negligence against Lender for consequent injuries.[40] Discomforted asks palsied Accommodator to take a cinder out of Discomforted's eye, knowing of Accommodator's unsteady hand. Due to the palsy, Accommodator injures the eye. Discomforted has no negligence action. And there are commercial dealings in which a buyer is entitled to no more than the amount paid; a buyer who is willing to purchase or rent a defective machine or house with knowledge of the defects may not, at least in some cases, be heard to complain about resulting hurts.[41]

38. 29 Cyclopedia of Law and Procedure 519 (1908).

39. See, e. g., Maryland State Fair and Agricultural Soc. Inc. v. Lee, 29 Md.App. 374, 348 A.2d 44 (1975). See also, Bullington v. Texas Elec. Serv. Co., 570 F.2d 1272 (5th Cir. 1978); Parker v. Highland Park, Inc., 565 S.W.2d 512 (Tex.1978).

40. Borrower may have rights under a no-fault statute.

41. Under some circumstances, some courts might compensate a buyer for breach of warranty or on a modern products liability theory.

Chapter IX

LIABILITY WITHOUT PROOF OF FAULT

Table of Sections

§ 1. TRESPASSING ANIMALS

Rancher's cow breaks out of its pasture and invades Farmer's cornfield, where it eats and tramples crops. At common law, Rancher was responsible for the damage done even though Rancher used utmost care to keep the animal home. Stockmen are obliged to fence their cattle in, at their peril. This common law "fence-in" rule is honored in most eastern states.[1]

Several policy justifications have been suggested for stockmen's liability without fault under the fence-in rule:

(1) Cattle properly restrained seldom escape; when cattle do escape, likelihood that their keeper was at fault is high; so escape is circumstantial proof of fault. If further proof of fault were required, plaintiffs often would be unable to muster it—rural areas do not abound in disinterested witnesses. Were stockmen's excuses heard, they often could and would fabricate them. The fence-in rule can, but seldom does, produce liability without fault; if, however, liability depended on proof of fault, many careless stockmen would not be held.

Criticism: Cattle do escape even when reasonable care is used to restrain them. Stockmen have incentives other than avoidance of liability to keep their animals confined—recapture is itself a burden, cattle at large are subject to risks of injury not present in pastures and barns, etc. Perhaps the fence-in rule visits liability on many, rather than few, careful stockmen. When stockmen have failed to use due care, proof of their negligence is often possible. Some stockmen guilty of negligence will

1. See, e. g., Wells v. Howell, 19 Johns. 385 (N.Y.1822).

not compound their fault by committing or suborning perjury. The number of careless stockmen who would escape liability if their fault had to be proved might not be high—particularly if proof of escape were held to be *prima facie* proof of negligence calling for an affirmative showing of the owner's *due care*.[2]

(2) The risk of damage to crops results from bringing stock into the community. Stockmen are in business for profit. Since prosecution of their profitable business creates the risk, they should foot the bill.

Criticism: The risk results from raising stock in communities in which crops are grown; but it also results from growing crops in communities in which livestock are raised. These two profitable kinds of enterprise are properly conducted in the same neighborhood. Neither alone creates the risk; the risk arises from juxtaposition of the two. Of course crops do not leave their fields and injure cattle, and cattle do leave their pastures and injure crops. Farmers can, themselves, take steps to keep animals out. It may "seem natural" to blame animate cattle for the damage and then identify them in law with their owners. But if the law holds careful stockmen for damage escaping cattle do to crops, proximity of crops threatens pocketbooks of stockmen as much as proximity of cattle threatens physical safety of crops. The position which favors farmers seems to rise from an emotional feeling that cattle raisers should bear losses, rather than a forward-looking policy reason for shifting losses to them.

Stockowners should be liable for the fodder value of crops eaten. If their cattle are sustained and fattened on fodder belonging to others, they are unjustly enriched unless they pay the fodder value of what the cattle eat. But liability under the fence-in rule often requires a stockman to pay much more than the fodder value of crops consumed—estrays in a truck garden may do hundreds of dollars of damage and yet eat only the fodder equivalent of a few dollars' worth of hay.

(3) Stockmen are better risk bearers than many land occupants whose property is invaded by estrays. Stock are raised for profit; estrays may damage kitchen gardens, lawns, etc. Stockmen can and probably will consider the risk as a business cost to be passed on to consumers. A land occupant who is not raising produce for market is unable to pass such damage on.

2. For example, proof of driving on the wrong side of the road is often held to cast a burden of explanation on the driver of the errant vehicle. See Pfaffenbach v. White Plains Express Corp., 17 N.Y.2d 132, 269 N.Y.S.2d 115, 216 N.E.2d 324 (1966).

Criticism: The relation between cattle prices and ranching costs is a complicated question of economics, and the ability of stockmen to pass such a cost on to consumers is not easily demonstrated. Stock is sometimes kept for domestic purposes—milk of a family cow as well as produce of a kitchen garden goes to the family table.

(4) An appropriate remedy of land occupants—impoundment —will not work unless stockmen are liable without fault for damage done by their trespassing cattle. Since ancient times, cattle "taken damage feasant" may be seized and held for security for the damage they do while trespassing.[3] This right to impound would be virtually worthless if it depended on the fault of the stockman. If land occupants could not impound with assurance that the stock might be held for security for damage done, they would be likely to drive stock off to be rid of them. The stock may then trespass on other lands and damage other property. But if impounders are fairly sure that they will be paid for their trouble and compensated for their losses, they have a strong incentive to hold trespassing stock. So liability without fault, coupled with the remedy of impoundment, has special value; it results in termination of a risk. This function, coupled with whatever values inhere in the first three less satisfactory explanations, seems to be sufficient justification for the fence-in rule.

When the remedy of impoundment is not available, usually the owner or custodian of trespassing livestock is not liable without fault. If a driven animal eludes its drover, runs off the highway, and damages adjoining land before it is brought under control, the landowner may not rush out and impound the animal. The law does not pit drover against land occupant in a struggle for custody of a wayward beast. Further, the drover is not liable for damage the beast does unless its trespass is the result of the drover's negligence.[4]

The fence-in rule applies to many kinds of livestock—cattle, horses, sheep, swine, etc. It does not usually apply, absent a statutory change, to petstock—dogs and cats. Those who allow their dogs and cats to run at large are not, at common law, liable for their entries on the land occupied by others. Furthermore, impoundment of petstock (though permitted by statute in some states and by ordinance in some cities) is not often a useful rem-

---

3. See 3 W. Holdsworth, A History of English Law 281 (4th ed. 1935).

4. See, e. g., Tillett v. Ward, L.R. 10 Q.B. 17 (1882). See also, Vaclavicek v. Olejarz, 61 N.J. 581, 297 A. 2d 3 (1972) (no liability without fault for animal escaping onto highway and causing traffic accident). Contra, Wood v. Snider, 187 N.Y. 28, 79 N.E. 858 (1907) (drover liable without fault).

edy. Some cats and dogs are hard to catch; many of them would be poor security for damage done.

The fence-in rule for livestock was not practicable when the western plains were first settled. Cattle by hundreds of thousands grazed untended on open range. Agriculture was small by comparison. In great stretches of the Middle West, fencing materials were hard to come by; barbed wire had not yet been invented and fencing timber was scarce. Under these conditions it was not surprising that in early times most western courts repudiated the fence-in rule and left farmers to protect themselves by fencing cattle out.

Open range has almost vanished. Both pastures and fields are now usually enclosed by relatively inexpensive and effective fences, and livestock trespasses are few. Many courts have stuck by their earlier views; the fence-out rule has survived in states in which conditions no longer call for its use.

An exceptional animal which develops a talent for penetrating ordinarily sufficient fences is sometimes the subject of contemporary dispute. Such an animal is a great nuisance and usually should be sent to the slaughterhouse. If its owner is liable for its depredations he or she has a special incentive either to sell it to the butcher, or, if it is particularly valuable, to take special steps to keep it fenced in. In eastern states the fence-in rule, coupled with impoundment, supplies this incentive. In many western states the legislatures have developed a similar rule in the "lawful fence statutes." These statutes describe the kind of fence that should be used to keep stock out, and then provide that stockmen shall pay for damage done by animals that go through such a fence. A lawful fencer is usually entitled to impound and hold stock for the damage done.

In some western states, intrastate varieties of conditions have been recognized in local option statutes providing for county elections on whether or not stock should be allowed to run at large, whether or not herdsmen should be employed, on varying the specifications for lawful fences, and the like. These statutes are often calculated to affect civil liability.

§ 2. PERSONAL INJURIES PERPETRATED BY ANIMALS

Owners or harborers of livestock or petstock have a duty to use due care in handling their animals. Those who ride their horses into crowds may be liable to bystanders who get kicked. Masters who inexcusably set their dogs on others are liable for the bites those dogs take.

Once masters have knowledge ("scienter") that their domestic animals have especially vicious dispositions, they are responsible for attacks regardless of the care they take to prevent them. It is sometimes said that every dog has one bite and every bull one gore. This is not quite accurate; an owner who knows his or her beast is vicious cannot escape liability on the ground that previous attacks were thwarted; a peaceful beast that attacks when abused may be entitled to a second bite. Known vicious disposition is the significant fact.[5]

Many who keep vicious animals after knowledge of their disposition are at fault; such beasts should ordinarily be destroyed. But some nasty animals are valuable animals. Perhaps the scienter rule antedates development of high-priced breeding stock and was a good criterion of fault for virtually all cases arising in a remote past. A keeper of a valuable but vicious animal may suffer liability without fault under the scienter rule. But the owner who knows of a special risk of injury is in a position both (1) to take special precautions to minimize it, and (2) to make special arrangements to bear loss if the risk falls in. The owner alone can make the judgment that the animal is worth the risk involved; and if the risk is such that the owner cannot afford to take it, he or she should not be able to foist it off on others.

Most courts hold the owners of captive wild animals liable for personal injuries inflicted by their beasts even though they use due care to prevent attacks.[6] A plaintiff attacked by a pet bear need not show that its owner knew the bear was specially vicious. Defendants in these cases are like those who harbor domestic animals known to have specially vicious dispositions. Most wild animals are notoriously unreliable, even when they are raised in captivity and display none of the viciousness of their kind. If they are valuable to their keepers (as they are to circuses, zoos, and the like), the keepers should take special pre-

---

5. See Burns v. Janes, — R.I. —, 398 A.2d 1125 (1979) (evidence of dog's known vicious disposition admissible and of probative value). The significance of such evidence of viciousness is sometimes tempered by circumstances. For example, see Davis v. Bedell, 123 Vt. 441, 194 A.2d 67 (1963), in which a dog had barked and rushed at pedestrians but had never bitten one. Proof of these facts, coupled with proof that the harborer had said that she thought a boy had stoned the dog and made it ugly, was held sufficient to thwart defendant's motion for a directed verdict. For an example of greater responsibility in a Louisiana version of French civil law, see Holland v. Buckley, 305 So.2d 113 (La.1974).

6. Hansen v. Brogan, 145 Mont. 224, 400 P.2d 265 (1965). But see Cowden v. Bear Country, Inc., 382 F.Supp. 1321 (D.S.D.1974).

cautions and can be expected to plan to bear losses the wild animals may cause.

The law of contributory fault in cases in which an animal has inflicted personal injury follows expected patterns. Most courts hold that only when the victim's claim is based on negligence of the keeper is contributory negligence a defense. A claim under the scienter rule or the wild animal rule is not usually barred by mere negligence, but assumption of risk will bar the claims of victims who foolhardily subject themselves to attack.[7]

§ 3. LIABILITY FOR ESCAPING INANIMATE DESTRUCTIVE FORCE

In early English common law there was much support for the theory that actors should pay for harm done by their activity. The court in the famous Case of the Thorns [8] said in 1466, "though a man doth a lawful thing, yet if any damage do thereby befall another, he shall answer for it, if he could have avoided it." The words "could have avoided it" do not mean "would have avoided it by use of due care," for the court held the defendant liable without fault for accidentally dropping hedge clippings on a neighbor's land. The court expressed similar ideas on other types of accidental injury—including unintended, nonnegligent personal injuries. By the eighteenth century, English law veered away from liability for innocently caused harm for most injuries other than some sorts of damage to real property and disparagement of reputation. Fault was generally requisite to liability for most personal injuries and physical harm to property.[9]

In the mid-nineteenth century the notorious case of Rylands v. Fletcher [10] was decided. A mill owner ordered construction of a dam to get water power. The resulting reservoir was located over ancient abandoned coal mines. The mill owner had no reason to suspect that these old diggings did in fact lead into an operating colliery. When the dam was closed, water ran down old shafts and seeped into and flooded the colliery. The case had an

---

7. But see Carr v. Case, —— Vt. ——, 380 A.2d 91 (1977), in which the Supreme Court of Vermont held that an owner of a dog who knows the dog has vicious propensities has a duty to restrain the dog. Breach of that duty is negligence; hence, under Vermont's comparative negligence law, a bitten claimant's contributory negligence properly reduces the amount of recovery.

8. Y.B. 6 Ed. IV 7, pl. 18 (1466).

9. The harbinger of this tenet was Gibbons v. Pepper, 1 Ld. Raym. 38, 91 Eng.Rep. 922 (1695).

10. 3 H. & C. 774, 159 Eng.Rep. 737 (1865), rev'd, L.R. 1 Exch. 265 (1866) aff'd, L.R. 3 H.L. 330 (1868).

extended history and many opinions were written as it went through the English courts. Ultimately the mill owner was held liable. Two of the many opinions are more quoted than others:

(1) In the Court of Exchequer Chamber, Mr. Justice Blackburn said, "We think the true rule of law is, that the person who for his own purposes brings on his land and collects and keeps there anything likely to do mischief if it escapes, must keep it in at his peril, and if he does not so, is prima facie answerable for all the damage which is the natural consequence of its escape. He can excuse himself by showing that the escape was owing to the plaintiff's default; or perhaps that the escape was the consequence of a vis major, or the act of God." This view of strict liability was not surprising in a jurisdiction in which courts were committed to the proposition that unauthorized entries on land resulted in liability without fault in trespass actions. But note that Blackburn's analysis is broad enough to cover liability for damages to personal property and injuries to life and limb even though harm occurs without an entry on private real property.

(2) In the House of Lords the most influential opinion is Lord Cairns'. He agreed, substantially, with Blackburn, but added in limitation, "if, in what I may term the natural user of that land, there had been any accumulation of water . . . the plaintiff could not have complained . . . . On the other hand, if the defendants, not stopping at the natural use of their close, had desired to use it for any purpose which I may term a non-natural use . . . and if in consequence . . . the water came to escape and to pass off into the close of the plaintiff, then it appears to me that that which the defendants were doing they were doing at their own peril." He then classified the mill owner's use as non-natural and voted for liability. By "non-natural use" Cairns probably did not mean "artificial use." But he did not define the term. Perhaps he intended to distinguish between traditional use and novel use.

Some American courts purport to follow Rylands v. Fletcher. Blackburn's statement of the rule has often been applied. His recognition of act of God as a defense has also been followed; in a Minnesota case, a city whose storm sewers overflowed in an unprecedented rainstorm escaped liability on this ground.[11] Cairns' limitation to non-natural use has been honored from time to time; in a Missouri case,[12] an action for damage done to goods in a cellar by the bursting of water mains through which

---

11. Power v. Village of Hibbing, 182 Minn. 66, 233 N.W. 597 (1930).

12. McCord Rubber Co. v. St. Joseph Water Co., 181 Mo. 678, 81 S.W. 189 (1904).

a water company supplied its customers, the court held that water was "brought in by the method universally in use in cities, and is not to be treated as an unnatural gathering of a dangerous agent."

English courts developed another important limitation by holding that legislative permission to conduct an activity has the same effect as "natural use." In Northwestern Utilities, Ltd. v. London Guarantee & Accident Co.,[13] the rule of Rylands v. Fletcher was held inapplicable to a utility company whose gas escaped into a basement and exploded, on the ground that the company located and used its pipes in accordance with statutory permission.

Many American courts have tried to reject the holding of Rylands v. Fletcher, lock, stock, and barrel. One early leading case was Marshall v. Welwood,[14] a suit for property damages resulting from a bursting steam boiler. The trial judge charged the jury that the boiler user was liable without proof of fault. The appellate court viewed Rylands v. Fletcher as an anomaly in a law of torts in which most liabilities depend on fault. Comparing the case before it to a traffic accident, the court said, "if traffic cannot be carried on without some risk, why can it not be said with the same truth, that the other affairs of life, though they be transacted away from the highways, cannot be carried on without some risk; and if such risk is, in the one case, to be borne by innocent persons, why not in other?"[15]

But the idea that enterprisers should pay for all damages resulting from their enterprise has strong appeal, especially when even careful prosecution of an enterprise conducted for profit is freighted with risk. This appeal is heightened when the enterprise is novel.

Sometimes the problem of enterprise liability is discussed by courts in terms of a special type of activity. Blasting is a good example. The American holdings on liability of a blaster originally followed three different lines: (1) Some courts held a blaster liable for proximately consequent harms to persons and property without proof of fault and even though use of explo-

13. [1936] A.C. 108.

14. 38 N.J.L. 339, 20 Am.Rep. 394 (1876).

15. Other well-known sweeping repudiations of Rylands v. Fletcher are Moulton v. Groveton Papers

Co., 112 N.H. 50, 289 A.2d 68 (1972); Losee v. Buchanan, 51 N. Y. 476, 10 Am.Rep. 623 (1873); Turner v. Big Lake Oil Co., 128 Tex. 155, 96 S.W.2d 221 (1936): But see Schronk v. Gilliam, 380 S. W.2d 743 (Tex.Civ.App.1964).

sives was justifiable.[16]　(2) Other courts refused to distinguish between blasting and other, less hazardous enterprises and held that a blaster is not liable for any type of harm unless blasting was unjustifiable or improperly done.[17]　(3) Still other courts worked out an intermediate position by use of a trespass *q. c. f.* analysis. If a blast throws damaging rocks or debris on adjoining property, the blast is denominated an unauthorized entry and the blaster is held liable; but if the damages are done merely by concussion or vibration, they are not sufficiently "direct" to constitute a trespass and therefore the blaster is not liable unless fault is established. New York originally took this position, but has now abandoned it in favor of liability without fault for all damages proximately resulting from blasting.[18]

The focus of judicial discussion on blasting or other specific activities is, of course, much narrower than the principles announced in Rylands v. Fletcher. Blackburn and Cairns tried to generalize on all cases in which substances escape and do damage. Some courts took a wider view than courts which singled out a kind of activity, and yet a narrower view than that taken by Blackburn and Cairns; these courts focused on "extra-hazardous activities." In Exner v. Sherman Power Constr. Co., a contractor stored dynamite at the site of a large construction job; it exploded, damaged a nearby house and injured the householder, who sued for both his personal injuries and his property damage. The householder's proof of fault was technically deficient, but the court swept these deficiencies aside on the ground that the contractor was liable without proof of fault. The court said that blasting had been singled out as a type of activity entailing liability without fault and that there was no reason to distinguish between (1) intentional blasting explosions and (2) accidental explosions of stored dynamite intentionally stored where it could do harm. Then the court generalized further that "When a person engages in such a dangerous activity, useful though it be, he becomes an insurer. . . . When, as here, the defendant, though without fault, has engaged in the *perilous activity* of storing large quantities of a dangerous explosive *for use in his business*, we think there is no justification for relieving it of liability, and that the owner of the business,

---

16. See Federoff v. Harrison Constr. Co., 362 Pa. 181, 66 A.2d 817 (1949).

17. See, e. g., Klepsch v. Donald, 4 Wash. 436, 30 P. 991 (1892).

18. Spano v. Perini Corp., 25 N.Y. 2d 11, 302 N.Y.S.2d 527, 250 N.E. 2d 31 (1969).

rather than a third person who has no relation to the explosion, other than of injury, should bear the loss." [19]

Two California cases set a similar general pattern of liability for those engaged in extra-hazardous enterprises. In Green v. General Petroleum Corp.,[20] an oil producer's drilling, though careful, resulted in a "blowout," which threw oil, mud, sand and rocks on nearby property. The court held the producer liable on the ground that it acted with knowledge that injury might result to its neighbor. In Luthringer v. Moore,[21] an exterminator used hydrocyanic gas to rid a restaurant of cockroaches and poisoned a workman in an adjoining store. The trial judge charged the jury that the exterminator was liable without proof of fault. The appellate courts affirmed on the ground that the enterprise was ultra-hazardous, and therefore the enterpriser was liable for foreseeable injuries proximately resulting even from reasonably careful prosecution of the enterprise. Said the court of appeals, "the dangerous enterprise must 'pay its way' and the tendency of the courts is to impose liability for resulting injuries which are foreseeable within the risk created." The Supreme Court of California agreed.

The activities which are singled out for strict liability in these modern versions of Rylands v. Fletcher are variously characterized as "perilous," "ultra or extra-hazardous," or "abnormally dangerous." While reduction of great risks may, in some measure, result from these holdings, the flavor of judicial and academic discussions is barely tinctured with any thought of discouraging hazardous enterprise. The judicial rationalization seems to be that one who conducts a highly dangerous activity should prepare in advance to bear the financial burden of harm proximately caused to others by such an activity. Since nearly all ongoing doings are freighted with irreducible risks, this sort of strict liability is, following Lord Cairns' theory, usually said to be limited to extraordinary ("unnatural") activities. On this ground the courts have refused to extend liability without fault to injuries arising out of automobile accidents,[22] transmission of high voltage electricity,[23] and so on. Most courts are on occasion reluctant to find various high-risk activities dangerous

19. 54 F.2d 510 (2d Cir. 1931) (emphasis added).

20. 205 Cal. 328, 270 P. 952 (1928).

21. 181 P.2d 89 (Cal.App.1947) 44, 211 A.2d 705 (1965).

22. Caron v. Guiliano, 26 Conn.Sup. aff'd, 31 Cal.2d 489, 190 P.2d 1 (1948).

23. Bosley v. Central Vermont Public Service Corp., 127 Vt. 581, 255 A.2d 671 (1969).

enough.[24] And at least one court has, as late as 1972, refused to hold that any kind of abnormally dangerous activity is, as such, prosecuted at the risk of the enterpriser.[25]

§ 4. POLICY ANALYSIS OF ENTERPRISE LIABILITY WITHOUT FAULT

Long before Rylands v. Fletcher was decided, the trespass rule of strict liability for unauthorized entries had been enshrined as traditional English common law. When Rylands v. Fletcher was tried in Exchequer, Baron Bramwell, said that the flow of water into the mine was a trespassory entry. Baron Martin was unwilling to accede; he said the mine damage was "too consequential" to constitute an action for trespass *vi et armis*. For over a century and a half English tort law had been moving away from a theory of strict liability for acts, and while Martin did not repudiate the unauthorized entry test of trespass, he showed a distinct distaste for liability without fault. He said, "To hold the defendants liable would . . . make them insurers against the consequence of a lawful act upon their own land when they had no reason to believe or suspect that any damage was likely to ensue. . . . There is no better established rule of law than that when damage is done to personal property, and even to the person, by collision either upon the road or at sea, there must be negligence in the party doing the damage to render him legally responsible . . . I can see no reason why damage to real property should be governed by a different rule or principle than damage to personal property." The Chief Baron, Pollock, voted with Martin, and the colliery owner's claim was disallowed at the trial. Martin's reasoning was surely considered by the judges in Exchequer Chamber and the House of Lords when they reversed and held the dam building mill operator liable. It seems most unlikely that all of the appellate judges were concerned with only dry technical considerations. Their motivations, however, are lost to history; recent speculations concerning nineteenth century English judges' attitudes toward liability without fault have not borne fruit.

The American record is clearer. Many nineteenth century American jurists were hostile to the concept of liability without

---

24. Cf., Blake v. Fried, 173 Pa.Super. 27, 95 A.2d 360 (1953) (injury to spectator when wheel came off racing stock car and bounced over crash fence into grandstand). In Kosters v. Seven-Up Co., 595 F.2d 347 (6th Cir. 1979), the court held that the trial judge was in error when he instructed the jury that it could hold Seven-Up liable on a theory of absolute liability for engaging in inherently dangerous activity by enfranchising bottlers to sell a carbonated drink (Michigan law).

25. Moulton v. Groveton Papers Co. 112 N.H. 50, 289 A.2d 68 (1972).

fault, and Rylands v. Fletcher was not followed in many states. Such is the power of high "authority," however, that some states embraced the views of Blackburn and Cairns.

The forces that molded nineteenth century law are spent or changed. Society has become highly industrialized, and in this context, liability without fault does not appear to be as great an anomaly as it once was. Scholarly proponents (whose ideas are reflected in some legislation and an occasional judicial opinion) applaud imposing liability without fault on good risk bearers. Their argument usually runs this way: Actors who should know that their activity, even though carefully prosecuted, may harm others, should treat this harm as a cost of the activity. If the activity is a business enterprise, this cost item will affect pricing and will be passed on to consumers, spread so thin that no one will be seriously affected. If the activity is not a business enterprise, the actors should not prosecute it for their own purposes unless they are willing to foot the bill. Actors can normally control this cost item by getting liability insurance, which substitutes a fixed premium for the hazard of ruinous runs of bad luck. The economics of this argument is, of course, built on assumptions and oversimplifications, but the theory is a rough approximation of what happens in fact in some situations. Worker's compensation laws are a good example. They were bitterly opposed by many industrialists in the early years of this century, but their promise of more economic security for workers, reduced litigation, and predetermined awards appealed to organized labor, some captains of industry, and the public. Virtually all state legislatures have adopted some kind of worker's compensation law. Compensation claimants are usually poor risk bearers, and industry probably can pass on to consumers most of the costs of worker's compensation liability insurance.

But if defendants' risk bearing capacity is a good reason for shifting losses to them, plaintiffs' risk bearing capacity should be an even better reason for letting losses lie where they have fallen, thereby saving the expense of shifting the losses. The policy should be, then, one of shifting losses only from inferior to superior risk bearers.

No one has suggested that courts hear proof in each case on risk bearing capacities of the particular litigants. If such issues were drawn their trial would be long and costly and often beyond the competence of judge and jury. Proof of the affluence or poverty of litigants is generally excluded as irrelevant and prejudicial (though, of course, jurors and judges may be consciously or unconsciously influenced by their suppositions on these subjects). Our sense of justice is often offended when

claimants are favored merely because they happen to be disadvantaged and defendants are disfavored merely because they
happen to be more fortunate.

We are not so shocked, however, when courts or legislatures
deal with classes of persons to which litigants belong—injured
workmen, landowners who take cattle damage feasant, blasters,
those engaged in abnormally dangerous business, and the like.
Though liability without fault imposed on classes of defendants
to benefit classes of plaintiffs has drawn criticism, it nowadays
is not likely, as such, to provoke widespread outrage.

What kinds of litigants are superior or inferior risk bearers?
For example, Enterpriser is a construction contractor readying
a bid on a highway bridge that cannot feasibly be built without
blasting near houses and people. Even if Enterpriser were not
liable for blasting damages without proof of fault, Enterpriser
would be foolish to make this bid without taking into account
the cost of liability insurance; if someone were injured, the likelihood that negligence would be found is high. If Enterpriser
were liable without fault, insurance premiums might reflect the
increased risk entailed. Only financially irresponsible contractors can afford to take a chance of disregarding insurance premium costs, and for a number of reasons builders who are hard
up are not likely to get such a job. Since, therefore, the cost of
liability without fault will be taken into account in Enterpriser's
price, Enterpriser is a good risk bearer.

Enterpriser is the successful bidder, commences work and
blasts carefully, but nevertheless decimates Neighbor's nearby
chicken flock. Since chicken raisers as a class are not likely to
be injured by blasting, Neighbor cannot recoup this loss by raising prices for chickens and eggs. Of course all poultry production is threatened to some extent by other catastrophic risks—
epidemic disease, lightning, tornado, and the like, and many
poulterers may happen to carry insurance that will cover all or
part of this loss. Such risks may affect prices slightly, but
when disaster falls on a single farm, the farmer may be faced
with a substantial dead loss. Enterpriser is not only a good risk
bearer; Enterpriser is likely to be a better risk bearer than
Neighbor.

If Neighbor suffered bodily injuries, the conclusion might be
much the same. The financial shock of disabling personal injury is still disastrous for ordinary people. While many can bear
costs of minor injury, long-term disability and extended medical
expense will inflict losses that most individuals cannot afford—
unless and until health costs become more easily defrayed than
they now are. Even if Neighbor happens to be affluent or cov-

ered by one of the more generous fringe benefit industrial plans, Neighbor is not now likely to be as good a risk bearer as Enterpriser. The preponderant likelihood is that Enterpriser is the better risk bearer of the two.

Suppose the harm inflicted was damage to Neighbor's improved urban property—the roof was knocked off of Neighbor's warehouse. Nowadays nearly all city buildings are insured and most policies cover damage resulting from explosion. After Neighbor was compensated by the insurance company, the insurer would be subrogated to Neighbor's rights; liability without fault would result in the loss being shifted from property insurance company to Enterpriser. The risk carried by the property insurer is somewhat reduced, and premiums paid for insurance against explosion damage should be a little lower. But the claim against Enterpriser would be paid by Enterpriser's liability insurance carrier, which would therefore have to increase its rates. And the increase will inevitably be greater than the decrease of explosion insurance rates, because it will also include the total cost of shifting losses from one insurance company to the other. Both liability and property insurance rates are so pervasive in our economy that consumers are about equally affected by an increase in either.

From another point of view the warehouse owner is a superior risk bearer to the contractor. Property insurance is a better risk-distributing device than liability insurance for two reasons:

(1) Property owners can know about how much insurance they need and can buy a sensible amount; contractors insuring against liability never know how much they may need. Neighbor who owns a $40,000 warehouse, can come close to discerning its value and will probably buy $40,000 worth of insurance. Enterpriser must guess how much damage may occur. If Enterpriser's guess is too low, damage in excess of insurance policy limits must be borne by Enterpriser, who is likely to be a poor risk bearer for this loss. If Enterpriser's guess is too high, the bid may be too high to be awarded the contract, or Enterpriser may bear a wasteful burden.

(2) Property losses are adjusted more smoothly and promptly (on the average) than liability losses. Neighbor's policy provides for settlement of claims in various ways. If Neighbor and the insurer disagree on the actual cash value of the property destroyed, the insurer can rebuild; if loss is total and the policy is "valued," liquidated damages have been set in advance, etc. Neighbor's insurance company probably wants to hold the goodwill of its customers and has special incentives for dealing with them promptly and justly. But Neighbor is not a customer of

Enterpriser's liability insurer; settlement of a liability claim is more likely to result in dickering, delay, compromise settlement, and litigation. This is often true even when a property insurer is subrogated to a claim and is asserting it against a liability insurer.

In the warehouse case Neighbor is the superior risk bearer. But suppose that Enterpriser, instead of building a bridge, establishes a nitroglycerin factory near Neighbor's warehouse. The proximity of such a hazard may make the warehouse uninsurable; no insurance company following sound underwriting principles would keep such a risk at regular rates, if at all. By the same token Enterpriser will probably have difficulties in securing liability insurance; but Enterpriser still has the alternative of setting up reserves, becoming a self-insurer and passing costs on to customers. Neighbor, too, can become a self-insurer, but Neighbor will be unable to pass on the costs to customers, who surely would not pay more for storage next to a nitroglycerin plant than for storage in a safer place. Enterpriser is likely to be the better risk bearer in such a case.

Thus far discussion has centered on risks regularly a part of Enterpriser's business. Sometimes, however, a justifiably risky activity is sporadic or occasional and neither affects pricing nor is covered by insurance. A householder, for example, undertakes to cut a decayed tree close to a heavily traveled street, or a small resort owner blasts in building a private road. These venturers in hazardous activity may not be good risk bearers; they do not have opportunities to pass their losses on to consumers and are unlikely to have plans for bearing them.

The conclusion converged on is that those engaged in dangerous activities sometimes are and sometimes are not better risk bearers than those injured by the prosecution of the activities. The system of analysis used is based on speculation and assumption, but more scientific materials are hard to come by to justify some schemes proposed and adopted in this field. Discussion justifies the conclusion that a general system of enterprise liability or liability for abnormally dangerous undertakings is bound to saddle some kinds of defendants with losses they can bear no better than the kinds of plaintiffs compensated. Only courts discriminating wisely between classes of cases that are now lumped together can evolve a system in which losses are shifted only from classes of inferior risk bearers to classes of superior risk bearers. The discrimination called for collides with some widely held notions about evenhanded justice—notions not likely to fade easily or quickly. The function of making these discriminations is not going to be exercised well except by a judiciary trained to weigh economic facts and informed by experts who know much about the economics of accident loss. Perhaps progress cannot wait for better knowledge on which to build a more clearly politic system. Certainly the system of basing liability on fault is itself based on assumptions not always borne out by the facts.

§ 5. PRODUCTS LIABILITY WITHOUT FAULT

In Chapter VI we discussed the twentieth century manufacturers' (and other suppliers' of chattels) liability for negligence which expanded greatly in the five decades after 1916. We now turn to the more extensive liability without fault which has burgeoned for these defendants since 1962.

A wide extension of products liability was preceded by a prophetic concurring opinion in 1944. Escola v. Coca Cola Bottling Co.,[26] was a waitress' suit against a bottler for injuries inflicted by an exploding bottle, bought by her employer. The court upheld her verdict on the ground that she had established the bottler's negligence. In his separate opinion, Justice Traynor went on to say,

> [T]he manufacturer's negligence should no longer be singled out as the basis of the plaintiff's right to recover in cases like the present one.   .   .   .   [I]t should now be recognized that a manufacturer incurs an absolute liability when an article that he has placed on the market   .   .   .   proves to have a defect that causes injury   .   .   .   .   [P]ublic policy demands that responsibility be fixed wherever it will most effectively reduce the hazards   .   .   .   in defective products   .   .   .   .   [T]he manufacturer can anticipate some hazards and guard against the recurrence of others, as the public cannot.

Even though Traynor also says that manufacturers can bear risks of injury caused by defects better than consumers, he seems importantly concerned with risk *reduction* as well as with risk *distribution*.

Liability without fault for harm done by "abnormally dangerous activities," discussed at the end of this chapter's section 3, attaches only to uncommon activities that inevitably cause harm regardless of the actor's care. Traynor would not restrict products liability to either unusual products or inevitable injuries;

26. 24 Cal.2d 453, 150 P.2d 436 (1944).

he argues that one of the results of holding manufacturers of *common* products liable without fault for injuries resulting from dangerous defects will be, in the long run, a greater incentive to produce safer products which will *reduce* injuries. The other judges in Escola did not expressly agree with him.

The seminal case in products liability was decided sixteen years later, in 1960. In Henningsen v. Bloomfield Motors, Inc.,[27] Chrysler Motors Co., one of the defendants, was held liable without proof of fault for an injury that resulted from a dangerous defect in a Plymouth's steering assembly. The holding in Henningsen inspired a rapid spread of manufacturers' strict liability for injuries to consumers caused by defectively made products. The Henningsen opinion, however, was based on a theory of the manufacturers' implied warranty of freedom from dangerous defects—an implied warranty of "merchantability" or "suitability for the intended use." These contractual concepts had been long entrenched in the law of sales. The novelty of the Henningsen case was in its extension of warranty liability to victims who had made no sales contract directly with the manufacturer.

Justice Traynor, backed by the full California Supreme Court, made his next contribution to strict products liability shortly thereafter.[28] The California Supreme Court affirmed a judgment for injuries inflicted in a home workshop by a defectively designed power tool that had flung a chunk of wood, injuring the plaintiff hobbiest. A trial judge's instruction permitted the jury, if it found certain facts, to hold that the manufacturer had violated an *express* warranty. The manufacturer contended that since the plaintiff had not given the required statutory notice of breach of warranty, the jury should not have been allowed to consider the warranty issue. Traynor rejected the manufacturer's argument on the ground that strict liability *in tort* is available to consumers, and therefore the injured man was not obliged to conform to technical warranty law. Traynor's theory was restated in section 402A of the Second Restatement of Torts, which is now highly respected by most courts.[29]

---

27. 32 N.J. 358, 161 A.2d 69 (1960).

28. Greenman v. Yuba Power Products, Inc., 59 Cal.2d 57, 27 Cal. Rptr. 697, 377 P.2d 897 (1963). Strict liability for personal injuries extends to the manufacturer of a defective component part. See Roy v. Star Chopper Co., 584 F.2d 1124, 1134 (1st Cir. 1978).

29. Professor Prosser stated in Handbook of the Law of Torts 657–58 (4th ed. 1971) that two-thirds of the courts then had relied on § 402A. But see the rejection of strict liability for reasonable failures to appreciate design deficiencies contributing to injuries of automobile accident victims in Frericks v. General Motors

Some courts, however, have continued to hold that strict products liability law conforms in some ways to warranty contract law, rather than to tort law. For example, in Mendel v. Pittsburgh Plate Glass Co.[30] a bank's customer passed through a glass door and was injured by a defect existing when the door was installed. The injured man sued the door installer promptly, but more than six years after the original installation. The court held that the six-year statute of limitations (applicable to suits on contracts) had started to run when the bank accepted the door, and, therefore, the victim's suit was barred. The tort statute of limitations does not start to run until a victim is injured; had it been applied in this case, instead of the contract statute, the victim would not have been barred.[31]

Warranty theory, however, is especially awkward when an utter stranger to both sides of a sales transaction is injured by defects in the product sold. In Passwaters v. General Motors Corp.,[32] a car had injured a bicycle rider in a passing collision. The victim proved that rear-wheel hubcaps were decorated with flanges protruding three inches. The flanges caused the harm. The court held the manufacturer liable for the harm done by this dangerously defective design, even though the victim was in no sense a party to the sale of the car. The court relied on precedents in which strict liability was founded on tort theory. At least one court has taken the view that a claimant injured by a defective product may join tort and contract theories and en-

Corp., 274 Md. 288, 336 A.2d 118 (1975).

30. 25 N.Y.2d 340, 253 N.E.2d 207 (1969).

31. The contract limitations statute may sometimes be more favorable than the tort statute. If the accident happens shortly after the product is fabricated, a dilatory plaintiff may succeed, after a tort action is barred, in a contract action against which the statute has not yet run. See Sinka v. Northern Commercial Co., 491 P.2d 116 (Alaska 1971).

In Idaho Power Co. v. Westinghouse Electric Corp., 596 F.2d 924 (9th Cir. 1979), the court held that, under Idaho law, a large manufacturer who sold a defective voltage regulator to a power company was not liable for extensive fire damage proximately caused by the defect. The manufacturer had written a disclaimer in the contract of sale limiting its liability to the price of the product and exculpating itself from liability for "special, indirect, incidental, or consequential damages .   .   . whether   in   contract   or   tort .   .   .   ." The Court expressly held that such a disclaimer was effective because the buyer and seller were two large corporations of relatively equal bargaining strength.

32. 454 F.2d 1270 (8th Cir. 1972) (applying Iowa law). See also, Polk v. Ford Motor Co., 529 F.2d 259 (8th Cir. 1976) (applying Missouri law); Martin v. Ryder Truck Rental, Inc., 353 A.2d 581 (Del. 1976).

joy the benefits of both claims insofar as these benefits do not overlap.[33]

The outer boundaries of the concept "defect" are becoming more structured by case law as the months pass.[34] Usually causes of dangerous defects in product manufacturing are either sporadic failures in quality control during manufacturing processes or are unappreciated dangers in design.

A mishap caused by defective design or quality control can, of course, be the result of negligence, and fall under the Mac-Pherson doctrine of liability for negligent manufacture; for example, an assembly line employee may negligently connect parts of a steering mechanism too loosely. However, even when a steering mechanism is designed and fabricated with meticulous care at every stage, some defects may occasionally escape discovery and correction; a steering assembly in a new car may be defective without fault of the manufacturer. If, nevertheless, manufacturers must pay for all harm proximately caused by their dangerously defective products, they are likely to be more deeply and continuously concerned with safety, and, as a result, allocate resources to research and testing that will improve safety quality control and reduce dangerous design defects.[35] Those insurance companies that sell products liability policies also have become more interested in safety; many employ safety engineers whose inspections of factories affect underwriting and retention of risks. These insurance activities, in turn, induce manufacturers to turn out safer products.[36]

Of course a plaintiff suing a manufacturer in a strict products liability case must prove that the product that caused injury was dangerously defective when the manufacturer sent it to market, and did not become dangerous as the result of someone's later mishandling.[37] A product may not be legally "defective," even

---

33. Westerman v. Sears, Roebuck & Co., 577 F.2d 873 (5th Cir. 1978) (applying Florida law).

34. See two interesting California cases: Cronin v. J. B. E. Olson Corp., 8 Cal.3d 121, 104 Cal.Rptr. 433, 501 P.2d 1153 (1972), and Barker v. Lull Engineering Co., 20 Cal.3d 413, 143 Cal.Rptr. 225, 573 P.2d 443 (1978).

35. See Phillips v. Kimwood Machine Co., 269 Or. 485, 525 P.2d 1033 (1974).

36. See Wade, On the Nature of Strict Tort Liability for Products, 44 Miss.L.J. 825, 826 (1973).

37. Failure to meet this burden defeated the claimant in Latimer v. General Motors Corp., 535 F.2d 1020 (7th Cir. 1976). See Ford Motor Co. v. Cockrell, 211 So.2d 833 (Miss.1968), exemplifying a variety of proofs held adequate to establish quality control failure resulting in a dangerous defect; and see Corbin v. Camden Coca-Cola Bottling Co., 60 N.J. 425, 290 A.2d 441 (1972). In Moraca v. Ford

though it is likely to become unsafe as the result of improper maintenance.[38]   A product may, however, be defective even when it conforms to accepted standards of safety, when those standards do not eliminate dangerous defects.[39]

Upgrading products safety almost always costs money. This cost is likely to raise retail prices. Since the effects of strict products liability are inflationary, they tend to price the disadvantaged out of the market. This untoward effect of expanded products liability seems, however, to be outweighed by the reduction of harm to life and limb. The poor are particularly unable to bear the expense of devastating injury, and they especially need the enhanced protection and more easily collectable compensation afforded by manufacturers' liability without fault for harm done by dangerously defective products.

Similar considerations apply to the liability of some enterprisers not unlike manufacturers. In Schipper v. Levitt & Sons, Inc.,[40] a child was scalded when he turned on a faucet in the bathroom of a house built by a developer of a huge residential area. A defect in the design of the water heating system resulted in the accident. The house had been sold to a third party who, in turn, leased it to the child's family. The court said that the developer "was not unlike the manufacturers of automobiles, airplanes, etc., whose products embody parts supplied by others," and therefore strict liability should also be applied to this sort of product. Shortly thereafter, however, a court in the same jurisdiction refused to extend strict liability to a landholder who rented an apartment in a two-family house to the family of a child who was scalded as a result of a similar defect.[41] The court refused to find that an isolated lease of a single apartment imposed on the landlord the liabilities of the builder of a huge development; the court held the landlord was not strictly liable for the defect. Other activities, however, have been analogized to manufacturing and entail liability without proof of fault. Rent-a-car firms and truck lessors, for example, have been held

Motor Co., 66 N.J. 454, 332 A.2d 559 (1975), the court held that circumstantial proof of a defect in an automobile steering assembly may be adequate even though the specific defect is not identified.

38. See Mitchell v. Ford Motor Co., 533 F.2d 19 (1st Cir. 1976).

39. Mustang Fuel Corp. v. Youngstown Sheet & Tube Co., 561 F.2d 202 (10th Cir. 1977).

40. 44 N.J. 70, 207 A.2d 314 (1965).

41. Conroy v. 10 Brewster Ave. Corp., 97 N.J.Super. 75, 234 A.2d 415 (1967), cert. denied, 51 N.J. 276, 239 A.2d 664 (1968).

subject to liability for injuries caused by dangerous defects in their rented vehicles without proof of their negligence.[42]

Contributory negligence, it is often said, is a defense only to actions based on negligence. Since claims against manufacturers for physical harm caused by their defective products no longer require proof of negligence, legalistic logic can be used to infer that a victim's contributory negligence is no defense to the manufacturer of a defective product. The conclusion was rejected by the Supreme Court of New Jersey, the very court that a few years earlier had so influentially based strict liability on implied warranty.[43] Since under the MacPherson doctrine a negligent manufacturer-defendant could shield itself by proving the consumer's contributory negligence, surely, it can be argued, the non-negligent manufacturer should fare as well. Other courts seem better attuned to social needs. Heightening the manufacturers' on-going concern for safety underpins strict products liability; therefore, a more politic result is reached by disregarding the inadvertence of the consumer who negligently fails to discover a dangerous defect.[44] Kassouf v. Lee Bros., Inc.[45] is a good illustration. The claimant, while reading a newspaper, did not notice the peculiar taste of a wormy candy bar until she had eaten several bites, and, as a result contracted chronic ulcerated colitis. The victim's failure to use due care for her own safety, the court held, did not bar her claim; this was a victory for better quality control, more urgently needed than consumer nicety. When a state has adopted "comparative negligence" and reduces the awards to contributorily negligent plaintiffs, the sting of manufacturers' remaining liability for

---

42. Martin v. Ryder Truck Rental, Inc., 353 A.2d 581 (Del.1976); Cintrone v. Hertz Truck Leasing and Rental Service, 45 N.J. 434, 212 A.2d 769 (1965); Francioni v. Gibsonia Truck Corp., 472 Pa. 362, 372 A.2d 736 (1977). But see Smith v. Nick's Catering Service, 549 F.2d 1194 (8th Cir. 1977). Cf. Realmuto v. Staub Motors Inc., 65 N.J. 336, 322 A.2d 440 (1974) (extending absolute tort liability to seller of a defective used automobile); contra, Brigham v. Hudson Motors, Inc., — N.H. —, 392 A. 2d 130 (1978).

43. Maiorino v. Weco Prods. Co., 45 N.J. 570, 214 A.2d 18 (1965).

See also, Codling v. Paglia, 32 N. Y.2d 330, 345 N.Y.S.2d 461, 298 N.E.2d 622 (1973).

44. But see Pan Alaska Fisheries, Inc. v. Marine Constr. & Design Co., 565 F.2d 1129 (9th Cir. 1977), in which plaintiff was not an ordinary unsophisticated consumer.

45. 209 Cal.App.2d 568, 26 Cal.Rptr. 276 (1962). See also, Roy v. Star Chopper Co., 584 F.2d 1124 (1st Cir. 1978) (applying R.I. law). A Comment to the Restatement, Second, Torts § 402A says that contributory negligence should not be a defense to a strict products defect claim.

marketing defective products perhaps constitutes a sufficient incentive to make their output safe.[46]

Some authorities say, however, that a claimant who proceeds voluntarily to encounter a known unreasonable danger is guilty of a kind of contributory fault that should relieve the manufacturer of a dangerous product from liability.[47] Perhaps a typist who intentionally uses a defective and wobbly orange crate for a typing table should not be entitled to hold the crate maker for harm resulting when the crate's collapse drops a heavy machine on the typist's foot. The New Jersey court became unhappy with its view that the defense of contributory negligence would generally thwart products liability without fault; in retreating from that position, however, the court went further than favoring only careless, inadvertent consumers like the wormy candy eater. Bexiga v. Havir Mfg. Corp.[48] was a suit brought by a workman disabled while operating a punch press made by the defendant-manufacturer and installed in the plant where the victim worked. The victim's hand was crushed in the press. The accident would not have happened if the machine could punch only when both of the operator's hands were on safety buttons. The operator knew how the punch press worked, but attempted a hazardous correction of a misplacement. The court reversed the trial judge's dismissal of the suit, saying that while contributory fault may be a defense in some strict liability products cases, that defense is unavailable when policy and justice dictate otherwise. In this punch press case, said the court, the operator's careless ineptness was the precise eventuality that safety buttons were expected to prevent.[49] A divided court in Cepeda v. Cumberland Engineering Co.[50] retreated a bit from this position; it held that an employee who had knowledge of the danger in operating a machine from which the guard had been removed, who *appreciated* the seriousness of that danger, and who nevertheless *unreasonably* continued to run the risk of injury, could not recover from the machine's manufacturer even though the design defectively permitted operation when the guard was not in place.

46. See, e. g., Larue v. National Union Elec. Corp., 571 F.2d 51 (1st Cir. 1978). Compare Thibault v. Sears, Roebuck & Co., —— N.H. ——, 395 A.2d 843 (1978).

47. See W. Prosser, Handbook of the Law of Torts 671 (4th ed. 1971).

48. 60 N.J. 402, 290 A.2d 281 (1972).

49. But see Merced v. Auto Pak Co., 533 F.2d 71 (2nd Cir. 1976), in which the court discusses the complicated New York law on this subject.

50. 76 N.J. 152, 386 A.2d 816 (1978). See also, Thibault v. Sears, Roebuck & Co., —— N.H. ——, 395 A.2d 843 (1978).

In Mitchell v. Fruehauf Corp.,[51] the plaintiff was seriously injured when a trailer manufactured by the defendant fell over on the plaintiff's vehicle. The trailer, carrying hanging meat carcasses, overtook the plaintiff's small truck and was passing at fifty miles per hour on a left-swinging curve in the lane to the left of the plaintiff. The plaintiff's evidence tended to show negligent design; the trailer was built so that heavy beeves would swing free to either side from a beam centered under the length of the trailer's roof. On curves, carcasses would swing to the outside; as a result the trailer's center of gravity would shift outward as far as seventeen inches. This design, therefore, resulted in dangerous instabilities, well known to drivers. Various methods of keeping the beeves from swinging could feasibly have been adopted, but the trailer manufacturer had ignored the danger and practical methods of reducing risks of tipovers. At the trial the truck manufacturer offered evidence of contributory negligence, which the trial judge excluded. The trial judge entered judgment for a half million dollars on the jury's verdict. The case was governed by Texas law. The Fifth Circuit Court of Appeals said, "Since contributory negligence is no defense in a products liability action in Texas . . . plaintiff's conduct in this case is irrelevant, and therefore the trial court's [exclusionary] ruling was correct." This case seems to establish two points of interest: First, a manufacturer's liability for defective products may extend to a bystander; and second, even though a defect in a product results from its manufacturer's negligence, contributory negligence is no defense. This second point adds to the reasonableness of products liability. If a manufacturer not guilty of fault is deprived of the defense of contributory negligence, surely a negligent manufacturer deserves no better treatment.

§ 6. NO–FAULT AUTOMOBILE INSURANCE

The traditional common law of traffic accidents leaves many victims either with no legal remedy at all, or with a worthless cause of action. Since 1930 academics have argued from time to time for legislation changing the character of traffic accident reparation law; nearly all of these proposals have included some liabilities both without proof of the defendant's fault and not subject to the defense of contributory negligence. Reformers have based their objections to the tort system on factual research which produced this data: first, that claimants with trivial injuries often received redress greatly exceeding their out-

---

51.　568 F.2d 1139 (5th Cir. 1978).

of-pocket losses; second, that seriously injured victims who required protracted medical and rehabilitative care, or whose disability resulted in great losses of earnings, seldom were compensated for as much as half of their out-of-pocket losses, and often received no reparation at all; and third, that survivors of decedents killed in traffic faired as badly as seriously injured victims. Furthermore, disposition of most of the sizable claims took a long, long time.

According to the pioneer 1932 Columbia University report,[52] more than half of the owners of passenger cars carried no liability insurance, and claims against these motorists rarely had any value. Over the years, three state legislatures made automobile insurance compulsory; in the other forty-seven jurisdictions, legislation imperiled driving privileges of motorists who turned out to be financially irresponsible after an accident. As a result of these responsibility laws more than 90% of the drivers on the road were insured against liability in many states during the early 1960's. Widespread liability insurance produced a substantial increase in the number of small claims settled generously; deaths and serious injuries were also more likely to be redressed in some measure, but reparation for large losses was usually either woefully inadequate or withheld entirely. Administration of automobile liability insurance absorbed more than half of the amount of the premiums collected by the insurance companies; when all of the claimants' reparation received was added up, the sum rarely amounted to 45% of the total premiums dollars that all motorists had paid for their liability insurance.

The first legislation requiring no-fault insurance came in the 1970's. At this writing all state legislatures have substantial interest in no-fault proposals. Most of the plans enacted so far have provided for relatively small no-fault benefits and retained the tort law system to deal with all but minor claims. The United States Department of transportation has released more than a dozen volumes of data and analyses on the redress of traffic accident victims and, at this writing, bills are pending in Congress proposing substantial national minimums for state no-fault plans.

Large increases in liability insurance premiums stimulated the emergence of widespread interest in no-fault plans. In Massachusetts, at the governor's behest, Professors Robert Keeton

---

52. Columbia University Council for Research in the Social Sciences, Report by the Comm. to Study Compensation for Automobile Accidents (1932), summarized in Thurston, Book Review, 43 Yale L.J. 160 (1933).

and Jeffrey O'Connell drafted detailed legislation, which was whittled down and enacted in 1970. The Keeton-O'Connell proposals were discussed throughout the country, and, for the first time, some private insurance companies announced that they favored various plans for compulsory no-fault automobile insurance.

In 1972 the National Conference of Commissioners on Uniform State Laws (a quasi-official organ of the several states) approved a "Uniform Motor Vehicle Accident Reparations Act," which resembles the Keeton-O'Connell plan. The Uniform Act will probably affect future legislative developments. Its central themes are these:

(1) Limited redress for economic losses resulting from motor vehicle accidents is forthcoming even when the drivers inflicting harm have exercised due care and the victims' negligence contributed to their injuries. Payment of "non-fault benefits" is guaranteed by compulsory insurance.

(2) Victims are entitled to compensation, first, for all reasonable medical and rehabilitation expenses; and secondly, for earnings lost by reason of the automobile accident not exceeding $200 per week and subject to some reductions for other benefits received from other sources.[53]

(3) Car owners may elect to pay smaller premiums if they agree to various deductibles reducing some of their own and their families' no-fault benefits in various specified ways.

(4) The insurance policies exclude all no-fault payments to victims who intentionally hurt themselves and to car thieves injured while using stolen automobiles.

(5) No legislative change affects the common law liability of drivers who evade their legal duty to carry the no-fault insurance required by the plan or the liability of drivers who intentionally hurt their victims.

(6) Drivers are subject to full common law tort liability (with all of its usual limitations) for the victims' losses of *earnings* occurring more than six months after the date of their original injuries.

(7) Automobile accident victims sometimes linger after their accidents and then die. If a wrongful death statute entitles some survivors to recover for earnings lost between accident and death, survivors cannot recover more no-fault lost-earnings ben-

---

53. The subtractions include earnings from substitute employment, benefits from social security, workmen's compensation, and some savings on income tax.

efits than the victims themselves would have recovered for the period between their injury and death.[54]

(8) Ordinarily, victims whose injuries are minor are not entitled to any redress for pain and suffering. In some circumstances victims whose pain and suffering is extreme and who have tort claims against their injurers may recover something for pain and suffering. Tort actions for pain and suffering may be brought (subject, of course, to all the usual common law limitations on tort liability) if the victims were either killed, seriously and permanently disabled or disfigured, or totally disabled for more than six months. Even in these cases, most claims for pain and suffering are subject to a "threshold" requirement. (The act suggests a threshold of $5,000.) All damages less than the threshold are disallowed. Whenever the damages exceed the threshold, the award is reduced by the threshold amount.

(9) The compulsory insurance required by the Uniform Act not only provides for no-fault benefits payable to automobile owners, their families, others occupying their cars, and pedestrians; it also covers owners and other legitimate drivers of insured cars with insurance protecting them against any tort liability they may incur, up to limits of $25,000 per person per accident. Higher policy limits are available to owners willing to pay an extra premium.

The foregoing description of the Uniform Act is a generalized and abbreviated sketch. Since the official draft (with its notes and comments) is eighty-five pages long, this abridgment is, perforce, very incomplete. Much significant detail, and many important provisions are not mentioned.

Adoption of a no-fault plan is not likely to make drivers either more or less careful. As in the past, most redress paid to automobile accident victims under no-fault legislation will not come directly out of drivers' private resources. Justification of no-fault insurance, therefore, should be formulated in terms of risk bearing and risk spreading. Reduction of the risk of injury is not a goal of no-fault plans; insofar as a plan reduces risks of

---

54. The victim can in no event recover more than $200 per week for earnings lost during the first six months following the injury unless excess premiums have been paid by or for the victim. When disability continues thereafter, the driver, if liable in tort, will be obliged to pay for all earning loss beyond the first six months. When the victim is killed, a survivor with a statutory remedy can in no event receive a no-fault award for decedent's lost earnings in excess of $200 per week for the period between the accident and death. The survivor may, however, be able to recover whatever damages the wrongful death statute allows for the decedent's earning power extinguished by death.

harm by reducing the number of cars on the roads, that result is merely a by-product.

No-fault automobile insurance is often called "first party" (as distinguished from "third party") insurance. Under the Uniform Act, when a car owner or members of his or her resident family are injured in a traffic accident and seek no-fault benefits, they will look only to the owner's insurer and no other company will be involved. Since many traffic injuries fall into this class, many claims should be settled promptly and easily. Insurance companies want the reputation of dealing fairly with their own customers; no-fault benefits are specifically described so that insurance companies and their selected customers should, in most cases, readily arrive at settlements. Insurance companies whose underwriting takes into account the character and size of families can, to some extent, minimize the risks they take when writing a no-fault policy. If, however, the claimant is not a customer (i. e., a pedestrian, or a casual guest in the owner's car, or a victim with a tort claim falling under the tort liability insurance coverage included in the no-fault policy), the no-fault insurer will be thrown into negotiations with a stranger. Even its own customer's large claim for extended medical and rehabilitation expenses and long-term disabilities may generate a dispute. Risk selection is made still more chancy by a clause in the Uniform Act providing that the members of an insured family must look to their own company for no-fault benefits when injured while riding as non-paying guests in other cars. Only to a limited extent, then, do insurance companies writing no-fault policies enjoy the underwriting advantages ordinarily associated with the first party insurance.

A good compulsory no-fault plan can assure that all costs of both medical attention and rehabilitation will almost invariably be met, and that lost earnings and survivors' rights will not go entirely unredressed; these assurances have become more urgent because the recent great rise in premiums for tort liability insurance has enhanced the temptation of less affluent car owners to drive uninsured against liability.

Rates for the insurance required by the Uniform Act are likely to be somewhat lower than ordinary tort liability insurance. No-fault coverage can cost less because minor injuries will be readily settled for much smaller sums. Great economies will be effected by the massive reduction of liability for pain and suffering, by the severe limitation on recovery for lost earnings, and by the deductibles to which most insurance buyers will agree. The volume and the average settlement cost of minor accidents (which have heretofore accounted for about half of the tort liability insurers' payout and administrative settlement costs) will shrink enormously. Serious injuries must be especially serious before no-fault benefits or tort liability for lost earnings and pain and suffering become sizable. Even then an insurer's tort liability is reduced by no-fault benefits the victim has already collected or will thereafter receive. The threshold, if it is substantial, should greatly reduce total payments for pain and suffering.[55]

The premium economies to car owners that result from the Uniform Act seem desirable. The limitation on no-fault benefits of $200 per week for lost earnings (subject to both deductibles for small losses and higher benefits for higher premiums voluntarily paid by large earners who want more income stabilization protection) allows sensible freedoms to the "first party" insurance buyers. Most urban pedestrian victims (and their number is an enormous fraction of the casualties of urban driving) are very young or very old and are rarely severely injured. This class of victim, then, usually involves no serious earning loss problem—though, of course, there are tragic exceptions. All "third party" victims are compensated for lost earnings by no-fault benefits limited to an amount currently greater than the average American's earnings for the total period of their disability. When victims' disabilities last for more than six months, and when they would have been entitled to recover damages for lost earnings at common law, the $200 per week limitation on their reparation ends, and their tort claims run against defendants whose financial responsibility up to $25,000 is certain. No-fault benefits never reflect the "noneconomic detriment" from pain and suffering; this exclusion does not, of course, limit medical or rehabilitation expense incurred to alleviate pain, or recovery for earnings lost as the result of disabling pain. When, however, the injuries are serious and the victims have third party tort claims they may recover full damages for pain and suffering subject only to the "threshold" limitation. Total recoveries for the noneconomic detriment of pain and suffering will be drastically reduced. The idea of providing for reparation for pain and suffering is a considerate one, and perhaps an affluent society could afford it in every case. Unfortu-

---

55. One clause in the insurance policy required by the Uniform Act may, however, increase loss experience and add to the cost of compulsory insurance, i.e., tort liability insurance covering no less than $25,000 per person per accident. Since large claims are only a small fraction of all claims, however, the expanded cost chargeable to this provision should not raise premiums greatly; at the same time, it should benefit some claimants whose losses are disastrously large.

nately, widespread entitlement to these damages has enormously raised the cost of dealing with small claims, has rarely influenced the inadequate redress actually paid to nearly all victims who have been seriously injured and has greatly increased liability insurance premiums.

The economies that can be effected by adoption of the Uniform Act would result, in part, from administrative economies but also would, of course, be reflected to some extent in reduced benefits. The compulsory premiums, nevertheless, will be high enough to price some of the disadvantaged out of the automobile market. A car is a virtual necessity to some people and to others an important ornament of life. Expensive no-fault insurance may shrink desirable consumption of other goods (say, nutriments, books, etc.) by those in low income brackets. Affluent and commercial motor vehicle owners will enjoy the no-fault economies to the full. The poor, who have been driving uninsured, will feel the sting of compulsory insurance; many of them may be grounded. On the plus side for the walking and driving poor are the extensive benefits assured by the Uniform Act. These benefits will safeguard poor families from disastrous disruption when a family member becomes an automobile accident victim.

There are, of course, potent reasons for cutting back the use of internal combustion engine vehicles. Reduction of motoring, however, is not a major justification of no-fault automobile insurance; it is an undemocratic by-product with some widely beneficial social results.

A broken wrist may inflict the same loss whether caused by an automobile accident or falling downstairs. An adequate system of social security would entitle a wrist break victim to appropriate benefits in both cases.

The tort system compensates both kinds of victims only sporadically, inefficiently and unjustly. Wider reform than that suggested by the Uniform Motor Vehicle Reparations Act is probably needed by many other unfortunates whose personal injuries are unassociated with motor vehicle accidents. Sound social change is, however, often made piecemeal. When the worker's compensation acts replaced the common law of industrial accidents in the early decades of the twentieth century, many similar problems were, for the nonce, ignored. One of the then-great tort academicians, Professor Jeremiah Smith, wrote in 1914,[56]

---

56. Sequel to Workmen's Compensation Acts, 27 Harv.L.Rev. 235, 251, 365 (1914).

If the fundamental general principle of the modern common law of torts (that fault is requisite to liability) is intrinsically right or expedient, is there sufficient reason why the legislature should make the workmen's case an exception to this general principle? On the other hand, if this statutory rule as to workmen is intrinsically just or expedient, is there sufficient reason for confining the benefit to workmen alone . . .? Workmen's Compensation legislation will inevitably give rise to a plausible agitation for . . . further legislation.

As a matter of fact, the draftsmen of the first no-fault plan for automobile accidents, set out in the Columbia Report,[57] did take the worker's compensation acts as their model. Fortunately, the Commissioner's Uniform Act is based on more pointed studies of the current aspects of automobile accidents. Similar widespread studies are not yet available on the background and effects of much personal injury tort law. No-fault automobile insurance plans do suggest the desirability of considering other similar reforms.[58] Updating the law is, however, a slow process; ripe reforms should not be delayed because they fail to effectuate similar, but somehow different, less studied, and therefore less ripe reforms. The future influence of no-fault automobile insurance legislation on other areas of the law may well be salutory.

§ 7. RESPONDEAT SUPERIOR

In a great many tort suits for damages, the claimant has been hurt by an act of an employee of the defendant. The claimant often relies on the rule of respondeat superior to reach the master. That rule holds a master responsible for torts of his servant committed while acting within the scope of his employment, even when the master has used due care in the selection, instruction and supervision of the servant. This vast area of masters' liability without fault raises policy problems resembling those discussed in other sections of this chapter.

Perhaps the rule of respondeat superior took root when most servants were closely supervised and seldom committed torts in which their masters were not implicated. Even today employers are sometimes negligent in selection, instruction, or supervision

---

57. See note 52, supra.

58. At this writing, a crisis in medical malpractice tort law has led to proposals for no-fault insurance providing the sole awards to victims of health care accidents. See, e.g., Report of the New York State Special Advisory Panel on Medical Malpractice 57–62 (1976).

of their workers.[59] But exemplary employers are now often held liable for harm done by their servants even though the masters have exercised every conceivable precaution to prevent their servants' misconduct.

The proponents of the "entrepreneur theory" have justified this vicarious liability without fault on a superior risk bearing theory. They reason that an employee who commits a tort is usually judgment-proof; if the injured person must look to the employee for reimbursement, the victim will, as a practical matter, have no recourse at all. Servants are usually employed in business, and employers should consider this liability as a cost of their businesses and reflect that cost in their pricing.

Most employers are good risk bearers, but a small merchant who hires a clerk, a little farmer who hires a harvest hand, or a parent who hires a babysitter may not be.[60] Some kinds of plaintiffs injured by servants may be superior risk bearers; the rule of respondeat superior can be used by a subrogated insurance company of a large department store against a master whose servant breaks an insured plate glass window as well as by a poor pedestrian who is knocked down by a brewer's big truck. Impact of the doctrine is perhaps greatest in personal injury cases. The fringe of cases in which employers' risk bearing capacities are not superior to victims' may not be worth worrying about, and no-fault automobile insurance may diminish this fringe still further.

Why should liability be limited to cases in which servants are at fault? Practically no business can hope to operate indefinitely without injuries to someone, even though its servants always use due care. The injury inflicted on a customer who slips on a banana peel dropped by a stranger in a grocery store is not affected by whether or not the grocer's servants had a reasonable opportunity to discover and remove the peel, and the grocer is an equally good risk bearer in either case. However, a purpose other than shifting the loss to a superior risk bearer is served by holding masters for torts of their servants. The fact that servants are likely to be judgment-proof not only thwarts reparation of injured persons at servants' expense; it also protects servants from the financial sting of tort liability and its presumed discouragement of wrongful conduct. Employers have a considerable measure of control over the lives of their employees; an employee who commits a tort may be disciplined by discharge, refusal of letters of recommendation, withholding advancement,

---

59. See, e.g., International Distributing Corp. v. American Dist. Tel. Co., 569 F.2d 136 (D.C.Cir. 1977).

60. See, e.g., Slutter v. Homer, 244 Md. 131, 223 A.2d 141 (1966).

etc. If masters were not liable for their servants' failures to act with reasonable considerateness for the safety of others, they might have less incentive to discipline servants guilty of such lapses—particularly when a servant has been furthering the master's interests at the expense of others,[61] or when a master might be indulgent to a servant injuring others but in no way prejudicing or threatening the master's private interests.[62] Liability probably inspires discipline for misconduct that might not otherwise be forthcoming. Servants who cannot be reached by law directly are deterred from committing torts by threats of discipline evoked by the legal responsibility of their masters. This function of the doctrine of respondeat superior supplies both (1) a reason for liability even when the master's risk bearing capacity is not superior to that of the injured third person, and (2) a reason for hesitating to extend liability to losses resulting from servants' nonfaulty behavior, when shifting the loss will not have this disciplinary value.

The entrepreneur theory is also inadequate to explain another working of the doctrine of respondeat superior; the doctrine not only permits injured persons to hold masters for torts of their servants, it also usually has been held to bar masters from recovering damages for their own losses resulting from the combined negligence of their servants and third persons—even when the masters are personally innocent of all fault.[63] Certainly a wrongdoer who has injured an innocent person should not be relieved from liability on the ground that the innocent person is better able to bear the loss than the wrongdoer. But a bar against an innocent master which gives the master an incentive to discipline the wrongdoing servant makes sense. When by statute or admiralty rule contributory negligence is not an absolute bar but merely a basis for reducing recovery, reduction of the master's award of damages, giving the master an incentive to discipline the negligent servant, seems quite sensible indeed.

Much litigated has been the question of whether or not the employee was, at the time of the tortious misconduct, acting "in the scope of employment." Usually this point is clear—a servant either is or is not at work. But a wide band of fuzzy bor-

61. See, e.g., Mautino v. Piercedale Supply Co., 338 Pa. 435, 13 A.2d 51 (1940), in which a sales clerk illegally sold gun cartridges to a minor out of his master's stock.

62. See, e.g., Tri-State Coach Corp. v. Walsh, 188 Va. 299, 49 S.E.2d 363 (1948), in which the master's bus driver got into an altercation with a motorist and hit the motorist in the face.

63. One case is contra, Weber v. Stokely-Van Camp, Inc., 274 Minn. 482, 144 N.W.2d 540 (1966).

derline often makes this question arguable except when well settled by precedent.

In the nineteenth and early twentieth centuries, the courts tended to hold that the servant acted outside the scope of employment whenever the misdeed was not an ordinary incident of the servant's work, especially if the action was self-serving. For example, in Herr v. Simplex Paper Box Corp.,[64] an employee, while signing a receipt for gasoline, some of which had been spilled, struck a match to light his cigarette. Ignited fumes caused serious injury to the deliveryman. The Pennsylvania Supreme Court held for the master, saying that smoking was neither connected with the master's business nor of any service to him. The holding is hard to reconcile with the weight of modern authority. In 1968, for example, the Second Circuit Court of Appeals decided a case in which a drunken coastguardsman caused harm. He was returning to his dry-docked ship and playfully opened three valves on one side of the dry dock, sinking the dry dock. The owner of the dry dock sued the government for damages to the dock. Government attorneys argued that the seaman's misconduct was not committed within the scope of his employment because he was in no way trying to serve his master. The court rejected this argument and said that an enterprise cannot justly disclaim responsibility for accidents which may be fairly said to be characteristic of its activities. Therefore, the court continued, the inadequacy of the "motivation" test becomes apparent, and the sailor's conduct was not so unforeseeable as to make charging the government unfair.[65] However ten years later, in Rabon v. Guardsmark,[66] the Fourth Circuit, applying South Carolina law, considered whether a security agency was liable for a rape committed by one of its guards stationed in a building the agency had undertaken to protect; the court held that since the guard's assault was not to further his employer's business nor in the scope of his employment, the agency was not liable for the guard's intentional tort under the doctrine of respondeat superior. Judge Winter said, "A substantial factor in our decision is the usual deference on the part of the Supreme Court of South Carolina to the South Carolina legislature in matters involving a change in the common law." He cited South Carolina's stand-pat decisions in charitable immunity and products liability cases.

64. 330 Pa. 129, 198 A. 309 (1938).

65. Ira S. Bushey & Sons, Inc. v. United States, 398 F.2d 167 (2nd Cir. 1968).

66. 571 F.2d 1277 (4th Cir. 1978); and see the court's opinion in International Distributing Co. v. American Dist. Tel. Co., 569 F.2d 136 (D.C.Cir. 1977).

One of the special areas of masters' liability for servants' torts is raised when servants, entrusted with motor vehicles, go out of their way on their own affairs. If a servant barely and momentarily leaves the line of travel required by his or her assigned mission, intending to return almost at once, this slight "detour" is legally insignificant, and the employer is held responsible for tortious driving during the deviation.[67] When, however, a deviation is both substantial and made to serve the servant's own interests, courts tend to hold that the servant is outside the scope of employment while engaged in this "frolic." Frolicking servants, however, are rarely deserters and eventually turn back to their employment. Some courts have adopted tests for reentry into employment fairly easily applied to some kinds of cases. The New York Court of Appeals held that servants continue outside the scope of employment, even after they have decided to end their frolics, until they have evinced, by unequivocal action, that their dominant purpose is to return to their masters' business.[68] Other courts have held that servants, once they have left their authorized work area, do not, as a matter of law, reenter their masters' employment until they have actually returned to their assigned territory, even though they have long since turned away from their own affairs and are singlemindedly headed toward the accomplishment of their masters' business.[69] Other courts have qualms about rules so hard and fast. In cases in which frolicking servants have given up their diversion and are on their way back to the authorized route of travel, some courts have held that the issue of reentry into employment (so as to bind their masters for negligent driving) is a "question of fact" to be submitted to a jury.[70]

67. See, e.g., Leuthold v. Goodman, 22 Wash.2d 583, 157 P.2d 326 (1945).

68. See, e.g., Fiocco v. Carver, 234 N.Y. 219, 137 N.E. 309 (1922), a well-known Cardozo opinion. A truck driver deviated miles from his authorized route to visit his mother. In her neighborhood he got involved in a street carnival and gave rides to costumed, merrymaking youngsters. One child was injured by the driver's negligence after the driver had, as he testified, intended to and started to leave for his master's garage. He had not, however, rid himself of his truckload of celebrating children. Said Cardozo, "The field of duty, once forsaken, is not to be re-entered by acts evincing a divided loyalty and thus continuing the offense."

69. See, e.g., Aldcroft v. Prudential Ins. Co. of America, 104 R.I. 240, 243 A.2d 115 (1968).

70. See, e.g., Kohlman v. Hyland, 54 N.D. 710, 210 N.W. 643 (1926). "Reasonable men," said the court, "might well reach different conclusions as to whether the servant was within the area of probable deviation, and therefore within his employment, when the accident occurred. That question should have been submitted to the jury."

The "rule of insulation" protects from liability one who entrusts, tasks to an independent contractor. When a specialist is engaged for occasional services, the specialist is usually an independent contractor. A plumber who is called by a householder to open a clogged drain is not the householder's servant, but is an independent contractor—for whose torts the householder is not liable. The factual and legal independence of two parties is often clear, even though their dealings are daily and continuous; a milkman who routinely supplies dairy products at retail to a number of different customers is clearly an independent contractor.[71] When all of a contractor's work done is for one employer who allows the contractor great latitude in organizing and managing the contractor's business, but who, nevertheless, retains the power of financial life and death over the contractor, the line separating independent contractors from servants is harder to draw. Court holdings in these cases are difficult to reconcile.[72]

The employer of an independent contractor may incur liability for negligently subjecting a third person to the dangerous incompetence of the independent contractor. Those who hire others to do their work should exercise due care in selecting their nominees. Becker v. Interstate Properties [73] held that this duty extended to using due care to appoint a contractor with adequate financial resources to pay for torts committed while prosecuting the work assigned.

Even though a wrongdoer is clearly an independent contractor, the employer may be liable without fault for the indepen-

---

71. See F. Mechem, Outlines of the Law of Agency, 288 (4th ed. 1952).

72. Compare Turner v. Lewis, 282 S.W.2d 624 (Ky.1955), in which a mine operator, paid by the ton, was held not to be the owner's servant, but an independent contractor, with Frank v. Sinclair Refining Co., 363 Mo. 1054, 256 S.W.2d 793 (1953), in which a wholesale distributor, selling refiner's petroleum products to filling stations, using his own trucks and hiring his own servants, was held to be, himself, a servant of the refining company. See also, Mehlman v. Powell, 281 Md. 269, 378 A.2d 1121 (1977), in which the Court of Appeals of Maryland assumed that an emergency room doctor was an independent contractor rather than a servant of the hospital, but nevertheless held the hospital liable for a negligent diagnosis on the ground that the hospital impliedly represented that emergency room staff members were its employees and that a patient who relied on this representation could hold the hospital liable for their negligence. This case may, as a matter of traditional analysis, seem to sound more in contract than in tort; the result, however, seems politic because of the hospital's power over the doctor's future.

73. Becker v. Interstate Properties, 569 F.2d 1203 (3rd Cir. 1978) (applying New Jersey law).

dent contractor's tort. In Maloney v. Rath,[74] the owner of an automobile ran into the car ahead of him, inflicting personal injuries and property damages. Proof showed that the car's brakes failed without warning and that the driver neither knew nor had any reason to suspect that his brakes were not working. A repairman had installed a new hydraulic hose which activated the car's brake shoes. The hose was so emplaced that a front wheel rubbed against it. Just before the accident, friction ruptured the hose; all of the hydraulic fluid drained out of the braking system and left the brakes inoperable. The court held that even though the negligence injuring the plaintiff was the misconduct only of the mechanic, who was an independent contractor, the motorist was, nevertheless, liable without fault. The court relied on two widely recognized exceptions to the rule of insulation. (1) Statutory duties or duties of care incident to the exercise of statutory privileges are "nondelegable." The California Vehicle Code included a statute providing that all motor vehicles should be equipped with adequate brakes maintained in good order. (2) Whenever work fraught with substantial risk of injury to others is entrusted to an independent contractor, the employer has a "nondelegable duty" to guard the public from injury proximately resulting from negligent prosecution of that work. This second exception to the rule of insulation is not restricted to the exercise of privileges acquired by legislation or to failures to comply with legislatively required safeguards.

In the brake failure case, the repairman's enterprise seems to be the proper bearer and spreader of the risks of injury resulting from negligent work. The motorist employing him, though liable for the mechanic's negligence, has a right to indemnity against him.[75] Anyone who has a nondelegable duty to use care in an activity may nevertheless look to the independent contractor to whom the activity was entrusted for reimbursement for payments made for injuries resulting from the contractor's misperformance.[76]

Sometimes an employer of an independent contractor contracts out a risky part of an enterprise in order to determine its total cost in advance. Should the work farmed out happen to fall within an exception to the rule of insulation, the employer is reasonably sure of accomplishing this result only when the inde-

---

74. 69 Cal.2d 442, 71 Cal.Rptr. 897, 445 P.2d 513 (1968).

75. See Tipaldi v. Riverside Memorial Chapel, 273 App.Div. 414, 78 N.Y.S.2d 12, aff'd, 298 N.Y. 686, 82 N.E.2d 585 (1948).

76. Bardwell Motor Inn, Inc. v. Accavallo, —— Vt. ——, 381 A.2d 1061 (1977).

pendent contractor carries adequate liability insurance, naming the employer as an additional insured. Unless employers are willing to run a risk of liability for negligence, they should not send straw men to do work that may injure others. Since straw men are unable to respond to the claims of their victims, they will also be unable to satisfy their employers' claims for indemnity. The exceptions to the rule of insulation tend, therefore, to give the victims of negligently conducted enterprise a reliable source of reparation.

Chapter X

PRIVATE NUISANCE

Table of Sections

---

§ 1. SCOPE OF THIS CHAPTER

The legal meaning of the word nuisance sprawls. In one of its several common usages, however, the tort of nuisance specially resembles other torts. Whenever a land occupant's ongoing activity seriously and persistently[1] interferes with neighbors' enjoyment of their property, the disturber may be guilty of nuisance and subject to liability; the disturber may be ordered to desist, or to pay damages, or both. An old feckless legal saw states that landowners' activities may not interfere with their neighbors' rights, but that no action lies against those who conduct legitimate enterprises. This truism is of little value, since it lacks power to identify those particular land uses that (in the eyes of the law) constitute a nuisance and give rise to a private cause of action. Courts of law and equity have for centuries, however, protected some of the victims of their neighbors' un-

---

1. An isolated single occurrence is not, in legal language, properly characterized as a nuisance. See Uniroyal, Inc. v. Hood, 588 F.2d 454 (5th Cir. 1979).

259

reasonable land uses.[2]   Nowadays zoning and environmental protection laws have greatly reduced (but have not yet eliminated) nuisance litigation.   Newly empowered administrative agencies deal with undesirable land use; they sometimes are backed up by courts, and, at other times, courts use administrative help in the process of reaching or enforcing their own decrees. More of this later.

A rather extensive inventory of cases will, perhaps, orient us to the law of nuisance. The next several sections will exemplify the boundaries of private nuisance litigation when householders are harassed by: (a) commerce and industry, (b) municipal activities or operations, (c) eleemosynary institutions, and (d) other householders.   The inventory will continue with cases brought by harassed agriculturists and harassed industrialists.[3]

§ 2. HOUSEHOLDERS HARASSED BY COMMERCIAL AND INDUSTRIAL ENTERPRISES

In an Iowa case,[4] an industrialist established a "ready-mix" cement plant (catering to builders engaging in construction projects in the surrounding territory). For many hours every week excruciating noise and clouds of dust issued from the plant. Mixing and loading operations were conducted on a tract of land just outside of city limits, and less than four hundred feet from the house of the nearest complainant. The harassed householders had enjoyed clean quietude in their urban subdivision until the obnoxious cement mixing venture started up. The court held that the enterprise was a nuisance and enjoined its operation.[5]

2. See a book full of ancient nuisance actions, London Assize of Nuisance 1301–1431 (H. Chew & W. Kellaway ed.1973). Among several hundred entries, number 524, for example, dated Oct. 24, 1365, tells about a London resident who kept oxen, cows, and pigs that broke down walls of an abutting owner's property and excreted ordure that rotted the foundation of the adjoining house. An assize ordered the harborer to remove his animals.

3. In every instance, however, plaintiffs in private nuisance cases must have an estate in land. A leasehold is enough. See Salter v. B.W.S. Corp., 290 So.2d 821 (La. 1974). A child living with its parents on the parent's land may not sue on a nuisance theory. See Conlon v. Town of Farmington, 29 Conn.Supp. 230, 280 A.2d 896 (1971).

4. Helmkamp v. Clark Ready Mix Co., 214 N.W.2d 126 (Iowa 1974).

5. Of course, ready-mix plants are the common source of the concrete used in nearly all sizable construction projects. They have to be located somewhere. Thousands of them are no doubt properly located.   Their operation, however, seems factually, and therefore legally, incompatible with nearby dwellings. Compare Bates v. Quality Ready-Mix Co., 261 Iowa 696, 154 N.W.2d 852

Similarly, noisy nighttime activities of a freight forwarder, which disturbed occupants of an adjoining apartment house, were enjoined between eleven p.m. and seven a.m.[6] A commercial kennel, located in a residential neighborhood, that could house forty-six noisy and noisome dogs was also held to be a common law nuisance, and the court gave both money damages and injunctive relief.[7]

Nuisance litigation may be used to interdict obnoxious commercial intrusions not forbidden by zoning legislation. In Rutledge v. National Funeral Home of New Albany,[8] an action for an injunction, an undertaker was about to establish a mortuary. The residences in the nine blocks around the site of the proposed funeral home numbered over a hundred. Nine innocuous small businesses were located in this same area. The town had no zoning ordinance. Neighbors dwelling near the proposed site of the mortuary brought a nuisance action. The court enjoined the defendant from establishing the funeral home at that location.[9]

Sometimes, however, habitants of a residential area cannot get judicial relief from a nearby commercial venture harshly annoying to persons of reasonable tolerance. In Ritchey v. Lake Charles Dredging & Towing Co.,[10] the complainant built an expensive house in a beautiful, riverside residential area. The river was wide and navigable. Two shell yards operated on the opposite bank. These yards supplied tons of shell for projects such as road building. Shell was delivered to the yards by noisy tugs, loaded and unloaded by clattering, rasping machinery; these operations were supervised over powerful loudspeaker systems. A hundred thousand cubic yards of shell a year were delivered to the yards and resold to builders. The defendants used proper equipment, followed standard methods, and operated only between seven a.m. and five p.m., Mondays through Fridays. The appellate court said that even though the householder proved considerable annoyance, the trial judge was not in error when he ruled that the defendants were acting reasonably.[11] In-

---

(1967), in which the court enjoined operation of a ready-mix plant built only 270 feet from a residence. Both litigants were located in a residential district.

6. Altman v. Ryan, 435 Pa. 401, 257 A.2d 583 (1969).

7. Herbert v. Smyth, 155 Conn. 78 230 A.2d 235 (1967).

8. 203 So.2d 318 (Miss.1967).

9. Cf. Benton v. Pittard, 197 Ga. 843, 31 S.E.2d 6 (1944) (defendant enjoined from establishing a venereal disease clinic in a residential section).

10. 230 So.2d 346 (La.App.1970).

11. Accord, Horn v. Community Refuse Disposal, Inc., 186 Neb. 43, 180 N.W.2d 691 (1970), in which the court held the plaintiffs failed to show that a sanitary landfill located close to a number of houses

terferences with light, view, or radio and television reception are legally permissible; they are not private nuisances. For example, in Katcher v. Home Sav. & Loan Ass'n,[12] four householders lived on the edge of a deep ravine. They unsuccessfully sought to enjoin a subdivider from terracing the slope and thereafter building structures cutting off the complainants' spectacular view.

An as-yet-unpeopled area may have a potential residential use which is legally protected. In Meat Producers, Inc. v. McFarland,[13] the plaintiff's 645 acres of farmland lay near Dallas, Texas. On adjacent property the defendant established, at a cost of two million dollars, a feedlot big enough to hold thirteen thousand head of cattle. The acreage owner's expert witness testified that, were it not for the smell of the feedlot, the farmland could have been put to small acreage residential use. The expert witness also gave testimony on the resulting substantial devaluation of the acreage. The jury assessed appropriate damages for this devaluation. The appellate court held that the trial judge's judgment on the verdict was warranted by the law of nuisance. In Fortin v. Vitali,[14] the plaintiffs proved that a group of mushroom growers established their odoriferous industry out in the country ten to twenty years before residential neighbors moved into a nearby subdivision. The new neighbors soon objected to the defendants' stench and sought to enjoin the mushroom-growing. Eventually the residential plaintiffs got their injunction. Robie v. Lillis,[15] raises the problem of whether or not the area in question was, in fact, residential. That area was dotted with widely separated rural residences whose citizens objected to the commercial operation of an aluminum boat storage shed. Chief Justice Kenison said that when a householder settles in a built-up area where homes abound, his expectation that the neighborhoood will remain residential is warranted. But, Kenison continued, when tracts of vacant land are scattered throughout an area used only for residences, its householders should not expect, with great assurance, that the area's exclu-

---

was a nuisance. See also the similar holding in Bader v. Iowa Metropolitan Sewer Co., 178 N.W.2d 305 (Iowa 1970). In damage suits for nuisance, close questions of the reasonableness of the defendant's land use, *vel non,* are often tried before a jury; see Northwest Water Corp. v. Pennetta, 29 Colo.App. 1, 479 P.2d 398 (1970).

12. 245 Cal.App.2d 425, 53 Cal.Rptr. 923 (1961).

13. 476 S.W.2d 406 (Tex.Civ.App. 1972).

14. 15 Mich.App. 657, 167 N.W.2d 355 (1969) aff'd, 28 Mich.App. 565, 184 N.W.2d 609 (1970) (per curiam).

15. 112 N.H. 492, 299 A.2d 155 (1972).

sively residential character will endure. The Supreme Court of New Hampshire affirmed the trial judge's finding that the boat storage shed was a reasonable land use and, therefore, not a nuisance.

Some householders dwell in zones that are predominantly commercial or industrial. Where factories and processing plants abound, those who live in a forest of smokestacks cannot insist on all the niceties of sections replete with curtilages and dwellings; they may not, therefore, object to normal industrial uses. One such householder asked in vain for an injunction to stop a freight forwarder (who operated in East Bottoms, Kansas City —a long-time industrial area) from dispatching trash trucks at night, and from floodlighting his yards to deter vandalism.[16] At the opposite extreme are cases like Krulikowski v. Polycast Corp.,[17] brought against a manufacturer of plexiglass operating in an industrial area. This defendant polymerized methyl methacrylate; its plant released a nauseating stench. The odor sickened residents who lived in an enclave surrounded by factories. The court held the manufacturer was committing a nuisance and ordered it to take corrective action.[18]

§ 3. HOUSEHOLDERS' NUISANCE SUITS AGAINST GOVERNMENTAL UNITS

Municipal waste disposal activities distasteful to householders are one source of nuisance litigation. For example, in Wood v. Town of Wilton,[19] several residents challenged a town's plan to open a dump near their homes. Private haulers had been theretofore exporting Wilton's refuse to an adjoining town. The recipient town gave notice that it no longer welcomed Wilton's refuse. This development induced Wilton to appoint a citizens' committee (including the town's health officer and two engineers) to investigate and report on opening a local dump. The committee deliberated and recommended establishing a sanitary landfill to be located in a specified rural area which was zoned for low density residential use. The committee favored establishing the fill on a sixty-five acre wooded tract, which was crossed by some power lines and adjoined a railroad line. Con-

---

16. Leonard v. Gagliano, 459 S.W. 2d 732 (Mo.App.1970). See Harrison v. Indiana Auto Shredders Co., 528 F.2d 1107 (7th Cir. 1976).

17. 153 Conn. 661, 220 A.2d 444 (1966).

18. See Daigle v. Continental Oil Co., 277 F.Supp. 875 (W.D.La.1967) (carbon black plant emitting particulates on dwellings in an industrial area held liable for damages).

19. 156 Conn. 304, 240 A.2d 904 (1968).

sulting engineers verified this tract's suitability for a sanitary landfill. At a subsequent town meeting the electors discussed and approved a proposal to buy the land. After the land was bought a disposal plan was developed. Four of the sixty-five acres were swampy but surrounded by higher ground; this small swamp was to be filled. A two hundred foot buffer strip of trees masked the fill site. During filling operations a bulldozer was to spread and cover garbage. All refuse was to be topped with a layer of clean earth at day's end. The plan prohibited rubbish burning and dumping cars, tires, construction materials, rocks and brush. The state board of health endorsed the plan and the local planning and zoning commission issued a permit for the dump. On these facts the Supreme Court of Connecticut held that neighboring householders were not entitled to an injunction against implementation of the plan. The opinion says that only when a local government abuses its authority to deal with refuse (a power granted by the legislature) can the courts interfere with municipal disposal operations. The court added that judicial intervention would be proper if, after the plan was implemented, the dump turned out to be a nuisance. The point we should stress is that, in judging whether or not a municipal operation is a nuisance, the criterion is not "unreasonable land use" but "abuse of discretion." A town's discretionary power does not, for example, privilege it to annoy dwellers by dumping raw sewage at the site of its unfinished sewage treatment plant.[20]

Some municipal activities, though extremely disconcerting, may be justified by their urgency. In Gendels v. Water Tunnel Contractors, Inc.,[21] residents sought to enjoin New York city's independent contractor from blasting around-the-clock to build a tunnel; the tunnel, when completed, would carry acutely needed water into the city. The court refused to stop the continuous blasting on the ground that, once public necessity is clearly shown, temporary annoyance of residents is not enjoinable. Courts have held that mild annoyances resulting from blander public activities also do not abuse the discretion vested in municipal authorities; that justification was given as the ground for affirming a summary judgment in favor of a city that planned to build a public swimming pool near five apartment buildings housing many residents.[22]

---

20. Aguayo v. Village of Chama, 79 N.M. 729, 449 P.2d 331 (1969). See also, Webb v. Town of Rye, 108 N.H. 147, 230 A.2d 223 (1967), in which a municipal refuse burner harassed nearby householders.

21. 67 Misc.2d 138, 323 N.Y.S.2d 780 (1971).

22. Brent v. City of Detroit, 27 Mich.App. 628, 183 N.W.2d 908 (1970).

On the other hand, when governmental land use results in an easily abated annoyance, private neighbors may be entitled to injunctive relief; a board of education may, for example, be ordered to take steps to keep dust from spreading from its parking lot onto nearby residential property.[23]

In 1886, the Supreme Court of Georgia affirmed a trial judge's refusal to enjoin county commissioners from erecting the Savannah jail near dwellings of the several complainants.[24] The court said that the jail had to be built somewhere; the county commissioners had discretion in selecting its location. The commissioners had not, held the court, abused that discretion. Nearly seventy years later, another board of county commissioners (who were required by statute to take steps to control venereal disease) acquired a home in a residential district to house a venereal disease clinic; the complainant dwelt next door. The trial judge, who was apparently willing to respect the commissioners' judgment, denied a prayer for an injunction. The Supreme Court of Georgia said that this case and the jail case were not identical, and that they were not inclined to extend the holding in the jail case to these facts.[25] This court said nothing about respect owed to the judgment exercised by the commissioners in locating an unwelcome center for venereal therapeusis; the public nature of the clinic, the court said, was not inconsistent with holding it a nuisance in a residential area. Two of the six judges dissented without publishing opinions.

§ 4.   PRIVATE ELEEMOSYNARY INSTITUTIONS LOCATED IN RESIDENTIAL AREAS

Those who propose to locate nongovernmental public service projects in residential zones cannot be sure that their good intentions will inspire judicial approval. These institutions are not common law nuisances (even though nearby residents find them distasteful) unless courts hold their location to be unreasonable. In Nicholson v. Connecticut Half-Way House, Inc.,[26] the defendants drew up a plan to help released convicts reenter society. The convicts were to be housed in a middle class residential area, given guidance, furnished with jobs, and so on;

---

23. Wayman v. Board of Educ., 6 Ohio App.2d 94, 216 N.E.2d 637 (1964). The opinion said that a court of equity could require the board to take "reasonable precautions" to stop damaging a neighbor. No mention was made of the board's discretion.

24. Bacon v. Walker, 77 Ga. 336 (1886). Accord, Florida East Coast Properties, Inc. v. Metropolitan Dade County, 572 F.2d 1108 (5th Cir. 1978) (applying Florida law).

25. Benton v. Pittard, supra note 9.

26. 153 Conn. 507, 218 A.2d 383 (1966).

none were to be sexual deviates, drug addicts, or alcoholics. Twenty-nine residences were located on the block on which the halfway house was to be opened. Many children played in front of these homes. The Supreme Court of Connecticut dissolved the injunction granted by the trial judge. Mere fears that future inmates will commit crimes in the neighborhood and that the values of nearby houses may depreciate, said the court, do not constitute facts adequate to justify an injunction. The Supreme Court of Arkansas dealt with similar facts some six years later. In the Arkansas case, however, the suit was not brought until after halfway house activities were carried on for a time. The neighbors adduced proof that, even though the institution's rules excluded sex offenders and alcoholics, one resident had committed an "unlawful carnal abuse," and another was an inordinate drinker. Experts testified that the halfway house had depreciated the value of other dwellings on the block. The Supreme Court of Arkansas referred expressly to the Connecticut holding but refused to overturn the trial judge's injunction. They differentiated their case from the Connecticut holding on the ground that their plaintiffs had adduced proof of actual past events and real depreciation, and therefore had established both reasonable apprehension and realized devaluation.[27] The contrast between these two cases may be a distinction without a difference. Perhaps the Connecticut court opined that attempts to ameliorate our untoward penal practices in a quiet residential area may legally subject the neighborhood to the small risks of poor selection (almost sure to happen occasionally) and property devaluation (almost sure to result from the proximity of such halfway houses). Maybe the Arkansas court put the dangers to domestic security and property values above the importance of reclaiming errant convicts by settling them among ordinary families.

§ 5. INCOMPATIBLE RESIDENTIAL NEIGHBORS

A householder can, of course, get on a next-door neighbor's nerves without committing a legal nuisance. For example, in Slaird v. Klewers,[28] a city householder proved that his next-door neighbor built a swimming pool. The diving board, at each use, uttered a clunk. Floodlights shone over the fence and dispelled some of the evening darkness in the complainant's garden. A water-purifying chlorinator emitted a trace of odor. And so on. The court held these irritations did not add up to a legal nuisance. More substantial harassment can, however, constitute a

---

27. Arkansas Release Guidance Foundation v. Needler, 252 Ark. 194, 477 S.W.2d 821 (1972).

28. 260 Md. 2, 271 A.2d 345 (1970).

residential land use unreasonably annoying the neighbors.   A landowner may be required to remove or modify a spite fence.[29] An injunction may restrict the use of a loud air-conditioning water tower; and a dog owner, whose pet barked resoundingly at passersby from four to six-thirty a.m., was ordered to keep it indoors during sleeping hours.[30]   Violators of zoning and building ordinances sometimes commit wrongs actionable by their neighbors.[31]

§ 6.   RURAL AGRICULTURISTS AND RESIDENTS COMPLAINING OF COMMERCIAL OR INDUSTRIAL NUISANCES

In the classic case, Madison v. Ducktown Sulphur, Copper & Iron Co.,[32] decided by the Supreme Court of Tennessee early in the twentieth century, air pollution had killed timber and ruined crops.   The defendants were two copper companies who had roasted great masses of ore.   The burning piles gave off sulphurous fumes and noxious smoke which defoliated nearby hillbilly farms of small value.   At the time the method used was the only known way of extracting copper from ore.   One of the companies had tried to find a less destructive process, and had spent large sums on fruitless experiments.   Both companies admitted that they were liable for the harm done.   The Supreme Court held that a master should be appointed to hear all claims and determine the damages to which each claimant was entitled.   More than sixty years after the Ducktown decision, Wisconsin farmers were compensated for similar crop damages caused by sulphur escaping from an electric power company's coal-burning plant.[33]   A phosphate producer located its works in a Montana hinterland; its process threw off fluoride pollutants which, over a radius of fifteen miles, sickened ranch animals and afflicted vegetation.   The producer was ordered to pay more than a hundred thousand dollars for the harm already inflicted, and was subjected to further liability if its newly adopted safe-

29.   See, e. g., DeCecco v. Beach, 174 Conn. 29, 381 A.2d 543 (1977).

30.   Nair v. Thaw, 156 Conn. 445, 242 A.2d 757 (1968); Allen v. Paulk, 188 So.2d 708 (La.App. 1966).   See, also, Davoust v. Mitchell, 146 Ind.App. 536, 257 N.E.2d 332 (1970).

31.   See Cole v. City of Osceola, 179 N.W.2d 524 (Iowa 1970); and see

Levasseur v. Dubuc, 229 A.2d 201 (Me.1967).

32.   113 Tenn. 331, 83 S.W.2d 658 (1904).

33.   Jost v. Dairyland Power Cooperative, 45 Wis.2d 164, 172 N.W.2d 647 (1969).

guards failed to arrest damaging contamination.[34]   A chemical
company proposed to bury poisonous wastes at a place where
they might seep into a well on adjoining farmland; the Supreme
Court of Louisiana ordered that the inhumation be made in compliance with standards for safety established by expert testimony adduced at the trial.[35]

In Township of Bedminster v. Vargo Dragway, Inc.,[36] the defendants bought a twenty-seven acre tract of land on which they
built a thirty-two hundred foot "drag strip" costing more than
eighty thousand dollars.   For three years, from early April to
late November (weather permitting), the defendants conducted
more than sixty-five races every Sunday.   Racing started at
nine a. m. and went on until five p. m.   Cars "revving up" made
noise like the clamor of a chain saw.   The racket was loud
enough to prevent conversation in normal tones at the sixty
homes located within a mile of the strip.   Windows rattled, cattle were disturbed.   The enterprise attracted traffic that dis-
rupted church services two miles away.   The Supreme Court of
Pennsylvania affirmed the trial court's permanent injunction ordering the defendants to stop drag racing.   The opinion noted
(perhaps with commiseration) the defendants' large investment,
but went on to say that the builders had taken a calculated risk
that a court of equity would close them down to protect the owners of the surrounding homes against such harassment.[37]

In yesteryear no one would have thought that a poultry yard in
the country could be a nuisance.   Modern methods of raising
chickens and producing eggs, however, have changed all that.
Now tremendous numbers of birds are crammed into individual
cages and subjected to a manufacturing form of aviculture.
Such an assemblage of poultry is, at best, unwelcomed by neighboring farmers.   In Patz v. Farmegg Products, Inc.,[38] the complainant owned a substantial farm in what had been a typical
Iowa rural locality—until the defendant, a thousand feet from
the plaintiff's house, set up two chicken houses on four acres.
Prevailing winds brought nauseating odors from eighty thousand
birds to the farm, spring, summer, and fall.   The Supreme
Court of Iowa affirmed a twenty thousand dollar judgment for

34. Dutton v. Rocky Mountain
Phosphates, 151 Mont. 54, 438 P.2d
674 (1968).

35. Salter v. B.W.S. Corp., 290 So.
2d 821 (La.1974).

36. 434 Pa. 100, 253 A.2d 659
(1969).

37. See Bates v. Quality Ready-Mix
Co., supra note 5, enjoining a
noisy, dusty ready-mix cement
plant built in a district zoned for
agriculture but located close to a
suburban residence.

38. 196 N.W.2d 557 (Iowa 1972).

the farmer, saying that defendant's operation was not an agricultural activity incident to rural life.[39]

§ 7. INCOMPATIBLE EXURBAN, NON–INDUSTRIAL NEIGHBORS

In Mercer v. Brown,[40] both litigants were situated in an area zoned (and long used) for agricultural purposes. Many residents kept cows, a few hogs, and chickens. Several husbandmen ran dairy farms in the zone. The defendant bought land that had been used for fifteen years as a commercial hog farm; he expanded the operation considerably, and, at the time of the suit, he was raising seven hundred and fifty swine; he planned, furthermore, to increase his herd to fifteen hundred. He fed his hogs slaughterhouse offal, slops, and garbage. The defendant's experts testified that he ran a model hog farm and that he used modern approved methods conforming to state and county regulations. Nevertheless great stench and unpleasant noise emanated from this swinery. The trial judge refused to enjoin this large-scale hog-raising venture; in fact, he ruled that the defendant could further increase his herd by one-third. The trial judge did, however, enter a decree regulating the times and methods of handling the offensive hog food. The appellate court affirmed, saying that the appellants failed to show that the trial judge abused his discretion when he found the hog raiser's venture to be a reasonable exercise of his dominion over his land (provided he abided by the decreed regulations on feeding).[41] Non-agricultural activities, which would be nuisances in town, may be permissible in the country. A gun club, for example, operating without great noise and safeguarded against escape of missiles, may be a reasonable use of rural land.[42]

39. See Valley Poultry Farms, Inc. v. Preece, 406 S.W.2d 413 (Ky. 1966), in which the plaintiff recovered a judgment for damages even though the defendant showed that his plant conformed to the highest standards. Of course a chicken-raiser whose methods are suspect may be ordered to change them. See Gerrish v. Wishbone Farm of N.H., Inc., 108 N.H. 237, 231 A.2d 622 (1967); and compare Blue Ridge Poultry & Egg Co. v. Clark, 211 Va. 139, 176 S.E.2d 323 (1970), a case in which a million dollar chicken-packing plant poured out three hundred gallons of offensive polluted water per minute into a watercourse traversing neighboring land.

40. 190 So.2d 610 (Fla.App.1966).

41. Compare Schiller v. Raley, 405 S.W.2d 446 (Tex.Civ.App.1966), which held a cattle feedlot housing some eighty-five animals, located two and a half miles out of town, was not an enjoinable nuisance.

42. Oak Haven Trailer Court, Inc. v. Western Wayne County Conservation Ass'n, 3 Mich.App. 83, 141 N.W.2d 645 (1966), aff'd sub nom., Smith v. Western Wayne County

§ 8.　NUISANCE LITIGATION BETWEEN COMMERCIAL OR INDUSTRIAL NEIGHBORS

Legitimate industry, properly located, is seldom a common law nuisance to its commercial neighbors. Occasionally, however, a commercial venturer has a valid nuisance claim against a nearby industrial plant. In Greyhound Leasing & Financial Corp. v. Joiner City Unit,[43] the complainant owned and was extracting underground oil. Its oil lay at one end of a pool five miles long. Owners of the rest of the pool injected water into their oil sands at a point about a mile from the plaintiff's boundary. The water injection was a "secondary recovery" operation calculated to produce oil that would otherwise be lost. The water, however, was forced across the injectors' boundary and deprived the plaintiff of a substantial amount of its oil. The Tenth Circuit Court of Appeals affirmed a district court judge's award to the plaintiff of a half-million dollars. The Court of Appeals called the suit a common law action for nuisance; it relied on Oklahoma law, which for such suits expressly negates a need to prove "unreasonableness or carelessness" when private persons encroach on a neighbor's subsurface lands. (The relationship between fault and nuisance will be analyzed in the next section.)

Earlier we discussed a case in which a court held that floodlights in an area zoned for industry were not a legal nuisance to annoyed householders who dwelt among industries.[44] Operators of drive-in movies fare no better when commercial neighbors' illuminations interfere with screen images. Outdoor movies are said to be "specially sensitive" and, therefore, not deserving of the legal protection available to disruptions of more "normal" activities.[45]

§ 9.　NUISANCE AND FAULT

In standard legal usage a person whose behavior is "reasonably prudent" is not guilty of any "fault"—not even negligence. Some unreasonable conduct is intentionally wrong. A land occupant who builds a structure for no purpose other than harassing

Conservation Ass'n, 380 Mich. 526, 158 N.W.2d 463 (1968).

43. 444 F.2d 439 (10th Cir. 1971).

44. See Leonard v. Gagliano, supra, note 16.

45. See Lynn Open Air Theatre, Inc. v. Sea Crest Cadillac-Pontiac, Inc., 1 Mass.App. 186, 294 N.E.2d 473 (1973); Belmar Drive-In Theatre Co. v. Illinois State Toll Highway Comm., 34 Ill.2d 544, 216 N.E.2d 788 (1966). Compare Richmond Bros., Inc. v. Hagemann, 359 Mass. 265, 268 N.E.2d 680 (1971), in which a radio broadcaster unsuccessfully sought to enjoin the construction of a five story structure on adjacent land that would affect his signal.

a neighbor commits a private nuisance. A "spite fence" is, in modern law, a tort.[46] In an Idaho case, two businessmen occupied adjoining land. One built a fence two feet from the other's motel windows. The structure was eighteen feet high and eighty-five feet long. The builder painted a sign on the fence. The sign was an obvious pretext; it had no advertising value. The builder was motivated only by his ill will toward his neighbor. The court held the sign a nuisance and ordered the builder to cut it down to the height of a proper boundary fence.[47]

Some intentionally harassing land uses are not motivated by spite. They are, nevertheless, set on foot with foreknowledge that harm or discomfort will be suffered by those nearby. For example, operators of a Nevada cement factory, after five years of innocuous operation, decided to enlarge their plant. They installed a new kiln with "primary filtration" like that on their old kiln. The new kiln, however, was not equipped with any "secondary" filter. They planned to design a novel secondary filter for the new kiln after they had gathered data while running the new kiln with only a primary filter. Data-gathering continued for nineteen months during which they knew that the second kiln was emitting nine pounds of dust for each barrel of cement produced. This pollution harmed nearby ranches and their habitants. The court held that such wanton wrongdoing subjected the cement manufacturers to both compensatory and punitive damages.[48]

Land use may turn out to be a nuisance when harm was neither foreseen nor done with reckless disregard of the rights of those injured. Harm inadvertently resulting from negligent land use may constitute a nuisance. In an Oregon case,[49] a fruit grower proved the steady decline of his pear orchard. The trees sickened because the water table rose, inundating their roots. The rise of the water table resulted from seepage out of irrigation canals. When built, the sides and bottoms of these waterways were raw earth; later, the irrigation district paved the inner surfaces of the canals but left chinks through which seepage continued. The trial judge told the jury to return a verdict for the pear grower if it found that the irrigation district had con-

---

46. See W. Prosser, Handbook of the Law of Torts 598–99 (4th ed. 1971).

47. Sundowner, Inc. v. King, 95 Idaho 367, 509 P.2d 785 (1973).

48. Nevada Cement Co. v. Lemler, 89 Nev. 447, 514 P.2d 1180 (1973). See also, Dutton v. Rocky Moun-tain Phosphates, supra note 34, in which a manufacturer started up his phosphate plant knowing it was sure to damage nearby pastures and hay farms, and was held liable for large compensatory and punitive damages.

49. Furrer v. Talent Irrigation Dist., 258 Or. 494, 466 P.2d 605 (1970).

structed the canals negligently and if, as a proximate consequence, the trees languished. The Supreme Court of Oregon affirmed a twenty thousand dollar judgment on the ground that liability for nuisance could be predicated on negligence.[50]

Can innocent conduct subject a land user to liability without fault to neighbors for the harm done? A modern case clearly raising this legal question is Wright v. Masonite Corp.[51] One of the litigants owned a composition board factory, the other, a grocery store. The manufacturers sprayed some of their board with lacquer and varnish with no suspicion that their spray guns emitted minuscule whiffs of formaldehyde. The store was two hundred feet away. When the grocer detected a slight odor in his store, he began a search for the source of the smell. By the time the truth was known most of the groceries were ruined. The trial judge ruled that the manufacturer had no reason to suspect that it was tainting the grocer's stock. The Fourth Circuit Court of Appeals affirmed the trial judge's holding that, under North Carolina law, the manufacturer was not guilty of nuisance and the grocer had no cause of action. Chief Judge Haynesworth wrote the opinion. He relied on dicta found in two North Carolina opinions written in cases that held against defendants who knew they were emitting noxious pollutants, and were, therefore, guilty of nuisance. Said Judge Haynesworth, "[I]n every . . . North Carolina case . . . which has been brought to our attention, the invasion was clearly intentional . . . Since [in this case] there was no negligence and the invasion was unintentional . . . there was no private nuisance . . . ."

The Masonite manufacturer, it seems to us, has greater capacity than the grocer to absorb this loss and reduce this kind of risk. Were Masonite held liable, its liability insurance would probably reimburse it for all or part of the loss; the grocer's property insurance would not be likely to cover deterioration by contamination. Masonite and its insurers have whatever opportunity exists to discover and control this sort of ambuscade; its neighbors often will be taken unawares with no opportunity to avoid injury. The holding in the Masonite case may, therefore, not be followed either in North Carolina or other jurisdictions.[52]

50. Compare Macca v. General Telephone Co., 262 Or. 414, 495 P.2d 1193 (1972), holding a telephone company liable for negligently listing a householder's number as the night number of a florist, thereby subjecting him to many annoying phone calls. See also, Lerro v. Thomas Wynne, Inc., 451 Pa. 37, 301 A.2d 705 (1973).

51. 368 F.2d 661 (4th Cir. 1966).

52. Perhaps a still better candidate for liability is the manufacturer of the lacquers and varnishes. See Ch. IX § 5.

In an Alabama case [53] the authors of a nuisance impertinently intruded on land without any fault on the part of its occupant. The interlopers were beavers; they dammed a watercourse. The resulting pond backed up onto a neighbor's property, killed his trees, harbored mosquitoes and water snakes, etc. Since the dam was a "natural" phenomenon,[54] the court reluctantly called upon the lower riparian landowner to remove the dam at, perhaps, considerable expense. The court provided, however, that if defendant did not open the dam, he should allow the upstream landowner to have access to the dam and permit him to take appropriate steps. Does this decree impose liability without fault, or is it merely a unique instance of judicial compromise? A less onerous decree unconditionally required some landowners to remove a single tree that was likely to fall on their neighbors' property.[55] On appeal the defendants argued that they had not planted the tree and were, therefore, not obliged to remove it. The court said that an unsound tree near a boundary line is a nuisance which the owner of the *locus standi* may be required to abate whether planted or natural growth. This liability without fault, if such it is, does not seem arduous.

In some cases, past fault is unimportant and the question posed is the tolerableness of future consequences of a continued or projected land use. In Hilliard v. Shuff,[56] a gasoline dealer maintained fuel tanks so that they were likely to explode and damage his neighbor. The court ordered the dealer to take further precautions. In Salter v. B. W. S. Corp., discussed earlier,[57] an industrial concern proposed to bury poisonous chemical waste that might seep into its neighbor's well. The court ordered the concern to coat the burial pit so that the waste was unlikely to escape.

Those who accidentally take something that belongs to someone else ought either to return it or pay for it, even though they were without fault in erroneously believing that the acquisition was proper. Some nuisances are analogous to taking or using nearby land; this kind of nuisance subjects takers to liability, whether or not they were honest and reasonable in believing they were entitled to impose on their neighbors. In such cases, a complainant need not establish fault, though, of course if complainant does prove fault the case may be clearer; and, when

53. Roberts v. Brewer, 290 Ala. 329, 276 So.2d 574 (1973).

54. See Ch. VI, § 3.

55. Fabbri v. Regis Forcier, Inc., 114 R.I. 207, 330 A.2d 807 (1975).

56. 260 La. 384, 256 So.2d 127 (1971).

57. 290 So.2d 821 (La.1974).

that fault is egregious enough, the complainant may be entitled to punitive as well as compensatory damages.

When the defendant "takes" for public use, the taking may be an exercise of eminent domain. This kind of taking is not wrong, but obliges the taker to pay due compensation. For example, in Thornburg v. Port of Portland,[58] a city airport verged on the complainant's dwelling. This house was not under, but to one side of a glide path and near the end of a runway. The noise of landing jet planes was intolerable to all who lived in the complainant's home. The trial judge dismissed the plaintiff's suit on the ground that airplane noise, alone, is not a taking for public use, and therefore, under the Oregon constitution, the city was not obliged to compensate this almost dispossessed landowner. Justice Goodwin said, "[W]e must decide whether a [noise] nuisance can amount to a taking . . . . [T]he inquiry should have been whether the government had undertaken a course of conduct on its own land which, in simple fairness to its neighbors, required it to obtain more land so that the substantial burdens of the activity would fall upon public land, rather than upon that of involuntary contributors who happen to lie in the path of progress." The case was remanded with instructions to the trial judge ordering retrial of the taking issue. The word "taking," since it was used in the Oregon constitution, had a history of interpretation before the Port of Portland case; it had become a legal word of art. Three of the nine Oregon Supreme Court justices dissented from the court's holding on the ground that the constitutional term "taking" did not cover any nuisance whatsoever. We need not, however, dig into this arcane problem of constitutional interpretation because Justice Goodwin also rested liability on the city's use or exploitation of neighboring land.

In another line of cases courts have held that proprietors whose non-governmental activities are properly located and operated with due care must nevertheless pay for harassing their neighbors. For example, in Valley Poultry Farms, Inc. v. Preece [59] a commercial poultry raiser operated in an appropriate rural area not far from two dwellings; the plant's operations conformed to the highest standards of care and consideration.[60] Nevertheless, the neighbors were greatly disconcerted by early

58. 233 Or. 178, 376 P.2d 100 (1962).

59. 406 S.W.2d 413 (Ky.1966).

60. The state farm federation filed an amicus brief which stressed the importance of the state's poultry industry and which characterized the defendant's plant design as the best known. The jury found specially that the plant was carefully designed and operated.

morning noise, summertime odor, etc., which depreciated the value of their property. The appellate court affirmed a five thousand dollar judgment for the plaintiffs. The poultry raiser's liability does not rest on the ground that he acted improperly; the rationale of this case is that the devaluation of the neighboring property should be a cost of the poultry business, rather than a permissible invasion of the plaintiff's enjoyment of their property. In a sense, then, the defendant's only legal fault was that he was making an unpaid-for use of someone else's property. Similarly, in Jost v. Dairyland Power Cooperative,[61] farmers proved that an air-polluting power plant blighted trees and crops. The power company offered evidence of its due care in construction and operation of its plant. The trial judge sustained an objection to the admission of this evidence. The appellate court approved the exclusion and held that lack of negligence was no defense because the company's relentless invasion of the farmers' property, in itself, subjected it to liability for compensatory damages.[62] In Meat Producers, Inc. v. McFarland,[63] the case in which the plaintiff owned several hundred acres of exurban land which would have been suitable for small acreage residential use but for the malodor of a nearby, properly operated feedlot, the court awarded the acreage owner compensation for the feedlot's devaluation of his acreage. The court said (as Judge Robert Keeton would),[64] that some business ventures are reasonable only when those engaged in them pay for the harmful consequences inflicted on their neighbors.[65]

§ 10. THE EFFECT OF LEGISLATIVE AND ADMINISTRATIVE RULES ON LIABILITY FOR PRIVATE NUISANCES

State legislatures only occasionally enact laws that deal expressly with private nuisances; when they do, they rarely precisely identify impermissible land uses. One case in which the

61. 45 Wis.2d 164, 172 N.W.2d 647 (1969).

62. Compare Greyhound Leasing & Financial Corp. v. Joiner City Unit, supra note 43.

63. 476 S.W.2d 406 (Tex.Civ.App. 1972).

64. Keeton, Conditional Fault in the Law of Torts, 72 Harv.L.Rev. 1 (1959). The author, who was a professor of law when that was written has been recently appointed a federal district judge.

65. See Wagner v. Burlington Industries, Inc., 47 F.R.D. 146 (E.D. Tenn.1969), in which the court likened the vibration of a high-speed loom (which damaged an adjoining structure) to an air pollution nuisance, and ruled out the defense that the weaver used due care and skill. The court said the weaver could not so "appropriate" its neighbor's property to its own use.

specific terms of a statute did guide judicial action was decided by the Supreme Court of Wyoming in 1966. A clause of an enactment provided that an annoying exposure of dead animals or slaughterhouse offal within one-half mile of an inhabited dwelling is "a nuisance detrimental to public health." The statute did not, however, confer a private cause of action on residents subjected to such a stench. A processor of rabbit carcasses (who sold the meat to mink raisers and cured the hides) accumulated viscera and offal in his yard in uncovered barrels. A trailer court was located a block away; its occupants asked the court for a protective injunction. The trial judge refused relief. The Supreme Court of Wyoming reversed, saying that a legislative definition of nuisance could not be ignored merely because complainants should not have been annoyed or were not bothered enough to warrant a harsh injunction.[66]

In the same year, a New Hampshire papermaker polluted a waterway with smelly liquors and decaying waste. It tried to defend its practices in a private nuisance suit on the ground that a statute gave it a privilege to dump its refuse into the river. Fifteen downstream land occupants sued to enjoin this pollution. The manufacturer based its defense on a statute in which the legislature had characterized this waterway as a "class D" river, and further provided that no abatement order lay against polluters of class D rivers for three years. The Supreme Court of New Hampshire rejected this defense.[67] Even though the manufacturer committed no "public nuisance," said the court, the statute did not affect private nuisance suits for harassments not suffered by the public at large. Each of these holdings can be looked upon either as statutory interpretation of the enactments in question or as proper exercise of judicial power, performed with due deference to legislative intentions, but dealing with gaps in the legislation. Had the legislatures spoken clearly in these statutes on the subject of private nuisance suits, their manifested intentions would have foreclosed judicial options.

A Louisiana nuisance statute (1) prohibits land occupants from making any work which *causes damages* to a neighbor, but (2) allows an occupant to *inconvenience* a neighbor. In Daigle v. Continental Oil Co.,[68] a federal judge, applying Louisiana law, had to decide which of these two characterizations applied to a plant dropping "carbon black" on a small residential enclave

66. Hillmer v. McConnell Bros., 414 P.2d 972 (Wyo.1966).

67. Urie v. Franconia Paper Corp., 107 N.H. 131, 218 A.2d 360 (1966);

see also, Maykut v. Plasko, 170 Conn. 310, 365 A.2d 1114 (1976).

68. 277 F.Supp. 875 (W.D.La.1967).

located in a large industrial area. Carbon black settled incessantly and tenaciously on houses, cars, and gardens. This intrusion, said the court, was no mere inconvenience; the occupants of these blackened dwellings were therefore entitled to relief.[69]

Zoning ordinances sometimes narrow land uses permitted by the common law. In Shifflett v. Baltimore County,[70] a zoning ordinance excluded junkyards from residential areas. A junk dealer contended, unsuccessfully, that this ordinance was unconstitutional. The court held that separating junkyards and residences was a proper exercise of the police power.[71]

Harassers accused of nuisance sometimes contend that their conformity to zoning law justifies their activities. For example, the nighttime operations of a truck repair and service station were brightly lighted and noisy; the glare and sound irked residential next-door neighbors. The area had long been zoned for commercial uses and teemed with industrial activities. The court dismissed the dwellers' suit on the ground that the floodlighting and disquiet were appropriate in this area, which was legislatively declared to be an industrial zone.[72]

On the other hand, land uses expressly authorized by zoning laws have nevertheless been enjoined as private nuisances. In a

69. Compare Cole v. City of Osceola, 179 N.W.2d 524 (Iowa 1970), in which the court cited a statute allowing municipalities, in the exercise of their police power, to pass ordinances regulating land use; the statute declared that structures violating these ordinances were "nuisances," which courts might abate at the behest of either the municipality or any of its property owners. The city intervened in a private suit to enjoin departure from an ordinance; an injunction was granted.

The Oklahoma constitution provides for sweeping liability for noxious land use. See British-American Oil Producing Co. v. McClain, 191 Okl. 40, 126 P.2d 530 (1942).

70. 247 Md. 151, 230 A.2d 310 (1967).

71. But see Northwest Water Corp. v. Pennetta, 29 Colo.App. 1, 479 P.2d 398 (1970), in which the water company built a large standpipe in a residential zone. The trial judge ruled that the company's tower violated the zoning ordinance and, therefore, constituted a nuisance. He entered a $4,000 judgment on a jury verdict. The appellate court, however, held that the zoning ordinance was not ineluctably controlling, and ordered the trial judge to allow the jury to determine whether or not the company's tower was unreasonable in a residential zone.

72. See Harrison v. Indiana Auto Shredders Co., 528 F.2d 1107 (7th Cir. 1976); Leonard v. Gagliano, 459 S.W.2d 732 (Mo.App.1970). And see Mercer v. Brown, 190 So. 2d 610 (Fla.App.1966), in which the court held that legislative zoning of an area for agriculture authorized the operation of a well-run, large-scale, smelly hog farm. Compare Oak Haven Trailer Ct., Inc. v. Western Wayne County Conservation Ass'n, supra note 42, in which the court recognized that zoning laws were useful in deciding the suitability of the location of some unusual activities, i. e., a shooting club in an agricultural zone.

1972 Colorado case,[73] a householder kept a horse in a neighborhood zoned residential. The zoning law provided that horses might be kept in this residential zone. The trial judge found that even though the horse's owner exercised all reasonable care, the annoyance to the neighbors constituted a private nuisance. He ordered the defendant to remove the horse. Both of the appellate courts affirmed. The justification of this holding, if there is one, is that this zoning ordinance either does not or cannot affect private nuisance suits. This judicial disdain for legislative judgment, even though the ordinance's provision may be both substantively wise and technically defensible, seems unsound. If the horse owner had relied on the zoning law when he bought the property, his reasonable expectations were thwarted. Since the legislative body especially considered the very problem before the court, change should probably be made legislatively rather than by the court. A dissenting judge said that land use regulation may be better conceived when promulgated by a legislative body than when imposed by judicial decision; the courts, he opined, may hamper land use planning.[74] Of course sloppy land occupants, even though they conform to zoning law, may be so sloppy that they commit a nuisance.[75]

Municipal administrative decisions contrary to earlier enacted zoning ordinances are likely to be respected by courts unless they are capricious and constitute an abuse of discretion.[76]

When an administrative agency considers and authorizes a specific use of a particular plot of land, the meaning of its order rarely leaves room for judicial interpretation—especially when the permittee proceeds to make a use more noxious than that approved by the agency. In Ruppel v. Ralston Purina Co., [77] a Missouri Water Pollution Board authorized a turkey packer to build a plant on a designated industrial site. The permit allowed the packer to process eleven thousand birds a day, and specified that the packer could discharge fifty gallons of waste water per bird. It exceeded its permit and not only packed twenty thousand birds a day, but also discharged seventy gallons of waste water per bird. The waste water stood in open lagoons near the com-

---

73. Hobbs v. Smith, 177 Colo. 299, 493 P.2d 1352 (1972).

74. Compare the majority and the dissenting opinions in Green v. Castle Concrete Co., 181 Colo. 309, 509 P.2d 588 (1973), decided by the same court in the same state one year later. And see Harrison v. Indiana Shredders Co., 528 F.2d 1107 (7th Cir. 1976).

75. See, e. g., Cox v. Schlachter, 147 Ind.App. 530, 262 N.E.2d 550 (1970).

76. See Brent v. City of Detroit, 27 Mich.App. 628, 183 N.W.2d 908 (1970), and Wood v. Town of Wilton, 156 Conn. 304, 240 A.2d 904 (1968).

77. 423 S.W.2d 752 (Mo.1968).

plaining householder's dwelling. The overload exacerbated stench and attracted swarms of noxious insects. The Pollution Board ignored the householder's complaints, but a nuisance action got him a judgment for twenty-five thousand dollars in compensatory damages, plus fifteen thousand in punitive damages. This exemplifies judicial respect for administrative judgment on reasonable land use (which the Water Pollution Board itself had made and then inexplicably ignored).

An order issued by a less reluctant, but ineffective agency was superseded by judicial action in Roy v. Farr.[78] Several householders living in a residential area complained to the town's Board of Health about the defendant's discharge of raw sewage into a watercourse passing their dwellings. The health officer ordered the defendant to stop polluting the stream, and notified him that if his pollution continued, the Board would exercise its statutory authority to make changes in his disposal system at the defendant's expense. (The statute which conferred authority on the Board permitted, but did not expressly require, it to make and carry out such a threat.) The polluter ignored the Board of Health's order; the Board, however, did not carry through its threat. The offended householders brought an action asking the court to issue a writ of mandamus compelling the Board to abate this nuisance. The Supreme Court of Vermont issued the writ. Even though the Board's decisions to inspect and issue a remedial order were discretionary, said the court, once the Board got that far its failure to carry through was an arbitrary abuse of the Board's lawful authority.[79] The court justified its decision by saying that, if the writ were not issued, the plaintiff would be unjustly saddled with expense and subjected to delay incident to personal litigation.

At the other end of the spectrum are defendants who invoke administrative approval of their land uses to protect themselves from liability. In a Nebraska case,[80] a refuse-disposal company planned a sanitary landfill on a quarter-section of land. The Nebraska State Department of Health licensed the landfill, requiring that the licensee conform to the Department's landfill rules. Habitants, most of whom lived more than a mile away, asked the court to enjoin the licensee from carrying out its plan. The court relied on the Board's rulings and refused to enjoin the licensee.[81] Harrison v. Indiana Auto Shredders Co.,[82] was a di-

78. 128 Vt. 30, 258 A.2d 799 (1969).

79. See Schwarz v. Ferrara, 63 Misc.2d 135, 311 N.Y.S.2d 211 (1970).

80. Horn v. Community Refuse Disposal, Inc., 186 Neb. 43, 180 N.W. 2d 691 (1970).

81. See also, Hood v. Winding Vista Recreation, Inc., 222 Ga. 345,

82. See note 82 on page 280.

versity of citizenship case involving the nuisance law of Indiana. The Honorable Thomas C. Clark, retired from the United States Supreme Court, sat on the Seventh Circuit bench by designation and wrote the long and interesting opinion. The trial judge had enjoined the operation of an automobile shredding plant. The plant had been built on a plot of land zoned by the city-county council for the heaviest industrial use. The zoning law permitted scrap metal operations in areas so designated, conditioned on conformity to detailed regulations on air pollution, vibration, noise, health hazards, landscaping, etc. The defendant's witnesses testified without contradiction that after some start-up violations, the shredder conformed to all relevant codes and ordinances except the landscaping regulations. The circuit court held that although the landscaping requirements must be met, an order shutting down the plant was unwarranted.

In a previously discussed Louisiana case,[83] the State Board of Health granted a permit to a chemical company allowing the burial of poisonous chemical wastes. The plaintiff feared that buried poisons would seep into his well. Uncontradicted expert testimony tended to prove that, were the disposal pit lined with clay, the poisons could not leak out. The Supreme Court of Louisiana, apparently more impressed by the experts than by the Department of Health, ordered clay linings and permitted the company to bury its waste. This court's decision, apparently, turned on a point that the administrative agency had ignored; this holding exemplifies judicial supplementation of administrative action.[84]

There are times when an administrative license has nothing to do with whether or not a land use is reasonable. In Richmond Bros., Inc. v. Hagemann,[85] the plaintiff, who had been licensed by the Federal Communication Commission to operate a radio station at a specified location, sought to enjoin an abutting neighbor from erecting structures that would skew its signal. The court denied relief on the ground that the broadcaster's license conferred no right on it to control its neighbors' proper use of their own property.[86] Administrative permission to

149 S.E.2d 784 (1966), in which the court held that a planning commission's permit approving a proposed swim club in a residential area barred the neighbors' suit for an injunction.

82. 528 F.2d 1107 (7th Cir. 1976).

83. Salter v. B.W.S. Corp., Inc., 290 So.2d 821 (La.1974).

84. Compare Schiller v. Raley, 405 S.W.2d 446 (Tex.Civ.App.1966).

85. 359 Mass. 265, 268 N.E.2d 680 (1971).

86. See People ex rel. Hoogasian v. Sears, Roebuck & Co., 52 Ill.2d 301, 287 N.E.2d 677 (1972), an unsuccessful effort by property owners to stop the defendant from

develop property so that the development will interfere with a pleasing view is not needed to bolster the American common-law immunity from liability for obstructing light and air.[87]

Courts, on occasion, ask administrative agencies to investigate the facts of a case to be decided. In Dutton v. Rocky Mountain Phosphates,[88] the defendant had been an intentional and unreasonable air polluter, whose emissions of fluorine sickened livestock and blighted vegetation. The trial judge rendered a hundred thousand dollar-plus judgment for damages already inflicted; nevertheless, he found that the defendant had adopted safeguards adequate to stop future pollution, and, therefore, he entered no injunction. On appeal, the Supreme Court of Montana was unsure that the nuisance was arrested. It instructed the trial judge to determine whether or not, during the two years since the trial, the pollution had really ceased; it suggested that the trial judge appoint the State Board of Health, or some other inspection agency, to reinvestigate the amount of fluorine emitted by the defendant's works.

Those administrative agencies that are given authority to deal with problems of environmental control often ask for and receive judicial rulings putting force behind their orders.[89]

completing a 110-story Chicago building that would distort television reception on the plaintiffs' property. The builder's compliance with whatever zoning and building permits he had, of course, were not used to support the decision.

87. For example, in Katcher v. Home Sav. & Loan Ass'n, 245 Cal. App.2d 425, 53 Cal.Rptr. 923 (1961), four householders tried to enjoin the erection of structures that would obstruct their spectacular outlook over the San Fernando Valley. The claim was summarily dismissed. The appellate court's ground for affirmance was that, absent the adjoining landowner's covenant to refrain from obstructing the householders' views, they had no such easement.

A 1979 New Hampshire nuisance case, Heston v. Ousler, —— N.H. ——, 398 A.2d 536, reached a reasonable, but unprecedented contrary view. The parties to a nuisance suit owned abutting land on Lake Winnipesankee, a large locus of many summer homes. The de-

fendant extended his dock in such a way that the plaintiff could no longer see the lake from his house. A master found the defendant's obstruction of the view to be a nuisance and that reasonable land use required a thirty-foot "buffer zone" where neither party should be permitted to maintain dockage, a ruling that would preserve the view of both parties. The New Hampshire Supreme Court affirmed a decree that adopted the buffer zone and required the defendant to remove his dock. This novel holding seems to take little from the defendant, while greatly benefitting the plaintiff. On other facts, however, protection of one person's view may deprive a neighbor of too much. The nuisance criterion, "unreasonable land use," allows for sufficient flexibility if it is used wisely.

88. 151 Mont. 54, 438 P.2d 674 (1968).

89. See, e. g., United States v. Bishop Processing Co., 423 F.2d 469

§ 11. INJUNCTIONS AGAINST NUISANCE

Historically, "injunction" decrees were issued only "in chancery," i. e., by the Courts of Equity. "Abatements" of nuisances, however, were at times ordered by "common law" courts, and could be had without applying to an equity court.[90] Modern American courts tend to look on all decrees arresting nuisances as equitable, and, therefore, our judges issue injunctions only when chancery courts would have used that remedy.

One requisite of "equitable" jurisdiction over a case was the inadequacy of the plaintiff's remedies at common law. This limitation is exemplified by the 1973 case of Atchison, Topeka & Santa Fe Ry. v. Parmer.[91] Four ranchers alleged that dry grass, weeds and brush accumulated on the railroad's right-of-way where it adjoined their pastures; that the railroad's locomotives, as the result of improper maintenance, had set fires that damaged two of the plaintiffs' pastures. The trial judge ordered the company to remove growths of easily kindled trash from its right-of-way. The appellate court dissolved this injunction on the ground that the ranchers' remedy at law was adequate. The plaintiffs were, said the court, suitably protected against future harm by their rights to recover for damages inflicted by fire in actions at law. The trial judge's injunction, had it been approved, would have set the stage for contempt proceedings whenever one of the ranchers worried about the flammability of the roadway. The appellate court thought that claims for damages, if and when pastures happened to be burned, would be a simpler use of the judicial process.

Courts of equity are loath to shut down a useful, but annoying venture when a less drastic equitable decree will do justice to the complainants. In Hilliard v. Shuff,[92] for example, a truck-stop operator built gasoline storage tanks five feet from an adjoining residential lot. Explosive vapors issued from vents in these tanks, and created a fifteen foot wide danger area across the end of the complainant's backyard. The appellate court held

(4th Cir. 1970), in which Delaware and Maryland health agencies and the United States Department of Health, Education and Welfare jointly asked the court to help them suppress the stench emitted by an animal rendering plant. Diamond [Commissioner of Environmental Conservation of the State of New York] v. Peter Cooper Corp., 65 Misc.2d 823, 317 N.Y. S.2d 40 (1970), is a similar case.

90. See London Assize of Nuisance, supra note 2, at pp. xviii–xix.

91. 496 S.W.2d 241 (Tex.Civ.App. 1973).

92. 260 La. 384, 256 So.2d 127 (1971).

that the trial judge erred when, without giving thought to whether or not steps could be taken to make the tanks reasonably safe, he ordered the tanks removed. Similarly, in Krulikowski v. Polycast Corp.,[93] the trial judge ordered a plexiglass manufacturer to stop its emission of nauseating odor; nevertheless, he stayed the execution of his injunction for a time in order to give the manufacturer a chance to make its venture tolerable by building a ventilating system that would carry off the stench through a high stack. This tempered injunction was affirmed.

Some judicial attempts to correct harassment, rather than entirely forbidding an annoying activity, call for ongoing supervision. Continual oversight was, historically, uncongenial to equity's chancellors. In disregard of this tradition, one judge trying a nuisance suit brought by neighbors of a dusty, noisy automobile racetrack, ordered a complicated program to make the racetrack tolerable; he decreed a detailed schedule of racing, specific measures to alleviate dust and regulations on the use of floodlights; he further ordered that the case remain under his jurisdiction until he could review the effectiveness of his intricate decree. The appellate court found this judicial involvement distasteful and substituted an order enjoining the defendant from holding automobile races.[94] The Court said that earlier decrees qualifying injunctions did not call for such complex supervision.

There are, however, many authorities for injunctions that impose a substantial burden of supervision upon the trial court.[95] Whenever the major provocation of a nuisance is disquieting noise, courts tend to approve decrees ordering specified reductions in hum, racket, clatter, or bang.[96]

Sometimes judicial attempts to ameliorate nuisances without closing down the defendant's business are failures. For example, a protracted attempt in Michigan to reduce the incompatability of mushroom-growing and urban homemaking went awry.

93. 153 Conn. 661, 220 A.2d 444 (1966).

94. Jones v. Queen City Speedways, Inc., 276 N.C. 231, 172 S.E.2d 42 (1970).

95. In Kasala v. Kalispell Pee Wee Baseball League, 151 Mont. 109, 439 P.2d 65 (1968), the trial judge enjoined all Pee Wee League baseball games. The games had caused a wide variety of annoyances. The appellate court reversed on several grounds; it said, among other things, that a nuisance arising out of a legitimate activity justified a decree forbidding only its objectionable components. See also, Corporation of Presiding Bishop v. Ashton, 92 Idaho 571, 448 P.2d 185 (1968).

96. See Oak Haven Trailer Ct., Inc., supra note 42 (gun club); Nair v. Thaw, supra note 29 (noisy air conditioning); O'Neill v. Carolina Freight Carriers Corp., 156 Conn. 637, 244 A.2d 372 (1968) (noisy nighttime activities at a truck terminal).

The mushrooms, it seems, were raised in composted straw, wheat, and horse manure. These beds emitted an intolerable redolence. After householders' proof in 1965 of their exasperation the trial judge ordered growers to take specified measures calculated to reduce the smell. The growers conscientiously obeyed the decree, but more than a year later the smell was still intolerable. The trial judge then forbade further composting. The appellate court held that the injunction, which would close down the growers' enterprises was too drastic and instructed the trial judge to try harder to work out a less drastic solution.[97] Further deodorization proved unsatisfactory, and a year later the appellate court wistfully affirmed an order forbidding growers from composting.[98]

Sometimes courts merely order the operator of a nuisance to eliminate the noxious aspect of its process within a stated time; these decrees do not specify how the defendant should proceed, but threaten a closedown unless the operator finds a way to stop giving offense.[99] In one case,[1] the court ordered a dealer in coal to continue to implement its coal dust abatement program until a further hearing, which was to be held within the ensuing six months. The court ruled that, since economical and feasible dust control was possible, the court would retain jurisdiction, in hope that the problem could be solved without destroying the defendant's business. It seems, therefore, that the courts have become less obdurate; they no longer insist invariably on reaching an immediate decision at the end of trial when, at that time, the only definitive alternatives are either perpetual annoyance or business disaster.

§ 12.   "BALANCING THE EQUITIES"

In a Maine case[2] the plaintiff's claim was trivial, the defendant's wrong clear but inconsequential, and the remedy of mandatory injunction unjustly burdensome. These were the facts: The defendant built a house next door to the plaintiff's residence; his contractor set the house's foundations, in violation of

97. Fortin v. Vitali, note 14 supra and accompanying test.

98. Id.

99. See, e. g., Gerrish v. Wishbone Farm of N. H., Inc., 108 N.H. 237, 231 A.2d 622 (1967) (egg producer given three months to develop more hygenic chicken manure disposal); Cook Industries, Inc. v. Carlson, 334 F.Supp. 809 (N.D. Miss.1971) (cotton oil mill operator given a reasonable time, but not later than January 1, 1973, to quit offensive water pollution).

1. Biechele v. Norfolk & W. Ry. Co., 309 F.Supp. 354 (N.D.Ohio 1969).

2. Levasseur v. Dubuc, 229 A.2d 201 (Me.1967).

ordinances, an inch or so too close to the side and front lines of the lot. The plaintiff asked the court to order the defendant to move the foundations. The trial judge characterized the deviations as negligible and committed in good faith; the relief requested would, he said, be disproportionately harsh to any benefit it would confer on the plaintiff. He therefore gave the plaintiff a hundred dollar money judgment. The affirming appellate court said, "Plastic remedies of equity are molded to the needs of justice."

Should a small property owner have a right to shut down a truly annoying, but gigantic enterprise? The earlier-discussed classic case giving a less severe remedy is Madison v. Ducktown Sulphur Copper & Iron Co.,[3] decided early in the twentieth century. The complainants were seven hillbilly farmers subsisting on poor land worth little money. By comparison, the worth of the defendants' plants was enormous. The copper companies' smelting fires gave off sulphurous smoke seriously damaging the farmers. The companies had sought to eliminate their emissions of sulphurous smoke, but found no way short of shutting down. The two ventures had attracted a twenty-fold population increase; the smeltries purchased large supplies of local fuel; and their product was a boon to the nation. The Supreme Court of Tennessee refused to "blot out two great mining and manufacturing enterprises." The court ruled that its equitable powers included discretionary denial of injunctive relief in nuisance cases, even when the plaintiff is clearly entitled to money damages. This doctrine is often referred to as "balancing the equities" and has been asserted in many modern cases.[4]

Some courts purport to disavow the doctrine of balancing the equities. The New York Court of Appeals formerly took this posture. In 1970, however, that court expressly reversed a long line of cases; it held that a dust-emitting cement plant, built in a proper place at a cost of forty-five million dollars and using all available dust control devices, would be ordered to pay substantial damages to a number of neighbors but would not be enjoined from continuing its operations.[5] Other courts seem to re-

3. 113 Tenn. 331, 83 S.W.2d 658 (1904).

4. See, e. g., Daigle v. Continental Oil Co., supra note 18; Koseris v. J. R. Simplot Co., 82 Idaho 263, 352 P.2d 235 (1960); Storey v. Central Hide & Rendering Co., 148 Tex. 509, 226 S.W.2d 615 (1950).

5. Boomer v. Atlantic Cement Co., 26 N.Y.2d 219, 309 N.Y.S.2d 312, 257 N.E.2d 870 (1970). The court said that the judicial power in private litigation, should rarely be exercised for achieving public objectives beyond the rights and interests of the parties before it; the court said expressly that it was not foreclosing public health

ject the doctrine of balancing the equities in cases in which they grant limited injunctions requiring perpetrators of nuisances to seek out ways of reducing their offensiveness, but do not close them down entirely.[6] Of course, the doctrine of balancing equities has its limits; the operator of a costly plant did not, for example, fall under the protection of the doctrine when it polluted more than three hundred gallons of water per minute and dumped its offensive effluent into a watercourse that crossed the plaintiff's farm, a mile away.[7]

In one interesting case, the offended plaintiff was given his injunction, but was required to balance the equities by paying damages *to the defendant*! A developer bought up several contiguous ranches for a town site at a cost of fifteen million dollars. The new town, Sun City, Arizona, grew gradually from north to south, eventually approaching a sizable feedlot. When the town was a small and distant village, the feedlot's capacity was expanded to fatten thirty thousand cattle per year. The penned animals excreted a million pounds of wet manure a day. The thirteen hundred Sun City residential lots nearest to the feedlot were, not surprisingly, unsaleable. The developer sued to enjoin the feeder from continuing to fatten cattle on its premises. The Supreme Court of Arizona affirmed the trial judge's order closing down the feedlot; nevertheless, it remanded the case and instructed the trial judge to award the feeder appropriate damages for its cost of moving to a suitable new location.[8] The court justified its remand on the ground that the developer knew that his activity was likely to transform the feeder's lawful activity into a nuisance.

or other public agencies from taking appropriate action against the cement producers in the future.

6. In Gerrish v. Wishbone Farm of N.H., Inc., 108 N.H. 237, 231 A.2d 622 (1967), a six million dollar egg production plant emitted an intolerable stench. The trial judge enjoined the plant's method of manure disposal, but gave the operator three months to devise a less offensive method. The appellate court characterized the egg producer's invocation of the doctrine of balancing the equities as a contention that expensive smells should be allowed to continue. The court nevertheless said that if no better method of disposal was found in the three months allowed by the trial judge, the defendant could ask the trial judge for more time.

This case differs from Madison v. Ducktown Sulphur, Copper & Iron Co., supra note 3, in which the copper companies proved that they were unable to stay in business and avoid air pollution. The court in Gerrish opined that the egg company would probably find a way to become a more tolerable neighbor without reducing its productivity.

7. Blue Ridge Poultry & Egg Co. v. Clark, 211 Va. 139, 176 S.E.2d 323 (1970).

8. Spur Industries, Inc. v. Del E. Webb Development Co., 108 Ariz. 178, 494 P.2d 700 (1972).

One defendant maladroitly deprived itself of an opportunity to pay off a plaintiff at a small price, and as a result incurred the burden of a very onerous injunction. In Estancias Dallas Corp. v. Schultz [9] a householder complained of noisy air-conditioning equipment installed close to his dwelling. The machinery cooled fifty-five apartments in an eight-building complex. The noise generated was like that made by a helicopter or a jet aircraft. Had the builder originally installed eight smaller units (one for each of its buildings), the air-conditioning system would have cost an additional sixty thousand dollars. Replacement of the big tower with eight smaller ones would, at the time of the suit, have cost two hundred thousand dollars. Apparently the total value of the householder's property before the apartment complex was built was about twenty-five thousand dollars; the nuisance reduced that value by about one-half. Had some form of the doctrine of balancing the equities been applied to these facts, the apartment complex owner stood to lose around twelve or thirteen thousand dollars. The defense counsel, however, thoughtlessly moved to require the householder to elect his remedy, i. e., to choose between injunction or money damages. The householder opted for an injunction. The trial judge ordered the defendant to deactivate its noisy tower. The Texas Court of Civil Appeals affirmed; the appellate court refused to consider the doctrine of balancing the equities because defense counsel's tactics curtailed proof of damages. This injunction became a valuable asset to the householder; he probably sold it to the apartment owner for much more money than the amount of damages that he could have recovered.

The doctrine of balancing the equities does not privilege expensive and socially valuable enterprises to escape all liability for private nuisances; it merely protects some defendants from injunctions without diminishing their victims' rights to sue for any damages to which they may be entitled. In Cox v. Schlachter,[10] the defendant was a breeder of white mice used for research on cancer and malaria. The appellate court affirmed a judgment awarding damages to neighbors harassed by the smell of the defendant's half-million dollar mousery. The court said that though the business was vitally useful to all people, the defendant's lax and negligent sanitary procedures had nothing to do with the social import of his business.[11] In Meat Producers,

9. 500 S.W.2d 217 (Tex.Civ.App. 1973).

10. 147 Ind.App. 530, 262 N.E.2d 550 (1970).

11. See Furrer v. Talent Irrigation Dist., 258 Or. 494, 466 P.2d 605 (1970).

Inc. v. McFarland,[12] a feedlot operator was sued only for damages. The appellate court affirmed the plaintiff's substantial money judgment, saying that when liability for damages is in question, the defendant's interference with its neighbor may be unreasonable even though the public utility of the defendant's services are great and the harm it does is relatively small. Continuation of a useful activity, said the court, may be reasonable only if the venturer pays for the harm it does.[13]

§ 13. THE MEASURE OF MONEY DAMAGES FOR NUISANCE

When unreasonable land use persists for only a limited term, those who were harassed may be entitled to damages for the harm that was inflicted on them.

Sometimes the proof establishes special damaging circumstances entitling a plaintiff to unusual compensation. In one case, for example, a subdivider's half million dollar investment in lakeside land devalued when a fertilizer manufacturer polluted lake water and air. The manufacturer, after a time, stopped emitting pollutants. During the nuisance's persistence, the sales value of the unsold lots depreciated; the value of these lots, nevertheless, bounced back to its original level when the pollution ended. The court held that the developer was entitled to interest on the decrease in sales value during the period of pollution.[14]

More often, perpetrators of temporary nuisances are obliged to compensate their victims for the reduced rental value of the victims' property for the term of the nuisance.[15] The plaintiff has the burden of proving these damages and ordinarily carries this burden by adducing expert testimony.

In Davoust v. Mitchell,[16] (the case in which the defendant was ordered to keep his dog quieter and his kennel cleaner), the court ruled that, since the complainant proved no lost rental value, he could recover no money. There is authority, however, for recovery of "personal damages" without proof of reduced rental value. In Aguayo v. Village of Chama,[17] a number of household-

---

12. 476 S.W.2d 406 (Tex.Civ.App. 1972).

13. See also, Jost v. Dairyland Power Cooperative, 45 Wis.2d 164, 172 N.W.2d 647 (1969).

14. Wilson v. Farmers Chem. Ass'n, 60 Tenn.App. 102, 444 S.W.2d 185 (1969).

15. See, e. g., Wagner v. Burlington Industries, Inc., 47 F.R.D. 146 (E. D.Tenn.1969).

16. 146 Ind.App. 536, 257 N.E.2d 332 (1970).

17. 79 N.M. 729, 449 P.2d 331 (1969). But see Harrison v. Indiana Auto Shredders Co., 528 F.2d 1107 (7th Cir. 1976).

ers sued a municipality for damages; they proved only that the village, for a period of time, dumped raw sewage near the vicinity of their houses. The residents prayed for a judgment of ten dollars per household for each day of wrongdoing. The trial judge denied this prayer on the ground that the plaintiffs had offered no proof of reduced rental values. The Supreme Court of New Mexico held that the trial judge erred and remanded the case ordering the trial judge to award appropriate damages to the plaintiffs for annoyance and discomfort.

When victims of a nuisance, since abated, adequately prove that, during its course, the nuisance proximately caused various amounts of physical harm (to livestock, crops, and so on) appropriate compensation is, of course recoverable.[18]

When a complaint is filed soon after a nuisance starts and the court promptly gives injunctive relief, temporary damages is only a trivial issue. If, however, the court refuses, once and for all, to enjoin the nuisance and balances the equities (as it did, for example in Patz v. Farmegg Products, Inc.), the court should award the victim lump-sum compensation for all past and future injuries.[19] (The major item in calculating such an award is likely to be compensation for depreciation of the market value of plaintiff's property.)

Whether or not a nuisance is permanent may, itself, be a disputed question of fact. In Meat Producers, Inc. v. McFarland,[20] a cattle feedlot was a nuisance when in operation. At the time that the case was heard, because meat was cheap and cattle feed was dear, the lot was not in operation. The jury brought in a special verdict characterizing the nuisance as permanent. The court said that this finding justified the jury's substantial money verdict, based on testimony of decreased market value of the plaintiff's land.

Even though a land use results in devaluation of neighboring property, that land use may be reasonable, and, therefore, not a nuisance; the victim suffering such a loss may have no cause of action whatsoever. For example, in Bader v. Iowa Metropolitan Sewer Co.,[21] the defendant had built a sewage treatment lagoon near a speculator's exurban property, which the speculator hoped to subdivide. The lagoon was located and operated so

18. See Dutton v. Rocky Mountain Phosphates, 151 Mont. 54, 438 P.2d 674 (1968).

19. Patz v. Farmegg Products, Inc., 196 N.W.2d 557 (Iowa 1972). See Boomer v. Atlantic Cement Co., 26 N.Y.2d 219, 309 N.Y.S.2d 312, 257 N.E.2d 870 (1970); Valley Poultry Farms, Inc. v. Preece, supra note 39.

20. 476 S.W.2d 406 (Tex.Civ.App. 1972).

21. 178 N.W.2d 305 (Iowa 1970).

that, in the court's view, it was not an unreasonable land use, and therefore, not a nuisance. The speculator offered proof showing that because of the lagoon's proximity, a large fraction of his tract would not be bought for residential use and therefore was substantially devalued. Since his proof did not establish a nuisance said the court, the sewer company was not liable for this depreciation; the company was privileged to make this lawful use of its property without compensating its neighbor.[22]

In the Bader case, the sewage company built its lagoon on a forty-acre tract to the north of the speculator's land. Since only a twenty-two acre fraction of the speculator's eighty acre tract was depreciated by the lagoon, perhaps the sewer company should have sought out a tract slightly larger than its sixty acres, instead of foisting a substantial loss on its neighbor to the south. The company knew, or should have known, that devaluation would result. Judge Keeton would probably say that the sewer company was guilty of conditional fault in knowingly causing this loss without being willing to pay for the harm it perpetrated.[23] The economics of this situation are not easy. The ramifications of requiring the sewer company to pay a substantial sum for the depreciation of twenty-two acres may, perhaps, affect its rates, which in turn could devaluate other properties, and so on. When economic issues are so arcane, courts are bound to be tempted to rely on technical legal doctrine rather than run the risks of choosing between complicated and conflicting expert testimony.

The legal principle that tells courts to determine nuisance, *vel non*, before concerning themselves with depreciation of value of neighboring land, however, rests on only slight authority. That doctrine, favoring enterprise over status quo, has a nineteenth century ring; since it tends to ignore the ecological presumption in favor of the natural, it may not, therefore, remain twentieth century orthodoxy.

22. Compare Nicholson v. Connecticut Half-Way House, Inc., 153 Conn. 507, 218 A.2d 383 (1966).

23. See Keeton, supra note 64.

Chapter XI

MISREPRESENTATION

Table of Sections

---

§ 1. MISREPRESENTATION CONTRASTED WITH OTHER TORTS

False statements can be material events in the commission of many torts. The lie a poisoner uses to induce a victim to eat a poisoned tart is certainly a misrepresentation, but the case is tried as any other battery would be. When a grade crossing guard accidently waves a car into the path of a speeding train, the case concerns negligent misrepresentation but it is tried as any other negligence suit would be. Misrepresentation, as a separate tort, concerns misstatements which result in pecuniary loss. These torts occur when misinformants induce such losses by misstating important business facts.

These torts were not recognized until late in the eighteenth century, and the courts still appear cautious in this area. In an era of *caveat emptor*, sharp practice was not considered blameworthy, or, if blameworthy, not sufficiently so to justify the burden of large judgments. Though fair dealing appears to be valued more highly now than it was two centuries ago, this factor still inhibits liability in this area.

§ 2. THE FAULT REQUIREMENT—SCIENTER

In the 1789 case of Pasley v. Freeman,[1] it was first held that liars can be held liable for business losses their lies had proximately caused. Plaintiffs alleged that defendant had wrongfully and deceitfully encouraged them to extend credit to one Falsh, representing Falsh to be worthy of credit even though defendant knew him not to be; and in reliance on this lie, plaintiffs had sold Falsh valuable goods on credit and were unable to collect. The Court of King's Bench held this declaration stated a cause of action, but the judges were careful to limit their holding. Judge Ashhurst stated, "But it is said that if this be determined to be law, any man may have an action brought against him for telling a lie, by the crediting of which another happens eventually to be injured. But this consequence by no means follows; for in order to make it actionable, it must be accompanied with the circumstances averred in this count, namely, that the defendant, 'intending to deceive and defraud the plaintiffs, did deceitfully encourage and persuade them to do the act, and for that purpose made the false affirmation, in consequence of which they did the act.' . . . [T]he quo animo is a great part of the gist of the action." This case was a belated recognition that the common law principle of grounding liability on fault extends to misrepresentations inducing commercial loss.

Mere negligence was held insufficient to support liability in this area in the leading case of Derry v. Peek.[2] The directors of a tramway company published an offering circular (a "prospectus" in the jargon of corporate finance) to attract investors in the company's stock. The prospectus contained important misstatements. When the company failed, a stockholder who had relied on these misstatements sued the directors. They proved good faith and the case was dismissed. The Court of Appeals reversed on the ground that the directors were careless, and negligence was sufficient fault for liability. The House of Lords, however, agreed with the trial judge and reinstated his dismissal. Lord Herschell's opinion is most often quoted. He said, "First, in order to sustain an action of deceit, there must be proof of fraud, and nothing short of that will suffice. Secondly, fraud is proved when it is shown that a false representation has been made (1) knowingly, or (2) without belief in its truth, or (3) recklessly, careless [3] whether it be true or false. Although I

---

1. 3 Term.Rep. 51, 100 Eng.Rep. 450 (1789)

2. 14 App.Cas. 337 (1889).

3. Note that the context indicates that the word "careless" means "without caring" and does not mean "without due care."

have treated the second and third as distinct cases, I think the third is but an instance of the second, for one who makes a statement under such circumstances can have no real belief in the truth of what he states." The holding of Derry v. Peek— that liability depends on a showing of the misinformant's lack of belief in the truth of the misstatement—is often called by lawyers "the *scienter* [knowledge] requirement." In cases where *scienter* is required, liability cannot be based on mere negligence. But certain kinds of sloppiness somewhat similar to negligence have been held to satisfy the requirement of *scienter*.

In Hadcock v. Osmer,[4] defendant told plaintiff that "The Browns are good for what money you let them have," whereupon plaintiff lent $400 to the Browns. The defendant had no knowledge of the Brown's financial condition. They were, in fact, insolvent and unable to repay the loan. Defendant was held liable to plaintiff because he had represented that he had well founded knowledge of the Brown's condition when he had, at most, merely an unsubstantiated belief. Though he may not have intended to misrepresent the Brown's financial condition, he did knowingly misrepresent that he had a factual basis for his statement, even though he supposed he was speaking the truth.

This approach was extended in the landmark case of Ultramares Corp. v. Touche.[5] A firm of public accountants had certified a financial statement of the Stern company, stating, "[T]he said statement, in our opinion, presents a true and correct view of the financial condition of Fred Stern & Co., Inc." Though the statement represented the company to be sound, it was insolvent and unable to pay the plaintiff who had extended credit in reliance upon the accountants' certificate. The trial court dismissed a count for fraud, but the New York Court of Appeals reversed and remanded for a new trial. The creditor's proof tended to show that the accountants had ignored suspicious circumstances which came to their attention—circumstances which, if investigated, would have shown that the books examined contained fictitious statements about the company's assets. From this proof, Chief Judge Cardozo reasoned, "[T]hey may . . . be found to have acted without information leading to a sincere or genuine belief when they certified to an opinion that the balance sheet faithfully reflected the condition of the business." Thus, in some cases, proof supporting a finding of lack of due care is sufficient to satisfy the *scienter* requirement and sustain a finding of fraud. Proof tending to establish negligent-

4. 153 N.Y. 604, 47 N.E. 923 (1897).   5. 255 N.Y. 170, 174 N.E. 441 (1931).

ly incomplete investigations may tend to show that the reporters lacked belief in the truth of their reports; if a reasonable person would have been more cautious (either by investigating more carefully or by qualifying the reports), then the reporters may have known they were not cautious enough. Proof adequate to support a finding of negligence, therefore, may be sufficient to sustain a finding of fraud—even in the face of defendants' protestations from the witness stand that they honestly believed they had reported truthfully.

§ 3. NEGLIGENT MISREPRESENTATION

As noted above, the English courts originally held that negligent misrepresentation was not actionable. Most other courts agreed. Beginning late in the nineteenth century, a few courts began holding otherwise. The numbers have grown and, with the House of Lords finally agreeing in 1963,[6] the cause of action for negligence is now generally recognized. Undoubtedly this delay can be partially explained by the fact that many deserving victims of negligence could raise an inference of heedlessness and prevail in an action for fraud.

Some deserving plaintiffs could prove only negligence. In International Products Co. v. Erie R.R.,[7] for instance, the owner of stored goods wanted to insure them and asked the bailee the address of the warehouse in which they were stored. The bailees' agent apparently misread the records and gave the wrong address. When the goods burned, the owner suffered a total loss because its insurance only covered goods stored at the mislocation. The court held the bailee liable for its negligence and ruled that good faith was no defense.

Sometimes liability for negligence may not be appropriate. In Vartan Garapedian, Inc. v. Anderson,[8] a rug merchant asked an amateur collector of oriental rugs about the financial standing of a small retailer in the town where the amateur lived. The wholesaler extended credit on the strength of the amateur's favorable reply. In fact, the retailer had a poor credit reputation, although the amateur did not know it. The court held the amateur not liable for this misinformation, saying the amateur had "no duty of preparatory care or subsequent investigation." The court was impressed, also, by the rug merchant's failure to sup-

6. Heldey Byrne & Co. v. Heller & Partners Ltd., [1964] A.C. 465 (1963).

7. 244 N.Y. 331, 155 N.E. 662, cert. denied 275 U.S. 527, 48 S.Ct. 20, 72 L.Ed. 408 (1927).

8. 92 N.H. 390, 31 A.2d 371 (1943).

plement the amateur's report with a report from conventional credit sources.

There are many casual situations in which honest misinformants ought not to be held liable, even though a careful investigation by them would have prevented the loss. One making such an inquiry ought not to expect the informant to be thorough. The rug merchant's inquiry and questions asked of lawyers at social occasions are typical of such situations. The Second Restatement of Torts analogizes these situations to the gratuitous loan of a chattel. The lender's only duty is to disclose any known facts which may make the chattel unsafe for use.[9] Other analogies can be used to argue for the opposite result. A Good Samaritan must act carefully. A gratuitous bailee is liable for negligent damage to the goods. The mere fact that an act is gratuitous is not, in itself, an adequate reason for excusing its sloppy performance.

Renn v. Provident Trust Co.,[10] for instance, appears to be wrongly decided. A creditor of a nearly destitute debtor asked the trust company which administered a trust established by the debtor's grandfather's will for a copy of the will to see whether the debtor had any attachable interest in the trust. The trust company mistakenly sent a copy of a will executed by a different person of the same name. As a result, the creditor did not attempt to seek payment from the trust until other creditors of the debtor had exhausted the debtor's interest. The court held that the trust company was not liable to the creditor for this mistake. "It was not in the line of defendant's business to supply copies of wills to anyone. Trust companies are not the official repositories of such documents, not even of those under which they may act. They, as everyone else, must procure their copies from the register of wills on payment of the regular fee. They do not usually make it a practice to prepare copies for others . . . and it is not alleged that the practice of this defendant was otherwise. It was exceptional and a pure courtesy that it was done in this instance." The case has a superficial resemblance to the rug merchant case, but the differences are important. In both cases, the inquiry was gratuitous and the inquirer did not seek information from more traditional sources. It was surprising that the rug merchant did not supplement the amateur's report with a report from a credit bureau, a source with, presumably, a different data base. It would have been equally surprising if the creditor, believing he already had one copy of the will, had purchased a second copy from the register of wills. Moreover,

9. Restatement, Second, Torts §   10. 328 Pa. 481, 196 A. 8 (1938).
552, Comment c at 129 (1977).

it would be an imposition to require the amateur, who was not in the credit reference business, to make an investigation or speak at his peril; though it would not be an undue imposition to require a trust company, which must use its own files efficiently in its own business, to take care in searching its files when it offers their contents to others.

What authority there is suggests that news media are not liable for negligent misrepresentation.[11] The public demand for the latest news requires hasty publication and limits the amount of care which can be taken to assure accuracy. It may, therefore, be unreasonable for anyone to take large risks based upon the accuracy of an unverified news story. Moreover, the courts are concerned that a momentary lapse could create immense liabilities which would destroy daily news services.

Many of the desirable limitations on liability for negligent misrepresentation could be made by permitting recovery only when reliance was reasonable. Whether reliance is reasonable in any specific case is often a jury question, and the courts seem to have been reluctant to leave this matter to juries. Partially for this reason and partly to avoid crushing liabilities, the courts have attempted to permit only certain misinformants to be liable for negligence. The Second Restatement's formula is, "One who, in the course of his business, profession or employment, or in any other transaction in which he has a pecuniary interest, supplies false information for the guidance of others in their business transactions is subject to liability for pecuniary loss caused to them by their justifiable reliance upon the information, if he fails to exercise reasonable care or competence in obtaining or communicating the information."[12] This formula does not state accurately the holdings of the cases and has little predictive value. It states two tests: (1) whether the informant spoke in the course of business, etc., or (2) whether the informant had a pecuniary interest in the transaction. Certainly the trust company in the wrong-will case had no pecuniary interest

---

11. Jaillet v. Cashman, 235 N.Y. 511, 139 N.E. 714 (1923). A wire service misreported the holding of a Supreme Court case, causing the prices of certain stocks to decline temporarily. The mistake was corrected 45 minutes later. Meanwhile, plaintiff speculated on the market in reliance on the false report. He was unable to recover his losses from the wire service. Cf. MacKown v. Illinois Pub. & Printing Co., 289 Ill. 59, 6 N.E.2d 526 (1937) (Plaintiff could not recover for a skin injury caused by a dandruff remedy prepared according to a recipe published in defendant's newpaper. Presumably, had he suffered an economic loss because he had decided to market the remedy and concocted a large, worthless batch of it, he could not have recovered for the misrepresentation.)

12. Restatement, Second, Torts § 552(1) (1977).

in the transaction, but the information was given in a business context. Assume a person had stepped in off the street to the trust company's teller window, asking the teller to change a $100 bill, and the teller negligently misidentified the bill as a counterfeit. Would the trust company be liable under the first test or not liable under the second?

Courts will not hold casual informants liable for negligence. Amateurs who should not be expected to make thorough investigations will not be held liable because they did not report information such investigations would have revealed. Even experts answering inquiries at social occasions will not be expected to speak at their peril.

At the other extreme are business and professional informants who will be held liable for negligence, with an exception yet to be noted. It is not an undue imposition to require them to investigate carefully or speak at their peril. Though it is true that all casual informants act gratuitously, and most business and professional informants have either a pecuniary interest in the transaction or charge for their services, some business and professional information is given for nothing.

In between these two classes of cases are situations such as the wrong-will case, in which a somewhat casual inquiry occurs in a business context. The informant is not in the business of giving such information, and yet it may not be an undue imposition to require care. When the courts had doubts concerning the propriety of liability for negligent misrepresentation, these cases were decided for defendants. Now that negligence liability is more fully accepted, it will not be surprising if the courts decide these cases for plaintiffs.

The danger of crushing liabilities may override the above analysis in some situations. Generally, this problem has been handled by denying remote victims standing to sue for negligence. It may be that in the case of newspapers and similar media, this even technique will not provide enough protection. The number and magnitude of negligence claims, if recognized, may make daily news service impossible to provide profitably. Therefore, even though newspapers are in the business of providing information and do not do so gratuitously, it may be necessary to hold them immune from liability for negligence.

The general recognition of liability for negligent misrepresentation has not reduced the *scienter* requirement to a historical curiosity. Some plaintiffs who cannot recover for negligence may be able to recover for fraud if they can prove *scienter*. When a defendant's fault borders on heedlessness, therefore, it may be prudent for the plaintiff to accept the burden of proving *scienter*. Although most jurors understand the difference between crookedness and carelessness, many of them will have trouble distinguishing between heedless disregard of the truth and mere negligence. The added burden of proving *scienter*, therefore, may be more apparent than real. A jury which is willing to find negligence will often be as willing to find heedlessness, and plaintiff will avoid the risk that on appeal the court will hold that the defendant cannot be liable to the plaintiff for negligence.

§ 4. INNOCENT MISREPRESENTATION

Liability for misrepresentation without fault has developed only in connection with purchases and sales. Just as fault is not central to the law of contracts or property, fault has not been found necessary for misrepresentation liability between parties to a sale.

Before discussing these cases, it is necessary to review the commercial law response to misrepresentation. Seller represents that a crib contains 500 bushels of corn when it actually contains only 400 bushels. Seller offers the corn to Buyer for $1,000, the going price for 500 bushels. Buyer accepts. Seller has obtained a contract at $200 over the going price for corn. If Buyer is skilled at estimating quantities of corn and knew that Seller erred, Seller may justly enjoy the benefit of this bargain. If, however, Buyer relied on Seller's representation and mistakenly agreed to overpay, Seller has been unjustly enriched. Unless punitive damages are sought, the issue of Seller's fault is irrelevant.

In cases where the parties to a contract have made a mutual mistake or where one party's fraud has induced the other's mistake, commercial and property law have developed the following remedies:

(1) Courts with equity powers have decreed rescission of the transaction, cancelling the deal and, if a contract of sale has been partially or fully performed, have ordered both parties to return the subject matter of the contract, reestablishing the status quo.

(2) Common law courts adopted a similar remedy, permitting buyers to rescind such contracts, tender back the goods received, and recover the amount they paid the seller.

(3) While the contract is wholly executory, both common law and equity courts protect the person injured by the mistake from liability to the other party. In some instances this protec-

tion is extended on the theory that the misrepresentation prevented the making of a binding contract and, in others, that misrepresentation is a defense to a suit to enforce the contract.

(4) Common law courts developed an action for compensatory damages on a breach of warranty theory.

It often happened, in a suit for rescission, that the plaintiff alleged an intentional fraud but was able to prove only that the defendant had misspoken. Defendant then claimed victory because fraud had been pleaded but not proved. Equity courts, nevertheless, invariably ruled for the plaintiff. "Fraud" in equity included an assertion of the truth of a representation which in fact was untrue, even when the asserter reasonably believed the statement was true, when the statement was made to induce reliance by the other party to the bargain. The enormity of the defendant's fault was not relevant since the courts were merely attempting to undo unjust enrichment. When common law courts followed equity in permitting rescission, they also adopted this view. There were, then, two kinds of "fraud": (1) the tort defined in Derry v. Peek, which required *scienter*, and (2) the right to rescission, which did not. In a sizeable minority of jurisdictions, the requirements adequate for rescission spilled over into the law of torts.

For instance, in Ham v. Hart,[13] defendant had a well dug on her property that, according to the well digger's log, produced two gallons of water per minute. Shortly after the well was completed, she stopped using it. A few years later she sold the property to plaintiff and, relying on the well digger's log, represented that the well would produce two gallons per minute. After plaintiff took possession of the land, he discovered the well was worthless and spent over $2,000 to procure a source of water on the land. His suit against the seller was dismissed because the trial court found the defendant had made an honest mistake and there was no *scienter*. On appeal, the case was reversed, the court holding that the rescission test should be used in suits for damages; an honest mistake made in good faith could support a suit for misrepresentation. This was a desirable result. Plaintiff had paid for a water-producing well but had not gotten it. Defendant was unjustly enriched. Had plaintiff rescinded immediately upon discovering that the well was dry, justice would have been done; but after spending over $2,000 improving the property, he could be made whole only by an award of damages.[14]

---

13. 58 N.M. 550, 273 P.2d 748 (1954).

14. Not all jurisdictions have shown a willingness to permit

In some states the courts have justified liability for innocent misrepresentation by finding fictitious fault. In Chatham Furnace v. Moffatt,[15] plaintiff bought an inactive mine full of water and debris. The seller had told the buyer that after the mine was cleared of water and debris, a body of iron ore would be uncovered. In fact, the body of ore described lay outside the tract of land conveyed. The seller had relied upon an old survey that was in error. When the survey had been made, the seller then knew of this error; but, he testified, he had forgotten the history of the survey and had made his statement in good faith. The court found for the buyer, saying, "The charge of fraudulent intent, in an action for deceit, may be maintained by proof of a statement [of fact] made as of the party's own knowledge, which is false . . .; and in such case it is not necessary to make any further proof of an actual intent to deceive. The fraud consists in stating that the party knows the thing to exist when he does not know it to exist; and, if he does not know it to exist, he must ordinarily be deemed to know that he does not." By this fiction, deeming the misinformant to know he did not know, the court created fault where, in fact, there may have been none. Misrepresenters may honestly and reasonably believe they have knowledge and yet be mistaken; if such misrepresenters are liable, they are liable without fault. The seller in the Chatham case—if his evidence is believed—did not intentionally lie; and if a reasonable person can forget a fact once known, he may not have been negligent. This seller profited by his mistake, and rescission would not restore the status quo since the buyer would not recoup the expense of clearing the mine; therefore seller's liability for damages seems appropriate.

Though the Chatham case cited a rescission case as its oldest precedent, its holding is not a simple adoption of the criteria for rescission in tort cases. In Pybus v. Grasso,[16] plaintiff contracted to buy the premises at 15 Ashford Street from the defendant. Defendant gave plaintiff a quitclaim deed to "lot numbered 37" on a certain plat. Both parties tacitly assumed that lot 37 included the building at 15 Ashford Street, but three months later

---

strict liability for sellers' misstatements. The *Ham* case may well be prophetic, but at this writing, not in its own state. In Hockett v. Winks, 82 N.M. 597, 485 P.2d 353 (1971), an opinion devoid of facts so that it is impossible to know whether the buyer could have been made whole by rescission, the court said, "[I]nsofar as the opinion in *Ham* . . .

held that the principle of equity applicable to the rescission of contracts is applicable in the tort of deceit . . . we disavow and hereby overrule that opinion."

15. 147 Mass. 403, 18 N.E. 168 (1888).

16. 317 Mass. 716, 59 N.E.2d 289 (1945).

a survey showed that only a part of the building was on the lot described. The sale probably could have been rescinded on the basis of mutual mistake. Plaintiff, however, sued for damages on the theory of the Chatham case. The claim failed because the claimant did not prove the defendant asserted that the building was wholly on lot 37.

These suits against sellers are functional equivalents of suits for breach of warranty. For instance, in Bergenstock v. Lemay's G.M.C., Inc.,[17] an action for damages brought by a buyer of a second-hand truck, the seller had represented that the truck was manufactured in 1967 or 1968. In fact it was of 1966 vintage. Apparently there was little difference between trucks manufactured in those years. An experienced trucking firm that inspected the truck after purchase did not detect the error. Possibly the seller honestly and reasonably believed his statement. The buyer offered no proof of *scienter* or even negligence. The seller was nevertheless held liable under U.C.C. § 2–313(1)(a) & (b), which provides: "(a) Any affirmation of fact . . . made by the seller to the buyer which relates to the goods and becomes part of the basis of the bargain creates an express warranty that the goods shall conform to the affirmation . . . . (b) Any description of the goods which is made part of the basis of the bargain creates an express warranty that the goods shall conform to the description." Application of this warranty theory, well developed in common law before its codification in the UCC, can result in liability without proof of fault. Warranty law recognizes that a seller who profits from misstatement can incur liability though the seller is neither dishonest nor careless.

Why, then, were the dry well and misplaced iron ore cases characterized as suits for tortious misrepresentation instead of breach of warranty? This characterization appears to have been made to avoid difficulties with some rules of real property law. In the mislocated building case, the parties had contracted for the purchase and sale of the building at 15 Ashford Street, but the buyer was unable to recover for breach of that contract. The court said, "By the rules of law, when a deed is executed in pursuance of a contract for the sale of land, all prior proposals and stipulations are merged, and the deed is deemed to express the final and entire contract between the parties."[18]

17. —— R.I. ——, 372 A.2d 69 (1977).

18. Pybus v. Grasso, 317 Mass. 716, 718, 59 N.E.2d 289, 291 (1945). Note the peculiar use of the word "merge." Usually the word means the mixture of two or more things into something which has some attributes of each constituent. Here it means that the attributes of some constitutents disappear. "Superseded" would have been a

The rule which cancelled the prior written contract also destroyed warranties not repeated in the deed. Aside from conforming with real property law's traditional respect for form and ritual, this "merger" rule had the function of creating certainty as to the parties' obligations; the rule tacitly recognized that bargainers often make proposals during negotiations that are superseded by the agreement finally reached. It should also be pointed out that the rule does not apply to "collateral" undertakings, an exception which over the years has greatly narrowed the rule. But to avoid the merger issue entirely, in some jurisdictions plaintiffs and courts simply characterize real property disputes as tort claims arising out of misrepresentation rather than as contract claims for breach of warranty.

A similar development has occurred in contract law. A final writing intended by the parties to embody their contract may not be contradicted by earlier statements. This principle is usually referred to as the "parol evidence rule," although it excludes both previous writings and previous parol (oral) statements. As formulated by the U.C.C. § 2–202, the rule is: "Terms [which are] set forth in a writing intended by the parties as a final expression of their agreement with respect to such terms as are included therein may not be contradicted by evidence of any prior agreement or of a contemporaneous oral agreement but may be explained or supplemented . . . by evidence of consistent additional terms unless the court finds the writing to be intended also as a complete and exclusive statement of the terms of the agreement." The word "court" in the rule means "judge," and some courts have been mechanistic in deciding that the writing was intended to be the complete and exclusive statement of the terms of the agreement, looking only to the writing itself to see whether it has an appearance of completeness.[19]

better word, but "merged" is usual legal usage. For instance, contract clauses intended to cancel prior proposals and stipulations are called "merger" clauses.

19. A leading case explains:
"When the parties to a written contract have agreed to it as an 'integration'—a complete and final embodiment of the terms of an agreement—parol evidence cannot be used to add to or vary its terms. When only part of the agreement is integrated, the same rule applies to that part, but parol evidence may be used to prove elements of the agreement not reduced to writing.

"The crucial issue in determining whether there has been an integration is whether the parties intended their writing to serve as the exclusive embodiment of their agreement.

. . . .

"[Some] cases have stated that whether there was an integration is to be determined solely from the face of the instrument, and that the question for the court is whether it 'appears to be a complete . . . agreement.' . . . The

Assume a case in which a representation made early in negotiations may or may not have been withdrawn by the time the final writing (which did not mention the representation) was made. Plaintiff alleging the representation to be false may seek to avoid the parol evidence rule by suing for misrepresentation rather than breach of warranty. The effect of this tactic will be to transfer from the judge to the jury the task of deciding whether the earlier representation actually had been withdrawn. We cannot easily condemn this tactic. It is only an armchair guess that juries are less able than judges to try such matters.[20] In those jurisdictions where the judge will not hear evidence on this issue when the writing appears complete on its face, the tactic may be beneficial. The admissibility of evidence in the tort suit will not be so restricted.

In many cases, however, a representation may be superseded by later contract terms and yet affect the bargain. Sellers' assurances may induce buyers to accept risks they otherwise would not have accepted, at least not at the price agreed to. Had the

requirement [however] that the writing must appear incomplete on its face has been repudiated in many cases where parol evidence was admitted 'to prove the existence of a separate oral agreement as to any matter on which the document is silent and which is not inconsistent with its terms'—even though the instrument appeared to state a complete agreement. Even under the rule that the writing alone is to be consulted, it was found necessary to examine the alleged collateral agreement before concluding that proof of it was precluded by the writing alone. . . .

"In formulating the rule governing parol evidence, several policies must be accommodated. One policy is based on the assumption that written evidence is more accurate than human memory. . . . Another policy is based on the fear that fraud or unintentional invention by witnesses interested in the outcome of the litigation will mislead the finder of facts. McCormick has suggested that the party urging the spoken as against the written word is most often the economic underdog,

threatened by severe hardship if the writing is enforced. In his view the parol evidence rule arose to allow the court [that is, the judge,] to control the tendency of the jury to find through sympathy and without a dispassionate assessment of the probability of fraud or faulty memory that the parties made an oral agreement collateral to the written contract, or that preliminary tentative [written or oral] agreements were not abandoned when omitted from the [ultimate] writing. [Citations omitted.]" Traynor, C. J., in Masterson v. Sine, 68 Cal.2d 222, 225–227, 65 Cal. Rptr. 545, 547–548, 436 P.2d 561, 563–564 (1968).

20. This is not the place to discuss the advisability of trial by jury as a general matter; but it should be kept in mind that an oft-repeated justification for trial by jury is that judges may lack sufficient compassion to do justice for underdog litigants. That, too, is an armchair guess. In any event, if distrust of juries' ability to try questions of fact is well founded, it would seem there would be more important areas from which to exclude them than this one.

misrepresentation been intentional, there would be no difficulty in permitting a remedy, for the fraud would have vitiated the contract; but when the seller has made an innocent mistake, can recovery in tort be justified?

In Clements Auto Co. v. Service Bureau Corp.,[21] a computer service company offered to automate and computerize a wholesaler's bookkeeping, representing that the data control system would be virtually error free. The ultimate writing only dealt with payment and procedures (that the wholesaler would record all transactions on machine-readable tapes and forward them to the service company, that the service company would process the tapes to generate weekly and monthly reports to be returned to the wholesaler, etc.), omitting any reference to the assurance of accuracy. The writing also included a "merger clause" which stated that the service company made no warranties not set forth in the written document. When the system began, the wholesaler ceased using its old bookkeeping methods. The computer printouts in the new system were so full of errors that the wholesaler lost control of its inventory, and all attempts by the service company to correct matters failed because its computers were not capable of handling the mass of data. The wholesaler sued for breach of warranty and for misrepresentation. The suit for breach of warranty was dismissed because of the merger clause. The suit for misrepresentation, however, was successful.

Knowledgeable parties, dealing at arm's length, should be able to allocate the risks of a transaction between themselves; and once they have done so, they should be bound by that arrangement. If under such conditions, the wholesaler had agreed to accept the risk of failure, it should not have been able to recover from the service company, regardless of the label used to characterize its lawsuit. It would have contracted away all warranties omitted from the writing and would not be relying on any representations. Perhaps this is why the wholesaler was willing to sign a contract with a merger clause. If that had been the course of the bargaining, proof of that fact would show that the wholesaler no longer relied on the representation and would defeat the cause of action.

But perhaps the wholesaler intentionally accepted this risk because the service company represented that the risk was minimal. The company, a branch of I.B.M., was apparently expert in this area. The parties' subsequent bargaining, therefore, did not necessarily dispel the force of the service company's repre-

---

21.   444 F.2d 169 (8th Cir. 1971).

sentation. (If it had, the wholesaler may have felt it necessary to retain the old bookkeeping system until the new one proved itself; but the added expense may have affected the price it was initially willing to pay.) In other words, this bargain was not an arm's length transaction allocating risks between knowledgeable parties.[22] The service company was selling its expertise as well as its computer services and claimed a degree of expertise that, unfortunately, it did not have. The field was then new, and presumably the service company did not know its own limitations. However, there is as much reason to require a company to stand behind the quality of the advice that is part of the service it sells as it is to require sellers of goods to stand behind the quality of the goods they sell, and to hold it liable without proof of fault if it does not meet a certain minimum. This is, of course, a question of commercial law; but jurisdictions which desire to adopt this position find it useful to do so by developing their law of torts rather than disturbing contract precedents which no longer fit the times.

Although liability for innocent misrepresentation can be justified as a kind of liability for breach of warranty when the defendant sells goods or services to the plaintiff, a warranty analogy is not available when the defendant is not a party to the contract of sale. One court has said that there can be no such liability. It posited a case in which some one learned of a good investment opportunity in a mine owned by strangers. As a favor he passed the information to his friend, who invested and lost when the information turned out to be false. The court commented, "He [the misinformant] did no moral wrong. Indeed, from a moral point of view, his conduct was commendable, and, unless compelled to do so, the court should not announce a rule of law which penalizes commendable conduct."[23] Though the court is undoubtedly correct, the case assumed has not been litigated. All misinformants who have been sued have had an interest in the transaction.

In Tischer v. Bardin,[24] for instance, a thief had previously sold a number of stolen cars to an unsuspecting second-hand car dealer. On the day the plaintiff came to buy a car from the dealer, the thief had just arrived with another stolen car but

22. Note that under this theory, a merger clause would not be totally ineffective. Had the system made occasional errors, the wholesaler would not have been able to claim that the misrepresentation had caused it to agree to take an undue risk.

23. Aldrich v. Scribner, 154 Mich. 23, 117 N.W. 581 (1908).

24. 155 Minn. 361, 194 N.W. 3 (1923).

had not yet sold it to the dealer. Plaintiff saw the car and liked it. The dealer sold it to him on commission, representing that the thief owned the car. When the true owner reclaimed the vehicle, plaintiff sued the dealer to recover the purchase price. The trial judge excluded proof tending to show that the dealer spoke in good faith. The appellate court affirmed a judgment for the plaintiff on the theory that the dealer "was bound to know whereof he spoke or remain silent." Since the court was unwilling to try the fault issue, the dealer might not even have been negligent. Is liability justified in this case?

Had the plaintiff approached the dealer a day later, it is probable that the dealer would have already purchased the car from the thief and would be offering it for sale. Under these circumstances, if the plaintiff bought the car and then lost it to the true owner, the dealer would have been liable to the plaintiff on implied breach of warranty of title, without any proof of fault. The dealer would be required to return the purchase price received from the sale of something he did not own. The dealer was liable to suffer a loss when he bought the car from the thief, a loss which he would not be permitted to shift to an unsuspecting customer. And although the judgment against him would be for the price the purchaser paid, his out-of-pocket loss would be the lower price he had paid the thief.

Is the actual case significantly different? The dealer had to repay the entire purchase price, although his commission on the sale had been only a minor fraction of that price. His out-of-pocket loss is, again, the amount paid to the thief. Financially, the actual case and the hypothetical one reach very similar results, and it may be that this analogy to a sales case was in the court's mind when it permitted liability without fault.

§ 5. CONCEALMENT AND NONDISCLOSURE

Active concealment of a material fact has the same consequence as telling a lie. Sellers of a house permeated with the smell of dog urine were held liable to the buyers when they used deodorants to temporarily conceal the defect.[25]

Is simple nondisclosure a lie? In Swinton v. Whitinsville Sav. Bank,[26] defendant sold a house to plaintiff without disclosing that the house was infested with termites. The court held there was no cause of action: "There is no allegation of any false statement or representation, or of the uttering of a half truth which may be tantamount to a falsehood . . . . There is

---

25. Campbell v. Booth, 526 S.W.2d 167 (Tex.Civ.App.1975).

26. 311 Mass. 677, 42 N.E.2d 808 (1942).

nothing to show any fiduciary relation between the parties, or that the plaintiff stood in a position of confidence toward or dependence upon the defendant. So far as appears the parties made a business deal at arm's length. The charge is concealment and nothing more; and it is concealment in the simple sense of mere failure to reveal, with nothing to show any peculiar duty to speak."

As the court indicates, there are situations in which there is a duty to speak:

(1) Half-truths are, of course, really lies, since what is not disclosed makes other representations misleading. If a seller of a house knows a termite inspector has found the house is infested with termites, the seller may not tell a prospective buyer, "I have never seen any termites here," even if true, and not reveal the inspector's report. The seller's statement implies there is no such report.

(2) Honest statements later discovered to be false must be corrected. The seller of a house who has honestly told a potential buyer that the house is termite-free must inform the buyer if later termites are discovered before the transaction is completed.[27]

(3) Fiduciaries and others in positions of confidence and trust have a duty to inform those they serve. This is an amorphous category of relationships. Certain situations have been authoritatively resolved; others have not. Agents must inform their principals concerning matters within the scope of their agency. Partners must inform each other concerning the firm's affairs. Other relationships requiring such candor are attorney and client, bank and investing depositor, executor and beneficiary of an estate, insurer and assured, surety and principal, physician and patient, priest and parishioner, close family members, and guardian and ward.[28]

The fiduciary duties of corporate officials have often been the subject of litigation. Sachem, vice-president in charge of land management for Lithos, Inc., discovers that valuable minerals lie under the company's swamplands. Sachem may not purchase these lands from Lithos without first disclosing the discovery to higher corporate authority, since Sachem is an agent of the company. May Sachem turn this knowledge to profit by personally approaching Lithos stockholders who are ignorant of this find

27. See, e. g., Bergeron v. Dupont, 116 N.H. 373, 359 A.2d 627 (1976); Fischer v. Kletz, 266 F.Supp. 180 (S.D.N.Y.1967).

28. Restatement, Second, Torts, § 551, Comment f at 121 (1977).

and, without disclosure, purchase their shares at a price lower than they would have accepted had they been informed? A minority of courts have condemned this practice.[29] The majority view has been that corporate officers are only in positions of trust and confidence in managing the business, so their official responsibilities do not extend to trading in their companies' shares. Therefore, they have no duty to disclose business facts in connection with such transactions.[30] This view was tempered by an exception for "special facts," as when an officer, to prevent a shareholder from suspecting that an offer was prompted by good business news, sent another person to make the purchase. This was deemed to be active concealment of a material fact.[31]

There has been a trend away from the majority view, either by expansion of the "special facts" exception to include facts that are not very special,[32] or by outright adoption of the minority rule.[33] The entire matter, however, has been largely superseded by federal securities law. Securities and Exchange Commission Rule 10b–5, one of the many provisions adopted to increase public confidence in the securities market, has been interpreted to require corporate insiders either to disclose important business developments or to abstain from trading in their companies' stocks.[34] To enforce this rule, federal courts have permitted shareholders victimized by insiders' nondisclosure of material facts to recover their losses.[35]

---

29. Hotchkiss v. Fischer, 139 Kan. 333, 31 P.2d 37 (1934) (plaintiff stockholder, an impoverished widow, consulted a corporate president who showed her the company books, refused to tell her the value of her shares, but offered her a price of $1.25 per share, which she accepted three days before the president and the two other directors declared a dividend of $1.00 per share); Oliver v. Oliver, 118 Ga. 362, 45 S.E. 232 (1903).

30. Connolly v. Shannon, 105 N.J. Eq. 155, 147 A. 234 (1929), aff'd, 107 N.J.Eq. 180, 151 A. 905 (1930) (bank president, knowing that the bank would negotiate a merger with another bank yielding at least $2,500 per share, offered to purchase plaintiff's shares for $1,400, which offer plaintiff accepted).

31. Strong v. Repide, 213 U.S. 419, 29 S.Ct. 521, 53 L.Ed. 853 (1909).

32. So claimed in 3 L. Loss, Securities Regulation 1447 (3d ed. 1961), but comment, 35 U.Colo.L.Rev. 410 (1963) concluded that the majority rule was still strong. See Goodman v. Poland, 395 F.Supp. 660 (D.Md.1975), finding that the majority rule still applies in Maryland.

33. Weatherby v. Weatherby Lumber Co., 94 Idaho 504, 492 P.2d 43 (1972); Jacobson v. Yaschik, 249 S.C. 577, 155 S.E.2d 601 (1967).

34. SEC v. Texas Gulf Sulphur Co., 401 F.2d 833 (2d Cir. 1968), cert. denied sub nom., SEC v. Kline, 394 U.S. 976, 89 S.Ct. 1454, 22 L. Ed.2d 756 (1969). Matter of Cady, Roberts & Co., 40 SEC 907 (1961).

35. Blue Chip Stamps v. Manor Drug Stores, 421 U.S. 723, 730, 95

(4) A further exception, not mentioned in the *Swinton* case, has come into favor. Some facts are so significant that they must be disclosed, if known, by parties to a transaction. This was first recognized when nondisclosure created risk of personal injury or property damage. The seller of a termite-infested house, which appears sound but which the seller knows is dangerous to enter, must inform prospective purchasers of the danger.[36] This duty is now recognized when only economic loss is threatened. As commercial mores have changed, parties to business transactions have come to expect more candor. Negotiators do not always fence with each other. Often they try to reach a common understanding. In aid of this, each bargainer invites the other's trust. Under these circumstances, a failure to disclose very important matters is as misleading as a half-truth; it is tantamount to representing that the undisclosed matter does not exist.

Recognizing this, courts have imposed a duty upon bargainers to disclose important facts if they know that the other parties are about to conclude the transaction in ignorance of those facts, and if the other parties would reasonably expect disclosure of such facts during the course of bargaining.[37] The full ambit of this responsibility is not clear. There may be a difference between buyers and sellers. A coin expert who recognizes that an object being offered for sale by a coin dealer merely as a curious medallion is really a rare Roman coin may probably purchase the coin at a bargain price without disclosure. A coin dealer, however, may not knowingly let a customer purchase an imitation Roman coin at a very high price under the misapprehension that it is genuine. There is not any clear distinction between

S.Ct. 1917, 1922, 1923, 44 L.Ed.2d 539 (1975); Kardon v. National Gypsum Co., 69 F.Supp. 512 (E.D. Pa.1946). The courts have made it clear that this is not the adoption of an administrative standard in an ordinary tort action (analogous to the cases discussed in Ch. IV, § 7) but is a judicially constructed remedy to implement the purposes of the Securities Exchange Act. *Scienter* was held to be a necessary element of the cause of action in Ernst & Ernst v. Hochfelder, 425 U.S. 185, 96 S.Ct. 1375, 47 L.Ed.2d 668 (1976).

36. "When a seller [of land] knows of a hidden hazard that is not likely to be discovered by the buyer, the seller is under a duty to disclose the hazard." Chapter VI, § 4, supra.

37. "One party to a business transaction is under a duty to exercise reasonable care to disclose to the other before the transaction is consumated . . . (e) facts basic to the transaction, if he knows that the other is about to enter into it under a mistake as to them, and that the other, because of the relationship between them, the customs of the trade or other objective circumstances, would reasonably expect a disclosure of those facts." Restatement, Second, Torts, § 551(2) (1977).

matters trivial enough to make disclosure permissive and those important enough to require it. The Second Restatement of Torts calls matters which must be disclosed "facts basic to the transaction," and comments, "There are indications   .   .   . that with changing ethical attitudes in many fields of modern business, the concept of facts basic to the transaction may be expanding and the duty to use reasonable care to disclose the facts may be increasing somewhat."[38]

It is clear, however, that most courts would require a seller of a house who knows it to be infested by termites to disclose that fact. The *Swinton* case still may be good law in Massachusetts, but it is a relic of an earlier view of business ethics, out of tune with the times.[39]

§ 6.   THE REQUIREMENT THAT THE REPRESENTATION BE ONE OF "FACT" RATHER THAN "OPINION"

Many sellers puff their wares, and buyers often disparage property for which they are dickering. Such talk may fall far short of unfair trading and not constitute actionable misrepresentation. For instance, a seller of a farm represented that "There is no better land in Vermont." In holding this statement not actionable, the court said: "It is well established by the cases that a representation relied upon in such a case as this must be of fact, and not estimate or opinion, and that it must be of an existing fact   .   .   .   . The plaintiffs must have known that the statement was not to be taken literally. It was so obviously nothing more than a highly exaggerated estimate or opinion that the plaintiffs had no right to rely upon it." [40]

This fact-opinion distinction is misleading. As observed by Learned Hand, "An opinion is a fact, and it may be a very relevant fact; the expression of an opinion is an assertion of a belief, and any rule which condones the expression of a consciously false opinion condones a consciously false statement of fact. When parties are so situated that the buyer may reasonably rely upon the expression of the seller's opinion, it is no excuse to give a false one   .   .   .   . The reason for the rule [condoning some false "opinion" statements] lies, we think, in this: There are some kinds of talk which no sensible man takes seriously, and if he does he suffers from his credulity. If we were all scrupulously honest, it would not be so; but, as it is, neither party

38. Id., Comment 1 at 125.

39. Weintraub v. Krobatsch, 64 N.J. 445, 317 A.2d 68 (1974), and cases cited therein.

40. Nichols v. Lane, 93 Vt. 87, 89–90, 106 A. 592, 593 (1919).

usually believes what the seller says about his own opinions, and each knows it. Such statements, like the claims of campaign managers before election, are rather designed to allay the suspicion which would attend their absence rather than to be understood as having any relation to objective truth. It is quite true that they induce a compliant temper in the buyer, but it is by a much more subtle process than through the acceptance of his claims for his wares."[41] The problem, then, is not one of distinguishing between opinion and fact but between permissible puffing or "dealers' talk" and improper unfair dealing.

This is not so much a question of law as a question of mores in the marketplace, and mores change over the years. In Massachusetts, it was once held that the sellers of land did not commit fraud by falsely saying they had been offered a certain price for the property in the course of trying to substantiate the asking price. In 1952, the Massachusetts court decided this view was out of date and held such bargaining tactics actionable.[42] Some selling techniques which were once tolerated are now scorned, and some old permissive precedents, therefore, are no longer reliable.

Predictions. Sometimes the problem takes a special form, as when sellers paint a rosy picture of future value of their wares. In Leece v. Griffin,[43] a buyer of farmland was told that the property would provide an income of $2,300 per year, which it did not. The court characterized this statement as "a mere expression of an opinion in the nature of a prophecy as to the happening or non-happening of a future event" and hence not actionable. Most predictions, however, are more then mere opinions. They are often representations that some facts exist which make such predictions reasonable or, at least, that the informant knows no facts which make the prediction unlikely to be fulfilled. In this case it appeared that a major source of expected income was a new orchard that was just coming into production, and the buyer knew this fact. Had it been an established, productive orchard, such a prediction could have impliedly represented that the orchard had recently produced sufficient fruit to justify such an estimate. Or, had the prediction been made by an expert orchardist, it could have implied the existence of facts such an expert would rely on in making such an estimate.

41. Vulcan Metals Co. v. Simmons Mfg. Co., 248 F. 853, 856 (2d Cir. 1918).

42. Kabatchnick v. Hanover-Elm Bldg. Corp., 328 Mass. 341, 103 N. E.2d 692 (1952).

43. 150 Colo. 132, 371 P.2d 264 (1962).

A statement of intention to do future acts is similar to a pre-diction (that the act will be done) and similar to a statement of fact (that the speaker actually harbors the intention). In Edgington v. Fitzmaurice,[44] the directors of a company represented that the money raised by the sale of debentures was to be used to expand the company's plant; in fact they intended to use the money to pay the company's debts. The directors were held liable to an investor. Lord Bowen said, "There must be a misstatement of an existing fact, but the state of a man's mind is as much a fact as the state of his digestion." Most courts have adopted Bowen's view.

A few courts have been bothered when the action involved a statement of intention which is also a promise not enforceable in a contract action, because it would be excluded under the parol evidence rule or was not in writing as required by the statute of frauds. These worries are ill-founded, for neither the parol evidence rule nor the statute of frauds was designed to protect a deceiver from liability. Moreover, these suits are not merely suits to enforce contracts characterized as tort actions. In a contract action, mere proof of the promise and its nonperformance would be sufficient; in deceit, the plaintiff must also prove that the defendant had no intention to perform when the promise was made. Mere nonperformance does not prove such an intention. This greater burden of proof makes difficult those trumped-up claims which the statute of frauds and the parol evidence rule were designed to thwart.

Misrepresentations of Law. In Gormely v. Gymnastic Ass'n,[45] an enterpriser rented a hall for a public dance. He told the proprietor of the hall that he wanted to swell his profits by selling liquor and asked if he needed a license. The proprietor fraudulently said that his license would cover the enterpriser's liquor sales. The enterpriser was convicted of selling liquor without a license and brought an action for damages against the proprietor. The court dismissed the claim on the ground that the representation was a misstatement of law rather than a misstatement of fact—a clear triumph of doctrine over common sense, grounded on the fiction that everyone knows the law and therefore no one can be misled about it. Though this view is generally followed, a "law-fact" distinction has developed much like the "opinion-fact" one, making this rule a special example of the opinion rule.

Statements of fact, rather than law, are actionable. Thus, were it true that such liquor licenses permit liquor sales by

---

44. L.R. 29 Ch.D. 459 (1885).

45. 55 Wis. 350, 13 N.W. 242 (1882).

dance hall lessees, but the proprietor had no such license, the enterpriser could have recovered from the proprietor for his implied representation that he had a license. Or had the proprietor told the enterpriser that the legislature had recently passed a statute exempting one-night enterprises from the requirement of a license, that would be a misrepresentation of fact, not law. Only conclusions of law, such as predictions of how courts will react to a certain set of facts, are not actionable under this view.

Also, some misinformants occupy positions which do not permit them to claim this immunity. For instance, in Stark v. Equitable Life Assur. Society,[46] an insurance agent fraudulently misrepresented to a policyholder that he was not entitled to benefits which were due him. A policy clause discouraged insureds from employing counsel and invited them to put their trust in the company and its agents. The court said that a misrepresentation of law is actionable if either (1) the misinformant is specially learned on the subject and takes advantage of solicited confidence, or (2) the relationship between misinformant and victim is fiduciary or one of trust and confidence. The court said that the case fell within both of these exceptions.

§ 7. THE REQUIREMENT THAT THE MISREPRESENTATION CAUSED THE INJURY—RELIANCE

If the misrepresentation has not caused injury, plaintiff ought not recover. Purchaser is contemplating buying Blackacre from Vendor. Stranger, who is not involved in the transaction, fraudulently tells Purchaser that the premises contain a working well. Purchaser has seen the well and knows it to be dry but buys the land anyway. Stranger's attempt to deceive has failed. There has been no wrong and should be no liability. This is often stated as a requirement that the plaintiff must have relied upon the misrepresentation to recover. There are two difficulties with this proposition.

First, some victims of a falsehood may be completely ignorant of it. Securities markets are very sensitive to false information or the suppression of the truth. These factors may effect the price, to the injury of those who trade without knowledge of the truth, though the representation may never have come to their attention. In such situations, the causation requirement ought to be deemed to be satisfied if the false information or suppressed truth is material, that is, if it is of sufficient importance to play a role in the decisions of traders generally, so that the price re-

---

46. 205 Minn. 138, 285 N.W. 466 (1939).

flects the falsehood.[47] A similar situation can arise when a person relies on another's reputation, without specific knowledge of misrepresentations which have made that reputation. There is, however, scant recognition of this possibility in the cases.[48]

Finally, some courts have placed too narrow a meaning on "reliance." In Enfield v. Colburn,[49] a cheat tried to collect a false claim, representing to town officials that he had suffered an injury caused by a defect in a street. The town went to considerable expense to investigate and discovered that the claim was a fabrication. In a suit for the expenses of the inquiry, the court dismissed the complaint on the ground that the plaintiff town did not rely on the misrepresentation. But clearly the plaintiff had relied to some extent. While not completely accepting defendant's story, the town did assume that there was reason, at least, to investigate whether it was obligated to pay; defendant's claim for payment was also a representation that there were facts sufficient to justify such an investigation. It would have been possible, therefore, for the court to have permitted the plaintiff to recover without unduly undermining the reliance requirement.

Not only must plaintiffs have relied on a misrepresentation, they must have relied to their detriment. In the usual case, this added requirement poses no problem, but there are a few cases in which it does. In Day v. Avery,[50] the plaintiff was a partner in a law firm which merged with another. Under the plan of merger, he was to lose his position as sole supervisor of one of the firm's offices. He was not told of this plan but was told, in-

---

47. Though this point has not been recognized in common law suits for misrepresentation, it has been in suits for securities fraud under SEC Rule 10b–5. Affiliated Ute Citizens v. United States, 406 U.S. 128, 92 S.Ct. 1456, 31 L.Ed.2d 741 (1972).

48. In Hospes v. Northwestern Mfg. & Car Co., 48 Minn. 174, 50 N.W. 1117 (1892), creditors of a defunct corporation were held able to recover from subscribers to the corporation's stock who had not paid the amount represented. This misrepresentation was held to have given the corporation a false appearance of financial soundness, to the injury of those who thereafter gave the company credit. The stockholders objected that the complaint did not allege that the

creditors had specific knowledge of the improprieties. The court answered that the misrepresentation could injure creditors who were ignorant of it but had assumed the company to be creditworthy because of its general reputation, a reputation which had been created by the misrepresentation to others in the business community. This tort rationale, however, may be only a rationalization of a rule of corporation law, requiring investors to provide substantial capital to their corporations if they are to enjoy the benefits of limited liability.

49. 63 N.H. 218 (1884).

50. 548 F.2d 1018 (D.C.App.1976), cert. denied 431 U.S. 908, 97 S.Ct. 1706, 52 L.Ed.2d 394 (1977).

stead, that he would not be worse off because of the merger. Because he was not a member of the executive committee, either before or after the merger, which had full power to designate who was to head the office, and because his single vote could not have blocked the merger, it was held that he had not suffered injury by virtue of this lie. Plaintiff argued that had he known the truth, he would have campaigned for votes against the merger, but the court was unwilling to speculate that he would have succeeded.

Whether this is proper depends upon what alternate scenario seems likely. Had the senior members of the law firm felt compelled to tell the truth, they might have reformed the plan of merger so as not to injure plaintiff rather than suffer his attempts to block it. For this reason, among others, several federal courts have held that misinformed minority shareholders may have a cause of action against a majority shareholder who solicits their votes, concealing the disadvantages of the proposed transaction to the minority, even though the minority lacks sufficient votes to block the proposed transaction.[51]

Some misrepresentations are so trivial they could not have induced detrimental reliance.[52] Others are commercially irrelevant.[53] And some are so ludicrous as to raise doubt that they were believed.[54] Plaintiffs in these cases may be using these misstatements merely as pretexts for recovery after the deals turned sour, for reasons unrelated to the representations.

However, some individuals have idiosyncratic beliefs and desires. Others are unusually gullible. Upon proof of such facts, plaintiffs may recover for statements which probably would not have misled most persons. In Hyma v. Lee,[55] defendant, a professed medium and head of a spiritualist church, told plaintiff members of that church that voices of the dead recommended

51. These suits are under the federal securities statutes rather than the common law. See Mills v. Electric Auto-Lite Co., 396 U.S. 375, 385 n. 7, 90 S.Ct. 616, 622, 24 L.Ed.2d 593 (1970) where the federal cases are collected. Cases to the contrary are also cited, and the Supreme Court has expressly left the issue open.

52. See, e. g., Miller v. Protrka, 193 Or. 585, 238 P.2d 753 (1951) (motel represented as earning "over $40,000" annually actually had earned only $39,791.80 the previous year.)

53. See, e. g., Farnsworth v. Duffner, 142 U.S. 43, 12 S.Ct. 164, 35 L.Ed. 931 (1891) (misrepresentation that vendor of land was a Baptist, had been governor of a state and was now the president of a bank.)

54. See, e. g., H. Hirschberg Optical Co. v. Michaelson, 1 Neb. (Unoff.) 137, 95 N.W. 461 (1901) (lenses of eyeglasses represented to alter their shape to accommodate to the optical needs of the eyes.)

55. 338 Mich. 31, 60 N.W.2d 920 (1953).

certain stock not be sold. The plaintiffs' reliance, it was held, could support a cause of action.

§ 8. CONTRIBUTORY FAULT IN MISREPRESENTATION CASES

In jurisdictions which recognize contributory negligence as a defense in negligence cases generally, plaintiffs whose negligence concerning their own affairs contributes to their misapprehension may not recover from those who negligently misinform them.[56] In comparative negligence jurisdictions, plaintiff's contributory negligence probably will reduce their recovery in negligence misrepresentation cases in the same manner it does in other negligence cases. The matter has yet to come before the courts in those jurisdictions.

A few courts have held that plaintiff's negligence will bar recovery in a deceit action. As a judge of an intermediate appellate court in Georgia commented, smarting under the rule, "In seeking to choose between a fraudfeasor and a negligent party, the Georgia law unfortunately goes with the alleged crook."[57]

The majority view, however, is that contributory negligence is not relevant in cases of fraud. When the defendant has intentionally lied or acted heedlessly, with reckless disregard of the truth of the matter, plaintiff's failure to investigate will not bar recovery.[58] In Citizens Sav. and Loan Ass'n v. Fischer,[59] plain-

---

56. There are few cases: McAfee v. Rockford Coca-Cola Bottling Co., 40 Ill.App.3d 521, 352 N.E.2d 50 (1976); Vartan Garapedian, Inc. v. Anderson, 92 N.H. 390, 31 A.2d 371 (1943); Gould v. Flato, 170 Misc. 378, 10 N.Y.S.2d 361 (1938). One case holds to the contrary, but it is an aberrant case, unlikely to be followed. Neff v. Bud Lewis Co., 89 N.M. 145, 548 P.2d 107 (1976).

57. Cole v. Cates, 113 Ga.App. 540, 545, 149 S.E.2d 165, 169 (1966) (Hall, J., concurring.) In Goff v. Frank A. Ward Realty & Ins. Co., Inc., 21 N.C.App. 25, 203 S.E.2d 65 (1974), plaintiff was assured by a realtor that the sewage system of the house he was purchasing worked properly. In fact, raw sewage flowed across the backyard, as an inquiry of the neighbors would have revealed. In holding against plaintiff for not making sufficient inquiry, the court quoted from an earlier case that, "The policy of the courts is, on the one hand, to suppress fraud and, on the other hand, not to encourage negligence and inattention to one's own interest." The court gave no indication of how, when faced with these two policies that were irreconcilable in this situation, the policy of discouraging negligence attained primacy over the policy of suppressing fraud.

58. "[When] a party to whom a representation has been made had not made an investigation adequate to disclose the falsity of the representation, the party whose misstatements have induced the act [in reliance] cannot escape liability by claiming that the other party ought not to have trusted him." Davis v. Re-Trac Mfg. Corp., 276 Minn. 116, 119, 149 N. W.2d 37, 39 (1967).

59. 67 Ill.App.2d 315, 214 N.E.2d 612 (1966).

tiffs were falsely assured that the home they were buying was free and clear of any encumbrances. Though they did not search the public records, which would have revealed a mortgage on the property, they were able to recover for this fraud. Intentional wrongdoers usually cannot avoid liability by showing that the victims were careless of their own safety. The victim of a shooting can recover even though a prudent person would have fled and avoided injury.

The shooting hypothetical, however, is not a good analogy. The gunshot victim, though fully aware, is nevertheless shot. The alerted target of a lie is not deceived. Plaintiff's state of mind has a significance in deceit that it lacks in other tort cases. In Goff v. American Sav. Ass'n,[60] the contractor building a house negligently displaced a basement wall, causing it to bow and crack clear through. Plaintiff, the person for whom the house was being built, saw the damage and even helped the contractor shove the wall back into place. Thereafter, plaintiff was informed that the wall would never be watertight by a subcontractor and by an expert friend of the family, and the contractor refused to guarantee that the basement would be waterproof. An inspector for defendant savings association, which was financing the construction, assured plaintiff that the basement would not leak. When it did leak, plaintiff sued the association. In affirming a summary judgment for defendant, the court said that "no reasonable person in [plaintiff's] position and circumstances could have reasonably relied on the statements." The fact that something is palpably unbelievable is strong evidence that it was not believed. Courts are unwilling to credit a claim of reliance on a falsehood by one who has abundant notice of the truth. It is probable that plaintiff knew the basement might leak and accepted the risk.

In Williams v. Rank & Son Buick, Inc.,[61] a young man purchased a used car with many accessories, but air conditioning was not one of them. Claiming that he had been told the car was air-conditioned, he sued for deceit. He testified that air conditioning was very important to him and that this deceit, therefore, was particularly grievous. However, he had been permitted to fully inspect the car and had taken it on an hour and a half trial run. The court would not believe that he had not discovered the truth before he purchased the car. The fact that most individuals in plaintiff's situation would have discovered the truth is strong evidence that plaintiff has done so.

60. 1 Kan.App.2d 75, 561 P.2d 897 (1977).

61. 44 Wis.2d 239, 170 N.W.2d 807 (1969).

This would appear to support a rebuttable presumption, but the law has gone further. The Second Restatement of Torts comments, "[Plaintiff] is . . . *required* to use his senses, and cannot recover if he blindly relies upon a misrepresentation the falsity of which would be patent to him if he had utilized his opportunity to make a cursory examination or investigation." [62] Plaintiffs probably know what they would have discovered had they looked, but why cannot a particular plaintiff try to prove ignorance? If this were permitted, many plaintiffs would try. Whether they actually knew what was patent and understood what was obvious would be known only to themselves. Cogent evidence of their ignorance would be rare. Perhaps the courts are correct in not accepting their mere disclaimers.

Consider, however, Providence State Bank v. Bohannon.[63] Plaintiff bank was the victim of a check kiting scheme, whereby it permitted a company to deposit drafts drawn on a distant bank and to withdraw funds from the account before the instruments drawn on that other bank had cleared. It was induced to do this by misrepresentations that the company had a line of credit which guaranteed that the distant bank would honor such instruments. After some months, the distant bank stopped honoring such instruments and sent a notice of dishonor to plaintiff. Due to "stupidity or negligence," the officer of the bank who received this notice did not forward it to the bank's operatives. The company was, therefore, permitted to withdraw additional funds from its account for a short time thereafter, though in fact the account was depleted. In a suit against an officer of the company who had misrepresented that the company had a line of credit, the bank was unable to recover those withdrawals made after receipt of the notice of dishonor because it had notice of the truth and its reliance was deemed unreasonable. But there is no reason to believe that the bank intentionally accepted the risk of loss when it permitted the withdrawals. The bank officials were stupid, negligent, or both; but they ought not to be held to owe a duty to the deceiver to be wise or use due care. There was credible evidence that this plaintiff continued to rely on a misrepresentation after its falsity was manifest. In such cases, when the evidence is much more than a plaintiff's unbelievable disclaimer, defrauders ought not to be shielded by their victims' folly.

---

62. Restatement, Second, Torts, § 541, Comment a at 89 (1977) (emphasis added).

63. 426 F.Supp. 886 (E.D.Mo.1977).

§ 10. LIMITS OF LIABILITY FOR MISREPRESENTATION

Broker induces Investor to purchase Sahara Oil Company stock by falsely representing that the company has discovered oil in West Africa. A month later the company does make such a discovery but the West African government immediately nationalizes the company's assets and the stock becomes worthless. Is Broker's deceit the proximate cause of Investor's loss? Cases such as this occasionally occur. A generalized view of the facts which minimizes the freakishness of events leads to a judgment for the plaintiff;[64] a detailed view which emphasizes unusual events results in a judgment for the defendant.[65] Misrepresentation is not materially different from other torts in this regard.[66]

One aspect of the misrepresentation scope-of-liability problem has been particularly troublesome. Which foreseeable victims shall be deemed too remote to recover? Lumberer, in the busi-

---

64. See, e. g., Fottler v. Moseley, 185 Mass. 563, 70 N.E. 1040 (1904). Defendant broker lied concerning the market for a company's stock, thereby dissuading plaintiff from selling his shares. Shortly thereafter, a massive embezzlement at the company was disclosed, and the stock fell from $27 to $3 per share. "If the defendant fraudulently induced the plaintiff to refrain from selling his stock when he was about to sell it, he did him a wrong; and a natural consequence of the wrong, for which he was liable, was the possibility of loss from diminution in the value of the stock, from any one of numerous causes."

65. See, e. g., Boatmen's Nat. Co. v. M. W. Elkins & Co., 63 F.2d 214 (8th Cir. 1933). A county issued bonds to defendant without receiving any money, with the result that the bonds were not legal obligations of the county. The defendant falsely represented to the plaintiff that the bonds had been paid for, inducing the plaintiff to purchase the bonds. The defendant then cured the defect by paying the county. Thereafter, the state supreme court held the bonds void for a reason unrelated to these matters. "[T]he bonds . . . were rendered valueless because the decision of the Supreme Court of Arkansas, and not because the purchase price of the bonds had not been paid to the county treasurer at or prior to the time of the issuance of the county treasurer's false certificate. . . The wrongdoer could not possibly have contemplated that the wrongful issuance of this false certificate would result in a decision by the Supreme Court of Arkansas, holding the bonds void, nor indeed did it have any such effect."

66. Another causation problem which is not unique to the tort of misrepresentation can occur in the case of multiple tortfeasors. When two or more persons independently tell a victim the same falsehood, they are each liable although the same loss would have occurred had any one of them remained silent. Restatement, Second, Torts § 546, Comment b & Illustration 1 at 103 (1977). Compare Corey v. Havener, 182 Mass. 250, 65 N.E. 69 (1902) (two motorcyclists whizzed by a horse and wagon, one on each side, and the wagon driver was injured in the resulting runaway; both held liable.)

ness of purchasing and logging timberland, hires Surveyor to map Blackacre. Surveyor's map shows a valuable stand of timber to be within Blackacre's boundaries. Actually the timber is on adjacent land. Lumberer purchases Blackacre and hires Sawyer to cut the timber. The true owner of the timber obtains an injunction against the logging. Surveyor is liable to Lumberer. Is Surveyor also liable to Sawyer for lost wages?

It is well settled that had the timber been on Blackacre and been destroyed when Kindler negligently set it ablaze, Kindler would be liable to Lumberer but not to Sawyer. The line would be drawn to deny recovery by victims of the fire who had suffered no physical damage, only economic loss. This test is impractical in misrepresentation cases, because almost all victims have suffered only economic losses. Other techniques must be used.

Negligent Misrepresentation. In Glanzer v. Shepard,[67] a bean merchant had contracted to sell a shipment of beans to plaintiff at a specific price per pound. The seller hired defendant public weigher to certify the beans' weight. Defendant overstated the weight. Plaintiff relied on defendant's certificate. In an opinion by Cardozo, it was held that the weigher was liable to the buyer for the price of the beans that plaintiff had paid for but not received.

A few years later, Ultramares Corp. v. Touche,[68] came before the same court. As mentioned above, this case concerned the liability of an accounting firm which had certified as accurate financial statements showing that the Stern company was prosperous when it was, in fact, insolvent. The accountants, hired by Stern, were asked to supply multiple copies of the certified statement so that Stern could use it in various financial transactions. The accountants, however, were ignorant of the size or character of such transactions—whether they were to be bank borrowings, purchases on credit, etc. When Stern went bankrupt, plaintiff, who had relied on the statement in lending to Stern, sued the accountants for both deceit and negligence. As mentioned above, Cardozo remanded the deceit count for trial. He was unwilling, however, to let the negligence count stand. "If liability for negligence exists, a thoughtless slip or blunder, the failure to detect a theft or forgery beneath the cover of deceptive entries, may expose accountants to a liability in an indeterminate amount for an indeterminate time to an indeterminate class. The hazards of a business conducted on these terms are

67. 233 N.Y. 236, 135 N.E. 275 (1922). 68. 255 N.Y. 170, 174 N.E. 441 (1931).

so extreme as to enkindle doubt whether a flaw may not exist in the implication of a duty that exposes to these consequences."

Cardozo attempted to distinguish *Glanzer*, saying, "[T]he service rendered by the defendant in Glanzer v. Shepard was primarily for the information of a third person, in effect, if not in name, a party to the contract, and only incidentally for that of the formal promisee. In the case at hand, the service is primarily for the benefit of the Stern company, a convenient instrumentality for use in the development of the business, and only incidentally or collaterally for the use of those to whom Stern   .   .   . might exhibit it thereafter." This "primary benefit" analysis seems flawed. In fact, the public weigher expected to serve both buyer and seller, facilitating a transaction which each desired. Similarly, the accountants expected their services to be useful both to the Stern company and to those who deal with the company.

Such was the prestige of the *Ultramares* case that some courts read it as overpowering the principle of *Glanzer* in suits against accountants, holding them not liable for mere negligence even when they had been told their audits were to be used in a specific transaction with the plaintiff.[69] Since such cases do not raise the specter of "liability in an indeterminate amount for an indeterminate time to an indeterminate class," these courts have misread the opinion.

The Second Restatement's formulation of the rules of *Glanzer* and *Ultramares* limits liability for negligent misrepresentation "to loss suffered (a) by the person or one of a limited group of persons for whose benefit and guidance he [the informant] intends to supply the information or knows that the recipient intends to supply it; and (b) through reliance upon it in a transaction that he intends the information to influence or knows that the recipient so intends or in a substantially similar transaction."[70] "Intends" as used here really means "expects." The bean weigher only intended to perform a compensable service. He expected his certificate to be shown to the buyer, but he would not have been concerned had the sale been cancelled and the certificate discarded. In *Ultramares*, the accountants expected the Stern company to use the certified balance sheet in financial transactions. The Restatement attempts to exclude liability in the *Ultramares* type situation by limiting liability only to "the person or one of a limited group of persons" in a "trans-

---

69. Stephens Industries, Inc. v. Haskins & Sells, 438 F.2d 357 (10th Cir. 1971) (applying Colorado law); Investment Corp. v. Buchman, 208 So.2d 291 (Fla.App.1968).

70. Restatement, Second, Torts § 552(2) (1977).

action that [the informant] intends the information to influence or knows that the recipient so intends or in a substantially similar transaction."[71] But the expected transactions were all financial business deals. If Golddigger, seeking a wealthy marriage, had relied on the balance sheet in marrying into the Stern family, Golddigger's reliance would be beyond the accountants' expectations. The actual creditor-plaintiff in the case was part of a limited (though perhaps large) class of potential victims injured in a transaction of the kind expected to be influenced by the representation. If the class of expected transactions is stated generally enough, liability in an *Ultramares* situation will follow from the Restatement's rule. Since there can be no authoritative standard concerning the proper level of generality, the Restatement fails to provide much guidance.

In a famous dictum, Cardozo observed, "The risk reasonably to be perceived defines the duty to be obeyed."[72] This helps define the class of plaintiffs which may recover. Just as a footbridge need not be strong enough to support a convoy of trucks, information intended for one purpose need not be reliable enough for all purposes. Buyers of businesses need accurate financial statements to assess the value of the enterprises they are buying. Trade creditors need less reliability in deciding whether or not to advance credit. Indeed, they find it more economical to set aside a reserve for bad debts than to pay for careful independent audits of debtor firms. A buyer of a business, therefore, ought not to be able to recover from a credit bureau because the buyer, relying on the bureau's reports, paid more for an enterprise than it was worth. Similarly, the owner of a city lot who is putting in a vegetable garden does not require the lot's boundaries to be marked with the same precision as does the builder of an apartment house on the same lot. If the gardener hires a measurer to stake out the garden, a subsequent owner of the lot who sites an apartment house in reliance on the garden's boundaries ought not to be able to recover from the measurer if the structure is wrongly sited. But the converse cases are different. A creditor who relies on an audit for a would-be purchaser and a gardener who relies on the survey for a would-be builder ought not to be held to have misplaced their confidence. The reliability of the information was appropriate to their needs.

Moreover, large differences in the amount of risk do not always dictate a difference in the degree of care. The preflight

---

71. Id.

72. Cardozo, J., in Palsgraf v. Long Island R. Co., 248 N.Y. 339, 162 N.E. 99 (1928). See Chapter VII, § 4, at note 14 above.

check of a plane about to carry a tour of octogenarians ought to be done as carefully as one about to carry a professional football team, although the money damages for wrongful death caused by a crash in one case would be only a small fraction of those in the other. Similarly, an audit, represented as being done in accordance with generally accepted auditing standards, should be as free from error as such audits customarily are, and should be reliable for all classes of persons who generally rely on such reports. A survey to site a residence ought to be as accurate as one to site a high-rise. Consideration of the amount of risk, therefore, does not dictate that the class of persons who ought to be protected be described with great specificity. A high level of generality would appear to be proper in many cases, particularly when professional informants, such as accountants and surveyors, have been retained to exercise customary care in the performance of their services.

But it is not the law that "[t]he risk reasonably to be perceived defines the duty to be obeyed." In some situations, to compensate all reasonably foreseeable victims might burden wrongdoers out of proportion to their blame. It was with this in mind that Cardozo, in *Ultramares*, further limited recovery to "primary" beneficiaries of the service. And it is with this problem in mind that the "limited group of persons" eligible to recover under the Restatement formula must be defined. This requires an estimate of the size of the potential burden and the ability of the defendant to withstand, shift or insure that burden. In *Ultramares*, Cardozo's armchair guess was that the burden on accountants would be too great. Lately, that judgment has been questioned. Accountants may negligently fail to detect small errors fairly often, but such errors would not be material in most instances. The number of undetected large errors may be quite small, and although some could result in large judgments, such judgments could be covered by insurance.

Recently, by expanding the concept of "limited group of persons," courts that are uneasy concerning the *Ultramares* decision have held accountants liable for negligence on the basis of the Restatement formula.[73] In a much quoted opinion, the court

73. See e. g., Rhode Island Hospital Trust Nat. Bank v. Swartz, Bresenoff, Yavner & Jacobs, 455 F.2d 847 (4th Cir. 1972); Rusch Factors, Inc. v. Levin, 284 F.Supp. 85 (D.R.I.1968) (citing Restatement, Second, Torts § 552 as published in Tent. Draft No. 12, 1966); Aluma Kraft Mfg. Co. v. Elmer Fox & Co., 493 S.W.2d 378 (Mo.App.1973); Shatterproof Glass Corp. v. James, 466 S.W.2d 873 (Tex.Civ.App. 1971); Ryan v. Kanne, 170 N.W.2d 395 (Iowa, 1969). Seedkem, Inc. v. Safranek, 466 F.Supp. 340 (D. Neb.1977), held the plaintiff to be within the foreseeable and limited class who had standing to sue the negligent accountant employed to maintain a company's books,

in *Rusch Factors*, the earliest of these cases, said, "The wisdom of the decision in *Ultramares* has been doubted [citing law review commentaries], and this Court shares that doubt. Why should an innocent reliant party be forced to carry the weighty burden of an accountant's professional malpractice? Isn't the risk of loss more easily distributed and fairly spread by imposing it on the accounting profession, which can pass the cost of insuring against the risk onto the entire consuming public? Finally, wouldn't a rule of foreseeability elevate the cautionary techniques of the accounting profession? For these reasons it appears to this Court that the decision in *Ultramares* constitutes an unwarranted inroad upon the principle that '[t]he risk reasonably to be perceived defines the duty to be obeyed.' "[74] The court hesitated to go that far, holding only that the accountant was liable to plaintiff as the member of a foreseen and limited class of persons.

In Bonhiver v. Graff,[75] plaintiff insurance agency, worried by a rumor that an insurance company was insolvent, ceased doing business with the company and sought verification of the rumor from the state insurance commissioner. The commissioner assured the agency that the company was solvent, and the agency resumed selling the company's policies. In fact, the company had been the victim of a massive undetected embezzlement, was insolvent, and soon collapsed, causing the agency financial loss. The commissioner had based his assurance on an examination of the company. His examiners had relied on the working papers of an accounting firm that had been employed by the company to keep its books. The accounting firm knew that its working papers were being used in this manner. The firm was held liable to the insurance agency for negligently failing to discover the embezzlement. The court, adopting the Second Restatement rule, reasoned that the insurance commissioner was a member of the limited class with standing to sue, since the accountants knew his examiners were relying on their work. Since the commissioner had suffered no loss, the court followed the chain of causation to the plaintiff whom the commissioner had informed and permitted recovery. The court observed, "[T]he extent of an accountant's liability for malpractice is not settled. If that liability is to be drawn somewhere short of foreseeability, it must be drawn on pragmatic grounds alone." Pragmatic

merely because those books showed that the plaintiff had a substantial interest in the company. Plaintiff's loss occurred when he thereafter lent the company a susbtantial sum, relying on the books.

74. Rusch Factors, Inc. v. Levin, 284 F.Supp. 85, 91 (D.R.I.1968).

75. 311 Minn. 111, 248 N.W. 291 (1976).

grounds are difficult to articulate, and the court did not do so, simply stating that it felt the agency was in the class of victims who could recover. Yet, this is tantamount to holding that all whom the commissioner assured could recover. It does not appear that others inquired of him, but if the rumors had been rampant, all policy holders and agents might have inquired and been assured. Other courts, aware of this possibility, might have denied recovery in this case.

The trouble with the *Ultramares* rule was that it completely insulated some negligent misinformants from liability. It ought to be possible to prevent the excessive liability that would sometimes result from recognizing all remote victims' economic losses and yet not excuse, in effect, inexcusably careless misinformants. The *Bonhiver* court's willingness to follow the chain to the most proximate victim does this. Similarly, when an extension of the chain does not materially increase the burden, a remote victim ought to be compensated. For instance, if a title abstracter overlooks a cloud on the title or if a surveyor mislocates a boundary line, any subsequent owner ought to recover for this negligence. "Injury will ordinarily occur only once and to the one person then owning the lot."[76] But the entire context of the case must be considered. A title insurance company ought not to be liable to subsequent uninsured owners. Such companies take risks only for a fee and should not be held liable to foreseeable reliers who have not paid.[77]

---

76. Rozny v. Marnul, 43 Ill.2d 54, 250 N.E.2d 656 (1969) (surveyor). In Williams v. Polgar, 391 Mich. 6, 215 N.W.2d 149 (1974), a title abstractor was held liable to a subsequent owner.

In Texas Tunneling Co. v. City of Chattanooga, 329 F.2d 402 (6th Cir. 1964), the city hired defendants to prepare a report on the subsurface conditions in a hill through which a sewer was to be built. The report was to be made available to all contractors bidding on the project. Defendants were negligent and the successful bidder underestimated costs and lost money on the project. The court, citing *Ultramares*, would not permit the contractor to recover, because the defendants did not know who would rely on their report. In the similar case of M. Miller Co. v. Central Contra Costa Sanitary Dist., 198 Cal.App.2d 305, 18 Cal.

Rptr. 13 (1961), plaintiff recovered. An indeterminate number of indeterminate persons relied on the reports, and, presumably, all of them bid lower than they would have had they not been misled; but only the successful bidder suffered injury. Expanding the potential class of claimants would not expand the number of successful ones.

77. In fact, title insurers sometimes take risks without investigation, so that their willingness to insure cannot be deemed a representation concerning the state of title. See Walters v. Marler, 83 Cal.App.3d 1, 147 Cal.Rptr. 655 (1978). Cardozo apparently did not understand this, for he justified his holding in *Ultramares* by a parade of horrors, one of which was that unless his rule were adopted, "Title companies insuring titles to a tract of land, with knowledge that at an approaching auction the fact that

Intentional or Heedless Misrepresentations. In suits for deceit, the courts started with a very stringent rule. Misinformants were held liable only to those persons or classes of person they intended to inform and only for losses in the transactions or kinds of transactions they sought to influence. In Peek v. Gurney,[78] the directors of a company issued a fraudulent prospectus to attract subscribers for the company's stock. The company failed. Those stockholders who had purchased stock from the company in response to the prospectus would have had standing to recover from the directors. Plaintiff, though misled by the advertisement, delayed investing until all the stock had been sold. He then purchased the stock on the open market. He was denied recovery because the directors had not sought to induce such purchases. In Wells v. Cook,[79] a seller of sheep represented them to be healthy although he knew them to have a contagious disease. This representation was made to the buyer's agent, without thought of damaging the agent but merely as a way of lying to the buyer, the agent's employer. Shortly after the buyer had incorporated the sick sheep in his flock, he sold the flock to the agent. When the flock became ill, the agent sued the seller. Even though the lie had, in fact, been told to the agent, he could not recover because the lie was intended to be acted upon only by the principal.[80]

Over the years the scope of liability has widened. Again, *Ultramares* is the leading case.[81] Cardozo held that the record would support either a finding of negligence or a finding of *scienter*. On the latter assumption, that the accountants "acted without information leading to a sincere or genuine belief when they certified . . . that the balance sheet faithfully reflected the condition of the business," Cardozo held that the accountants could be liable to all who relied on the certification in any financial transaction with the business. "To creditors and investors to whom the employer [Stern] exhibited the certificate, the defendants owed a . . . duty to make it without fraud, since there was notice in the circumstances of its making the employer did not intend to keep it to himself."

they have insured will be stated to the bidders, will become liable to purchasers who may wish the benefit of a policy without payment of a premium."

78. L.R. 6 Eng. & Ir. App. 377 (1873).

79. 16 Ohio St. 67, 88 Am.Dec. 436 (1865).

80. In contrast, recall the doctrine of "transferred intent," which holds liable for battery one who strikes at one person but by chance hits another. Carnes v. Thompson, 48 S.W.2d 903 (Mo.1932), discussed above in Chapter VII, § 10.

81. Note 68, supra.

On the basis of *Ultramares* and similar cases, the Second Restatement limits the scope of liability for fraud to "the persons or class of persons whom [the misinformant] intends or has reason to expect" to react in "the type of transaction in which he intends or has reason to expect their conduct to be influenced."[82] This language is an attempt to expand the scope of liability beyond the narrow intentions of misinformants but to stop short of holding them liable for all foreseeable losses. To be liable to the persons injured, a misinformant "must have information that would lead a reasonable man to conclude that there is an especial likelihood that it will reach those persons and will influence their conduct."[83] The formula is not a particularly good one. The distinction between "reasonably foreseeable" and "especially likely" may be a difficult one to administer. A caveat to this section states, "The [American Law] Institute expresses no opinion on whether the liability of the maker of a fraudulent representation may extend beyond the rule stated in this Section to other persons or other types of transactions, if reliance upon the representation in acting or in refrainng from action may reasonably be foreseen."[84]

As we stated in the chapter on extent of liability, not all foreseeable victims are permitted to recover for negligence.[85] This is true for intentional torts as well. With that exception, the Institute's caveat is well taken. The liberalization occurring in negligent misrepresentation must necessarily be mirrored in de-

---

82. Restatement, Second, Torts § 531 (1977).

83. Id., Comment d at 68.

84. In a comment on this caveat, the Restatement specifically expresses no opinion on the continued vitality of the sick sheep case or cases like the false prospectus case.

See Citizens Bank v. C & H Constr. & Paving Co., Inc., 89 N.M. 360, 552 P.2d 796 (1976). A bank that had lent money to a corporation induced an officer of the corporation to sign a document giving the bank a security interest in the corporation's accounts receivable by misrepresenting the character of the document. On the basis of this security interest, the bank threw the corporation into receivership, halting its operations and putting it out of business. Another corporate officer, who was ignorant of this deception until the receiver was appointed, had previously guaranteed a debt of the corporation to a creditor, expecting that the corporation would pay that debt from the proceeds of its operations. When the receivership halted all operations, the creditor was left unpaid and collected from the officer on his guarantee. The bank was held liable to the officer for that amount plus punitive damages. Though the fraud had been practiced on the corporation and the officer had not relied on the misrepresentation, the court found that "[t]he damages suffered by [the officer] were the natural and probable consequences of the fraudulent conduct of Citizens Bank and his judgment is affirmed." This is a far cry from the sick sheep case.

85. Chapter VII, § 9.

ceit, for it would be senseless for the ambit of responsibility to be smaller in deceit than in negligence. Whether there can be a set rule, however, is not at all clear because the degree of blameworthiness varies considerably from one case of deceit to another.

Nader v. Allegheny Airlines[86] illustrates that even victims whose reliance the deceiver "has reason to expect" (in the Restatement's words) may not recover. Because a number of airline ticket holders can be expected not to show up for their flights, airlines attempt to minimize their losses by overbooking. Since the number of "no shows" cannot be predicted accurately, occasionally too many ticketed passengers show up for a flight and latecomers are denied passage. Though now airlines publicize this booking practice, for many years they did not, thereby misrepresenting that each ticket holder was assured a seat, Mr. Nader was "bumped" off a flight to Hartford and had to take a flight to Boston, instead. His Connecticut host had to provide transportation from Boston to Hartford and had to cancel a public meeting because of Mr. Nader's delay. Mr. Nader was permitted to recover compensatory damages, the extra amount he had to pay for the longer flight to Boston, but his host was denied standing to recover. "[F]oreseeability is not the test to be used in determining the class of third persons who may recover; otherwise, liability in a case such as this could become indeterminate." Yet the host's loss, in having to supply additional transportation, was probably more than merely foreseeable. Many travellers undertake to visit, and their hosts often undertake to meet and transport the travellers.

Any attempt to limit the burden of liability by denying recovery to remote victims must be somewhat arbitrary. The formula used in other areas of the law, denying standing to plaintiffs who have suffered only pecuniary loss, cannot be used here since all misrepresentation losses are pecuniary. The privity requirement proved too stringent. The formulae suggested by the Second Restatement are too nebulous to be administered with precision. As of this writing, no set rule exists and it may well be that no workable rule will ever be devised specifying which misrepresentation victims are too remote to recover.

---

86. 512 F.2d 527 (D.C.Cir. 1975), rev'd on other grounds, 426 U.S. 290, 96 S.Ct. 1978, 48 L.Ed.2d 643 (1976). See also, Roman v. Delta Air Lines, Inc., 441 F.Supp. 1160 (N.D.Ill.1977).

Chapter XII

DEFAMATION *

---

§ 1. THE "ABSOLUTE" PRIVILEGES

As the name implies, suits for defamation seek to vindicate injuries to reputation caused by published statements which tend to hold a person up to hatred, contempt, or ridicule, or cause the person to be avoided or shunned. As will be discussed more fully hereafter, this area of the common law had peculiarities not found in other branches of torts.

A solicitous concern for individuals' reputations comes into conflict with some very important social values. The threat of liability can have a chilling effect on expression. This was always recognized, and certain speakers and writers were deemed privileged; it was so important that they perform their functions that their utterances were not actionable or were actionable only in limited situations. Recently, there has been an expansion of this concept, a revolution in defamation law, as the courts have decided to protect freedom of the press and free speech from the full impact of orthodox defamation law. As a result, this body of law is best understood by first examining exceptions to liability. We start with the "absolute" privileges, those which bar all liability whether the vilification was made viciously, negligently, or reasonably and honestly.

Participants in governmental proceedings are usually not subject to civil liability for any damage they do to the reputations of those they defame. As a rule, these immunities are absolute; the vilifier is not liable in tort, even though the defamation has

* An earlier version of this chapter appeared as C. Morris, Modern Defamation Law, Copyright 1978 by The American Law Institute.

Reprinted with the permission of the American Law Institute-American Bar Association Committee on Continuing Professional Education.

been deliberately and mendaciously planned to destroy the standing of someone the calumniator knows has an unblemished character.

Easiest to justify is the immunity enjoyed by state and federal legislators for defamations spoken or filed during floor debates, in the course of committee hearings, in reports on proposed enactments, and so on. The federal and most state constitutions expressly protect legislators and those who testify before their committees against any civil liability for defamations made public during legislative proceedings or circulated in official reports.[1] When our federal and state constitutions were adopted, the founders chose to favor legislative processes untrammeled by threats of lawsuits brought by victims of character assassination—even when this choice protected malicious abusers of the legislative privilege. At least one court has absolutely privileged legislative proceedings without reference to any constitutional sanction.[2] The limits of a legislator's absolute immunity exclude press conferences and broadcasting defamations.[3]

An absolute privilege has, in some states, been extended even to participants in local legislative bodies, like city councils.[4] In many states, however, the courts have refused to go so far in protecting disparagers; they have adopted the theory that sacrifices of deserved reputations exact too great a price for free speech of aldermen and other enactors of local rules who subvert their offices; these courts hold that local lawmakers are subject to civil liability for defamation when they abuse their privilege to speak out.[5]

The common law has long promoted free speech during judicial proceedings by a protective covering of absolute privilege to defame. Judges announcing aspersions from a trial or appellate

---

1. W. Prosser, Handbook of the Law of Torts 781–82 (4th ed. 1971). See Restatement, Second, Torts § 590 (1977). A witness may lose his privilege if his defamation has no relation to the proceeding. Id. at § 590A.

In Hutchinson v. Proxmire, —— U.S. ——, 99 S.Ct. 2675, 61 L.Ed.2d 411 (1979), the Supreme Court held that the "speech or debate" clause in the federal constitution which absolutely privileges members of Congress does not apply to newsletters or press releases sent out by members of Congress which repeat defamatory matter in the members' speeches or their insertions into the Congressional Record.

2. Jennings v. Cronin, 256 Pa.Super. 398, 389 A.2d 1183 (1978).

3. Hutchinson v. Proxmire, —— U.S. ——, 99 S.Ct. 2675, 61 L.Ed.2d 411 (1979).

4. See, e. g., Larson v. Doner, 32 Ill.App.2d 471, 178 N.E.2d 399 (1961).

5. See, e. g., McClendon v. Coverdale, 203 A.2d 815 (Del.Super. 1964). Restatement, Second Torts prefers this view. See id. at § 590, Comment c at 254 (1977).

bench enjoy freedom from civil liability.[6] Litigants,[7] lawyers,[8] witnesses,[9] and court reporters [10] need not pay damages to those whom they defame, regardless of the malicious falsity of statements promulgated during judicial proceedings—so long as their utterances were in any way relevant to the matter litigated. The privilege of participants in lawsuits applies to many defamations, written or spoken, in pretrial proceedings as well.[11]

The executive branch, too, is absolutely immune from civil liability for defamations promulgated in the exercise of its functions.[12] In the federal establishment, even lower level executives are absolutely privileged when they spread defamations while acting in their official capacity. Many, though not all, state courts, however, hold that lesser state and local administrators are civilly liable for *abuse* of their privilege to defame others while performing their duties.[13] State law does nevertheless extend an absolute privilege to major state officials who defame while acting within the scope of their offices.[14]

The governmental absolute privileges are not, of course, intended to be perquisites of those political rogues who attain office. Immunity is thought to embolden and invigorate officials who dare to govern well; some officials might be overly wary if they were threatened with liability for disparagements let fall while performing their duties. Other checks induce some restraint; outrageous misconduct may result in censure or, in ex-

6. See, e. g., LaPlaca v. Lowery, 134 Vt. 56, 349 A.2d 235 (1975); Restatement, Second, Torts § 585 (1977).

7. See, e. g., Brown v. Shimabukuro, 118 F.2d 17 (D.C.Cir. 1941); Restatement, Second, Torts § 587 (1977).

8. See, e. g., Mohler v. Houston, 356 A.2d 646 (D.C.App.1976); Restatement, Second, Torts § 586 (1977).

9. See, e. g., Massey v. Jones, 182 Va. 200, 28 S.E.2d 623 (1944); Restatement, Second, Torts § 588 (1977).

10. See, e. g., Lowenschuss v. West Pub. Co., 542 F.2d 180 (3rd Cir. 1976).

11. See, e. g., Adams v. Peck, 43 Md.App. 168, 403 A.2d 840 (1979).

12. See, e. g., Lombardo v. Stoke, 18 N.Y.2d 394, 276 N.Y.S.2d 97, 222 N.E.2d 721 (1966). Cf. Colpoys v. Gates, 118 F.2d 16 (D.C. Cir. 1941), holding that a United States marshall enjoyed no privilege to defame his deputies after they had been dismissed, since his public discussion of the former deputies did not occur when he was exercising his executive functions.

13. Walker v. Cahalan, 542 F.2d 681 (6th Cir. 1976) (applying Michigan law); Ranous v. Hughes, 30 Wis.2d 452, 141 N.W.2d 251 (1966); Carr v. Watkins, 227 Md. 578, 177 A.2d 841 (1962). Cf. Paul v. Davis, 424 U.S. 693, 96 S.Ct. 1155, 47 L.Ed.2d 405 (1975).

14. See, e. g., Matson v. Margiotti, 371 Pa. 188, 88 A.2d 892 (1952); Cf. Restatement, Second, Torts § 591 (1977); and notes 9 and 10 supra.

treme cases, impeachment. Voters may refuse to return vilifiers to office. Nonofficial traducers taking part in government proceedings run risks of criticism and, in some extreme cases, may become subject to criminal liability for perjury or obstruction of justice. The media and private individuals, as shall be seen later, have wide, though not absolute, privileges to criticize public officials.

The common law absolute privilege covering disparagements made privately to the detractor's husband or wife may be, at this writing, less impregnable than the absolute privileges protecting participants in governance. Though courts until now have not questioned the matrimonial privilege, few decisions uphold it. Earlier opinion writers relied on the fiction that man and wife are one person and held that private conversation between spouses could not constitute the publication of a slander. Prosser ridiculed this quaint figment and said that the justification of matrimonial absolute privilege lies in "the very confidential character of the relation"; [15] in the 1971 edition of his Handbook of the Law of Torts, only one of the decisions he cites was handed down as late as the second half of the twentieth century. [16] The federal district judge who handed down the opinion in that case said, "A communication from husband to wife in the absence of a third person is not publication, and is not actionable as slander, whatever the motive may be . . . ." This opinion expresses no social concern for the privacy of intranuptial communications. The absoluteness of spouses' privilege to defame serves legal technicality more than justice. Perhaps a plaintiff who can overcome the other difficulties put in the path of modern defamation claimants, soon to be discussed, will be able to persuade some court to temper the absoluteness of this interspousal privilege.

§ 2. THE CONSTITUTIONAL REVOLUTION IN DEFAMATION LAW

Before 1964, many defamation claimants recovered substantial judgments, even though their disparagers were innocent of fault and the claimants themselves made no offer to prove any economic loss. When a defendant could not establish some privilege, which was often the case, demonstration that the defendant had made derogatory comments about the plaintiff to third per-

---

15. W. Prosser, Handbook of the Law of Torts 785 (4th ed. 1971). See also Restatement, Second, Torts § 592 (1977).

16. Dyer v. MacDougall, 93 F.Supp. 484 (E.D.N.Y.1950).

sons frequently entitled the claimant to at least an award of "general damages," which could be quite substantial.

The prerevolution inconsequence of a defamer's innocence is exemplified by Owens v. Scott Pub. Co.[17] In that case, Owens was a school board member who had sued a newspaper for publishing an editorial attacking his honesty in office. When both parties rested on their proof, the newspaper publisher asked the trial judge to tell the jury that, even though the charge in the editorial was false, the defendant deserved a verdict if before publication, the paper had carried out a fair and impartial investigation of Owens' conduct and consequently had honestly and reasonably believed that the editorial was true. The trial judge refused to give any such instruction, and the school board member prevailed at the trial. On appeal, the Washington Supreme Court held that the trial judge's refusal had been proper. The appellate opinion stated, "The newspapers have assumed the responsibility of bringing matters of public interest into the open. The public is entitled to such information. But such information should be true. [To hold the contrary] would create too great a temptation, during the heat of a . . . crusade against waste or corruption in government, to be too careless in their search for truth."[18] Only nine short years before the United States Supreme Court was to differ greatly from this Washington holding, the Court refused to grant certiorari in the *Owens* case.[19]

The Supreme Court started its turnabout in expanding the freedoms of speech and press in 1964, when it decided New York Times Co. v. Sullivan.[20] This libel case was predicated on an advertisement published by the Times. The advertisement had protested treatment of southern blacks who engaged in nonviolent protests. Sullivan was the Police Commissioner of Montgomery, Alabama; he brought a libel suit based on two paragraphs in the advertisement. The first of these paragraphs stated that after black college students had sung "My Country,

17. 46 Wash.2d 666, 284 P.2d 296 (1955), cert. denied, 350 U.S. 968, 76 S.Ct. 437, 100 L.Ed. 840 (1956).

18. About three-fourths of the states had so viewed the law in cases in which defendants were sued for publishing defamatory facts about public officials or candidates for office. The leading case for the contrary minority view was Coleman v. MacLennan, 78 Kan. 711, 98 P. 281, (1908), approving a jury charge like the one requested but distained in *Owens*. The United States Supreme Court mustered eight other states that followed Kansas law as set out in *Coleman*. See New York Times v. Sullivan, 376 U.S. 254, 280 n. 20, 84 S.Ct. 710, 726, 11 L.Ed.2d 686 (1964).

19. 350 U.S. 968, 76 S.Ct. 437, 100 L.Ed. 840 (1956).

20. 376 U.S. 254, 84 S.Ct. 710, 11 L.Ed.2d 686 (1964).

'Tis of Thee" on the steps in front of the State capitol, truck-loads of armed policemen encircled both their campus and dining halls. The second paragraph set out instances of police violence and intimidation inflicted on Dr. Martin Luther King, Jr., that is, that Dr. King had been arrested seven times on charges of speeding, loitering, and similar offenses.

Commissioner Sullivan contended that since he was responsible for the oversight and supervision of all Montgomery police operations, the statements about improper police activities had libeled him personally. Commissioner Sullivan called witnesses who purported to substantiate this theory by testifying that they had seen the Times advertisement and had read all or some of the paragraphs about police conduct as references to commissioner Sullivan.

The Times admitted slight inaccuracies in the advertisement. The students had not sung "America"; they had sung "The Star Bangled Banner." Their dining hall had not been padlocked. The police had not surrounded the campus; they had deployed near the campus in large numbers. The police had arrested Dr. King four, not seven, times.

The Commissioner did not try to prove any financial loss. The Times had sent only thirty-four copies of the edition carrying the advertisement into Montgomery County.

The Times proved that it maintained an Advertising Acceptability Department. The department's manager testified that since the advertisement had borne endorsements of well-known people whose reputations he had had no reason to question, he accordingly had entertained no suspicion of falsity. The Times had therefore done nothing to check the accuracy of the advertisement.

The case was heard first in an Alabama state trial court. The trial judge told the jury that (1) the statements were libelous in themselves; (2) the Times and the advertisement's endorsers had not been privileged to publish such statements; (3) the jury should therefore decide whether the statements had been made "of and concerning" Commissioner Sullivan, and if the jury so decided, the jury should consider the words false, malicious, and not privileged; and (4) the jury should presume that Commissioner Sullivan had suffered general damages and that the jury could award punitive damages, even though the amount of actual damages had been neither shown nor found. The judge said, however, that punitive damages would not lie for mere carelessness.

The Times requested an instruction telling the jury that punitive damages should not be awarded unless the jury found that the newspaper had actually intended to inflict harm upon the Commissioner or had been guilty of "gross negligence or recklessness." The trial judge refused to give this instruction. The trial judge also refused to instruct the jury to separate its awards of general and punitive damages. The jury brought in a verdict for $500,000, the amount for which Commissioner Sullivan had prayed.

The trial judge rejected the contention of the New York Times that his rulings in these jury charges abridged freedoms of speech and press guaranteed by the first and fourteenth amendments to the Constitution.

The Alabama Supreme Court sustained the trial judge's jury instructions in all respects and affirmed the lower court's judgment on the $500,000 verdict. In its opinion, that court said, "We think it common knowledge that the average person knows . . . [the] police . . . are under the control and direction of a single commissioner. In measuring the performance or deficiencies of such groups [as the police], praise or criticism is usually attached to the official in complete control of the body."

The United States Supreme Court unanimously reversed the Alabama courts.

Mr. Justice Brennan, writing for six members of the Court, said that the Court, for the first time, was addressing itself to the constitutional limits on the States' authority to award damages in a libel action brought by a public official against a critic of the official's conduct while exercising his duties.

Only nine years earlier, the Court had refused to consider the identical problem presented in *Times* when it was raised in the *Owens* case.[21] Thirty-three years earlier, the Court handed down its opinion in the famous constitutional case of Near v. Minnesota,[22] in which the Court held a Minnesota statute unconstitutional. That statute had purported to allow Minnesota courts to enjoin a newspaper from printing scandalous and malicious articles that the newspaper had been on the verge of publishing. The holding in *Near* had forbidden prior restraint of the publication of defamations. Chief Justice Hughes said that the American free press guarantee was designed to renounce the prior restraint of English censorship, but that "*the common law rules that subject the libeler to responsibility for . . . pri-*

21. See note 17 supra.

22. 283 U.S. 697, 51 S.Ct. 625, 75 L.Ed. 1357 (1931).

vate injury, are not abolished by the protection extended in our Constitutions." [23]

Times changed the common law as long perceived by most state courts.[24] Mr. Justice Brennan said that Alabama common law had allowed the Times only one defense—truth. Alabama allowed fair comment only when the underlying facts were true; a commentator who failed to prove truth was subject to liability for general damages, and even consideration of a commentator's good motives was a ground only for mitigating punitive damages.

"We consider [the Times] case," said Mr. Justice Brennan, "against the background of a profound national commitment to the principle that debate on public issues should be uninhibited, robust, and wide-open, and well may include . . . sharp attacks on government and public officials . . . . [E]rroneous statement is inevitable in free debate, and . . . it must be protected if the [constitutional] freedoms of expression are to have . . . 'breathing space' . . . ." Fear of incurring damages, said Mr. Justice Brennan, even though truth is a defense, may seriously inhibit free speech.

The First and the Fourteenth Amendments, Mr. Justice Brennan continued, require a federal rule barring any government official from succeeding in a damage suit for defamatory criticisms unless the plaintiff establishes that the critic was guilty of "actual malice." Actual malice, as defined in the *Times* opinion, exists only when the defamer either knows the statement is an untruth or speaks in "reckless disregard" of probable falsity.[25] Four years later, the Court refined its requirement of reckless

---

23. Near v. Minnesota ex rel. Olson, 283 U.S. 697, 715, 51 S.Ct. 625, 630, 75 L.Ed. 1357 (1931) (emphasis added).

24. The bell-weather decision widely followed up to 1964, but repudiated by *Times*, was Post Pub. Co. v. Hallam, 59 F. 530 (6th Cir. 1893). The opinion in *Hallam* was written by William Howard Taft, later President of the United States and Chief Justice of the Supreme Court of the United States.

25. See Restatement, Second, Torts § 580A, Comment a at 214 (1977).

Even so lowly a public servant as a secretary to a small-town director of public works, who sued a news-

paper for stating that she lacked secretarial skill and was excessively absent from her work, was required to establish *Times* malice in Grzelak v. Calumet Pub. Co., 543 F.2d 579 (7th Cir. 1975). Compare the opinion of Brennan, J., in Rosenblatt v. Baer, 383 U.S. 75, 86 S.Ct. 669, 15 L.Ed.2d 597 (1966), where he said nine years earlier, "[T]he 'public official' designation applies at the very least to those among the hierarchy of government employees who have, or appear to the public to have, substantial responsibility for or control over the conduct of governmental affairs." Id. at 85. Restatement, Second, Torts § 580A, Comment b at 215.

disregard to mean "sufficient evidence to permit the conclusion that the defendant in fact entertained serious doubts as to the truth of his publication."[26]

Mr. Justice Brennan characterized the *Times* restrictions on liability as tending to redress an imbalance, in that *Times'* protection of political critics partially offsets the official's absolute privilege to defame others in the course of exercising official duties. The Alabama court's *presumption of malice* was not, of course, a substitute for the requirement of *proof of malice* conforming to the *Times* definition.

The Supreme Court's duty in applying the federal constitution, Mr. Justice Brennan continued, extends beyond elaboration of principles; the Court must also, in proper cases, "make certain that those principles are constitutionally applied." *Times*, he said, was such a case. Consequently, the Court searched the whole record and found that proof of actual malice was inadequate, since it did not impugn the Advertising Acceptability manager's good faith in believing that the advertisement had been substantially correct. Even if Commissioner Sullivan had shown that the newspaper had been negligent, his case would still fall short of establishing the recklessness required to show malice, as defined in *Times*.

Mr. Justice Brennan also found that Commissioner Sullivan's proof was constitutionally defective in another respect. The Commissioner's evidence did not support a finding that the advertisement had made derogatory statements "of and concerning him". Since on its face the advertisement had made no reference to the Commissioner as an individual, it could not reasonably have been read to involve the Commissioner in its statements about police activities. An impersonal attack on governmental operations was not, in itself, a libel of the official responsible for those operations.

Three Justices concurred in reversing the Alabama courts, but they would have created a still more extensive constitutional protection for free speech and free press. They said the First and Fourteenth Amendments interdicted all defamation suits whatsoever against any critic of governmental activities. They would grant an immunity to defamers of officials, even when they maliciously speak falsely and know that they are disseminating untruth. None of these three judges still sits on the Court.

26. St. Amant v. Thompson, 390 U. S. 727, 731, 88 S.Ct. 1323, 1325, 20 L.Ed.2d 262 (1968).

The United States Supreme Court took its next step to extend its protection of the freedoms of expression in Associated Press v. Walker.[27] Walker was a retired United States Army general who had become a well-known advocate of resistance to desegregation. When a federal court ordered the University of Mississippi to admit its first black student, the University's officials became defiant, and the court then ordered a large number of federal marshalls to enforce its decree. The campus became embattled. In reporting the event, the Associated Press sent a dispatch to its subscribers stating that the General had taken command of rioters and had led a charge against the marshalls.

General Walker sued the Associated Press for disseminating this dispatch, alleging that inaccuracies in its story had libeled him. At the libel trial, the General testified that his only activity had been futile counseling of white student rioters to adopt peaceful processes; he denied having taken any part in the attack upon the marshalls.

Walker's libel suit was filed in a Texas state court. The trial judge refused to honor a $300,000 verdict for punitive damages for Walker, but entered judgment on the jury's verdict of $500,000 for compensatory damages. The *Times* rule, said the Texas trial judge, applied only to defamations disparaging public officials, and the General had retired from office before the Associated Press sent out the defamatory dispatch. Accordingly, under Texas law, Walker was entitled to recover compensatory damages, even though he made no showing that the Associated Press had been actuated by *Times* malice. Associated Press appealed to higher Texas courts; those courts stood by the trial judge's ruling.

All nine Justices of the United States Supreme Court found that the Texas judgment violated the Associated Press' constitutionally protected freedom of the press. Five Justices joined in an opinion asserting that the *Times* malice requirement had to be met by all "public figures," including those who held no public office at the time when they were defamed. The four concurring Justices stated they, too, would not allow "public figures" to recover for defamation unless they had established their detractor's fault; they were, however, willing to accept proof short of *Times* malice, provided that the public figure plaintiff proved that the defendant had departed substantially from the standards of investigation ordinarily adhered to by responsible publishers. This minority espousal of a relaxed measure of

27. Decided with, and under the title of, Curtis Pub. Co. v. Butts,   388 U.S. 130, 87 S.Ct. 1975, 18 L. Ed.2d 1094 (1967).

fault in public figure cases has had no judicial support since *Walker*.

The Supreme Court decided Curtis Pub. Co. v. Butts[28] as a companion case to *Walker*; both cases were considered in the same opinion. Curtis, in its weekly magazine, The Saturday Evening Post, irresponsibly spread abroad a story accusing Butts of secretly divulging plays that Georgia University's football team had planned to use in a forthcoming game against Alabama. Mr. Butts, even though he had directed Georgia's athletic program, had not been employed by the University of Georgia. Butts had worked for the Georgia Athletic Association, a private corporation that, by statute, was not an agency of the State of Georgia. The court in which this libel suit was initiated found in favor of Mr. Butts.

In the *Butts* case, however, the Supreme Court was not considering the holding of a state court; it was reviewing the judgment of a United States Court of Appeals. That judgment upheld the action of a United States District Court. When, therefore, five Supreme Court Justices voted to sustain this federal judgment, the Court approved Mr. Butts' entitlement to collect his award. Four of those five Justices who voted for affirmance did not support their votes by stating that Butts had established *Times* malice; they affirmed on the ground that Curtis had departed from the standards of investigation adhered to by responsible publishers—a test of constitutionality that, in the succeeding ten years, has fallen into disuse. Only the fifth vote for affirmance was cast by a Justice who said Butts had proved *Times* malice. Two of the dissenting Justices, who had previously said that the *Times* rule was applicable to public figures, nevertheless refused to find that Butts had proved *Times* malice. The two remaining Justices said that *Times* protection of freedom of the press was inadequate and that the press should not be civilly liable for defamation under any circumstances whatsoever.

The best that can be said for *Butts*, as a Supreme Court authority supporting a public figure's right to recover damages for defamation if, and only if, the Plaintiff establishes *Times* malice, is that only three Supreme Court Justices said that such was the law; whereas in the companion case, *Walker*, five Justices disallowed a public figure's state court recovery because the plaintiff had not established *Times* malice. In spite of the analytical weakness in the underpinning of Butts' *success*, five judges had acceded to Walker's *defeat* on the ground that the

28. Id.

Times malice requirement should be extended to public figure cases. (Certainly, public figure defamation plaintiffs should not be saddled with burdens any heavier than those borne by public official defamation plaintiffs.) In post-*Butts* cases, public figures suing in defamation have invariably been met with rulings that the establishment of *Times* malice is a sufficient and necessary proof of fault,[29] and recently all nine Supreme Court Justices assumed that a public figure must establish *Times* malice to recover for a newspaper libel.[30]

Logically, the next problem that was bound to be put to the Supreme Court was whether or not the *Times* rule applied to defamatory remarks referring to private persons in the course of discussing matters of public concern. The Court considered this problem, but was unable to muster a majority view until it decided Gertz v. Robert Welch, Inc.[31] in 1974—ten years after *Times* and seven years after *Walker.*

29. See Hotchner v. Castillo-Puche, 551 F.2d 910 (2d Cir. 1977); [William F.] Buckley v. Littell, 539 F.2d 882 (2d Cir. 1976), cert. denied, 429 U.S. 1062, 97 S.Ct. 785, 786, 50 L.Ed.2d 777; Brewer v. Memphis Pub. Co., 538 F.2d 699 (5th Cir. 1976); [Johnny] Carson v. Allied News Co., 529 F.2d 206 (7th Cir. 1976). Cf. Orr v. Argus-Press Co., 586 F.2d 1108 (6th Cir. 1978), in which the court held that the libel plaintiff was a public figure *for the limited purpose* of reporting his arrest and indictment, which involved a matter of general public interest. See also Restatement, Second, Torts § 580A, Comment c at 216–17 (1977). The court not only required a public figure plaintiff to establish *Times* malice in Wolston v. Reader's Digest Ass'n, Inc., 578 F.2d 427 (D.C.Cir. 1978), but also held that whether or not a particular plaintiff is a public person is a question of law to be decided by the court and is not a jury question.

30. Herbert v. Lando, 41 U.S. 153, 99 S.Ct. 1635, 60 L.Ed.2d 115 (1979). In that case, a retired U.S. Army general received widespread media attention for accusing his superiors of covering up Vietnam war atrocities. His charges were reported in a CBS television program, "60 Minutes."

Herbert sued CBS and others, alleging that the program falsely and maliciously pictured him as a liar. The issue before the Supreme Court was whether or not the plaintiff could use pretrial procedures to inquire into CBS' editorial processes. Mr. Justice White, writing the majority opinion, said, "*New York Times* and its progeny made it essential to proving liability that [some] plaintiffs focus on the conduct and state of mind of the defendant. To be liable, the defamer of . . . public figures must know or have reason to suspect that his publication is false . . . . Inevitably, unless liability is to be completely foreclosed, the thoughts and editoral processes of the alleged defamer would be open to examination." Id. at 1641. Thus Mr. Justice White concluded that the first amendment's protection of freedom of the press did not cloak publishers or broadcasters with an immunity allowing them to block questions about their editorial activities.

31. 418 U.S. 323, 94 S.Ct. 2997, 41 L.Ed.2d 789 (1974). See Restatement, Second, Torts § 580B, Comments c & d at 223–25 (1977); Comment g deals well with proof. Id. at 227–28.

Gertz was a lawyer. Among his clients had been relatives of a man murdered by a policeman, and Gertz had been retained to bring a wrongful death action against that policeman. Robert Welch, through a corporation named for him, published a monthly magazine that was designed to be an "outlet for the views of the John Birch Society." For several years, this magazine had intermittently accused radicals of trying to discredit local policemen with the hope that a national law enforcement agency would eventually supplant local police forces and serve a Communist dictatorship. Welch commissioned an article on the policeman's trial for murder, a maneuver he believed would bolster suspicion of the conspiracy. The resulting article, entitled "Frame Up," purported to divulge that the policeman had been convicted on Communist-inspired perjured testimony. The article charged that Gertz was the Communist who had engineered this dastardly conviction.

Welch and his staff had made no effort to check the truth of the article's charges against Gertz. A foreword to the article stated that the author had extensively researched the murder trial. Gertz' picure, captioned, "Elmer Gertz of the Red Guild harasses Nuccio," was printed with the article.

Gertz was well known in some circles, but neither the trial judge nor the Supreme Court looked upon him as a public figure.[32]

At the trial, Welch denied that he had had any knowledge of the article's falsity when he published it. He testified that he had relied on both the author's reputation and his own experience with the accuracy and authenticity of the author's former contributions to Welch's magazine.

The jury found a verdict for Gertz, but on Welch's motion for a judgment notwithstanding the verdict, the trial judge ruled that Gertz had not established *Times* malice, and granted the motion. The theory behind this ruling was that, even though Gertz was not a public figure, the article had discussed a matter of public concern; therefore, the constitution protected Welch from liability unless he had been guilty of *Times* malice.[33] The judges who heard Gertz' appeal to the Seventh Circuit enter-

32. Compare Hotchner v. Castillo-Puche, supra note 28, where a successful writer who published a memoir about his friend Ernest Hemmingway was characterized by the court without comment as a "public figure" in a defamation action against another Hemmingway biographer.

33. This theory was, three years earlier, the plurality view in the Supreme Court of the United States in Rosenbloom v. Metromedia, Inc., 403 U.S. 29, 91 S.Ct. 1811, 29 L.Ed.2d 296 (1971). Many courts adopted it before the *Gertz* decision was handed down.

tained doubts about the trial judge's finding that Gertz was not a public figure; but even assuming that the trial judge had been correct, they held that liability for publishing the magazine article depended on a showing of *Times* malice.

The Supreme Court reversed the circuit court's ruling and remanded the case for retrial. Gertz' verdict had been returned by jurors given the prerevolutionary instruction that had allowed them to assess "presumed" damages against Welch without finding him guilty of any fault. The Supreme Court opined that, even when matters of public concern are discussed, the states may not impose liability without fault for defamation; each state may, however, set up its own standard for measuring the fault that subjects a discussant to liability, as long as that standard requires a showing of fault at least as grave as negligence. The Court also held that the federal constitution forbade the states to award judgments for "presumed or punitive damages, at least when liability is not based on a showing of [either] knowledge of falsity or reckless disregard for the truth."

The holdings in *Gertz* departed radically from English common law and the judicially announced defamation law of most of the several states. Before the revolution, many (though not all) American courts had held that unprivileged defamatory statements uttered during discussions of matters of public concern were actionable, even though the disparager was not at fault; moreover, the sullied victim was entitled to substantial "general damages" for vindication and compensation, albeit no specific financial losses were proven or even provable.[34]

The Supreme Court applied *Gertz* two years later in Time, Inc. v. Firestone.[35] The Firestone suit grew out of an item in Time magazine which had stated, "DIVORCED. By Russell A. Firestone, Jr., 41, heir to the tire fortune; Mary Alice Sullivan Firestone, 32 . . . on grounds of extreme cruelty *and adultery* [italics added] . . . in West Palm Beach, Fla. The . . . trial produced enough testimony of extramarital adventures on both sides, said the judge, 'to make Dr. Freud's hair curl.' "

In 1964, the Firestones' marriage was coming apart, and Mary Alice had sued for separate maintenance. Russell filed a counterclaim, praying for a divorce on two grounds: extreme

---

34. See, e. g., Cassidy v. Daily Mirror Newspapers, Ltd., [1929] 2 K. B. 331. The American authorities are discussed in the previous edition of this book. C. Morris, Morris on Torts 284 et seq. (1953).

35. 424 U.S. 448, 96 S.Ct. 958, 47 L. Ed.2d 154 (1976).

cruelty and adultery. The trial judge handed down an opinion mentioning racy tales of both spouses' wayward sex exploits told by witnesses for both parties and expressing the judge's doubts about the credibility of these witnesses. The divorce court judge concluded, nevertheless, that "neither party [was] domesticated"; he granted Russell's prayer for divorce and entered an order requiring Russell to pay Mary Alice specified alimony. The judge's opinion did not state explicitly the ground or grounds for divorce on which he had based his judgment. The statutory law of Florida provides, however, that when a husband is granted a divorce on the ground of his wife's adultery, she is not to be given alimony.

At the trial of the libel suit brought in a Florida court by Mary Alice against Time magazine, the publishers of Time made a showing that they had exercised considerable caution before they published the item. The Florida trial judge sent this libel case to the jury without instructing it that Time's liability depended on fault; he charged the jury that the magazine could be held liable if it found the article defamatory, untrue, and a proximate cause of injury to Mary Alice. The jury found for her and awarded her a $100,000 verdict. Judgment was entered on this verdict.

The Florida Supreme Court affirmed the $100,000 judgment. Its opinion stated that Time magazine's erroneous publication was, in itself, clear and convincing evidence of the negligence required by *Gertz* for liability; that, since the divorce court's award of alimony had impliedly ruled out adultery, a careful reading of that court's decree would have revealed that the sole ground for divorce had been extreme cruelty; and that the item was thus a flagrant example of journalistic negligence.

The United States Supreme Court reversed and remanded. The Court spoke through Mr. Justice Rehnquist.[36] He first refused to characterize Mary Alice as a public person. He then said the record did not show, at any point in the litigation, that a Florida court had made a conscious determination of the publisher's negligence; he therefore remanded the case to the Florida courts for a proper trial of that issue. This remand rejected the Florida Supreme Court's finding that negligence on Time's part had existed, since reading the decree with due care would have informed Time that the one ground of the divorce had been extreme cruelty. Though it is said that everyone knows the law, Time magazine could not have been presumed to know the *legal effect* of adultery in Florida's divorce law.

36. Id.

One of the three dissenting Justices had difficulty in characterizing the notorious and newsworthy Mrs. Firestone (whose protracted litigation had come to the attention of many Floridians as well as the residents of several other states) as a private person—that is, one entitled to maintain a libel suit without establishing *Times* malice.[37]

The Supreme Court holdings previously discussed all exercised the Court's function as the guardian of the press' rights to free speech and freedom under the Constitution. The Court directed

37. In Wolston v. Reader's Digest Ass'n, — U.S. —, 99 S.Ct. 2701, 61 L.Ed.2d 450 (1979), defendant published a book in which Wolston was falsely identified as a Soviet spy. Defendant won a summary judgment on the ground that Wolston was a public figure. Holding Wolston was not a public figure, the Supreme Court reversed. Sixteen years earlier he had failed to respond to a grand jury subpoena and had received a one year suspended sentence. At that time, the matter was reported in the press because Wolston was the nephew of an admitted Soviet agent and the grand jury was investigating espionage activities. Writing for six members of the Court, Justice Rhenquist quoted from *Gertz* the two ways an individual could become a public figure: "[1] For the most part those who attain this status have assumed roles of especial prominence in the affairs of society. Some occupy positions of such persuasive power and influence that they are deemed public figures for all purposes. [2] More commonly, those classed as public figures have thrust themselves to the forefront of particular public controversies in order to influence the resolution of the issues involved." It was admitted that the first test did not apply to Wolston; he had been a totally private person before and after the subpoena incident. Nor did he thrust himself into events to influence them. It appeared he was motivated by reasons of health. "Petitioner's failure to appear . . . and [his] citation for contempt were no doubt 'newsworthy,' but the simple fact that these events attracted media attention is not conclusive of the public figure issue. A private individual is not automatically transformed into a public figure just by becoming involved in or associated with a matter that attracts public attention." The Court specifically rejected "the further contention . . . that any person who engages in criminal conduct automatically becomes a public figure for purposes of comment on a limited range of issues relating to his conviction . . . . To hold otherwise would create an 'open season' for all who sought to defame persons convicted of a crime." Two Justices concurred on the ground that even if Wolston were a public figure at the time of the incident, he had lost that status in subsequent sixteen years of private life. Justice Brennan dissented.

Cf. James v. Gannett Co., 40 N.Y.2d 415, 386 N.Y.S.2d 871, 353 N.E.2d 834 (1976), in which the New York Court of Appeals distinguished a publicity-seeking plaintiff from Mrs. Firestone and held her affirmative action was the essential step underlying the category "public figure." But see Rosanova v. Playboy Enterprises, Inc., 580 F.2d 859 (5th Cir. 1978), in which the court held that a publicity-eluding plaintiff who had been often referred to in various publications as involved in organized crime had become a "public figure" in spite of his personal passion for anonymity, because his activities aroused a legitimate interest in his possible misdeeds.

the Florida courts to try the issue of Time magazine's negligence in *Firestone* and did not direct the Florida courts to try the fault issue by the standard of *Times* malice. In *Firestone*, the Court followed *Gertz* and held that Florida could compensate a newsworthy private person damaged by a negligent magazine that was not guilty of *Times* malice.

Contrast this to what happened in a Colorado case. Walker v. Colorado Springs Sun, Inc.,[38] had been tried before the *Gertz* opinion was handed down. The suit was brought by the Walkers, proprietors of an antique shop. They sued the Sun, its publisher, and one of its reporters. The Walkers proved they bought some wares that they had no reason to believe had been stolen. The property had, in fact, been taken by thieves from the unoccupied house of a woman confined to a nursing home. A friend of this woman tracked down the property and conferred with the Walkers, but he did not come away with the stolen articles. The Good Samaritan then related his conversation with the Walkers to a Sun reporter, who thereafter interviewed the elderly woman, the district attorney, and the police. Subsequently, the reporter wrote a feature article, based on his interviews, which tended to defame the Walkers. The Sun not only published the reporter's article, but followed it for weeks with clearly defamatory material that more pointedly disparaged the Walkers. The trial judge submitted the case to the jury, instructing that it could award compensatory and punitive damages to the Walkers if it found that the publications were false and that they had been published either with knowledge of their falsity or with reckless disregard for the truth. The jury returned a verdict for the Walkers, allotting them $29,200 compensatory damages and $9,900 punitive damages. The trial judge entered a judgment on this verdict against all three defendants.

The Colorado Supreme Court had written, but not issued, its opinion in this case when the *Gertz* opinion was published in United States Law Week. Thereupon, the court ordered counsel to file new briefs within sixty days and set a date for further oral arguments. Thereafter, the Colorado Supreme Court handed down a decision affirming the trial judge's rulings to the effect that the Walkers were private persons and that the newspaper's publications had involved matters of public concern. The court noted the *Gertz* opinions expressed willingness to allow any state to adopt a standard requiring fault greater than negligence; the court said, "We hold that, when a defamatory statement has been published concerning one who is not a public offi-

38. 188 Colo. 86, 538 P.2d 450 (1975), cert. denied sub. nom., Woestendiek v. Walker, 423 U.S. 1025, 96 S.Ct. 469, 46 L.Ed.2d 399.

cial or a public figure, but the matter involved is of public or general concern, the publisher of the statement will be liable to the person defamed if, and only if, he knew the statement to be false or made the statement with reckless disregard for whether it was true or not." These words convey the same meaning as the words used in *Times* to define actual malice; the Colorado court, however, eschewed both the word "malice" and the federal requirement that "reckless disregard" be found only in cases in which the disparager had serious doubts about the truth of the statement in issue. Applying its announced standard, the Colorado Supreme Court concluded that the judgment against the Sun and its publisher should be affirmed; the court held that the jury instructions had been proper and that the Walkers' evidence had supported the verdict. The court reversed the holding against the reporter, however, and rendered judgment for him on the ground that the verdict against him had not been supported by proof of sufficient fault.

The conclusion supported by the Colorado holding is that, in some circumstances, a state court can afford greater freedom of expression to a defendant than the minimum required by the constitutional cases that abolished liability without fault in defamation law.[39] There will be several further occasions to demonstrate that *Times*, *Walker*, and *Gertz* contracted liability for defamation but conferred no new rights on defamation plaintiffs whose claims fail under state law. Some states, in private persons' libel suits, have not exercised *Gertz'* permission to give the press more freedom than *Gertz* did;[40] these states, at this writing, seem to represent the majority view.

According to the *Gertz* opinion, when a private plaintiff sues for defamation, "the States may not permit recovery of presumed or punitive damages, *at least when liability is not based on a showing of knowledge of falsity or reckless disregard for the truth.*"[41] This rule, as has been said earlier, was at odds

---

39. Thus far, New York, like Colorado, has required private persons to produce evidence of fault greater than negligence when defamations were published in discussing matters of public concern. Commerical Programming, Unlimited v. Columbia Broadcasting Systems, 50 A.D.2d 351, 378 N.Y.S.2d 69 (1975). See also, Chapadeau v. Utica Observer-Dispatch, Inc., 38 N.Y.2d 196, 379 N.Y.S.2d 61, 341 N.E.2d 569 (1975).

40. See Martin v. Griffin Television, Inc., 549 P.2d 85 (Okl.1976); Taskett v. King Broadcasting Co., 86 Wash.2d 439, 546 P.2d 81 (1976); Troman v. Wood, 62 Ill.2d 184, 340 N.E.2d 292 (1975); Stone v. Essex County Newspapers, Inc., 367 Mass. 849, 330 N.E.2d 161 (1975).

41. Gertz v. Robert Welch, Inc., 418 U.S. 323, 349, 94 S.Ct. 2997, 3011, 41 L.Ed.2d 789 (1974) (emphasis added).

with pre-*Times* common law.   The *Gertz* opinions' treatment is quoted more fully in the footnote.[42]

The United States Supreme Court has set no guidelines, however, to confine the states' allowances of actual damages.   When the *Firestone* $100,000 Florida judgment was reviewed by the United States Supreme Court, Time magazine pointed out that, on the eve of trial of her libel suit, Mrs. Firestone had withdrawn her claim "for damages to her reputation; " this maneuver, Time magazine contended, put her in a posture inconsistent with the *Gertz* requirement that defamation plaintiffs prove actual damages.[43]   Mr. Justice Rehnquist replied, "Florida has obviously decided to permit recovery for other injuries without regard to measuring the effect the falsehood may have had upon a plaintiff's reputation.   .   .   .   [In *Gertz*] we made it clear that States could base awards on elements other than injury to reputation, specifically listing 'personal humiliation, and mental anguish and suffering' as examples of injuries which might be compensated consistently with the Constitution upon a showing of fault." [44]

42. In his opinion, Mr. Justice Powell stated:

"The common law of defamation   .   .   .   allows recovery of purportedly compensatory damages without evidence of actual loss.   .   .   .   [T]he existence of injury is presumed from the fact of publication. Juries may award substantial sums as compensation for supposed damage   .   .   .   .   [T]he states have no substantial interest in securing for plaintiffs such as   [*Gertz*] gratuitous awards of money damages far in excess   of   actual   injury   .   .   .   .

"We also find no justification for allowing awards of punitive damages against publishers and broadcasters held liable under state-defined standards of liability for defamation.   .   .   .   [T]he private defamation plaintiff who establishes liability under a less demanding standard than that stated by *New York Times* may recover only such damages as are sufficient to compensate him for actual injury." Id. 350–51.

43. Time was probably relying on cases like Terwilliger v. Wands, 17 N.Y. 54, 72 Am.Dec. 420 (1858). Terwilliger sued for slander. At that time, the imputation of sexual irregularity on which he sued was not slander per se in New York; accordingly, Terwilliger could not prove actionable slander unless he adduced evidence of special damages. He attempted to meet this requirement by showing that, as a result of the slander, he became ill, took to his bed, and was unable to work his farm. The court held he failed to prove special damages, stating that since the slander was not shown to cause anybody to have treated the plaintiff any differently from what they otherwise would have done, the emotional disturbance was not enough. "Special damages," said the court, "must flow from impaired reputation." Id. at 63.

44. Time, Inc. v. Firestone, 424 U.S. 448, 460, 96 S.Ct. 958, 968, 47 L. Ed.2d 154 (1976). But see Restatement, Second, Torts § 623.

The Supreme Court did not expressly hold in either *Gertz* or *Firestone* that the states must allow damages for emotional upsets resulting from negligently issued defamations. According to *Firestone*, however, unless the states choose to restrict damages, jurors can constitutionally make multi-thousand dollar awards in appropriate cases to compensate private plaintiffs for emotional upset proximately caused by defamations published in good faith in negligently inaccurate reports on matters of public concern.[45] The chilling effect that *Firestone* may have on an unpopular reporter of derogatory news of public interest has not made the United States Supreme Court shiver.

To repeat, *Gertz* outlawed punitive damage awards to those defamed, "at least," said Mr. Justice Powell, "when liability is not based on a showing of knowledge of falsity or reckless disregard for the truth. . . . [J]uries assess punitive damages in wholly unpredictable amounts. . . . [J]ury discretion to award punitive damages unnecessarily exacerbates the danger of media self-censorship. . . . [T]he private defamation plaintiff who establishes liability under a less demanding standard than that stated by *New York Times* may recover only such damages as are sufficient to compensate him for actual injury." [46]

Nearly all the states recognized that, on a proper occasion, a defendant could be found liable for punitive damages. Ordinarily no state instructed jurors that they could award punitive damages against a defendant whose fault was no worse than negligence; only a wrong more flagrant than a mere failure to use due care justified such an award. In unprivileged defamation cases, in which the common law had allowed liability without proof of any fault, some courts were likely to echo the ancient saw to the effect that the defendant's malice was presumed once the other elements of a plaintiff's defamation case had been established. Some common law courts treated presumed malice as an appropriate basis for punitive damages.[47] However, this fictitious malice has long been rejected as a ground for awarding punitive damages by most common law courts.[48] Seven

---

45. 424 U.S. 448, 458, 96 S.Ct. 958, 967, 47 L.Ed.2d 154 (1976).

46. Gertz v. Robert Welch, Inc., 418 U.S. 323, 349–50, 94 S.Ct. 2997, 3011–12, 41 L.Ed.2d 789 (1974).

47. In the Supreme Court of Alabama's opinion in *Times*, the court saw nothing awry in the clause in the trial judge's jury charge:

"[W]here as here, the Court has ruled [the advertisement] is libelous per se then punitive damages may be awarded by the jury . . . ." New York Times Co. v. Sullivan, 273 Ala. 656, 679, 144 So.2d 25, 43 (1962).

48. See, e. g., Corrigan v. Bobbs-Merrill Co., 228 N.Y. 58, 126 N.E. 260 (1920); see also General Mo-

months after the *Times* opinion was handed down, the Court announced its refusal to review a Minnesota libel judgment that included a punitive damage award based on proof of malice.[49]

Gertz did not encourage state courts to allow punitive damages, even after *Times* malice had been established. Four state courts turned their backs on the English common law practice of allowing punitive damages on any occasion; these four states outlawed punitive damage awards in all tort litigation.[50] Massachusetts was one of these four. Post-*Gertz*, the Massachusetts Supreme Judicial Court held that punitive damages were not recoverable in any defamation case—regardless of whether or not the plaintiff had established the defendant's malice.[51] Although the opinion seemed specially to formulate Massachusetts defamation law, closer examination reveals that it merely followed long-established Massachusetts general tort law.

Buckley v. Littell [52] illustrates the current law of punitive damages. William Buckley proved that Littell had written a book criticizing political extremists, one of whom had been the conservative publicist Buckley. Among Littell's dispraisals was the statement that Buckley, like the author and critic Westbrook Pegler, had lyingly defamed many people who could take him to court for his lies. The trial judge found that Littell had made this aspersion either with knowledge of its falsity or in reckless disregard of its untruth. Buckley offered no evidence to show that Littell's defamations had caused him to suffer humiliation, anxiety, or financial loss. The trial court awarded one dollar to Buckley for actual damages and $7,500 in punitive damages. Although the Second Circuit Court of Appeals reduced the punitive damage award to $1,000, the court found no constitutional bar to punitive damage awards once *Times* malice has been shown. Other courts have made rulings in accord with the *Buckley* view on punitive damages.[53]

tors Corp. v. Piskor, 277 Md. 165, 177, 352 A.2d 810, 817 (1976) (post-*Gertz*).

49. Loftsgaarden v. Reiling, 267 Minn. 181, 126 N.W.2d 154, cert. denied, 379 U.S. 845, 85 S.Ct. 31, 13 L.Ed.2d 50 (1964).

50. W. Prosser, Handbook of the Law of Torts 9 (4th ed. 1971).

51. Stone v. Essex County Newspapers, Inc., 367 Mass. 849, 330 N.E. 2d 161 (1975).

52. 539 F.2d 882 (2d Cir. 1976), cert. denied, 429 U.S. 1062, 97 S. Ct. 785, 786, 50 L.Ed.2d 777 (1977).

53. Appleyard v. Transamerican Press, Inc., 539 F.2d 1026 (4th Cir. 1976), cert. denied, 429 U.S. 1041, 97 S.Ct. 740, 50 L.Ed.2d 753 (1977); Davis v. Schuchat, 510 F. 2d 731 (D.C.Cir. 1975); Walker v. Colorado Springs Sun, Inc., 188 Colo. 86, 538 P.2d 450, cert. denied, 423 U.S. 1025, 96 S.Ct. 469, 46 L.Ed.2d 399 (1975). One case which denied punitive damages on constitutional grounds, even if

The ambit of the propriety of punitive damage awards at common law, in those states that permitted their recovery, is a little fuzzy. The traditional state formulations, whatever their past history, have been expressly superseded in defamation cases by the *Gertz* opinion, which has forbidden awards of punitive damages, "at least when liability is not based on a showing of knowledge of falsity or reckless disregard for the truth." These words, then, should be the standard controlling those trial judges' rulings that either allow or forbid juries to assess punitive damages. When juries are to try the issue of whether or not punitive damages should be allowed, the *Gertz* test should be incorporated in their instructions.[54] However, in at least one jurisdiction (Arkansas), an award of punitive damages may not be made without a showing that the defendant was not only guilty of reckless disregard for the truth, but also actuated by personal spite.[55] This holding, of course, does not infringe constitutional rights to free speech.

Before 1964, truth was a "defense" in defamation cases—which meant that falsity would be assumed unless the defendant pleaded affirmatively that his aspersion was true and then came forward at the trial with evidence of its truth. Once all the proof was in, the defendant had the burden of convincing the court that the disparagement was true. The revolution changed all this: the United States Supreme Court has, by implication, allocated an issue of falsity to the plaintiff by holding that plaintiffs have no cause of action unless they establish the defendants' fault. Public officials or public persons are required by *Times* and *Walker* to establish *Times* malice; and private persons are required by *Gertz* to establish at least negligence. These constitutional burdens requiring plaintiffs to demonstrate the defendants' fault make no sense unless the plaintiff shows that the disparagement was untrue. Statements of defamatory truth are not actionable as either libel or slander. Some state courts have expressly recognized this constitutional reallocation of the burdens on the truth issue.[56]

Times malice were proved, was reversed on appeal. Maheu v. Hughes Tool Co., 384 F.Supp. 166 (C.D.Cal.1974), rev'd, 569 F.2d 459 (9th Cir. 1978).

54. This was the court's view in Marchesi v. Franchino, 283 Md. 131, 387 A.2d 1129 (1978).

55. Luster v. Retail Credit Co., 575 F.2d 609 (8th Cir. 1978).

56. See, e. g., General Motors Corp. v. Piskor, 277 Md. 165, 352 A.2d 810 (1976). See also Restatement, Second, Torts § 613, Caveat & Comment at 307 (1977). Contra, Corabi v. Curtis Pub. Co., 441 Pa. 432, 453, 273 A.2d 899, 910 (1971) (but untenable). But see Moyer v. Phillips, 462 Pa. 395, 407, 341 A.2d 441, 447 (1975) (Roberts, J., concurring).

In another way the United States Supreme Court has disfavored def-

Statements of "opinion," in themselves, would not support a defamation claim at common law before the revolution. The courts were expecially permissive to critics passing judgment on art put on public view [57] and literature distributed to public readership.[58] Courts refused to become supercritics of those who evaluate pictures, performances, poems, and the like, even when an unqualified scoffer belittled a work of great merit. This critic's license was no early recognition of a freedom of expression; in 1808, Lord Ellenborough, unconcerned with both our first amendment and English impediments imposed by censors, had rationalized the immunity this way: "Every man who

amation plaintiffs, with a theory based on constitutional grounds. In most civil cases, the country over, the performance of a litigant bearing a burden of proving some fact is adequate once that fact is established by "a preponderance of the evidence"—that is, proof found strong enough to make the sought-for conclusion more probable than not. In *Times,* Mr. Justice Brennan says: "We must 'make an independent examination of the whole record,' so as to assure ourselves that the judgement does not constitute a forbidden intrusion on the field of free expression. . . . [W]e consider that the proof presented to show actual malice lacks the convincing clarity which the constitutional standard commands, and hence that it would not constitutionally sustain the judgment for [Commissioner Sullivan] under the proper rule of law." 376 U.S. at 285–86, 84 S.Ct. at 728–29.

At least two United States Courts of Appeal have published opinions indicating that *Times* malice, when an issue, must be proved by the plaintiff with "convincing clarity" —a burden which sounds (and probably is, on occasion) more difficult to carry than proof by "a preponderance of the evidence." See Arnheiter v. Random House, Inc., 578 F.2d 804 (9th Cir. 1978); Alioto v. Cowles Communications, Inc., 519 F.2d 777 (9th Cir. 1975), cert. denied, 423 U.S. 930, 96 S.Ct. 280, 46 L.Ed.2d 259; Wasserman

v. Time, Inc., 424 F.2d 920, 921 (D.C.Cir. 1970), cert. denied, 398 U.S. 940, 90 S.Ct. 1844, 26 L.Ed.2d 273; but see Corabi v. Curtis Pub. Co., 441 Pa. 432, 456–67, 273 A.2d 899, 911–12 (1971), and compare Maheu v. Hughes Tool Co., 569 F. 2d 459 (9th Cir. 1978). In many cases the burden to prove malice "with convincing clarity" may be no more difficult than adducing a "preponderance of the evidence"; a trial judge who believes that a plaintiff's evidence can preponderate will seldom believe that that evidence is not clear and convincing. Plaintiff's counsel may, on occasion, run an unnecessary risk by successfully obtaining a "preponderance of the evidence" instruction, inviting reversal on appeal. Jurors who believe plaintiff's witnesses and doubt defendant's showing of good intentions are likely to find the plaintiff's proof clear enough to convince. See Restatement, Second, Torts § 613, Comment f at 309 (1977).

57. See the ill-fated claim put forth in a libel suit in Cherry v. Des Moines Leader, 114 Iowa 298, 86 N.W. 323 (1901) (newspaper published a scathing, sardonic criticism of a corny vaudeville act).

58. Carr v. Hodd, 1 Camp. 355, 170 Eng.Rep. 983 (note *nisi prius* 1808) (ridicule of plaintiff's travel books illustrated with ludicrous caricatures of plaintiff a-traveling).

publishes a book commits himself to the judgment of the public, and anyone may comment on his performance." [59]

The common law courts showed less leniency to commentators who had uttered adverse remarks about an individual's competence in his daily work, office, or profession. In 1930, the New York Court of Appeals reviewed a football coach's libel judgment against a newspaper. The paper had published its sports reporter's article challenging the plaintiff's coaching abilities.[60] The court found that the article's characterization of the football team's play as "antique," was opinion and, therefore, not actionable. However, the reporter's charge that the coach had not developed his players' abilities was held to be factual enough to subject the newspaper to liability for defamation. When a medical publicist called a notorious doctor "a charlatan and a quack," he escaped liability for defamation under Texas law only by adducing proof held by the court to justify his opinion.[61]

Political name-calling could be costly before the revolution. A "Good Government League," for example, published a circular advising voters against supporting a particular candidate "because in the last legislature he championed measures opposed to the moral interests of the community." The Michigan Supreme Court held the circular libelous because the League "did not state what measures were supported, and [the League's] opinions of that particular conduct, but said generally and unqualifiedly, as a fact, that [the candidate] had arrayed himself against the moral interests of the community, which, if true, should discredit him with any voter who believed the statement." [62]

Compare this last quotation with the Pennsylvania Supreme Court's legal analysis in Clark v. Allen,[63] decided less than eight months after the *Times* opinion came down. Senator Joseph Clark, then running for reelection, initiated libel proceedings after political foes had circulated a letter in which they stated "we are shocked at Joe Clark's . . . . [Americans for Democratic Action] approved voting record with its Communistic tendencies." Chief Justice Bell noted that cases in his

---

59. Id. at 360, 170 Eng.Rep. at 985.

60. Hoeppner v. Dunkirk Printing Co., 254 N.Y. 95, 172 N.E. 139 (1930).

61. Brinkley v. Fishbein, 110 F.2d 62 (5th Cir. 1940), cert. denied, 311 U.S. 672, 61 S.Ct. 34, 85 L.Ed. 432.

62. Eikhoff v. Gilbert, 124 Mich. 353, 83 N.W. 110 (1900). Compare Orr v. Argus-Press Co., 586 F.2d 1108 (6th Cir. 1978) (reviewing decision of E.D.Mich. court).

63. 415 Pa. 484, 204 A.2d 42 (1964).

court had previously held that "referring to any American Citizen as a Communist, or knowingly a member of a Communist organization, or engaging in Communist activities, is libelous per se." The Chief Justice continued nevertheless, "Governed by the decision and guided by the opinion in New York Times Co. v. Sullivan, we hold *as a matter of law*, that the averments contained in the aforesaid letter are *not libelous* . . . ." Senator Clark alleged that the defendants had acted maliciously, a charge admitted by the defendants' demurrer; on oral argument, the Senator asked leave to amend his complaint by alleging "actual malice." This request was refused. The court's final footnote states, "Since the statements were not libelous, it is unnecessary to consider whether they were made with actual malice." Accordingly, the Pennsylvania court characterized odious political name-calling as privileged free speech.

A similar result was reached in Buckley v. Littell,[64] the libel case already mentioned, in which a critic of totalitarianism had called Buckley not only a lying defamer, but also a fascist, a fellow traveler with the radical right, and a disseminator of items picked up from openly fascist journals. The court called these epithets "opinion" and relied on the dictum in *Gertz*,[65] stating that since ideas and opinions can never be false, they therefore cannot be malicious in the sense in which malice is defined in *Times*. Political labels said the court, cannot be looked upon as statements of fact because their meanings in political debate are imprecise. Thus vociferous utterances of "nonfactual" political propaganda are licensed by Supreme Court protection of robust debate under the intendment of the first amendment.

No doubt the courts will characterize some expressions of general disregard as opinion, even when spoken out of political contexts. When someone is called "stupid," "mean," "stingy," "unlikeable," or any number of more colorful equivalents, courts are likely to classify these invectives as opinion and, therefore, not actionable in defamation.

§ 3.   WHAT SURVIVES THE REVOLUTION?

At one time, truth may not have protected its publisher from liability for defamation. Old books stated the greater the truth, the greater the libel, in accordance with the theory that scandal should be reported to the authorities for appropriate action and

---

64. 539 F.2d 882 (2d Cir. 1976), cert. denied, 429 U.S. 1062, 97 S. Ct. 785, 50 L.Ed.2d 777 (1977).

65. 418 U.S. at 339–40, 94 S.Ct. at 3006–07. Cf. Restatement, Second, Torts § 566, Comment c, Illustration 2 at 174, Comment e at 176 (1977).

not be spread abroad. Sometime later, but long before *Times*, defamation actions would not lie against those who spoke the truth. A disparagement of ignoble misconduct could misstate insignificant detail and yet be truthful enough to protect the utterer from liability for defamation. For example, in the 1936 case of Fort Worth Press Co. v. Davis,[66] a newspaper reported that a public official had wasted $80,000 of the taxpayers' money on a worthless project. Proof showed an expenditure of only $17,500. The Texas court held, however, that truth was adequately established, since no less opprobrium attached to wasting $17,500 than would attach to wasting $80,000.[67] A defamation may, nevertheless, expand upon a discreditable fact to the point that a kernel of truth is so overlaid with falsity that the defamer is subject to liability.[68]

If Busybody should traduce Thinskin, face-to-face, but in isolation from all other human beings, Thinskin's reputation would not be affected by Busybody's scurrility. In such a situation, no action for defamation would lie. The common law formulated this dimension of liability by requiring defamation plaintiffs to prove "publication," which may have been oral or written, to a third person. Nothing in the modern protection of free speech has dispensed with this requirement.[69] Legal publication could be established only by a showing that the disparager had been guilty of negligence or greater fault—a precursor of the *Gertz* fault requirement in one narrow area of common law defamation. Weidman v. Ketcham [70] is a good illustration of this fault requirement. An individual had written a letter accusing the addressee of theft. Although the writer had sent his missive by mail in a sealed envelope, the letter had been opened by a third person. The addressee, however, could adduce no proof showing that, under the circumstances, the writer should have known the letter was likely to have been intercepted and read by a third

---

66. 96 S.W.2d 416 (Tex.Civ.App. 1936). See also, Orr v. Argus-Press Co., 586 F.2d 1108 (6th Cir. 1978).

67. Proof that the newspaper put the figure at $80,000 maliciously (as defined by *Times*) would probably make no difference.

68. Restatement, Second, Torts § 581A, Comment c at 236 (1977).

69. In the 1969 case of McGuire v. Adkins, 284 Ala. 602, 226 So.2d 659 (1969), the court held that,

even though the plaintiff had alleged publication "in the presence and hearing of diverse persons," his complaint was defective since it failed to state "when, where and to whom the slander was published"—a clear indication that the issue of publication is still alive and doing well in Alabama. Id. at 603, 226 So.2d at 660–61. Compare Restatement, Second, Torts § 577 (1977).

70. 278 N.Y. 129, 15 N.E.2d 426 (1938).

person. The addressee's suit was dismissed on the ground that traducers incur no liability in defamation unless they either intend publication or negligently allow their disparagements to become published. One who is defamed has no libel or slander claim for an "unpublished" canard that becomes known by third persons. Vilifiers who know their disparagements are false, but use due care to prevent publication, are not subject to liability.

The old books said that a disparager's careless or intentional communication to only a single third person was publication enough to subject the disparager to liability. This element of liability existed, it was said, even if the one person made privy to the defamation was the claimant's spouse. In 1970, the Michigan Supreme Court expressed satisfaction with this minimal publication.[71] Mr. Justice Black said, "[A] defamation, though uttered or dramatized in the presence [only] of one's spouse . . . constitutes some evidence of publication. [I. e., proof capable of supporting the plaintiff's claim on that issue]. . . . [T]he husband knew she was innocent. But that [knowledge] does not . . . affect the cause except as it may bear upon the recoverable amount of the plaintiff's damages. We may fairly presume that, in the uneven course of marital life, the humiliation suffered . . . is more likely to be recalled—and brooded over—than if the event in question had occurred in the presence of strangers then and strangers forever." This judicial observation sounds more like an outline for a short story than a justification for allowing a defamation claim, especially in light of the *Gertz* requirement that the defamation plaintiff establish actual damages.[72]

One who repeats a canard is usually held to have republished it, even if the talebearer accurately ascribes the aspersion to the original utterer. One common form of repetition, however, does not result in liability, even though the republisher knows that the aspersion is false. For example, if a newspaper publishes a full and fair report of Smith's trial for murder, the paper incurs no liability for stating that the accused testified at the trial that he saw Jones commit the crime. Even though the newspaper

---

71. Bonkowski v. Arlan's Dept. Store, 383 Mich. 90, 174 N.W.2d 765 (1970).

72. See text accompanying notes 35–37, supra, the discussion of the *Firestone* case in which the Supreme Court of the United States approved a recovery to a plaintiff who waived damages to her reputation. *Quaere*: if the plaintiff's reputation goes completely unimpaired, has a defamation been published? Historically, the function of the action on the case for defamation was primarily to clear title to the plaintiff's reputation and only secondarily to compensate the plaintiff for harm proximately caused by the cloud cast on it.

publisher knows the testimony is perjured, the paper is still privileged to repeat it. This common law privilege to make a full and fair report of public proceedings was well recognized long before the revolution and has not been narrowed by it.[73] The privilege extends to publicizing legislative, judicial, and administrative activities. Reports about open meetings in which matters of public concern are discussed are also privileged.[74] The details are thoroughly covered in Prosser's Handbook of the Law of Torts.

The common law privilege to make full and fair reports, however, usually gave no comfort to the pre-*Times* reporter who made a mistake. In a Maryland case [75] decided five years earlier than *Times,* a newspaper had misreported that proceedings before a county commissioners' meeting revealed that the sheriff's records of "booked prisoners" were *incomplete.* The newspaper reporter attending that meeting had misunderstood an investigator's statement to the commissioners to the effect that these records were *complete.* The court held that the privilege to publish accounts of public meetings protected only substantially correct accounts; therefore, the newspaper was liable to the sheriff as a matter of law.

After *Times,* however, the Supreme Court expanded the privilege relating to reports of public proceedings. In Time, Inc. v. Pape,[76] decided in 1971, the Court reviewed a defamation suit brought against Time magazine. Time had published an article that dealt with a report on police brutality released by the Civil Rights Commission. One item in the Commission's report referred to an incident involving one Pape, a Chicago Deputy Chief of Detectives. The report included a summary of *allegations in a petition* filed by citizens who had brought a suit against Pape; these allegations specified abuses that had been inflicted by Pape. Time magazine, however, repeated the substance of these allegations as *findings of fact* by the Civil Rights Commission. The writer of the magazine article testified that she was aware she had omitted the word *alleged* from the article, but also testified that she thought the Time article was true. The Supreme

73. W. Prosser, Handbook of the Law of Torts 830–33 (4th ed. 1971). See also Restatement, Second, Torts § 611 (1977).

74. Lulay v. Peoria Journal-Star, Inc., 34 Ill.2d 112, 214 N.E.2d 746 (1966) (report on Health Department's hearing involving violations in plaintiff's food store); Bray v. Providence Journal Co., 101 R.I.

111, 220 A.2d 531 (1966) (report of school committee meeting during which chairman challenged a teacher's veracity).

75. Brush-Moore Newspapers, Inc. v. Pollitt, 220 Md. 132, 151 A.2d 530 (1959).

76. 401 U.S. 279, 91 S.Ct. 633, 28 L.Ed.2d 45 (1971).

Court held that the detective had not proved *Times* malice and that, therefore, Time magazine was entitled to judgment. The Court's opinion in *Pape* thus put defamatory interpretations of public proceedings involving a public official on the same basis as other statements of fact about a public official—that is, it applied the rule requiring proof of *Times* malice.[77] Public figures defamed by misreports of public proceedings will fare no better than public officials, since the Supreme Court put retired General Walker, who had become a public figure by taking a prominent position on desegregation matters, in the same legal position as public officials.[78]

In *Firestone*, the Court viewed inaccurate reports of public proceedings defaming a private individual as simply special cases falling under the *Gertz* rule; the *Firestone* decision had approved the Florida theory that negligence on the part of Time magazine was, constitutionally, fault sufficient to justify liability. The Massachusetts Supreme Judicial Court anticipated *Firestone* by several months. That court held, in Stone v. Essex County Newspapers, Inc.,[79] that all the *Gertz* limitations on defamation liability apply whenever a newspaper is sued for misreporting a private person's criminal trial. The newspaper article in question in *Stone* had misidentified the plaintiff, a private person, as the accused. Liability for misreporting a public proceeding has, in these ways, been limited by the newly enunciated constitutional protections of the freedoms of speech and press.

There is an Arkansas case[80] that should receive special mention. A newspaper published an article about civil litigation involving a private person. This litigant sued the newspaper for libel, alleging that the article contained defamatory misstatements, had many omissions, and added unwarranted insinuations of its own. When the case went to the jury, the trial judge charged that the plaintiff was entitled to a verdict only if he had proved the newspaper's actual malice. The jury returned a verdict in favor of the newspaper. The Arkansas Supreme Court held that the jury had been charged improperly and remanded the case for retrial. The court stated that judicial proceedings were susceptible of exact reporting, and that, therefore, defamation plaintiffs need not prove malice. Newspaper reports of ju-

---

77. Cf. Wharen v. Dershuck, 264 Pa. 562, 108 A. 18 (1919) (a much earlier case in which one state court tolerated an inaccurate report of a public proceeding).

78. See, e. g., Orr v. Argus-Press Co., 586 F.2d 1108 (6th Cir. 1978).

79. 367 Mass. 849, 330 N.E.2d 161 (1975); Compare Restatement, Second, Torts § 611, Comment b at 298 (1977).

80. Jones v. Commercial Printing Co., 249 Ark. 952, 463 S.W.2d 92 (1971).

dicial proceedings were privileged under "the present [1971] rule," only if those reports were complete, impartial, and accurate.

The Arkansas court's view, it seems, is repudiated by the Supreme Court for public officials like Pape, who, as a police officer, had to prove *Times* malice, and for private litigants like Mrs. Firestone, who, on remand, had to establish negligence to be entitled to her judgment. The *Walker* case, in which Walker's Texas judgment was overturned, also involved a public event and concerned an inaccurate news report. Since the Supreme Court held against Walker because of the absence of *Times* malice, it seems unlikely that the requirement of *Times* malice would be relaxed for public figures when a news item involves a judicial proceeding. After *Gertz*, decided three years later than the Arkansas case, it seems doubtful that a false defamatory newspaper report of any public proceeding, court trials included, could, under the federal constitution, be held actionable without some proof of fault.

In a Kansas pre-*Gertz* case, a newspaper reported falsely that the plaintiff had pleaded guilty of cruelty to animals. The defendant paper moved for and received a summary judgment on the ground that the plaintiff was not ready to prove *Times* malice, but merely offered to come forward with proof of negligence. *Gertz* was decided before the Kansas summary judgment was considered on appeal. The Kansas Supreme Court remanded the case on the ground that the plaintiff's offer to prove negligence met the *Gertz* requirement of fault.[81] *Gertz*, however, does not invalidate state law requiring the victim of defamatory misreporting to prove that the publisher was guilty of fault more flagrant than negligence. The Kansas court knew it could no longer sanction the state's traditional liability without fault for defamatory misreports of judicial proceedings. The trial judge sought to meet the fault requirement by compelling the victim of defamatory misreport to establish that the publisher had acted with malice. The Kansas Supreme Court, however, chose to ride the press with tighter rein. The court reduced the plaintiff's burden to prove fault to the constitutional minimum —that is, negligence. Thus Kansas, more fervent in vindicating the reputations of its private citizens maligned by misreports of judicial proceedings than the federal constitution allows, subsequently reduced that protection by only so much as was necessary to accord with what the newly interpreted federal constitu-

---

81. Gobin v. Globe Pub. Co., 216 Kan. 223, 531 P.2d 76 (1975).

tion requires. The Kansas court could have given the Kansas press more leeway than it did.

The term *malice,* as used in the nineteenth century, denoted some instances of unbecoming behavior not included in *malice* as defined in *Times.* In the 1879 case of Stevens v. Sampson,[82] for example, a plaintiff brought a defamation suit against a lawyer who had made derogatory remarks about the plaintiff during an earlier legal proceeding. The plaintiff did not sue for the defamatory remarks that had been made in court—probably because they were absolutely privileged. Some time later, however, the lawyer had repeated his courtroom utterances in preparing an accurate account of the trial—an account that he had sent to a newspaper. The paper had then published this account. Thereupon, the plaintiff filed his defamation suit against the lawyer, who pleaded a privilege to publicize legal proceedings. The jury, asked to consider whether or not the lawyer had acted maliciously, entered a special verdict stating that he had been actuated "by a certain amount of malice." The court held that since he had abused his privilege by acting with malice, he accordingly was liable for defamation.

If this lawyer had knowingly used his absolute privilege at the trial to vilify an innocent man and had then incited republication in order to spread his smear more widely, his conduct was certainly unappealing. The special verdict, however, fell far short of establishing that such was the case. The lawyer may have been motivated by spite but have sent his dispatch without having any reason to suspect the falsity of the statements he had made at the original trial. Lord Justice Bramwell, one of the three judges who unanimously held the barrister liable, had qualms. He said, "Suppose a reporter for the press bore malice toward a person, a party to an action, and published a fair report of proceedings injurious to him. I incline to think that, as he would be performing a kind of duty, it ought to be taken that he is acting under privilege. . . .[83] However, I only throw this out as a suggestion, and it is unnecessary to decide the point. There is a plain distinction [!] between that case and the present where the defendant is a volunteer."

This common law view of malice as hatred, irascibility, personal dislike, or spite has been outmoded by *Pape.* After the Supreme Court's toleration of an inaccurate report of public proceedings, our courts would be, it would seem, unlikely to con-

82. 5 Ex.Div. 53 (1879).

83. The Supreme Court of the United States agrees on first amendment grounds. Cox Broadcasting Corp. v. Cohn, 420 U.S. 469, 95 S. Ct. 1029, 43 L.Ed.2d 328 (1975).

demn an accurate one, even if made by a spiteful volunteer. The constitutional condemnation of widespread liability without fault in the states' defamation laws has limited the states' power to hold any defendant liable for defamation to those cases in which the plaintiff, if an official or public person, established that the defamer knowingly spoke falsely or spoke with reckless disregard for truth. Under the Constitution as expounded in *Gertz,* any state that chose to do so could extend the ambit of liability for defaming private persons a little further; recoveries may be allowed, provided that the state's laws required the plaintiff to show at least negligent disregard for the truth. None of the constitutional cases, however, permitted a state court to substitute bare spite as fault adequate for liability when the hateful defamer was not guilty of the requisite form of intentional, reckless, or negligent disregard for truth. Of course, a defamer who is actuated by animosity may be tempted to lie or recklessly or negligently fail to speak the truth. It is at least theoretically possible, however, that a spiteful defamer's animus will not induce less care before the mistaken disparagement is uttered. Spite may have some evidentiary value in proving constitutional fault. But spite in itself is not a legally operative fact establishing defamation liability under the Constitution. The common law of defamation, as will be seen later, often tended to treat spite as substantively significant. The revolution, however, has turned defamation law away from this substantive law result. Ulterior motive is not the legal equivalent of intended, reckless or negligent disregard for truth.

Dealers selling or circulating defamatory newspapers, books, and magazines that had been published by others were not usually treated as republishers of libel by common law courts. They have seldom been sued in defamation in modern times. Bottomly v. F. W. Woolworth & Co.[84] was decided in 1932. Bottomly, who had been defamed in a magazine, sued a merchant who had sold copies of the libelous issue. The court dismissed Bottomly's case on the ground that dealers distributing libelous material published by others incurred no liability unless they knew or had reason to suspect that they were dealing in libelous publications. The law does not require disseminators to employ readers to scan their wares for libel. Perhaps distributors are seldom sued for libel because their fault is rarely susceptible of proof. Absent such proof of fault, the evidence required by the Supreme Court in the first amendment cases would be fatal to defamation plaintiffs in future litigation.

---

84. 48 T.L.R. 521 (1932). See also Restatement, Second, Torts § 581(1) & Comments b, d, & e at 232–34 (1977).

Spoken defamation is slander; written or printed defamation is libel. When slander is recorded on records, tapes, or sound tracks, it becomes libel.[85] At common law, the distinction was important because slander was not actionable without proof of "special damages," except when the spoken slur fell into one of three or four arbitrary classes of disparagements. Plaintiffs seldom could adduce evidence of special damages, but such proof was not needed if the slanderer had imputed that the plaintiff (1) had committed a crime involving moral turpitude; (2) had had syphilis or leprosy, (3) had been unfit to practice his or her trade, office, or profession; or, in some jurisdictions, (4) had been an unchaste woman. Many serious aspersions fell outside these four classifications and were therefore not characterized as "slander per se." Kluender v. Semann [86] exemplifies one such case. A gossip had said that the plaintiff took narcotics to the extent that his mind was affected and that, consequently, he was incapable of telling the truth. The court dismissed this claim on the ground that the imputation in itself did not accuse the plaintiff of any crime and the plaintiff's failure to prove special damages was fatal to his claim.

The ambit of common law special damages included less than the "actual damages" required by *Gertz*. Special damage, says Prosser, was "temporal damage . . . pecuniary in its nature. Thus, while the loss of customers or business, or a particular contract or employment, of an advantageous marriage, will [do] . . . it is not enough that the plaintiff has lost the society of his friends and associates . . . ." [87] To repeat, all the constitutional cases were calculated to enhance free expression by cutting down, in various ways and under certain circumstances, the inhibiting threats of large liabilities for defamation; none of these cases required the states to alter their defamation laws to enlarge the rights of those whose reputations were unjustly impaired. Therefore, when a slander suit would not have succeeded for lack of proof of special damages before *Times, Walker, Butts,* and *Gertz*, nothing in these more recent cases was calculated to improve the slander plaintiff's claim.[88]

85. Whether defamatory broadcasts were libel or slander was formerly a much debated and confused matter. Section 568A of the Second Restatement of Torts provides: "Broadcasting of defamatory matter by means of radio or television is libel, whether or not it is read from a manuscript." Many states, however, have adopted statutes to the contrary.

86. 203 Iowa 68, 212 N.W. 326 (1927).

87. W. Prosser, Handbook of the Law of Torts 760–61 (4th ed. 1971).

88. But see the dicta in Metromedia, Inc. v. Hillman, 285 Md. 161, 400 A.2d 1117 (1979).

On the contrary, the *Gertz* ruling that disallows "presumed damages," at least when *Times* malice has not been proved, curtailed prerevolution liability for slanders that previously fell within the arbitrary classes of slander *per se*, for which "general damages" were recoverable at common law.

In the nineteenth century, the courts did not require any *libel* plaintiff to prove special damages; [89] plaintiffs could offer evidence of special damages if they had it, hoping thereby to recover a larger judgment. Libel plaintiffs could, however, establish a claim without the least itemized showing of special damages, and yet be entitled to an award of "general damages."

In the twentieth century, some state courts decided to distinguish between writings that were libelous on their face and writings that conveyed their libelous meanings only to readers knowing extrinsic facts about the plaintiff. These courts called explicit canards *libel per se* and tacit canards *libel per quod*. *Libel per quod* was not actionable in these states unless the claimant could prove special damages, that is, injuries like those necessary in slander cases falling outside of the arbitrary classes. In 1970, for example, William Barrett's widow brought a libel suit against the decedent's brother and the mortician who buried him. The brother had delivered an obituary to the mortician, who in turn had sent it to the local newspaper. The brother knew that the death notice described the decedent as a bachelor. The widow learned about this misdescription, and before its release she complained to both defendants. They ignored her complaint and allowed the obituary to appear in print without correction. Some of the people who read the obituary consequently believed that the widow had illicitly cohabited with the decedent. The widow admitted she could prove no special damages. She contended, however, that since illicit cohabitation was a crime in Rhode Island, the obituary was libel *per se*.[90] The trial judge

---

89. See, e. g., Cassidy v. Daily Mirror Newspapers, Ltd., [1929] 2 K. B. 331.

90. In some of the states that required proof of special damages to support a recovery for libel *per quod*, Mrs. Barrett's contention would be correct; that is, in these states, whenever a libel *per quod* was shown to fall within one of the slander *per se* categories, the state law allowed recovery without a showing of common law "special damages," and conse-

quently, if the plaintiff's proof of damages satisfied the *Gertz* rule on damages, a post-revolution recovery could follow. See, e. g., Wegner v. Rodeo Cowboys Ass'n, 417 F.2d 881 (10th Cir. 1969), cert. denied, 398 U.S. 903, 90 S.Ct. 1688, 26 L.Ed.2d 60 (1970) (expounding Colorado law).

In Louisiana a libel *per quod* is not actionable unless the defamed plaintiff proves malice. See Makofsky v. Cunningham, 576 F.2d 1223 (5th Cir. 1978).

rejected her argument and entered a summary judgment for the defendants; this judgment was affirmed by the Rhode Island Supreme Court.[91]

Once again, the United States Supreme Court first amendment cases neither expanded liability for defamation nor conferred any additional rights on defamation plaintiffs. Rhode Island in no way contravened the constitutional rights of the widow, a private person, when its court refused to recognize her claim under state law because she suffered no special damages. Rhode Island could, however, have retreated from the much criticized minority view and have reinstated the common law's indifference to whether or not libel appeared on the face of the writing. Such a retreat, nevertheless, would not excuse plaintiffs like the widow from meeting the more rigorous constitutional requirement of proving damages acceptable under *Gertz*. Since in the *Barrett* case the defendants were arguably guilty of *Times* malice, the widow might have recovered a substantial sum but for the Rhode Island libel *per se* rule.

In a Maryland case decided nine years after Barrett, the court was inspired by *Gertz* to favor a plaintiff who, before the revolution, might have been barred by the rule requiring common law special damages in a libel *per quod* case. A district court judge, pursuant to a Maryland statute, certified questions about Maryland libel law. The district judge asked the Maryland Court of Appeals (1) whether or not Maryland continued to distinguish between libel *per se* and libel *per quod* ; and (2) if the distinction was still recognized, did Maryland still require pleading and proof whenever knowledge of extrinsic facts is needed to perceive the defamatory meaning of a libel. It was constitutionally possible for Maryland to restrict liability to the same small scope as Rhode Island had retained in the *Barrett* case. The Maryland court, however, said that after *Gertz* "we have no need to involve ourselves in the controversy . . . relative to libel *per se* and libel *per quod*." The court adjured any distinction between statements defamatory on their face and statements that were defamatory in the light of extrinsic facts. The court also adopted the statement in *Gertz* to the effect that, though in private plaintiffs' cases the plaintiff has the burden of establishing "actual injury," that requirement is not limited to out-of-pocket expenses, but includes proof of "impairment of reputation and standing in the community, personal humiliation,

---

91. Barrett v. Barrett, 108 R.I. 15, 271 A.2d 825 (1970). See also Electric Furnace Corp. v. Deering Milliken Research Corp., 325 F.2d 761 (6th Cir. 1963).

and mental anguish and suffering." [92]   In this Maryland case, then, the court was uniquely inspired (but not required) by the revolution to relax a state limitation on recovery for defamation.

Before *Times* and its sequelae, the common law recognized conditional privileges, which could be lost by abuse, to defame either to benefit the hearer or to protect the defamer's own interests.

Richardson v. Gunby [93] illustrates the first of these two privileges.   The defendant was a banker who had written a defamatory response to an inquiry about the standing of a corporation and its officers.   The court held that the occasion was privileged, and the banker incurred no liability to the defamed corporate officer who had made no showing of abuse of privilege. The rationale for such a privilege was this: If the banker could not answer without subjecting himself to liability for defamation, he might well be disinclined to respond.   Exchange of commercial information facilitates trade and might accordingly promote prosperity.

The privilege to speak for the hearer's benefit was not confined to information advancing commerce and industry.   The old books said that the privilege covered all statements made by any speaker who had a "legal, moral, or social duty" to inform.   The privilege protected agents reporting information to their principals to safeguard the principals' interests; immediate members of a family counseling one another on marriage, divorce, and the like; members of a church congregation considering the fitness of their minister; and former employers discussing the character and qualifications of their erstwhile servants with those considering hiring them.   The best of friends, however, were likely to find themselves unprivileged when meddling in each other's affairs; such was the fate, for example, of an amicable informer who took it upon himself to tell a wife about reports of her overseas husband's love life. [94]

Some question has arisen about whether or not agencies that sell business information are entitled to be privileged.   In MacIntosh v. Dunn, [95] an English case, the court held that they are not; most American courts, in contrast, have held that they are, at least when responding to a subscriber's inquiry about the like-

92. Metromedia, Inc. v. Hillman, 285 Md. 161, ——, 400 A.2d 1117, 1121 (1979).

93. 88 Kan. 47, 127 P. 533 (1912); see Restatement, Second, Torts § 595 (1977).

94. Watt v. Longsdon, [1930] 1 K.B. 130;   see Restatement, Second, Torts § 595(2), Comment j at 273–74 (1977).

95. [1908] A.C. 300.

lihood that prospective customers will pay their bills.[96] There is widespread doubt, however, about whether or not a commercial credit agency is privileged when it disseminates defamations to subscribers who have not made a specific request for information about the precise person who is defamed.[97]

The privilege to protect the defamer's own interests is exemplified by Browne v. Prudden-Winslow Co.,[98] in which a salesman sued his former employer for writing to customers the employee had previously served to tell them that the salesman had been discharged for dishonesty. The company thus tried to thwart efforts to lure away its customers to the discharged employee's new ventures. A New York court dismissed this libel suit on the ground that the former employer had a privilege to defame in self-defense. This common law privilege was applicable in many similar cases, such as accusations made in attempts to recover stolen goods, attacks on the credibility of defamers who had previously disparaged the attacker, a joint owner's charge that another joint owner had mismanaged the property or business, and so on.

The First Amendment holdings, again, do not expand liability; the revolution has not restricted free speech that is *allowed* by state law privileges. On the other hand, liability under state law for abuse of privilege may discourage free speech, and thereby run afoul of the constitutional holdings.

Common law abuse of conditional privilege consisted of either excessive publication or malice. In some states, lack of probable cause was a legally adequate substitute for malice.

The abuse representing excessive publication was found in a 1930 Texas case.[99] The defendant, a storekeeper, suspected a shopper of stealing a pair of bloomers. In the presence of other customers, he loudly and angrily accused her of theft. On proof of these facts, the storekeeper was found guilty of abusing his privilege, since he unreasonably published his suspicions to other customers without any interest in the matter. Reasonable disclosures to third persons, however, are not excessive publica-

---

96. See, e. g., Watwood v. Stone's Mercantile Agency, 194 F.2d 160 (D.C.Cir. 1952); and cf. Luster v. Retail Credit Co., 575 F.2d 609 (8th Cir. 1978) (applying Arkansas law).

97. See the equally divided court's opinions in Barker v. Retail Credit Co., 8 Wis.2d 664, 100 N.W.2d 391 (1960). See Restatement, Second,

Torts § 595, Comment h at 271–73 (1977).

98. 195 App.Div. 419, 186 N.Y.S. 350 (1921); see Restatement, Second, Torts §§ 594–596 (1977).

99. Perry Bros. Variety Stores, Inc. v. Layton, 119 Tex. 130, 25 S.W.2d 310 (1930); see Restatement (Second) of Torts § 604 (1977).

tions; accordingly, in appropriate circumstances, dictating to a stenographer, sending a telegram and even publishing accusations in a newspaper have been held not to constitute legally excessive publication.[1]

Privileged defamers who publish excessively will thereby lose their privilege. Since excessive publication is unreasonable, it is therefore, at the least, a negligent failure to use due care to prevent unconcerned strangers from seeing or hearing the aspersion. The Maryland Court of Appeals, in a recent case, held that the defendant's excessive publication was fault enough to justify liability under *Gertz*. General Motors Corp. v. Piskor,[2] decided in 1976, involved a nineteen-year old factory worker who sued his employer for defamation. The worker proved that he had manned a post on an automobile assembly line in a General Motors plant. His demeanor aroused the suspicion of the foreman in charge of radios and tape recorders, which are small, valuable items that can easily be stolen. The foreman telephoned his suspicions to a security officer at an exit "guard shack," a plate glass enclosure where guards routinely inspected packages and handbags carried out by departing workers. The plaintiff testified at the trial that he had caught a glimpse of the suspicious foreman pointing him out to the guards; that two guards had tried to stop him, but he had shaken them off; and that other guards had blocked his departure and forced him back toward the glass enclosure. The workman indignantly asked the guards whether he was being called a thief, but the guards hustled him into the shack, saying they wanted to establish his identity. At first, he resisted the guards' demands that he open his jacket; afterward, he submitted to a thorough search. The investigation established that the workman had not been purloining any company property. The guard shack interlude lasted about a half hour, during which one shift of workmen left and another came in. Large numbers of employees saw what was going on, and many slowed down as they passed the shack in order to watch the commotion.

The trial judge submitted a slander claim to the jury, who returned a verdict for the plaintiff. The intermediate court held that the evidence of slander and abuse of privilege was adequate for submission to the jury; the opinion, however, declared that *Gertz* was not in point, since this case did not involve a matter

---

1. See W. Prosser, supra note 1, at 793; Restatement, Second, Torts § 604 (1977).

2. 277 Md. 165, 352 A.2d 810 (1976); Compare Restatement, Second, Torts § 580A, Comment h at 221, and § 580B, Comment f at 226 (1977).

of public concern or of general interest. The Maryland court of last resort granted a request to review this case further. The court referred to and approved a statement in one of its earlier opinions to the effect that the court "read *Gertz*" as applicable to any private person's defamation claim, whether or not the claim was of public concern or of general interest. On the issue of excessive publication, the Maryland court said that a conditional privilege to defame may be abused by excessive publication to third persons and that the standard by which excessiveness is to be judged is negligence. The case was remanded for a retrial, with directions that the jury's instructions should conform to *Gertz* law on burden of proof, negligence, and damages.[3] A defamation plaintiff who is either a public official or a public figure must prove *Times* malice to recover. It follows that in some circumstances, excessive publication might or might not enter into a case requiring proof of actual knowledge of falsity or proof of reckless disregard for truth.

A privilege, it was said traditionally, was lost not only when abused through excessive publication but also when the privileged defamer was actuated by common law malice. This issue often arose when the defamers spoke to protect their own or others' interests. In Zeinfeld v. Hayes Freight Lines, Inc.,[4] for example, the defamation plaintiff alleged that he had applied for mortgaging financing and had given his former employer as a reference; the employer's response to the lender's inquiry, maliciously and in bad faith, had cast doubt upon the applicant's honesty. The employer filed an answer alleging that his letter, written in good faith, had been truthful as far as he knew. After the plaintiff filed a reply denying the employer's affirmative allegations, the employer moved for a judgment on the pleadings. The trial judge granted this motion. The Illinois Supreme Court remanded the case with instructions to try the issues of good faith and lack of knowledge of falsity. Of course, there is no holding in the constitutional cases *requiring* the Illinois courts to allow recovery when Illinois law protects the responding employer from liability. The opinion can possibly be interpreted, however, to have held that the former employee was

---

3. On retrial, the *Gertz* rule on damages might be a stumbling block to recovery. The workman did not lose his job, and he stayed on with General Motors after the guard shack episode. Conceivably, publication was excessive enough to constitute *Times* malice and subject General Motors to an award of punitive damages. See the *Buckley* case, supra note 52.

4. 41 Ill.2d 345, 243 N.E.2d 217 (1968). See also, Johns v. Associated Aviation Underwriters, 203 F.2d 208 (5th Cir.), cert. denied, 346 U.S. 834, 74 S.Ct. 38, 98 L.Ed. 356 (1953).

entitled to recovery if the letter writer had been accurate but motivated by spite.

In any event, some prerevolutionary common law courts clearly held that spite was the legal equivalent of malice and that, consequently, a spiteful detractor abused the privilege to protect the hearer's interest even if the dispraisal was factually correct. In Tanner v. Stevenson,[5] the disparager had written to the State Superintendent of Education about a public school teacher's disrepute. Because of the nature of the superintendent's duties, the writer was conditionally privileged to send him such information. The court held, however, that he abused that privilege and would incur liability if he had been actuated by spite—even though he honestly and reasonably believed what he had written. This view of the law has not survived the revolution; a defamer's honest and reasonable belief is inconsistent with both *Times* malice and *Gertz* negligence. According to the Supreme Court, the Constitution requires the states to give public official or public figure defamation plaintiffs the burden of proving *Times* malice and to give private person plaintiffs the burden of proving at least *Gertz* negligence.[6] Ill will, in itself, constitutes neither knowledge of untruth nor reckless or negligent disregard for truth.[7]

At common law, defamations were assumed to be false unless the defendant-traducer established their truth. The revolution abolished defamation liability without fault and instead assigned to defamation plaintiffs the burden of proving *Times* malice in some cases or at least *Gertz* negligence in others. A plaintiff cannot establish that a defendant has been guilty of knowingly, recklessly, or negligently uttering an untruth without proving that the utterance was untrue. If a defamed plaintiff must establish falsity in order to recover damages against an unprivileged defendant,[8] the plaintiff must accordingly have just as heavy a burden when the defendant enjoys the protection of any common law privilege.

In some common law cases, a conditionally privileged defamer is not deemed to have abused the privilege, even though the traducer knew or greatly suspected the substantial falsity of the canard reported. For instance, fiduciary agents often have express or implied duties to report important business information to their principals. Should such agents hear someone say that one

---

5. 138 Ky. 578, 128 S.W. 878 (1910).

6. Marchesi v. Franchino, 283 Md. 131, 387 A.2d 1129 (1978).

7. See Luster v. Retail Credit Co., 575 F.2d 609 (8th Cir. 1978).

8. See text accompanying note 56, supra.

of their principals' bankers, creditors or suppliers is facing financial disaster, and if they fully and accurately report such stories to their principals, adding those doubts of their own for which they have any basis, they should incur no liability for making reports they are required by law to make. Similarly, a parent should incur no liability for repeating to a son or daughter gossip, the truth of which the parent doubts, about the person the child is engaged to marry—so long as the parent at least makes a full and fair report. Insofar as the common law has restricted liabilities in such cases, first amendment law should tend further to support, rather than inhibit, these freedoms of speech. Nonetheless, whenever abuse-of-privilege common law would impose liability on the ground of fault as flagrant as *Times* malice, liability for abuse of privilege does not violate the Constitution.[9]

Before the revolution, courts in some states held that privileged defamers were guilty of abusing their privilege if they lacked "probable cause" for believing the defamation that had prompted the suit; a corollary defined *probable cause* as honest and *reasonable* belief in the truth.[10] Although an honest but unreasonable belief in the truth could on occasion be reckless, it also could be merely negligent. When a private person brings a libel or slander suit, the constitutional requirement of proof of fault is satisfied, according to *Gertz*, if the plaintiff proves negligence. The states may require proof of fault more flagrant than negligence, but cannot accept proof of lesser fault.

Gertz has not purported to be satisfied with spite as a substitute for negligence. The holding in the 1975 Wisconsin case of Calero v. Del Chemical Corp.[11] may accordingly have offended the Constitution as expounded in *Gertz*. Calero, an accountant, had worked for Del Chemical. He sued Del and one of its executives for making several defamatory statements that had hindered him from getting appropriate employment for a number of years. Del's executive had discharged Calero on three grounds: (1) he had been about to start an enterprise to compete with

9. See Restatement, Second, Torts § 602 (1977); see, e. g., Jacron Sales Co. v. Sindorf, 276 Md. 580, 350 A.2d 688 (1976) (*semble*) (Held: a charge of dishonesty made to plaintiff's employer, by an agent of plaintiff's former employer who had no basis for believing what he said, abused the speaker's privilege. Inspired by, but not required by, *Gertz*: since the disparaged man was a private person, negligence would have been fault enough.)

10. See, e. g., Williams v. Kroger Grocery & Baking Co., 133 Pa.Super. 1, 1 A.2d 495 (1938), aff'd, 337 Pa. 17, 10 A.2d 8 (1940). See also, Jacron Sales Co. v. Sindorf, 276 Md. 580, 350 A.2d 688 (1976).

11. 68 Wis.2d 487, 228 N.W.2d 737 (1975).

Del, (2) he had tried to lure some of Del's key personnel into his new enterprise; and (3) he had copied some of Del's confidential records to use in his new enterprise. Calero explained the falsity of these charges when initially called upon to clear himself; nevertheless, he was immediately dismissed. Calero gave testimony at the trial that tended to show that the charges were unfounded. The executive codefendant admitted that he had had no personal knowledge of the charges of Calero's disloyalty; he further testified that he had based each ground of dismissal on "office information" that had been reported to him. He explained that he had made no attempts to verify the reports because he had had no reason to entertain doubts about the veracity of his informants. Other evidence established that the executive had repeated the charges of disloyalty to several prospective employers who had inquired about Calero. The trial judge rendered a judgment for Calero for $19,000 after the jury returned a verdict awarding Calero $7,000 for loss of income, $3,000 for injury to his feelings and reputation, and $9,000 for punitive damages. On appeal, the Wisconsin court noted that the defendants' procedural ineptness had virtually obliterated their rights to review; nevertheless, the court decided to consider the merits of the case. The court stated, "[W]e are not dealing with a conditional privilege based on First Amendment principles, but rather with one based on a public policy favoring the encouragement of a free exchange of information [in response to an] inquiry by a prospective employer to a former employer. In such a case one must prove only 'express malice' which is a defamatory statement motivated by ill will, spite, envy, revenge, or other bad or corruptive motive. . . . In the case before us there is no matter of general or public interest; there is no involvement of the media. . . ."

The court's requirement of "express malice" differed from the concept of *Times* malice. The court made no reference to the defendant's knowledge of falsity or reckless disregard for truth. Nor did the court require the plaintiff to establish even so much fault as the lack of due care required to prove *Gertz'* negligence. Perhaps a reasonable jury, if instructed to try the issue, would have found that the irascible executive, though obdurately angry, was nevertheless not guilty of reckless or even negligent disregard for the truth; conceivably he may not have been unreasonable in relying on "office information" in answering the inquiries of prospective employers. This Wisconsin court, it seems, was in a dilemma created by the constitutional decisions providing that spite alone is not the kind of fault that should deprive a defamer of freedom of speech: If the court wished to use the traditional word *malice* to describe the fault needed for abuse of privilege, it would be obliged to change its meaning to *Times* malice; if the court viewed that course as overly tender to conditionally privileged defamers of private plaintiffs, it could abandon that kind of malice and adopt the *Gertz* rule requiring negligence or lack of probable cause as the criterion of abuse.

Even when the plaintiff is a private person, state courts can constitutionally reject the lack of probable cause criterion, which includes negligence, as a measure of fault insufficiently flagrant to constitute abuse.[12] *Gertz requires* at least negligence for liability but *permits* the states to use *Times* malice to determine whether or not a conditionally privileged defendant has abused his privilege.

The courts in every state but Georgia and Idaho have held that agencies in the business of gathering and selling information, such as credit reporting agencies, enjoy a conditional privilege when they respond to their customers' requests for information.[13] Of course, this privilege is subject to abuse. When a subscriber asks any agency to furnish information about an applicant for credit, and the agency returns a defamatory answer either knowing that the answer is false or with reckless disregard for the answer's truth, the agency is clearly guilty of abuse of privilege.[14]

A New Jersey intermediate court considered, post-*Gertz*, a credit rating agency case on appeal. The agency had reported to a financial company, to which the plaintiff had applied for a mortgage loan, that certain judgments had been entered against the plaintiff. The agency's report was false; the plaintiff's loan application was rejected as a result. The trial judge held that the plaintiff's proof raised no issues requiring jury trial and dismissed the suit. The Appellate Division of the New Jersey Superior Court remanded the case with instructions that, on retrial, an abuse of privilege issue should be submitted to the jury. The jury should be charged, said the appellate court, that the agency was subject to liability unless it had had *reasonable* grounds or probable cause for believing the truth of its report.[15]

12. See, e. g., Retail Credit Co. v. Russell, 234 Ga. 765, 218 S.E.2d 54 (1975).

13. See, e. g., Dun & Bradstreet, Inc. v. Robinson, 233 Ark. 168, 345 S.W.2d 34 (1961).

14. See, e. g., Johns v. Associated Aviation Underwriters, 203 F.2d 208 (5th Cir. 1953) (applying Texas law).

15. Krumholtz v. TRW, Inc., 142 N.J.Super. 80, 360 A.2d 413 (1976). The agency that reported to the prospective loan company relied on another enterprise that specialized in searching judgment rolls and reporting judgments to its

Since this claimant was a private person, the test of fault to be used on retrial would conform to the holding in *Gertz*.[16]

§ 4. RETRACTION

Mr. Justice Schaefer, in a 1975 Illinois case, acknowledged the constitutional holdings abolishing the states' power to inflict liability without fault on defamation defendants, and then referred to articles in the Illinois Constitution. He went on to say, "The constitutionally recognized interest of the individual in his reputation is not and can not be measured solely in terms of monetary compensation. . . . [T]he individual has an interest in preserving and restoring his reputation through an authoritative and publicly known determination that an injurious statement about him is in fact false." [17]

The reduction of the scope of defamation liability by *Times* and its sequelae has cut back the boundaries of legal liability for defamation; perforce, it has simultaneously reduced the incentive of many mistaken detractors to avoid or meliorate the risk of money judgments by issuing full and fair retractions. Few people happily and pleasantly publicize their serious mistakes when they have little to gain from printing corrections and apologies. The revolution in defamation law, by reducing the danger of liability and the size of judgments, has diminished the pressure to retract.

In earlier times, the victims of inadvertent libel by the media often got retractions as a matter of course once a defamatory mistake had been called to the publisher's attention. Fairness and such legal pressure that have survived the revolution can still, on occasion, produce corrections. The Philadelphia Inquirer regularly publishes a short feature headlined "Clearing The Record"; on March 24, 1977, the paper corrected two mistakes: a minor error in an obituary and a mistake in Indira Gandhi's family tree. These items were followed by the paper's standard statement of its intention to be fair and accurate, a request that mistakes be reported, and a promise to investigate and correct

clients; this enterprise sent word to the defendant agency that a judgment had been entered against a building firm, and in that judgment the applicant for a loan was listed as "r/a." R/a is an abbreviation of registered agent, and does not indicate any judgment liability on the part of the person so designated. The judgment reporting firm wrote to the credit reporting agency telling the agency that it had been issuing reports listing "r/a's" as judgment debtors, and advised them to clear their records.

16. Cf. Retail Credit Co. v. Russell, 234 Ga. 765, 218 S.E.2d 54 (1975); see Restatement, Second, Torts § 580B, Comment e at 225 (1977).

17. Troman v. Wood, 62 Ill.2d 184, 195, 340 N.E.2d 292, 297 (1975).

errors. On February 19, 1977, the New York Times published: "Sequel. A few weeks ago in an episode of 'Phyllis,' the television series . . . a fictitious member of the San Francisco Board of Supervisors made a wisecrack to the effect that another supposedly fictional 'Supervisor Mendelsohn' had been fooling around with a secretary. It turns out that there was a real Supervisor Robert Mendelsohn in San Francisco and, he said, he was embarrassed by what the 'Phyllis' producers later called the 'merely coincidental' use of the name Mendelsohn. Now the producers plan to work in an apology to Mr. Mendelsohn in the February 27 episode of the show. 'The exact wording of the apology is being worked out by our attorney, and Mr. Mendelsohn's lawyer' said a 'Phyllis' spokesman." Unfortunately for the maligned Commissioner, the program's attorney knew about the *Times* malice requirement, and, accordingly, the apology was a bit casual and without much contrition.

It has long been the law that defendants sued for libel may offer proof of their retractions. Before the revolution, when "general damages" could be recovered even without proof of fault, a number of defendants retracted to "mitigate" the general damage award.[18] A diminished incentive to retract still persists in some cases after the revolution. *Gertz* allows—but does not require—the states to award to private plaintiffs who otherwise satisfy *Gertz* rules damages for "actual injury," a term that embraces "impairment of standing in the community." Since a retraction may diminish the stigma that would otherwise result from the original disparagement, it could consequently reduce the "actual damages" that might otherwise be recoverable.[19]

Courts have held that stubborn or negligent failure to retract constitutes misconduct faulty enough to sustain liability. Vigil v. Rice,[20] a 1964 New Mexico case, arose out of a medical report

18. See, e. g., Francis v. Lake Charles American Press, 241 So.2d 73 (La.App.1970), modified, 262 La. 875, 265 So.2d 206 (1972), appeal dismissed, 410 U.S. 901, 93 S.Ct. 961, 35 L.Ed.2d 265 (1973).

19. See Stone v. Essex County Newspapers, Inc., 367 Mass. 849, 330 N.E.2d 161 (1975).

20. 74 N.M. 693, 397 P.2d 719 (1964). See also, Mahnke v. Northwest Publications, Inc., 280 Minn. 328, 160 N.W.2d 1 (1968), in which a police official won a substantial verdict. The trial judge charged the jury, since the plain-

tiff was a public figure, that they could not find for the official unless they found *Times* malice— without taking the newspaper's refusal to retract into account. The newspaper appealed; the official did not; the retraction instruction, therefore, was not an issue on appeal. Nevertheless, the appellate court said, "Under the circumstances of this case, we think the failure to retract . . . underscored defendant's reckless attitude as to the consequences of what had been published and the jury was entitled to take that fact into consideration." Id. at 344, 160 N.W.2d at 11. Cf. West's Ann.

about a crippled schoolgirl. The girl's parents had asked the school authorities to provide instruction for her at home; the authorities consequently sent a medical practitioner to examine her. The doctor falsely and capriciously reported that the girl was pregnant; he thereafter brushed aside demands for a retraction. The trial judge instructed the jury that this doctor's report was privileged; if this doctor had acted maliciously, however, he had abused and therefore lost his privilege and incurred liability justifying awards of both compensatory and punitive damages. The jury returned a verdict assessing actual damages at $2,000 and allowing $5,000 more as punitive damages. The appellate court affirmed the judgment entered on this verdict, saying that proof of the doctor's unwarranted refusal to retract tended to show he had been actuated by malice. The doctor's behavior approached the level of *Times* malice and seems to prove his knowledge of falsity or, at the least, his reckless disregard for the truth. If malice was so understood at the trial, the holding is consonant with the constitutional cases.

Once a defamer properly retracts, even though the stigma of the slur may not completely disappear, litigation is unlikely to result in further vindication of the defamed person. A proper retraction is published promptly and prominently, and is full, fair, and apologetic.[21] When litigation nevertheless follows such a retraction and damage issues are submitted to a jury, the jury should be instructed that little or no damages should be awarded to effect further exculpation. In the past, trial judges usually charged on retraction only in general terms; the standard instruction recognized only that a retraction, though not a complete defense, may be considered in mitigation of damages. Such a charge left defense counsel to their own persuasive devices to convince the jury not to overlook a retraction's exculpatory effects.

For over a hundred years, various state legislatures have intermittently enacted retraction statutes designed to protect the press, and subsequently broadcasters, from excessively large judgments once they have retracted a defamation. Most of the earlier legislation accomplished little; the statutes either were interpreted so that the common law was left intact or were held to be unconstitutional.[22] In the latter part of the twentieth century, many American judges have been more likely to deem stat-

Cal.Civ.Code, § 48a(2) (statutory provision to the contrary).

21. See Allen v. Pioneer Press Co., 40 Minn. 117, 41 N.W. 936 (1889) (opinion of Mitchell, J.).

22. See Morris, Inadvertent Newspaper Libel and Retraction, 32 Ill. L.Rev. 36 (1937). And see Madison v. Yunker, —— Mont. ——, 589 P.2d 126 (1978).

utes valid unless compelling arguments make unconstitutionality clear. An example of special interest is the California Supreme Court's 1950 ruling on the constitutionality of a retraction statute that greatly favored retracting newspaper publishers and broadcasters. In Werner v. Southern California Associated Newspapers,[23] a paper reported Werner's conviction and subsequent sentencing in a felony case. Werner brought a libel suit, alleging in his petition that the newspaper had known its report was false but had published it anyway, intending to disgrace and defame him. The trial judge dismissed the petition on the ground that the plaintiff failed to conform to § 48a of the California Civil Code, which limits newspapers' liability for libel to special damages, except when the maligned person calls upon the newspaper to retract and this demand is ignored. The statute defines *special damages* as loss "in respect to property, business, trade, or occupation." On appeal, the victim unsuccessfully contended that the statute offended both the federal and state constitutions. Since those defamed seldom can prove special damages as defined by section 48a, retracting newspapers or broadcasters rarely incur liability for defamation—even if their original disparagement has been made with fault sufficient to satisfy the applicable federal constitutional requirement. The constitutional cases only contract state defamation liability; thus the California statute, which does not expand common law liability, has been unaffected by the revolution.

An Oregon statute much like the California enactment differs only in providing that a victim of media defamation who neither demands a retraction nor shows that the publisher intended to vilify the plaintiff may recover only the special damages established. The Oregon Supreme Court held that the statute contravened neither the Oregon nor the United States Constitutions. Consequently, a plaintiff who did not allege either intentional vilification or special damages failed to state a cause of action.[24] In 1962, the United States Supreme Court refused to review the Oregon holding.[25]

More will be said later about both the value of apology and the desirability and constitutionality of state retraction statutes that might be drafted with the revolution in mind.

23. 35 Cal.2d 121, 216 P.2d 825 (1950).

24. Holden v. Pioneer Broadcasting Co., 228 Or. 405, 365 P.2d 845 (1961), cert. denied, 370 U.S. 157, 82 S.Ct. 1253, 8 L.Ed.2d 402 (1962).

25. Id.

§ 5.   COUNSELING CLAIMANTS

A dishonored client who wants a lawyer to file a libel suit may be actuated by several different motives. The client may want compensation for financial losses caused by the slur. Usually the victim is outraged and would like to make the harasser squirm. Sometimes the complainant wants to grab a chance to receive a great deal of money. Perhaps the most decent goal of a person dishonored is an urgent need for exculpation and vindication. These motives seldom occur singly, and a defamed client often hopes to reach more than one objective.

Counsel representing a smeared client whose major motive is the rehabilitation of reputation must proceed with circumspection. When vindication is the client's principal need, the wisest course may involve sacrificing other objectives in order to get a prompt, prominent, and full retraction. An out-and-out apology will often neutralize dishonor more effectively than successful litigation ending in a substantial judgment. An early and large money settlement without complete retraction is often unthinkable to one who urgently needs to clear his or her name; even though the dishonored person widely publicizes the settlement, the rancorous vilifier may, in reply, circulate the imputation that the victim seemed willing to sell honor for a price. Sometimes, especially when the defamation results in heavy financial losses, the astute counsel for a claimant may be able to persuade the libeler both to retract and to pay for all or part of the harm done. Even after the revolution, the claimant who can muster clear proof of both falsity and substantial damages still has at least a chance of establishing enough fault to satisfy the suitable constitutional requirement. The risk of incurring both liability and legal expenses in such a case may bring the libeler around not only to publishing a retraction but also to paying for all or some of the claimant's financial loss. Retraction, however, does not always protect one defamed from suffering extraordinarily large damages, recoverable only through litigation.[26]

When a disparaged person brings and loses a defamation suit, further resort to litigation will probably reestablish or reenforce the plaintiff's disrepute. The technical reasons for losing a libel suit are many and are rarely understood by the public. An honorable person who has been defamed can lose a case on a number of grounds that have nothing to do with the plaintiff's deserved reputation. The victim can be defeated by the libeler's constitu-

---

26.   See, e. g., Luster v. Retail Credit Co., 575 F.2d 609 (8th Cir. 1978).

tional privileges of freedom of expression, the libeler's common law privilege, the plaintiff's inability to prove the right kind of fault or to establish the right kind of damages, and so on. The besmirched plaintiff's acquaintances, once the libel suit is lost, are likely to believe that the defamation was true; a plaintiff's ironclad proof of falsity is overshadowed when the court awesomely dismisses the case. Most claimants who genuinely desire a rehabilitated reputation should be advised not to sue when risk of failure is substantial.

A claimant who desires to litigate must be prepared, once started, to fight all the way to the end. The plaintiff must stand ready to appeal if the case is lost at the trial, since subsidence may imply an admission that the disparagement was true.

Counsel should view with special caution a proposal to bring suit on a subtle or somewhat trivial defamation. Like any witness, a disparaged plaintiff who takes the stand is subject to impeachment by cross-examination intended to show acts of misconduct evincing bad moral character;[27] conviction of a crime involving moral turpitude, if such has been the case;[28] or bad reputation for truth and veracity.[29] Even one who can prove all elements of a postrevolution libel case may not be well served when his or her past has been less than perfect. The litigant's opponent may offer proof calculated to show that the claimant's "actual damages" could have resulted from widespread knowledge of misdeeds having no relation to the defendant's disparagement. Only plaintiffs with good records are likely to come out of a libel suit with better reputations than they had going in. Oscar Wilde unwisely sued on a libel that was proven true. The civil suit's sequel was an indictment, and Wilde was convicted. His two years' experience in prison is reflected in his woeful Ballad of Reading Gaol.

Defamation plaintiffs who collect substantial judgments have not necessarily acted in their best interests. Slurs are often less damaging than the derided person fancies. Defamations, like most communications, seldom are fully apprehended; many people who hear or read aspersions neither clearly identify the person affronted nor remember the scorn for long. Those well acquainted with the victim will generally not believe false accusations. Litigation, at its various stages and over a substantial

27. See Georgia v. Bond, 114 Mich, 196, 72 N.W. 232 (1897). See also, C. McCormick, Handbook of the Law of Evidence 82 (2d ed. 1972).

28. See C. McCormick, Handbook of the Law of Evidence 85 (2d ed. 1972).

29. Id. at 90.

period of time, republicizes the defamation. Fragments of trials and appeals are reported as they happen. Many who know that legal proceedings are in progress never follow their entire course; others who read about a final judgment often forget who won. When a defendant vigorously contests a suit for publishing a defamation, some people will sententiously say that so much smoke without some fire is unlikely.

The well-known victim of prominent and persistent vilification may have little to lose, other than legal costs, by bringing a libel suit. Some litigation victories are newsworthy and easily understood; they are especially exculpatory and reparative when judgment awards the plaintiff substantial damages. There are, then, only a modicum of cases in which counsel should recommend filing a defamation suit and prosecuting it vigorously to its conclusion.

§ 6. POLICY CONSIDERATIONS

When the Supreme Court decided *Times* and embarked on a decade of filling out and limiting the policy enunciated there, the Court undertook unprecedented checks on civil litigation for defamation. This innovative development significantly enlarged the various freedoms of expression. Why did the nineteenth century and two-thirds of the twentieth century pass before the Supreme Court nurtured a fresh growth of first amendment freedoms? Perhaps the answer is embedded, at least in part, in a sudden surge in the size of some libel verdicts, most notably those awarded by jurors inflamed by racial and cultural antipathies of mid-twentieth century America. In *Times* itself, the Alabama jurors were not full of compassion for the sophisticated New York newspaper that had published a full-page advertisement berating the Old South for injustice to blacks. These jurors did not hesitate to award $500,000 against the New York Times, the verdict which Sullivan had alleged in his petition to be the appropriate one.

Earlier in the twentieth century, defamation verdicts against newspapers were likely to fall within the $5,000–$40,000 range, even when awards included general "presumed" damages were augmented by punitive damages. Before the revolution, most newspapers and some broadcasters carried limited, but fairly adequate liability insurance that supplied coverage sufficient for those days.[30] The immoderate $500,000 judgment in *Times* was

---

30. "[Libel and slander insurance] . . . is [in 1951] relatively inexpensive. . . ." Footnote: "One firm, Employers Rein- surance Co. of Kansas City, offers an 'excess' policy whereby the assured pays damages up to a certain amount and the insurer pays

a jarring event, quickening the response from the Supreme Court. Repugnance against official English censorship, it has been said,[31] originally inspired American constitutional protections of free expression. The large Alabama judgment in *Times*, entered after publication, was calculated to induce self-censorship by those whose words were likely to inflame a jury as unbridled as the one in *Times*. Since the effect of defamation laws of the states could induce prior self-censorship resembling the first amendment interdiction, it was clear that defamation law now needed radical change.

Of course, the constitutional limitations on defamation liability, recognized mainly in *Times*, *Walker*, and *Gertz*, do not abolish all actionable libel and slander. The area in which the states may properly award damages for defamation has, however, been greatly reduced; and when damages are recoverable, they are now often curtailed in various ways. Contingent fee lawyers invited to invest their time and skill on defamation cases no longer respond with enthusiasm. And few are the clients who are willing and able to pay their lawyers—win or lose—for prosecuting a questionable defamation claim. Only wealthy defamation victims are likely to get their days and months in court; and they, moreover, seldom profit much, even when they succeed in establishing both the constitutionally requisite fault and damages.[32]

The satisfying gains achieved in the freedoms of speech and press have been accompanied by a less welcome loss. Many innocent victims of vilification who could formerly go to law for vindication and compensation no longer have legal remedies. Furthermore, the majority of defamers who are advised that they will probably not be held liable for publishing particular slurs are not likely to go overboard in making detailed, prominent, and completely exculpatory apologies, if indeed they retract at all. Certainly, the immune detractor will seldom be gen-

. . . excess. For example . . . a daily newspaper of approximately 5,000 circulation can take out insurance against libel damages of $25,000 in excess of $1,000 for approximately $130 a year." 28 Emory Univ.Journalism Q. No. 4 (Fall 1951). Quoted from article by Newell and Pickerell.

31. See Near v. Minnesota ex rel. Olson, 283 U.S. 697, 51 S.Ct. 625, 75 L.Ed. 1357 (1931) (opinion of Hughes, C. J.).

32. In Buckley v. Littell, 539 F.2d 882 (2d Cir. 1976), cert. denied, 429 U.S. 1062, 97 S.Ct. 785, 50 L. Ed.2d 777 (1977), the plaintiff paid lawyers who pressed his case through a Federal District Court trial and fought the defendant's appeal through the Second Circuit. The plaintiff's modified judgment was for a thousand and one dollars, as fabulously unprofitable as A Thousand and One Nights (Unexpurgated) is interesting.

erous to the point of compensating his victim for any financial losses caused by the canard.

The Supreme Court has barred another kind of palliative to those defamed. On the day that the Supreme Court decided *Gertz*, it also held a Florida retraction statute unconstitutional in Miami Herald Pub. Co. v. Tornillo.[33] The Florida enactment provided that when a newspaper "assails the personal character" [of a candidate for public office] . . . "or otherwise attacks his official record" [the newspaper must] "publish without payment" [a reply submitted by the candidate disparaged]. The Court held this statute unconstitutional under the first amendment, with Chief Justice Burger writing for the Court. "The Florida statute," he said, "exacts a penalty on the basis of the content of a newspaper . . . . [T]he penalty . . . is exacted in . . . the cost in printing . . . and materials and in taking up space that could be devoted to other material the newspaper may have preferred to print . . . . Faced with [these] penalties . . . editors might well conclude that the safe course is to avoid controversy . . . [and consequently] political and electoral coverage would be blunted or reduced." The Chief Justice added, "Even if a newspaper would face no additional costs . . . the Florida statute fails to clear the barriers of the First Amendment because of its intrusion into the function of editors . . . . The choice of materials to go into a newspaper . . . constitute[s] the exercise of editorial control and judgment . . . ." The Burger opinion may imply that all retraction statutes enacted by state legislatures are also unconstitutional; any legal pressure put upon a newspaper to publish a retraction is an "intrusion into the function of editors" and may distort "the exercise of editorial judgment."[34]

The unconstitutional Florida reply statute should, however, be distinguished from those retraction statutes that permit defamers to ignore appeals for retraction; such enactments are different in nature from the Florida statute, which obliged newspapers to open their columns, gratis, for replies. In *Tornillo*, two concurring Justices said that the decision to hold the Florida statute unconstitutional did not encompass the constitutionality of retraction statutes. *Times* and its progeny have not inhibited

---

33. 418 U.S. 241, 94 S.Ct. 2831, 41 L.Ed.2d 730 (1974).

34. Another minor check on state defamation law: An Oklahoma statute allowing all successful defamation plaintiffs to recover at least $100 plus costs (even when plaintiff establishes no actual damages) is unconstitutional under *Gertz*. Martin v. Griffin Television, Inc., 549 P.2d 85 (Okl.1976).

the states from further constricting the liability of those libelers who recant.

The California retraction statute does not order editors to heed or even listen to appeals for retraction. Such behavior will deprive editors only from enjoying the statutory benefits conferred on retractors.[35] The protection conferred by the California statute, however, has probably induced some retractions that might not otherwise have been forthcoming. Professor Albert C. Pickerell, an inquisitive teacher of journalism at the University of California at Berkeley, surveyed disclaimers of California newspapers published in 1956–57,[36] using a clipping service that scanned all California newspapers. The service sent him some one thousand items, most of which merely corrected nondefamatory errors. Eighty-four items were significant retractions of vexatious libels. These retractions gave to those libeled exculpation far more effectual than that represented by delayed judicial vindication. Insofar as those vilified were prejudiced in business or employment, they still had legal claims for compensation despite the fact of the retraction; the retraction only protected the libeler from liability for either emotional upset or punitive damage. Professor Pickerell says, "All of the retractions appear to stem from inadvertent libel. There was a certain amount of carelessness [committed by employees of the newspapers in some of the eighty-four instances]."

Those of the eighty-four who were libeled could now, under *Gertz*, recover no proven damages unless they also established fault at least as serious as lack of due care. Any of the eighty-four who were either public figures or governmental officials could at present, under *Walker* and *Times*, recover no damages unless they proved *Times* malice. Even so, the media should be interested in lobbying for retraction statutes that, like the California enactment, would protect them, once they had retracted, against liabilities still recoverable—that is, those for pain and suffering, permitted under *Firestone*, or those awarded in punitive damages, as awarded in *Buckley*.

State legislatures should not limit their concern to the media's freedom of expression. Nonmedia defamers willing to make suitable and prompt public apology deserve as much freedom of speech as publishers and broadcasters. Legislation should protect all retracting defamers against liability for either pain and suffering or punitive damages, even though their original can-

---

35. West's Ann.Cal.Civ.Code, § 48a.

36. The California Publisher, Retraction Study " . . . In Substantially as Conspicuous Manner." (Sept. 1958 pub. by the Cal. Newspaper Publishers Ass'n, Sacramento).

ards had been carelessly or maliciously uttered. Such legislation
would have two virtues: It would induce the best available form
of vindication for many who have been unjustly maligned, and it
would militate against self-censorship tending to suppress robust
free expression. At the same time, proper retraction statutes
would not reduce, and would perhaps strengthen, the remaining
constitutional claims for clearly needed compensation for loss of
profits and earnings.

Chapter XIII

MALICIOUS PROSECUTION AND FALSE IMPRISONMENT

Table of Sections

Some children, preferring retort to retaliation, say, "Sticks and stones will break my bones, but names will never harm me." This recognition of the futility of demanding redress for defamation now befits most of their elders, who must live with the modern restrictions on liability for libel and slander. The ancient remedies for malicious prosecution and false arrest, however, have not been cut back on constitutional grounds; victims disgraced by either of these misdeeds still enjoy wide protection of tort law. Though occasionally malicious prosecution and false imprisonment litigation result in enormous judgments, most successful claimants usually enjoy only moderate awards.

§ 1. MALICIOUS PROSECUTION

Meanwretch told a district attorney that Scruple stole Meanwretch's wallet. The report was a hateful falsehood told by Meanwretch with the intention of hurting Scruple. As a result, Scruple was tried for larceny, but, fortunately, acquitted.

Scruple thereafter sues Meanwretch in a tort action for the malicious prosecution. Meanwretch is at fault and should be liable. Scruple should be and is entitled to recover financial losses proximately caused by the prosecution—the cost of defense (attorneys' fees, outlay for bail bonds, and the like), compensation for time unprofitably and unpleasantly spent while in the custody of the law and in defending the charge, plus any other special damages legally consequent to the unfounded prosecution. In those jurisdictions that allow punitive damages for heinous fault, juries are permitted to assess them against defendants like Meanwretch.[1]

---

1. Punitive damages were recovered in Western Union Telegraph Co. v. Thomasson, 251 F. 833 (4th Cir. 1918). Failure to instruct the jury properly on its authority to levy punitive damages was held to be

Scruple, it was formerly said, would be entitled to a substantial "general damages" award for injury to reputation even if Scruple offered no proof of any items of loss or expense (which would seldom be the case).[2]

Perhaps the principal value of civil responsibility for malicious prosecution is the vindication afforded victims defamed by outrageously unfounded accusations of crime.[3] In Gertz v. Welch,[4] the court forbade recovery of "presumed damages" awarded for injury to a libel plaintiff's reputation. At this writing, five years after *Gertz*, no counterpart to this constitutional reduction of liability has appeared in malicious prosecution litigation. On the contrary, a Maryland court held, post-*Gertz*, that a malicious prosecution plaintiff was entitled to a judgment even though he offered no evidence of special damages.[5] If Scruple was convicted of a crime and the conviction stands, Scruple cannot maintain a civil action for malicious prosecution. Malicious prosecution plaintiffs may succeed only after criminal proceedings have terminated in their favor. Proof of Scruple's acquittal, of course, meets this requirement.[6]

reversible error in Chavez v. Sears, Roebuck & Co., 525 F.2d 827 (10th Cir. 1975) (applying Oklahoma law). See also, Dunn v. Koehring Co., 546 F.2d 1193 (5th Cir. 1977); Bertero v. National General Corp., 13 Cal.3d 43, 118 Cal.Rptr. 184, 529 P.2d 608 (1975). Compare Park v. Security Bank & Trust Co., 512 P.2d 113 (Okl.1973).

2. In Schwartz v. Boswell, 156 Ky. 103, 160 S.W. 748 (1913) an action was brought, maliciously and falsely charging that a partisan bystander joined into a fistfight. The defendant contended that, since the plaintiff neither alleged nor proved damage to his reputation, the trial judge should not have told the jury that the plaintiff could be given an award for injury to his standing in the community. The Kentucky appellate court said that damage to the plaintiff's reputation should be presumed to have resulted from his arrest.

In malicious prosecution suits, plaintiffs are entitled to prove that newspapers carried stories about criminal charges filed against them. Burke v. Watts, 188 Cal. 118, 204 P. 578 (1922).

3. Prosecution for some minor misdeed like obstructing a highway may not involve serious opprobrium. See Adams v. Bicknell, 126 Ind. 210, 25 N.E. 804 (1890). Arrest, however, may result in disgrace, even when made for some minor misdeed not involving moral turpitude. Cf. Nelson v. Hill, 30 N.M. 288, 232 P. 526 (1924). Expense and outrage resulting from unpardonable false charges of crime should subject the accuser to civil liability even when the accused's reputation is not impaired.

4. 418 U.S. 328, 94 S.Ct. 2997, 41 L.Ed.2d 789 (1974).

5. Krashes v. White, 275 Md. 549, 341 A.2d 798 (1975). See also Bertero v. National General Corp., 13 Cal.3d 43, 118 Cal.Rptr. 184, 529 P.2d 608 (1975).

6. In Cuthrell v. Zayre of Virginia, Inc., 214 Va. 427, 201 S.E.2d 779 (1974) a shopper accused of shoplifting put up a fight, and thereafter was charged with petty larceny and disorderly conduct. She was acquitted of theft, but convicted of disorderly conduct. Held: The conviction did not bar

Proof that charges were dropped also meets this requirement, except when Scruple either pleads with the state's attorney for mercy in spite of guilt,[7] or escapes prosecution by initiating a compromise such as proposing to deliver over property in return for dismissal of charges.[8] Should Scruple leave the state and forestall extradition by convincing foreign authorities that the charge was baseless, the accuser incurs no liability for malicious prosecution unless the original charge has been dismissed.[9]

We shall see later that in some states under some circumstances, courts allow the victim of unwarranted non-criminal proceedings to recover damages proximately caused by those proceedings. Since a defendant in a civil proceeding cannot, when filing an answer to the plaintiff's complaint, show a favorable termination, the defendant *ipso facto* is not entitled to file a cross action for damages for injuries that have or will result from the civil proceeding.[10]

Favorable termination of a criminal prosecution tends to vindicate the accused. If Scruple offers proof of innocence so irrefutable that the trial judge directs an acquittal and pronounces, as the state's representative, regret that so honorable a person should have been brought to trial, Scruple may have no need of further exculpation.

Acquittals, however, are not as such a pronouncement of innocence; an acquittal, standing alone, formally implies only that the accused's guilt was not established beyond a reasonable doubt. A prosecutor's nolle prosequi of a charge before or during trial may often be based on some ground other than the prosecutor's belief in the accused's innocence. Those maliciously prosecuted may often need vindication not afforded by favorable termination. To recover civil damages for malicious prosecu-

---

her right to recover for malicious prosecution for theft.

7. See, e. g., Bickford v. Lantay, 394 A.2d 281 (Me.1978); Green v. Warnock, 144 Kan. 170, 58 P.2d 1059 (1936). Cf. Hammond Lead Products, Inc. v. American Cyanamid Co., 570 F.2d 668 (7th Cir. 1977) (civil suit which was dismissed without prejudice held, nevertheless, an adequate basis for malicious prosecution liability).

8. See, e. g., Cimino v. Rosen, 193 Neb. 162, 225 N.W.2d 567 (1975); Singer Sewing Machine Co. v. Dyer, 156 Ky. 156, 160 S.W. 917 (1913).

9. See Cowan v. Gamble, 247 S.W. 2d 779 (Mo.1952).

10. This is illustrated by Nataros v. Superior Court of Maricopa Cty., 113 Ariz. 498, 557 P.2d 1055 (1976), a civil action based on fraud. The accused filed a cross action, alleging that the accuser's suit was a malicious prosecution. Held: Cross action dismissed as premature. The court said that if the defendant were allowed to offer proof that the fraud suit was filed maliciously and without probable cause, this evidence might unduly prejudice the jury against the civil plaintiff.

tion, a plaintiff must establish that the defendant initiated prosecution "without probable cause"—that is, without reasonable grounds for suspecting the accused's guilt. The defendant in a malicious prosecution suit is entitled to offer evidence of the plaintiff's guilt even though the criminal court has acquitted the accused, and when the defendant establishes by a preponderance of the evidence that, despite acquittal, the plaintiff was guilty, the plaintiff is not entitled to civil damages. After an accused's reputation has been tarnished by a criminal trial ending in a jury finding that guilt had not been proved beyond a reasonable doubt, a malicious prosecution judgment against the accuser establishes both that the accuser, though afforded a second opportunity to muster some evidence that the accused had committed a crime, still failed to show a probability of guilt, and that the accuser did not have a reasonable suspicion in the first place.

Some victims of unfounded prosecution who deserve vindication, nevertheless, cannot maintain actions for malicious prosecution. When Scruple has been convicted on perjured testimony, Scruple has no claim for damages for malicious prosecution so long as the conviction stands. Innocent victims of perjury are deprived of vindication not because they are guilty; they cannot maintain civil actions because many guilty convicts might seek this easy form of review to impugn their convictions. Scruple's worthy claim, therefore, cannot be heard without entertaining many meritless claims. Otherwise, a criminal occasionally might be able, in a civil action, to discredit the administration of the penal law; furthermore, were all convicts entitled to challenge their accusers in malicious prosecution actions, many criminals probably would escape accusation.[11] Everyone, therefore, has a qualified privilege to instigate criminal proceedings.

The proof of fault required to establish liability for malicious prosecution is two-headed. An accuser is subject to civil liability only if the accusation was both prompted by "malice" and was made without probable cause.

Want of Probable Cause. In Stohr v. Donahue,[12] the defendant, a manufacturer of specialized farm machinery, discharged the plaintiff who had been his sales agent. Several days after the agency was terminated, the former agent moved the manufacturer's machines to new consignees and thereafter accepted nearly three thousand dollars from a new consignee. The plaintiff had no authority, even before his discharge, to accept pay-

---

11. See Keithley v. Stevens, 142 Ill.App. 406 (1908), aff'd, 238 Ill. 199, 87 N.E. 375 (1909).

12. 215 Kan. 528, 527 P.2d 983 (1974).

ments. The defendant learned that the machines had been moved and payments had been made to his discharged agent. Inquiries addressed to the discharged agent by registered and unregistered mail produced no response and were either returned as undeliverable or ignored for some twenty-five days. The employer then called on the authorities to prosecute the former agent. The agent was brought to trial and acquitted, and thereafter he brought a malicious prosecution suit against his former employer. The appellate court, on the ground that the agent had failed to prove want of probable cause at the time the employer instigated the prosecution, affirmed the trial judge's judgment for the employer. The "test" of probable cause that courts usually purport to apply is this: An accuser does not lack probable cause to initiate criminal proceedings when belief of the accused's guilt would be entertained by a reasonably prudent and cautious person acting in similar circumstances. Even when actuated by malice, an accuser who has probable cause incurs no liability.[13]

At the opposite extreme are cases like Wilson v. Thurlow,[14] in which an informant had told the accuser that a certain man had indecently exposed himself on a certain road; the accuser's sole grounds for pressing charges were that the accused was black and was hauling a load of corn over the road mentioned by the instigator's informant. The court ruled that proof of these facts showed want of probable cause.

There are some few situations in which a criterion other than reasonably founded suspicion has been used as a test of probable cause.

In Parli v. Reed,[15] a landowner entertained suspicions that a builder who was working for him was about to sneak off with money collected for completed construction, but without paying his workmen and material suppliers (whose unpaid claims would become liens on the landowner's property). The landowner charged the builder with crime; thereafter the builder sued for malicious prosecution. The Kansas court ruled that the landowner lacked probable cause, since the suspected facts constituted no crime in Kansas. The court treated this accuser, who misapprehended the law, as though he knew the law, disregarding the reasonableness of his misapprehension. Most courts have

13. See Western Union Telegraph Co. v. Thomasson, 251 F. 833 (4th Cir. 1918), in which the accuser may have been motived more by a desire to get back property than a desire to see a guilty man convicted.

14. 156 Iowa 656, 137 N.W. 956 (1912).

15. 30 Kan. 534, 2 P. 635 (1883).

taken a different view; in one case a lawyer who had excusably misconstrued a criminal statute did not subject himself to liability for malicious prosecution. The court held he had had probable cause to institute a prosecution for acts that he had erroneously thought were covered by that statute.[16] While most people do not, of course, know the subtleties of the law, the average person nevertheless can make some unreasonable mistakes of law.[17]

Several courts have held that a conviction at criminal trial reversed on appeal conclusively establishes probable cause unless the accuser prevailed by perjury or bribery.[18] These courts have reasoned that when a criminal trial court has convicted an accused, the reasonableness of the accuser (who has resorted to neither perjury nor bribery) must be inferred. Most convictions, including those reversed, are in fact based on proof from which guilt could reasonably be suspected. Once a case is brought to trial, however, the very fact that it has been brought to trial has some tendency to counteract the presumption of innocence and to suppress, if it exists, the accuser's lack of probable cause. Magistrates, police judges and pickup juries do sometimes jump to unwarranted pronouncements of guilt. Some more exalted trial judges have been motivated by bias against some or all prisoners in the dock. A reversed conviction damages the convict even more than an immediate acquittal. When, therefore, a charge has been made originally with malice and without probable cause, the defamed, detained, humiliated, expense ridden, innocent victim should not be deprived of a malicious prosecution claim. Several courts, though they recognize that an initial conviction should be given proper weight, also have given appropriate weight to proof that tended to show that the accuser lacked probable cause when lodging the charges.[19]

---

16. Whipple v. Gorsuch, 82 Ark. 252, 101 S.W. 735 (1907). The court said that an excusable misapprehension of the law should not be treated differently from an excusable mistake of fact. See also, Nyer v. Carter, 367 A.2d 1375 (Me.1977); Siegman v. Equitable Trust Co., 267 Md. 309, 297 A.2d 758 (1972). Cf. Welch v. Kinchla, 577 F.2d 767 (1st Cir. 1978), a civil case in which the defendant attached plaintiff's property under a statute later held unconstitutional.

17. See Burke v. Watts, 188 Cal. 118, 204 P. 578 (1922).

18. See, e. g., Brewster v. Woodward & Lothrop, 530 F.2d 1016 (D. C.Cir. 1976); Broussard v. Great A. & P. Tea Co., 324 Mass. 323, 86 N.E.2d 439 (1949). And see Williams v. City of New York, 508 F. 2d 356 (2d Cir. 1974) applying New York law; Smith v. Anderson, 259 Ark. 310, 532 S.W.2d 745 (1976). A similar result was reached in a suit for maliciously bringing a civil suit, in Nagy v. McBurney, —— R.I. ——, 392 A.2d 365 (1978).

19. See, e. g., Lind v. Schmid, 133 N.J. 255, 337 A.2d 365 (1975); MacRae v. Brant, 108 N.H. 177,

In Ohio the courts have held that proof of a grand jury's indictment is *prima facie*, but rebuttable, evidence that the accuser had probable cause;[20] in Oregon an indictment has been held to be some evidence of probable cause.[21] The Supreme Court of Florida, nevertheless, has held proof showing that the accused was bound over for trial by a justice of the peace conclusively established probable cause.[22] Twenty years later, Florida refused to give force to the accuser's proof that the accused was bound over when the accused proved that the justice of the peace ordered committal, not because the justice had found probable cause, but because the accused had refused to give his accuser a release in exchange for dismissal of the criminal proceeding.[23]

Virtually all courts have held that accusers establish probable cause conclusively whenever they prove that, before instigating prosecutions, they have made full and fair disclosure of all their knowledge about the case to lawyers who thereupon advised them to file charges.[24] A vexed person who, on the verge of instigating a criminal proceeding, consults a lawyer, may be in no frame of mind to disclose some facts that throw doubt on the guilt of the person the accuser wants prosecuted. Cross-examination of client and lawyer may bring out the client's lack of objectivity and candor during the consultation. Juries have more than once found that accusers lacked probable cause even though they sought counsel before making charges.[25]

A private accuser who harbors doubts about the guilt of the person that the accuser officially charges with crime does not have probable cause even though the accuser's knowledge would

230 A.2d 753 (1967); Johnston v. Byrd, 279 Ala. 491, 187 So.2d 246 (1966).

Alabama stands by Johnston v. Byrd, but a civil judgment is conclusive of probable cause, absent fraud, perjury, or other serious impropriety during the trial. Jordan v. Empiregas, Inc., 337 So.2d 732 (Ala.1976).

20. Hruska v. Severance Specialty, Inc., 498 F.2d 796 (6th Cir. 1974).

21. Lampos v. Bazar, Inc., 270 Or. 256, 527 P.2d 376 (1974).

22. Gallucci v. Milavic, 100 So.2d 375 (Fla.1958).

23. Rodgers v. W. T. Grant Co., 341 So.2d 511 (Fla.1977).

24. See L. B. Price Mercantile Co. v. Cuilla, 100 Ark. 316, 141 S.W. 194 (1911). The privilege to file a civil proceeding on advice of counsel protects the suitor against liability for bringing the suit. See, e. g., Hernon v. Revere Copper & Brass, Inc., 494 F.2d 705 (8th Cir. 1974); Lewis v. Crystal Gas Co., 532 P.2d 431 (Okl.1975).

25. See Page v. Rose, 546 P.2d 617 (Okl.1976); Bertero v. National General Corp., 13 Cal.3d 43, 118 Cal.Rptr. 184, 529 P.2d 608 (1975); Lampos v. Bazar, Inc., 270 Or. 256, 527 P.2d 376 (1974); Varner v. Hoffer, 267 Or. 175, 515 P.2d 920 (1973); Hendrie v. Perkins, 240 Ky. 366, 42 S.W.2d 502 (1931).

convince a reasonable person that the accused is guilty. In the classic case, Connery v. Manning,[26] a lender prosecuted a property owner who made false representations to obtain a mortgage loan. The borrower, in his financial statement, exaggerated his property's *assessed* value. Before the lender pressed charges, the lender was told that the mortgagor misunderstood the word, *assessed*, and had given his honest opinion on the actual value of the property when he had answered a question on assessed value. The judge who tried the civil action for malicious prosecution directed a verdict for the defendant on the ground that the accidental misrepresentation would have led a reasonably cautious person to conclude that the borrower intended to deceive. On appeal, the court held that the proof raised an issue that should have been tried by the jury: Did the mortgagee in fact believe that the borrower intended to deceive?[27] A peace officer may, however, have probable cause to start a criminal proceeding against a person whenever the officer receives a credible report that the person charged has committed criminal acts, even though the officer personally has formed no firm conviction that the accused is guilty.[28]

Whether or not a private accuser's reasonable belief that the accused is *probably* guilty of crime constitutes a privilege to institute criminal proceedings seems to be an open question. The accuser is certainly privileged to make a full and fair report to the authorities, but a citizen of a cautious turn of mind who prefers to suspend judgment should hesitate to instigate prosecution when there is belief only that the accused has probably committed a crime.

In damage suits for torts other than malicious prosecution, jurors often decide whether or not a defendant's behavior should be characterized as reasonable; jurors sitting in personal injury cases in which the defendant's acts and omissions are not in dispute may be asked to determine whether or not the defendant's conduct was negligent. The procedure for trying an issue of want of probable cause in a malicious prosecution action nevertheless is different. When the facts are not in dispute, the issue of want of probable cause is for the court, and the trial judge must decide whether or not the plaintiff has proved that

---

26. 163 Mass. 44, 39 N.E. 558 (1895).

27. See also, Bertero v. National General Corp., 13 Cal.3d 43, 118 Cal.Rptr. 184, 529 P.2d 608 (1975);

Dodson v. MFA Ins. Co., 509 S.W. 2d 461 (Mo.1974).

28. See Slade v. City of Phoenix, 112 Ariz. 298, 541 P.2d 550 (1975).

the defendant lacked probable cause.[29] When the facts are in dispute, the trial judge is not allowed to define probable cause abstractly and let the jury apply that definition to the facts as the jury finds them; the trial judge is obliged to give more specific instructions telling the jury what legal effect attaches to resolutions of disputes of fact bearing on the defendant's want of probable cause. An instruction giving the jury no more concrete guidance than "the reasonably prudent and cautious person" test is in error.[30] Whenever proof is complicated or subtle, the trial judge may be able to do little more than first focus the jury's attention on critical times and places, and then tell the jury to determine, once the jury decides what happened at each disputed event, whether or not the facts if found would convince a reasonably cautious person of the accused's guilt.[31] One court has suggested that, in complicated cases, the trial judge should consider asking the jury to return special verdicts on each factual issue bearing on probable cause, so that the trial court, thereafter, is enabled to give proper legal effect to the jury's findings about what the defendant did and what significant circumstances existed.[32]

Malice. The courts often have said that even though an accuser lacked probable cause to believe that the accused was guilty, there is no liability for damages for malicious prosecution unless the plaintiff has established that the accuser maliciously pressed charges. Thus, a dunderhead, actuated by a desire to bring a guilty person to justice, can escape liability for rashly instigating criminal proceedings against an innocent person, even when belief in the accused's guilt is utterly unreasonable.

In some cases the courts have favored foolish accusers. Griswold v. Horne [33] was a case in which an elderly couple instigated

29. Smith v. Tucker, 304 A.2d 303 (D.C.App.1973). See also, De Salle v. Penn Central Transportation Co., —— Pa.Super. ——, 398 A.2d 680 (1979); Rose v. Reinhart, 194 Neb. 478, 233 N.W.2d 302 (1975).

The court held the same way in a suit for maliciously instituting a civil suit, in Carroll v. Kalar, 112 Ariz. 595, 545 P.2d 411 (1976). See also, Hernon v. Revere Copper & Brass, Inc., 494 F.2d 705 (8th Cir. 1974).

30. See, e. g., Burke v. Watts, 188 Cal. 118, 204 P. 578 (1922) in which the instruction was: If the accuser knew that the accused

took the chattels under a good faith claim of title, then the accuser did not have probable cause for charging theft. See also, Lampos v. Bazar, Inc., 270 Or. 256, 527 P.2d 376 (1974). But see the old case of Gulf, C. & S. F. Ry. v. James, 73 Tex. 12, 10 S.W. 744 (1889).

31. See Schwartz v. Boswell, 156 Ky. 103, 160 S.W. 748 (1913).

32. Gustafson v. Payless Drug Stores Northwest, Inc., 269 Or. 354, 525 P.2d 118 (1974).

33. 19 Ariz. 56, 165 P. 318 (1917).

prosecution for theft. The accused was their youthful companion, whom they had theretofore treated like an adopted daughter before they unjustly charged her with stealing some trifles. She was exonerated and brought suit for malicious prosecution. The Arizona Supreme Court reversed her judgment for damages on the ground that the trial judge had failed to charge the jury clearly that the accused could not succeed unless she had established bad faith; the court said that the jury as instructed might have found against the old people even though it found that these accusers had believed their accusation was true.[34]   The justification of the rule of this case is that wrongdoers might escape prosecution if accusers lay themselves open to liability whenever jurors find that their honest belief of guilt is undiscerning.

The requirement of proof of malice has not always been so understood. Some accusers, who may well have believed their accusations have, nevertheless, been held liable for malicious prosecution. Judges have often approved of statements like this: While want of probable cause may not be inferred from spite, malice may at times be inferred from want of probable cause. This idea was incorporated in the trial judge's charge in the case against the elderly couple; the appellate court held that its incorporation was improper. Other courts have, however, approved malicious prosecution judgments against defendants whose accusations were made too hastily.[35]   In Wilson v. Thurlow,[36] the case in which the accuser charged a black with indecent exposure when all he know about the matter was that a third person had reported some black's exhibition in the general vicinity, the court held that proof of such a glaring lack of probable cause was an adequate basis for inferring malice. The proof tended to show, circumstantially, that the accuser may not have believed that the man he had charged was the guilty person. If the accuser did believe the accused guilty but was held liable for malicious prosecution on the ground of the inanity of his self-persuasion, then the case is at odds with the *Griswold* case,[37] in which the elderly couple escaped liability.[38]

Some courts have expressly held that the instigator's credulity about the accused's guilt did not preclude a finding that the ac-

---

34. See also, Nyer v. Carter, 367 A.2d 1375 (Me.1977).

35. See, e. g., Gustafson v. Payless Drug Stores Northwest, Inc., 269 Or. 354, 525 P.2d 118 (1974).

36. 156 Iowa 656, 137 N.W. 956 (1912).

37. Cited in note 33, supra.

38. See also, Montgomery Ward & Co. v. Keulemans, 275 Md. 441, 340 A.2d 705 (1975) in which the accuser pressed charges overhastily.

cuser acted with malice. In Callahan v. Kelso,[39] neighbors' relations became acrimonious; one, without probable cause, charged that the other stole his turkeys. The accuser testified that he believed the accused took his foul with criminal intent. The appellate court, passing on the adequacy of proof of malice, said that the accuser "appeared to believe" he had the right to call his neighbor a thief. While honest belief in the accused's guilt protects an accuser from liability, a captious or reckless belief, said the court, is not an honest one. In Hugee v. Pennsylvania R. R.,[40] the court held that the jury could infer malice from want of probable cause and that malice is not limited to spite; malice, said the court, includes reckless disregard of truth evidenced by pressing charges with undue haste and on insufficient grounds.[41] In an old case in which an accuser believed that bloodhounds could not only track and identify a quarry from one place to another, but also had the ability to smell out their quarry's guilt, the court held that the accuser's want of probable cause to believe in the quarry's guilt constituted malice as a matter of law.[42] On the other hand, a showing of mere clerical negligence may prove want of probable cause, but it does not prove malice.[43]

Any private accuser who presses charges without in fact entertaining a belief in the accused's guilt is guilty of malice. An accuser who did not know which one of several suspects had committed the crime, but pressed charges against the accused to find out who was guilty, not only lacked probable cause, but was also guilty of malice.[44] There are, however, instances of malice that are neither disbelief in nor reckless disregard of the truth of the accusation made. When accusers who lacked probable cause tried to enforce the payment of a disputed claim or the de-

39. 170 Mo.App. 338, 156 S.W. 716 (1913).

40. 376 Pa. 286, 101 A.2d 740 (1954).

41. Cf. Vander Linden v. Crews, 231 N.W.2d 904 (Iowa, 1975), holding that while private accusers need not prove spite to establish malice, when public administrative officials press charges in the exercise of their offices, they are subject to liability for malicious prosecution only if they were primarily inspired by spite; when accusing administrators' purposes in instigating prosecution are otherwise proper, they are privileged even though they harbored some resentment or indignation toward those accused. See also, Williams v. Crews, 564 F.2d 263 (8th Cir. 1977).

42. Tucker v. Bartlett, 97 Kan. 163, 155 P. 1 (1916). See also Krol v. Plodick, 77 N.H. 557, 94 A. 261 (1915).

43. Wesko v. GEM, Inc., 272 Md. 192, 321 A.2d 529 (1974). Compare O'Toole v. Franklin, 279 Or. 513, 569 P.2d 561 (1977).

44. Glover v. Fleming, 36 Md.App. 381, 373 A.2d 981 (1977).

livery of property by instigating a criminal prosecution, their belief in the guilt of the accused did not protect them from liability.[45]

A malicious prosecution action cannot succeed when the defendant sued did not set the prosecution going. Whenever a person has made full disclosure about the possible commission of a crime to the authorities the informant is not the instigator of a malicious prosecution, even though he or she has signed formal charges at the behest of the authorities; the legal responsibility for the prosecution is taken by the authorities rather than by the informant. The accused has no common law action against the state's attorney or the magistrate issuing an arrest warrant for reasons similar to those that justify the absolute privileges of judges and lawyers who publish libel in the exercise of their functions.[46] When a person warps or shades knowledge of the facts in a report to the authorities the informer is subject to liability for malicious prosecution.[47]

Should the authorities refuse to act, no prosecution has been set afoot, and consequently no malicious prosecution action will lie. The accused's only hope is that the accuser will be liable for defamation; all courts have held that accusations of crime are

---

45. See, e. g., Wadkins v. Digman, 82 W.Va. 623, 96 S.E. 1016 (1918); Suchey v. Stiles, 155 Colo. 363, 394 P.2d 739 (1964); Kitchens v. Barlow, 250 Miss. 121, 164 So.2d 745 (1964).

46. Prosecuting attorneys' absolute immunity against liability for malicious prosecution has long been recognized at common law. The leading case is Gregoire v. Biddle, 177 F.2d 579 (2d Cir. 1949) cert. denied, 339 U.S. 949, 70 S.Ct. 803, 94 L.Ed. 1363.

Imbler v. Pachtman, 424 U.S. 409, 96 S.Ct. 984, 47 L.Ed.2d 128 (1976) held that the Civil Rights Act, 42 U.S.C.A. § 1983, made no inroads on state attorneys' immunities for undertaking prosecutions. The Second Circuit Court of Appeals did, however, hold that administrative officers could be subject to liability for serious financial loss resulting from malicious prosecution of administrative proceedings. Economou v. U. S. Dept. of Agriculture, 535 F.2d 688 (2d Cir. 1976). The Third Circuit has held that law enforcement officers who served process on an accused and threatened prosecution for purposes of extortion, enjoyed no common law immunity, and were subject to liability for damages under the Civil Rights Act, 42 U.S.C.A. § 1983. Jennings v. Shuman, 567 F.2d 1213 (3rd Cir. 1977).

47. Rose v. Whitbeck, 277 Or. 791, 562 P.2d 188 (1977). Compare Noell v. Angle, 217 Va. 656, 231 S.E.2d 330 (1977), in which the defendant's candor in his report protected him from liability. In Bickford v. Lantay, 394 A.2d 281 (Me. 1978), an accuser urged the chief of police eight times and insisted that the chief arrange for a prosecution. The chief told the accuser that he believed no criminal prosecution was warranted; whereupon the accuser circulated a letter criticizing the chief's performance of his office. The chief gave in and followed this accuser's demand. Proof of this behavior, coupled with other evidence of irate behavior, was held to support a finding of malice.

privileged. In a few jurisdictions the privilege to accuse falsely is conditional and subject to abuse; consequently, if false charges are made recklessly or in bad faith, the accuser may incur liability for libel or slander.[48] In most jurisdictions the privilege is absolute.[49] This view seems preferable; prosecuting attorneys and grand jurors seldom air accusations on which they are unwilling to act. When the story leaks out, the accuser often has retold it personally in an unprivileged context, and the accuser (or some other repeater) may be subject to liability for defamation.

A witness testifying before a grand jury or at a criminal trial incurs no liability for malicious prosecution, even when the testimony is perjured.[50] Courts may make this distinction between false witnesses and false accusers because a suit against a witness called an action for malicious prosecution seems inappropriate. There is, however, a reason for the distinction that is more substantial than this misnomer. Accusers are self-starters; their impetus should be sober and well-founded. Many witnesses do not appear voluntarily; sometimes they are reluctant to testify even after they are called to the stand. Were there a threat of civil liability for damages in a malicious prosecution suit brought against a mere witness by an outraged, money-seeking plaintiff, that threat could tend to stifle important testimony needed in criminal trials.

If Meanwretch has pressed criminal charges against Scruple, and, as a result, a warrant is issued for Scruple's arrest, what are Scruple's rights when the warrant is never executed? Some courts have said that no prosecution is started until arrest and therefore Scruple cannot maintain an action for malicious prosecution.[51] Other courts have held that issuance of a warrant for arrest is prosecution enough and an accuser may be subject to liability even though the accused is never taken into custody.[52] The better result is to hold that a malicious prosecution plaintiff need not prove arrest; issuance of a warrant for arrest is a public act likely to be reported in the press and,

48. See Miller v. Nuckolls, 77 Ark. 64, 91 S.W. 759 (1905).

49. See Bryant v. Commonwealth of Kentucky, 490 F.2d 1273 (6th Cir. 1974); Hott v. Yarbrough, 112 Tex. 179, 245 S.W. 676 (1922).

50. "[T]he necessities of a free trial demand that witnesses are not to be deterred by fear of tort suits, and shall be imune from liability."

W. Prosser, Handbook of the Law of Torts 837 (4th ed.1971).

51. See Mitchell v. Donanski, 28 R. I. 94, 65 A. 611 (1906). Compare Larocque v. Dorsey, 299 F. 556 (2d Cir. 1924); Cooper v. Armour, 42 F. 215 (2d Cir. 1893).

52. See, e. g., Ballard v. Cash, 191 Ky. 312, 230 S.W. 48 (1921).

therefore, likely to result in damages to the person whose arrest has been ordered, even though the order has been ignored.

Courts disagree on whether or not proceedings in a court lacking jurisdiction to try an accused on the charge will subject the accuser to liability for malicious prosecution.[53] Dismissal of an unfounded criminal charge on the ground that the court in which the charge was lodged lacked jurisdiction neither vindicates the accused nor compensates for legal expenses, lost time, humiliation and other damages resulting from the prosecution. The accused, says Prosser, should not have a malicious prosecution action dismissed on the ground that the charge was brought before a court lacking jurisdiction, "with the consoling assurance that he never really was prosecuted at all; nor is it any less a prosecution because it is successfully defended on the law rather than the facts."[54]

The courts are also divided on whether or not plaintiffs who maliciously file civil suits incur liability. In some American jurisdictions, Meanwretch risks liability for damages by maliciously instituting a civil action without probable cause.[55] Most courts, however, take the view that, subject to some exceptions, the malicious institution of civil proceedings is not a tort.[56] The courts denying liability do so because they fear that the evil done by deterring claimants from seeking their day in court outweighs the evil of the damages likely to result from malicious filing of civil cases without probable cause. The cost of unprofitable civil litigation is high; therefore spiteful unfounded civil litigation is comparatively rare. When, however, civil litigation is maliciously instituted and bootless, it may result in various kinds of damages to a successful defendant. Honest claimants (who almost invariably are advised by counsel) are not likely to give up their rights to be heard because of the possibility that they may be held liable for malicious prosecution; if the courts were careful to restrict liability to cases in which civil litigants either knew their claims were false or were recklessly and inex-

---

53. A malicious prosecution action will not lie, Berger v. Saul, 113 Ga. 869, 39 S.E. 326 (1901). Contra, Kuhnhausen v. Stadelman, 174 Or. 290, 148 P.2d 239 (1944); Sutor v. Wood, 76 Tex. 403, 13 S.W. 321 (1890).

54. W. Prosser, Handbook of the Law of Torts 836 (4th ed. 1971).

55. See Hammond Lead Products, Inc. v. American Cyanamid Co., 570 F.2d 668 (7th Cir. 1977); Bertero v. National General Corp., 13 Cal.3d 43, 118 Cal.Rptr. 184, 529 P.2d 608 (1975); Slee v. Simpson, 91 Colo. 461, 15 P.2d 1084 (1932).

56. See, e. g., Ammerman v. Newman, 384 A.2d 637 (D.C.App.1978); Buck v. Gale, 271 Or. 90, 530 P.2d 1248 (1975).

cusably indifferent to the defects in the claim asserted, the danger of silencing honest claimants would be small.[57]

Most courts do hold malicious users of civil litigation liable for so doing when the proceedings result in detention of the person or property of the victim.[58] A litigant who maliciously files a multiplicity of suits may incur liability even though the filing of the first suit would not have been actionable.[59]

In Melvin v. Pence,[60] the court held that a malicious instigator of an administrative proceeding to consider revocation of a detective's license incurred liability to the detective. The court said that this accusation to an administrative board did not differ from instigating a criminal prosecution. Judge (later Justice) Rutledge stressed the financial losses that the detective suffered while the proceeding had barred him from practicing his vocation for nearly a month. The Supreme Court of Oregon has held that an accuser who had lodged a complaint of serious misconduct in the University of Oregon's student court was subject to liability if the accused could establish specific financial loss.[61]

Suppose Lender lends a car to Borrower for an evening. The car is not returned that night; the next morning Lender can find neither Borrower nor the automobile. Lender reports the loss to the police, who three days later find the car in a remote place and badly damaged. Borrower, who was injured when the car was smashed up, is released from a country hospital sometime thereafter. Lender comes to believe that the car was wrecked two days after Borrower had agreed to return it, and presses criminal charges against Borrower for larceny by bailee,

---

57. See Robinson v. Goudchaux's, 307 So.2d 287 (La.1975), in which a claimant who filed a suit for debt with complete want of probable cause was held liable for his unwarranted litigation.

58. See, e. g., Black v. Judelsohn, 251 App.Div. 559, 296 N.Y.S. 860 (1937), in which the victim was arrested for contempt when an injunction was issued against him; Nassif v. Goodman, 203 N.C. 451, 166 S.E. 308 (1932), in which the victim's property was tied up by bankruptcy proceedings. (The Bankruptcy Act, 11 U.S.C.A. § 303(i), now specifically provides for liability in this situation, to be imposed by the bankruptcy court.) Compare O'Toole v. Franklin, 279 Or. 513, 569 P.2d 561 (1977); Wesko v. GEM, Inc., 272 Md. 192,

321 A.2d 529 (1974); Lowe v. Root, 166 Mont. 150, 531 P.2d 674 (1974).

59. Soffos v. Eaton, 152 F.2d 682 (D.C.Cir. 1945); Weisman v. Middleton, 390 A.2d 996 (D.C.App. 1978). Compare Perry v. Arsham, 101 Ohio App. 285, 136 N.E.2d 141 1 O.O.2d 266 (1956). Contra, Pye v. Cardwell, 110 Tex. 572, 222 S. W. 153 (1920).

60. 130 F.2d 423 (D.C.Cir. 1942).

61. Donovan v. Barnes, 274 Or. 701, 548 P.2d 980 (1976). See also, Ring v. Ring, 102 R.I. 112, 228 A. 2d 582 (1967) conditioning liability for malicious filing of any civil suit on a showing of "special damages."

a statutory crime in the state where both parties live and all relevant events occur. Suppose Borrower is tried and acquitted on the ground that the wreck occurred on the evening of the bailment and thereafter sues Lender for malicious prosecution. If Borrower establishes that Lender had no grounds whatsoever to believe that the wreck occurred after the agreed-on period of the borrowing, Borrower will probably win the malicious prosecution suit. Suppose, however, that while the criminal charges are still pending, Borrower sues Lender for abuse of process. Suppose further that Borrower neither claims innocence nor that Lender knew or should have known that the accident occurred during the period for which the car was lent. Instead, Borrower offers to prove that Lender demanded payment for the damages to the car on the ground that they resulted from the bailee's negligent driving. When payment was not forthcoming, Lender lodged the larceny charge and thereafter offered to withdraw the charge if and when Borrower tendered money to pay for repairs. Lender may be not only subject to criminal liability for compounding a felony, but may also be subject to civil liability for damages, provided Borrower can establish that the criminal suit was instigated primarily for the ulterior purpose of collecting the claim. Lender may be liable for abuse of process even though Borrower has not been acquitted and even though Lender has probable cause to believe that the accident happened long after the bailment had expired.[62]

---

62. See, e. g., Thrifty Rent-A-Car v. Jeffrey, 257 Ark. 904, 520 S.W.2d 304 (1975); see also Sarvold v. Dodson, 237 N.W.2d 447 (Iowa, 1976), in which plaintiff alleged in his petition that he entertained a belief that the defendant policeman had so acted that he should be dismissed from the force, and made charges of defendant's misbehavior to the authorities. In retaliation the defendant instigated proceedings which resulted in plaintiff's commitment to a mental hospital for evaluation and treatment of plaintiff's alleged mental disease. The defendant, alleged the plaintiff, "did not file said information for the sole purpose of obtaining treatment for Plaintiff but maliciously filed same for the collateral and ulterior purpose of having Plaintiff . . . confined so that [the plaintiff] could not pursue his efforts [to get the defendant discharged] and to destroy [the plaintiff's] credibility." The plaintiff prayed for damages proximately caused. The Supreme Court of Iowa held that the plaintiff had alleged facts constituting a cause of action for abuse of legal process and that the plaintiff need not establish either that the defendant lacked probable cause or any malice other than malicious use of process for an improper purpose. And see Jennings v. Shuman, 567 F.2d 1213 (3rd Cir. 1977) (applying Pennsylvania law); Mayer v. Walter, 64 Pa. 283 (1870).

§ 2. FALSE IMPRISONMENT

Some restraints are illegal arrests that purport to enforce the criminal law; others are unprivileged detentions unrelated to law enforcement. The legal aspects of the latter are simpler and will be considered first.

Joker has perversely barred the door to the room in which Victim is asleep. Victim awakes and demands release. Joker refuses and laughs.

If Victim cannot get out by using some other reasonably safe exit, Joker, unless some special privilege exists, has falsely imprisoned Victim and is liable for damages, even though the detention was both short and caused Victim no financial loss. Victim's cause of action is a modern survival of trespass *vi et armis* for false imprisonment, closely related to actions for assault and battery, unlawful entry on land, etc. Victim is therefore entitled to "compensatory damages" for the time lost and mental distress suffered.[63] In most jurisdictions Joker is subject to liability for punitive damages, since Joker's wrong was both intentional and oppressive. If Victim could have left the locked room either by another door or, without appreciable risk of injury, through a window then, since there was no confinement in fact, Victim has no claim for false imprisonment. One who has not been detained, but has unreasonably entertained a belief that restraint would occur if an attempt was made to leave, has not been falsely imprisoned.[64] An action for false imprisonment will not lie against a wrongdoer who has closed off one avenue or direction of movement but left impeded travelers free to go wherever else they wished; for example, in the classic Bird v. Jones,[65] Queen's Bench held that a usurper of a stretch of public highway overlooking a boat race, allowing entrance only to those who paid the usurper a fee, did not falsely imprison a traveler who wanted to go down the wrongfully closed road. Some other form of action might have succeeded against the usurper; in Cullen v. Dickinson,[66] the court held that high-handed city officials who had decided young girls should not be admitted to public dances incurred liability, under reformed procedure, to a girl who was turned away from a dance hall. This liability was not,

---

63. Griffin v. Clark, 55 Idaho 364, 42 P.2d 297 (1935), held that practical jokers were liable for false imprisonment; the award was, in the main, compensation for personal injuries incurred.

64. Riggs Nat. Bank v. Price, 359 A.2d 25 (D.C.App.1976).

65. 7 Q.B. 742, 115 Eng.Rep. 668 (1845).

66. 33 S.D. 27, 144 N.W. 656 (1913).

however, the equivalent of the common law action for false imprisonment.

When a private person has locked someone in, there is no liability for false imprisonment unless the restraint was inexcusable. For example, in Wood v. Cummings,[67] the custodian of a bankrupt's assets had allowed a creditor to come into the shop in which the bankrupt's goods were stored. When the creditor's business was ended, he discovered that the door to the shop had been locked from the outside during his visit. The custodian had explained to the creditor that he suspected that the creditor had brought along confederates who would make trouble; the custodian had immediately signalled to his sentry, who had instantly unlocked the door to let the creditor out. The court said that since the custodian had no intention to detain the creditor, he could not be held liable for false imprisonment. Merchants and tradesmen are privileged momentarily to detain customers to collect for goods sold or services rendered, but an unreasonably harassing detention constitutes a false imprisonment.[68] Creditors do not have a lien on the persons of their debtors. In Gadsden General Hospital v. Hamilton,[69] the court held that a hospital which had detained a patient until her bill was paid had falsely imprisoned her.

Most detainers who commit false imprisonments intend to restrain their victims. One negligent detention subjected a careless defendant to liability;[70] though the court that characterized the suit as an action for false imprisonment, its opinion was written sixty years after the forms of action distinguishing between intentional trespass and negligence were abolished.[71]

67. 197 Mass. 80, 83 N.E. 318 (1908).

68. Jacques v. Childs Dining Hall Co., 244 Mass. 438, 138 N.E. 843 (1923) (restaurateur liable for detaining customer half an hour to investigate the accuracy of her bill); Woodward v. Washburn, 3 Denio (N.Y.) 369 (1846) (bank liable for capricious detention of a customer).

69. 212 Ala. 531, 103 So. 553 (1925).

70. Talcott v. National Exhibition Co., 144 App.Div. 337, 128 N.Y.S. 1059 (1911).

71. In Harnik v. Levine, 106 N.Y.S. 2d 460 (Mun.Ct.N.Y.1951), aff'd,

202 Misc. 648, 115 N.Y.S.2d 25 (1952), a doubleparker was held liable for inconveniencing a motorist who could not move his car; the decision was reversed at 281 App.Div. 878, 120 N.Y.S.2d 62 (1953). The court said that the claimant's delay was too short to constitute a nuisance and that the plaintiff had not established any actionable damages (prerequisite for a recovery in a suit to negligent misconduct). A bank was held liable in Mouse v. Central Sav. and Trust Co., 120 Ohio St. 599, 167 N.E. 868 (1929), for negligently dishonoring a check whose drawer, as a consequence, was arrested. In Sullivan v. County of Los Angeles, 12 Cal.3d 710, 117 Cal.Rptr. 241, 527 P.2d 865 (1974), the California Supreme Court said,

Lack of positive acts intended to restrain may not, under some circumstances, defeat an action for false imprisonment; a refusal to afford release from restraint may be sufficient detention. A yacht owner who ignored his guest's request to be put ashore at the agreed end of a voyage, or a car-driving Lothario who disregarded a maiden's demand that he stop the car and let her out have both been held guilty of false imprisonment.[72]

Can a person be falsely imprisoned without knowing it? In the classic English case, Herring v. Boyle,[73] a schoolmaster refused to release a young boarding school pupil until his mother paid tuition in arrears. On the ground that the child had been oblivious of his improper detention, the court found that he was not falsely imprisoned. In several jurisdictions the mother could have recovered both compensatory and punitive damages; an action based on the ancient authorities allowed parents recovery for "loss of their child's services," in which juries were permitted to redress improper deprivation of parents' custody of their children.[74] In at least one American case, a kidnapping parent has been held liable for falsely imprisoning his small child;[75] no mention was made of the four-year-old's understanding of the impropriety of her asportation. In a 1919 English case,[76] the majority opinion stated that company detectives who had guarded the door of a room to prevent the escape of an employee suspected of theft, falsely imprisoned the suspect even though he had been unaware of their presence and purpose. The defamatory implication of the guards' action (seen by third parties) may have influenced the court's decision. In Whitman v. Atchison, T. & S. F. Ry.[77] a train passenger knew he was detained but did not realize the impropriety of his outrageous detention. The passenger had been hurt while getting off the train. The conductor had told him that he was required by law to remain at the scene of the accident until he signed a statement; the injured man had complied and his treatment was delayed for

"Under California common law the jailer has long been held liable for false imprisonment if he . . . should have known of the illegality of [an] imprisonment." Contra, Garber v. U. S., 578 F.2d 414 (D.C.App.1978).

72. Yacht case: Whittaker v. Sandford, 110 Me. 77, 85 A. 399 (1912). Car case: Cieplinski v. Severn, 269 Mass. 261, 168 N.E. 722 (1929).

73. 1 Cr. M. & R. 377, 149 Eng. Rep. 1126 (1834).

74. See, e. g., Steward v. Gold Medal Shows, 244 Ala. 583, 14 So. 2d 549 (1943), a case in which a circus harbored a young runaway boy; and see W. Prosser, Handbook of the Law of Torts 882–84 (4th ed. 1971).

75. Robalina v. Armstrong, 15 Barb. (N.Y.) 247 (1852).

76. Meering   v.   Grahame-White Aviation Co., 122 L.T.R. 44 (Ct. of App. 1919).

77. 85 Kan. 150, 116 P. 234 (1911).

twenty minutes. The court found he had been falsely imprisoned.

Judges have often said that imprisonment implies either actual physical restraint or threat of force if the captive should attempt to get free. In the yacht case (in which the passenger claimed that the captain refused to allow her to go ashore at the end of the agreed-on voyage),[78] the passenger had withdrawn from a strange cult led by the captain. The leader's evidence had tended to show that he tried to keep the backslider aboard only by questioning her rejection of the faith. The court approved the trial judge's instruction that told the jury to hold against the apostate only if it found she was not detained merely by moral persuasion but by the leader's withholding of physical means of disembarking. However, some detentions that have resulted from disadvantages that might have been incurred by departure have been characterized as false imprisonments. In National Bond & Investment Co. v. Whithorn,[79] a finance company hired strong-arm men to repossess cars of delinquent borrowers. These henchmen tracked down a car buyer in arrears and halted him on a busy street. When the delinquent balked when they asked that he turn over his car to them, they attached their wrecker to the front end of the car and dragged it off with the delinquent in it. The automobile buyer knew he was free to go his own way without his car. The loan company was held liable for compensatory and punitive damages for the false imprisonment of buyer.[80]

Some protested losses of freedom may not be actionable. A person in danger, though ignorant of the fact, may resist being carried to safety by a rescuer, but the rescuer will not incur liability for abridging the victim's freedom.[81]

Good intentions coupled with bad judgment can result in officious intermeddling. Courts take a dim view of confinement without use of legal process on suspicion that the victim is men-

---

78. Whittaker v. Sandford, 110 Me. 77, 85 A. 399 (1912).

79. 276 Ky. 204, 133 S.W.2d 263 (1938).

80. See also, Griffin v. Clark, 55 Idaho 364, 42 P.2d 297 (1935) (false imprisonment by threat of separating a traveller from her baggage, causing her to make outcry to avoid detention); Jacques v. Childs Dining Hall Co., 244 Mass. 438, 138 N.E. 843 (1923)

(diner charged with presenting cashier an improper bill; she stayed to clear her name).

81. See State v. Hemphill, 162 N.C. 632, 78 S.E. 167 (1913). This is a case holding that such a defendant incurs no criminal liability. We have found no civil cases in point, perhaps because those so served will not sue their rescuers, or because contingent fee lawyers see no likelihood of profitable litigation under these circumstances.

tally disturbed. In a nineteenth century case,[82] a daft person agreed to be escorted to the home of friends in an adjoining state; when departure time came, however, she repudiated the plan, resisted the trip, and was carried off by force. The Supreme Court of New Hampshire held that she had been falsely imprisoned. Forty years later, a woman exhausted by caring for her ailing husband called in a trained nurse to take charge; the overtired woman seemed to the nurse and attending doctor to be a nuisance in the sickroom and badly in need of a rest. When the wife fainted the nurse gave her a shot of morphine, and she was carried off to a sanatorium and forcibly detained for two weeks. The Supreme Court of Illinois held that, absent commitment proceedings, even insane people cannot be deprived of their liberty except when they are endangering their own lives or the lives of others.[83] In 1950, Judge Henry W. Edgerton, a noted champion of civil liberty, wrote the court's opinion in Jillson v. Caprio.[84] A psychiatrist had called on the police to imprison the plaintiff in a mental hospital. Congress had passed a statute that authorized arrest of alleged insane persons in Washington, D.C., before commitment only after (1) a person of unsound mind had been apprehended wandering about in the street or a public place, or (2) when two or more responsible residents had made affidavits swearing that, for specified reasons, they believed a person unfit to be at large, and when thereafter two physicians examined that person and certified that the person should not be allowed to remain at liberty but should be subjected to treatment likely to improve the unsound mental condition. In Jillson, Judge Edgerton said, "In providing protection for persons whose relatives think or pretend to think they require restraint because of mental illness, Congress necessarily struck a balance between individual liberty and public safety. A policeman or psychiatrist may think Congress should have drawn the line in a different place . . . [E]ven the most reasonable belief that [persons imprisoned] will do harm in the future does not justify doctor or layman in arresting [them] without statutory authorization and without a warrant. [The psychiatrist's] calling neither defeats the [incarcerated woman's] claim to damages nor reduces its amount." None of the above cases imposes liability without fault; the proper way of

82. Keleher v. Putnam, 60 N.H. 30 (1880).

83. Crawford v. Brown, 321 Ill. 305, 151 N.E. 911 (1926). In Maxwell v. Maxwell, 189 Iowa 7, 177 N.W. 541 (1920), a son confined his 78-year old father, who had shown signs of senile dementia; the court held the son was subject to liability for false imprisonment unless he could prove that his father was in fact insane.

84. 181 F.2d 523 (D.C.Cir. 1950).

imposing commitment on those whose sanity is suspect is to abide by proceedings calculated to protect sane eccentrics from being caged like madmen (which some say is a growing practice in governments disdaining dissent).

False Arrest. Citizen suspects that Paragon has committed a crime. Citizen makes full and fair report to a magistrate of all the relevant facts known to Citizen about Paragon's doings. The magistrate, in the exercise of official power, in good faith issues a warrant directing a peace officer to arrest Paragon. The peace officer, as ordered, takes Paragon into custody. Paragon is innocent and is released.

Paragon has no cause of action against anyone for (a) defamation, (b) malicious prosecution, or (c) false imprisonment. Paragon has no defamation action because Citizen, the magistrate, and the peace officer are absolutely privileged to utter defamatory remarks in pretrial criminal proceedings. Paragon has no malicious prosecution claim against the magistrate or police officer because an action for malicious prosecution lies only against a private person who makes an accusation of crime.[85] Full disclosure to the magistrate protects Citizen from liability for malicious prosecution. A false imprisonment action will serve Paragon no better. In Bohri v. Barnett,[86] a peddler had been acquitted of hawking his goods without a license. He contended that the ordinance requiring a license was unconstitutional and on that ground brought false imprisonment actions against the warrant-issuing justice of the peace, the arresting officer, and the prosecuting attorney. He lost because the officials were privileged and his accuser had not arrested him.

The immunity of officials issuing warrants for arrest and peace officers executing those warrants is not so sweeping as their immunities from liability for defamation and malicious prosecution. Magistrates are probably subject to common law liability if they issue warrants for arrest in bad faith.[87]

---

85. If the proceedings went to trial, Paragon would have no action against the absolutely privileged prosecuting attorney. Powell v. Seay, 553 P.2d 161 (Okl.1976).

86. 144 F. 389 (7th Cir. 1906).

87. We have found no cases in which adequate proof of bad faith in issuing a warrant for arrest was offered; but there have been holdings in favor of warrant issuers avoiding liability after proving good faith, in which good faith was treated as a defense. See, e. g., Brooks v. Mangan, 86 Mich. 576, 49 N.W. 633 (1891). See a Civil Rights Act (42 U.S.C.A. § 1983) case, Keeton v. Guedry, 544 F.2d 199 (5th Cir. 1976), in which the plaintiff sued a justice of the peace for issuing a warrant for the plaintiff's arrest. The court held the Justice incurred no liability because, said the court, "he clearly believed that criminal conduct possibly had occurred."

Both the warrant-issuing magistrate and the arresting officer incur liability when the magistrate acts without color of authority. In Heller v. Clarke,[88] a Milwaukee, Wisconsin justice of the peace had issued a warrant for arrest in utter disregard of a statute divesting all Milwaukee justices of the peace of jurisdiction to act in any criminal proceeding. The court held that the justice committed a false arrest since he acted "wholly without jurisdiction;" the court also held that the arresting officer, who had executed the warrant, also incurred liability because the magistrate's lack of jurisdiction was apparent on the face of the warrant. The justice of the peace's liability seems proper; for a magistrate to issue a warrant for arrest utterly beyond his jurisdiction should be inexcusable. Justices of the peace are not expected to be highly learned in all branches of the law, but they should know the rudiments of their own jurisdiction. The rule visiting liability on magistrates for issuing arrest warrants utterly beyond their jurisdiction is, then, a sound concrete standard describing a magisterial fault. A policeman or constable acting in executing a valid warrant incurs no liability for making the arrest authorized by that warrant.[89] The *Heller* case, however, held that the Milwaukee warrant, issued by a magistrate acting outside of his jurisdiction, did not protect the arresting policeman. If the policeman made this arrest in bad faith, his liability was justifiable. Though policemen ordinarily can know and act in conformity to legal principles, should they always incur liability whenever they make an arrest on any warrant which on its face exceeds the issuing magistrate's legal jurisdiction? In some circumstances a policeman's failure to be versed in knowledge of the legal ambit of a warrant-issuing magistrate's jurisdiction ought to be excused; the rule of the *Heller* case may, therefore, occasionally subject an arresting officer to unmerited liability without fault. When, however, the circumstances should alert an arresting officer to a warrant's invalidity, the officer should and does incur liability for executing that warrant.[90]

An officer of the law authorized by a warrant to make an arrest runs still other risks of liability. Certainly an officer incurs liability when he or she negligently arrests the wrong person.[91] Due care to identify the person arrested does not pro-

88. 121 Wis. 71, 98 N.W. 952 (1904).

89. Rodriquez v. Ritchey, 556 F.2d 1185 (5th Cir. 1977); Slade v. City of Phoenix, 112 Ariz. 298, 541 P.2d 550 (1975).

90. Woodward v. District of Columbia, 387 A.2d 726 (D.C.App.1978).

91. See, e. g., McCollan v. Tate, 575 F.2d 509 (5th Cir. 1978); State ex rel. Anderson v. Evatt, 63 Tenn. App. 332, 471 S.W.2d 949 (1971); Boies v. Raynor, 89 Ariz. 257, 361 P.2d 1 (1961).

tect an officer from liability when he or she arrests a person not bearing the exact name set out in the warrant.[92] In Kratzer v. Matthews,[93] an officer held a warrant to arrest a man likely to escape before the officer could take him into custody. A superior telephoned to a second officer and ordered him to detain the man until the warrant-bearing officer arrived. The second officer incurred liability for false arrest for obeying his superior's command, on the theory that a warrant does not authorize arrest unless the officer displays the document at the time he takes the person named into custody.[94]

Arrest Without Warrant. The perimeter of the privilege to arrest without warrant has been the subject of legislation in every state in the Union; no lawyer dealing with the privilege should proceed without due regard to applicable statutes. Many of these statutes are, however, legislative restatements of common law rules. The survey which follows may be usefully orienting, but the great likelihood of statutory variation should be kept in mind.

Before turning to the common law limitations on arrest without warrant, we should note that some arrests, with or without warrant, may violate constitutional rights. Constitutional rights of free speech and lawful assembly may be invaded when, for example, demonstrators are taken into custody; such arrests may subject arresting policemen and their municipal employer to substantial damages.[95]

At common law the police were privileged to arrest without warrant those whom they reasonably suspected had committed a felony; they incurred no liability without fault to innocent prisoners (even though no felony had been committed), so long as

---

92. In Holmes v. Blyler, 80 Iowa 365, 45 N.W. 756 (1890), a constable executing a warrant for the arrest of Martin had taken Holmes into custody. In Holmes' action for false arrest, the constable offered evidence tending to show that he had reasonably believed Holmes to be Martin; this tender of proof was rejected as irrelevant. In West v. Cabell, 153 U.S. 78, 14 S.Ct. 752, 38 L.Ed. 643 (1894), the magistrate had intended to authorize the arrest of the man actually taken into custody, but got the man's initials wrong. The arresting officer incurred liability.

93. 233 Mich. 452, 206 N.W. 982 (1926).

94. An officer who reasonably suspects a person of having committed a felony (and therefore, as we shall soon see, is privileged to arrest without warrant) nevertheless commits a false arrest if he or she displays a defective warrant and purports to execute it. Elwell v. Reynolds, 6 Kan.App. 545, 51 P. 578 (1897).

95. See, e. g., Tatum v. Morton, 562 F.2d 1279 (D.C.Cir. 1977).

each arrest was made with probable cause to believe the person taken into custody had committed a felony. Of course this privilege extends to an officer who sees a felonious act and proceeds to arrest the actor. An arrest made by a witness who has seen acts believed to be criminal may nevertheless be based on an unreasonable conclusion, and the arrestor may therefore incur liability.[96]

Police may catch felons in the act of committing a crime; but many arrests by officers are made for misdeeds committed out of their presence. In Eberhart v. Murphy,[97] a sheriff of one county made an arrest on the strength of a letter from another county's prosecuting attorney; the letter said the man had committed grand larceny. The Supreme Court of Washington held that since the sheriff acted with probable cause, he incurred no liability. Similarly, in Grau v. Forge,[98] a patrolman proved that a fifteen-year-old boy sought him out and complained of being robbed at gunpoint. The officer and boy combed the neighborhood until they came upon a man whom the boy identified as the robber. The court held that these facts justified the policeman's arrest of the man. Some courts are not so permissive in sanctioning an arrest merely on a stranger's uninvestigated statements.[99] A peace officer also may have probable cause to delay a suspect for monetary relevant questioning and therefore incur no liability for such an interrogation.[1] If, however, the delay is unreasonably prolonged, the officer will incur liability.[2]

When an arresting peace officer uses force which is unreasonably cruel or deadly, the officer may incur liability for such a battery under modern state statutes or newly developed common law.[3] Some defendants found guilty of inordinate arrests also have been held liable under the Federal Civil Rights Acts.[4]

---

96. See, e. g., Dellums v. Powell, 566 F.2d 167 (D.C.Cir. 1977); Montgomery Ward Co., Inc. v. Keulemans, 275 Md. 441, 340 A.2d 705 (1975). Compare Harrison v. May Dept. Stores Co., 381 A.2d 610 (D.C.App.1977).

97. 110 Wash. 158, 188 P. 17, rev'd, 113 Wash. 449, 194 P. 415 (1920).

98. 183 Ky. 521, 209 S.W. 369 (1919).

99. See, e. g., Butler v. Goldblatt Bros., Inc., 589 F.2d 323 (7th Cir. 1978) (applying Illinois law).

1. See Lansburgh's Inc. v. Ruffin, 372 A.2d 561 (D.C.App.1977).

2. See Marshall v. District of Columbia, 391 A.2d 1374 (D.C.App. 1978).

3. See the opinions and citations in Schumann v. McGinn, 307 Minn. 446, 240 N.W.2d 525 (1976). See also, Jones v. Wittenberg Univ., 534 F.2d 1203 (6th Cir. 1976).

4. See, e. g., Jones v. Marshall, 528 F.2d 132 (2d Cir. 1975).

Want of probable cause is a plaintiff's issue in a malicious prosecution suit; that is, the plaintiff must (1) come forward with evidence tending to prove that the accuser did not have legally sufficient reason to believe that the accused was guilty and (2) convince judge and jury that this evidence establishes lack of probable cause. In a suit for false arrest without warrant, however, probable cause is the defendant's issue; the defendant has both the burden of coming forward with evidence of probable cause and the burden of persuasion.[5] In another respect, however, procedure in false arrest and malicious prosecution cases is identical. When facts relating to probable cause are not in dispute, the trial judge, rather than the jury, must decide whether or not the party who has the probable cause issue has carried the burden of proof; when facts bearing on probable cause are disputed, the trial judge is obliged to tell the jury how its resolution of each specific issue of fact should affect its finding on the existence of or lack of probable cause for arrest. In the Kentucky case of arrest made after the identification of a gunman by a fifteen-year-old holdup victim, the jury was charged that the patrolman was not liable if he had reasonable grounds to believe his prisoner had committed a felony. The Supreme Court of Kentucky held that the trial judge erred in submitting the probable cause issue to the jury. The court said that even if reasonable jurors could differ on whether or not the undisputed facts established probable cause, since the facts were undisputed, the trial judge should have decided the issue himself. The court concluded that the trial judge should have found that the officer had had probable cause to make the arrest.[6]

An officer does not have probable cause to arrest when all that is known is that a reputable citizen believes the arrested person has committed some unspecified crime. In Laster v. Chaney,[7] for example, a plantation manager telephoned the sheriff, gave him only an automobile license number, and asked him to stop the car and hold the driver. The sheriff carried out this request, without other basis for suspicion. The man arrested was utterly innocent and gave the arresting sheriff full and credible explanations of his past doings. The Supreme Court of

5. See McCollan v. Tate, 575 F.2d 509 (5th Cir. 1978); Dellums v. Powell, 566 F.2d 167 (D.C.Cir. 1977); Broughton v. State, 37 N. Y.2d 451, 373 N.Y.S.2d 87, 335 N. E. 310 (1975).

6. Grau v. Forge, 183 Ky. 521, 209 S.W. 369 (1919). Compare Woodward v. District of Columbia, 387 A.2d 726 (D.C.App.1978).

7. 180 Miss. 110, 177 So. 524 (1937).

Mississippi held the sheriff lacked probable cause to arrest; the court said mere belief in the bare possibility that a man has committed some sort of an unnamed felony does not justify his arrest.

Those who commit "breaches of the peace" in the presence of an officer may be arrested without warrant. In Lynn v. Weaver,[8] a landlord, while collecting rent, got into a fistfight with his tenant. Police arrived during the affray and carted the combatants to jail. The arrest was proper. If the landlord was acting in privileged self-defense, his arrest nevertheless was lawful; police are not obliged to inquire into the merits of street fighters' actions before arresting them. In most jurisdictions, officers may not without warrant arrest for breaches of the peace committed before they came on the scene. When an officer comes within view of a fight and the fighters run away, the officer is entitled to give chase and take the combatants into custody. The officer loses this privilege once pursuit is no longer "fresh;" the officer cannot quit the chase and make a privileged arrest the next time he or she happens to encounter one of the fighters.

Doubt shrouds the authority of officers to make arrests without warrant when they witness crimes that are neither a felony nor a breach of the peace. Statutes privileging some such arrests are not uncommon. Officers who believe they are taking a person into custody for a misdemeanor committed in their presence, run a risk both that they have seen aright and that they understand the law. If the person arrested is not guilty, the officer may be excused for acting in good faith.[9]

Officers also may run the risk of understanding criminal law when they arrest a peron on suspicion that they are apprehending a felon. Some crimes are fairly serious and yet not felonies; a policeman who knows that most heinous crimes are felonies may arrest an offender who committed only a serious misdemeanor. Such a mistake of law has been a misfortune suffered by officers who did not know, for example, that conspiracy to commit an illegal abortion,[10] or that exhibitionistic indecent

8. 251 Mich. 265, 231 N.W. 579 (1930). See also, Hunter v. Clardy, 558 F.2d 290 (5th Cir. 1977).

9. See, e. g., Dellums v. Powell, 566 F.2d 167 (D.C.Cir. 1977). Contra, under Nebraska statute, Linn v. Garcia, 531 F.2d 855 (8th Cir. 1976). Compare Schulz v. Lamb, 591 F.2d 1268 (9th Cir. 1978).

10. Scott v. Eldridge, 154 Mass. 25, 27 N.E. 677 (1891).

exposure [11] were at the time misdemeanors. In the indecent exposure case, two other officers who drove the arrested man to headquarters were held to be the arresting officer's joint tortfeasors.[12]

A private person may make a "citizen's arrest." Citizen incurs no liability for arresting Innocent for felonious theft of silver from Citizen's home when the felony has actually been committed by someone and Citizen has probable cause to suspect Innocent.[13] Even when the authorities have probable cause to suspect Innocent, however, if Citizen complies with the police's telephoned request to hold Innocent until an officer can come, Citizen may be subject to liability for false arrest.[14] Citizen's lack of knowledge can lead to liability for Innocent's false arrest; for example, if Citizen bought silver on credit, and the creditor properly repossessed it during Citizen's absence, in some jurisdictions Citizen is not privileged to arrest Innocent for stealing the silver even though Citizen reasonably believed that Innocent had stolen it.[15] Most shoplifting involves theft of articles of small value, and a citizen storekeeper who reasonably, but mistakenly, detains a shoplifter for petty theft may incur liability.[16] In some states, however, citizens' arrests for either felony [17] or for shoplifting petty thefts [18] are privileged when made with probable cause. Section 102A of the Second Restate-

11. Cook v. Hastings, 150 Mich. 289, 114 N.W. 71 (1907).

12. See also, Schulz v. Lamb, 591 F.2d 1268 (9th Cir. 1978), in which a police officer who happened upon the scene of resistance to arrest, and who assisted the arresting officer without knowledge of the facts that preceded the false arrest, was held liable for his participation.

This result seems impolitic. Do we wish to discourage peace officers from coming to the aid of other officers discovered in trouble? Will this liability discourage wrongdoing? Is liability of the officer who initiates the false arrest an adequate remedy?

13. Burns v. Erben, 40 N.Y. 463 (1869). (Incidentally the court held that since the facts bearing on probable cause were undisputed, that issue should be decided by the trial judge.) In Enright v.

Gibson, 219 Ill. 550, 76 N.E. 689 (1906), the court held that a citizen's arrest for felony was privileged only if the arrested person was actually guilty; this theory was created judicially and thereafter promulgated legislatively.

14. See Casserly v. Wheeler, 282 F. 389 (9th Cir. 1922).

15. See the opinion in Great A. & P. Tea Co. v. Paul, 256 Md. 643, 261 A.2d 731 (1970); Thorne v. Turck, 94 N.Y. 90 (1893).

16. See Gill v. Montgomery Ward & Co., 284 App.Div. 36, 129 N.Y.S.2d 288 (1954); Szymanski v. Great A. & P. Tea Co., 79 Ohio App. 407, 74 N.E.2d 205, 35 O.O. 177 (1947).

17. See Missouri Pac. R. R. v. Quick, 199 Ark. 1134, 137 S.W.2d 263 (1940).

18. Prieto v. May Dept. Stores Co., 216 A.2d 577 (D.C.App.1966). See

ment of Torts grew out of the serious need to deter shoplifting.[19] The section provides, "One who reasonably believes that another has tortiously taken a chattel upon his premises, or failed to make due cash payment for a chattel purchased or services rendered there, is privileged, without arresting the other, to detain him on the premises for the time necessary for a reasonable investigation of the facts." Whether or not this proposition was, in fact, a restatement of common law at the time it was adopted by the American Law Institute in 1965, it is likely to affect the law in jurisdictions lacking legislation calculated to deal with shoplifting.

In one other situation the common law has long privileged a citizen's arrest for a misdemeanor; a citizen may arrest a peacebreaker for a breach of the peace committed in that person's presence.[20]

Citizens seldom collar and drag a suspect off to jail. Whenever citizens merely tell officers what they know, and thereafter the officers undertake on their own responsibility to make an arrest, the informants are not subject to liability for false imprisonment.[21] Whenever a citizen demands an arrest, the officer who does the citizen's bidding is acting for the demandant, and the citizen can incur liability.[22] For more than a century, American courts have held that suspects who voluntarily

Neisner Bros., Inc. v. Ramos, 326 A.2d 239 (D.C.App.1974), in which the department store was held liable because it detained the plaintiff as a shoplifter without having probable cause.

19. In Great A. & P. Tea Co. v. Paul, 256 Md. 643, 261 A.2d 731, 738 (1970), the court said, "[S]hoplifting may be regarded as the price merchants pay for the success of modern merchandising; goods alluringly displayed to stimulate 'impulse buying' inevitably also stimulate 'impulse taking.'" We hereby add that any cost of merchandising is likely to be added to the price honest customers must pay.

20. See Baltimore & O. R. R. v. Cain, 81 Md. 87, 31 A. 801 (1895).

21. See Butler v. Goldblatt Bros., 589 F.2d 323 (7th Cir. 1978);

Meering v. Grahame-White Aviation Co., 122 L.T.R. 44 (Ct. of App.1919).

22. In Ehrhardt v. Wells Fargo & Co., 134 Minn. 58, 158 N.W. 721 (1916), an express company's detective helped a sheriff question the sheriff's prisoner, suspected, without probable cause, of complicity in a hold-up. The sheriff asked the detective what he wanted done with the man. The detective replied, "Better hold him for further examination." Held: express company liable for false imprisonment. In Palmer v. Maine Central R.R., 92 Me. 399, 42 A. 800 (1899), a conductor mistakenly thought that a passenger was using a non-transferable ticket—a misdemeanor; the conductor induced a constable to arrest the passenger. Held: railroad liable for false arrest.

go to the police station to clear themselves are not arrested.[23]   A person can, however, be arrested without being touched; an arrest is consummated when an officer tells a person that he or she is under arrest and that person submits—even though the arrested person is not required to go along with the officer.[24] Some who are accosted are not arrested; for example, in Atlantic & Pacific Tea Co. v. Billups,[25] a storekeeper's clerk ran after a customer who had left the store and mistakenly accused her of taking a two-cent piece of candy without paying for it; the clerk demanded that she come back to the store, but after some bickering she went on her way. The court held that because she was not restrained, she was not falsely arrested. A few years later the same court tried another similar case, Ashland Dry Goods Co. v. Wages.[26] A customer bought a cap for her child, put it on his head, and put his old cap in her handbag. The store's rules required that all purchases be wrapped. A floorwalker saw the customer put an unwrapped object in her purse and suspected that she had shoplifted. He questioned her and disbelieved her. He then grabbed the bag out of her hands and searched through it. He took the old cap, wrapped it, and then handed both the wrapped package and her purse to the customer. The customer testified that she had not left the spot lest the floorwalker put something into her purse and accuse her of stealing it. In a false imprisonment suit, the storekeeper contended that the customer was not restrained and therefore had not been falsely imprisoned. The court found proof of detention sufficient for liability.

Many, probably most, defendants held liable for false arrest for crime are guilty of conduct that should be discouraged. Only a few plaintiffs who sue for damage for false arrest are detained for long. Jury verdicts, therefore, are likely to allow only small compensation for lost time. Juries are permitted to add compensation for indignity and pain and suffering.[27] In the remote past these damages were seldom large, but wrongfully

23. Marshall v. District of Columbia, 391 A.2d 1374 (D.C.App.1978); State ex rel. Powell v. Moore, 252 Miss. 471, 174 So.2d 352 (1965); see Brushaber v. Stegemann, 22 Mich. 266 (1871).

24. See Martin v. Houck, 141 N.C. 317, 54 S.E. 291 (1906); Boies v. Raynor, 89 Ariz, 257, 361 P.2d 1 (1961).

25. 253 Ky. 126, 69 S.W.2d 5 (1934).

26. 302 Ky. 577, 195 S.W.2d 312 (1946).

27. See Marshall v. District of Columbia, 391 A.2d 1374 (D.C.App. 1978).

inflicted indignity may nowadays result in substantial verdicts.[28] In most jurisdictions an outrageous false imprisonment can subject the arrestor to liability for substantial punitive damages.[29] Parrott v. Bank of America Nat. Trust & Sav. Ass'n [30] is an example of a 1950 false arrest judgment for thirty thousand dollars. Often, as in the Parrott case, a major incentive for suing for false arrest is vindication. When those who have arrested the plaintiff are found liable for a substantial sum, the judgment tends to convince the plaintiff's friends and acquaintances that the arrest was groundless. Under some circumstances, those who arrest a guilty person may be subject to liability. The guilty, however, seldom sue, and when they do they are not likely to recover enough to make litigation worthwhile.

There seems to be little reason for holding peace officers or citizens liable without fault for reasonable mistakes made while making arrests. Perhaps we should fear tyranny masked by smiling evidence of sweet reasonableness. Consider, however, these cases.

(a) An officer of the law executing a warrant excusably gets the wrong person. Why should we disregard the officer's excuse? We do not hold an officer without warrant when an arrest is made with probable cause for suspecting an innocent person of committing a felony. There are no policy grounds for distinguishing between these two good excuses for mistaken arrests.

(b) Neither arresting officers nor arresting citizens escape liability for making reasonable mistakes of law. When an officer who has excusably failed to recognize a fatal defect on the face of the warrant he or she has executed, or when an officer or a citizen has reasonably supposed a serious misdemeanor is a felony, liability may be predicated on the arrests. These results are not surprising in light of the other contexts in which courts have held mistakes of law inexcusable, but they add to the bulk of judicial missteps made by courts who insist that in all circumstances everyone knows the law.

---

28. See Neisner Bros. Inc. v. Ramos, 326 A.2d 239 (D.C.App.1974), in which a falsely suspected shoplifter's judgment was predicated on proof that her mental disturbance had resulted in protracted insomnia which had occasioned fifteen medical consultations.

29. See Atkinson v. Dixie Greyhound Lines, 143 F.2d 477 (5th Cir. 1944), cert. denied, 323 U.S. 758, 65 S.Ct. 92, 89 L.Ed. 607.

30. 97 Cal.App.2d 14, 217 P.2d 89 (1950).

(c) Perhaps the most unsound false arrest liability without fault is that incurred by a citizen who reasonably, but mistakenly, believes that a felony has been committed and has probable cause for believing that the prisoner has committed it. An innocent victim of arrest for felony is likely to have suffered the same damages whether or not someone else has committed the felony for which the innocent person has been arrested. A reasonably prudent citizen who has made an excusable mistake of fact is, nevertheless, reasonably prudent, and does not deserve the burden of liability.

TABLE OF CASES

References are to Pages

References are to Pages

INDEX

DEFENSE OF PROPERTY
Animals, privilege to kill, 37.
Chattels, 37.
Mechanical devices, 38–39.
Molliter manus imposuit, 36.

DESTRUCTION OR USE OF PROPERTY TO PREVENT DISASTER, 39–42
Private interests protected, 40–42.
Public interest protected, 39–40.

DUE CARE
See Negligence.

DUTY
Criminal statutes and civil no-duty rules, 146–151.
Extent of liability for negligence, 159, 161–162.
No-duty rules, 126–153.
    Concrete standards of fault, 126–127.
    Exoneration of faulty behavior, 127.
    Land occupants, 132–140.
    Landlords, 140–142.
    Rescue, see Rescue.
Nondelegable duties, 157.
Products liability, evolution of negligence law, 141–145.

EMERGENCY
    See also Necessity.
Medical treatment without consent, 26.
Negligence, 50.

EMOTIONAL DISTURBANCE, 191–196

EMPLOYERS
See Independent Contractor; Vicarious Liability.

ENTERPRISE LIABILITY
Entreprenuer theory, 252–254.
Policy, 232–237.
Products liability, 237–243.
Vicarious liability, 252.

EQUITABLE RELIEF
Misrepresentation, 298–299.
Nuisance, 282.

EVIDENCE
    See also Burden of Proof; Negligence, Proof of negligence and due care.
Causation in fact, proof of, 155–158.
Medical malpractice, expert testimony, 55–58.
Res ipsa loquitur, 117–125.

EXPLOSIVES
Liability without proof of fault, 229–232.
Policy analysis, 14–15.

EXTENT OF LIABILITY
Actual cause, proof of, 155–158.
    Circumstantial evidence, 157–158.
    Expert testimony, 156–157.
Blame and extent of liability, 199–200.
Certainty of the law on scope, 185–187.
    Specialized rules, 185–186.
Contributory negligence, 208–210.
Damages, recoverable, proof and extent of, 178–179.

†